THE PSYCHOLOGY
OF ADOLESCENCE

THE PSYCHOLOGY
OF ADOLESCENCE

★

MARVIN POWELL
NORTHERN ILLINOIS UNIVERSITY

THE **BOBBS-MERRILL** COMPANY, INC.
A SUBSIDIARY OF HOWARD W. SAMS & CO., INC.
Publishers • INDIANAPOLIS • NEW YORK

TO MY WIFE RITA
AND TO
JEFFREY, LINDA, AND LAURA

Contents

vii

Preface

The topic of adolescence is of great interest to almost everyone, even to those who have no direct involvement with teen-agers. The general purpose of this book is twofold: (1) To present the most recent research relating to the various areas of adolescence discussed herein; and (2) to present the adolescents' viewpoint concerning these areas. It is my belief that this approach will clarify the thinking of those who are generally interested in the topic and will be of particular value to those directly involved with adolescents.

All too often, today's textbooks present research studies done twenty or thirty years ago, and the reader is led to believe that those results are still meaningful today. Yet, it is well recognized that we live in a constantly changing society and that the adolescent of today is appreciably different from the counterpart of thirty years ago. Certainly, many of the leisure-time activities of teen-agers in the 1960's differ considerably from those of thirty years ago. The greater availability of automobiles and the development of television have brought about many changes in uses of leisure time. Entirely new vocational areas have opened up, and the importance and value of advanced educational training are increasingly felt as fewer jobs than ever are available to the younger, untrained individual. Educational practices, especially at the secondary-school level, are being criticized, with much concern expressed over the alleged failure of schools to meet the adolescents' needs.

In addition to the "practical" changes that have occurred in our society, there has been new thinking about areas that were thought to be thoroughly understood. The changing concepts covering intelligence may force us to redo or at least re-evaluate all the previous studies in this area and perhaps reject certain concepts that have long been accepted.

Most studies of adolescence have given, in a sense, the adult view of the nature of adolescence. It is quite obvious, however, that the adolescent's point of view must be considered, since it is his perception of the situation that causes him to react as he does. For some time now, the author has invited groups of teen-agers to discuss their viewpoints with his graduate students. These teen-agers usually poll large groups of their age mates and report their feelings to our classes. The author decided to use this double approach in order to show the reader both points of view and the way in which they interrelate. The balance of research and teen-age viewpoint varies according to the topic. In the areas of social attitudes, values, and the like, more emphasis may be placed on the adolescents' point of view because of the limited amount of research available, while in the area of intellectual development the reverse will be true.

The author feels strongly that this kind of synthesis will offer more useful information to both the professional and the layman who have reason to be interested in or concerned with adolescent development and behavior. Parents, guidance counselors, teachers, psychologists, social workers, and others who deal closely with adolescents must be thoroughly aware of these relationships if they are to function successfully in their work with teen-agers.

A book such as this one could have been written only with the help of many people who have given both constructive criticism and encouragement. The author wishes to offer his appreciation to the administration of Northern Illinois University for allowing him the time to work on this book. Nancy Tait, my graduate assistant, was particularly valuable in helping locate original references and typing the rough drafts from my somewhat illegible scrawl. Thanks are also expressed to Mrs. Karen Taylor and Miss Sally Kenyon, our departmental secretaries, who typed much of the manuscript during their free time. Finally, I would like to acknowledge my wife's efforts in reading and rereading my various drafts and in making essential corrections in the grammatical structure of this book. Her patience and understanding were most valuable during sometimes difficult periods of this effort.

September 1963   MARVIN POWELL

CHAPTER 1

Adolescence: The "Between" Years

Since the publication more than fifty years ago of the monumental two-volume work on adolescence by Stanley Hall (1904), there has been increasing interest in this portion of the life span. Many studies have been made on the subject, but in spite of all this work no definition of adolescence has yet been universally agreed upon. Because of the changes that have taken place in our society, definitions that may have been adequate twenty years ago are no longer acceptable, and definitions that are acceptable today may well be useless twenty years hence.

DEFINITIONS AND CONCEPTS

Many attempts have been made to designate the period of adolescence in terms of time limits. The descriptions of the beginning of adolescence relate to a fairly limited time span, but those indicating its end show much more divergence. The following lists illustrate this.

Beginning of Adolescence	*End of Adolescence*
Puberty	When sexual development is complete
One year prior to puberty	At the end of the teen-years
Time of first menstruation (girls)	When physical growth ceases
At the beginning of the teen-years	At graduation from high school
When the growth spurt begins	
At entrance to junior high school (seventh grade)	
	At marriage
	When economic independence is achieved
	When emancipation from parents is achieved
	When emotional and intellectual maturity is achieved
	At age twenty-one (legal definition)

Obviously, there is considerable agreement as to the beginning of adolescence, since the items in that list fall within a limited time period —between the ages of eleven and fifteen for most adolescents. The designations indicating the end of adolescence, however, cannot be confined to any single time period. The first four items refer to events occurring between the ages of fifteen and nineteen, but no age can be directly associated with the next four. If these are to be used as criteria, we can safely say that some individuals will remain adolescent throughout their entire lives.

Adolescence has further been described as: a period during which maturity is attained; a period of transition between childhood and adulthood; a period during which an emotionally immature individual approaches the culmination of his physical and mental growth; a time of "rebirth"; etc. In general, there is fairly universal agreement that puberty does mark the beginning of adolescence. To date, no equally acceptable term has been found to describe its culmination.

However it may be defined, the adolescent period is a source of much interest and concern to adults and to adolescents themselves. Although subsequent research has never completely substantiated Hall's point of view, part of the frame of reference he established is widely accepted. His concept of adolescence as a "rebirth" has been rejected, but his emphasis upon adolescence as a time of "storm and stress" still has a great deal of influence on those who deal with adolescents. Even those who do not accept this rather extreme point of view agree that emotionality is apparently heightened during this period.

This heightened emotionality results from the complex interaction of a variety of factors. Thus it is most difficult, if not impossible, to establish cause-and-effect relationships for many adolescent behavior patterns. This is not to suggest that the appearance of certain patterns is inherent in the process of physical growth; rather, these result from the impact of the culture on the developing individual. Adolescent behavior, like behavior in general, is the result of cultural, social, biological, and physical forces acting on the individual while they interact with one another.

We would expect that if society made no unusual or unnecessary demands on the individual as he approaches and enters the adolescent time period, heightened emotionality would not be present. Mead's early study (1928) of Samoan youngsters illustrated this point very well. In the sense in which we use it, the term adolescence was meaningless to the Samoans, and the heightened emotionality pattern was not present. Little was heard about problems of adolescence in Europe during the period preceding World War II. Because of the educational and economic structure of Europe at that time, most young people finished their schooling early and immediately sought employment. During Hitler's regime in Germany, adolescents were supervised by the government and were under complete control. The penalties for failure to conform to the rigidly structured rules were most severe. In pre-World War II Japan, the society was strongly patriarchal, and conformity to the family rules was strictly enforced. Any act by a teenager that was not within this pattern would bring shame to the family, and this was to be avoided at all costs. If adolescent problems existed in any of these situations, they were seldom discussed in the research literature. Such problems were handled within the family; in public, "the less said the better." The studies that were reported were primarily concerned with the physiological rather than the psychological aspects of development.

UNIVERSALITY OF THE PROBLEMS RELATED TO ADOLESCENCE

For many years, the whole concept of adolescence as a problem period was restricted to America. Relatively few of the studies available from other cultures, primitive or civilized, indicated the presence of a similar situation. Since the end of World War II, however, more and more studies on the problems of adolescence in other countries have appeared. Many changes have occurred in the educational, vocational, and social processes in these countries that are very similar to changes that had taken place and are still taking place in our own country. As the cultural similarities increase, so, too, do the similarities of the problems of adolescence.

Numerous recent studies of adolescence done in various foreign countries point up these increasing similarities. There are still differences in the ways that adolescents view and react to these problems in different societies, but the same problems admittedly exist.

Suellwold (1959) used an adaptation of the SRA Youth Inventory, Form S (Science Research Associates, 1959), on present-day youth in Germany. Frequency of responses to the various items by the German and United States samples were compared. Most problems covered by this inventory were chosen by equal percentages of both national groups. There were, of course, differences that reflected the different values in the two cultures. For example, German young people responded oftener to such statements as: "I am afraid of failure and humiliation," and "My parents criticize me too much." The American adolescents were more often bothered by such problems as: "I want people to like me better," and "I want to feel important to society or to my own group," etc.

Störring (1958) has written generally on the topic of the status and needs of German youth. He stresses the present-day acceleration of physical development, as contrasted with that of the last generation, as having had an important influence on personality adjustment. He further feels that such acceleration has created discrepancies in physical, emotional, and intellectual functioning. German young people today tend to be dependent on family and peer-group relationships and are a concrete, action-oriented group. Their exaggerated need to conform with the peer group is responsible for a general instability in goals. There is also evidence of problems related to maternal overprotection and lack of parental encouragement.

Okaji (1958) studied Japanese youth in an attempt to determine what changes in the adolescent's attitudes toward life resulted from group discussion. He contrasted the responses of high-school students to an attitude scale with those of a group of adults. Both groups were favorable toward an "uneventful," easy, and *petit bourgeois* way of living, and both manifested "constructive, spiritual, and social-centered attitudes." Both students and adults reacted negatively to a fatalistic way of living, and the author concluded that such an attitude toward life was not characteristic of the groups studied. Okaji also concluded that instability of adolescent attitudes was indicated by the significant changes in attitude that resulted from group discussions.

The presence of adolescent problems in Egypt was demonstrated by El Koussy (1960). In a study of rural and urban Egyptian adolescents, he found no fundamental differences between his groups and what is known about European and American groups. The stresses, the strains, the moodiness, the clumsiness, etc., were all apparent. The boys seemed more interested in family solidarity, orderliness, and quietness than did the girls. Resentment of parental authority and a strong dislike of family adherence to old customs were noted.

Even in a country such as Poland, which is under the control of an authoritarian government, the problems are apparent. Brzezinska (1960) tried to determine the factors that influence the attitude of present-day Warsaw youth. About 30 per cent indicated displeasure with the influence of the school, the home, and the society, while 22 per cent expressed disappointment. Eighteen per cent were concerned about the lack of opportunity for having a good time. Despite the emphasis on clubs, cultural groups, and various organizations, about half the group did not believe that youth organizations offered much possibility of help in solving their problems. Even though these findings may be somewhat biased because of the political structure in which they were conducted, the problems of adolescents are still quite apparent and are similar to those of American adolescents.

As societies that until very recently were relatively primitive move rapidly in the direction of becoming organized civilized countries, the problems of adolescents seem to increase. Although little investigation has been done in the many new African countries that have suddenly come into being, it is probably safe to assume that among the many problems confronting these nations will be the difficulties experienced by adolescents.

It would thus appear that the various problems associated with adolescence are no longer a strictly American phenomenon. Indeed, as more and better evidence becomes available it seems more and more likely that many of these problems are universal. Today the unrest expressed by students in foreign societies, notably in Central and South America, and recently in Hungary, is the first sign of general unrest in the whole society. The importance of youth and its effect on the culture have become more and more obvious.

There are, of course, differences in the kinds and the severity of the problems, since many specific problems are peculiar to the society in which they exist. Hsu, Watrous, and Lork (1961) illustrate this point in a study that compares Chinese boys and girls aged fourteen to nineteen, living in Hawaii, with adolescents in Chicago. They found appreciably more turbulence among the American white youth than among the Chinese-Americans. Juvenile delinquency rates in Chinese neighborhoods in the United States had previously been found to be very low as compared with those in white neighborhoods. The differences indicated in both cases seem to result from the somewhat different family structure in which Chinese-American adolescents are reared.

A more detailed discussion of the influences of culture on personality development appears in Chapter 5 of this book. The studies summarized here are mentioned simply to emphasize the increasing worldwide awareness of the adolescent and his problems. These studies do suggest that adolescent conflicts are more externalized in some societies than in others. However, the situation in the more authoritarian societies, where conflicts may appear to be less frequent because they are not overt, is different from that in societies like the Samoan, in which conflict is relatively lacking.

THE ADOLESCENT IN AMERICAN SOCIETY

In a recent article, Gardner (1957) has pointed out that adolescents are being thrust into a group of societies which are beset with the same conflicts that they are. American society is in reality a whole host of societies, which he believes indicates a glaring lack of set values and standards. He does not seem surprised that, in a country plunged into national adolescence, the adolescent has difficulty in solving his problems. The point is perhaps somewhat overstated, yet many agree with it, and there is increasing concern over the general societal conflicts in regard to social morality.

Rather than stressing only the societal aspects, however, adolescence must be considered in terms of physiological, social, and emotional development. Davis, Gitelson, Maxwell, and Ross (1949) held a round-table discussion of adolescent problems in the present culture. They felt that there are three main requirements to be met in order to prepare the adolescent for competition in an adult world: (1) sexual control; (2) long schooling; and (3) postponement of marriage until the educational requirements of a good marriage have been met. These requirements present a dilemma for parents, who need a good deal of calm and understanding to help adolescents meet them. Rube (1955) has also stressed the fact that there is no over-all single problem of adolescence. Rather, there is a series of very complex, intricate problems of a cultural, psychological and/or sociological nature, many of which influence pubescence. It is these factors rather than constitutional ones that bring forth problems. Rube does suggest, however, that these conditions need not result in unhappiness or severe problems.

The Prolongation of Adolescence

To those already concerned about the problems of adolescence, the apparent prolongation of its time span is a further source of anxiety. The period of transition between puberty and recognized maturity is now appreciably longer than it was fifty years ago. Actually, this period has been lengthened during each of the last five decades, and it is probably safe to assume that this pattern may continue in the future. To the degree that such prolongation postpones the achievement of maturity and adult status, it creates and maintains many problems.

Many changes in our society have brought about this prolongation. Compulsory schooling is now required in most states until the individual reaches at least the age of sixteen, and there is considerable pressure for an extension to eighteen. For those who wish further schooling the prolongation is even greater. For example, an individual seeking a career in medicine may require as much as twelve years of education and training beyond high school before he is ready to start medical practice—four years of undergraduate training, four years in medical school, at least one year of internship, and about three years of residence in his field of specialization. A person so trained may be thirty years old before he goes out on his own.

Such extended educational endeavor tends to keep the individual from early achievement of some of the goals previously mentioned as associated with adulthood, i.e., economic independence, marriage, etc. However, increasing numbers of young people do marry and manage to support themselves even while they are completing their education.

Obviously, though extended education may be a cause of prolonged adolescence, it does not have to be.

The changing economic situation in our country has also been responsible in at least two ways for prolonging adolescence. First, more money is available to adolescents than was true, even relatively, twenty-five years ago. In many cases this money comes from the parents in the form of allowances or gifts. Because the adolescent can usually count on the home environment to provide for his needs and even offer some luxuries, he does not have to seek employment in order to obtain money for these purposes. This often leads to greater dependence on the home and consequently an extension of the period of adolescence.

The second way in which economic change affects the prolongation of adolescence is by the reduction in vocational opportunities for individuals who leave school early, and even for those who complete their high-school education. The increasing growth and strength of the labor unions have contributed to this situation. As the unions strive to keep older workers employed longer, there is necessarily less opportunity for young people. Some occupations are virtually closed to youngsters, and fewer and fewer apprenticeships are available in those that are still open. This situation may change somewhat if older workers begin retiring earlier, thus making room for younger people. However, increased automation may impede this trend. Many industries that are automating have agreed to keep their present workers employed but will not replace them when they retire. Such industries as the railroads, which once employed very large numbers of young people, have eliminated formerly essential jobs. Thus the employment opportunities for untrained young people are very poor.

The pressure previously mentioned to prolong compulsory education is in a sense a result of this employment situation. The school helps to keep unemployed youngsters "off the street" and should offer training that will better enable them to find employment when they graduate. How well this need is being met by the schools is discussed in detail later (see Chapter 13).

We may be more aware of the prolongation of the adolescent time period today, but some of the factors involved have been present previously. During the depression era of the 1930's, employment was limited and salaries for the available jobs were very low. Consequently, it was most difficult for adolescents to achieve economic independence. Often, as a result of this economic situation, marriage had to be postponed indefinitely. Although there were some studies of the problems of teen-agers of that period (notably Bell's, 1938), there was less general interest than there is today. Perhaps the fact that employment problems were so widespread kept the particular needs of adolescents from being of too great concern.

CLASSIFICATIONS OF ADOLESCENTS

Even if the beginning and end of the adolescent time period could be agreed upon, it would still not be possible to generalize about all adolescents over the entire time span. For purposes of study, various subdivisions must be made. Probably the most important are the division according to sex and the division according to age.

Sex Differences

There are major differences between the sexes in rate of development, which although present during childhood are most obvious during adolescence. It is generally agreed that girls mature mentally and physically earlier than boys do. Even at the beginning of the first grade (at about six) girls more often than boys are ready for the introduction of reading. These kinds of differences are so apparent that it has been suggested that the age of entering school be delayed one year for boys as compared to girls (Topp, 1961).

In most cases the differences noted during childhood increase during adolescence. This increase is most apparent in the area of physical development. Stuart (1946) finds girls to be one year ahead of boys in physical development at age nine and two years ahead at age twelve. The advantage to the girls has been most often noted in the age at which pubescence is reached (Shuttleworth, 1949; Greulich and Pyle, 1950). The characteristic in which this advanced development is most obvious to the observer is height. Simmons (1944) has clearly demonstrated that between the ages of eleven and thirteen girls are usually taller than boys (see Figure 3, page 32).

Although physical differences are important determinants of behavior at various age levels, the problems that arise may be influenced by cultural patterns. Some of these cultural patterns may be the result of the physical differences, i.e., because girls mature earlier they resemble adults sooner and therefore are treated more like adults than boys are. Other patterns are not physically based but result from the different expectancies the culture has for the sexes. Girls are expected to be "little ladies" early in childhood, while boys are allowed to be aggressive and boisterous even into adolescence. As a result of the years of such conditioning, adolescent girls appear more docile and accepting, while adolescent boys appear obstreperous and more difficult to control.

Once these differences have developed, they in turn bring about other cultural responses that may cause problems. This is fairly obvious in the "female-centeredness" of American elementary and secondary schools. Generally, teachers of both sexes seem to give preferential treatment to girls (Topp, 1961), and girls are considered better students. This attitude is reflected in the academic grades assigned to the two sexes; girls generally receive better grades than boys do. During the early elementary school years, this difference could, of course, result from the early maturity of girls, but in high school the differences are probably more culturally oriented. There is some evidence to suggest that from grade four up there are no significant differences in achievement as measured by objective standardized tests (Powell *et al.,* 1962), and that boys, therefore, have actually learned as much as girls. Apparently, then, teachers, in assigning grades, are as much influenced by the overt behavior of individuals as by actual achievement.

Harris (1959) repeated an earlier study done by Symonds (1937) relating to sex differences in adolescent problems and interests. In a comparison of the two studies, significant changes appeared in fifteen of the issues involved. These issues, considered both as problems and as interests, were mostly concerned with love and marriage, family relations, mental health, and study habits. Concern with health, manners, recreation, and safety had apparently lessened. The sex differences, which changed appreciably in rank over the twenty-year period, reflect the greater interest of boys in recreation and money. Girls showed greater interest in social relationships, personal attractiveness, and (most recently) in love and marriage and family relationships. According to their own reports, mental health and personal attractiveness seemed to be greater problems for girls than for boys. Harris feels that there is less consistency today than in the earlier study between the order of issues considered as problems and their order considered as interests.

Sex differences are apparent in, and relate to, all the areas discussed in this book. In certain areas, such as physical and heterosexual development, they play a major role. In other areas, such as religion and intellectual development, they are perhaps less influential but definitely present.

Age Groupings

No less important than the differences between the sexes in understanding various aspects of development are differences within the sex groups, particularly the age differences. In the literature there is generally a differentiation between the younger adolescent and the older adolescent, or between early and late adolescence. Quite often this differentiation is related to school levels, with junior-high-school students considered as younger or early adolescents (Cameron, 1938) and high-school students as older or late adolescents (college students are often included in this latter group). The differentiation is also often related to ages, with the ten- to fourteen-year age group defined as the early adolescents and the fifteen- to nineteen-year age group as the late ones (Milner, 1949; Valadian *et al.,* 1961). Hurlock (1955) has differentiated among three periods based on age: preadolescence, from ten to twelve years; early adolescence, from thirteen to sixteen years; and late adolescence, from seventeen to twenty-one years.

Powell (1955) has studied age and sex differences in degree of conflict in seven areas of adjustment. He has found the usual two-year differences between the sexes and has also noted the different ages at which conflict appears and at which it reaches a maximum in each sex (see Table 8, Chapter 5). It is evident from this study that some adjustment areas are sources of concern fairly early in adolescence, while others become problems later. This study, which covers the range from ten to thirty years of age, also demonstrates that in certain areas conflict continues into adulthood, while in other areas the major concern is generally restricted to the teen years.

Studies have also been made to determine the differences that exist between those reaching pubescence early and those reaching it late (see Chapter 2 for a detailed discussion of this topic). Mussen and Jones (1957) have studied attitudes of late- and early-maturing boys and find substantial differences, generally favoring the early-maturers. The early-maturers tend to "present a consistently favorable personality picture with regard to . . . important social variables." Even though the differences in physique largely disappear, the psychological pattern relating to the age at which they appear often carries over into adulthood. In order to understand adolescence better, both age differences and sex differences must be considered, and the interaction of these variables is also most important. Early-maturing boys do differ in a number of ways from late-maturing boys, and early-maturing boys are also appreciably different from early-maturing girls.

STUDYING THE ADOLESCENT

Even the foregoing brief discussion of adolescence should have made it obvious that a good deal of research on this topic is needed. Whenever problems arise in relation to human development, efforts should be made to determine why they arise and how they should best be treated. The main question involved is whether the time span defined as adolescence can be studied as a separate period or must be closely related to the preceding period of childhood and the succeeding one of adulthood. Dennis (1946) does not feel that a psychology of the teen age is appropriate or reasonable unless we are prepared also to develop psychologies of the twenties, thirties, forties, etc. Many people believe that adolescence is just one part of the total life span and that the behavior of all human beings, regardless of age, is governed by the same general laws. There is also evidence to suggest that conditions affecting the child's development will have definite influences on the adolescent's development.

Although these arguments have some truth in them, a general over-all knowledge of behavior is not sufficient for specific situations within a given age group. An adolescent's anxiety about maturing late physically is appreciably different from the problems that a younger child may have about physical development. The adolescent's concern about his genital development is unlike any problem of this sort encountered by the younger child or even by the adult.

Ausubel (1954) points out the parallel situation in the field of medicine. Here, the emphasis is more and more on specialization, with fields such as pediatrics evolving. The increasing awareness that children and adults react differently to disease and that some diseases are peculiar to or more damaging in children helped bring about such specialization.

Perhaps the best reason for treating adolescence as a "separate" period is based on the distinctive biological changes which occur during that time span. These changes, as well as the psychological changes that accompany them, are appreciably different from changes in other periods of the life span. The occurrence of the menarche, for example, may bring about greater physical and psychological changes than does the menopause.

Perhaps the simplest justification for the study of the adolescent period is in terms of the applicability of the knowledge gained to everyday problems. Whether adolescence is a unique time period is really not the major point to be considered. Adolescence is widely recognized by layman and expert alike as a period during which the individual is confronted by many problems of interpersonal relations, and since such problems do exist they should be investigated as fully as possible.

Methods of Study

There are few specific methods or techniques of research that are peculiar to studies of the adolescent. The Symonds Picture-Story Test (1948), which is described later, is one of the very few instruments designed specifically for such use. Most of the methods employed are usually applicable to studies of children and of adults. Standardized tests may have been structured for different grade levels, i.e., grades

1-3, 4-6, 7-9, 10-14, but this differentiation is based on grade levels, not age spans. Nonetheless, results of tests so differentiated are useful in comparing one group to another and in investigating sex differences at any level.

Even though the same methods and techniques are used at other age levels, a brief review of those most frequently employed with adolescents is worth including. Most studies can be categorized as either longitudinal or cross-sectional.

LONGITUDINAL STUDIES. These studies are scientifically more precise because certain controls can be established and maintained. Basically, a longitudinal investigation is concerned with studying characteristics in an individual or group of individuals over an extended period of time. If our concern is with the adolescent age span, such a study might well start with a group of ten eleven-year-olds who would be followed up until they were eighteen or nineteen. Since exactly the same individuals are being studied throughout, the controls established at the beginning of the study can be maintained easily, and the group can be precisely described.

Until fairly recently, very few longitudinal studies covering the adolescent period were reported. The failure to employ this method was caused by practical rather than technical or scientific considerations. Such studies are very costly financially and are also quite time-consuming. When little is known about a field, the desire to get information quickly is foremost in the minds of investigators. Rather than waiting eight or ten years for complete results, earlier researchers often chose to use approaches that obtain data more quickly. A more technical problem—that of keeping the sample intact—was also a source of difficulty to earlier investigators. If a study was started with fifty youngsters, only twenty of them might still be available to the investigator ten years later.

There have been some notable longitudinal studies over the years, including the Berkeley Growth Study, the California Adolescent Growth Study, the studies of Gesell at Yale, and the studies of the Fels Institute. Fortunately, more studies of this nature are being reported and are currently in progress. The Berkeley Growth Studies originally involved young children; the subjects have now been studied for some twenty-five years. The California Adolescent Growth Studies have concerned themselves only with the longitudinal investigation of the adolescent years. Increasing numbers of universities have set up research centers, usually well financed, to carry on longitudinal studies of the development of the human organism in general, and study of the adolescent is not being neglected in these centers.

CROSS-SECTIONAL STUDIES. This type of study may yield the same general results as a longitudinal study. However, since cross-sectional studies cannot be as precisely structured, the results will probably be somewhat less reliable. Basically, cross-sectional research involves studying characteristics in different groups of individuals at different age levels. For example, one would select fifty ten-year-olds, fifty eleven-year-olds, fifty twelve-year-olds, and so on, up to fifty nineteen-year-olds. Then, by using the proper tests and measuring instruments, one could demonstrate the growth or development of a characteristic from age ten through age nineteen. Such information would be available in a relatively short period of time and would not be too costly. The main difficulty is in matching the groups so that they would be considered comparable. Obviously, one could not use fifty ten-year-olds from a high socioeconomic group, fifty eleven-year-olds from a low socioeconomic group, etc. The meaningfulness and usefulness of the results would depend greatly on the degree to which the various samples are comparable.

The curves representing the development of the characteristic studied will vary somewhat with the approach used (see Figure 1), but the direction and acceleration of the two curves are generally quite similar. The curve based on the longitudinal study is smoother, representing the control of the sample that is inherent in this kind of study. The more jagged curve, based on the cross-sectional approach, reflects the lack of complete comparability between the groups.

USE OF NORMATIVE DATA. Normative data may be acquired through the use of either longitudinal or cross-sectional studies, with the latter having been more frequently employed. Such data are used to establish a frame of reference that describes a given characteristic as it is peculiar to or related to a given age. Norms are usually based on arithmetic averages determined from a wide range of scores of individuals in the age bracket studied. For example, it may be said that the average eight-year-old boy weighs 65 pounds. This average was derived from the weights of a group of eight-year-old boys whose weights ranged from 45 to 90 pounds. No one of the boys involved may actually have weighed 65 pounds, but, nonetheless, that is the norm for that age level.

Normative data are of great value, since they show us the general patterns of growth and development and the comparability of various aspects of growth. This in turn helps us know what to expect from members of a given group in motor patterns, intellectual functioning, physical development, etc. Although the norm does not describe the individual case, it is of value in considering the individual. By knowing whether or not he deviates from the norm and how great such deviation may be, we may better understand certain aspects of his behavior.

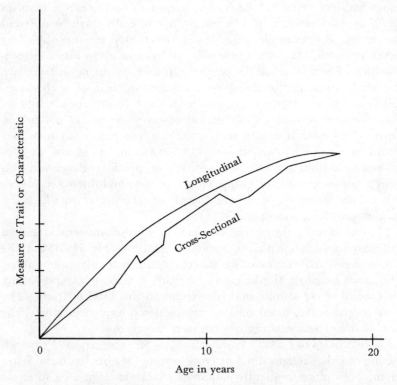

FIGURE 1. Curves based on longitudinal and cross-sectional studies of the same
characteristic

For example, the average height of sixteen-year-old boys is 5 feet,
8 inches. A sixteen-year-old individual being studied is only 5 feet,
4 inches tall. The fact that he deviates from the norm may be a source
of emotional involvement to him. The investigator's awareness of the
norm enables him to recognize the deviation and may, in turn, help
him to understand the individual boy's problem and offer appropriate
aid.

The whole concept of what is "normal" is often a confusing one,
particularly in considering the complex human organism. No individual is likely to be average in all his characteristics. An individual
who is of average height for his age may be below average in weight
and above average in intelligence. In using normative data, one can
only compare each characteristic with its own norm.

Bayley (1955) has expressed the opinion that knowledge of the normal features of development is essential for the full understanding of emotional and personal factors in children. She has presented significant data from the California-Berkeley Growth Study to show that interpretation of pathologic behavior is best made in the light of normal behavior. Bayley (1956) also points out the importance of individual differences in the temporal process—that is, the different rates at which development and differentiation of structure and function occur.

In studying the individual who deviates from the norm, we may still find that the general pattern of development approximates the norm but at a higher or lower point (see Figure 2). As Figure 2 shows, the general curves for those who continue to deviate are similar to the average curve. Some may deviate initially but later catch up to or fall back toward the average.

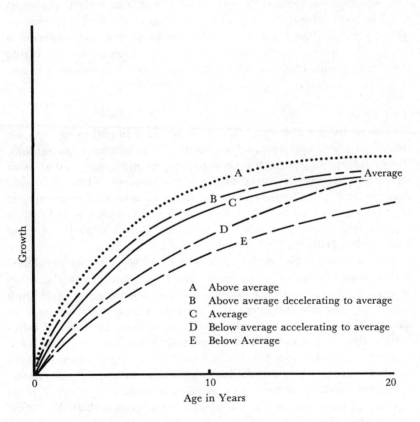

FIGURE 2. How individual growth patterns approximate the average growth curve

CULTURAL NORMS. Deviations from normative data based on objective measurements are relatively easy to illustrate and, within limits, to understand. However, many subjective norms that are of particular concern to adolescents are difficult to assess or explain. These are the so-called "cultural" or "societal" norms, which everyone seems to understand implicitly, yet which no two individuals may define in the same way. These norms, too, are constantly re-evaluated by the individual as he grows to maturity, and his interpretation of their influence on his development may change appreciably. What is the norm for femininity or masculinity? What is the norm for beauty, attractiveness, or handsomeness? The so-called norm for each of these characteristics may exist solely as the individual views them. A girl whom others regard as beautiful may see herself as unattractive. Her own interpretation of this norm causes this judgment, and to change it the norm may need to be reinterpreted to her.

As will be demonstrated throughout this book, many of the problems of adolescents arise from their interpretations of these cultural norms. These often deviate from the adults' interpretations, thus offering a source of conflict. Often neither adults nor adolescents can define these norms adequately even to themselves, and the problem of communication between the groups is thus intensified.

Techniques

Some of the specific research techniques used in gathering data for studies of the adolescent are outlined in the following paragraphs. These are not of course the only techniques used, nor, as has been mentioned, are they restricted to use with adolescents. This discussion does not attempt to include the more technical aspects of experimental methodology and/or design. For the reader who wishes to familiarize himself with these, a number of excellent sources is available (Van Dalen, 1962; Hillway, 1956; Good, 1959; etc.).

QUESTIONNAIRES. G. Stanley Hall is credited with having developed this approach, along with his many other contributions to the study of people. A questionnaire enables the investigator to acquire from large and generally representative samples a substantial amount of data relating to one or more characteristics. Almost any kind of information that an individual can relate about himself or about his view of how others react can be obtained in this way. Questionnaires may be used to acquire very specific information concerning a single characteristic or mode of behavior, or to acquire gross data about a large number of patterns. In the initial investigation of a relatively unexplored area the collection of gross data by means of questionnaires is valuable. When such data have been analyzed and more refined investigation is needed, a more specific and carefully structured questionnaire may well be used for this purpose.

There are different kinds of questionnaires and different ways of structuring them. In one type of questionnaire, the respondent may be asked to give his view about certain characteristics, modes of behavior, political parties, etc. Such a questionnaire might be called an "opinionnaire," since the respondent is not necessarily expected to be an "expert" in the area being questioned. In other cases the respondent is asked to answer questions about himself. A questionnaire of this type is usually referred to as an "inventory." Many modern-day paper-and-pencil personality and interest tests are inventories. In still other cases a questionnaire may be administered to individuals who are considered experts in the area under question and who answer on the basis of actual knowledge rather than personal opinion.

The questionnaire may be structured in a number of ways in terms of the kind of answer the investigator seeks. The respondent may be requested to give a detailed answer to a question such as "What do you think are the common problems of adolescents?" He may simply be asked to answer yes or no to such questions as "Do you think teen-agers find acne a major problem?" He may be asked to express his reaction to such a statement as "The peer group has greater influence on the teen-ager than the parents do" by choosing among a list of responses: strongly agreeing; mildly agreeing; mildly disagreeing; or strongly disagreeing.

A rather serious drawback to the use of questionnaires is the danger that the individual may not give a truthful response. This problem has been particularly apparent in the use of paper-and-pencil inventories of personality. If the results of the inventory may have a direct bearing on the individual's future, he may deliberately falsify his answers. If, for example, an individual taking such a test as part of an employment interview sees the question "Do you have frequent headaches?" he may immediately say, "No." He may have a splitting headache at that very moment but fear that a response of "Yes" might well jeopardize his possible employment. More often, however, falsification is unconscious. An individual is so familiar with what is or is not socially acceptable that he often responds on this basis rather than in terms of his real feelings. Most people would respond "No" to the question "Do you hate your mother?" simply because hating one's mother is not socially approved. Even an individual who did hate his mother would probably have so repressed this feeling that he would feel perfectly honest in answering, "No."

One must therefore critically examine questionnaire studies, particularly those of adolescents, whose conflicting ideas and doubtful interpretations of cultural norms may color their responses to the extent that they become meaningless. Even the instruments that have "lie" scales or validity checks are far from foolproof; and results based on these scales, too, should be critically evaluated.

INTERVIEWS. Although the interview has been used most often in clinical work, many feel it is a most valuable research technique. In face-to-face interaction, a trained interviewer may ask the person being interviewed to pursue an answer further or base the next question on an earlier response. Interviews are often based on prepared questions, but the interviewer is allowed flexibility in stating or restating them. An obvious advantage is that if the respondent does not adequately comprehend the question, it can be clarified; this would not ordinarily be possible with a questionnaire. Today, with recording equipment available, any biases that the interviewer might have can be negated. The recorded interview can be the basis for ratings by independent observers, against whose judgments the interviewer can check his own ratings. A bias caused by some aspect of the respondent's appearance, for example, could not be reflected in the independent raters' judgments. Another advantage over the questionnaire is the fact that a skilled interviewer can assess the sincerity of the responses. However, he has no way of judging the accuracy of the respondent's memory. In accumulating interview information for case studies, researchers have often found that the memories of the individuals questioned do not always bring forth accurate accounts of a given situation.

OBJECTIVE AND/OR STANDARDIZED TESTS. Tests of this type are specifically constructed as measures of short but rather general samples of behavior. A test of perhaps one hour's duration gives us information about the individual that helps us to understand the characteristic measured and even to predict its development.

For example, intelligence tests are used to measure the individual's capability for learning, while achievement tests are used to measure what he has learned. The score derived from each test may tell us a number of general things about the individual, and the interrelationship of the two scores may offer still further information. An adolescent who has an IQ of 135 may be gifted, should be well above average in achievement at his present school level, and would usually be capable of success at higher educational levels, including the level of professional schools. An eighth-grader who scores at the 50th percentile on an eighth-grade achievement test should be expected to continue at an average level of achievement for his grade level. Suppose, however, that both these scores were received by the same individual. Can we now say that we have a very bright individual who is achieving well below his level of ability? If the scoring is by national norms, in which an average IQ is 100 and the 50th percentile indicates average eighth-grade achievement, then the answer is probably "Yes." If, however, we are using norms based on the student's own eighth-grade group, the answer would vary according to the structure of the group. Suppose the average IQ of his class is 135. Then a 50th-percentile score based on the results of that class means he is working up to the level of his ability in terms of the group with which he functions. To evaluate tests of this kind, therefore, both the norms of the test and the specific norms used in the sample under discussion are important.

Objective tests in order to be useful must be reliable and valid. (For a detailed discussion of these topics, see Lindquist, 1951.) If a test is to be useful for general application, the sample on which it was standardized should have been as representative of the total population as possible. Most of our modern-day intelligence and achievement tests do meet these various standards. Personality and interest are also generally well structured but require careful interpretations, as we suggested in the previous discussion of inventories.

Much valuable research evidence has been accumulated by use of objective group tests. Such evidence has been useful in establishing various growth and developmental trends. High-school guidance programs make wide use of group test results for counseling and vocational guidance. However, since group tests are designed to measure behavior characteristics of groups, very special care must be used when their results are applied to individuals.

PROJECTIVE DEVICES. These techniques are most often employed as measures of personality structure. They were devised to negate the effects, already mentioned, of the individual's knowledge of the socially approved answer. Projective devices present a relatively unstructured situation to which the individual can respond freely. There is no apparent right or wrong answer, and the situations do not present any threat.

The Rorschach Ink Blot Test is probably the best-known projective test and one that illustrates the point; there is nothing right or wrong or threatening about an ink blot.

Many projective devices were developed for use with adults, and a substantial number have been developed for use with children. One of the few developed especially for the adolescent is the Symonds Picture-Story Test. It consists of cards showing figures, usually adolescents, in various situations. The respondent tells the story that the picture suggests to him. It is assumed that the adolescent identifies with the adolescent figure on the card and is actually telling the story about himself.

Although projective techniques are being widely used to investigate various aspects of personality and behavior, they cannot be considered as precise measuring instruments. The scoring is generally very subjective, which may be useful to an individual clinician but makes the results very difficult to quantify for precise statistical analyses. A good deal of research is needed to establish the reliability and validity of these devices if they are to be useful research tools. Although a great many studies involving these instruments are presented in this book, the reader is cautioned to be aware of the deficiencies of these techniques.

CASE STUDIES. The case study is an attempt to gather any and all information that can be acquired about a given individual. This approach has been widely employed in psychological clinics, but it can be useful in accumulating information about any individual. It involves subjective as well as objective information. For an adolescent the data gathered might include such objective measures as height, weight, IQ, achievement scores, health records, etc. The subjective data would include interviews with parents, academic grades, teachers' reports, etc. In addition to gathering data from the school and the home, information could be gathered from the child's peers and from other agencies with whom the child might have contact (Y.M.C.A., juvenile court, church organizations, etc.). The individual developing a case study might carefully observe the child in a variety of situations or interview him in an attempt to add the child's point of view to the other information acquired.

Various refinements of the techniques discussed, as well as numerous other investigative tools, are useful in research relating to adolescence. Some of these will be discussed in various portions of this book as they relate to specific studies in the various areas.

A GENERAL FRAME OF REFERENCE

Judging by such books as Salisbury's *The Shook-Up Generation* (1958), everyone seems to be interested in adolescents for one reason or another. Parents would like to know as much as possible about their adolescent children and are especially interested in how to "get along" with them. School personnel are interested in many aspects of adolescent development. Problems of physical growth, intellectual development, emotional disturbances, vocational planning, and development of interests are all part of the schools' interaction with the adolescent. Juvenile courts want to find out what patterns of child and adolescent behavior are likely to lead to juvenile delinquency. Manufacturers of cosmetics, apparel, and accessories are very much concerned about adolescent interests as they relate to marketing (*The New Yorker,* 1958; *Consumer Reports,* 1957). Medical personnel and psychologists are concerned about the adolescents' physical and/or mental health. Every adolescent is also very much interested in learning more about himself and about his peer group.

Specific aspects of adolescent development and behavior will be discussed in detail in later chapters. However, some general frames of reference are needed here for a better understanding of the strivings of the adolescent. These points of reference, developmental tasks, or goals provide the broad bases for understanding the adolescents' behavior. Although these points of view are presented individually, the reader should be aware that they interrelate and interact with one another in establishing the total picture of adolescence. Each of the tasks may also be considered either as a single complex task or as a group or series of smaller tasks.

Perhaps the best-known frame of reference is that presented by Havighurst (1953) in his book on human development and behavior. He lists the following ten major developmental tasks of adolescence:

(1) achieving new and more mature relations with age-mates of both sexes;
(2) achieving a masculine or feminine social role;
(3) accepting one's physique and using the body effectively;
(4) achieving emotional independence of parents and other adults;
(5) achieving assurance of economic independence;
(6) selecting and preparing for an occupation;
(7) preparing for marriage and family life;
(8) developing intellectual skills and concepts necessary for civic competence;
(9) desiring and achieving socially responsible behavior;
(10) acquiring a set of values and an ethical system as a guide to behavior.*

Each of these tasks is discussed in terms of the nature of the task, the psychological basis, the cultural basis, the social class structure, and the educational implications. The developmental tasks of childhood and adulthood are also presented, thus giving the reader a total picture of the complex aspects of human development.

Horrocks (1962) has presented five major points of reference from

*From *Human Development and Education* by R. J. Havighurst (New York: David McKay Co., Inc., 1953), by permission of the author and publisher.

which he feels adolescent growth and development should be viewed. Adolescence, he says, is a time:

(1) of physical growth and development;
(2) when group relationships become of major importance;
(3) of seeking status as an individual;
(4) of intellectual expansion and development, and academic experience;
(5) of development and evaluation in values.*

Within limits, these five points of reference seem to include each of Havighurst's developmental tasks. The interrelationships of these tasks can easily be noted as they are combined into various aspects of Horrocks' points of reference.

Gardner (1957) presents four different developmental tasks that he considers crucial for adolescents:

(1) modification of their unconscious concept of parental figures;
(2) need for assumption of appropriate standard of morality;
(3) identification with biologically determined sex role;
(4) permanent decisions and choices as to educational and occupational future.

Gardner seems particularly concerned about the second task, assumption of appropriate standards for morality. He feels that it is indeed difficult for the adolescent to solve his conflicts in regard to social morality in a society that is itself in conflict.

Any one of these three frames of reference is appropriate as an indication of the goals the adolescent must achieve in order to reach adult status. When these tasks have been accomplished they are then followed by other developmental tasks of adulthood, just as they were preceded by developmental tasks of childhood. Failure to accomplish any one of these tasks during adolescence may make it impossible for the individual to attempt the adult task which follows.

THE ADOLESCENT VIEWS ADOLESCENCE

Many of the earlier studies of adolescence were reported from an adult frame of reference. Adolescents were, of course, the subjects studied, but the interpretation of the results does not always reflect the way the adolescent actually views the situation. For example, many adults assume the existence of a dominant and widespread youth culture. This view regards the influence of the peer culture as more important to

* Adapted from *The Psychology of Adolescence* by J. E. Horrocks (Boston: Houghton Mifflin Company, 1962), by permission of the author and publisher.

the teen-ager than are adult values, which it may cause him to reject. Elkin and Westley (1955) challenge this assumption from findings in interviews with a group of adolescents in Montreal. The teen-agers did not appear to be independent and rejecting of adult values, and there is more continuity than discontinuity in their socialization. Although youth-culture elements do exist, they are less dominant than accepted family and authority guidance patterns. Boyer (1959) has further substantiated the point of view that parents are the teen-agers' most influential reference group. Rose (1956) has also investigated the importance of different membership reference groups. He studied four groups of rural high-school students in Minnesota and found that the family was the most frequently mentioned and presumably the most important reference group.

Recently, investigators have shifted the emphasis toward seeking information directly from adolescents. It is now accepted that the adolescent's own perception of his situation is at least as important as the adult's perception of him. This difference in perception is in fact responsible for much of the conflict between the adolescent and the adult. A simple everyday situation may illustrate this point. Sixteen-year-old John is told to go to the store by his mother. After some initial grumbling, he does as he was told, grumbling all the way to the store and still complaining after he returns. He is then given a lecture on his lack of cooperation, etc.

There are two ways of viewing this situation. Despite the complaining, John has done what he was told to do. His mother is annoyed by his attitude, which may seem to her an attempt to flout her authority. She reprimands him for this attitude, as she perceives it, and seems to forget that he actually obeyed her. John finds the reprimand unjust since in his perception of the situation the important fact is that he did go to the store.

This is not to suggest that the adolescent's perception is always the correct one, and that the adult's perception is always wrong. Each may have an unrealistic view of the role of the other that may increase misunderstanding between them. Often, too, adolescents think that adults undervalue and depreciate them, while the adults expect the teen-agers to overestimate their own maturity (Hess and Goldblatt, 1957).

The adolescent does not always have a clear concept of specific adult roles and therefore often has an unrealistic view of these roles (Hobart, 1958; Chapman, 1956; Crane, 1956). Often these unrealistic viewpoints are based on "idealistic" patterns of behavior as the adolescent perceives them rather than on the practical situation in which the adult actually finds himself. In studies of occupational choice, for example, teen-agers are often found to have a rather distorted view of an occupational field, very unlike the perception of the adult who is actually in the field.

Many factors influence the perceptions of the adolescent and the degree to which these perceptions vary from the adult view. Among these factors are sex, age, and physical maturity.

Disagreement between adolescent boys and girls was revealed in Payne's study (1956) on whether or not wives should work after marriage. Seventy-eight per cent of the boys were opposed to wives working, while 92 per cent of the girls indicated that they expected to work after marriage.

Perceptions change considerably with age. The younger adolescents' perception of the adult world differs from the older adolescents' view. The older adolescent is treated more like an adult himself and becomes increasingly involved and accepted in adult activities. Thus, the "secrets" of adulthood are more readily available to the older adolescent because of this acceptance. In general, girls appear to approximate adult standards at an earlier age than do boys.

The physical maturity of the individual is another influential factor, not always correlated with chronological age. The adolescent, male or female, who looks like an adult physically has a better chance of gaining adult acceptance than one who still has childish physical characteristics. Thus, an early-maturing adolescent, although young chronologically, is more readily accepted than a chronologically older late-maturer. Since girls mature physically about two years earlier than boys, this factor affects them sooner.

Evaluation of Adolescents' Comments

Almost every textbook written about the adolescent has presented certain views expressed by teen-agers themselves. This author has found that the same comments reappear in discussions with adolescents of all kinds. The following typical statements are presented and discussed to help the reader comprehend the feelings of individual adolescents. "I resent being categorized as an adolescent, as though the term meant something bad. A lot of adults seem to think all adolescents are juvenile delinquents."

This viewpoint is widely held among teen-agers and to some extent justified. The term "adolescent" does seem to create a negative response in most adults. Parents of younger children look forward with great concern to this stage in their children's development. They seem to expect that once this crucial stage is reached their calm, serene household will become a shambles. The adult culture does little to conceal this kind of reaction from the adolescent, and the adolescent may come to feel that he is expected to be emotionally disturbed.

It is also true that many adults do use such terms as "juvenile delinquent" too freely. This is a legally defined term correctly used only to describe those few whose socially deviant behavior actually involves law-breaking. Certainly the large majority of adolescents will never perform deviant acts of this nature. "If you read what is written about them, you think all adolescents are troublemakers."

Unfortunately much of what is written about adolescents is negative. Newspapers and magazines devote much space to stories of delinquency, unsuccessful teen-age marriage, automobile accidents involving adolescents, etc. They seldom feature the good deeds of teen-agers, which far outnumber the negative ones. Occasionally a feature story in a newspaper will deal with a positive aspect of adolescence, but the good behavior is often made to sound atypical. The reader should be aware that only a small percentage of adolescents is involved in the negative activities that are so widely publicized. "Parents think we have no respect for them, and that we fight with them constantly. Sure, we have arguments, but we don't think they're serious."

Here again we see a difference in the perceptions of the adult and the adolescent. Many adults are firmly convinced that their opinions are not respected as much as those of the peer group. The adolescent does not actually respond this way, as demonstrated by a number of research studies. Parental influence diminishes during adolescence, but usually not to the extent expressed by parents. The comment about conflict in the home is also well documented. Teen-agers are generally less concerned about or emotionally involved with arguments with parents than the parents are. "I can't seem to talk to my parents any more. We just don't talk the same language."

This comment may be much more important than it seems at first glance, since a similar comment is usually made by parents. It would appear that there is often a breakdown in communication at this stage. It is not simply that adults fail to understand the adolescents' jargon. Too often, they feel that the adolescent, because his experience is so much more limited, just doesn't know what he's talking about. "My parents tell me to choose my own vocation, and don't even like to discuss it with me."

This may be a true statement, but the adolescent may not understand why the parent reacts this way. So much has been written about parents' forcing children into occupations of the parents' choice that many today seem to lean over backward to avoid doing this. The adolescent, however, may take their attitude as evidence of lack of interest.

School guidance counselors are particularly aware of this situation, and often may help alleviate the problem by interpreting between parents and adolescents.

AN OVERVIEW

Most adolescents are not seriously concerned about their passage through this particular time span. Many experience a very pleasant, positive developmental pattern with relatively few anxieties. Others have severe problems relating to some areas of development and no problems in other areas. Some—relatively few—suffer severe conflict in all areas of adjustment and find the adolescent period a very painful one.

The reader must keep in mind that the kind of childhood the individual experienced will have much to do with his functioning as an adolescent. An individual who was well adjusted and secure during childhood is very likely to remain well adjusted during adolescence. He may have problems, but he will probably handle most of them adequately. On the other hand, the individual who was poorly adjusted during childhood will probably continue to be maladjusted through adolescence and even into adulthood.

REFERENCES

AUSUBEL, D. P. *Theory and Problems of Adolescent Development*. New York: Grune and Stratton, 1954.

BAYLEY, NANCY. "Normal Growth and Development." In Hoch, P. H., and Zubin, J., *Psychopathology of Childhood*. New York: Grune and Stratton, 1955.

BAYLEY, NANCY. "Individual Patterns of Development." *Child Development*, 27, 800-818, 1956.

BELL, H. M. *Youth Tell Their Story*. Washington, D.C.: American Council on Education, 1938.

BOYER, W. H. "A Survey of Attitudes, Opinions and Objectives of High School Students in the Milwaukee Area." *Journal of Educational Sociology*, 32, 344-348, 1959.

BRZEZINSKA, ZOFIA. "The Attitude of Today's Youth Towards Life." *Psychologia Wychawawcza* (Warsaw), 3, 150-166, 1960.

CAMERON, W. J. "A Study of Early Adolescent Personality." *Progressive Education*, 15, 553-563, 1938.

CHAPMAN, A. W. "Attitudes toward Legal Authorities by Juveniles." *Sociology and Social Research*, 40, 170-175, 1956.

CONSUMER REPORTS. "Teen-age Consumer." *Consumer Reports*, 32, 139-142, 1957.

CRANE, A. R. "Stereotypes of the Adult Held by Early Adolescents." *Journal of Educational Research*, 50, 227-230, 1956.

DAVIS, ALLISON, GITELSON, MAXWELL, WILLIAM, HENRY, and ROSS, HELEN. "Adolescents in American Culture." *University of Chicago Round Table*, no. 576, 1949.

DENNIS, WAYNE. "The Adolescent." In Carmichael, L., ed., *Manual of Child Psychology*, pp. 633-666. New York: John Wiley & Sons, Inc., 1946.

ELKIN, F., and WESTLEY, W. A. "The Myth of Adolescent Culture." *American Sociological Review*, 20, 680-684, 1955.

EL KOUSSY, A. H. "The Characteristics of Rural and Urban Adolescents in Egypt." *Vita Humana*, 219, 226, 1960.

GARDNER, GEORGE E. "Present-day Society and the Adolescent." *American Journal of Orthopsychiatry*, 27, 508-517, 1957.

GOOD, C. V. *Introduction to Educational Research*. New York: Appleton-Century-Crofts, 1959.

GREULICH, W. W., and PYLE, S. I. *Radiographic Atlas of Skeletal Development of the Hand and Wrist*. Stanford: Stanford University Press, 1950.

HALL, G. STANLEY. *Adolescence*, 2 vols. New York: Appleton-Century-Crofts, 1904.

HARRIS, DALE B. "Sex Differences in the Life Problems and Interests of Adolescents." *Child Development*, 30, 453-459, 1959.

HAVIGHURST, R. J. *Human Development and Education*. New York: Longmans, Green and Co., 1953.

HESS, R. D., and GOLDBLATT, I. "The Status of Adolescents in American Society: A Problem in Social Identity." *Child Development*, 28, 459-468, 1957.

HILLWAY, T. *Introduction to Research*. Boston: Houghton Mifflin, 1956.

HOBART, C. "Some Effects of Romanticism during Courtship on Marriage Role Opinions," *Sociology and Social Research*, 42, 336-343, 1958.

HORROCKS, J. E. *The Psychology of Adolescence*. Boston: Houghton Mifflin, 1962.

HSU, FRANCIS L. K., WATROUS, BLANCHE G., and LORK, EDITH M. "Culture Pattern and Adolescent Behavior." *International Journal of Social Psychiatry* (London), 7, 33-53, 1960-61.

HURLOCK, E. B. *Adolescent Development*, 2nd ed. New York: McGraw-Hill Book Co., Inc., 1955.

LINDQUIST, E. F., ed. *Educational Measurement*. Washington, D.C.: American Council on Education, 1951.

MEAD, MARGARET. *Coming of Age in Samoa*. New York: William Morrow & Co., 1928.

MILNER, E. "Effects of Sex Role and Social Status on the Early Adolescent Personality." *Genetic Psychology Monographs*, 40, 231-235, 1949.

MUSSEN, P. H., and JONES, M. C. "Self-conceptions, Motivations, and Interpersonal Attitudes of Late and Early Maturing Boys." *Child Development*, 28, 243-256, 1957.

NEW YORKER. "Profiles—a Caste, a Culture, a Market," II. *The New Yorker*, 34, (Nov.), 57, 1958.

OKAJI, ICHIRO. "Studies on Characteristics of Adolescents' Attitudes toward Life." *Japanese Journal of Educational Psychology,* 5, 7-13, 1958.

PAYNE, R. "Adolescents' Attitudes toward the Working Wife." *Marriage and Family Living,* 18, 334-339, 1956.

POWELL, MARVIN. "Age and Sex Differences in Degree of Conflict within Certain Areas of Psychological Adjustment." *Psychological Monographs,* vol. 6, no. 387, 1955.

POWELL, MARVIN, O'CONNOR, H. A., PARSLEY, K. M., and DEUTSCH, M. In press. "Are There Really Sex Differences in Achievement?" *Journal of Educational Research,* 1963.

ROSE, A. M. "Reference Group of Rural High School Youth." *Child Development,* 27, 351-363, 1956.

RUBE, P. "Adolescence: I. Is There a Problem of Adolescence?" *American Journal of Psychotherapy,* 9, 503-509, 1955.

SALISBURY, H. E. *The Shook-Up Generation.* New York: Harper & Brothers, 1958.

SCIENCE RESEARCH ASSOCIATES *Youth Inventory, Form S.* Chicago: Science Research Associates, 1959.

SHUTTLEWORTH, FRANK K. "The Adolescent Period: A Pictorial Atlas." *Monographs of the Society for Research in Child Development,* vol. 14, 1949.

SIMMONS, K. "The Brush Foundation Study of Child Growth and Development: II. Physical Growth and Development." *Monographs of the Society for Research in Child Development,* vol. 9, no. 1, 1944.

STÖRRING, G. E., and LÖWNAU, H. W. *"Problematic der Jugend in der Gegenwart"* (Concerning the Problem of Youth in the Present). *Praxis der Kinderpsychologie und Kinderpsychiatrie* (Goettingen), 7, 1-8, 1958.

STUART, H. C. "Normal Growth and Development during Adolescence." *New England Journal of Medicine,* 234, 666-672; 693-700; 732-738, 1946.

SUELLWOLD, FRITZ. "Empirical Studies concerning Problems of Adolescents in Germany and the U.S.A." *Psychologische Rundschau* (Basel), 10, 49-66, 1959.

SYMONDS, P. M. "Changes in Sex Differences in Problems and Interests of Adolescents with Increasing Age." *Journal of Genetic Psychology,* 50, 83-89, 1937.

SYMONDS, P. M. *Symonds Picture-Story Test.* New York: Teachers' College, Columbia University, 1948.

TOPP, R. F. "Let's Stop Down-grading Boys." Chicago: *Chicago Sunday Tribune Magazine,* Dec. 3, 1961.

VALADIAN, ISOBELL, STUART, H. C., and REED, R. R. "Studies of Illnesses of Children Followed from Birth to Eighteen Years." *Monographs of the Society for Research in Child Development,* vol. 26, No. 3, 1961.

VAN DALEN, D. B. *Introduction to Educational Research.* New York: McGraw-Hill Book Co., 1962.

CHAPTER 2

Physical Development
and the Physical Self-Image

The physical changes that occur in the period of adolescence, and especially the marked sexual changes, have already been mentioned among the reasons for regarding this period as distinct in the life of the individual. In addition to the actual physical changes, the psychological and emotional reactions that these changes produce are significant in the behavior patterns of the adolescent. In order to understand these reactions, it is first necessary to understand the nature of the physical changes.

PHYSICAL DEVELOPMENT

In spite of variations in defining the span of the adolescent time period, most authorities have agreed that it is correct to place its beginning at or near the advent of pubescence. This event indicates the beginning of the physiological changes that are peculiar to part of the life span and that occur in all geographic locales, regardless of society or culture. The term pubescence includes the great variety of bodily changes that occur in association with the sexual maturation of the human organism. These changes, all of which take place at about the same time in the individual's development, although each has its own rate, are primarily responsible for the differentiation between the adolescent and the younger child.

That these changes in height, weight, tissue, and endocrine functions are universal is evidence of the genetic nature of pubescence. Nevertheless, there is sufficient variability within the realm of the hereditary influences to permit different phylogenetic factors to appear at different times and at different rates in two individuals reared in the same geographic locale. The age at which girls reach the menarche is a good illustration of this point, with the average for this event generally about thirteen, but with a range varying from ten to as high as eighteen (Shuttleworth, 1949). However, an early study by Gould

(1932) pointed out a positive relationship between age of maturity of girls and that of their mothers.

The onset of pubescence in boys is far more difficult to assess since there is no such clear-cut indication as the menarche. Studies of osseous development (Greulich and Pyle, 1950) have been used extensively to show the characteristic picture of the development of the skeleton, and such studies have clearly demonstrated that boys develop later than girls do. There is irregularity in osseous development in some individuals, and in such cases it may be difficult to assign an exact osseous age. However, it is relatively easy to recognize those who are either advanced or retarded in osseous age as related to their chronological age. Recently Pyle, Stuart, Cornoni, and Reed (1961) reported on the ages of onset and completion of ossification of twenty-one centers and presented a Skeletal Maturity Chart to provide graphic norms for boys and for girls for comparison of age of onset and age of completion, with a Skeletal Age (hand) Graph for use with individual children. Prediction seems to be somewhat more accurate for girls than for boys. The difference between the sexes in this respect can be noted from these charts.

More recent studies have indicated the existence of a relationship between tooth calcification formation and other maturational factors. Lewis and Garn (1960) found positive but insignificant correlations between tooth formation and general growth in infancy, with the correlation becoming appreciably higher as adolescence approaches. These authors have also found sex differences in tooth calcification. They set up five stages of calcification for mandibular molars and premolars, and found that girls were advanced in each stage, particularly in the later ones. Girls, as compared to boys, are well advanced in tooth calcification by the tenth year. This particular difference in development cannot be attributed to the time of the sex-hormone secretion, as are many other growth patterns.

In extensive studies of puberty, based on direct observations of a relatively homogeneous British population consisting of 850 boys and 900 girls, Hogben et al. (1948) investigated the following criteria of puberty: axillary hair; pubic hair; voice; mammary glands; and physical measurements. Of these criteria, enlargement of the neck was found to be the most characteristic of male sexual development, and widening of the pelvic region was found to be most characteristic of female sexual development.

Individual Patterns of Development

In most studies of growth and development, the stress has been laid on structural and functional processes and the differences between the two. Bayley (1956) strongly urges that the individual differences in the temporal processes also be considered, since as structure and function develop and become differentiated from each other, they do so at different rates and at different times. In presenting mental and physical data from measures and observations of children from birth to twenty-five years, she indicates that each child's pattern of growth is unique.

Tyler (1957) has further emphasized this point with his findings, which, like Bayley's, were based on youngsters involved in the California Adolescent Growth Studies. From extensive analysis of the relationships between the growth patterns for five boys, he concluded that intra-individual differences are as much marked as are interindividual differences. These intra-individual differences cannot be attributed solely to the effects of cyclical growth in physical characteristics.

Much normative data relating to adolescent growth and development are available that provide a general frame of reference but make individual deviations from the norm even more striking by comparison. The reader will be wise to remember that the "average" adolescent is only a hypothetical creature, since no single individual is likely to be average in all the multitude of developmental processes involved in the growth of the complex human organism.

PHYSICAL GROWTH

So much research in the area of physical development has been done since the early part of this century that it would seem to have been thoroughly explored. Yet within the last decade more investigators than ever have concerned themselves with studies in this area, often using newly developed techniques more precise than those available to earlier investigators.

According to Tuddenham and Snyder (1947), three major trends in recent research in physical growth emphasize: (1) longitudinal investigation of the same children over a long period of time; (2) investigation of morphological variations among individuals, and of relationships between physique, temperament, disease, and physical capacity; and (3) integration of research findings from various sources. This last-mentioned aspect of research has become even more important as increasing numbers of studies of adolescents in other societies are becoming available. Tuddenham and Snyder reviewed the studies done during the 1940's and discussed research dealing with the influences exerted upon growth by geographical, racial, socioeconomic, temporal, disease, heredity, prenatal, and pubescent factors. They further reported studies on growth in stature and weight; studies on growth of the head, pelvis, extremities, skeletal ossification, dentition, and body tissues; and also studies on evaluation of progress in physical status and growth, physique and morphological variation, and contributions to the theory and techniques of research.

Shock (1947) has indicated that from 1944 to 1947 areas in which research on physiological factors in development was most active were: the influence of prenatal conditions upon fetal and neonatal development; the developmental effects of anoxia at birth; the effects of diet upon growth and development of the individual; and the physiological factors in the development of the adolescent. Jensen (1950) reported that between 1948 and 1949 alone six hundred pertinent studies were published on the metabolic functions of the endocrine glands.

This would appear to be an overwhelming amount of research in this area, yet most of the studies reported in this chapter have been done since the above-mentioned reviews appeared. Despite the tremendous body of information already available, much more research is necessary to develop even greater understanding of the problems related to the physical aspect of adolescent development.

In studies of physical growth for any period in the life span, curves are presented that are based on averages in order to show general development trends. As was previously suggested, such curves must be

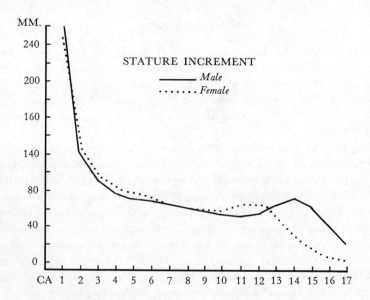

FIGURE 3. Stature increment according to chronological age
From Simmons (1944), by permission of the author and the Society for Research in Child Development

interpreted carefully, since the developmental pattern for any given individual may vary tremendously from the average. Caution is particularly necessary in viewing growth during the adolescent time period because of the differences in development between those who mature early and those who mature late.

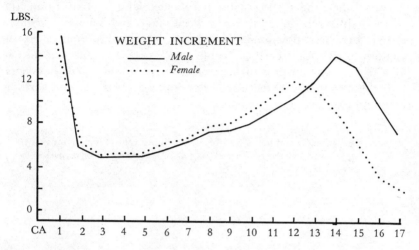

FIGURE 4. Weight increment according to chronological age
From Simmons (1944), by permission of the author and the Society for Research in Child Development

Height and Weight

Typical of the curves of adolescent development are those reported by Simmons (1944) in his study of the average growth figures obtained from repeated measurements of the height and weight of a large number of adolescents (see Figures 3 and 4). The sample in his study was chosen from better-than-average socioeconomic levels, but his averages resemble those presented in a number of earlier studies (Dearborn and Rothney, 1941; Ministry of Health of Canada, 1942). In the data relating to height in Figure 3, there appears to be a sharp decrease in the growth rate from the first to the second year, with the curves almost reaching a plateau during the early school years. The curve for females starts to accelerate at about age nine and shows a slight increase to age twelve, where it again decelerates. For boys the acceleration in the curve appears about two years later, at age eleven, and continues to rise until age fourteen, when it too decelerates. These curves rather clearly illustrate the often-observed fact that, between the ages of eleven and thirteen, because of earlier maturation, girls are taller than boys.

The data for weight presented in Figure 4 shows a somewhat different picture, particularly during the adolescent period. Again, as was true of height, the greatest deceleration takes place between the first and second years, with the curves then almost reaching a plateau until the fifth year. There is a rather steady acceleration of the curves from this point until age twelve for the males and age fourteen for the females, when the curves again sharply decelerate. Here, again, the two-year difference in maturing between males and females is evident.

Meredith and Boynton (1937) have developed norms based on eighteen body measurements. Table 1 shows sex differences in the age at which maximum growth occurs in the areas measured; and here, too, the two-year differential in development between the sexes is readily apparent.

TABLE 1. Segmental and sex differences according to year of maximum growth
Extracted from Meredith and Boynton (1937), by permission of the authors and Human Biology

	Year of maximum growth	
Measurement	*Boys*	*Girls*
Weight	15	12
Height	14	12
Sitting height	15	12
Shoulder breadth	14	12
Pelvic breadth	—	13
Hip breadth	14	—
Thoracic circumference	14	11

Hansman and Maresch (1961) have reported findings on skeletal maturation based on the extensive longitudinal growth study of the Child Research Council. They have attempted to remove the stigma of "retarded bone age" by demonstrating the wide variability of carpal ossification compatible with health, as well as the sex differences in ossification. Girls had eight visible carpal centers by eleven years of age, while these centers were not all visible for boys until fourteen years of age. Children whose skeletal ages are consistently above the group median by more than twelve months are early-maturers, while those whose skeletal age is twelve months below the group median are late-maturers. Those within twelve months above or below the group median are a variable group of average- , early- , and late-maturers.

Boys who mature very early, and to a lesser degree those who mature later than average, show less variation in stature than those who are only somewhat early in adolescent development. Except in the case of those who mature very early, these variability differences are paralleled in the heights of the mothers and fathers. For those who mature very early, there is far less variability in height than is found among their parents (Livson and McNeill, 1961).

Solley (1960) has plotted chronological age, weight, and height, and combinations of these measures, as reflected in body shape, body, developmental age, and ratio of physical development. These were plotted over a five-year period for children in grades one to eight on the Wetzel Grid (a graph on which height and weight are plotted and from which future growth is predicted). Among other findings, it was reported that the number of development levels achieved by the student in a given period of time is a significant factor in marked deviations in growth curves from normal during the same period. Excessive changes in physique and in speed of growth were reflected significantly in ratio of physical development. Some correlations among factors included in the study increased and others decreased as grade levels increased. Some doubt was cast on the value of developmental level as an improved measure of body size.

Differences in Growth Patterns

A good deal of research has been devoted to the marked physical differences between children of the same chronological age, particularly in relation to the age at which the spurt in development begins and ends, and to the magnitude of this spurt. Davenport (1926) first reported these differences, and many later studies have explored and developed these areas further. The Shuttleworth study (1938) showing yearly increments of gain for different groups of girls selected on the basis of their chronological age has become almost a classic and has been reproduced in many textbooks written on adolescent psychology. These studies serve to emphasize further the point that children move through their adolescent growth period at widely different chronological ages. However, the pattern of growth for any particular measurement follows the same sequence regardless of when the sequence begins. This applies equally for both sexes in height, weight, and almost all other measurable dimensions, particularly since there appears to be considerable conformity between the patterns of height and weight and these other dimensions.

Muhsam (1947), in his re-analysis of data from an earlier study, also shows the correlation in growth. Selected results showed that: (1) growth during different periods is "compensatory," i.e., girls who grow more than average during one period grow less than average during another; (2) growth of girls can be divided into two periods, one in late childhood and the second during pubescence, with evidence demonstrating that those who grow much during one year of either period, grow much during the whole period, with the converse also being true;

(3) for weight, both growth and the compensatory effect begin one or two years later than for height.

Ellis (1947) studied 208 boys on the basis of maturity (i.e., whether nonpubescent, pubescent, or adolescent), comparing the mean height and weight of boys in a higher-maturity grade with those of boys of the same age but less mature. Height and weight of pubescent boys are greater than for nonpubescent boys, and height and weight for adolescent boys are greater than for pubescent boys, when all the boys are of the same chronological age. Boys reaching puberty late are on the average smaller and lighter than their earlier-maturing contemporaries.

Shuttleworth's (1937) study offered evidence of the variability in age of reaching maximum growth, demonstrating the age range between the earliest- and latest-maturing individuals, and the sex differences that exist. Fewer than 4 per cent of the girls studied reached the maximum between $10\frac{1}{4}$ and $10\frac{3}{4}$ years, and fewer than 4 per cent reached a maximum between $14\frac{1}{4}$ and $14\frac{3}{4}$ years, while more than 50 per cent of the group reached the maximum between $11\frac{3}{4}$ and $13\frac{3}{4}$ years. The pattern for boys was essentially similar, but the maximums were reached about two years later by boys.

Environment and Growth

Not only can one find substantial variability among individuals within one geographic locale, but there are also differences among individuals in different locales and even in different regions within a geographical area. Whitacre and Grimes (1959) reported on measurements of more than 6000 boys and girls in four cities in Texas, two in the northern part of the state and two in the southern part. They found that the children from the two southern cities were larger on each of the eleven measures used for all ages combined, and for each age separately. Since the differences in food consumption, socioeconomic level, and other variables could be ruled out as possible influences, these authors proposed that climatic variations between the cities be considered as possible reasons for the differences.

Using samples more widely separated geographically, Foll (1958), in a study of a large group of children from Upper Burma, who ranged from ten to fifteen years of age, found the average age of the menarche to be 14.4 years, which is generally later than the averages previously mentioned. Ellis (1950) compared Nigerian girls with a control series in Great Britain and found the Nigerian girls to be significantly later in reaching the menarche than the British girls. The degree of maturity of Nigerian schoolboys of various ages, however, was essentially similar to that of the control boys in Britain.

Although these studies seem to confirm the earlier findings of Mills

(1937) that pubescence appears earlier in temperate areas than in northern and tropical climates, there is still much disagreement about the effects of climate. Mueller (1932), in a study of Japanese girls, did not find an earlier menarche for these girls than for North American girls; he also noted that studies done in India, Egypt, and Japan have also failed to demonstrate the effects, if any, of climatic conditions on early or late pubescence.

Socioeconomic factors, as they relate to various aspects of development, have been studied by a number of investigators. Binning (1958) studied three groups of Saskatoon school children between the ages of six and fifteen. Groups 1 and 2 came from districts that were relatively similar, while group 3 came from a district that was different ethnically and lower socioeconomically. The children in district 3 were generally shorter and lighter than those of like age in the other two districts. Keddie (1958) studied growth factors of Scottish children of different socioeconomic groups at ages five, nine, thirteen, and sixteen. He found a variety of differences in height and weight, generally favoring the upper socioeconomic group, and concluded that although differences of stature between children of different socioeconomic classes may have been reduced in recent decades, the differences may still be greater than is generally realized.

There is, perhaps, more agreement on the relationship of nutrition to early or late development than on the other factors thus far discussed. Breckenridge and Vincent (1955) have devoted considerable space in their book to the topic of nutrition as it relates to physical growth and have concluded that adequate diet is not only related to physical growth but to behavior and mental performance as well. Greulich (1958) feels that good nutrition and generally favorable environmental conditions hasten the onset of pubescence to some extent, with the converse also true. He compared stature, weight, sitting height, and skeletal age of more than 800 American-born Japanese children living in California with the corresponding characteristics of a group of children of the same age and sex living in Japan. The California children were more advanced in all these characteristics than the comparable children in Japan, with these differences being of even greater magnitude than he had anticipated. It would appear that these differences must be attributed to the less adequate diet and the less than optimal environmental conditions existing in Japan.

Henton (1958) has further emphasized the part the environment plays in development in his attempt to find racial differences in the age of the menarche in children living in the same geographic locale. He studied 133 white girls and 801 Negro girls attending school in Montgomery, Alabama, and found no significant difference in the mean age of menstruation in the two groups. The generally equal nutrition and similar environment afforded the two racial groups apparently negate any differences that might have been present if the American girls had been compared with African Negro girls.

ORGANIC GROWTH

Ausubel (1954) has presented schematically the different types of physical changes and their interrelationships, grouping the physical changes that occur at puberty into three levels according to the antecedent factors that bring them about (see Figure 5). This kind of representation

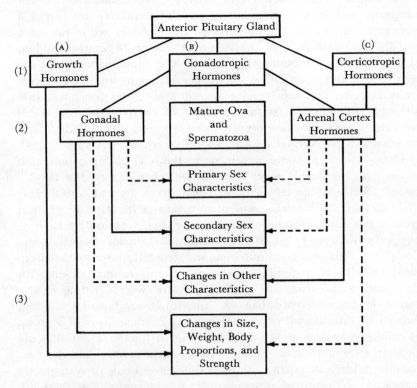

FIGURE 5. Types of physical changes occurring during pubescence and their interrelationships

From Ausubel (1954), by permission of the author and Grune and Stratton

would perhaps convince the layman of the "painfulness" of the adolescent growth period, particularly if he views it from a sociological point of view, in which the major concerns center around the relationships of the various organic changes to the demands of the society in which the child is growing up. Biologically, too, the emphasis may be placed on the "stressfulness" of development, but in terms of physiological imbalances in body structure and function related to hormonal development and to skeletal development. A combination of the sociological and biological points of view would probably best describe these disturbances, when and if they occur.

Eichorn and McKee (1958), using physiological data from the Adolescent Growth Study, have attempted to test the hypothesis that adolescence is characterized by a temporary decrease in physiological stability. They found an increase in intra-individual variability for systolic and diastolic blood pressure and for pulse rate from age twelve to age seventeen or eighteen, but a decrease in variability of basal metabolism rate. There was little systematic change in variability in body temperature. Aside from these changes, there was no evidence of heightened variability for the girls, and only slight indication was found for the boys.

These same authors (McKee and Eichorn, 1953) also attempted to study seasonal variations in physiological functions through an analysis of the basal metabolism rate, oral body temperatures, basal pulse rate, respiratory rate, and systolic blood pressure. There was evidence of a fall in basal metabolism and pulse rates during the spring, followed by a rise in these rates in the autumn. Some evidence, although less clearcut, of an opposite effect in body temperature was found for boys but not for girls.

In an earlier study of instability in the physiological processes, Shock (1946) found marked fluctuations in basal metabolism coinciding with the beginning of the puberal cycle; an increase and then a decrease in pulse rate for girls just before the menarche; and an increase and then a leveling off in systolic blood pressure. These changes do not appear to be cause for any great concern; they are commonplace and are normally shown in the process of adjusting to this new phase of more rapid growth.

McKee and Eichorn (1955) have attempted to find evidence that might confirm a general hypothesis of growth and rhythm. They carefully examined intra-individual correlations between several indices of physical and physiological growth in adolescents. Although between 40 and 50 per cent of the cases showed a pattern of interrelationships identical with the pattern indicated by the group data, the relationships were not sufficiently great to support the concept of general growth rhythms.

The development of the endocrine glands and the resulting endocrine problems in adolescence have been studied by a number of investigators. Richardson (1949) has done a brief survey of endocrine disorders in adolescence that touches on the early onset of adolescence with premature puberty, disorders of adolescence associated with the onset of puberty, delayed puberty in girls, disorders of the breasts in girls, delayed puberty in boys, breast changes in boys, obesity in adolescence, and the thyroid gland and adolescence.

Most of these areas of disturbance are discussed to some extent in various portions of this chapter, but with the general emphasis on the psychological rather than the physiological problems. This type of emphasis is suggested by Gordon (1948) in his study of obesity, short stature, tall structure, gonadal disturbance, gynecomastis, and thyroid disturbances. Although these are endocrine problems, he feels that the disturbances related to them are not inherent but are due primarily to environmental factors, particularly emotional ones. These disturbances, therefore, may be helped not only by endocrine therapy but by good mental hygiene and if necessary by psychotherapy.

PHYSICAL FUNCTIONING

The numerous and rapid changes that have been described as taking place in the physical organism naturally affect function to some degree. The areas that have been most studied are the general health of adolescents, including their susceptibility to disease, and the effects of rapid growth on physical strength and motor coordination.

Adolescent Health and Disease

There has often been undue alarm concerning the physiological changes previously discussed, and older reference sources, such as Diven's "Peculiarities of Disease in Childhood" (1923), pointed out that there were many dangers to health resulting from the changes, including the appearance of mental disorders. It now seems apparent that this point of view was very much overstated and overemphasized, yet casual observation of the adolescent may still lead one to support such a concept. The presence of acne, the disproportionate development of the body, the apparent awkwardness, and the presence of excess fat could easily be regarded as indicating difficulties in development. If, however, the physiological reasons for the presence of these characteristics are clearly understood, there is not great cause for serious concern. Although such characteristics may not be sources of physical disturbances, they are often the basis for psychological problems in relation to the physical self-concept of the individual. This aspect of adjustment is discussed in detail later in this chapter.

There are, however, some problems of health and disease more or less peculiar to the adolescent time period, and some that are more serious in adolesence than in earlier childhood. Mumps, for example, is much more serious during adolescence than during childhood, since it can cause sterility, particularly if there is bilateral testicular swelling. Heart damage, perhaps incurred earlier in childhood, may restrict the adolescent's physical activities, and his adjustment to these restrictions may result in social or emotional problems. Some diseases, including diphtheria, seem to be more common with adolescents than with younger children or adults; young children are more likely to be immunized against such diseases, while adolescents have not developed an adult immunity. Tuberculosis has been found to be a frequent cause of death among adolescents, especially during the later adolescent period, and this fact appears to have some relationship with certain aspects of gonadal secretion (Ausubel, 1954).

General hormonal imbalance, which is most common during adolescence, also seems to be related to the greater prevalence of diabetes and goiter conditions at that period and may well be related to the presence of acne. Such imbalance, as well as other conditions of the organism, also seems to be related to menstrual difficulties, such as pain, irregularity of flow, etc., which girls encounter even after the menstrual cycle has become well established. Although many of the difficulties encountered by adolescent girls in pregnancy are psychological in nature, physiological factors, such as toxemia, have been related to such disturbances.

There are adolescents, just as there are younger children and adults, who are characterized as "delicate." This term is used to describe individuals who without a diagnosis of any specific disease are considered physically unfit to live a full, active life (Hunter, 1949). Such chronic subnormal health has often been related to nutritional difficulties, but evidence from findings based on limited diets imposed by rationing during World War II does not seem to support this as a meaningful reason. Possibly there are cardiac-vascular difficulties associated with this condition that are not yet sufficiently understood. Hunter suggests that from the psychosomatic standpoint the condition may be the resultant of a subconscious desire on the part of the child and the parent for a prolongation of infantile dependency. This same thought has been expressed by others and tends to emphasize the emotional rather than the physical aspects of such "delicateness." Although only a very small portion of the adolescent population is so diagnosed, the condition is well worth noting and deserves further investigation.

Despite the incidence of the various ailments and difficulties discussed, the adolescent period cannot be regarded as unusually subject to illnesses, particularly as compared to earlier childhood. Bayer and Snyder (1950) have studied the illness experience of 126 normal chil-

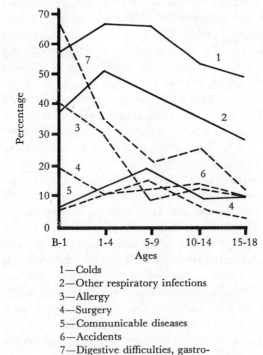

1—Colds
2—Other respiratory infections
3—Allergy
4—Surgery
5—Communicable diseases
6—Accidents
7—Digestive difficulties, gastro-
     intestinal and abdominal
     disturbances

FIGURE 6. Disease rates at different ages
        From Bayer and Snyder (1950), by permission of the authors and Child
        Development

dren over an eighteen-year period and have compared their findings
with national and local public-health statistics wherever available.
Every period of childhood was found to have its special health hazards,
but none of them appeared too serious when ordinary care was given,
and there was no striking increase in the number and severity of illnesses during adolescence (see Figure 6). Most recently Valadian,
Stuart, and Reed (1961) have done an extensive longitudinal study of
the illnesses of 134 children who were followed up from birth to age
eighteen. The data, presented in Figure 7, further demonstrate the
fact that there are no substantial increases in disease and illness during
adolescence. Nonetheless these authors have done an extensive analysis
of those illnesses that are present during early adolescence (ages ten to

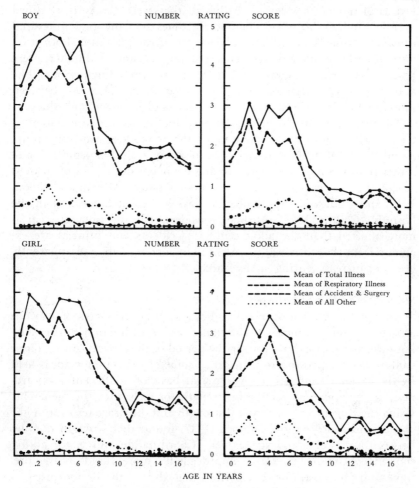

FIGURE 7. Means for total illnesses and for three groups of illnesses by year of age
*From Valadian, Stuart, and Reed (1961), by permission of the authors and
the Society for Research in Child Development*

fourteen) and late adolescence (ages fourteen to eighteen). For the most
part the differences in illness experiences between early and late adolescence were not great, although some sharp differences did exist. In
each of the two time periods, boys had a considerably larger number of
total illnesses than did girls.

Boys had about the same number of respiratory illnesses during each
period, but somewhat fewer girls had them during the late period.
Generally, the number of communicable diseases is much lower for
both boys and girls in adolescence than during the preceding periods
(two to six years and six to ten years); most of these diseases were classi-

fied as of moderate severity. Although they were generally classified as mild illnesses, boys had about three times as many gastrointestinal illnesses during early and late adolescence as the girls did. Both sexes were alike in number of accidents and surgery, and again there were fewer cases during adolescence than during the preceding periods. The authors of this study stress the importance of the variations between individual children in the various categories of both age and illness.

The mortality rate during adolescence doubles for the fifteen-to-nineteen-year age group as compared to the ten-to-fourteen-year group. Ausubel (1954) feels that one should analyze the "morbidity" rate rather than the mortality rate. Basing his belief on studies of sickness during the war years as it relates to school absence (Altman and Ciocci, 1945) and studies of the number of days in bed at home and in the hospital (Collins, 1945), Ausubel considers that the preadolescent is more affected than the adolescent. If accidents and injuries are excluded from the statistical reports, the incidence of disease apparently does not increase during adolescence.

Strength and Coordination

An appreciable number of studies has been reported on various aspects of strength, motor performance, and coordination during adolescence, and particularly during the period of the growth spurt. These studies have helped to prove incorrect some of the common ideas held by the layman concerning the physical basis of adolescent awkwardness, or the apparent decline in strength for girls after the menarche. Using the Rogers test for physical strength and the Brace tests for motor ability and coordination, Dimock (1937) found that strength doubles between age twelve and age sixteen. Coordination and motor ability showed continuous moderate improvement, more rapid in the prepubescent and postpubescent periods than during the period just preceding maximum growth. There was no real evidence that awkwardness is associated with rapid growth. The data from Espenschade's extensive study (1940) of adolescent performance on a series of motor performance tests are presented in Figure 8 and show rather clearly that the mean performance for boys on the tests increased steadily, with an increment pattern similar to that of growth in standing height. Girls showed an increase up to about age thirteen, but little change, and in some instances an actual decline, thereafter. The plateau or decline shown for girls may have a cultural rather than a physical cause. There were, of course, marked differences in all tests and within both sexes, but after age 13.8 boys surpassed girls in all the tests, with the difference increasing with age.

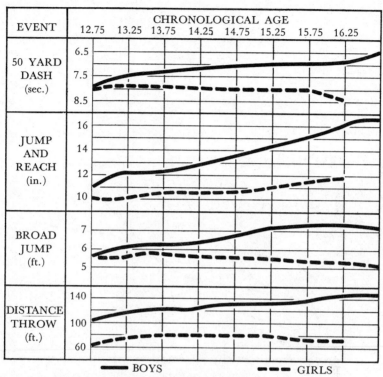

FIGURE 8. Increase in athletic skills during adolescence
From Espenschade (1940), by permission of the author and the Society for Research in Child Development

Jones (1949) analyzed semiannual records of 89 boys and 87 girls (ages 11 to 17.5) on right grip, left grip, pull, and thrust, as measures of dynamometric strength. The effect of early and late sexual maturing was noted, with a comparative study of the puberal growth spurt in strength as a maturity indicator. Correlational methods, group comparisons, and individual case studies were used in studying the personal and social significance of physical ability (see Figure 9). Jones sought results that could be applied in educational guidance. To obtain a strength index, Willgoose (1950) used a battery of strength tests that involved the essential large-muscle groups of the body. He reported a positive correlation between this index and motor coordination during adolescence as measured by the standing broad jump, the 30-yard crab race, and the 50-yard dash.

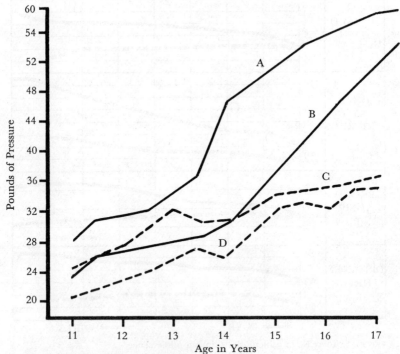

FIGURE 9. Maturity and strength
From Jones (1949), by permission of the author and University of California Publications in Child Development

Muscular fatigue of 200 boys and girls ranging from eight to seventeen years of age was studied by Rich (1960). He found that the older children were stronger and exhibited greater fatigue. At age eight boys and girls had equal rates of strength-loss per muscle contraction. Older boys tended to reach fatigue level more rapidly than younger children, because they exerted more strength initially, but older girls reached their fatigue level more slowly.

In an extensive study done in Finland, Ghesquiere (1958) investigated the physical performance of 177 boys between ten and twenty-one years of age in relation to their height, weight, and age. The physical performance measurements included vital capacity, expiratory force, maximum breathing capacity, hand grip, back lift, and vertical jump. Regression analysis was used to determine the dependence of performance scores on height and weight; and it was observed that by keeping the data constant within the range of one year the effects of age are partially cancelled out. With age held constant, the improvement in hand grip seems to be entirely dependent on gain in weight, while the major factor for the vertical jump is height. Vital capacity, maximum breathing capacity, and back lift are determined by both height and weight but to a varying extent. Ghesquiere has attempted to develop several prediction monograms where the average performance can be forecast on one year's age group, given height and weight.

SEXUAL MATURATION

The wide range of variability in development discussed previously is most evident in the appearance and size of the primary and secondary sex characteristics. The end result of the development of the primary sex characteristics is the capability to reproduce. This pattern is well developed by the end of adolescence, as is evidenced in the male difference of structure in motile spermatazoa in the semen. There seems to be about a four-year spread in the difference in development in testicular growth between advanced and retarded boys.

Male Sex Characteristics

For the male, the primary sex characteristics are the testes, epididymus, the seminal vesicle, the prostate, the genital passages, and the penis. The secondary sex characteristics, which include the pubic, axillary, and facial hair and the quality of the voice, appear at different intervals after the rapid growth of the primary sex organs has begun. These changes, and the bone and muscle changes associated with them, continue well into the postpubescent stage.

Although biologically the development of the primary sex characteristics is of major importance, there is greater concern among adolescents about the appearance of the secondary sex characteristics because these are more obvious to the observation of their peers. This emotional concern is discussed later in this chapter.

The appearance of the secondary sex characteristics was studied by Greulich (1942), who demonstrated the sequential development of hair in the male, which appeared first in the pubic region, followed by the presence of axillary hair, and then the appearance of the facial hair which starts on the upper lip and then spreads medially. Another pattern of this sort that sometimes appears later is the change in the hairline on the forehead, where the hair starts to recede.

The patterns associated with the change in the voice and with development of the breast area are also important. The voice change, so very obvious to the listener, has usually been completed by about age fifteen, when a stable, deep tone is achieved. Apparent development in the breast region, although not present in all adolescent males and variable in those in whom it does appear, is usually caused by development in the tissue structure underlying the areola and usually disappears in later adolescence, although it may continue into adulthood.

Female Sex Characteristics

The primary sex characteristics of the female are the uterus and the ovaries. These have not been as thoroughly studied as the growth of the penis in the male, but the growth pattern is apparently similar: slow development during the prepubescent period and most rapid development during postpubescence. An early study by Harris and others (1930) indicated that the ovaries have attained only 30 per cent of their ultimate weight at the time of the menarche. Apparently the full growth of the ovaries and of the male testes is not required for reproduction to be possible.

The secondary sex characteristics of the female include the pelvis and hips, the breasts, pubic hair, and axillary hair, which develop in that order. Greulich and Thomas (1944) have studied pelvic development by means of X rays and found that the pelvis grows slowly and symmetrically during the prepubescent period, and rapidly with considerable change in shape during pubescence, requiring about eighteen months to complete its development. The rounding out of the hips is caused by the broadening of the pelvis and by the increased fat in the subcutaneous tissue in this area of the body. These changes generally occur after the first signs of breast development, are well along at the time of the menarche, and end soon after this time.

The breast seems to develop in three stages, the bud stage at about eleven or twelve years of age, followed by the development of the "primary breast," and finally the enlargement of the breast into the "mature" breast. Usually the girl is in the primary stage when menstruation first occurs, but she could be in either of the other two stages at this point. Breast size and rate of breast development, although biologically determined, are sources of much psychological concern to females, since the development is obvious to the view of others.

There is less extensive hair growth for females than for males, and the axillary hair appears appreciably later than the pubic hair. Facial hair, although present, is usually not very obvious, although if extensive facial hair occurs, it may become a source of emotional concern for the female. Just before the axillary hair appears, the sweat glands enlarge; the characteristic odor associated with these glands becomes pronounced in early adolescence. An increased perspiration related to the menstrual cycle is particularly noticeable during menstruation.

The sebaceous glands increase in size and activity during puberty, and the development and activity of these glands may be related to the presence of acne during adolescence. There seems to be more activity in these glands than is appropriate for their size, and they fail to drain properly. As a result blackheads form, and continued activity by the glands after the opening has been blocked causes pimples. Small hairs also develop in the hair follicles associated with the sebaceous glands, and acne often results. This condition may be partly caused by an excess of male hormone.

THE PHYSICAL SELF-IMAGE

Obviously, this discussion has not covered all aspects of physical growth and development, and there are many other research studies relating to these topics besides those cited. The material presented was chosen to give the reader a fairly comprehensive overview of major aspects of physical growth and development and to enable him to understand better the complexity of this kind of growth in adolescence.

Although this information is of great value, it is perhaps more important to be aware of the individual psychological and emotional reactions that result from these developmental patterns and the changes therein. More and more, we are becoming aware that it is important to know not only how the individual grows and develops, but how he views and responds to such growth and development. Too often, the adult who has reached a state in which physical changes are almost imperceptible and whose image of his physical self has become reasonable and realistic is unable to understand why an adolescent is deeply concerned about some physical characteristic or change that now seems to him unimportant or meaningless. The remainder of this chapter is concerned with adolescents' reactions to the various physical growth patterns as they perceive these in relation to themselves.

Concepts of the Ideal Physical Self

It is characteristic of all human beings to have a physical self-image. During most of the life span, this image changes slowly because the changes in the body are relatively imperceptible and can pass unnoticed. During adolescence, however, such rapid changes take place in the body proportions, size, facial appearance, and development of the primary and secondary sex characteristics that the individual must make major adjustments in his body image, and the rapid changes cause increased concern about reaching some culturally determined ideal.

The adolescent's physical self-image is based to a large extent on cultural norms, and particularly on the interpretation of these norms that is accepted as the standard by the peer group. Thus girls often have a culturally accepted image of femininity represented by some glamorous movie or television star, and boys often select an athlete as the ideal masculine image, although they too are often influenced by actors who are considered "masculine" men. These images are rather generally perceived as ultimate goals that may be reached in adulthood, and the more immediate ideal physical image is likely to be based on the physique of another adolescent. A well-developed, well-groomed adolescent girl is often the ideal physical image for other adolescent girls of the same age and may be even more of an ideal to younger girls. A well-built, athletic, handsome male adolescent serves as the physical self-image for his peer group and for younger males. Not only are the physiological aspects of the ideals' development important, but their way of dress and caring for their hair and the kind of physical activities in which they engage are all imitated by those who seek to be like them.

Yet these very adolescents who serve as ideal physical figures to others are not always pleased with certain aspects of their own development, a fact well worth noting and illustrating.

John G. is sixteen years old, six feet tall, and weighs 170 pounds, all solid muscle. To most of the other males in his tenth grade he is the ideal physical specimen, one whom most of them would like to resemble. John has been an excellent athlete, well coordinated and graceful, and greatly interested in sports. Despite all this, John is very unhappy with his own development and feels that something is wrong with the way he is growing. Evidence of this disturbance first became apparent to others when John suddenly dropped off the various athletic teams and even refused to attend the required physical-education class. He finally admitted that the reason for all this was unwillingness to take showers with the other boys, which was due, he sheepishly admitted, to his feeling that his genital organs were undersized.

This example will illustrate the difficulty of identifying some of the problems that may arise as a result of physical growth. To the adult or peer group observer, John appears to have all the qualities, physical and otherwise, needed to make a good adjustment, and only a very perceptive individual could have understood why he reacted as he did.

Emotional Effects of Deviations from the Ideal

Since the importance of bodily change to the adolescent is a major factor in the development of his self-image, one can accept the fact that deviations from some "cultural" norm can cause emotional difficulties. Every six months Stolz and Stolz (1944) questioned a number of the children involved in the California Adolescent Growth Study about any worries they might have about physical growth. Some 30 per cent of the boys expressed concern about lack of size, fatness, poor physiques, lack of muscular strength, and/or unusual facial features. The boys also expressed concern about acne, skin blemishes, bowed legs, and size of genitalia. Of the girls, almost 46 per cent gave evidence of body anxieties. Girls were generally concerned with being too tall or too short, being fat, having unusual facial features, squinting, needing to wear glasses, being thin, and having small breasts. The authors feel that these percentages are minimal and that more adolescents than the study showed have some degree of disturbance at one time or another in the adolescent growth period.

Frazer and Lisonbee (1950) investigated the response of teen-agers to descriptions of their physiques and the concern they felt about these characteristics. Their results are presented in Table 2.

TABLE 2. Per cent of 580 tenth-grade boys and girls giving descriptions of their physiques and per cent expressing concern about the characteristic described*

From Frazier and Lisonbee (1950), by permission of the authors and School Review

Description	Per cent so describing themselves		Per cent expressing concern	
	Boys	Girls	Boys	Girls
Thin	21	16	22	48
Heavy	13	30	3	55
Short	26	27	39	22
Tall	28	22	4	49
Development early	19	24	6	15
Development slow	17	13	40	36

*This table is read as follows: 21 per cent of the boys and 16 per cent of the girls described themselves as thin; 22 per cent of the boys and 48 per cent of the girls so describing themselves expressed concern about this characteristic.

There has been much investigation of the emotional effects of pubescence on the individual's adjustment. In particular, the studies of the time at which the menarche occurs have offered valuable information concerning the effects of this event on the individual girl's self-image. Cultural factors, of course, have a good deal of influence on how the individual responds to the changes related to pubescence, and these factors vary appreciably in different countries (Abel and Joffee, 1950). There is general agreement that puberty is a sociological phenomenon, not one caused by constitutional factors alone. However, these cultural influences and effects need not result in unhappiness, feelings of inadequacy, and/or neurosis in the individual (Bondy, 1956).

Hubble (1958) has discussed the problems of puberty without specifically defining the term. He finds that among boys the practice of masturbation, variations in strength of sexual impulse, and occurrence of transient homosexuality are concomitant manifestations of normal sexual development, and warns adults against making any reaction to these activities that might cause serious problems to develop. As an illustration, many adults still tell their teen-age sons that masturbation can result in insanity. This statement is a misconception with no factual basis, but it can be frightening to a youngster who because of natural sex impulses is beginning to indulge in this kind of activity. Thus what might be a relatively normal behavior pattern becomes highly emotionally involved, and serious psychological disturbances may result.

TIMING OF PUBESCENCE

The timing involved in reaching pubescence is of major importance in the development of the adolescent's self-image. This self-image is likely to be based to a large extent on how others, particularly adults, respond to him. Thus, an indivdual who reaches pubescence early is more likely to be treated as an adult by adults because of his size and level of development. The late-maturer, on the other hand, remains relatively small and underdeveloped during the early teens, and adults tend to treat him more as if he were a child. However, except when athletics are involved, the adults' view is not based on size alone. A study by Latham (1951) of more than 800 male junior-high-school students' choices of leaders illustrates this point rather well. The students were first classified by the Crampton Criteria, according to level of sexual maturity, and then were rated by their teachers as to leadership, with the ratings subdivided into three categories: elective, appointive, and athletic leaders. At ages thirteen and fourteen consistent significant differences were found among the athletic leaders, with more of the mature than the immature boys listed as leaders. In the nonathletic leader categories, however, there were no clear discriminations between the physically mature and the immature boys.

The prestige of adolescent girls in relation to developmental maturity was studied by Faust (1960), who found that level of physical development was an important factor in all three junior-high-school grades. In the sixth grade the traits significantly correlated with prestige were most frequently ascribed to girls who were "prepuberal," but in grades seven, eight, and nine girls who were physically accelerated received the preponderance of favorable reputation scores. It would appear from these findings of these latter two studies that during the junior-high-school years girls are more concerned with physical maturity than are boys.

Jones and Bayley (1950) also discuss the relationships between physical maturing and behavior. They find that those who are physically accelerated are usually accepted and treated both by adults and by other children as more mature. As a result, such youngsters seem to have relatively little need to strive for status. The accelerated boys were rated as more physically attractive, neater, less animated, less "affected," less inhibited, and more relaxed. The physically retarded boys, on the other hand, continue to exhibit many forms of relatively immature behavior, partly because of the tendency of others to treat them as "little boys." They continue to strive for status and particularly try to counteract their physical disadvantage in some way: through withdrawal; greater activity; and better academic work. Although these authors strongly stress the physical effects of maturing on behavior, they also point out the multiplicity of factors, psychological and cultural as well as physical, which contribute to the formation of the personality patterns.

Projective techniques have been employed to investigate the emotional states and level of adjustment of early- and late-maturing individuals. Jones and Mussen (1958) administered the Thematic Apperception Test to a group of seventeen-year-old girls, of whom about half had been consistently accelerated and about half were retarded in physical development. Generally, the early-maturing girls seemed to have lower scores on the category "negative characteristics," indicating that they had more favorable self-concepts. These findings would indicate that late-maturers of both sexes have less adequate self-concepts than the early-maturers. These authors also stress the psychological and cultural factors involved in personality development and point out that the pattern of these influences varies for each individual.

Davidson and Gottlieb (1955) employed the Rorschach Test as a measure of emotional maturity in a group of premenarcheal and post-menarcheal girls. The means reported on all the scoring tests used were in the direction of greater maturity for the physically more mature group with only one category (relating form and color) yielding a statistically significant difference.

Smith and Lebo (1956) examined self-concept as revealed through projective materials in relation to pubertal status (pubic hair rating). Their findings, based on a sample of pubescent males between the ages of twelve and fifteen, were as follows: (1) The subjects showed a marked positive relationship between items of a revised Vineland Social Maturity Scale and pubic hair status. Chronological age and pubic hair status showed a less significant relationship. (2) Prepubescent and postpubescent males differed significantly in certain projective aspects of their human-figure drawings. (3) Self-attitudes in the area of hetero-sexual development in relation to parents showed a closer relationship to chronological age than to pubic hair ratings.

THE IMPORTANCE OF PHYSIQUE

Important as is the timing of pubescence in the development of the physical self-image, the physique that finally results is equally impor-tant. Whether the process is completed early or late, the final self-image will be determined when physical growth stops. From the beginning of the growth spurt until its end, the adolescent will be very much con-cerned with his physique and will strive to develop it to the fullest.

The importance of his physique to the adolescent is suggested in Hanley's study (1951) of the relationship between physique and repu-tation. He studied two groups of boys aged sixteen to twenty to deter-mine whether correlations between their junior-high-school School Reputation Test scores and components of their mature somatotypes were in agreement with the earlier study of Sheldon (1942). The results indicated an association between physique and reputation, but the relationship was not as strong as the earlier study had suggested. Deno (1953) found that boys are more likely to admire the culturally approved strongly masculine physique with its V-shaped symmetry than the physique of another adolescent. Her study offers only slight support to the generalization that the boys with the most admired physique tend to be socially favored.

Schonfeld (1950) reported the effects of inadequate masculine phy-sique on personality development of adolescent boys, based on observa-tions of boys ranging in age from nine to sixteen. These boys all pre-sented personality difficulties relating to physical inadequacy. His re-sults suggest that apparent or actual delay in the onset of maturation, failure of the growth spurt at adolescence, or inadequacy of masculine development may lead to a variety of difficulties.

The height that is attained is a most important factor in the development of the physical self-concept. Again, timing is important, and the sex difference in growth also plays a major role. The problems related to height are usually temporary for those individuals whose height changes appreciably during adolescence but are more permanent for those who continue to deviate from the culturally accepted norm.

Shortness

That shortness is considered a handicap among young adolescent boys is related to two factors: the culturally developed preference of girls for boys who are "tall and handsome," and the precocity of physical development of girls in relation to boys in early adolescence. At this time girls tend to seek the companionship of boys older than themselves, rather than to accept the advances of those their own age who still look and act like small boys. Ausubel (1950) also finds shortness a real handicap for junior- or senior-high-school boys who seek prestige through athletics or team games. Short boys never succeed in achieving representation in popular sports in proportion to their incidence in the total population. It is equally unusual to find older adolescents or even young adults who are short in stature involved in team sports, and the presence of a short player on most professional athletic teams is a rarity.

In social situations, especially social dancing, the short boy's position is untenable, since both boys and girls prefer a situation where the boy is at least as tall as the girl or taller than she is. Self-consciousness about his shortness, therefore, may cause a boy to develop some degree of timidity or shyness in his behavior, which may isolate him at least temporarily from his peer group.

Many boys who are relatively short during early adolescence do grow to at least average height or better during their growth spurt. Where such growth does take place, there is an accompanying change in the physical self-image and a good adjustment pattern is usually achieved. Those who remain short, however, find it harder to make a good adjustment to their size and often employ compensatory mechanisms. Although it is not necessarily true, most adults think of short males as being highly aggressive and verbal, and as using these attributes to compensate for lack of height. This stereotype exists because short, aggressive males are readily noticed, but the short male may react in other ways. Many short individuals will withdraw as their means of compensating, and since such behavior is much less obvious than aggressiveness, they go relatively unnoticed.

Shortness in females is not a great handicap either during adolescence or later. The short but otherwise well-developed young adolescent girl has little difficulty in attracting attention from boys. She has, in fact, a wider range to choose from since she will not "tower over" the young adolescent boys. The short girl is usually considered "cute" or "petite" and has little or no difficulty in being accepted by her peers.

Tallness

Being too tall is more of a problem for girls than for boys. Even height well above the average is acceptable for males, and "the taller the better" is often the case. Tallness is a desired attribute in some sports, especially basketball, in which the boy of even average height has little chance of becoming a member of a team. In professional basketball, even an individual who is six feet tall is considered too short. The tall male's total physique is to some extent a factor in determining how well he will be accepted. If he is well built in relation to his height, as is often the case, he will be readily accepted. The individual who is very tall but also very thin, i.e., the "beanpole," may have some difficulty in developing a positive physical self-image.

For girls the opposite condition prevails. While the girl who is below average in height usually is accepted, the girl who is well above the average often has difficulty gaining acceptance. Tallness in girls is still not a generally accepted cultural standard of femininity. The tall girl often has great difficulty in her heterosexual relationships and, unless she is willing to date boys shorter than she is, is rather restricted in the choice of males she can date. Very often, even the boys who would be tall enough prefer to go out with shorter girls. Girls who reach a height of over 5 feet 8 inches have not only dating problems but also difficulty in finding clothing and accessories properly designed to fit them.

Fortunately, some positive changes in attitude toward the taller girl seem to be developing. Instead of trying to conceal their height by wearing flat shoes, many tall girls now actually try to accentuate their height. More and more clothes and shoes for the tall girl can be found in department stores instead of being available only in a few specialty stores. Socially, too, the tall girl is finding herself more acceptable, although often this acceptance is only by other tall people. "Skyscraper" clubs have been organized in many places; they will accept only tall girls and boys as members, and such organizations now offer social opportunities to the tall girl that were not readily available previously.

Despite these gains, excess height is still a major concern to the female, and development of a positive self-image is difficult, especially during the teen years. Many of those tall girls who do make a good adjustment to their height do so in adulthood, often after experiencing a highly difficult period of adjustment during adolescence.

Fatness

Just prior to and during the early stages of pubescence there is a period during which about 25 per cent of all children show a tendency toward fatness. Since fatness is not a culturally approved characteristic, the individual with excess fat is subjected to jibes and unpleasant nicknames. The emotional effects resulting from such treatment are often negative, and their influence on the individual's adjustment may carry over into adulthood. Excess fat is particularly handicapping to boys during the early adolescent years because of their great interest in participation in active games. Of particular concern to boys is the increased development of fatty tissue in the breast region, which gives the impression that the breasts are developing. At a time when the individual is striving for a masculine physical image, the presence of an apparently feminine characteristic of this sort is most disturbing.

Girls, too, suffer emotionally from excess weight, because the cultural norm calls for slenderness in women. Part of the problem is socially oriented, since the fat girl will usually withdraw from social situations rather than suffer possible ridicule. Girls will often try severe dieting in an attempt to eliminate their excess fat and at times actually almost starve themselves.

Although there may occasionally be glandular causes for excess fat, the most common cause of obesity in adolescence is increased intake of food. Lowrey (1958) feels that this increased intake is due to underlying psychological changes, while Burch (1958) contends that some of the psychological aspects may be the result of the overweight condition, which in turn is due to a variety of underlying disturbances in appetite and weight regulation. Both these authors feel that diets and reducing are not enough; the parents and family, as well as the adolescent, must be educated to better understanding. It should be noted that a child's weight during preadolescence will relate to his weight during adolescence. Those who were fat as children often remain fat during adolescence and into adulthood. Such individuals, of course, have more difficulty in losing weight than do those whose excess fat appears only during adolescence. Sometimes, however, those who were fat as children have made some kind of adjustment to their obesity that keeps them from becoming greatly disturbed about this condition as they grow older.

Fortunately, only a few of that original 25 per cent will still be fat after high-school graduation. The great majority will have lost the excess fat and will fall within the normal weight range.

Voice Change

Another common problem relating to physical growth and development is that of the changing voice. This is usually a lesser problem because adolescents realize that it is temporary and will pass. The voices of both boys and girls deepen somewhat as they mature, but girls are seldom concerned about this. For boys the change in pitch may be great, accompanied by an embarrassing inability to regulate and maintain a constancy of pitch. The breaks in the voice often occur when the boy is excited or under tension. Unfortunately, the sound produced usually is humorous to the listener, and his amusement may actually increase the tension of the adolescent speaker. Boys have been known to "skip" school on days when they think they will have to recite, rather than risk being laughed at. Adults can help minimize this problem by refraining from showing amusement and by not forcing the uneasy adolescent into a position where his temporary malfunction will be conspicuous.

PROBLEMS RELATED TO PHYSICAL FUNCTIONING

Some of the problems associated with the physical self-image relate to function. Adolescents are concerned with health, strength, and coordination, all of which often affect their social activities and their standing with their peers.

Concern with Health

In this modern age of "miracle" drugs and of increased medical-psychological knowledge, problems of the adolescent relating to health are less severe than was the case twenty years ago. While there are still individuals who suffer from diseases and physical malfunctions, such problems are generally less severe during adolescence than was previously thought. Even with such enlightenment, however, there are relatively few facilities exclusively designed for medical treatment of teen-agers. One of the few clinics of this type was established at the Kaiser Foundation Hospital Medical Center in Oakland, California. Here, teen-agers are treated with a special understanding of their psychological problems, and results are most effective (Roth, Weissman, and Linden, 1958). Another such clinic has been established at the Boston Children's Hospital. The program there is entirely devoted to treatment and study of young people age twelve to twenty-one, and the clinic is also used for training physicians in the care of adolescents

(Gallagher, 1954). There is relatively little psychiatric care available to adolescents, since many psychiatrists feel that these youngsters are too disturbed emotionally as a result of their adolescence to respond well to treatment.

Although progress in providing health education for teen-agers is being made, they are still much concerned about their health needs and show great interest in topics relating to bodily health. Schaller (1960) administered an inventory for determining the health needs and interests of high-school students to 501 students, 100 parents, 20 health educators, and 17 doctors. His conclusions indicated that there is a common core of interest among high-school students, and that the expressed needs of boys and girls are appreciably different. The students were generally concerned about understanding more about harmful habit-forming substances and learning more about the importance of activity and rest. They wanted more information about the structure and function of the human body, about community health services and facilities, and about the official and voluntary health programs. They did not feel, however, that these subjects should be included in high-school health courses.

Girls are particularly interested in and concerned about various aspects of health related to the menstrual cycle. They are interested in knowing how much rest and what kinds of activities they should have during the menstrual period. Many girls even today still need to be assured that menstruation is a completely normal function of the body and is in no way indicative of any physiological malfunction. Special attention should be given to those whose menstrual cycles are irregular since concern about this situation may lead to emotional upset. Studies have demonstrated that brighter girls who fully understand the "whys" and "wherefores" of menstruation are freer from psychological stress than those who are not well prepared (Dalton, 1960). There is much agreement that a good deal of the physical discomfort accompanying menstruation in many girls is the result of emotional stress that is often related to a poorly developed self-image.

Physical Skills

There has been a good deal of controversy over the issue of whether or not awkwardness in adolescence is biologically or socially determined. In the studies discussed earlier in this chapter evidence was presented that indicates a consistent gain in gross motor aptitude with age for boys during the adolescent period. Although girls do not show a comparable gain, neither do they show any loss in aptitude or any awkwardness. Most of the boys' apparent awkwardness does seem to be the result of their involvement with new activities, such as dancing, where lack of skill is often the cause of "razzing" from which embarrassed self-consciousness results. Dennis (1946) also points to the "size-age illusion" as a contributing cause. The early-maturing child who undergoes an early growth spurt "is perceived as older and hence arouses expectations of agility and skill above average for his age." His failure to perform adequately at this "expected" level is often misinterpreted as awkwardness.

Ausubel (1950) agrees in part with this kind of interpretation but feels that biological variables are relevant. Growth in size and strength takes place in spurts and precipitates too sudden a need for acquiring new patterns of physical coordination. He indicates that studies of growth curves usually show that gain in muscle mass precedes gain in muscle strength, which in turn precedes the gain in gross motor skill.

Probably most important in this respect is the adolescent's own self-concept. If he thinks he is awkward, whether the cause be physical or social, he becomes more and more self-conscious and as a result appears to be even more awkward.

Strength and motor ability are important aspects of development and relate to other aspects, specifically to personality development. Boys whose strength develops early and rapidly and who are well coordinated, with good motor ability, often have opportunities available to them that those less able or those not yet developed cannot attain. Because a boy is physically developed and able to participate in athletics, he may be "looked up to" by others in his age group. He may also be afforded some opportunities for leadership that are denied the less endowed boys. Merriman (1960) has shown the relationship between personality traits and motor ability. The Phillips Jump, Chins, and Run (JCR) Test and the California Psychological Inventory were administered to more than 800 high-school boys, and boys with high JCR scores scored significantly higher than boys with low JCR scores on the poise, ascendancy, intellectual, and interest-mode parts of the CPI. Generally, motor skills are acquired at different rates and in different degrees, and if developmental needs of children in the realm of these skills are to be met, adequate time and competent instruction must be provided during the time that these skills are maturing.

Girls are somewhat less concerned about their physical strength. As was previously mentioned, they seem to reach a plateau in physical strength at about age fourteen, the cause of which is generally interpreted as cultural rather than physical. Girls are apparently aware that they are not supposed to be as strong or as athletically inclined as boys and therefore fail to demonstrate any increase in strength after early adolescence. From a purely physical point of view, it seems logical to assume that there is an increase in strength for girls and that its failure to show up in studies is socially oriented. Perhaps the greater participation of women in active sports at the present time may cause this picture to change in future studies.

REACTIONS TO SEXUAL DEVELOPMENT

The changes and patterns of development associated with sexual maturation are usually anticipated pleasurably and accepted with pride by most adolescents. They are also a major source of concern for quite a few adolescents, particularly those who deviate from the norm. Most girls, for example, look forward eagerly to the onset of menstruation, though there may also be much dread and embarrassment associated with the event. Many of the more serious problems relating to menstruation arise later, but the initial menstrual period is usually accepted quite unemotionally. Generally, the members of both sexes welcome the presence of the primary sex characteristics; the secondary sex characteristics, being for the most part more obvious to observers, are often sources of far greater emotional concern.

There is, however, a sex difference in the relative importance of the development of the primary and secondary sex characteristics as they relate to emotional adjustment. Boys generally are more concerned with primary sex characteristics; and girls, with secondary sex characteristics.

Male Genitalia

For boys, the source of greatest concern is the development of the major sex organ. The difference between boys and girls in this respect is probably due to the fact that the penis is an external organ, whereas the major female sex organs are internal. Because of its external location, the male sex organ can be compared with the genitalia of other males, and herein often lies the basis of an emotional problem. There is a widespread belief, which is completely unsubstantiated by any research, that the size of the external genitalia is closely associated with masculine virility and potency. Young adolescents are very much impressed with this thought and are, therefore, deeply concerned with the growth of their own sex organ. Ausubel (1954) feels that the seriousness of this problem is not truly appreciated, since the adolescents who are thus disturbed are unwilling to admit this concern even to themselves.

Boys also have other concerns related to their genitalia. Often they will be upset about nocturnal emissions and/or erection of the penis. The nocturnal emissions, a normal pattern of functioning, are often accompanied by sex dreams, and these may in turn lead to feelings of guilt or shame. Erections of the penis usually cause mixed feelings. Pride at this evidence of virility is accompanied by concern that there will be inability to control erections, which in the young adolescent can be produced by very slight stimulation. This latter concern may cause a male student to be unwilling to stand to recite in front of a class.

Male Facial Hair

The secondary sex characteristic that seems most important to boys is the development of facial hair. Teen-age boys eagerly look forward to the presence of facial fuzz, and their first shave, although usually not even needed, is a source of great pride. A late-maturer's lack of facial hair growth is the subject of much ridicule by his earlier-developing peers. This, however, is not too serious a matter, since facial hair will eventually appear and with it will come a feeling of increased virility in the individual.

Female Breasts

For girls, the secondary sex characteristic that is probably the greatest source of emotional difficulties is the development and size of the breasts. A generation or so ago, early-maturing girls were often concerned about breast development if it occurred as early as eleven or twelve years of age. It was not unusual to see such an early-maturer wearing loose-fitting clothes and walking "slumped over" in an attempt to conceal this development. This is not often the case today; in a culture where the female breast is virtually eulogized, the early-developing girl is more likely to try to accentuate her development by wearing tight-fitting clothes and walking erect.

For the late-maturer or for the girl whose breasts are relatively small even when they are fully developed, a number of emotional problems may arise, partly as a result of a rather poor physical self-image. These youngsters are often victimized by advertisements of products that purport to help breast development but which in fact usually have no results and may even cause further frustration when the desired result does not materialize. Artificial aids such as padded brassieres and other types of "falsies" are often employed by girls seeking to enhance their physical status. Although such artificial aids seem to have some positive effect as far as the peer group's reaction is concerned, they are also quite likely to cause even more concern for the individual using them. The adolescent girl usually worries about others finding out that artificial aids are being employed and as a result will avoid almost any situation that might lead to such discovery.

The concern about small breasts is not restricted to adolescence, although the difficulty usually begins during that period. Many adult females still continue to be concerned about breast size and respond to these concerns in much the same way as do adolescent girls.

Physical Development and Problems Related to Sex

Sex-maturing brings with it a number of serious problems that are not merely physically oriented. Many problems of this type are discussed in Chapter 7 (Heterosexual Development), but it should be emphasized here that such problems are often based on the way the individual developed physically and the kind of physical self-image that was based on such development. Curiosity, worry, and ignorance about sexual maturing and its implications are common in our society and are the source of many of the problems most often encountered by the adolescent.

PROBLEMS RELATED TO PHYSICAL APPEARANCE

In addition to the problems relating to such physical growth factors as height, weight, and fatness which have been discussed, there are many other problems to be found in the development of the adolescent's physical self-image. These relate primarily to physical handicaps, physical defects, and the general area of physical appearance. For purposes of this discussion, physical handicaps are defined as physically based malfunctions that in some way impair the ability of the individuals to perform normal motor or perceptual tasks. Physical defects are defined as characteristics of the individual that are physically normal but deviate from the cultural norm. Such defects usually do not impair physical performance, although the psychological reaction to them may keep the individual from normal physical activities. Physical appearance has to do with the over-all appearance of the individual, as both he and others view it, and includes personal appearance and grooming.

Physical Handicaps

The degree of emotional reaction that accompanies physical handicaps varies in relation to the extent to which the handicap is obvious to the observer. A shortened leg that causes an obvious limp, a badly deformed hand, or a "hunched" back is more likely to cause serious emotional problems than are such defects as a partially malformed foot or a twisted elbow, which can be concealed from the view of others. Defects that require the use of artificial aids such as braces, thick glasses, or hearing aids may also create emotional reactions that are related as much to the obvious presence of the aid as to the handicap itself. The emotional problems that arise for the adolescent in relation to these various kinds of handicaps have at least two bases. First, the handicaps may actually keep him from doing many of the things the members of his peer group are doing because he is physically unable. Second, the poor self-image, which may result from viewing his handicaps as more paralyzing than they actually are, may cause him to withdraw from peer interaction for fear of being ridiculed or rejected. Actually, members of the peer group are seldom concerned about the handicap and are ready and willing to accept him.

Physical handicaps often occur early in life, and in such cases the problems and the adjustments to them occurred long before adolescence. The emotionality may be increased somewhat during adolescence, but not to any appreciable degree.

Arthur J. was born with a badly malformed left hand which could not be corrected through surgery. As a child, he was constantly confronted by the curiosity of adults and other children about this characteristic and became most self-conscious. In his early school years, he tried to keep the hand hidden from others and avoided physical activity as much as possible. He soon became aware that his peers were not ridiculing or rejecting him because of this defect, but were in fact actually sympathetic. By the time he was twelve years old he had made a good adjustment to this handicap and was no longer deeply troubled by it. He started playing tennis, and even became a member of the school tennis team.

If the handicap appears during adolescence, for example the result of an accident, it may cause a good deal of emotional disturbance. In such cases the individual must make a series of new adjustments, both physical and social, to the handicap, and he will often develop feelings of inadequacy. The seriousness of the emotional problem varies with the degree to which the handicap restricts the individual's physical activity. Such an individual will benefit greatly from counseling and psychotherapy, which should be administered along with the treatment of the physical problem.

Wenar (1958) investigated the difference in depth of psychological disturbance between handicapped and nonhandicapped adolescents who needed professional help. The Rorschach was administered, and the data were treated statistically and also evaluated by means of a rating scale. The results indicated that the handicapped youths tended to be somewhat healthier and to have more vitality, inner resources, and creativity, but were more sensitized to potential dangers in their environment. Wenar concluded that physical handicaps cannot be equated with psychological disturbance.

Physical Defects

The adolescent's concern with physical defects, either real or imagined, is often not obvious to others. The adolescent may feel that some physical characteristic is unusual, but the peer group and adults with whom he has contact may consider it perfectly normal.

Frazier and Lisonbee (1950) investigated items of self-description checked by more than 500 adolescent boys and girls and the amount of concern expressed about these items. The results of this study, presented in Table 3, show many of the characteristics that can be dis-

TABLE 3. Items of self-description checked by 10 per cent or more of 580 tenth-grade boys and girls, with amount of expressed concern
From Frazier and Lisonbee (1950), by permission of the authors and School Review

	Boys			Girls	
Item of description	*Per cent checking*	*Per cent of concern*	*Item of description*	*Per cent checking*	*Per cent of concern*
Blackheads or pimples	57	51	Blackheads or pimples	57	82
Lack of beard	34	2	Heavy eyebrows	24	11
Heavy eyebrows	27	1	Freckles	23	24
Scars, birthmarks, moles	20	13	Oily skin	22	52
Irregular teeth	17	39	Scars, birthmarks, moles	22	30
Heavy lips	14	5	Glasses	21	31
Protruding chin	13	6	High forehead	19	8
Ears stick out	13	6	Too round face	19	21
Oily skin	12	27	Too homely	18	42
Freckles	12	—	Dry skin	16	43
Heavy beard	11	13	Irregular teeth	16	42
Glasses	11	23	Thin lips	15	13
Dark skin	10	4	Low forehead	13	3
Receding chin	10	4	Too long nose	11	23
Gaps in teeth	10	26	Too big nose	11	44
Too long nose	10	8	Receding chin	10	13
Too thin face	10	15	Odd-shaped nose	10	23
Too large ears	10	8			

turbing to adolescents. A number of these characteristics, such as freckles, glasses, too round a face, heavy beard, too high a forehead, are probably not considered defects by others. However, if the adolescent himself is concerned about them, they are as much defects in his own self-image as are blackheads, pimples, or other noticeable blemishes. It may be noted that these are primarily facial defects which cannot be easily concealed from others. A detailed discussion of some of these characteristics follows.

ILL-SHAPED NOSES. One of the most disturbing of all instances of asynchrony in adolescent growth is the early and sudden spurt in the growth of the nose. Often this growth is corrected by corresponding growth in other facial features, but if not its disproportionate size is one of the related causes of homeliness in both men and women. Such an outstanding characteristic may bring forth ridicule that is often cruel, though perhaps unintentionally so.

Donald P. had a large hooked nose even as a child. When he was a child, this was not too disturbing to him, although it was a source of ridicule by his peer group. In early adolescence the problem became rather severe, and Donald withdrew to a degree from heterosexual contacts, even refusing to go to his high-school graduation dance. His contacts with members of his own sex, however, were relatively good, which probably kept the maladjustment from becoming even more serious. During World War II Donald was a member of the Air Force and received another temporary jolt. He had to be especially fitted with a custom-made oxygen mask, since none of the standard sizes would fit. In the Air Force, however, Donald finally made a good adjustment to this problem when he realized that others were not actually rejecting him. He also found that much of the ridicule came from others whose noses were as unattractive as his own.

The problem of the oversized or otherwise unattractive nose is usually more severe for females than for males since facial attractiveness is more important to females. Plastic surgery on the nose has become relatively common and has been a highly successful method of alleviating or even eliminating this problem. Strangely enough, females respond much more favorably in terms of personality change as a result of plastic surgery than do males. Apparently, the male can learn to live with this defect more effectively than can the female.

BIRTHMARKS, MOLES, AND SCARS. The degree to which these characteristics cause emotional disturbance varies with their size and their location. A small birthmark or mole on the face is often not unattractive and may actually be considered attractive. At one time women actually used artificial molelike marks to accentuate their beauty. Girls are more often disturbed by the presence of hair growing out of a mole than by the mark itself. If the blemish is large or oddly located it may be a source of much concern. Examples are scars on the face and the purple type of blemish that covers a fair portion of the face and is obvious to all. Here again modern medical techniques have made it possible for such blemishes to be removed or concealed, thus minimizing the emotional disturbance. This medical treatment must often be followed up with extensive counseling, particularly when the emotional problem has built up over a long period.

ACNE. Perhaps the most common problem of early adolescence is the presence of acne. Empirical evidence may be lacking, but many feel that this defect is an important determinant of social unpopularity during adolescence. The concern involved is apparent in members of both sexes, but the experience is probably more traumatic for girls.

The basic cause of acne still defies complete explanation, but most explanations presuppose a "hormonal imbalance." The hormones most related to such "imbalance" seem to be those of the adrenal-pituitary-gonadal group. The greater incidence of acne among boys is probably due to the fact that in the male hormonal stimuli are spent chiefly on the sebaceous glands rather than, as in the female, on breast development.

The actual importance of acne to adolescents is obvious in their willingness to experiment with every conceivable remedy suggested for eliminating or disguising this condition. Often these attempts at self-treatment actually intensify the situation by reinfecting other blackheads. Since even minor skin eruptions can cause a certain amount of social disability, a condition like acne can be almost paralyzing, particularly because the individual often thinks that there is no recovery from this skin condition in the foreseeable future. Stolz and Stolz (1944), after cataloguing the major somatic deviations of adolescence, conclude: "Of all items mentioned, acne seems to be the only one which almost universally causes emotional difficulties for an adolescent boy or girl."

With increased medical and dental knowledge and with the greater awareness of cosmetic effects, many of the problems relating to facial characteristics can be eliminated or greatly alleviated. Protruding ears can be "pinned back"; long noses can be shortened; receding chins can be built up, etc. The concern about having to wear glasses can be relieved in many cases by contact lenses. Although braces on the teeth may cause some temporary physical and emotional difficulties, these are less disturbing than having permanently irregular or distorted teeth. Unusual hair growth on the face can be permanently removed by means of electrolysis.

All these techniques may have great value, but they are not always necessary in order for an individual to make a good adjustment. When some of these techniques are employed, they often must be followed up with counseling or psychotherapy if the emotional problems that had previously developed are to be fully alleviated.

Personal Appearance

The over-all physical appearance of the individual has much to do with the impression he makes on others. A neatly dressed, well-groomed adolescent evokes a more favorable response from adults than an un-kempt one does. Good grooming, neatness of dress, and erect posture may actually compensate in part for certain negative characteristics and even focus attention away from them. For example, if a very tall girl tries to conceal her height by slumping, she actually calls more negative attention to herself. If, on the other hand, she walks erect, actually accentuating her height, people will be favorably impressed with her "bearing" and her height will not be a disadvantage.

The patterns governing mode of dress and grooming for the adolescent are usually set by the peer group. Thus, if some adolescent females adopt ankle bracelets as a desirable accessory, the rest of the group immediately starts wearing them. If a "crew cut" becomes the accept-able hair style for the male adolescent, all of them will blossom out in "crew cuts." Very often, parents and school authorities do not accept these patterns and will bring pressure on adolescents to change a cer-tain pattern. They fail to realize that the adolescents' desire to be like others carries over to dress, and that this conformity is just another effort to identify with the group.

A problem that still exists today, although it is not as disturbing as it was in the depression era of the 1930's, relates to the availability of proper clothing. Adolescents have been known to leave school be-cause they cannot afford to dress as the others do. Some schools require that all students dress alike, even requiring uniforms in some instances, so that differences in apparel will not create problems. Other schools enforce rules governing what is and what is not appropriate attire. Such rules may prevent the wearing of odd-type attire from getting out of hand.

Fads in dress and grooming are nothing new and usually pass quickly. All too often a fad that would otherwise die out maintains itself as a reaction against adult attempts to squelch it. Adults would probably be wise to ignore most of these fads until such fads lose their popularity.

Good grooming is very important, and the well-groomed individual is well thought of. Even a homely individual who is well groomed may be described as "striking" and accepted or even sought out socially. Again, this type of appearance may actually minimize the effect of negative characteristics.

Manufacturers of accessories and aids for the correction of malfunc-tions have become style-conscious. Glasses, long a bugaboo to teen-agers, have been designed to be attractive and often becoming. Some are so ornate as to become conversation pieces. Hearing aids can now be concealed in the earpieces of glasses or even encased in ornate earrings, thus coming relatively unnoticeable.

If adolescents have the opportunity to learn how to dress and how to make the most of their positive characteristics, they are better able to function with their peers. Fortunately, more attention is now being paid to such training both in the home and in the schools. There has been decided improvement in this area over the last two decades, and such improvement can be expected to continue to alleviate some of the problems adolescents have encountered. In many schools, courses are now offered in the correct use of cosmetics and the proper way to dress. Girls are taught to dress their hair becomingly in relation to their facial structure in order to accentuate their positive physical attributes. Even penal institutions housing teen-agers now often have extensive programs designed to show the adolescents how to bring out their good points and conceal or minimize negative characteristics.

REFERENCES

ABEL, T. M., and JOFFEE, N. F. "Cultural Backgrounds of Female Puberty." *American Journal of Psychotherapy,* 4, 90-113, 1950.

ALTMAN, I., and CIOCCI, A. "School Absence Due to Sickness in the War Years." *Child Development,* 16, 189-199, 1945.

AUSUBEL, D. P. "Problems of Adolescent Adjustment." *Bulletin of the National Association of Secondary School Principals,* 34, 1-84, 1950.

AUSUBEL, D. P. *Theory and Problems of Adolescent Development.* New York: Grune and Stratton, 1954.

BAYER, LEONA M., and SNYDER, MARGARET. "Illness Experience of a Group of Normal Children." *Child Development,* 21, 93-120, 1950.

BAYLEY, NANCY. "Individual Patterns of Development." *Child Development,* 27, 800-818, 1956.

BINNING, G. "Earlier Physical and Mental Maturity among Saskatoon Public School Children." *Canadian Journal of Public Health,* 49, 9-17, 1958.

BONDY, CURT. "Puberty as a Socio-Cultural Phenomenon." *Praxis der Kinderpsychologie Kinderpsychiatrie* (Goettingen), 5, 198-201, 1956.

BRECKENRIDGE, M. S., and VINCENT, E. L., *Child Development.* Philadelphia: W. B. Saunders Company, 1955.

BURCH, HILDE. "Psychological Aspects of Obesity in Adolescents." *American Journal of Public Health,* 48, 1349-1353, 1958.

COLLINS, S. D. "Sickness and Health: Their Measurement, Distribution, and Changes." *Annals of the American Academy of Political Science,* 237, 152-163, 1945.

DALTON, KATHARINA. "Schoolgirls' Behavior and Menstruation." *British Medical Journal* (London), 2, 1647-1649, 1960.

DAVENPORT, C. B. "Human Metamorphosis." *American Journal of Physical Anthropology*, 9, 205-233, 1926.

DAVIDSON, HELEN H., and GOTTLIEB, LUCILLE. "The Emotional Maturity of Pre- and Post-menarcheal Girls." *Journal of Genetic Psychology*, 86, 261-266, 1955.

DENNIS, W. "The Adolescent." In Carmichael, L., ed., *Manual of Child Psychology*. New York: John Wiley & Sons, Inc., 1946.

DENO, EVELYN. "Self-identification among Adolescent Boys." *Child Development*, 24, 269-273, 1953.

DIMOCK, H. S. *Rediscovering the Adolescent*. New York: Association Press, 1937.

DIVEN, J. "Peculiarities of Disease in Childhood." In Abt, I. A., ed., *Pediatrics*, vol. II. Philadelphia: W. B. Saunders Co., 1923.

EICHORN, DOROTHY H., and MCKEE, JOHN P. "Physiological Instability during Adolescence." *Child Development*, 29, 255-268, 1958.

ELLIS, RICHARD W. B. "Age of Puberty in the Tropics." *British Medical Journal* (London), 1, 88-89, 1950.

ELLIS, RICHARD W. B. "Growth in Relation to Maturity." *Edinburgh Medical Journal*, 54, 269-283, 1947.

ESPENSCHADE, A. "Motor Performance in Adolescence." *Monographs of the Society for Research in Child Development*, 5, 49-53, 1940.

FAUST, MARGARET S. "Developmental Maturity as a Determinant in Prestige of Adolescent Girls." *Child Development*, 31, 173-184, 1960.

FOLL, C. V. "Physical Development of School Girls in Upper Burma." *Archives of Diseases of Childhood*, 33, 452-454, 1958.

FRAZIER, A., and LISONBEE, L. K. "Adolescent Concerns with Physique." *School Review*, 58, 397-405, 1950.

GALLAGHER, ROSWELL J. "A Clinic for Adolescents." *Children*, 1, 165-170, 1954.

GARN, S. M., and LEWIS, A. B. "The Sex Difference in Tooth Calcification." *Journal of Dental Research*, 37, 561-567, 1958.

GHESQUIERE, JOSEPH L. "Interdependence Analysis of Physical Performance and Growth in Boys." *Annales Paediatriae Fenniae* (Helsinki), suppl. 11, 1958, 140 pp.

GORDON, HARRY J. "Endocrine Problems in Adolescence." *Rocky Mountain Medical Journal*, 45, 127-133, 1948.

GOULD, H. N., and GOULD, M. R. "Age of First Menstruation in Mothers and Daughters." *Journal of the American Medical Association*, 98, 1349-1352, 1932.

GREULICH, WILLIAM W., et al. "Somatic and Endocrine Studies of Puberal and Adolescent Boys." *Monographs of the Society for Research in Child Development*, 7, no. 3, 1942.

GREULICH, WILLIAM W. "Growth of Children of the Same Race under Different Environmental Conditions." *Science*, 127, 515-516, 1958.

GREULICH, WILLIAM W., and PYLE, S. I. *Radiographic Atlas of Skeletal Development of the Hand and Wrist*. Stanford: Stanford University Press, 1950.

GREULICH, WILLIAM W., and THOMAS, J. "Growth and Development of Pelvis of Individual Girls before and after Puberty." *Yale Journal of Biology and Medicine*, 17, 91-97, 1944.

HANLEY, CHARLES. "Physique and Reputation of Junior High School Boys." *Child Development,* 22, 247-260, 1951.

HANSMAN, CHARLOTTE F., and MARESH, MARION M. "A Longitudinal Study of Skeletal Maturation." *American Medical Association Journal of Diseases of Children,* 101, 305-321, 1961.

HARRIS, J. A., PATERSON, D. G., JACKSON, C. M., and SCAMMON, R. E. *The Measurement of Man.* Minneapolis: University of Minnesota Press, 1930.

HENTON, COMRADGE L. "A Comparative Study of the Onset of Menarche among Negro and White Children." *Journal of Psychology,* 46, 65-73, 1958.

HOGBEN, HAMILTON, WATERHOUSE, J. A. J., and HOGBEN, LANCELOT. "Studies on Puberty. Part I." *British Journal of Social Medicine,* 2, 29-42, 1948.

HUBBLE, DOUGLAS. "The Problems of Puberty." *British Medical Journal* (London), 1, 191-193, 1958.

HUNTER, T. A. A. "The 'Delicate' Adolescent." *Practitioner* (London), 162, 275-279, 1949.

JENSEN, KAI. "Physical Growth and Physiological Aspects of Development." *Review of Educational Research,* 20, 390-410, 1950.

JONES, HAROLD E. *Motor Performance and Growth: A Developmental Study of Static Dynamometric Strength.* University of California Publications in Child Development, I, 1-181, 1949.

JONES, MARY COVER, and BAYLEY, NANCY. "Physical Maturing among Boys as Related to Behavior." *Journal of Educational Psychology,* 41, 129-148, 1950.

JONES, MARY COVER, and MUSSEN, P. H. "Self-conceptions, Motivations and Interpersonal Attitudes of Early- and Late-maturing Girls." *Child Development,* 29, 491-501, 1958.

KEDDIE, J. A. G. "The Heights and Weights of Scottish Children of Different Socio-economic Groups." *Medical Officer* (London), 1, 101-106, 1958.

LATHAM, A. J. "The Relationship between Pubertal Status and Leadership in Junior High School Boys." *Journal of Genetic Psychology,* 78, 185-194, 1951.

LEWIS, A. B., and GARN, S. M. "The Relationship between Tooth Formation and Other Maturational Factors." *Angle Orthodontist,* 32, 70-77, 1960.

LIVSON, NORMAN, and MCNEILL, DAVID. "Variability in Male Stature as a Function of Adolescent Maturation Rate." *Science,* 133, 708-709, 1961.

LOWREY, GEORGE H. "Obesity in the Adolescent." *American Journal of Public Health,* 4, 1354-1358, 1958.

MCKEE, JOHN P., and EICHORN, DOROTHY H. "Seasonal Variations in Physiological Functions during Adolescence." *Child Development,* 24, 225-234, 1953.

MCKEE, JOHN P., and EICHORN, DOROTHY H. "Relation between Metabolism and Height and Weight during Adolescence." *Child Development,* 26, 205-212, 1955.

MEREDITH, H. V., and BOYNTON, B. "Transverse Growth of Extremities: Analysis of Girth Measurements for Arm, Forearm, Thigh, and Leg Taken on Iowa City White Children." *Human Biology,* 9, 366-403, 1937.

MERRIMAN, J. BURTON. "Relationship of Personality Traits to Motor Ability." *Research Quarterly of the American Association for Health, Physical Education and Recreation,* 31, 163-173, 1960.

MILLS, C. A. "Geographic and Time Variations in Body Growth and Age at Menarche." *Human Biology,* 9, 43-56, 1937.

MUELLER, H. "Enkele waarnemingen imtrent den groci van het beenderenstelsel en imtrent de geslachterijkkeid van Javaansche meisjes." *Mededeelengen van Dienst de Volkgezondherd in Nederlandsch-Indie,* 21, 48-63, 1932.

MUHSAM, H. V. "Correlation in Growth." *Human Biology,* 19, 260-269, 1947.

PYLE, S. I., STUART, H. C., CORNONI, J., and REED, R. B. "Onsets, Completions and Spans of the Osseous Stage of Development of Representative Bone Growth Centers of the Extremities." *Monographs of the Society for Research in Child Development,* 26, no. 1, 1961.

RICH, GEORGE Q. "Muscular Fatigue Curves for Boys and Girls." *Research Quarterly of the American Association for Health, Physical Education, and Recreation,* 31, 485-498, 1960.

RICHARDSON, JOHN S. "The Endocrines in Adolescence." *Practitioner* (London), 162, 280-286, 1949.

ROTH, ARTHUR, WEISMANN, ARTHUR, and LINDEN, CORINNE. "A Plan for Medical Care for Adolescents." *Pediatrics,* 25, 86-89, 1958.

SCHALLER, WARREN E. "Health Needs and Interests as a Basis for Selecting Health Content in Secondary Schools." *Research Quarterly of the American Association for Health, Physical Education, and Recreation,* 31, 512-522, 1960.

SCHONFELD, WILLIAM A. "Inadequate Masculine Physique as a Factor in Personality Development of Adolescent Boys." *Psychosomatic Medicine,* 12, 49-54, 1950.

SHELDON, W. H. *The Varieties of Temperament.* New York: Harper & Row, 1942.

SHOCK, NATHAN W. "Some Physiological Aspects of Adolescence." *Texas Reports on Biology and Medicine,* 4, 289-310, 1946.

SHOCK, NATHAN W. "Physiological Factors in Development." *Review of Educational Research,* 17, 362-370, 1947.

SHUTTLEWORTH, F. K. "Sexual Maturation and the Skeletal Growth of Girls Age Six to Nineteen." *Monographs of the Society for Research in Child Development,* 2, no. 5, 1937.

SHUTTLEWORTH, F. K. "The Adolescent Period: A Pictorial Atlas." *Monographs of the Society for Research in Child Development,* 3, no. 3, 1938.

SHUTTLEWORTH, F. K. "The Adolescent Period: A Pictorial Atlas." *Monographs of the Society for Research in Child Development,* 14, 1949.

SIMMONS, K. "The Brush Foundation Study of Child Growth and Development. II. Physical Growth and Development." *Monographs of the Society for Research in Child Development,* 9, no. 1, 1944.

SMITH, WALTER D., and LEBO, DELL. "Some Changing Aspects of the Self-concept of Pubescent Males." *Journal of Genetic Psychology,* 88, 61-75, 1956.

SOLLEY, WILLIAM H. "Relationship of Selected Factors in Growth Derivable from Age-Height-Weight Measurements." *Research Quarterly of the Association for Health, Physical Education, and Recreation,* 31, 92-100, 1960.

STOLZ, H. R., and STOLZ, L. M. "Adolescent Problems Related to Somatic Variations in Adolescence." *Forty-third Yearbook, National Society for the Study of Education, Part I.* Chicago: University of Chicago Press, 1944.

STUART, H. C. "Normal Growth and Development during Adolescence." *New England Journal of Medicine,* 234, 666-672; 693-700, 1946.

TUDDENHAM, READ D., and SNYDER, MARGARET M. "Physical Growth from Birth to Maturity." *Review of Educational Research,* 17, 371-379, 1947.

TYLER, FREDERICK. "Organismic Growth." *Child Development,* 28, 55-63, 1957.

VALADIAN, I., STUART, H. C., and REED, R. B. "Studies of Illnesses of Children Followed from Birth to Eighteen Years." *Monographs of the Society for Research in Child Development,* 26, No. 3, 1961.

WENAR, CHARLES. "The Degree of Psychological Disturbance in Handicapped Youth." *Exceptional Children,* 7, 7-10, 1958.

WHITACRE, J., and GRIMES, ETHEL T. "Some Body Measurements of Native-Born White Children of Seven to Fourteen Years in Different Climatic Regions of Texas." *Child Development,* 30, 177-209, 1959.

WILLGOOSE, CARL E. "The Relationship of Muscular Strength to Motor Coordination in the Adolescent Period." *Journal of Educational Research,* 44, 138-142, 1950.

CHAPTER 3

Intelligence and Achievement

Unlike the growth spurt in physical development, the curve of intellectual development shows no striking changes during adolescence. Nonetheless, a consideration of intellectual development during this time period is of great importance. During adolescence the individual is becoming more and more effective in dealing with his environment and is expanding his ability to interpret it. Previous learning and activity are being reorganized into new concepts and related to new learning. At this time the individual's intellectual development becomes more closely related to his plans and goals for education and future vocation. Bayley (1955) defined intelligent behavior as "a dynamic successsion of developing functions, with the more advanced and complex functions in the hierarchy depending upon the prior maturing of earlier simpler ones," thus emphasizing the increased complexity of developing intellectual patterns.

Although there are numbers of definitions of intelligence, the one proposed by Stoddard and Wellman (1934) seems to be as comprehensive and inclusive as one might desire. They define intelligence as "the ability to undertake activities that are characterized by (1) difficulty; (2) complexity; (3) abstractness; (4) economy; (5) adaptiveness to a goal; (6) social value; and (7) the emergence of originals. A person is intelligent to the extent that he is given habitually to such mental activity." This definition includes both the theoretical and functional aspects of intelligence and indicates effectively the complex interrelationships involved. The shorter definition of intelligence by Wechsler (1958) as "the aggregate of global capacity of the individual to act purposefully, to think rationally, and to deal effectively with his environment" is also a good workable definition, which in a sense includes the variables presented by Stoddard.

THE GROWTH OF INTELLIGENCE

During the last decade, thinking concerning the growth and development of intelligence has changed considerably. Particularly, these changes have been in terms of the age at which intellectual growth

74

ceases. In his original standardization of the Stanford-Binet scale, Terman (1916) presented the point of view that intelligence reaches a peak at age sixteen, with the acceleration of the curve beginning to slow down at about age twelve or thirteen. Not only were the 1916 and 1937 revisions of the Stanford-Binet scale based on this viewpoint, but many of the group intelligence tests were and still are so based. The early studies on intelligence had mostly children and young adolescents as subjects, with few if any adults being included. The early Jones and Conrad study (1933) of adult intelligence as measured by the Army Alpha Test indicated that intelligence continued to develop until between age nineteen and age twenty-one. Rapid growth in intelligence continued until age sixteen, and then the curve negatively accelerated until age nineteen to twenty-one. In an earlier study, also involving the use of the Army Alpha Test, Hart (1924) had concluded that the peak was reached at about sixteen or seventeen. Wolman (1947/48) found a continuous development of intelligence (based on the results of the Terman-Merrill scale) after the sixteenth year of age, with negative acceleration of the growth curve appearing at that point.

Watts (1958) investigated the effects of age and practice on intelligence-test performance through the annual testing of a group of British grammar-school girls. The mean scores showed improvement over each of the seven test periods from ages eleven to eighteen. No group had reached the maximum in mental growth by the end of the study. Watts felt that age was important but that practice might be even more involved in this increase.

Thorndike (1948) used the American Council Examination as an indicator of intelligence for 1004 individuals from 13.5 to 20 years of age. The linear solutions derived from this data indicated that the point of zero gain in intelligence was reached at 25 years, 9 months. The quadratic solution showed this point to be reached at 21 years, 6 months. Either way the gain continued until at least the twentieth year.

Measures of Adult Intelligence

The Wechsler-Bellevue test was specifically designed to measure adult intelligence, since Wechsler (1958) felt that the sixteen-year-old limit of most other tests precluded accurate measurement of adult intelligence. His findings, based on the Wechsler-Bellevue Full Scale, are presented in Figure 10. These findings indicate a continual growth to age twenty, with the negative acceleration beginning at about age fifteen.

Nisbet (1957) attempted to investigate improvement in test performance over an interval of twenty-four years with a group of graduates from the University of Aberdeen. The test, a shortened form of the Simplex Group Tests, was originally administered in 1930–1933 and

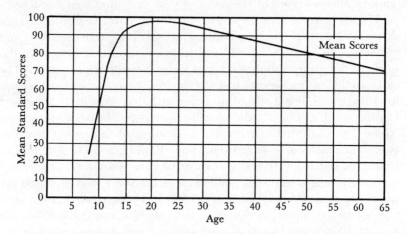

FIGURE 10. Curve of Mental Growth and Decline—Bellevue Full Scale. Ages 7–65

Adapted from D. Wechsler (1958), by permission of the author and Williams and Wilkins

was readministered in 1955 when the graduates had reached an average age of forty-seven. There was significant improvement in all but one of the fourteen subtests. These findings support those other studies which show no decline in test performance up to the late forties.

A group of fifty-year-old men who had taken the Army Alpha as college freshmen some thirty years before were retested with the same instrument by Owens (1953). He found a general increase in ability at this later age, with the greatest increase appearing on the information test. The least gain was in the arithmetic area. There is no reason to believe that the ceiling had been reached at age fifty, and further retesting might have shown continued increase.

Bayley and Oden (1955) repeated a concept-mastery test, generally considered to be a very difficult test, on a gifted group ranging in age from twenty to fifty, who had originally been tested twelve years previously. Again, there was an increase for all groups tested, but the amount of increase varied with the area measured and with age. The scores, which were expressed in Standard Deviation units for each subtest, showed the greatest increase in the Synonym-Antonym portion and an increase about one-half as great in the Analogies portion. For the older subjects the gains in the Analogies portion were less than for the younger group.

Recently, Bayley (1955) presented numbers of individual curves of intelligence based on data from the Berkeley Growth Study. These data show continual growth up to at least age twenty-seven, and possibly beyond this point. She further attempted to fit the curves presented by Owens and the scores on Terman's Concept Mastery Test to the Berkeley Growth Study curve. The result was a fifty-year curve incorporating the best features of both tests. Generally, it appeared that the greatest portion of adult growth in the factors measured occurs between twenty and twenty-five years, with growth continuing beyond this level in smaller but relatively constant increments.

The most recent study concerning growth and/or decline in intelligence with age has been reported by Bradway and Thompson (1962). These investigators have also found continuation of mental growth into adulthood. They were able to plot mental age against chronological age for the years two through five, the years eleven through fifteen, and the years twenty-seven through thirty-one. There was some indication of a leveling-off or even of a slight drop in the curve during this latter period. This may be partially due to the ceiling effect of the Stanford-Binet Scale (which only allows for a maximum IQ of 152 for an adult). However, analysis of variance was applied to the data and to data based on the Wechsler Adult Intelligence Scale (WAIS) on the same subjects, and the variation with chronological age did not approach significance. The point at which growth terminates and at which the curve may start to decline was not determined by the data.

Bradway and Thompson (1962) have investigated the increase in abilities from adolescence to adulthood. Since their findings and those of other investigators have shown that such an increase does exist, they wished to identify the kinds of abilities that increase most. The various items on the Stanford-Binet were evaluated and then grouped into the

TABLE 4. Comparison of four subscales on increase from adolescence to adulthood
From Bradway and Thompson (1962), by permission of the authors and Journal of Educational Psychology

| | | Rank order among 26 items | | Mean of increases in per cent |
Scale	Number of items	M	Median	passing
Vocabulary	8	8.1	7.3	43.7
Reasoning				
Abstract	6	9.9	11.8	42.2
Practical	7	17.4	18.0	25.1
Memory	5	21.0	22.0	18.7

categories presented in Table 4. Memory items showed the least gain, and abstract reasoning and vocabulary the greatest. The authors feel that this finding offers further support to the conclusion "that growth of functions dependent on continued learning and on the building of concepts is more likely to continue into adulthood than is growth of memory and performance function."

This investigation points up the fact that the shape of the curve of mental growth varies according to the kind of test used to measure such growth. If the test used is very heavily weighted in items measuring vocabulary, the curve derived from such test results will differ from the curve derived from a test heavily weighted in performance items.

Adult intelligence scores can be predicted with some degree of accuracy from scores obtained as adolescents. It is difficult, however, to predict the amount of gain that takes place from adolescence to adulthood, apparently because the gain varies in relatively small amounts within the total framework of intelligence. Bradway and Robinson (1961) feel that the amount of gain is not dependent on educational level, level of initial mental age, or level of ancestral intelligence. Adolescent girls with high IQ's have been found to increase less in mental age than girls who test lower, or than males at any level.

The possibility that an individual's educational background may have some relationship to increase or decline in abilities has been investigated to some extent. Vernon (1948) tested large groups of children in an attempt to determine changes in abilities from age fourteen to twenty years. His findings showed that: (1) General intelligence shows a very slight increase from fourteen to seventeen in boys leaving school, a greater increase in those who receive further schooling. (2) A decrease starts after seventeen among men in lower-grade occupations, but the level is maintained to a later age in more "intellectual" occupations. (3) Unless there is further education, educational attainments decline rapidly from fourteen. (4) Even without any technical education, there is a marked increase in ability at mechanical and spatial tests and in some performance tests. These results seem to indicate that abilities continue to develop largely in relation to the extent to which they are used.

Current studies are still involved with more precise attempts to measure the age at which a ceiling in intellectual growth is reached, and the final answer is not yet known. It is possible that intellectual growth, or at least certain aspects of it, may continue well into the adult years. This is difficult to spell out in detail because we still have insufficient knowledge concerning the various so-called factors involved in the structure of intelligence. Even where such factors have been isolated and/or defined, our current instruments are often not sensitive enough to measure them adequately.

THE STRUCTURE OF INTELLIGENCE

At present, partly because of our lack of specific knowledge in this area, we seem to be without a truly adequate theory of the intellect. The theories thus far propounded can be divided into those favoring the concept of "general intelligence" and those separating intelligence into various specialized factors.

The "General" Concept

In the early part of this century, Spearman (1927) proposed a theory that called for a very high degree of mental organization. He felt that all mental activity demands the exercise of a special characteristic which he terms "mental energy." Its place in the realm of the mind is considered to be analogous to that of physical energy in the field of physics. Spearman designates this attribute of mind as the "general factor" (g), which is possessed by all individuals and enters into all mental activity. Both the degree of g and the extent to which it enters into mental activity vary from individual to individual. Within this general framework there are also other factors, s factors, which are specific to particular situations, while g is common to all.

Although many authorities, especially those who develop intelligence tests, still follow the "general" intelligence concept presented by Spearman (1927), there is increasing concern about the adequacy and accuracy of such an approach. There is increasing interest in the study of special abilities, particularly as they relate to academic success in fields like science and mathematics. Nonetheless, the "general" factor theory is still defended by many as being the most meaningful, at least in terms of present knowledge. In an article published in Norway, Stern (1956) defended this concept. He believes that g is identified in all manifestations of human intelligence, that it can be identified, and that it is not a superintellective factor. It is the interaction and coupling of mental phenomena that result in a new level of mental organization, and on this level of organization the concept of intelligence emerges. Stern feels that human memory, for example, cannot be considered singly or in isolation, but only as associated with other intellectual factors. This would indicate a level of mental organization that can be identified with the phenomenon of mind.

Burt (1953) further defends the hypothesis of "an innate, general, cognitive ability" and feels that this concept has been clearly verified by vigorous statistical analysis. He contends that the substantially innate character of general intelligence, when conceived in terms of the hypothesis of multifactor inheritance, is consistent with Mendelian principles of "particulate" inheritance and segregation. Evidence indicates that at least 75 per cent of the measurable variance in intelligence is attributable to differences in genotype.

Concepts Involving Separate Factors

Thurstone (1946) generally disagreed with the concept of general intelligence, favoring instead a concept of primary mental abilities. He conceived of a number of intelligences, each relatively separate and distinct from the others. He developed a test, the Primary Mental Abilities Scales (1950), to measure these various types of intelligence. His analysis of the results of this test indicated that these factors were not unrelated, since they overlapped to some degree. This area of overlap or interrelation is defined as a "second-order factor" and is in some respects a general factor. It is far less important in the scheme of things than Spearman's general factor, and Thurstone still preferred to emphasize the importance of the primary mental abilities. These primary mental abilities, extracted from his factor analytic studies, include a space factor, a number factor, a verbal factor, a word-fluency factor, a memory factor, an inductive factor, and a deductive factor.

A somewhat different concept has been proposed by Garrett (1946). He feels that "abstract or symbol intelligence changes in its organization as age increases from a fairly unified and general ability to a loosely organized group of abilities or factors." In a sense, he seemed to be attempting to combine the Spearman and Thurstone points of view. Doppelt (1950) failed to confirm this hypothesis in a factor-analysis study of the results on the Differential Aptitude Tests administered to 200 boys and 200 girls aged thirteen to seventeen. He found a general reasoning factor and three additional factors. The percentage of variance accounted for by the general factor was substantially the same at all age levels, and the relationships between the general factor and the original variables showed very few significant changes from age level to age level. Doppelt concluded that, for both sexes, the general factor tends to maintain rather than to lose its importance as age increases.

There does seem to be evidence indicating that there are different factors involved in intellectual functioning. These are not necessarily separate, unique factors and they may even be part of, or at least within the framework of, a general factor. Wechsler (1950) has described cognitive, conative, and nonintellective factors. The cognitive factor includes abstract-reasoning, verbal, spatial, numerical, and other specific factors. The conative factor involves such elements as drive, persistence, will, and some aspects of temperament. The nonintellective factors include capacities and traits which are really factors of personality *per se*. Guilford (1959) also finds three factors: (1) basic processes or operations (cognition, memory, convergent thinking, divergent thinking, and evaluation); (2) material or content (figural, symbolic, semantic); and (3) products (units, classes, relations, systems, transformations, and implications).

The Verbal Factor in Intelligence Testing

The verbal factor has been the most widely studied of all the factors. Wesman (1949) thinks that further research may show that there are several verbal factors, but for the moment goes along with the concept of a single verbal factor. Davis (1949) feels strongly that the verbal factor should be narrowly defined as an index of both range and precision of word meanings and suggests that it be measured by means of cleverly contrived multiple-choice items. He feels that this factor would then be distinguished from the reasoning abilities involved in terms of the work-analogy type or of the opposites type. These reasoning abilities are probably important enough to be assigned separate names.

There may have been a tendency in most intelligence tests to place too much emphasis on the verbal factor. Lorge (1949) feels that intelligence tests should "stress the processes underlying intellectual performance." A departure from the heavy overload of verbal content in intelligence tests is needed if we are to understand better the average behavior of individuals. This is particularly true if we are to use E. L. Thorndike's concept (1926) of manipulating things and dealing with people.

CONSTANCY OF THE IQ

For some time the thought has prevailed that the IQ is constant, i.e., it changes very little. It was believed that, within the limits of the accuracy of the measuring instruments, a child's IQ at age eighteen could be predicted from his IQ at age eight. A recent study by Meyer (1960) demonstrates the stability of the Primary Mental Ability Test administered to a group of eighth-graders and to the same group when they were in the eleventh grade. He concluded that prior measure of a particular ability predicts subsequent performance on that ability better than the total score. Patterns of subscores in grade eleven seem to be clearly dependent upon subscore patterns obtained in the eighth grade.

Generally, however, a definite change in this point of view has come about, primarily as the result of findings based on carefully structured longitudinal studies. Bayley (1949) still felt there was evidence for constancy in studies she reported in the late 1940's. She found that by school age (six years) the prediction of the general level of intelligence is fairly stable, with, however, considerable individual differences in stability at all ages. The stability was particularly evident when Sigma scores were used, but test-norm IQ's showed much wider fluctuation.

Honzik, MacFarlane, and Allen (1949) investigated the stability of test performance over a sixteen-year period. They administered mental tests to a large group of children at various ages between twenty-one months and eighteen years. Group prediction was good over short periods. During the school years, 60 per cent of the group showed IQ changes of 15 or more points, 31 per cent showed changes of 20 or more points, and 9 per cent showed changes of 30 or more points. The changes generally demonstrated a regression toward the family socio-economic status. Because of the marked fluctuation shown by many children, the authors concluded that a single test score should not be put to predictive use.

Recently, however, Bayley (1956), using longer-term findings derived from the Berkeley Growth Study and other evidence, has also cast doubt on this concept. Hilden's longitudinal study of intellectual development (1949) further investigated the concept of constancy and predictability of the IQ. He felt that the highest score prior to puberty seemed most representative of midadolescence trends. There was also a slow but reliable rise in IQ's over the period studied.

Clarke and Clarke (1953) examined more than 100 adolescent and adult defectives who had been tested a year or more previously. They reported large IQ increments over this time period, and hypothesized that these changes are related to early home environments. The results showed that intellectual retardation among deprived people is not necessarily either permanent or subject to reversal. Considerable change in intellectual level may occur during the course of individual development. Perhaps the point of view expressed by DeGroot (1955) would be of value to the reader. He feels that if IQ's are computed by the original method—mental age/chronological age—no constancy can be expected. If some constant index of intelligence is needed, he suggests the use of percentile norms or standard scores within age groups. In other words, the actual IQ score may change from one test to another, but the individual's rank within a group remains relatively constant.

The recent study by Bradway and Thompson (1962) offers evidence that an individual's intelligence in relation to that of others of his own age may be more stable than studies mentioned above

TABLE 5. Correlations between test scores at the several administrations
From Bradway and Thompson (1962), by permission of the authors and Journal
of Educational Psychology

Test	1941 S-B (L)	1956 S-B (L)	1956 WAIS Full	1956 WAIS Verbal	1956 WAIS Performance
1931 S-B (L and M)	.65	.59	.64	.60	.54
1941 S-B (L)		.85	.80	.81	.51
1956 S-B (L)			.83	.89	.46
1956 WAIS Full				.87	.84
1956 WAIS Verbal					.59

have indicated it to be. The results of Bradway's and Thompson's study are presented in Table 5. The correlation of .64 between the 1931 testing of the group as preschoolers and the 1956 testing as adults was statistically reliable, and was not far removed from the .65 correlation between preschool (1931) and adolescent (1941) test results. The correlation of .80 between the adolescent (1941) Stanford-Binet and the adult (1956) WAIS is also worth noting. "Apparently whatever the Stanford-Binet measures at preschool and at adolescence is still being measured by the WAIS in adulthood."

It seems rather obvious that there is a need for further exploration of the concept of constancy of the IQ. There is reason to believe that few, if any, of our present-day measuring instruments possess the sensitivity to evaluate properly this aspect of intelligence. More specialized instruments designed to measure the various factors in adult intelligence are needed if this problem is to be resolved.

INTELLIGENCE IN RELATION TO HEREDITY AND ENVIRONMENT

For some years there has been a good deal of controversy concerning the relative effects on intelligence of heredity and environment. There is no question that both are involved, but the degree of involvement of each has been investigated by many researchers.

Hereditary Aspects

A number of investigators have emphasized the hereditary aspects of intelligence. Burt (1955, 1958) concluded that more than 80 per cent of the total variance in intelligence is attributable to genetic factors.

He felt, too, that even nonintellectual factors influencing mental performance are not solely environmental but are themselves genetic variations. This substantially innate character of intelligence is consistent with Mendelian principles of "particulate" inheritance and segregation, Burt stated, if it is conceived in terms of the hypothesis of multifactor inheritance.

Piaget (1950) has also taken a strong genetic point of view. He stated that, in the field of purely intellectual process, the same notion or operation is manifested during the child's development in a sequence of distinct constructions or reconstructions, the continuity of which is functional only in opposition to structural differences. Knehr (1950) has conceived of intelligence as flexibility, which in turn is "the limitation imposed on behavior by the existing structural elaboration."

There is, on the other hand, a number of studies that purport to demonstrate the influence of environment. Most notable of these is the study done by Skeels and Skodak (1949), who did a ten-year follow-up of 100 children placed for adoption in 1936. These adopted children are "consistently and unmistakably superior" to their natural parents. The above-average mental development of the children adopted in infancy has been maintained into early adolescence. The intellectual level of these adopted children is equal to or surpasses the mental level of true children in family environments that are similar to the environments offered by these foster parents. The unanswered question is whether these children would have reached the same intellectual level had they remained in the kind of environment that the "true" parents might have offered.

Honzik (1957) compared her findings on two groups of children reared by their own mothers with the data reported by Skeels and Skodak and found great similarity in the results. The parent-child resemblance in ability follows the same age changes in the two studies, even though the true parents were not involved in the Skeels-Skodak group, which suggests to Honzik that the existing relationship is largely due to genetic factors. These factors apparently become manifest in the child during the later preschool years. Honzik feels that the similarity of the parent-child resemblance in both groups indicates that "parental education" *per se* is not an environmentally important factor. The parent-child correlation that was obtained seems to reflect individual differences that are genetically determined.

Conway (1958) suggests that differences in intellectual level are due both to environmental and genetic factors. In spite of the improvement in social conditions in recent years, he finds that the differences among the average levels for various social classes are much the same as they were previously. While the average level of children from the lower occupational groups is lower than that of other groups because of their numbers and the wide range of individual variation, these groups provide a larger number of able children than the higher groups. Apparently a multifactor process of inheritance combined with the effects of social mobility is needed to account adequately for all the observed data.

Determining Effects of Environment

Perhaps the argument can best be resolved for the reader in the following statement: Heredity may set the limits for intellectual functioning, but the environment determines whether or not any individual reaches his limit. To date, we cannot manipulate heredity through matched mating or other means. We can, however, manipulate the environment in many ways. Basically, the argument centers around differences in structure and in function within the structural limit. For example, the height an individual will reach is genetically determined, and under normal environmental conditions that limit should be reached. Some form of extreme environmental deprivation, like inadequate diet, however, may keep the individual from reaching this limit. Another illustration, which involves athletic ability, may further clarify this point:

Currently, a number of athletes have run a mile in less than four minutes, a feat that only a decade ago was considered almost impossible. Perhaps the capability for such a feat was always present, but the environmental situation was not. Better methods of training, better track facilities, and even better nutrition may have made this feat possible. However, unless the actual capacity is present in a given individual, it is unlikely that any amount of training will enable him to accomplish this task.

So it is, too, with intelligence. An individual may have the capacity to function at an IQ level of 140, but his environment may not afford him the opportunity to reach this level. He may, because of environmental deprivation, function at an IQ level of 100 or so, much lower than his structural characteristics would allow. The following brief case study may better illustrate this point:

John R. was an apparently average student with a group-test IQ of about 100. His academic achievement was at about the level one might expect for this IQ, yet a number of his teachers felt he was more capable than either his IQ or achievement indicated. He was given an individual intelligence test by a psychologist who was able to establish excellent rapport with him. The result of this test showed John's IQ to be 135, confirming the teachers' feelings about his capability. Why was he testing and performing at a lower level? Careful investigation revealed that he was a very poor reader, with a well-developed emotional problem relating to his reading skill.

Thus we can see how an emotional problem, which is an environmental factor, can keep an individual from functioning at a level that he is capable of reaching.

This case study brings out another important point. The emotional difficulty also caused John to do poorly on the test that purported to measure his capability. Quite often the interference of an environmental problem makes it impossible to assess the level of potential functioning. If John's teachers had not noticed occasional "flashes of brilliance" and called for additional testing, his actual ability level might never have been discovered. Even such additional testing may often fail to uncover the true potential. It is safe, therefore, to assume that numbers of students function at a lower level than they should, but that teachers are often unaware of the situation because the environmental difficulty that causes the poor achievement also causes the students to do poorly on the test of their capability.

Actually, one would expect a youngster who scores low on an achievement test also to score low on an intelligence test, since most present-day intelligence tests are really just achievement tests. Most of these tests do not measure innate capacity, but what the individual has learned in his environment.

If we are able to assess actual capability and it proves to be well above the level indicated by an individual's achievement, we are then faced with the problem of properly manipulating the environment to bring achievement to the capability level. In order to do this effectively, we must first determine what the environmental problem is and then decide how best to overcome it. Perhaps the individual had poor instruction in basic skills and needs only some remedial work to bring him to his proper level. Perhaps the difficulty is emotionally based and psychotherapy must be recommended. Or perhaps there is a number of interrelated factors that must be identified and corrected. In each case, manipulation of the environment is necessary to bring forth the desired result.

MEASURING INTELLIGENCE

In Chapter 1 we discussed briefly some of the general measuring instruments used in assessing adolescent development. Because knowledge of an individual's intellectual capability is extremely important, some specific discussion of the instruments used to evaluate this trait is included at this point. The reader is also referred to the excellent books in the area of measurement that cover this topic in detail (Lindquist, 1951; Cronbach, 1960; Anastasi, 1961).

Individual Intelligence Tests

The intelligence tests most commonly administered to individuals are the Stanford-Binet (1937 or 1960 Revisions) and the Wechsler Adult Intelligence Scale (WAIS). These tests should be administered only by well-trained and experienced personnel who are particularly adept at establishing rapport with others, particularly with young people. Although these tests are called intelligence tests, it is unlikely that they directly measure the actual "potential" with which the individual is born. Rather, they tend to measure actual performance as an indirect measure of potential. As we suggested earlier, such intelligence tests are really only general achievement tests. Consequently, they are strongly affected by the individual's environmental experiences as well as by innate factors.

The Stanford-Binet score is strongly based on the individual's verbal facility. This, of course, penalizes an individual who has had poor verbal experiences, i.e., one who has a bilingual background, parents who use poor language, a hearing impairment, or reading difficulties. Verbal facility does relate to some degree, however, to prediction of school success, since most school learning areas are highly involved with verbal skills.

It has also been suggested that the Stanford-Binet measures only a very general kind of intelligence rather than specific factors, that its greatest precision is found for the earlier age levels, and that, consequently, it is a less effective measure for adolescents. The 1960 revision of the test has attempted to correct this to some degree up to age eighteen, but many still prefer the WISC and/or WAIS for the adolescent and young adult levels. These latter tests also eliminate the mental age concept that is the basis for the IQ as derived from the Stanford-Binet.

One of the major reasons for the popularity of the Wechsler scales as opposed to the Stanford-Binet is that these scales include both a verbal scale and a performance scale. The performance scale is considered to be one of the most important performance tests available. The total-scale IQ measures about the same things as the Stanford-Binet, as is evidenced by the .82 correlation between the two (Krugman *et. al.*, 1951). The verbal scale by itself correlates .74 with the Stanford-Binet, while the performance scale correlates only .64. The performance scale makes this test applicable for individuals who lack verbal facility and for whom, therefore, the Stanford-Binet is inappropriate. Thus, if a person does appreciably better on the performance tests than on the verbal test, we might assume he may have a language handicap or a limited educational background, or that he may perhaps be deaf or hard of hearing.

The Wechsler scales have been claimed to be useful in clinical diagnoses. Although there is some evidence to warrant this claim (Schafer, 1948), for our purposes the test should be considered primarily as a general measure of mental ability. In the hands of a skilled clinician, its diagnostic value may be great, but it is administered more often than not by psychometrists or school psychologists who lack diagnostic skills.

Again, it must be emphasized that the results of both the Stanford-Binet and the Wechsler tests are influenced by cultural factors. Both, in a sense, are measures of what the individual has been exposed to environmentally. However, although they are not, therefore, true measures of an individual's potential, they are still valuable predictors of future behavior. In particular, they remain fairly good predictors of both present and future academic success.

Group Intelligence Tests

Because it is usually both impractical and costly to administer large numbers of individual intelligence tests, group tests are much more widely used. In such large group situations as a school system or the armed forces, group tests may be useful. They are not very costly and do not require specially trained administrators. Although group tests are usually as reliable and often as valid as individual tests, their administration cannot be as precisely controlled, and scores for any given individual may be greatly in error. If large groups are to be broken into smaller groups on the basis of different levels of ability, group tests are most useful instruments for selecting the individuals who should be placed in the various groups. However, if the results are used to determine the specific ability of individuals, the results will be less valid. The standardized procedures involved in administering such tests make no allowance for the individual. If the subject fails to understand the directions, has a headache, forgot his glasses, or the like, his individual result may be quite inaccurate.

Most of the group intelligence tests currently used purport to be measures of general intelligence. In this sense the total score of the test is usually more meaningful than any part scores that may be offered. Even the part scores, such as language scores and/or performance scores, are measures of general rather than specific factors. Generally, the scales most popularly used are primarily verbal scales. In school situations this is legitimate, since verbal facility is one of the major factors involved in predicting school success. In situations in which the environmental experiences of the group vary widely, a nonverbal type of test may be more useful. For example, the Raven Matrices, a nonverbal test, was used in Britain during World War II to help minimize the rejection of personnel whose education had been poor. Cronbach (1960) feels, however, that the purely nonverbal score has one special function in school testing: "It calls attention to pupils who have good reasoning ability but who are below standard in reading and verbal development."

The California Test of Mental Maturity (1936-1951), a popularly used group test currently available, is a good example of the typical group intelligence test. Like the Stanford-Binet, it measures general ability. Separate language and nonlanguage IQ's are available, although the differentiation between the two is not clear. This breakdown may serve to help identify those having some language difficulty, reading problem, or poor educational background. Generally, however, the total IQ is the most reliable and probably the most meaningful. The authors also offer a profile based on subtests, but since the validity of these subscores is questionable, this profile probably should not be used.

Perhaps even more than the individual tests, the group tests are influenced by cultural and environmental factors. They are in a sense achievement tests and can often be used for the same purposes. The mental test is generally more useful than the achievement test, particularly when the students have had different educational backgrounds.

Many test-developers today recognize the difficulty of differentiating intelligence tests from achievement tests. As a result, they seem to be placing even more emphasis on achievement type tests as predictors of school success. (The relatively new School and College Ability Tests illustrate this point.)

Brief mention should be made here of the SRA Primary Mental Abilities Test (1950). This test is being widely used in public education, despite the fact that experts in the field consider it still to be an experimental instrument (Anastasi, 1961; Cronbach, 1960). It purports to measure specific mental abilities and is based on a different theoretical framework from that of the general intelligence tests. Although a total IQ is available, it does not mean the same thing as the total IQ on scales measuring general ability.

Recently, too, there has been increasing emphasis on attempts to develop "culture-free" intelligence tests. Such instruments might truly measure potential and could be used equally well with a college graduate or a native of a primitive tribe. To date, no test that actually achieves this goal has been developed. The Cattell Culture Fair Test is a widely used test that makes this attempt, but it is influenced to an appreciable degree by cultural factors. Scale 1 of this test seems to be as much influenced by culture as the Stanford-Binet, although Scale 2 seems to be less influenced by culture.

SEX DIFFERENCES IN INTELLIGENCE AND ACHIEVEMENT

For some time now there has been evidence indicating that girls are slightly superior to boys during early adolescence (Conrad, Jones and Hsaio, 1933; Freeman and Flory, 1937). Generally, this evidence seems related to the earlier maturation of girls, and the difference is less apparent during later adolescence when boys have "caught up" maturationally. Certain areas currently measured by intelligence tests show even greater differences between the sexes. Girls generally are superior in the verbal items involving vocabulary, memory, language manipulation, and the like, while boys are superior in performance items involving spatial relations, mechanical abilities, and numerical manipulations. Havighurst and Breese (1947) administered the Thurstone Primary Mental Abilities test to a large group of thirteen-year-olds. Girls excelled the boys in the number factor, work fluency, reasoning, and memory, while boys excelled girls in the space test. On the verbal comprehension test, there was no significant sex difference.

More boys are found at both the high and low extremes of the distribution of intelligence (Terman and Oden, 1947). At the high end of the scale, this may result from the operation of cultural factors that tend to depress girls' scores. The differences at the lower end of the scale cannot be easily explained and are still the source of further investigation.

Many currently used intelligence tests are constructed to minimize sex differences. This variable has been considered rather difficult to assess, and little attention has been given to it. Bradway and Thompson (1962) feel that this was one of the more important aspects of their study. Table 6 demonstrates their findings that females achieved a higher mean score than males on all three administrations of the Stanford-Binet. In 1931 and 1941 the differences between the sexes was significant beyond the .01 level of confidence. From 1941 to 1956, however, the male scores increased significantly more than did the female scores, seeming to indicate that beyond adolescence females do not increase their scores as much as males do.

These authors further investigated the relation between IQ at adolescence and continuation of education for the total group. They found no significant sex difference in means in the 1941 group for those who completed their education with high-school graduation, or attended but did not graduate from college. For those who did graduate

TABLE 6. Sex differences on the Stanford-Binet
From Bradway and Thompson (1962), by permission of the authors and Journal of Educational Psychology

Test	Male	Female	Difference
1931 L-M			
N	51	59	
M	108.5	115.8	−7.3
SD	14.4	13.3	
$CR*$			2.79
1941 L			
N	52	59	
M	107.9	116.1	−8.2
SD	19.0	13.7	
$CR*$			2.58
1956 L			
N	52	59	
M	121.6	125.7	−4.1
SD	19.6	10.6	
$CR*$			1.36

*A value of 2.57 is significant beyond the .01 level and a value of 1.96 beyond the .05 level.

from college, the mean IQ for both sexes is higher than for those who did not graduate. The lack of other substantial studies of sex differences in IQ makes it difficult to relate these findings to any other frame of reference. As Bradway and Thompson suggest, there is a need for further study in this important area.

Sex and School Grades

These sex differences become even more noticeable when one deals with academic achievement as reflected in school marks. Girls seem to be better students at all grade levels than do boys. Even in areas where boys seem to excel intellectually, girls frequently receive better academic grades; i.e., girls not only receive better grades in reading, which might be expected, but frequently also receive better grades in arithmetic, which would not be expected. This has become so obvious to all that there have even been recommendations made to start boys in school a year later than girls (see page 8).

Achievement test results, however, do not present the same picture (Powell *et al.*, 1962). True, girls do seem to excel in areas such as reading vocabulary and reading comprehension, but they are not necessarily superior in arithmetic reasoning. Even where significant differences do exist, they do not seem to warrant holding boys back a year. These results may be suspect, since achievement tests measure what has been learned, and learning may well be influenced by the classroom environment, which generally favors girls.

Again, as was suggested earlier, there is reason to believe that these apparent differences between the sexes are not true differences but are the result of cultural artifacts. Teachers, both male and female, seem to favor girl students over boy students. This subjective feeling is reflected in criteria for grading students and accounts for the fact that girls generally receive better grades than boys do. Thus, students seem to be graded as much on the basis of overt behavior as on actual achievement. Girls are more obedient, less boisterous, more controlled, and generally better behaved in the classroom environment than boys are. Even their early advantage in an area like reading may have these behavioral overtones. Because young girls as compared to boys are rather restricted in physical activities and overt physical expression of aggression, they may resort to solitary activities such as reading. That they spend more time at this kind of activity helps account for their greater proficiency.

The reverse of this general situation is often apparent at the college level, where the instructors seem to favor the male over the female student. At this level the male is also likely to be more highly motivated toward success, especially in relation to his future occupation. Further, it seems safe to assume that by this time the male has definitely "caught up" to the female maturationally, thus negating differences resulting from the different levels of earlier maturation.

INFLUENCE OF SOCIOECONOMIC STATUS

The relationship between environmental background and the development of intelligence has already been mentioned several times in this chapter. This relationship is particularly important, especially since the instruments used to measure intelligence are heavily influenced by environmental experiences. Further, relationships between IQ and socioeconomic and/or vocational level have been found to exist. Davis, in a study (1948) of social-class influences upon learning, further emphasizes this by pointing out that most intelligence tests favor the child from the middle-class home environment. Generally, the findings indicate that children from high socioeconomic levels are consistently superior to those coming from homes lower in the socioeconomic scale (Shuttleworth, 1940). Similarly, the early studies by Asher (1935) and Wheeler (1942) indicate that deprived environments depress the IQ so that it not only fails to rise but actually declines. Reymert and Hinton (1940) have demonstrated that an improvement in the environment can and does raise the IQ of those who come from deprived backgrounds. The Skodak and Skeels study (1949), previously mentioned (see page 84), further demonstrates this point.

Too often this relationship between IQ and socioeconomic status is interpreted as meaning "the rich get richer . . . ," but this is not really the case. Those who have achieved a high socioeconomic level, usually as a result of their own higher intellect, offer higher-level environmental experiences to their children than do those on a lower socioeconomic level. Two children with the same IQ might well function at different levels academically because of different environments. Perhaps the following case description will illustrate this point.

John G., whose father is an M.D. and whose mother was a teacher, enters the same school as Arthur N., whose father is a semiskilled laborer with an eighth-grade education and whose mother was a clerk with only seven years of educational experience. In the first grade John was far superior to Arthur in most subjects and appeared to be appreciably brighter. At the end of the first grade both boys were given individual intelligence tests and, much to the surprise of the teacher, both had IQ's of 135. The difference in achievement obviously was related to the differences in the environmental experiences that the two sets of parents offered. John's parents read to him extensively, took trips to local and distant points of interest, discussed "adult" topics with him, encouraged him to question and seek information, and impressed him with the importance of education. Arthur's parents seldom read to him, discouraged his questions, made few trips, and were rather uninterested in his academic achievement. When the school authorities became aware of Arthur's high IQ, they tried to make Arthur's school environment as much like John's as possible. Even with this kind of effort, the boys became more different with increasing age. By the tenth-grade level in school John was one year advanced for his age, while Arthur was one year retarded and was planning to drop out of school.

Despite the efforts of the school, Arthur's general environmental background resulted in his apparent failure. His parents' lack of concern about education, their failure to encourage his academic work, and their own restricted environment kept Arthur from functioning at the level of which he was capable. The following study shows the possible effect of a positive change in environment on an individual who was initially very much like Arthur:

Bill R. was the child of parents of whom neither had finished the ninth grade or had full-time employment. Bill's IQ in the second grade was 123, but his actual achievement was far below this level. When he was in the fifth grade, his mother deserted him and the court decided to place him in a foster home. The foster parents were a childless professional couple who almost immediately accepted Bill as though he were their own. Bill was exposed to situations completely new to him and responded quickly. When he was retested in the seventh grade, his IQ was 138 and his academic achievement was compatible with this score.

These are, of course, rather unusual cases; the majority of children from socioeconomicaly low homes are generally average or below in intelligence. In such cases, a change in environment would probably not have the extreme effect described above. Yet even a duller child may live in an environment that fails to offer him the opportunity to reach the limit of even his lesser potential. For example, a child may have an actual potential of about 90 IQ but because of environmental deprivation may never function above a level of IQ 75.

Cultural Differences

Various aspects of family background and intelligence have been investigated. Havighurst and Breese (1947) administered the Primary Mental Abilities test to a group of thirteen-year-olds in a typical Midwestern community. Children of higher socioeconomic status tended to do better in all the tests than did those of lower family social status. In a later article, Havighurst (1949) discussed the cultural background, particularly as it is reflected in socioeconomic status and the IQ. He indicates that there are systematic differences in the experiences of the upper-middle class and the lower class that might be expected to result in different levels of performance on intelligence tests. These cultural differences are categorized into four areas: (1) cultural differences in home and family life; (2) cultural differences in neighborhood and community life; (3) cultural differences in school experience; and (4) cultural differences in motivation for test performance.

Himmelweit (1948) studied intelligence and family size. He found that even in a highly selected sample of college students, large families tend to have a higher proportion of lower intelligence than do small families. These negative correlations operated equally in all socioeconomic groups. They were not affected by the relative homogeneity of educational background or of socioeconomic factors and could not be explained by differences in opportunity. Nisbet (1953) further explored the relationship between family size and environment. His findings tended to confirm the hypothesis that limited contact between parents and children in large families seems to retard verbal development and as a result seems to depress test scores.

The high correlation between intelligence test scores, educational levels, and socioeconomic variables must be seen against fertility differentials. Anastasi (1959) feels that these differentials vary from their own group patterns for families that move upward socially, that come from high fertility areas, for postwar marriages, and for highest income groups. She feels that methodological considerations, such as sampling, physical factors modifying reproduction, changes in educational level and in tests used from generation to generation, conceal the clarity of the trends. Therefore, the genetic and environmental contributions affecting fertility are most difficult to unravel.

Getzels and Jackson (1962) in their studies relating to creativity have also found relationships with family background. They studied two groups of adolescents: (1) those exceptionally high in intelligence (IQ) but not in creativity; and (2) those exceptionally high in creativity but not in intelligence. The groups were found to differ in intellective and social behavior and to have their source in differing environments. One group was characterized by parental vigilance over academic performance, while the other focused upon less visible qualities, such as the child's openness to experience and his values, interests, and enthusiasms. Getzels and Jackson feel that there is a need for more investigation of the ways in which types of cognition are shaped by types of family structure.

Family relationships to intelligence are not peculiar to American society. Ginsberg (1951) found statistically significant differences between higher, middle, and lower socioeconomic status groups in a study done in five cities in Brazil. She also found that males scored better than females on an adapted version of the Terman Group Test of Intelligence and that there were differences between whites and Negroes or Indians.

Stenquist and Lorge (1951) have commented on the implication of cultural differences for test-makers and test-users. Stenquist dealt with the question of whether or not intelligence tests are unfair to children of low cultural level. He felt that the school must broaden its educational aims and objectives: "As the school is the epitome of our culture, tests should be the epitome of the schools." Lorge strongly urged that the test-maker should make the test-user aware that intelligence and measurement of social status are related.

Some studies have attempted to determine whether certain extreme environmental situations, such as war, have any effect upon intelligence. DeGroot (1948) found that Dutch children averaged four points lower in IQ's in the postwar years than in the prewar years. This may, of course, have been result of the setback suffered by the educational program during the war. This type of evidence seems to show that the

IQ reflects any conditions that alter the rate of mental development, particularly environmental conditions.

RELATIONSHIP BETWEEN INTELLIGENCE AND ACHIEVEMENT

Earlier in this chapter the high correlation between intelligence and achievement was discussed briefly. Although some part of this high relationship is a result of the similar structure of the tests used to measure these variables, some investigators feel that the relationship is nonetheless meaningful. Frandsen (1950) investigated the relationship between the Wechsler-Bellevue Intelligence Scale and school achievement for a group of relatively superior high-school seniors. He found that the results of the whole scale and also of various subtest combinations were effective in predicting academic achievement. There was a .69 correlation for both the full-scale IQ's and the verbal scale IQ's with the grade-point averages over a three-year period. By also using various subtest combinations, he found correlation with academic achievement ranging from .60 to .71.

Bolton (1947) agrees that intelligence-test scores have value in predicting achievement, but he feels that several tests should be used rather than one. Not only will the use of more intelligence tests facilitate educational guidance, but it will also allow for better prediction in the different achievement areas. For example, he found the Pintner Non-Language Test useful in predicting achievement in courses in safety, health, mechanical drawing, printing, English, and clothing and foods.

Green (1953) related intelligence-test scores to five measures of learning for a group of eleventh-grade pupils. The correlations ranged from —.14 to +.33. However, the correlations between the five learning tests and school marks ranged from —.02 to +.30, while IQ scores correlated .54 with school marks, thus appearing to be a better over-all predictor of academic success than were the five learning tests.

In order to determine the factors involved in intelligence and achievement, Driscoll (1952) administered a number of tests of general ability to a group of high-school juniors. The three factors that were found to underlie the performance of the tests were identified as cognitive, verbal, and numerical. Roesslein (1953) found differential patterns of intelligence traits in his study of high- and low-achieving high-school boys. The chief differences found were an integrating factor (a preponderance of the cognitive *g*) and superior abstract reasoning favoring the high-achievers. Gough (1953) constructed a sixty-four-item achievement scale to measure academic achievement of high-school students. This scale correlated .44 with grade average and .26 with IQ.

The IQ itself correlated .47 with grades, and the multiple correlation of the achievement scale and IQ was .62 in relation to the grade-point average.

The IQ apparently may be used to predict success in specific subject areas. Since most intelligence tests have a high verbal content, they correlate well with verbal skill areas such as English and social studies. Sister Rosilda (1951) has also found a moderate relation between IQ and algebra achievement, which is less verbally oriented. The correlation between IQ and algebra achievement in a large group of high school students was .42. Obviously, such a correlation does not make for perfect individual prediction, but from it one could make general predictions of the achievement of fairly large groups of students; i.e., generally bright students will achieve better in algebra than average or dull students.

On such evidence as that just cited, the IQ apparently continues to be a relatively good predictor of academic success up through the high-school level. Generally, this holds true even for those experiencing emotional difficulties, except of course for extreme cases. Nonetheless, this author feels that achievement tests are as good predictors as intelligence tests and may be more useful because they relate more directly to areas of school instruction.

INTELLIGENCE AND ADJUSTMENT

There are many misconceptions concerning the relationships between intelligence and emotional adjustments. For example, one often hears it said that there is only a fine line between genius and insanity, and generally the gifted individual is thought to be emotionally unstable. At the other end of the scale, the layman erroneously feels that the dull or retarded individual makes up for his lack of intelligence by being skilled in motor tasks such as woodworking or machine operation, and thus usually makes a good adjustment. The onset of pubescence, with its accompanying emotional problems, is often regarded as the time when intellectual functioning is most affected.

Educators do indicate that there is frequently a drop in academic grades when students enter junior high school. This is usually interpreted as being the result of increased emotionality related to pubescence. One might suggest that it could simply be due to the change in structure from the self-contained classroom at the elementary level to the departmentalized structure of the junior high school. Once students adjust to this change, which is usually by the second grading period, the achievement level usually comes back up. It is, of course, possible that a young adolescent who is somewhat disturbed emotionally will become more upset as a result of this transition and will therefore continue to function poorly academically.

Anxiety

There has been a number of studies that indicate the relationship between intelligence and adjustment, particularly the adjustment dimension of anxiety. There has been particular concern that many bright students fail to live up to their potential in life situations because of emotional problems. Edelston (1950) investigated this hypothesis and concluded that wide variations exist in the origin and nature of these deleterious influences. In his discussion of the relative parts played by intellectual capacity and emotional factors in achievement, he concludes that "the limitations of an emotional nature are more rigid than is usually accepted."

Sarason (1956) investigated the effects of anxiety and defensiveness on intellectual performance. His results do not show significant changes in intellectual performance as a result of anxiety. However, those subjects who scored low in defensiveness did perform more poorly on the measure of achievement and had poorer grade-point averages. These students also evidenced the adverse effects of self-criticism on their performance.

The relationships of achievement, personality, and interest to scores on an interpretation-of-the-data test were investigated by Fattu and Fox (1949). They found that ability to interpret data was related to intelligence and achievement. The adjustment and interest scores also showed some relationship, but of a "distinctly lower order of association." Apparently intelligent functioning was not affected appreciably by level of adjustment. The study by Phillips *et al.* (1960) of the influence of intelligence on anxiety and attitudes toward self indicated that anxiety did tend to produce dissatisfaction with self and others, but these relations were modified when the intelligence of the subjects was considered. The relationship between anxiety and attitudes toward self and others seems to be dependent to some extent on the intelligence of those studied.

Morgan *et al.* (1960) used the Children's Manifest Anxiety Scale to examine the relationship between anxiety and achievement at different ages. Although there was some doubt as to the adequacy of the instrument used, the results did indicate an apparent relationship between the preadolescent growth spurt and increased anxiety for girls. The high-achieving and probably most intelligent girls reached a peak in anxiety earlier than their low-achieving peers. Once pubescence is reached, the high-achieving girls seem to become more stable. Boys did not show a comparable pattern, but such a pattern may occur at later levels than grades four, five, and six, which were investigated in this study.

It is not unusual for an emotionally disturbed student to be a high-achiever, and in fact his compulsive drive to attain high grades may actually be a part of his pattern of disturbed behavior. In some cases, achieving well academically may be the only source of satisfaction and success for a student who is frustrated in other environmental circumstances. The following case study may illustrate this point:

Joseph G. was a tall, thin, generally unattractive sixteen-year-old. He possessed few, if any, friends and seemed to be the butt of most of the practical jokes of his classmates. He was known as the "brain" of the class, since his grades were excellent, but his peers seemed to consider this further evidence of his being a "grind." Most of his teachers were pleased with his academic achievement and often singled him out for special praise, pointing him out to the others as an example they might well emulate. This, in turn, caused the peer group to reject Joseph more than ever.

In a discussion with the school guidance counselor, Joseph indicated that he was rather disturbed emotionally, and he was referred to a local mental-health clinic. Here it was found that he was seriously concerned about his rejection by the peer group and compulsively sought to receive high grades as a partial compensation. At least his academic achievement did bring him praise from teachers and other adults.

With the help of the clinic staff, Joseph developed a good deal of insight into his own behavior and began to "blossom out" socially. As he became more and more accepted by the peer group, his grades began to drop off somewhat, and his compulsive study habits changed to a more relaxed, almost casual pattern. Although he continued to achieve at a high level, it was no longer his only source of satisfaction.

This study is not meant to suggest that high achievement is generally indicative of emotional maladjustment. If, however, this situation occurs, the emotional disturbance may go unrecognized, especially in the school setting. Teachers are usually pleased with the high-achiever and consequently often fail to recognize the kind of disturbance presented in this illustration. By praising such an adolescent and by making him an example for the others, they may actually increase the degree of disturbance.

THE GIFTED ADOLESCENT

Today's space-age preoccupations have created increased concern about identifying the gifted individual and then affording him the opportunity to achieve at the level of his capability. In order to do this effectively, it may be necessary to change our present views concerning the aims of education. Bartlett (1949) feels that with our present orientation toward attempting to include the integration and maturing of the emotional and physical aspects of all individuals, we may actually be penalizing the exceptionally intelligent. The very intelligent students are actually "far too teachable for their own good and there is often a tendency to exploit their intellectual responsiveness." Since these are the potential leaders of the next generation, he feels that we should do all we can to help them "develop right values and a sound attitude both toward their own abilities and to the responsibilities to the community which these gifts entail."

Identifying the Gifted

One of the difficulties encountered in this area is that of identifying the gifted individual. There is not yet general agreement as to how this can be done most effectively. IQ alone is not a satisfactory criterion, since the cut point above which a student is considered gifted may range from 125 to 140. The relative importance of grades, achievement-test results, teachers' judgments, etc., has not yet been evaluated, and the best combination of these factors needed for effective selection is still not determined.

Pegnato and Birch (1959) set up seven methods for screening out the gifted in a junior-high-school population of 1400 students. The seven methods included: teacher judgment; honor-roll listing; creative ability in art or music (based on teacher choices); student council membership; superiority in mathematics (teacher choices); group-intelligence-test results; and achievement test results. Seven hundred eighty-one students selected on these bases were then tested individually with the Stanford-Binet. Ninety-one adolescents of this group exceeded the criterion of giftedness, on this test an IQ of 136 or higher. The authors found that the combination of the group intelligence test and the group achievement test predicted 96.7 per cent of these gifted students. Further, they found some indication that group intelligence tests help to locate gifted children who do not show their ability in their academic marks or in the group-achievement-test results.

Once the gifted have been identified, the problem of adequately meeting their needs in the educational environment arises. Barbe (1954) points out that while there are various provisions for the gifted, there is little agreement as to the relative merits of acceleration, enrichment within the classroom, and homogeneous groupings. Few, if any, attempts have been made to structure well-designed, controlled research studies to investigate these methods and determine which have been most effective. Homogeneous grouping, for example, has been in operation for more than thirty years, but few have attempted to evaluate its usefulness.

Leadership Training

Concern has been expressed not only at the failure of the gifted to reach their potential academically, but also at their failure to attain the level of leadership of which they appear capable. Cassel and Haddox (1959) studied leadership in a group of typical ninth-grade students and a comparable group of gifted ninth- and eleventh-graders. Two leadership tests, the Leadership-Q-Sort Test and the Leadership Ability Test, were used to assess this characteristic. In the Q-Sort Test, a set of phrases covering various personality characteristics related to leadership were sorted into piles ranging from most descriptive to least descriptive by the subjects. No significant difference was found between the groups on the LQT Scores. There was a statistical difference for decision pattern for LAT Scores, with the gifted students exhibiting scores more closely approximating those of democratic leaders. The authors feel there is a need for training programs for leadership development in our high-school curriculum. Such programs should help able students enter adult roles in the community better prepared to exhibit leadership values and patterns more comparable to those of demonstrated leaders.

It is unfortunate that so little has been done to help the gifted adolescent to achieve his proper level academically and to exhibit his leadership qualities. Many do, of course, succeed in reaching these levels despite the lack of assistance by the schools. However, failure of early identification and inappropriate school curricula have penalized many to the degree that their potential is never realized. This in turn penalizes the society in which they function, since they fail to make the contributions to that society of which they might be capable.

THE ADOLESCENT'S CONCERN WITH INTELLIGENCE

Adults, particularly educators, have expressed much concern that adolescents are not interested in intelligence and intellectual achievement. Many able teen-agers seem to work below their capacity in order to avoid such labels as "brain," "grind," or "bookworm," which have unpleasant connotations to that age group. Superior intelligence and its overt demonstrations do not seem to be of great value in peer group acceptance. It seems odd, however, that adults should question this kind of attitude toward intelligence, since they too seem to be suspicious or nonaccepting of high intellect. Until very recently such terms as "egg-head" were applied to bright individuals, and the "intellectual" was considered to be somewhat odd.

This general attitude has changed somewhat since the appearance of the first Russian Sputnik. Whether or not the layman really understands the gifted individual, at least he now accepts him as a necessary part of society. However, such recognition and/or acceptance are still related to the individual's field of endeavor. The importance of the intellectual's contribution in science and mathematics is now recognized, but it is doubtful that such acceptance is as readily accorded to the philosopher, to the poet, or to those who function generally in the humanities.

The attitude of adolescents toward the intellectual performance of their peers expresses something of this change in orientation. They, too, are more accepting of the demonstration of ability in science and mathematics, but continue to view with some degree of suspicion the individual who is gifted in English, art, music, and the like.

High Achievement as a Social Handicap

Evidence of this peer attitude can often be found by examining the achievement of gifted students. There is of course tremendous variability in achievement even among the gifted, in terms of both achievement-test results and academic grades. However, an appreciable discrepancy often exists between these two measures, with the achievement-test scores correlating highly with the IQ but the academic marks being much lower than would be expected in terms of the IQ. When this is the case, it is quite possible that the adolescent is achieving in class at a level below his capability in order to avoid condemnation from his peers. Such a child is not truly an underachiever, since his achievement-test scores indicate that he is actually learning at the level of his capability. He seems to seek to be "average" in his classroom performance so as not to be singled out as the "brain" or class intellectual.

This tendency of bright students to seek "averageness" is often noted as they continue into college. The "gentleman's C" seems to be the golden mean for a large number of college students who are capable of far better grades. Even at this academic level, acceptability to the peer group appears to be more related to extracurricular activities than to academic achievement. Perhaps this situation develops in an attempt to avoid the cultural stereotype of the gifted individual's being socially inept and emotionally unstable. Actually, this stereotype is highly fallacious, since Terman's studies of the gifted (1947) demonstrate that they are generally both socially skilled and emotionally stable. Nonetheless, the adolescent seeking to avoid this stigma is quite likely to spend as much of his time as possible demonstrating his social capabilities, while at the same time de-emphasizing his intellectual ability.

Brumbaugh's study (1955) of the attitudes of preadolescent children toward brightness indicates that intelligence is not really involved in their choices. These children did not select those with higher IQ's as the ones whom they considered bright. The author concluded: "If you are a pleasant person, eleven-year-olds think you are bright." The same point of view carries over into adulthood. We adults all too often feel that the individual with a pleasant "personality" is a bright person. Similarly, the bright individual who is somewhat withdrawn socially is seldom credited with being as intelligent as he is.

There is an appreciable sex difference operating in this area, with females being even more likely than males to conceal high intelligence. Here again a strong cultural factor seems to be the major influence. The study of Bradway and Robinson (1961) mentioned earlier in this chapter (see page 78) seems to indicate that even intelligence-test results may be depressed for the very bright girl. The peer group seems even less willing to accept the girl "brain" than the bright boy. Girls seem to learn fairly early in their school careers that the overt display of high intelligence is not particularly approved, especially by males. A teen-age girl rarely becomes popular with members of the opposite sex because she is highly intelligent and shows it.

The Responsibility of the Schools

The failure of our schools to provide challenging programs for the gifted may also be responsible for their failure to achieve at the level of their high capability. Since the bright child seldom has to work very hard to acquire high marks, he may fail to develop good study habits during his early school career. He may then be somewhat penalized in high school and college by these poor study habits. Nonetheless, his high level of intelligence is generally sufficient to enable him to complete his education, although he may not benefit from it as much as he could or receive grades commensurate with his ability.

MacLean (1954) feels that we are actually discriminating, probably unintentionally, against the various levels of intelligence of children in our schools. Not only do we fail to offer adequate programs for the academically superior students, but we also tend to ignore those with outstanding talent in the clerical, mechanical, or artistic areas. With present-day research more clearly differentiating mental abilities and special aptitudes of the individual, more should be done in the schools to assist the development of these abilities. Certainly, individuals of all intellectual levels who drop out of school prior to high-school graduation often do so because the school fails to meet their needs. A more detailed discussion of the problems of the adolescent in school is presented in Chapters 12 and 13.

Present-Day Motivations Toward Achievement

As was pointed out earlier, the advent of the space age has done much to make the bright adolescent a more respected member of the peer group and the adult society. It has become apparent to all that, if we are to compete effectively against other societies, there is a need for more highly trained personnel, from technicians to scientists. The adolescent has become aware of new and interesting fields of endeavor and also of the requirements that must be fulfilled to achieve success in these fields. He recognizes that his desire to become a physicist, engineer, space expert, or even a psychologist is not only approved but actually encouraged. Even the less gifted individual is well aware of the need for achievement at as high a level as possible if he is to find a place in a highly complex and increasingly competitive labor market.

A number of other practical considerations is also motivating adolescents to achieve at the level of their capability. Young people are aware that colleges are becoming increasingly selective in their admissions, and that they must compete for admission against an increasing large number of other applicants. Despite the increasing emphasis on special tests (College Board examinations, etc.) for admission, the adolescent is well aware that his high-school grades are also carefully considered. He has also become more aware of the special requirements related to various fields and seeks to improve his background in these areas. For example, some years ago most students took only the minimal required high-school courses in mathematics, often because they were ignorant of the need for mathematics in their chosen field. An individual considering psychology as his vocation might assume that he would have little need for mathematics. Too late, he would find out that he would have to take a number of courses in statistics, for which a good mathematics background is invaluable. Increased knowledge about occupations, as well as the general relation of mathematics and science courses to our space-age technology, has caused increased numbers of students to take as many mathematics courses as their high school offers. Many colleges are now offering special courses in advanced mathematics to advanced high-school students.

Another practical consideration that has helped motivate the gifted individual is the change in status and in financial remuneration accorded some occupations. Physics, chemistry, and mathematics, as well as fields like psychology, anthropology, and sociology, have become well known to the layman and are considered to have very high status. The teen-ager today is highly aware of and interested in the research orientation of these occupations. He no longer thinks of a researcher as an isolated individual working on some obscure project that may never reach fruition, but views him as a highly trained person involved in complex interactions with others on a variety of meaningful projects.

The financial problems involved in attaining advanced training and/or advanced academic degrees are not as great as they were twenty or thirty years ago. Tremendous numbers of subsidies are available, both in industry and at the university level, to those seeking advanced knowledge. Young people are aware that training in some fields is available at no cost to them, and, in fact, some further payment is often available to assist them in meeting living costs. The occupational and/or academic areas that do not offer such subsidies are often hard pressed for candidates. This has been especially noted by medical-school admissions officers, who find that they are receiving fewer applications than ever before. Bright students who might have chosen medicine are now likely to seek Ph.D.'s in fields where assistantships, fellowships, and other financial aids are available. Since many of these other fields have as high a status as medicine, the financial aid may be the most attractive feature in recruiting candidates. The medical profession, well aware of this problem, is currently taking steps to develop equally good subsidy programs.

All these circumstances have had a positive influence on students' achievement. Students know that, to gain admission to these subsidized programs, they must achieve at the highest level their capability allows. Thus, they are beginning to acknowledge the need for and value of intellectual functioning and attainment. Some of the biases against the "egghead" still exist, but if our present rate of progress continues, these should slowly disappear. Even if they should continue, we must strive to make all people, especially the gifted, aware of the increased need for a high level of achievement. Perhaps teen-agers so enlightened will be more influenced to work harder in order to achieve the goals of which they are capable. One might well hope that this kind of drive will actually become more important to the adolescent than the social approval of his peers, or better still, that high-level achievement and overt intellectual functioning will become one of the variables involved in peer acceptance.

REFERENCES

ANASTASI, ANNE. "Differentiating Effect of Intelligence and Social Status." *Eugenics Quarterly*, 6, 84-91, 1959.

ANASTASI, ANNE. *Psychological Testing*, 2nd Ed. New York: Macmillan, 1961.

ASHER, E. J. "The Inadequacy of Current Intelligence Tests for Testing Kentucky Mountain Children." *Journal of Genetic Psychology*, 46, 480-486, 1935.

BARBE, WALTER B. "Are Gifted Children Being Adequately Provided For?" *Educational Administration Supervision*, 40, 405-413, 1954.

BARTLETT, E. M. "The Handicap of High Intelligence." *Mental Health* (London), 8, 71-74, 1949.

BAYLEY, NANCY. "Consistency and Variability in the Growth of Intelligence from Birth to Eighteen Years." *Journal of Genetic Psychology*, 75, 165-196, 1949.

BAYLEY, NANCY. "On the Growth of Intelligence." *American Psychologist*, 10, 805-818, 1955.

BAYLEY, NANCY, and ODEN, M. H. "The Maintenance of Intellectual Ability in Gifted Adults." *Journal of Gerontology*, 10, 91-107, 1955.

BOLTON, FLOYD B. "Value of Several Intelligence Tests for Predicting Scholastic Achievement." *Journal of Educational Research*, 41, 133-138, 1947.

BRADWAY, K. P., and ROBINSON, N. M. "Significant IQ Changes in Twenty-five Years: A Follow-up." *Journal of Educational Psychology*, 52, 74-79, 1961.

BRADWAY, K. P., and THOMPSON, C. W. "Intelligence at Adulthood: a Twenty-five Year Follow-up." *Journal of Educational Psychology*, 53, 1-14, 1962.

BRUMBAUGH, FLORENCE. "What Is an IQ?" *Journal of Experimental Education*, 23, 359-363, 1955.

BURT, SIR CYRIL L. "The Evidence for the Concept of Intelligence." *British Journal of Educational Psychology* (London), 25, 158-177, 1955.

BURT, SIR CYRIL L. "The Inheritance of Mental Ability." *American Psychologist*, 13, 1-15, 1958.

CASSEL, RUSSELL N., and HADDOX, GENEVIEVE. "Comparative Study of Leadership Test Scores for Gifted and Typical High School Students." *Psychological Reports*, 5, 713-717, 1959.

CLARK, W. W., and TIEGS, W. T. *California Test of Mental Maturity*. Los Angeles: California Test Bureau, 1936-1951.

CLARKE, A. D. B., and CLARKE, A. M. "How Constant is the IQ?" *Lancet* (London), 265, no. 6791, 877-880, 1953.

CONRAD, H. S., JONES, H. E., and HSAIO, H. H. "Six Differences in Mental Growth and Decline." *Journal of Educational Psychology*, 24, 161-169, 1933.

CONWAY, J. "The Inheritance of Intelligence and Its Social Implications." *British Journal of Statistical Psychology* (London), 11, 171-190, 1958.

CRONBACH, LEE J. *Essentials of Psychological Testing*, 2nd ed. New York: Harper & Row, 1960.

DAVIS, A. *Social-class Influences upon Learning*. Cambridge, Mass.: Harvard University Press, 1948.

DAVIS, FREDERICK B. "Delimiting the Verbal Factor." *Proceedings of the 1948 Conference on Testing Problems, Educational Testing Service*, 50-51, 1949.

DEGROOT, A. D. "Demasque van de IQ constantie" (Unmasking IQ Constancy). *Nederlandische Tidschrift voor de Psychologie en Haar Grensgebredden* (Amsterdam), 10, 532-537, 1955.

DEGROOT, A. D. "The Effects of War Upon the Intelligence of Youth." *Journal of Abnormal and Social Psychology*, 43, 311-317, 1948.

DOPPELT, JEROME EDWARD. "The Organization of Mental Abilities in the Age Range 13 to 17." *Teachers College Contributions to Education*, no. 962, 1950.

DRISCOLL, JUSTIN A. *Factors in Intelligence and Achievement.* Washington, D. C.: The Catholic University of America Press, 1952.

EDELSTON, H. "Educational Failure with High Intelligence Quotient: A Clinical Study." *Journal of Genetic Psychology*, 77, 85-116, 1950.

FATTU, NICHOLAS A., and FOX, WILLIAM H. "Scores on the Interpretation of Data Test: Their Relation to Measures of Achievement, Personality and Interest." *Bulletin of the School of Education, Indiana University*, 24 (3), 1949.

FRANDSEN, ARDEN N. "The Wechsler-Bellevue Intelligence Scale and High School Achievement." *Journal of Applied Psychology*, 34, 406-411, 1950.

FREEMAN, F. N., and FLORY, C. D. "Growth in Intellectual Ability as Measured by Repeated Tests." *Monographs of the Society for Research in Child Development*, 2, no. 2, 1937.

GARRETT, H. E. "A Developmental Theory of Intelligence." *American Psychologist*, 1, 372-378, 1946.

GETZELS, JACOB W., and JACKSON, PHILLIP W. *Creativity and Intelligence.* New York: John Wiley and Sons, Inc., 1962.

GINSBERG, ANIELA MEYER. "Comparacao entre os resultadoes de um tests de nivel mental aplicado em diferentes grupos etnicos e socials" (Comparison of the Results of a Test of Mental Level Administered in Different Ethnic and Social Groups). *Arquivos Brasileiros de Psicotecnica*, 3(4), 27-44, 1951.

GOUGH, HARRISON G. "What Determines the Academic Achievement of High School Students?" *Journal of Educational Research*, 46, 321-331, 1953.

GREEN, CLINTON WALLACE. "The Relationship Between Intelligence as Determined by Intelligence Tests and the Ability to Learn as Determined by Performance on Learning Tests." *Journal of Educational Research*, 47, 191-200, 1953.

GUILFORD, J. P. "Three Factors of Intellect." *American Psychologist*, 14, 469-479, 1959.

HART, H. "Slowing up at Growth in Mental Test Ability." *School and Society*, 20, 573-574, 1924.

HAVIGHURST, ROBERT J. "Culture and the IQ." *Purdue University Studies in Higher Education*, no. 69, 42-53, 1949.

HAVIGHURST, ROBERT J., and BREESE, F. H. "Relation between Ability and Social Status in a Midwestern Community: III. Primary Mental Abilities." *Journal of Educational Psychology*, 38, 241-247, 1947.

HILDEN, ARNOLD H. "A Longitudinal Study of Intellectual Development." *Journal of Psychology*, 28, 187-214, 1949.

HIMMELWEIT, H. T. "Intelligence and Size of Family: Their Relationship in an Adult Group of High Education Standard." *Eugenics Review*, 40, 77-84, 1948.

HONZIK, MARJORIE P. "Developmental Studies of Parent-Child Resemblance in Intelligence." *Child Development*, 28, 215-228, 1957.

HONZIK, MARJORIE P., MACFARLANE, JEAN W., and ALLEN, L. "The Stability of Mental Test Performance between Two and Eighteen Years." *Journal of Experimental Education,* 17, 309-324, 1948.

JONES, H. E., and CONRAD, H. S. "The Growth and Decline of Intelligence." *Genetic Psychology Monographs,* 13, 223-298, 1933.

KNEHR, CHARLES A. "Intelligence as Structural Limitation and Potential." *Journal of Psychology,* 29, 165-171, 1950.

KRUGMAN, J. L., *et al.* "Pupil Functioning on the Stanford-Binet and the Wechsler Intelligence Scale for Children." *Journal of Consulting Psychology,* 15, 475-483, 1951.

LINDQUIST, E. F., ed. *Educational Measurement.* Washington, D.C.: American Council on Education, 1951.

LORGE, IRVING. "Why a Verbal Factor?" *Proceedings, 1948 Conference on Testing Problems, Educational Testing Service,* 45-46, 1949.

MACLEAN, MALCOLM S. "Are We Discriminating against Intelligence?" *Educational Leadership,* 12, 85-89, 1954.

MEYER, WILLIAM J. "The Stability of Patterns of Primary Mental Abilities among Junior High and Senior High School Students." *Educational and Psychological Measurement,* 20, 795-800, 1960.

MORGAN, E., SUTTON-SMITH, B., and ROSENBERG, B. G. "Age Changes in the Relation between Anxiety and Achievement." *Child Development,* 31, 515-520, 1960.

NISBET, JOHN D. "Family Environment and Intelligence." *Eugenics Review,* 45, 31-40, 1953.

NISBET, JOHN D. "Intelligence and Age: Retesting with Twenty-four Years' Interval." *British Journal of Educational Psychology,* 27, 190-198, 1957.

OWENS, W. A., JR. "Age and Mental Abilities: A Longitudinal Study." *Genetic Psychology Monographs,* 48, 3-54, 1953.

PEGNATO, CARL V., and BIRCH, JACK W. "Locating Gifted Children in Junior High Schools: A Comparison of Methods." *Exceptional Children,* 25, 300-304, 1959.

PHILLIPS, BEEMAN N., HINDSMAN, EDWIN, and JENNINGS, EARL. "Influence of Intelligence on Anxiety and Perception of Self and Others." *Child Development,* 31, 41-46, 1960.

PIAGET, JEAN. "Perception et Intelligence" (Perception and Intelligence). *Bulletin du groupe d'étude psychologie,* University of Paris, 4(1-2), 25-34, 1950.

POWELL, M., O'CONNOR, H. A., and PARSLEY, K. M. In press. "Are There Really Sex Differences in Achievement?" *Journal of Educational Research* (a), 1963.

POWELL, M., O'CONNER, H. A., and PARSLEY, K. M. In press. "Further Investigation of Sex Differences in Achievement." *Journal of Educational Research* (b), 1963.

REYMERT, MARTIN, and HINTON, R., JR. "The Effect of a Change to a Relatively Superior Environment upon the IQ's of One Hundred Children." In *Intelligence: Its Nature and Nurture, 39th Yearbook, National Society for the Study of Education, Part II.* Chicago: University of Chicago Press, 1940.

ROESSLEIN, CHARLES G. *Differential Patterns of Intelligence Traits Between High Achieving and Low Achieving High School Boys.* Washington, D.C.: Catholic University of America Press, 1950.

ROSILDA, SISTER M. "Is an IQ an Index to Algebra Ability?" *Journal of Educational Research,* 44, 391-393, 1951.

SARASON, IRVIN G. "The Relationship of Anxiety and 'Lack of Defensiveness' to Intellectual Performance." *Journal of Consulting Psychology,* 20, 220-222, 1956.

SCHAFER, R. *The Clinical Application of Psychological Tests.* New York: International University Press, 1948.

SHUTTLEWORTH, F. K. "The Cumulative Influence on Intelligence of Socioeconomic Differentials Operating on the Same Children over a Period of Ten Years." *Thirty-ninth Yearbook of the National Society for the Study of Education,* Part II, 275-280, 1940.

SKODAK, MARIE, and SKEELS, HAROLD M. "A Final Follow-up Study of One Hundred Adopted Children." *Journal of Genetic Psychology,* 75, 85-125, 1949.

SPEARMAN, C. *The Abilities of Man.* New York: Macmillan, 1927.

STENQUIST, JOHN L., and LORGE, IRVING. "Implications of Intelligence and Cultural Differences; as Seen by a Test-user; as Seen by a Test-maker." *Teachers College Record,* 54, 184-193, 1951.

STERN, ALEXANDER W. "The Nature of G and the Concept of Intelligence." *Nordisk Psykologi* (Copenhagen), 8, 202-209, 1956.

STODDARD, G. D., and WELLMAN, B. L. *Child Psychology.* New York: Macmillan, 1934.

TERMAN, L. M. *The Measurement of Intelligence: An Explanation of and a Complete Guide for the Use of the Stanford Revision and Extension of the Binet-Simon Intelligence Scale.* Boston: Houghton Mifflin, 1916.

TERMAN, L. M., and ODEN, M. H. *Genetic Studies of Genius: Vol. IV, The Gifted Child Grows up.* Stanford: Stanford University Press, 1947.

THORNDIKE, E. L., *et al. The Measurement of Intelligence.* New York: Teachers College, Columbia University, 1926.

THORNDIKE, ROBERT L. "Growth of Intelligence During Adolescence." *Journal of Genetic Psychology,* 72, 11-15, 1948.

THURSTONE, L. L. "Theories of Intelligence." *Scientific Monthly,* 62, 101-112, 1946.

THURSTONE, L. L., and THURSTONE, T. G. *Primary Mental Abilities Scales: Primary, Elementary and Intermediate.* Chicago: Science Research Associates, 1950.

TOPP, R. F. "Let's Stop Down-grading Boys." *Chicago Sunday Tribune Magazine,* Dec. 3, 1961.

VERNON, P. E. "Changes in Abilities from 14 to 20 Years." *Advancement of Science,* 5, 139, 1948.

WATTS, KATHLEEN P. "Intelligence Test Performance from 11 to 18: A Study of Grammar School Girls." *British Journal of Educational Psychology,* 28, 112-119, 1958.

WECHSLER, DAVID. "Cognative, Conative, and Non-intellective Intelligence." *American Psychologist,* 5, 78-83, 1950.

WECHSLER, DAVID. *The Measurement and Appraisal of Adult Intelligence,* 4th ed. Baltimore: Williams and Wilkins, 1958.

WESMAN, ALEXANDER G. "Verbal Factors." *Proceedings, 1948 Conference on Testing Problems, Educational Testing Service,* 52-53, 1949.

WHEELER, L. R. "A Comparative Study of the Intelligence of East Tennessee Mountain Children." *Journal of Educational Psychology,* 33, 321-334, 1942.

WOLMAN, B. "Hitpathut hasekhel b'gil han' urim" (The Development of Intelligence in Adolescence). *Hahinukh,* 21, 131-148, 1947/48.

CHAPTER 4

Personality and Culture

One of the major difficulties involved in any discussion of personality is trying to define the term itself in a simple, meaningful manner. To the layman, the word is usually associated with an individual's overt display of socially oriented skills, particularly his ability to interact effectively with others. Thus, an individual who is socially adroit and who is readily accepted by others in social situations is said to have "a lot of personality." Those who lack such skills and who may therefore avoid or be excluded from social contact are considered to have personality problems.

This effect of overt behavior can also be noted when an adjective descriptive of some outstanding characteristic is associated with the term "personality." A person who demonstrates a good deal of overt aggressive behavior is said to have an "aggressive" personality, while a shy, retiring individual may be said to have a "submissive" personality. If this kind of description of an individual's personality is used, one can also evaluate personality subjectively as good or bad.

In an extensive review of the literature, Allport (1937) was able to identify some fifty different definitions, and since that time more have come into being. These can be grouped into a number of broad categories, no one of which is completely acceptable. Perhaps the viewpoint offered by Hall and Lindsey (1957) that "personality is defined by the particular empirical concepts which are part of the theory of personality employed by the observer" is worth noting. These authors further state: "Personality consists concretely of a set of values or descriptive terms which are used to describe the individual being studied according to the variables or dimensions which occupy a central position within the particular theory utilized." Since the studies relating to adolescent personality fall into a number of different theoretical frameworks, such a viewpoint should help the reader to evaluate these.

If a definition to which the reader may relate the various studies discussed herein is needed, the frame of reference proposed by Sears (1948) may be useful. Personality is viewed as a complex pattern in which the biological needs and drives are modified in accordance with the formalized patterns of a society's behavior. These patterns are transmitted by the adults to the young and are based on accepted systems established in the society. Here one can readily see the relationship between the cultural influences under which the child is reared and the personality pattern he will develop.

In societies where the formalized patterns of behavior and the value systems are clearly defined, the problems of adolescence may be minimal or nonexistent. If American society, as Gardner (1957) believes, is really a whole host of societies with a glaring lack of set values, it is easy to understand the difficulty the adolescent faces in developing his personality.

THE DEVELOPMENT OF PERSONALITY IN CHILDHOOD AND ADOLESCENCE

Since personality development is a continuous process, one must briefly review its early development in order to understand the changes, if any, that occur during adolescence. Many believe that the personality of an individual is rather well developed and structured during childhood, possibly as early as age five or at least by age nine, and that little or nothing can be done later to change these basic patterns. While we cannot disagree concerning the influence of the early environment on the development and organization of the personality, it does seem reasonable to expect continual reorganization to take place through a good deal of the individual's life span. If it is true that the American adolescent is influenced by a whole set of societies, rather than one, one might well conclude that each of these societies has some impact on the reorganization of his personality.

Heredity and Environment

It has been rather well established that the individual's behavior is based on the interaction of maturation and learning, for which terms we may substitute heredity and environment. This viewpoint is equally applicable to the more inclusive area of personality. At our present limited stage of knowledge, which results primarily from the relative subjective character of the instruments used to measure personality, the importance of these variables is difficult to determine. One can, of course, use the approach of Sheldon and Stevens (1942), which describes personality structure on the basis of hereditary-constitutional factors, or the almost opposite approach of Davis and Havighurst (1946), which strongly stressed social-cultural factors. Although both points of view probably have much merit, neither can be studied under the kinds of controlled situations needed to offer final proof in support of one or the other. Actually the social-cultural influence can be more readily investigated, since these patterns can be manipulated to some minor degree, whereas the genetic determinants that operate at the time of conception cannot.

Shirley (1933) studied the personality manifestations of twenty-five babies during the first two years of life. She concluded that there are definite personality differences present at the time of birth and that these children showed consistency in their behavior patterns as they grew older. She feels that such an early appearance of these patterns and the consistency of the patterns indicate a permanence of personality traits. These factors as well as the relationship of these traits to familial traits strongly support the concept of the influence of heredity. Neilon (1948) followed up this study with fifteen of Shirley's original group fifteen years later. The judges attempted to match personality sketches with those presented in the earlier study and were able to do so at a statistically significant level. Although Neilon concluded that personality similarities in an individual do seem to persist, there was evidence of considerable fluctuation in some of the children.

Body Type and Temperament

There have been many scientific attempts to relate body morphology to personality characteristics. Before any scientific studies of these relationships were made, the layman accepted a number of common body-characteristic–temperament stereotypes: "Fat people are jolly"; "Redheads are hot-tempered"; "Short individuals are aggressive"; etc. Such assumptions seem to imply that each temperament trait is directly related to the specific physical characteristic, and that the presence of the physical characteristic insures the presence of the temperament pattern. Since, as we have already stated, body type does seem to be an inherited characteristic (see page 29), the supposedly related temperament type should also be primarily inherited.

Sheldon's attempts (1940, 1942) to relate body type and temperament have been the most ambitious of any to date. Using three basic body types—endomorph, mesomorph, and ectomorph—he devised a seven-point rating scale indicating the degree to which the individual is of one type and the accompanying degrees of the other two types. A 6-1-1 rating, for example, indicates a strongly endomorphic type, while a 2-5-2 rating would indicate a predominance of mesomorphic tissue. Sheldon then identified three temperament components—cerebrotonia, somatotonia, and viscerotonia—that seem to be present in adult men, and that correspond with the components of physique. Table 7 shows the correlations between these physical and temperament components.

TABLE 7. Intercorrelations and intracorrelations between the primary components of physique and temperament
From Sheldon (1942), by permission of the author and Harper & Row, Publishers, Inc.

	Viscerotonia	Mesomorphy	Somatotonia	Ectomorphy	Cerebrotonia
Endomorphy	+.79	−.29	−.29	−.41	−.32
Viscerotonia		−.23	−.34	−.40	−.37
Mesomorphy			+.82	−.63	−.58
Somatotonia				−.53	−.62
Ectomorphy					+.83

N = 200

Although these correlations are rather high, more investigation of such relationships is needed before one can definitely assume that heredity-constitutional factors are the basic determinants of these relationships. At our present stage of knowledge one might assume that cultural factors may bring about the development of certain temperament traits in relation to certain body types; i.e., because an individual is very short and fat, the culture, especially his peer group, may respond to him in a certain fashion. He, in turn, learns to respond appropriately to their reactions, and his temperament develops accordingly. The fact that Sheldon's high correlations were based on studies of *adult* men does not negate this possibility. These learned temperament patterns would be well established by adulthood. We must point out, however, that Sheldon's methods are somewhat subjective, since he gives his own ratings to both personality and physique. Certainly there is still a need for far more research before we can be certain that strong relationships exist between temperament and body type.

The Impact of the Culture

Mead (1947) has long emphasized the importance of cultural impact on personality development. She points out that certain personality characteristics are inevitable when the individual grows up in a homogeneous culture that changes slowly, if at all. The rapidity of social change today has eliminated many of the continuing features for most people. The personality of an individual developing under the tremendous cultural strain created by our American society today would be expected to be different from that of an individual who lived in the Samoan culture of some forty years ago.

For the adolescent in particular, the impact of the culture seems of major importance. Barnes (1956) has stated that "anywhere in the world adolescence is what the culture makes it." Any environment in which a child lives and develops seems to influence his personality to some degree. The basic cultural environment of the home probably has the earliest and greatest impact on personality development, but many other environments interact to restructure and reorganize these early patterns. The neighborhood, the school, the peer culture, the community, and other influences all aid in the further development or redevelopment of the individual's behavior patterns.

Perhaps the soundest viewpoint is an eclectic one, involving interaction of both heredity and environment, without great concern over which is more important. From the preceding presentation, the reader should readily see that neither the genetic nor the environmental approach by itself suffices to explain behavior. We must be aware that culture is influenced by biological and geographical conditions and can never really become an independent source in itself (Bidney, 1947).

PERSONALITY DEVELOPMENT IN OTHER CULTURES

Ever since Mead's early studies (1928) of the Samoan culture, which indicated that the concept of adolescent "storm and stress" was completely foreign to the Samoans, there has been increased interest in studying teen-agers in societies other than our own. Results of studies made of other relatively primitive societies, as well as of more civilized societies, all demonstrate the impact of a given culture on the development of the adolescent's personality.

Primitive Cultures

Although Mead (1947) suggested that homogeneous societies seem inevitably to bring forth certain personality characteristics among their members, Wallace (1947) did not find this to be the case with the Hupa Indians of California. His results reveal a diversity of personality traits despite the rigid impositions of the Hupa culture. Underwood and Honigman (1947) compared the personality development of children in a Haitian peasant community and among the Kaska Indians. Both groups seem to handle the basic drives with relative tranquility, yet the Indians become taciturn, individualistic adults, while the Haitians are sociable, warm, expressive, and insecure. These differences are attributed to the variation in the continuity of training and the concomitant secondary effects that tend to prolong or contract the desirability of remaining a child. Apparently the greater rigidity of the Indian structure results in the type of adult personality found.

Cohen (1955) found that adolescence in a Jamaican community was a period almost entirely free of "storm and stress." The "adolescent conflict" actually appears at the end of adolescence and during the early years of adulthood. The conflicts were rather typical of those we expect to find in our own teen-agers: avoidance of parents; formation of close friendships; and preoccupation with criticisms from almost everyone.

In many primitive societies the puberty rite is still practiced. One of the underlying bases for this ritual is the assumption that it has a definite influence on the individual's later development. Wallace (1947) reported on the puberty rite of Mohave Indian girls. Although these rites are familial rather than public, they are generally similar to those of other Yuman tribes. The rite involves a four-day period of seclusion during which various restrictions are placed upon clothing, eating, and general deportment. It is strongly believed that a girl's actions in response to these restrictions will influence her future.

Civilized Societies Other Than Our Own

The positive influence of the culture is equally obvious in complex civilized societies. Although there seem to be many similarities between modern societies in England, West Germany, France, etc., there are still some essential differences, especially in child-rearing practices. These basic practices, which do much toward structuring the individual's personality, become a source of conflict as major changes impinge on the major society. Fried and Fiske (1949) interviewed German young people to appraise the prospects of democratizing them. The questions dealt with social attitudes and personal outlook. Males wanted to be master of the household, while women wanted a husband who "understands" them. Sixty-eight per cent believed in training children by punishment, shaming, or contempt. Although half the respondents professed to favor democratic government, they had no real conception of basic democratic functions. They still possessed strong ties with the "Fatherland" and wanted to be governed by strong leaders. They were willing to admit their political immaturity, deference to authority, and inability to compromise, which were fostered by the autocratic governments that formerly ruled their country.

The situation that exists in postwar Japan is a good example of the effect of rapid social change on a society, and particularly on its youth. The imposition of democracy on the Japanese society has forced a change in structure that has broken down many of the formal old traditions. Generally, the older individuals react more slowly to such change, since they are rather "set" in the old ways. The young people, because they are more flexible, are immediately attracted by the greater freedoms of the new situation and attempt to take advantage of them immediately. The old authoritarian family structure is challenged, and conflict results. The youth group further seeks to take full advantage of privileges, such as advanced education, that had been previously denied it. As young people continue to take advantage of all these opportunities and to broaden their environmental background, they draw even further away from the old patterns of behavior, and the gap between generations widens. Japanese youth has become highly Westernized and has as a result brought into the society patterns of behavior that were originally foreign to it. Unfortunately, negative patterns arise along with the positive; the previously relatively unknown problems of juvenile delinquency, for example, are now fully apparent.

Suellwold (1959) has compared German youth to American adolescents and finds differences of the kind that are generally assumed to differentiate both cultures. Problems identified by the German youth included such comments as, "I am afraid of failure or humiliation," and "My parents criticize me too often."

An attempt to investigate the hypothesis that an individual's degree of neurosis is a function of culture was made by Hsu (1952). He administered Thurstone's Neurotic Inventory to a group of 144 Chinese students in America and a group of 110 Chinese students who had never been in America but could read English. The group living in America showed a significantly lower neurotic score than the group that had never been in America. There was also a negative relationship between the length of residence in America and the neurotic scores. The author feels that "the existence of a universal neurotic trait is denied." The Chinese living in America apparently make a fairly good initial adjustment to this culture. The fact that they are students, however, indicates that they are probably above average in ability. This may be a major factor in their adjustment.

A study of letters written by partially Westernized young adults in China revealed such problems of social change as revolt against the parental generation and the lack of accepted patterns (Chin, 1948). There was a strong belief in self-improvement through education to replace the former strong support of familial groups. Personal problems were projected outward, and there was a constantly recurring emphasis on the desire to participate in social progress. The rapid transition of this culture was obviously a source of many problems and conflicts relating to personality development. It would be most interesting to re-examine the feelings of these same semi-Westernized individuals today to find out how they have reoriented their feelings toward the communistic philosophy under which they now function. It seems probable that this rather rapid transition has created further conflict, forcing a restructuring of many of their earlier personality and behavior patterns.

Barschak (1951) studied happiness and unhappiness of girls in four different cultures: those of England, Germany, the United States, and Switzerland. More than three-fourths of the members of each group indicated that they considered themselves happy in both childhood and adolescence (except for the German girls living in Berlin). More than one-third of each group rated themselves as unhappy in adolescence. The reasons given for either condition varied according to the culture. National differences were present, but not to the degree one might have expected. It appears that these cultures today are relatively similar to one another and that, as this similarity increases, so do the similarities of the problems of the adolescents.

Cultural differences within a total society have been studied to determine their effect on adolescent development. El Koussy (1960) studied the characteristics of groups of urban and rural adolescents in Egypt. Although urban-rural differences were present, the similarities of the groups were more striking. The general patterns were similar to those typically found in other European cultures and in American society. The strains, the stresses, the changeability, the moodiness, the clumsiness, the feelings of self-respect and elation, the pride and vanity, and the feelings of guilt and self-abasement were all present in both groups. The rural group did relate more closely to the traditions standard in the dominant culture, such as gaining the approval of God, parents, teachers, and older people. Acceptance by peers was of only minor importance. The author points out that the cultural lag is quite marked in such a country as Egypt.

Danziger (1960) reported the results of a study in which Japanese high-school students from both rural and urban areas were asked to choose the personality models they thought ideal. Two major categories of the ideal personality were identified: (1) personalities drawn from the immediate private sphere (family, school, friends); and (2) those drawn from public life (past and present community and national leaders). Thirty-five per cent of the total choices were of the former category; 65 per cent, of the latter. Danziger found that choice of model tended to be associated with family income and that subjects from the higher-income families tended to prefer models from private life (57 per cent). These differences are probably related to class differences in child-rearing practices in the various income groups.

CULTURAL DIFFERENCES WITHIN THE AMERICAN SOCIETY

Ethnic Minority Groups

The concept of the United States as the melting pot of the world is well worth considering in relation to adolescent personality development. Our society is a tremendous mixture of subcultures, many of which still maintain their "old world" patterns of behavior. An adolescent growing up in one of these groups is influenced by a number of cultures impinging on him. At home the major influences operating on him may be those of the old-world culture. In the neighborhood he may have a combination of the old and the American cultural influences interacting. In the school he may be primarily under American cultural influences. If these patterns are fairly similar, the conflicts of the adolescent will not differ greatly from those of a comparable teen-ager wholly reared in the home offering a typical American pattern of behavior. If, however, there are some basic disagreements between the old-world and the American cultural patterns, the adolescent reared in such an environment will probably exhibit far greater conflict than the youngster who is exposed to a single cultural pattern.

Some years ago, when fairly large numbers of children were being born to parents who were immigrants, there was greater recognition of the problems of these cultural conflicts. As we move into the second and third generation of the American-born descendants of these immigrant groups, we seem to feel that these subcultural impacts lessen and even disappear. While this is true to some extent, it must be emphasized that a number of the original "foreign" patterns may continue to carry forward to each succeeding generation and still come into conflict with the mainstream of the American culture. The degree to which this carry-over continues may relate to socioeconomic level, geographic locale, religious background, etc. For example, if the descendants of the immigrant group achieve socioeconomic levels higher than those of their forebears, they probably are influenced more by the "American culture" than by the old-world carry-overs. Those who remain at the lower socioeconomic levels probably maintain a fairly large number of the old-world patterns. If the geographic locale consists primarily of the descendants of a particular cultural group (as does New Ulm, Minnesota, which is largely populated by the descendants of German immigrants), many of the patterns of the original culture may be maintained. If these descendants live in areas that are made up of many groups with no single major emphasis, the influence of the original patterns may be minimal.

Glad (1947) studied the drinking patterns of a group of eleventh- and twelfth-grade American-Jewish and American-Irish males. Reactions and attitudes toward alcohol were measured through questionnaires, rating scales, and interviews. The data support the thesis that the difference in inebriety rate between the Jewish and the Irish in America is explicable in terms of differences between the groups that were probably present among their ancestors. The Jewish group tended to drink for socially and symbolically instrumental reasons, while the

Irish tended to use alcohol for personally and socially affective consequences.

The decline of Chinatowns in this country illustrates the kind of breakdown in a subcultural pattern that can come about when the over-all American culture makes an impact on it. As long as the Chinatowns remained relatively isolated from the culture, they continued to preserve their old-world culture. During World War II, many of the young people reared in the rigid environments of Chinatowns were drafted and were then exposed to broader cultural patterns. When they returned, many were unwilling to function in the same old-world manner. Their rebellion, in addition to the influences of other outside forces such as the advent of television, resulted in major changes. Lee (1949) feels that Chinatowns have been affected by (1) change in the economic, social and political structure of the large community of which Chinatowns are a part; and (2) the population composition of the larger community. She suggests four factors that may affect existing Chinatowns and help hasten their decline: (1) occupation invasion and succession; (2) decline of the Chinese population; (3) social change; and (4) ecological invasion and succession. Generally, it appears that as Chinese youngsters sought greater occupational, social, and economic growth, they rejected the restrictions of the Chinatown.

Apparently, as once-isolated minority groups come into greater and more intimate contact with the cultural patterns of a majority group, they take over certain of the larger group's patterns. Briggs (1954) attempted to investigate this type of situation with a group of Japanese-American boys who were compared with a control group of Caucasian boys. No significant differences were found between the two groups in degree of father dominance, degree of authoritarianism, or parents' feelings about the youths' companions. The Japanese boys felt that they "talk back" more often than the Caucasians do. This may reflect some of the cultural conflict between the two generations. Although they felt freer to talk back, the Japanese also indicated fewer arguments with their families. This seems to support the general view that differences of opinion are not permitted in the Japanese family. On the whole, there apparently was less flexibility in families represented by the Caucasian group than in those of the Japanese group. One might assume that the Japanese families work at conforming to what they feel are Caucasian culture patterns.

Sometimes the minority group manages to maintain its separate identity by isolating itself from the larger community. The Amish in this country, for example, have managed to maintain their old patterns to an appreciable extent, although they have often been in conflict with the larger community as a result. The Amish adolescent has been affected particularly in terms of school attendance. The various states usually require school attendance longer than the Amish feel is necessary. The younger Amish child usually attends Amish-directed schools, but the adolescent who remains in school generally attends a high school in the larger outside community. He is, therefore, exposed to values and patterns of behavior that are often in conflict with those of his relatively closed group. The conflicting value systems of the two societies that impinge on him often develop in such an adolescent more intense conflict than is felt by one exposed to only one cultural pattern.

There are also situations in which the minority group is a relatively large one and its cultural patterns have been a relatively accepted part of the majority pattern. This seems to be the situation with the Chinese-Americans living in Hawaii. Hsu *et al.* (1960/61) compared Chinese-American teen-agers reared in Hawaii with white teen-agers reared in Chicago. They found a relative lack of turbulence among the Chinese-Americans and a relative abundance of it among the white Americans. These differences were associated with the differences in childhood experiences, parental attitudes, the role of the peer groups, and the demands of the wider society. Such a study might well be repeated twenty years hence, when Hawaii has become more integrated into the total American society and the Chinese-American group even more assimilated. It seems likely that the results would approximate those of the study of the Japanese-Americans previously discussed.

Other Cultural Factors

Besides its ethnic diversity, there are other cultural differences in the American society. The socioeconomic class to which the individual belongs, the geographic locale in which he lives, the urban or rural character of his environment, and the home and immediate family are all major forces involved in personality development.

Hathaway *et al.* (1959) reported the results of a study of 15,000 rural and urban ninth-grade students in a Minnesota school who were tested with the Minnesota Multiphasic Personality Inventory. Generally, the rural children were more inclined toward feelings of shyness, self-depreciation, and suspicion of others. The urban children were less self-critical, less suspicious of the motives of others, and more likely to express feelings of rebellion against authority.

The fact that these urban-rural differences are still so apparent may be surprising to many laymen. There appears to be a general feeling that urban-rural differences have been disappearing as a result of better transportation, better communication (especially television), and the movement toward suburban living. However, the rural family may actually be striving harder to maintain its patterns of behavior as a reaction against these factors which are impinging on them.

Havighurst and Taba (1949) sought to determine the extent to which character development is influenced by the social environment and the extent to which it is influenced by the individual's personal make-up. The study involved 144 sixteen-year-old "Prairie City" youngsters of various social-class levels. Low positive relationships were found between character reputation and social environment and personality, but these were too low to be of predictive value. It was generally concluded that "moral character cannot usefully be studied apart from the total personality."

In their studies of cultural pressure and achievement, Child and Bacon (1955) also stress the importance of parental attitude. They feel that differences in parental attitude, depending on social-class factors, may even affect the way in which a parent regards a child's report card. Thus, it would appear that a child whose lower-class parents are relatively unconcerned about his achievement is also unconcerned about his achievement, while children whose middle-class and upper-class parents constantly stress the importance of grades may become compulsive in their desire to achieve at a high level. A significant relationship between the emotional patterns of adolescents and the disciplinary patterns they experienced in living with their parents was also reported by Peck (1958).

Numerous studies have attempted to investigate personality patterns related to scholarship. McArthur (1954) found that boys who had attended public schools consistently achieved higher college grades than those who had attended private schools. The author feels that this is a reflection of the differences in dominant value systems among the American subcultures as these values affect the personality. Such differences are described as the "being" vs. "doing" orientations of the Eastern upper class and the lower-middle class, respectively.

Heist et al. (1961) set up a series of hypotheses relating to personality and scholarship that were tested on two groups of National Merit Scholarship students. The educational institutions that these students were attending were ranked as high or low in the production of future scholars and scientists. Students of high ability attending highly productive institutions were generally found to have patterns of traits, values, and attitudes that were more closely related to serious intellectual pursuits than were those of students of high ability attending less productive institutions. One might wonder whether the students' traits influenced their choice of institution or whether their traits and attitudes developed as a reflection of the environment offered by the institution.

The influence of community interaction upon a self-governing adolescent group was studied by Grambs (1956). His is a report of part of the Youth Community Participation project, which attempted to analyze specific community settings in which youth groups were to function. The author suggests three generalizations based on his findings: (1) "Civically oriented self-governing youth groups probably cannot develop or survive without community help and localized institutional support." (2) "The broader American culture predisposes groups toward prescribed organizational forms, group procedures and group goals." (3) "Many adolescents perceive adolescents as persons judged by the community as being bad unless and until proven good."

Differences in Treatment of the Sexes

In the American culture, as well as in most of the subcultures of which the total society is comprised, the standards applied to the two sexes vary considerably. Lynd and Lynd (1937) have suggested that the two sexes might almost be considered as subcultural groups, since they are treated as differently as the members of two different minority groups might be. From birth boys and girls are treated differently, and differences in treatment increase as they develop into adulthood. Boys are expected to be rather boisterous, physically aggressive, and athletically inclined. They play with guns, athletic equipment, and other "masculine" types of toy. Girls are taught, almost from the beginning, to be "little ladies" and are given "feminine" types of toy, such as dolls, to play with. A boy who plays with dolls is viewed with concern by his parents, as is the girl who becomes a "tomboy."

In adolescence the double standard becomes even more apparent. Boys may stay out later than girls (even colleges impose "hours" on girls but are relatively lenient in respect to curfews for males). Male adolescents are allowed more sexual freedom than are females and are generally protected far less than are the members of the so-called weaker sex.

The differences between the sexes resulting from this kind of cultural impact are obvious in all the areas of development discussed in this book. We have already noted sex differences in the physical and intellectual areas of development (Chapters 2 and 3) and will continue to stress these differences in the discussions of interest, social development, vocational choice, and the like.

Mussen (1961) has suggested that there is a good deal of stability in the degree of adoption of the traditional masculine or feminine sex-role interests over a fifteen-year period. These interests also carry over into adulthood, as is evidenced by the fact that those having the highest feminine-interest scores in adolescence scored higher in their early thirties on scales purporting to measure (1) nonmasculine interests, (2) dominance, and (3) capacity for status.

Bronfenbrenner (1961) discussed the possibility of changes in children's personalities as a function of changes in the child-rearing practices of American parents. He found that working-class parents differentiated their behavior on the basis of the child's sex more than the middle-class parents did, the former being more rigid with the females than the males. Torgoff (1958) reported similar findings in his study of social class and parental response to sex differences. Kohn (1959), in a study of parental values as related to social class, also stressed sex differences. He found that middle-class and working-class parents had similar ideas about what they wanted to see in their children's behavior according to the child's sex.

Culture and Conflict

In summary, it must be emphasized that these studies strongly reinforce the importance of culture on personality development. If we fully understand the influences of the over-all American culture, the community culture, the neighborhood culture, the ethnic culture, and the family culture as they interact on the individual, the tremendous complexity of personality development is readily apparent. Further, an awareness of the ways in which these various environments interact with and sometimes against one another will help to explain the conflicts that often confront the adolescent as he tries to function within these patterns.

ASSESSING PERSONALITY

Many of the results of early studies of adolescent personality were based on paper-and-pencil personality inventories and/or temperament tests. These results have often been found to be contaminated by the tendency of the respondent to give the socially approved response rather than to indicate his true feelings (see Chapter 1). Nonetheless, such instruments are widely used, particularly because they may be given to large groups with relative ease of administration and scoring. If the test administrator has carefully instructed the individuals in the group as to the purpose of the test and the need for them to consider their responses carefully, and the results are used cautiously, a good deal of useful information can be gathered from such tests.

Feiveson (1953) felt that personality schedules or tests are most valuable in helping an individual evaluate himself and that they also serve as strong motivators for class activities. Damrin (1947) felt that students generally do tend to give truthful responses to such scales. She tested a group of high-school girls with the Bell Adjustment Inventory, first with the usual signed form and later in a way that made the students feel that their papers could not be identified. The differences between the signed and the unsigned responses were very slight, a fact that Damrin interpreted as suggesting that the students replied truthfully. Her data, therefore, seems to contradict the belief that girls admit maladjustment more readily when they think their responses are anonymous.

Use of Projective Techniques

The most recent research studies dealing with adolescent personality have tended toward the use of projective techniques (see Chapter 1). Since projective techniques present relatively unstructured situations that have no socially approved answers, the individual is supposedly able to respond freely to a nonthreatening situation. Some of the findings concerning adolescent personality obtained by studies employing these projective instruments are presented here.

THE RORSCHACH. Abel (1948) has discussed the use of the Rorschach test as a valuable instrument for the study of culture. She considers it an essential part of the equipment of any anthropological expedition and summarizes reports of major findings of studies in Europe, Morocco, South Africa, Samoa, and the East Indies, and among several different North and South American Indian groups. While cultural and language differences create many problems in methods of administration, inquiry, and interpretation, Abel nonetheless feels that the Rorschach method holds promise of becoming one of the most valuable tools in the study of culture.

Obviously, in such situations, care must be exercised in assessing the Rorschach results. For example, Newman (1955) studied the Rorschach protocols of Otomi Indian boys and girls, ages thirteen to twenty, from Mexquital Valley in Mexico. "By tracing the relationship of the central tendency (median) of each determinant to other determinants as well as to the personality structure as a whole, for both groups and individuals, trends were established whereby the significance of the Rorschach determinants emerged as a function of the cultural matrix." Newman carefully noted cultural differences and the implications for personality theory.

Similar care must be exercised when using the Rorschach to study adolescent personality. While there are established norms for adults and for children, the norms for the adolescent age group have not been thoroughly developed. McFate and Orr (1949) have conducted a longitudinal study of a group of children's Rorschach protocols at four different levels during the adolescent period. In their first report on this study they deal with the frequency of the occurrence of single-scoring variables. Results indicated that the average use of R (productivity of response), K (depth or vista response), M (movement response), F (form response), P (popular response), H (human response), and A (animal response) increased with age for both sexes. There was a decrease in the use of FM (form-movement responses) and CF (color-form responses; form-major determinant). Throughout the four ages there were increases in the percentage of adolescents using d (small detail) and Dd (fine detail). Girls were both qualitatively and quantitatively more responsive than boys. A greater number of the boys scored on the anxiety indicators, while girls consistently used color variables more.

THE THEMATIC APPERCEPTION TEST. Another test that has been widely used in studies of the adolescent, although it was originally devised primarily for use with adults, is the Thematic Apperception Test (TAT). Henry and Farley (1959) attempted to determine the validity of the TAT as an instrument for studying adolescent personality. A blind interpretation was made of the TAT records of a group of adolescents who had been studied by the clinicians doing these interpretations. The interpretation was matched against statements obtained from a large group of psychological instruments designed to measure their behavior at overt, subjective, and projective levels. The authors concluded that: (1) the TAT is a valid diagnostic instrument; (2) it is reliable when used for personality assessment; (3) it can predict in all behavioral areas with varying degrees of accuracy; and (4) it tends to reflect the current conscious and unconscious concerns of the individual rather than the purely unconscious and deeply repressed sources of these concerns. These are strong claims, indeed, and there is reason to suggest that they are not truly demonstrated in this study. If the blind interpretation of the TAT records had been made by clinicians who did not know the subjects, the results might have differed appreciably. Stern (1951) has also supported the use of the TAT for studying the adolescent's personality structure. His study demonstrated that manifestations of the Oedipus complex, the need for tenderness, sexual craving, and various perversions are present in the adolescent.

Mussen (1953) analyzed TAT protocols of white and Negro lower-class boys and scored these in terms of various categories (fifty) of need and press. A press is a property or attribute of a person or object that facilitates or impedes the efforts of an individual to reach a goal. Mussen found the following significant differences: Negro boys' stories showed more aggressive press from the environment, mild verbal aggression from heroes; they displayed less interest in having friendly relations with others and seemed relatively indifferent to achievement. The white boys had more feelings of rejection, showed more extreme hostility, saw others as respecting them, were interested in establishing friendly relations, and wanted to achieve at a creditable level. The author carefully points out that the interpretation of TAT stories can be useful and meaningful only when the cultural background of the individual is fully considered.

OTHER TESTS. Butler and Marcuse (1959) attempted to determine whether the Draw-A-Person Test was as useful with children, adolescents, and young adults as with adult groups. The test was administered to 810 boys and 934 girls between the ages of five and eighteen. The subjects above the age of eight responded to the DAP in the same way as adult groups do. The results were interpreted generally as reflecting a growing awareness among females of the dominance of the male sex in contemporary Western civilization. To the degree that the DAP is a useful technique in general, it is appropriate for use with adolescents.

A modified form of Raven's Controlled Projection Test has been used in an attempt to measure differences in responses by two cultural groups (Kaldegg, 1948). A group of German and a group of English secondary-school boys were tested, and the major differences between the groups were noted. The results indicate that: (1) the English boys are more detached, while the German boys deal with the test as a serious life situation; (2) the German boys dislike cowards, while English boys dislike bullies, ruffians, and girls; (3) English boys show less anxiety than the Germans do over school work and wrongdoing; (4) German boys show strong agreement in the use of corporal punishment for any offense, while English boys show a greater tendency to make punishment fit the crime. Generally, this test does appear to be sensitive enough to determine cultural differences and may be useful for evaluating teen-age groups.

The Symonds' Picture-Story Test is one of the few projective devices specifically for use with the adolescent. Anderson and Anderson (1951) feel that the Thematic Apperception Test adequately covers the age group for which the Picture-Story Test is designed, and there is therefore no need for a special test for adolescents. However, the Symonds' Test does appear to be useful, and it includes some pictures that seem to bring forth stories very specifically related to adolescent problems. The results of this test also seem to relate rather well to the results of the Rorschach. Symonds and Jensen (1961) did a thirteen-year follow-up on a group of young men and women who had originally been given the Symonds' Picture-Story Test and the Rorschach. The 1940 and 1953 themes were then compared in terms of both dynamic and formal characteristics. There was a marked persistence of themes in fantasy over the thirteen-year interval and also a high degree of consistency in overt personality.

Limitations of Projective Techniques

While the present author agrees that a well-trained clinician may find projective techniques valuable in diagnosing individual deviations in behavior, he questions their value as research techniques. As pointed out earlier, these techniques are far too subjective, and the results are difficult to quantify. Further, they are often based on theoretical considerations that have yet to be proved correct, and many of these theoretical conditions are not widely accepted. Before these techniques can be readily used as research tools, far more study is needed to determine their validity and reliability and to make them less subjective.

CHARACTERISTICS AFFECTING PERSONALITY

Physical Characteristics

We pointed out in Chapter 2 that patterns of physical development seem to have some effect on the individual's physical self-concept, or, more broadly stated, on his personality structure. Schonfeld's study (1950) of boys who presented personality difficulties relating to physical inadequacy suggests that apparent or actual delays in the onset of sexual maturation, failure of the growth spurt at adolescence, or inadequacy of masculine development may lead to a variety of difficulties. The adolescent's awareness of his deviation from the group pattern is an important factor in the development of these difficulties.

Mussen and Jones (1957) attempted to study the relative effects of early and late maturation on the self-concepts of boys. The TAT was administered to two groups of seventeen-year-old boys, one of which had been consistently accelerated physically during adolescence and the other of which had been consistently retarded. The data indicated that the generally unfavorable sociopsychological environment that the physically retarded encounter seems to have adverse effects on their personalities. The retarded group showed more evidence of negative self-conceptions than did the early-maturers, who generally appeared to be self-confident. The groups were similar in their needs for achievement and personal recognition.

Wenar (1953) attempted to determine the effect of a motor handicap on personality, in relation to the effect of level of aspiration. Subjects were categorized into three groups: nonhandicapped, moderately handicapped, and severely handicapped; and all were given a level-of-aspiration task to perform that involved five trials of puttings pegs in a pegboard. There was no significant tendency for the handicapped to set higher or lower goals for themselves when all five trials were combined. There was, however, a significant change in pattern of goal-setting from trial to trial, with the nonhandicapped group progressively lowering their level of aspiration. In contrast, the handicapped groups showed an initial lowering followed by a reversal toward setting higher goals as the task continued. The author interpreted this as meaning that the handicapped child when faced with a motor task can maintain a realistic attitude toward his capabilities for only a limited period; he then begins to aim at what he would like to do rather than what he is capable of doing.

Emotional Characteristics

Cattell (1959) investigated second-order personality factors such as anxiety and extroversion in two samples of thirteen-year-old boys and girls who were given the High School Personality Questionnaire. While they showed an over-all similarity to the adult factor profiles for extroversion and anxiety, there were a number of significant differences explainable in terms of psychological development. Children are less concerned with internal conflict associated with defects of personality integrations and more concerned with situational stresses. Cattell feels that further study of psychological development through factor-analytic procedures is extremely worthwhile.

Janis and Fesbach (1954) studied anxiety predisposition associated with individual differences in responsiveness to fear-arousing communications. Two groups of high-school students, categorized as high-predisposed and low-predisposed, were given an illustrated lecture on dental hygiene that was presented in two forms, one containing a strong fear appeal, the other containing little fear-arousing material. The high-predisposed group was influenced less by the strong appeal than by the minimal appeal.

High-school students who later became schizophrenic were found to differ significantly from a randomly selected control group of their peers in the manner in which they were perceived by their school staff and in certain phases of their school record (Bower *et al.*, 1960). Boys developing schizophrenia tended to have less interest in girls, group activities, and athletics. They showed fewer leadership skills and were more submissive, anxious, dependent, and careless than the average boy. In almost all cases, their ratings on over-all mental health and school adjustment were significantly poorer than those of the control group, although they were usually not perceived as major problems or as being emotionally disturbed. Most of the preschizophrenics could be generally characterized as tending toward the shut-in, withdrawing kind of personality.

Intellectual Factors

One might generally assume that the brighter the individual, the more aware he is of the many ways in which his culture impinges on him and the more able he is to develop characteristics that enable him to function effectively within his environment. Terman and Oden (1959) feel that the gifted group involved in their study was at least as well adjusted as the general population. Although this aspect of development is more difficult to assess objectively than are such characteristics as achievement, the gifted group does not appear to differ significantly in personality and adjustment problems. In excessive use of alcohol, homosexuality, and delinquency, the gifted were well below the general rate. Generally, desirable traits seem to go together, and the relationship between intelligence and emotional stability is a positive one.

Lightfoot (1951) has also studied the personality characteristics of a group of relatively bright and a group of relatively dull individuals. She found significant differences, with the bright group showing more positive traits. Reid, et al. (1959) studied a group of "creative" and a group of "noncreative" seventh-graders to determine whether the groups differed in certain cognitive and other personality characteristics. The performance by the creative group on the cognitive measures involving intelligence and achievement tests were similar to those reported for adults. Creative children seemed to be less anxious than the noncreative.

The concept that good things go together may result in a sort of generalization effect in these studies. For example, Bentley and Springer (1953) studied the relationship between vision and adolescent personality and found some indications that good vision and good personality adjustment relate to each other positively. Apparently physical size, intellectual level, socioeconomic level, etc., all relate to personality development.

DEVELOPMENT OF THE SELF-CONCEPT

The development of the physical self-image as one aspect of total development was discussed in Chapter 2. However, this is only a part (although a most important one) of the total goal of the adolescent, i.e., the development of an over-all self-concept. Here, again, we are confronted with the problem of learning the way in which the adolescent views himself and his relationships to the environment surrounding him. His view of this environment is subject to change, especially as he moves from early to late adolescence, and as these environmental frames of reference change, so does the self-image.

Wittenberg (1959/60) categorizes adolescents into two general groups. The larger group prefers play to work and tends to avoid the socially, economically, and culturally significant aspects of living. However, this group is greatly influenced by mass media and promotion campaigns, and these bring them into contact with the very social climate that they wish to avoid. The second and smaller group is generally more sophisticated and informed and copes with the social climate by more or less open defiance and rebellion. These are the young people who criticize social injustices and fight against racial discrimination and poverty. The author feels that this is their way of rationalizing their own unresolved conflicts. They are also better informed than the other group on the social and economic aspects of their culture. The second group now seems to be increasing in numbers.

Choice of Ideal Figures

The development of a healthy positive self-concept seems to present great difficulties for the adolescent. The society in which he is reared has a major influence on this aspect of development, since the self-ideal is often based on his perception of what that society considers the ideal individual. Generally, the developmental trend is characterized by identification in early childhood with a parental figure; an intermediate stage of romanticism and glamour, which is omitted by some children; and a stage in late adolescence in which the ideal figure is a composite of many desirable qualities (Havighurst and MacDonald, 1955). These authors find the same pattern present in American children and in a group of New Zealand children.

MacDonald (1954) asked large groups of New Zealand boys and girls, aged nine to sixteen, to write briefly on "The person I would like to be like." All age groups chose parents, glamorous adults, attractive adults known to them, and composite or imaginary characters. The first and third categories declined in percentage with age, the second increased and declined, and the fourth increased. Wheeler (1961), in a study of Western Australian youth, also attempted to investigate this developmental trend. He also found that the number of parental figures chosen decreased as the subjects increased in age, while the number of imaginary characters and composites increased. Although this cannot be said to be a universal pattern, it does seem to be present in many modern-day civilized societies.

Glockel (1960) asked 1251 German youths, aged ten to twenty-one, to respond to the questions: "What person do you want to be like?" and "What person would you least like to be?" He classified their responses into three categories: (1) persons with whom the subject had direct contact; (2) famous people, both real and fictitious; and (3) generalizations and abstractions that did not refer to any one individual. His findings indicated that younger children, girls, and elementary-school children select more persons in the first category. Older children, boys, and secondary-school children select their self-ideal more often from the second category, with girls preferring movie stars and the boys athletes, scientists, and politicians. With increase in age the emphasis changes from concrete and obvious characteristics to psychological qualities and abstract values.

Frequently, the young adolescent can verbalize the characteristics he does not like or the people he does not want to resemble more clearly than those he does. He has not yet clearly crystallized the ideal self-image, but he does know what he hopes to avoid. Again, the characteristics to be avoided can often be found in an individual whom the child knows or about whom he has been told. "Uncle Ben" may constantly be pointed out to the child as possessing highly undesirable traits, and the child does not want to be like "Uncle Ben."

Even the patterns that the child purports to want to follow are ambiguous. He may see a certain characteristic as being present in a number of his ideal figures, but he sees only its overt and sometimes superficial patterns. In the child's perception, two people who are at opposite ends of the scale of a certain characteristic may appear very much alike. The child may also be influenced by the role a given ideal figure plays without realizing that the individual is not as he is often portrayed.

All these factors may occasionally lead to the development of unrealistic self-ideals, especially among younger adolescents. This lack of realism is often as much a result of the individual's failure to see himself as he is as it is of his distorted perception of figures in his environment. Until the individual becomes aware of his own real strengths and weaknesses, he will have difficulty finding the ideal figure with which he can truly attempt to identify.

Adolescence is often viewed as the time of life when the individual reaches a crisis in his attempts to construct a stable self-image, and as a result there is some diffusion in identity. Generally, there is an indication of lack of continuity between past and present self-pictures, a high degree of anxiety, less certainty about present dominant personal characteristics, and fluctuation in feelings about self (Bronson, 1959). Anderson (1959) attempted to study the consistency of the self-concept in a group of eighth-grade pupils and reported that there was evidence of much fluctuation and/or inconsistency in the functions being measured by the tests he used.

An attempt to measure the stability of the adolescent self-concept was made by Engel (1959). She retested a group of lower-middle-class and middle-class students who had originally been tested two years earlier, when they were in the eighth and tenth grades. There was a .53 correlation in the measures of self-concept over the two-year period, which would indicate relative stability. Subjects whose self-concept was negative at the first testing were significantly less stable in self-concept than those who initially indicated a positive self-concept. Further, Engel found that positive scores on self-concept increased significantly between the two testings for the tenth and twelfth grade subjects. The present author feels, however, that there is generally more inconsistency than consistency in adolescents' self-concepts.

Accuracy of the Self-Concept

As the image of the ideal changes with increasing age, so, too, does the adolescent's self-concept. The accuracy of the self-concept varies with age, usually becoming more precise as the individual grows older. DeJung (1959) used the Syracuse Scale of Social Relations to measure the awareness a member of a group has of how he is being rated by his peers. He found a tendency toward increasing accuracy with increasing age from grades five to eleven, with a slight decrease at grade twelve. Within most grades, neither mental age nor chronological age was found to be related to accuracy of self-role perception.

The accuracy of self-estimates by sixth- and eleventh-grade pupils was also studied by Brandt (1958). He obtained self- and peer-estimates of performance and the results of actual performance in arithmetic fundamentals, spelling, vocabulary, broad jumping, strength of grip, and baseball throwing. The author's findings support "the idea that self-concept is an organized and organizing dynamic within personality structure." He reports a .32 correlation between intelligence and accuracy of self-estimate but finds only a slight relationship between performance ability and accuracy. The accuracy of self-rating tended to increase over the grade span studied.

Hanlon et al. (1954) administered the California Test of Personality and a modified Q-Sort technique to high-school students to measure the relationship of adjustment and the congruence of self and ideal-self. They found an over-all tendency toward congruence of the two concepts of self and a positive correlation between self-ideal congruence and total adjustment. There was no significant relationship among intelligence, age, and self-ideal congruence. The measures of adjustment also showed no relationship to intelligence or age. The authors propose that a correlation of less than .27 between the self-concept and the ideal-self may be an indicator of maladjustment.

The discordance between the adolescent's conception of himself in relation to his peers is a necessary stage in development, Zazzo (1960) concluded from a study of 87 young men enrolled in a teacher-education program. These subjects saw their peers as more socially at ease, more stable, and generally more relaxed than they saw themselves as being. Zazzo felt that the conception the adolescent has of other adolescents serves as an incentive for self-development. Kojima (1957) administered a modified sentence-completion test to a group of adolescents in an attempt to study the relationship between their own and others' attitudes. This test was constructed on the basis of Murray's "need-press" theory, and an attempt was made to specify the active and passive parts in the situations described. The correlation between the subjects' aggressive reaction to others and others' reactions to them was .48. In corresponding passive situations it was .60. In general, the adolescent's expectation of other persons' attitudes seems to be related to his own reaction to others in the same circumstances.

Amatora (1955) compared self-evaluation in personality of teachers and pupils. One hundred teachers, 500 boys, and 500 girls were asked to give self-judgments on twenty-two scales consisting of many personality variables. The teachers' self-opinions were higher than the boys' on all scales, and higher than the girls' on all but three scales. The girls' self-opinions were higher than the boys' on all but three scales; on these three scales the boys' were higher than the girls' but lower than the teachers'. As one might expect, the adults, as the most mature group, had the highest self-estimates, while the boys, who are generally the least mature, have the lowest.

In a study of evaluations of adolescent personality by Egyptian adolescents and adults, Kamel (1947) reported the results of ratings on forty-five traits. Boys from fourteen to eighteen show a decrease in desire to serve society and an increased interest in social life, aggressive behavior, day-dreaming, frankness, materialism, and care for appearance. Girls in the same age range show an increase in social interest, talkativeness, and care for personal appearance, and a loss of interest in gymnastics and religion.

The differences adolescents perceive between themselves and their peers were also investigated by Zazzo (1960). A group of 198 male adolescents, aged fifteen to nineteen, was given a questionnaire in which each was to assign traits to four groups: adolescent boys, adolescent girls, men, and women. About one-half of the group was then interviewed and asked to dissociate the self-image from that of the peer group. The subjects tended to see others as having more audacity, desire for rank, and self-assurance, and as attaching more importance to appearing intelligent. They viewed themselves as liking more solitude; attaching more importance to friendship, love, and professional success; and being more revolted by social injustice. Those under seventeen, those living at school, and those with close friends saw less difference between themselves and the group than did older adolescents, those living at home, and those with fewer close friends.

CULTURE AND PERSONALITY AS VIEWED BY THE ADOLESCENT

Ethnic and Religious Factors

The adolescent is often well aware of his cultural background, particularly if it deviates from the norms of the total American society. If he is a member of an ethnic or religious minority group, especially one whose standards and codes come into conflict with the total society, he is likely to have more conflict than a teen-ager who is part of a majority group. It is often during the teen years that the cultural conflicts become obvious for the first time. The following case study serves to illustrate this type of situation:

Paul R. was born in a large city in a neighborhood composed almost entirely of Italian-Americans, many of whom had been born in Italy. Paul's parents were American-born, but both sets of grandparents, who also lived in this neighborhood, had been born in Italy. A large proportion of Paul's age-mates were bilingual, as was Paul himself, and Italian was spoken by these children as well as English.

Paul attended an elementary school within his neighborhood where 85 per cent of the children came from the same kind of environmental background. In elementary school, he seemed to be well adjusted both socially and emotionally and had many friends. The junior high school that he attended after completing elementary school was also within his neighborhood but drew its students from other neighborhoods as well. Still, more than 50 per cent of the students were Italian-Americans, and most of Paul's friends were children with whom he had attended elementary school. However, the high school he attended was not in his old neighborhood but in a suburb to which his parents had moved. Fewer than 10 per cent of those attending this school were of Italian extraction, and most of Paul's new friends were not part of that group. Paul began to show some signs of social maladjustment but still managed to get along effectively with his peer group.

When he went to college, more conflict became apparent. Although he was often invited to spend a vacation with a close college friend, he never accepted such an invitation, nor did he ever invite any of his friends to his own home. Although he had a number of friends, he showed increasing signs of social and emotional disturbance, to the degree that he was referred to the college psychiatrist.

During the discussions with the psychiatrist it became apparent that Paul was afraid of being "different" and did not want to be identified as a "foreigner." He indicated that this reaction had started in high school and had become intensified in college. His refusal to accept invitations to his friends' homes was based on the fear that he wouldn't know how to act. His failure to invite his friends to his home was based on a fear that his parents' patterns of behavior were too "old-world" and different from those his friends would expect.

Obviously this situation is not unique. Even today, many of our large cities are still segregated into neighborhoods where one ethnic group predominates. Many children like Paul attend elementary schools in which many of the students have a common ethnic background. Although the junior high school often draws students from a broader environment, the neighborhood ethnic groups are still well represented. High schools usually are far more heterogeneous, drawing from wider areas and containing relatively small numbers from any given ethnic group. At the college level this heterogeneity of home background is even greater, and often no single ethnic group is large enough to predominate. By this stage the total culture has greater impact than the subculture.

The elementary or junior-high pupil has little or no reason to feel different because he is generally with others like himself. It is in high school and even more in college that his awareness of the ways in which his subculture differs from the total culture grows. If he sees these two cultural patterns as conflicting with each other, he, in turn, shows evidence of conflict. He may choose to identify with his subculture or to reject it in favor of the total American culture, but in either case he will have some conflict before making the final adjustment.

One might expect these types of conflicts to become less frequent in the future. With relatively little immigration and with the majority of children being born to American-born parents, old ethnic patterns should logically disappear. However, while this may be true to some extent, it is doubtful that such subcultural patterns will ever break down completely. We may not be as much aware of an individual's ethnic background today as we might have been fifty years ago, but some awareness still persists and probably will continue to be present.

We are still very much aware of differences between and within religions, though we no longer directly associate ethnic groups with religion. We now know that not all Irish are Catholics, not all Germans are Lutherans, etc., but are more or less aware that Catholics, Protestants, Jews, etc., are different from one another. Even within the same religion, there are various divisions with differing theologies and codes of behavior. Episcopalians, Baptists, Methodists, etc., are all Protestants, yet they hold different beliefs within this total framework. There is reason to believe that these various religious differences affect adjustment in the same way as did the ethnic differences previously discussed, although the effects may be less serious. For example, a child who has attended parochial schools through high school may have some adjustment problems if he attends a nonsectarian college. Even if ethnic differences ultimately disappear, it is unlikely that religious differences ever will, and religion will probably continue to be a basis for cultural differences in America. Religion and the problems associated with it are discussed in more detail in Chapter 9.

Personality Characteristics

When the adolescent discusses personality at all, he usually uses the word as a layman does, describing a friend as having a "lot of personality," or as being a "personality kid," etc.; that is, he thinks in terms of behavior rather than of a total pattern. The teen-ager wants to be identified as having a pleasing personality and is usually very much aware of the characteristics that the peer group considers negative. He does not want to be identified as shy, bossy, talkative, overly aggressive, silly, etc., since any of these adjectives would be related to having a "poor personality." On the other hand, to appear suave and sophisticated, or "smooth," is apparently highly desirable.

Another desirable characteristic is good humor, especially the ability to "take a joke." This is particularly important with the peer group, which often has its own private jokes and regards a sense of humor as a "must." However, the attempt to be humorous cannot be carried to an extreme, and the "clown" is more likely to be rejected than accepted.

Perhaps it would be correct to say that the adolescent is concerned with overt behavior traits rather than with inner personality. Honesty, kindness, courage, etc., are characteristics that the adolescent views as being highly desirable in others and in himself. Generally, a characteristic such as aggressiveness is not acceptable. Feinberg, Smith, and Schmidt (1958) asked 2400 adolescents from all socioeconomic groups to describe the traits that they felt led to acceptance or rejection. Intelligence, fairness, honesty, and conscientiousness all were regarded as positive, and noisiness and conceit were considered negative. The children of the lower- and middle-income groups considered aggressiveness as irrelevant. Goertzen (1959), in a study of 1773 boys and girls, found that the group considered aggressive behavior more objectionable than nonconforming or withdrawing behavior.

Personality and character traits become increasingly important to the adolescent as he becomes concerned with social and heterosexual development. As he interacts with a more varied group of members of his own and the opposite sex, he becomes increasingly aware of those traits that are desirable and those that are undesirable. In order to achieve acceptance and popularity within his peer group, he strives to develop characteristics that the group approves and at least to conceal any unacceptable traits that he may possess. These various characteristics will be discussed in detail in Chapters 6 and 7.

REFERENCES

ABEL, THEODORA M. "The Rorschach Test in the Study of Culture." *Rorschach Research Exchange* (now *Journal of Projective Techniques*), 12, 79-93, 1948.

ALLPORT, G. W. *Personality.* New York: Holt, Rinehart & Winston, Inc., 1937.

AMATORA, SISTER MARY. "Comparisons in Personality Self-evaluation." *Journal of Social Psychology,* Nov., 315-21, 1955.

ANDERSON, CHARLES C. "The Many Voices: A Preliminary Investigation into the Consistency of the Self Concept." *Alberta Journal of Educational Research,* 5, 7-15, 1959.

ANDERSON, H.H., and ANDERSON, GLADYS L. *An Introduction to Projective Techniques.* Englewood Cliffs, N.J.: Prentice-Hall, Inc., 1951.

BARNES, MELVIN W. "The Nature and Nurture of Early Adolescents." *Teachers College Record,* 57, 513-521, 1956.

BARSCHAK, ERNA. "A Study of Happiness and Unhappiness in the Childhood and Adolescence of Girls in Different Cultures." *Journal of Psychology,* 32, 173-215, 1951.

BENTLEY, CHARLES S., and SPRINGER, DONALD A. "The Role of Certain Visual Phenomena in Adolescent Personality Adjustment." *American Journal of Optometry,* 30, 227-243, 1953.

BIDNEY, D. "Human Nature and the Cultural Process." *American Anthropology,* 49, 375-399, 1947.

BOWER, ELI M., SHELLHAMER, THOMAS A., and DAILY, JOHN M. "School Characteristics of Male Adolescents Who Later Become Schizophrenic." *American Journal of Orthopsychiatry,* 30, 712-729, 1960.

BRANDT, RICHARD M. "The Accuracy of Self Estimate: A Measure of Self-concept Reality." *Genetic Psychology Monographs,* 58, 55-99, 1958.

BRIGGS, DENNIE L. "Social Adaptation among Japanese-American Youth: A Comparative Study." *Sociology and Social Research,* 38, 293-300, 1954.

BRONFENBRENNER, U. "The Changing American Child—A Speculative Analysis." *Merrill-Palmer Quarterly,* 7, 73-84, 1961.

BRONSON, GORDON W. "Identity Diffusion in Late Adolescents." *Journal of Abnormal and Social Psychology,* 59, 414-417, 1959.

BUTLER, R. L., and MARCUSE, F. L. "Sex Identification at Different Ages Using the Draw-A-Person Test." *Journal of Projective Techniques,* 23, 299-302, 1959.

CATTELL, RAYMOND B. "Anxiety, Extraversion and Other Second-Order Personality Factors in Children." *Journal of Personality*, 27, 464-476, 1959.

CHILD, IRVIN L., and BACON, MARGARET K. "Cultural Pressures and Achievement Motivation." In Hoch, P. H., and Zubin, J., eds., *Psychopathology of Childhood*. New York: Grune and Stratton, 1955.

CHIN, AI-LI S. "Some Problems of Chinese Youth in Transition." *American Journal of Sociology*, 54, 1-9, 1948.

COHEN, YEHUDI A. "A Contribution to the Study of Adolescence: 'Adolescent Conflict' in a Jamaican Community." *Samiksa* (India), 9, 139-172, 1955.

COHEN, YEHUDI A. "Character Formation and Social Structure in a Jamaican Community." *Psychiatry*, 18, 275-296, 1955.

DAMRIN, DORA E. "A Study of the Truthfulness with Which High School Girls Answer Personality Tests of the Questionnaire Type." *Journal of Educational Psychology*, 38, 223-231, 1947.

DANZIGER, KURT. "Choice of Models among Javanese Adolescents." *Psychological Reports*, 6, 346, 1960.

DAVIS, ALLISON, and HAVIGHURST, R. J. "Social Class and Color Differences in Child-Rearing." *American Sociological Review*, 11, 698-710, 1946.

DE JUNG, J. E. "Measurement of Accuracy of Self-Role Perceptions." In Juddleston, Edith M., ed., *The Sixteenth Yearbook of the National Council on Measurements Used in Education*. New York: National Council of Measurements Used in Education, 1959.

EL KOUSSY, A. H. "The Character of Rural and Urban Adolescents in Egypt." *Vita Humana*, 219, 226, 1960.

ENGEL, MARY. "The Stability of the Self-concept in Adolescence." *Journal of Abnormal and Social Psychology*, 59, 211-215, 1959.

FEINBERG, M. R., SMITH, M., and SCHMIDT, R. "An Analysis of Expressions Used by Adolescents at Varying Economic Levels to Describe Accepted and Rejected Peers." *Journal of Genetic Psychology*, 93, 133-148, 1958.

FEIVESON, PHILIP. "The Value of a Personality Inventory in a Self-Appraisal Course on the Secondary Level." *California Journal of Educational Research*, 4, 69-72, 1953.

FRIED, EDRITA G., and FISKE, MARJORIE. "The Dilemmas of German Youth." *Journal of Abnormal and Social Psychology*, 44, 50-60, 1949.

GARDNER, GEORGE E. "Present-day Society and the Adolescent." *American Journal of Orthopsychiatry*, 27, 508-517, 1957.

GLAD, DONALD DAVISON. "Attitudes and Experiences of American-Jewish and American-Irish Male Youths as Related to Differences in Adult Rates in Inebriety." *Quarterly Journal of Studies on Alcohol*, 8, 406-472, 1947.

GLOCKEL, HANS. "Eine Vergleichsuntersuchung zur Frage jugendlichen Idealerlebens" (A Comparative Study of the Self-ideal in Youth). *Psychologische Rundschau* (Goettingen), 11, 1-20, 1960.

GOERTZEN, S. M. "Factors Relating to Opinions of Seventh Grade Children Regarding the Acceptability of Certain Behaviors in the Peer Group." *Journal of Genetic Psychology*, 94, 29-34, 1959.

GRAMBS, J. D. "The Community and the Self-Governing Adolescent Group." *Journal of Educational Sociology*, 39, 94-105, 1956.

HALL, C. S., and LINDSEY, G. *Theories of Personality*. New York: John Wiley and Sons, Inc., 1957.

HANLON, THOMAS E., HOFSTAETTER, PETER R., and O'CONNOR, JAMES P. "Congruence of Self and Ideal Self in Relation to Personality Adjustment." *Journal of Consulting Psychology*, 18, 215-218, 1954.

HATHAWAY, STARKE R., MONACHESI, ELIO D., and YOUNG, LAWRENCE A. "Rural-Urban Adolescent Personality." *Rural Sociology*, 24, 331-346, 1959.

HAVIGHURST, ROBERT J., and MACDONALD, DONALD V. "Development of the Ideal Self in New Zealand and American Children." *Journal of Educational Research*, 49, 263-273, 1955.

HAVIGHURST, ROBERT J., and TABA, HILDA. *Adolescent Character and Personality*. New York: John Wiley and Sons, Inc., 1949.

HEIST, PAUL, MCCONNELL, T. R., MATSLER, FRANK, and WILLIAMS, PHOEBE. "Personality and Scholarship." *Science*, 133, 362-67, 1961.

HENRY, WILLIAM E., and FARLEY, JANE. "The Validity of the Thematic Apperception Test in the Study of Adolescent Personality." *Psychological Monographs*, 73(17), 1959.

HSU, E. H. "The Neurotic Score as a Function of Culture." *Journal of Social Psychology*, 34, 3-30, 1952.

HSU, FRANCIS L. K., WATROUS, BLANCHE G., and LORK, EDITH M. "Culture Pattern and Adolescent Behavior." *International Journal of Social Psychiatry*, 7, 33-53, 1960-61.

JANIS, IRVING L., and FESBACH, SEYMOUR. "Personality Differences Associated with Responsiveness to Fear-Arousing Communications." *Journal of Personality*, 23, 154-166, 1954.

KALDEGG, A. "Responses of German and English Secondary School Boys to a Projection Test." *British Journal of Psychology* (London), 39, 30-53, 1948.

KAMEL, MAHER. "Evaluations of Adolescent Personality by Adolescents and Adults." *Egyptian Journal of Psychology*, 3, 33-54, 1947.

KOHN, M. L. "Social Class and Parental Values." *American Journal of Sociology*, 64, 337-351, 1959.

KOJIMA, KENJIRO "Jiko-tasha taido no kankei ni tsuiteno KenKyū: Busho Kanseihō no yoru hōkoku" (A Study of the Relationship between Self and Others' Attitudes: a Study with Sentence Completion Method). *Japanese Journal of Educational Psychology*, 5, 52-45, 1957.

LEE, ROSE HUM. "The Decline of Chinatowns in the United States." *American Journal of Sociology*, 54, 422-432, 1949.

LIGHTFOOT, GEORGIA FRANCES. "Personality Characteristics of Bright and Dull Children." *Teachers College Contributions to Education*, 969, 1-136, 1951.

LYND, R. S., and LYND, H. M. *Middletown in Transition*. New York: Harcourt, Brace, 1937.

MACDONALD, DONALD V. "The Development of the Ideal Self in New Zealand Children." In Havighurst, Robert J., ed., *Studies of Children and Society in New Zealand*. Christchurch, N.Z.: Canterbury University College, Department of Education, 1954.

MCARTHUR, CHARLES. "Personality of Public and Private School Boys." *Harvard Educational Review*, 24, 256-262, 1954.

MCFATE, MARGUERITE Q., and ORR, FRANCES G. "Through Adolescence with the Rorschach." *Rorschach Research Exchange* (now *Journal of Projective Techniques*), 13, 302-319, 1949.

MEAD, MARGARET. *Coming of Age in Samoa*. New York: William Morrow and Co., 1928.

MEAD, MARGARET. "The Implications of Cultural Change for Personality Development." *American Journal of Orthopsychiatry*, 17, 633-646, 1947.

MURRAY, H. A., et al. *Explorations in Personality*. New York: Oxford, 1938.

MUSSEN, PAUL H. "Differences Between the TAT Responses of Negro and White Boys." *Journal of Consulting Psychology*, 17, 373-376, 1953.

MUSSEN, PAUL H. "Some Antecedents and Consequences of Masculine Sex-Typing in Adolescent Boys." *Psychological Monographs*, 75, no. 2, 1961.

MUSSEN, PAUL H., and JONES, M. C. "Self-Conceptions, Motivations, and Interpersonal Attitudes of Late- and Early-Maturing Boys." *Child Development*, 28, 243-56, 1957.

NEILON, PATRICIA. "Shirley's Babies after Fifteen Years: A Personality Study." *Journal of Genetic Psychology*, 73, 175-186, 1948.

NEWMAN, R. E. "The Application of the Rorschach Technique to a Primitive Group." *Zeitschrift für Psychologische Diagnostick* (Goettingen), 3, 187-222, 1955.

PECK, ROBERT F. "Family Patterns Correlated with Adolescent Personality Structure." *Journal of Abnormal and Social Psychology*, 57, 347-350, 1958.

REID, J. B., KING, F. J., and WICKWIRE, P. "Cognitive and Other Personality Characteristics of Creative Children." *Psychological Reports*, 5, 729-737, 1959.

SCHONFELD, WILLIAM A. "Inadequate Masculine Physique as a Factor in Personality Development of Adolescent Boys." *Psychosomatic Medicine*, 12, 49-54, 1950.

SEARS, ROBERT R. "Personality Development in Contemporary Culture." *Proceedings, American Philosophical Society*, 92, 363-370, 1948.

SHELDON, W. H., and STEVENS, S. S. *The Varieties of Temperament*. New York: Harper and Row, 1942.

SHELDON, W. H., STEVENS, S. S., and TUCKER, W. D. *The Varieties of Human Physique*. New York: Harper and Row, 1940.

SHIRLEY, M. M. *The First Two Years: A Study of Twenty-five Babies' Personality Manifestations*. Minneapolis: University of Minnesota Press, 1933.

STERN, E. "Recherches sur la psychologie de l'adolescent à l'aide du Thematic Apperception Test de Murray" (Studies in Adolescent Psychology by Means of Murray's Thematic Apperception Test). *Schweizerische Zeitschrift für Psychologie und ihre Andwendung* (Basel), 10, 26-42, 1951.

SUELLWOLD, FRITZ. "Empirical Studies Concerning Problems of Adolescents in Germany and the U.S.A." *Psychologische Rundschau* (Basel), 10, 49-66, 1949.

SYMONDS, P. M., and JENSEN, ARTHUR R. *From Adolescent to Adult*. New York: Columbia University Press, 1961.

TERMAN, L. M., and ODEN, M. H. *The Gifted Group at Mid-life: Thirty-five Years' Follow-up of the Superior Child.* Stanford: Stanford University Press, 1959.

TORGOFF, I. *Parental Developmental Timetable.* Paper presented to the American Psychological Association, 1958. Detroit: Merrill-Palmer Institute, mimeographed, 1960.

UNDERWOOD, F. W., and HONIGMAN, I. "A Comparison of Socialization and Personality in Two Simple Societies." *American Anthropologist,* 49, 557-577, 1947.

WALLACE, WILLIAM J. "The Girl's Puberty Rite of the Mohave." *Proceedings, Indiana Academy of Science,* 57, 37-40, 1947.

WALLACE, WILLIAM J. "Personality Variation in a Primitive Society." *Journal of Personality,* 15, 321-328, 1947.

WENAR, CHARLES. "The effects of Motor Handicap on Personality: I. The Effects of Level of Aspiration." *Child Development,* 24, 123-130, 1953.

WHEELER, D. K. "Development of the Ideal Self in Western Australian Youth." *Journal of Educational Research,* 55, 163-167, 1961.

WITTENBERG, RUDOLPH M. "Young People Look at Society." *Child Study,* 37(1), 16-20, 1959-60.

ZAZZO, BIANKA. "L'image de soi comparée à l'image de ses semblables chez l'adolescent" (The Self-Image of the Adolescent Compared to His Image of Peers). *Enfance,* nos. 2-4, 9-141, 1960.

CHAPTER 5

Emotionality, Anxiety, and Adjustment

To some extent most of the chapters in this book deal with different problem areas and the adolescent's adjustment to them. There is some degree of emotional stress involved with physical growth, social development, vocational planning, religion, etc., and these and other areas are covered in detail in separate chapters. Nonetheless, there is need for a general discussion of the over-all problems, anxieties, and disturbances of adolescence, and the various adjustments that the individual can make. Even those who question the "storm and stress" concept in its extreme form do agree that there is substantial evidence of the presence of heightened emotionality during the teen-years.

EMOTIONALITY AS A GENERAL STATE

There is even reason to suspect that this heightened emotionality is a rather general state, not specifically related to any one area of adjustment. This author used reaction time as a measure of conflict in an investigation (1955) of age and sex trends in emotional conflict of adolescence in seven areas of psychological adjustment: parent-child relationships, emotional tendencies, heterosexual relations, physical appearance, religion, vocational outlook, and social acceptability (see Tables 8 and 9). In each area girls showed evidence of conflict earlier than boys, confirming other evidence of their relative advancement.

The results for both sexes seemed to indicate that intensity of conflict is at a maximum during the adolescent years, as compared to both preadolescence and early maturity, in all areas except vocational outlook. Conflict in this latter area also reaches a maximum during adolescence but continues to be present through early adulthood. Although controls were imposed to minimize any generalization effect, the author feels that a general over-all pattern of conflict may exist. Within this general situation the degree and intensity of conflict may vary in the individual adjustment areas.

Most people apparently do think of adolescents and their problems

TABLE 8. *d* Test of statistical significance of differences in the difference scores between males and females at various age levels to words drawn from the various pyschological adjustment areas (Values of Fisher-Behrens *d*)

From Powell (1955), by permission of the author and Psychological Monographs

Adjustment area	Age in years									
	10	11	12	13	14	15	16	17	21–25	26–30
Parent-child relationships	1.34	.54	1.10	2.95*	.26	.36	.37	.09	.40	.98
Emotional tendencies	.84	1.54	1.79	6.20*	.79	.59	.17	1.56	.68	.41
Heterosexual relations	.34	.99	3.20*	6.18*	1.71	.20	1.46	1.94	.75	1.03
Physical appearance	.57	.58	2.01	6.13*	.57	.18	.56	.87	.61	1.07
Religion	.74	2.46*	1.32	2.35*	.69	.69	1.37	.07	.34	.06
Vocational outlook	1.11	1.79	.39	1.14	1.07	1.20	.08	.69	.01	.85
Social acceptability	1.07	3.04*	3.31*	4.50*	3.30*	.44	2.98*	3.35*	.79	.55

*.05 level of confidence

144

TABLE 9. *d* Test of statistical significance of age differences in the difference scores in the various areas of psychological adjustment, by sex
(Values of Fisher-Behrens *d*)
From Powell (1955), by permission of the author and Psychological Monographs

Stimulus area	Sex	10 vs. 11	11 vs. 12	12 vs. 13	13 vs. 14	14 vs. 15	15 vs. 16	16 vs. 17	17 vs. 21–25	21–25 vs. 26–30	15 vs. 17
Parent-child relationships	Male	1.05	.00	2.53*	1.83	.47	.08	1.26	2.90*	.09	—
	Female	.43	1.87	3.75*	1.51	.67	.04	.17	2.86*	.25	—
Emotional tendencies	Male	.77	.38	1.79	5.52*	.26	.53	.44	3.26*	.26	—
	Female	1.27	3.26*	6.08*	3.45*	.41	.13	.70	5.66*	.00	—
Heterosexual relations	Male	.63	1.13	2.38*	4.32*	2.14	.89	1.47	3.57*	.16	2.46*
	Female	.61	3.20*	4.84*	2.33*	.21	.93	1.59	6.54*	.20	—
Physical appearance	Male	.81	.13	.52	3.79*	1.13	1.16	.88	3.02*	.03	—
	Female	.19	2.93*	5.45*	1.07	.42	1.44	.17	4.79*	.62	—
Religion	Male	.07	1.15	2.86*	2.20*	.04	.56	.23	3.28*	.40	—
	Female	1.42	2.15*	3.67*	2.78*	.17	.37	1.01	6.24*	.03	—
Vocational outlook	Male	.21	1.62	.67	3.71*	2.40*	.83	.38	.76	.53	—
	Female	3.12*	.47	2.83*	3.64*	.21	.31	.18	.04	.28	—
Social acceptability	Male	1.81	3.20*	3.12*	3.41*	2.99*	2.37*	.29	4.89*	.34	2.80*
	Female	1.80	3.15*	5.52*	3.97*	.47	.87	.02	6.01*	1.06	—

*.05 level of confidence

145

in general rather than specific terms. The mere mention of the word "adolescent" seems to conjure up a picture of a high-strung, inconsistent, unstable individual. This point of view, therefore, seems to call for the general discussion that follows. The reader must realize that many of the "abnormalities" discussed in this chapter are "abnormalities" only in the eyes of adults. What often seem to adults to be serious behavior disturbances are relatively common in adolescence and are far less serious than the adult may assume. If one carefully considers these patterns within the framework of adolescent norms, they are often not abnormal in any sense of the word.

Many general discussions of adolescent problems have appeared in the professional literature during the last decade. Josselyn (1951) described a number of characteristics of adolescent behavior in an attempt to develop a theory in regard to this age group. She gave particular attention to the effect of earlier conflicts upon the behavior of the adolescent and also discussed the significance of the "family triangle" in the adolescent's attempt to gain security. Leonard (1954) also discussed tension areas in adolescents, stressing their "perplexities," "trigger" emotions, and their needs. This discussion was particularly oriented toward YMCA youth workers to point out the limitations they face.

Varying Interpretations

Although there seems to be a fair amount of agreement among researchers as to the emotionality of the adolescent, interpretations of the causes vary appreciably. There is also disagreement concerning the frequency of conflict and the severity of the disturbances that appear. Frick (1955) was critical of the needless repetition of research and the continual differences of opinion that have arisen from these interpretations. In the following paragraphs a number of points of view are presented to help the reader better understand these differences of interpretation.

Rube ("Adolescence, I," 1955) feels that the child's emotionality is reorganized under the influences of puberty and of leaving the parental milieu, both events that occur during adolescence. He proposes that it is this reorganization which gives the impression that the adolescent's personality is a personality in the making. There is no single problem of adolescence, as such, but rather a series of very complex, intricate problems interacting with one another. Luchins (1954) discussed the diversity in conceptions of adolescence and urged more study of individual cases. He suggests that the difficulties of the period might be eased by: (1) early marriage; (2) adult discussion and action to minimize intra-institutional and interinstitutional conflict; and (3) a search for socially useful outlets for youthful energy.

The importance of the dual desire of adolescents for independence (to be self-governing) and dependence (to obtain assurance and approval) was emphasized by Resnick (1953). He feels that punishment should be reasonable and corrective and that adolescents should gradually be freed from control. Lowrey (1955) discussed the major characteristics of adolescence, including psychosexual frustrations, ego problems, and peer relations. He lists as adolescent defenses increased ambivalence in all attitudes, increased hostility toward adults, flight into adventure, increased fantasy formation, seeking the protection of the peer group, and increased egocentricity.

The roles of daydreaming and the image of the self in adolescents were considered by Rube ("Adolescence, II," 1955). He suggests that "day-dreaming in adolescence is the necessary process of re-organization and re-evaluation of the image of one's self." This process enables the individual to test reality and to visualize the ambitions and wishes that he had previously stored in his inner world.

Doherty (1948) believes that the normal adolescent should possess such characteristics as an individual point of view and behavior; qualities of leadership within the group; critical judgment, tending in later adolescence to become more constructive; self-control and self-discipline; and complete adjustment to his own sex. She also believes that adolescents should have an interest in a definite career and the ability to modify this choice of career if such modification is necessary. They should also have a general interest in hobbies, world topics, religion, music, art, and independent reading; should be concerned with living and reaching forward to maturity; and should have the ability to adjust to people of totally different types. If problems arise in these latter areas, she strongly recommends that the adolescent be referred for psychiatric help at an early age.

Rao (1948) stated that a scientific approach in dealing with adolescent boys and girls should involve (1) recognition of individual differences; and (2) an effort to discover exactly why the adolescent is manifesting whimsical, rebellious, melancholic, or self-conscious behavior. He suggested that the right approach in controlling adolescent behavior is through gaining a willing and cooperative submission rather than through overawing discipline. The energy and enthusiasms of teen-agers should not be suppressed but rather sublimated, and monotony should be minimized through diversion and relaxation.

The Field-Theory Approach

The present author feels that the field-theory approach to adolescence presented by Lewin (1939) offers a frame of reference that is still most appropriate. Lewin's concept of this life-space is expressed in the formula: "Behavior-Function of person and environment = Function of life-space (BE = F(P,E) = F(LSP)." He summarized his discussion as follows:

"(a). The basic fact concerning the general situation of the adolescent can be represented as the position of a person during locomotion from one region to another. This includes (1) the widening of the life-space (geographically, socially, and in time perspective) and (2) the cognitively unstructured character of the new situation.

"(b). Somewhat more specifically, the adolescent has a social position 'between' the adult and the child, similar to a marginal member of an underprivileged minority group.

"(c). There are still more specific factors involved in adolescence, such as the new experiences with one's own body, which can be represented as the baffling change of a central region of the established life-space.

"From this representation one can derive conceptually:

"I. The adolescent's shyness, sensitivity, and aggressiveness, owing to unclearness and instability of ground (follows from a, b, and c).

"II. A more or less permanent conflict between the various attitudes, values, ideologies, and styles of living (follows from b).

"III. Emotional tension resulting from these conflicts (follows from a, b, and c).

"IV. Readiness to take extreme attitudes and actions and to shift his position radically (follows from a, b, and c).

"V. The 'adolescent behavior' should appear only if the structure and dynamic of the field is such as represented by a, b, and c. The degree and particular type of behavior should depend upon the degree of realization of this structure and upon the strength of the conflicting forces. Above all, the degree of difference and of separation between adults and children which is characteristic for a particular culture is important; also, the extent to which the particular adolescent finds himself in the position of a marginal man. According to field theory, actual behavior depends upon every part of the field. It follows that the degree of instability of the adolescent should be greatly influenced also by such factors as general stability or instability of the particular individual."*

Generally, the present author does not agree that adolescence is or must be a time of "storm and stress." He feels that it is a period of generally heightened emotionality resulting from this "marginal" position. While adolescents may occasionally develop severe adjust-

* Quoted by permission from "Field Theory and Experiments in Social Psychology; Concepts and Methods" by Kurt Lewin, *American Journal of Sociology,* 44 (1949), pages 868-896.

ment problems, they are usually able to cope effectively with their environments, and many of the problems that they do develop will be alleviated by the time they reach adulthood.

ADOLESCENT EMOTIONALITY IN OTHER CIVILIZED SOCIETIES

We pointed out in Chapter 1 that the problems of adolescence are no longer peculiar to the American society. Many studies on this topic have been reported from foreign countries; most of these emphasize the presence of heightened emotionality during this age span. The interpretations from these studies are also varied and often contradictory of one another, but the general conclusions seem very similar to those in studies of American teen-agers.

Germany

Buytendijk (1958) feels that young people in Germany seek to know the meaning of existence, which results in their searching for security. The unrest of that search is counteracted to some degree by belief, trust, and hope. This latter aspect is, he feels, the true security, but is itself in turn ground for unrest. Bornemann (1958) has written of the problems of the German adolescent of our time. He analyzed the impact of historical political changes upon adolescents in Germany and described five distinctly different youth generations: (1) the romantic youth movement of the earlier part of this century; (2) the politicizing youth of the pre-Nazi period; (3) the Nazi youth movement; (4) the disillusioned youth of the post-World War II period; and (5) the present youth, characterized by an objective, functional, utilitarian approach toward reality. He concludes that this present youth generation is exposed to too much mental and emotional stimulation, accompanied by an acceleration of physical maturity but lacking a correspondingly accelerated mental and emotional development. The present-day problems of adolescents in Germany are brought about by changes in (1) family life; (2) vocational and industrial life; (3) community, public, and political life; and (4) the widely observed phenomenon of acceleration of physical maturity. Bornemann discusses in detail the attitude of German youth toward family, school, work, leisure time, means of mass communication, youth organizations, the opposite sex, and the legal structure.

The status and needs of youth in the German culture were also discussed by Storring and Lownau (1958), who feel that acceleration of physical development, as contrasted with the development of the last generation, has strongly influenced adjustment by creating a marked discrepancy between physical, emotional, and intellectual functioning.

They feel that young people today are very dependent on family and peer group relationships. The instability of their goals is related to an exaggerated need to conform to and fit in with the peer group. Parents' failure to encourage self-realization contributes to the teen-agers' insecurity. Muchow (1950) proposes that the intractability of early adolescence in Germany is the expression, not of a legitimate psychophysical phase of development, but of a deep gulf between the structure of the child's emotional pattern of maturation and the modern environment. This environment, with its "mechanization," forces the juvenile back into the "inner exile" of his childhood world for far too long a period.

Debesse (1949), writing in a Dutch journal, has also criticized the idea of crises in development. He thinks that the egotistic mentality of the adolescent is not opposed to sociability, which at this age is still subjective.

Israel

Gitlin-Bitensky (1954) attempted to give a psychological and sociological explanation to the entity of adolescent problems in Israel. She considered adolescence in terms of a crisis between adolescents and adults, and also discussed sexuality and sex education, the way to independence, crystallization of ego, the way out of the crisis, youth community, and transition from adolescence to adulthood. These areas are, of course, similar to those considered as sources of conflict in other geographic locales. Eisenstadt (1958) discusses the appearance of a new type of juvenile behavior that is found in many countries and to some extent in Israel. This negative behavior, expressed by an increase in juvenile delinquency, is reported as typical for youth from well-to-do homes and appears to arise out of boredom. This phenomenon is a result of institutionalization of social and national ideologies. Because of this situation, youth is not able to look at its future as different from the present, and thus seems to demonstrate Riesman's "cult of immediacy."

Communist Countries

The problems of adolescence are well known even in Communist-dominated societies. The explanation of interpretation of these problems has been fitted into Marxian psychology in an effort to de-emphasize the difficulties. Baley (1950) wrote a self-critical discussion of his own *Psychology of Adolescence,* which was written twenty years earlier as a study of Polish youth, and which suggested the universality of adolescent problems. The author, now functioning under Communist influence, considered that his original work represented the bourgeois psychology of adolescence and that his generalizations of the "classical" psychology of adolescence were often hasty and imprudent, pertinent only for some social classes of Western civilization. His revised position was that these concepts are not universally valid; that mental development during the puberty age has a quite different course both among primitive peoples and in a socialistic society. Marxian psychology, he said, explains the dynamics of this period and the molding of its structure in definite conditions of the new social existence.

This explanation rather obviously follows the "party line" and is an attempt to deny the existence of the problems of adolescence. Nonetheless, much evidence is available from newspaper and magazine sources to indicate that the problems of adolescents living under the Communist regime are in many ways similar to those of youngsters in Western societies. The conflicts of Iron Curtain youth might well be expected to be even more severe than those of their Western counterparts, as a result of governmental as well as parental controls.

Increase in Adolescent Problems

Recognition of the problems related to adolescence appears to be world-wide, although these problems are not actually universal. There are still some primitive societies where adolescent disturbances are unknown, but these are becoming increasingly rare. As the newly formed nations become more civilized and structured, the problems of their adolescents will probably become intensified. Better education, more industrial development, mechanization, etc., all seem to be factors that speed the appearance of the areas common to adolescent conflict. Thus, even though the explanations and interpretations may differ, many common problems do exist and are generally recognized.

There is, perhaps, a need for a redefinition of "youth" and a radical change of educational methods, which should be based on scientific research. The youth period has been prolonged, and the attitude of adults toward youth has changed. The adolescent's adjustment, particularly in rapidly changing cultures, has become more and more difficult. If we are thoroughly to understand the development of the new youth we must study carefully and analyze critically those patterns that are conflict-producing (Szcepanski, 1959).

THE GENERAL PROBLEMS OF ADOLESCENCE

The adolescent's heightened vulnerability to stress is not inherent. Rather, it has been suggested that adults evoke his maladaptive behavior by expecting it, by encouraging him to face life as they think it is rather than as he finds it, by prolonging his immaturity, and by modeling inadequate values and attitudes (Pitt, 1954). Generally the adolescent is entering an uncertain, complicated, and troubled world in which it is most difficult for the adult to help him understand the problems of achieving independence, of engagement and marriage, of finding a job, and of building a philosophy of life (Ojemann, 1954). This difficulty is intensified by the fact that many adults are also baffled by these problems.

The school, like the home, seems to be a source of teen-age problems. Remmers and Shimberg (1949), in a study of high-school youth, found the school environment to be a major problem source. Cary (1948) administered the Mooney Problem Check List to ninth- , tenth- , eleventh- , and twelfth-graders, asking them to double-check the problems that concerned them most. The items double-checked most frequently were those that concerned the school situation. Marked differences in degree of conflict have been reported among those who left school early as opposed to those who completed their educations. With the raising of the school-leaving age, this distinction may well lose its significance. Ogilvie (1949) feels that a continuation of this pattern of requiring children to remain in school longer may lessen some of the problems of adolescence. While this is probably a correct assumption, enforced school attendance may at the same time increase the intensity of some other problems. Chapters 12 and 13 are devoted to an exploration of the educational structure and the teen-age problems relating to it.

Adolescents have a number of goals to attain, and the attainment tends to be impeded by a variety of cultural factors. The lack of opportunity for emancipation may lead to a prolongation of dependency. Inability to establish a healthy identification with the parent of the same sex may be a major cause of disturbance. Failure of the child "from early infancy to relate himself to small units of society . . . specifically his family," gives, in the opinion of Kirkpatrick (1952), cause to worry over the ability of the developing adolescents to grow up capable of assuming their place as world citizens.

Most adults are greatly concerned about the alleged rebellion of the adolescent. Anderson (1948) has defined adolescent resentment of authority as lying between downright revolt and the normal dislike we all have of being directed or crossed in our desires by someone in authority. Colm (1951) feels that the preadolescent child needs to rebel to some degree from the standards and values of his parents if he is to grow into a healthy adult. Parents, however, must maintain their role in order to give the child the firmness and stability he needs.

Burt and Howard (1952) factorized the correlations among twenty-four conditions reported among 273 maladjusted adolescents. Only a small general factor was found. The first bipolar factor indicates a broad classification into environmental conditions and personal conditions, respectively, and a cross-classification into intellectual conditions and emotional conditions. The authors concluded that cases of maladjustment can hardly be regarded as forming a single relatively homogeneous group. In a sense this seems to substantiate the present author's belief in the existence of a pattern of heightened emotionality during the teen-years.

Many of the difficulties discussed here are common to physically handicapped youngsters as well as to the nonhandicapped. Johnson (1953) suggests that the similarities in the difficulties encountered by both groups are greater than the differences. The differences must, of course, be realistically taken into account, and the degree of conflict in relation to the same problem area may vary appreciably in the two groups.

SPECIFIC PROBLEMS

The specific problems of adolescents and a number of factors correlated with these problems have been investigated by a number of researchers. Socioeconomic factors, sex differences, emotional adjustment, and intellectual level all bear on the presence of the problems of this age group. Although many different problem areas have been identified, it is often difficult to assess their significance, since frequency of appearance is not directly correlated with degree of seriousness.

Lent (1957) used Rotter's Incomplete Sentences Blank to survey the number, type, and distribution of problems of each age group of 425 junior- and senior-high-school students. The problems most frequently identified were designated as personal-psychological, study-learning, social-psychological, and home-family relationships. Here, again, the most frequently appearing problems cannot be assumed to be the most serious ones.

Similar problems concerning adolescent difficulties were mentioned by male students and their teachers in Catholic high schools (Finn, 1950). There were significant grade-level patterns apparent: generally problems were less frequent after tenth grade; school-life problems showed irregular decrease from grades nine through twelve; vocational problems increased with grade level; family-life, personality-adjustment, and financial problems appeared with similar frequencies at all grade levels; boy-girl problems were more numerous in grades ten and twelve. No dissimilarities from school to school were noted among the five schools studied.

Causes of Worry

Family and school problems seem to appear consistently in most of the studies. Stacey (1955) found that 15 seventeen-year-old girls with IQ's ranging from 50 to 79 ranked these two areas first on a "worries"

inventory. Next in importance as sources of worry these girls listed
personal inadequacy, economic problems, and imaginary or unreason-
able items. Last in importance were problems related to physical health
and punishment, in that order.

Angelino *et al.* (1956) discussed the relationship of socioeconomic
status and age to the fears and worries of 1100 children aged nine
through eighteen. Their data showed a positive relationship between
socioeconomic background and the number and kinds of reported
fears. Fears related to safety caused greatest concern at ages nine
through eleven and nine through twelve for lower- and middle-class
boys respectively. Boys reached a peak in this area at ages eleven and
twelve. The economic and political category showed a sharp increase
from sixteen to eighteen, with upper-class boys showing a bit more
concern at earlier ages. Table 10 summarizes the socioeconomic differences for both sexes and all ages.

TABLE 10. Summary of means for the total number of fears and worries indicated
by both boys and girls from two differing socioeconomic levels in
each of ten categories
From Angelino et al. *(1956), by permission of the authors and The Journal Press*

	Boys		Girls	
Category	Upper S-E (N=179)	Lower S-E (N=383)	Upper S-E (N=178)	Upper S-E (N=390)
1. Safety	1.07	1.05	.87	1.30
2. School	1.32	1.06	1.39	1.14
3. Personal appearance	.04	.02	.06	.17
4. Natural phenomena	.28	.13	.25	.35
5. Economical and political	.49	.44	.40	.27
6. Health	.26	.16	.34	.20
7. Animals	.20	.51	.22	.64
8. Social relations	.43	.37	.63	.58
9. Personal conduct	.28	.22	.27	.28
10. Supernatural	.04	.04	.09	.04

Angelino and Shedd (1953) also studied changes in fears and worries
in relation to chronological age. Each category studied showed increases and decreases from one age group to another. At ages ten,
eleven, and twelve there seemed to be a preponderance of fears connected with animals, but by age thirteen there was a shift to fears connected with school. At age fifteen economic and political interests appeared, and these increased through age eighteen. Contrary to expectation, social relationships, personal appearance, and personal conduct
did not appear to be as important as earlier studies had indicated.

The California Test of Personality and the Mooney Problem Check

List were administered to a group of eighth-grade pupils by Pflieger (1947). The correlations, some of which were negative, indicated that a poorly adjusted student will check a greater number of concerns. A significant proportion of those students were concerned about health, school, earning money, and success in life. The author feels that there is an advantage in administering both these tests, since the correlations were not high enough to warrant the use of either test by itself.

Aggression

Mandel (1959) studied aggressive behavior in a group of boys ten to sixteen years old. A factor-analytic study of the data yielded four factors in aggression: enmity; proximity of others; inhibition or control; and dominance drive. He found aggression was also related quantitatively and qualitatively to position in a sociogram and to situational frustration. He concluded that aggression is not only a reaction to frustration (factor of enmity) but may also arise spontaneously (factors of dominance drive and need for contact with others). Aggressive behavior was usually directed downward in the "pecking order," except for teasing and insolence.

OVEREMPHASIS OF EMOTIONAL PROBLEMS

Again, we must point out that many of the problems mentioned by teen-agers are relatively mild ones. Since many researchers ask only to have problems listed, the subjects respond in these terms. Most of the research, therefore, is designed to bring out negative characteristics, and very few studies are done in which adolescents have the opportunity to show the positive aspects of their development. One such study, by Wall (1948), illustrates this point. He asked his female subjects to indicate both happy and unhappy experiences that they had in childhood and adolescence. They reported twice as many happy experiences in childhood as unhappy ones, and an almost equal number of happy and unhappy experiences during adolescence. The fields of experience investigated included family, school, personal future, social environment, physical environment, games, and interests.

It should also be re-emphasized that many of the problems of adolescence are not caused by biological factors but are united with puberty by cultural circumstances and the influences of the social environment. The roles that children and adolescents wish to assume demonstrate the force of these influences. Cobb (1954) found that boys' wishes are more "in the direction of personal achievement and self-aggrandizement," while those of girls tend more "in the direction of social and family relations and personal characteristics." These are obviously socially oriented goals based on the individual's cultural experiences.

Situational Problems

Certain areas of difficulty are situational and may arise relatively seldom for a given individual. Brooks (1960) reinforced this point in a study of factors in rigidity. She administered to a group of fifteen-year-olds a battery of concept-formation tests designed to measure Einstelling effects (a preparedness for a particular kind of stimulus) as a function of certain situational variables. She hypothesized that the Einstelling effects would vary with the complexity of task, type of task, and also with the habituating and nonhabituating character of prior problems. The evidence does indicate that rigidity of behavior is related to some extent to the complexity of the task. The general conclusion was that situational factors are important variables in rigidity of behavior.

Antecedent events also appear to have some effect on the individual's reaction to a current situation. Steisel and Cohen (1952) structured a study to determine whether differences in degrees of failure, defined in terms of independently controlled antecedent events rather than in terms of the subject's responses, could be shown to have a reliable effect upon responses. Their results generally indicated that "failure experiences were followed by a lowering of aspiration levels, and more severe failures resulted in a greater drop than did mild failure." Generally, the teen-ager's success or failure in the antecedent event seems to have a good deal of influence on his performance of future events.

Competition

Much stress has been laid on the emotion-producing effects of competition, and organized competition for youth has been criticized on this basis. For example, a good deal of criticism has been directed toward the highly competitive aspects of Little League and Middle League baseball. Skubic (1955) structured an experiment "designed to collect objective data regarding the effects of competition of boys between the ages of nine and fifteen" who were involved in these activities. Responses in the organized game structure were compared with responses of the same boys in softball competition in physical-education classes. Galvanic skin-reflex tests were used to measure the emotional excitation of the subjects. Generally, there was no evidence to suggest any greater emotional excitation in the organized League games than in the physical-education games.

Effect of Films

Wall and Simpson (1950) attempted to study the impact of commercial films on the social and psychological development of early teen-agers.

Amusement, enduring satisfaction, and a feeling of ultimate goodness were the commonest reactions, while sadness, fright, and desire for more wealth were least often reported. These same authors (1951) concluded that "the content of the film does seem much to determine the responses made" and that "the cinema provides a powerful stimulus to the fantasy life."

Relationships among Problems

Misconceptions sometimes arise about the relationships of certain behavior patterns. Teachers, for example, often feel that cheating on tests is an indication of emotional disturbance or neuroticism. Keehn (1956) attempted to measure the relationship among cheating, neuroticism, and extroversion in a group of eleven- to thirteen-year-olds. If answers to more than three out of twenty-four questions on an arithmetic test were changed, it was assumed to be cheating. A twenty-item questionnaire was given to measure extroversion and neuroticism. Most of the subjects who were rated as extroverted were also rated as neurotic. Differences in cheating between high and low neurotic groups were not significant. However, those rated low in neuroticism and extroversion cheated significantly less frequently than those with high scores on these measures. Thus, the author concludes that extroversion is more related to cheating than neuroticism is.

Cigarette smoking is also thought by many to be an indicator of emotionality, particularly among teen-agers. Horn *et al.* (1959) found two relatively independent factors associated with a high proportion of smoking: (1) a correspondence with family practices as indicated by parental smoking; and (2) a syndrome of personal factors characterizing inactive students who tend to be scholastically unsuccessful and who have lower academic goals. However, these factors did not account for the significantly higher proportion of smokers found in a Catholic parochial school.

If nothing else, these studies demonstrate the need for caution when attempting to generalize about adolescent behavior. The specificity of certain patterns, the situational aspects related to behavior, sex differentials in behavior, socioeconomic differences, all make it difficult to define adolescent behavior *per se* in clear terms. Even when common patterns of behavior are present in all adolescents, they vary in degree of intensity and in frequency of appearance.

Pregnancy

Certain extremes in behavior are often interpreted by laymen as common indicators of disturbance. Pregnancy among adolescent girls is one such pattern. Fleck (1956) does confirm that adolescent pregnancy does seem to be a major symptom of maladjustment. Although 25 per cent of his samples were not adolescents chronologically, they were found to be emotionally immature with respect to sexual and family problems: 54 per cent were deprived of one or both parents, Among the conclusions of this study were: that girls who seek agency support are immature and are not good candidates for assuming the mother role; and that pregnancy is a symptomatic act often brought about almost unconsciously as a neurotic solution during adolescence. These conclusions are quite valid, but one must remember that only a very small minority of adolescent girls, even among those who have severe emotional problems, become pregnant.

Physical Handicaps

Adolescents who have physical handicaps or disabilities are also considered to have more emotional difficulties than their nonhandicapped peers. Cruickshank (1952) analyzed the responses to a sentence completion test by a group of adolescents having cardiac, orthopedic, and neurological handicaps and compared them with responses of a similar group of nonhandicapped youngsters. His findings indicated that the handicapped children "see themselves as having more fears and more feelings of guilt" than do the nonhandicapped.

A further investigation of the relationship of psychological disturbance and physical handicaps in adolescence was reported by Wenar (1958). He hypothesized that there was no significant difference in the depth of psychological disturbance between handicapped and nonhandicapped adolescents needing professional help. His results suggested that the handicapped youths tend to be somewhat healthier, with more vitality, inner resources, and creativity, but are more sensitized to potential dangers in their environment. His general conclusion was that physical handicap cannot be equated with psychological disturbance.

THE ROLE OF THE SCHOOL IN EMOTIONAL ADJUSTMENT

Although Chapters 12 and 13 of this book are entirely concerned with the adolescent and the school, some brief discussion of this area seems warranted at this point. Most of the studies of fears or worries discussed previously do indicate that the school is a frequently mentioned source of conflict. We do not suggest that the school climate is likely to cause severe disturbance in an adolescent who is otherwise well adjusted, but rather that those adolescents who are already somewhat disturbed emotionally may become more upset in the school environment. Some frustration may arise even in a well-adjusted individual if the school fails to satisfy his needs, but severe disturbance is unlikely to result from this usually temporary frustration.

Recognition of Problems

School personnel have become increasingly aware of the necessity of understanding the "whole" child if the educative process is to be completely successful. It is well recognized that an emotional problem may interfere with effective learning, and failure to learn may, in turn, intensify the emotional difficulty. Teachers are being better educated to recognize the different symptoms of disturbance, especially those which are considered serious. For example, teachers formerly were likely to consider boisterous children as more maladjusted than withdrawn children. The latter appeared to be well behaved and seldom caused any disturbance in class. As a result they were seldom noticed by the teacher. Teachers are now more aware of such children and recognize that withdrawal may be a more serious symptom than overt aggressive behavior. However, teachers still seem to be more concerned over pupils who disrupt the classroom environment. Clark (1951) asked 181 elementary-school teachers to respond to a paired-comparison annoyance questionnaire containing thirty-five behavior items. Most annoying to these teachers was pupil behavior that affected the functioning of the pupil group. Generally, behavior affecting the teacher more or less directly was less annoying.

There is room for a good deal of improvement in teachers' ability to recognize problems relating to pupil adjustment. Graham (1947) reports the results of a workshop demonstration in which teachers made observations on the personal and social adjustment of a group of high-school students who had taken the California Test of Personality. Generally, the teachers felt that the test results accurately described the students they had observed, but were unable to cite specific behavior that had led them to the conclusions they had drawn. The workshop seemed to be valuable in increasing the intensity of the teachers' interest in the pupils with an emphasis on securing more adequate information. Further, these teachers seemed to give greater attention to personal and social orientations than they had prior to the workshop.

Andrew and Lockwood (1954) attempted to determine how teachers evaluate the mental health of their students. They administered an eleven-item mental-health rating scale to teachers of a random sample of 10 per cent of the children in the Battle Creek schools. Of these students, 19 per cent were judged to be maladjusted, and 2 per cent as severely maladjusted. Poor adjustment seemed to be associated with low socioeconomic status, low intelligence, and broken homes. There was no apparent relationship between adjustment and grade in school, family size, or race.

Whether the problem child should remain in school or be allowed to quit and start work is a very practical question. Such children remain problems when and if they become part of the working force. Since business and industry seldom offer the possibility of adequate guidance for such persons, their problems probably will be intensified. Therefore, it is generally suggested that such children should remain in school for the longest possible time, and that the schools have a responsibility to provide a maximum of individual guidance (Fornwalt, 1947).

Teachers must be careful not to single out children with handicaps as necessarily being maladjusted. In a study done by Zintz (1951) teachers were asked to rate handicapped and nonhandicapped children in grades six, seven, and eight on a test of twenty-one behavior traits. Generally, they rated the handicapped as less aggressive, more withdrawing, and behaving in a less socially acceptable manner than the nonhandicapped. While this study is undoubtedly accurate, one must be aware that a teacher's response is subject to bias. If teachers have a stereotyped picture of the handicapped youngster as being "different," their responses may be based on this stereotype rather than on the actual behavior of the individuals being rated.

Guidance in the Classroom

In order to serve the best interests of both "average" and maladjusted students, classroom situations should be diagnosed by means of sociometric tests, students' compositions about their worries, socio-drama, interviews with parents, and direct observation. After such diagnosis, techniques which may be employed to help children are: reading stories about typical problems and encouraging discussion by the class; grouping the students according to their sociometric choices; socio-drama; projects for teachers aimed at helping to integrate studies with adult work; and enlarging the curriculum so that no area of subject matter assumes isolated emotional significance (Elkins, 1951).

The thesis has been proposed that every teacher is a teacher of psychology, who regards all-around adjustment as a major objective of education. As a means of helping the adolescent understand himself and behave in a mature way, Reid (1951) suggests the use of unfinished stories or pictures which present a normal teen-ager in a usual situation that calls for a solution. Individual and group guidance is then accomplished through free discussion. The subject matter is designed to relate to the changing patterns of the students' lives, with the aim of preventing emotional disturbances. The present author feels that the objective of every teacher's being a teacher of psychology is a good one, but that this goal is not yet attained. Most teachers do not have sufficient psychological training to interpret such techniques or to guide adequately discussion concerning them.

Schools are attempting to foster the optimum development of all children. This is being done in part by applying the findings of research in areas such as individual differences, personality growth, and the learning process. The key to good mental health in the classroom is, of course, the teacher. The teacher must, therefore, have health of mind and freedom from fear in order to help children develop healthy attitudes. Children who fail in school usually have personality problems, and poorly adjusted children fail to do as well as they should in school work (Cason *et al.*, 1950).

MEASUREMENT OF EMOTIONALITY AND ADJUSTMENT

In Chapter 4 the measuring instruments used to assess various aspects of personality were discussed. These same instruments are also used to measure emotional disturbance and level or degree of adjustment. Results of some of the studies employing these tests for this particular purpose are reported in the following paragraphs. The reader must keep in mind the problems associated with the use of the instruments, especially those in which the respondent's knowledge of the socially acceptable answers can influence the results. Walters and Zaks (1958) also have warned that the use of adult norms to interpret adolescent inventory protocols may result in inaccuracies in the findings.

Rorschach Evaluations

The Rorschach has been and is being widely used to assess emotionality. Ives *et al.* (1933) have attempted to determine the "incidence of Rorschach 'neurotic' and 'adjustment' signs in a population of normal adolescents." Their subjects included eleven- , thirteen- , fifteen- , and eighteen-year-olds. They report that "the incidence of many signs currently used to diagnose neurosis was found to be considerably higher than would be expected if the signs were truly indicative of neuroses." Five or more "neurotic" signs were found in more than one-third of the eighteen-year-olds. The patterns appeared to be relatively stable, since eleven of the fourteen "neurotic" signs were present at all the ages studied. As a result of these findings the authors question "the validity and usefulness of these 'neurotic' signs as a diagnostic technique with adolescents." Further, they did not find the seventeen "adjustment" signs occurring with the frequency that would be expected in a group of well-functioning adolescents. They recommend that more attention be given to sex differences in the "neurotic" and "adjustment" signs, since their findings showed girls demonstrating fewer "neurotic" and more "adjustment" signs than boys. The results of the correlations of "adjustment" signs and interview ratings of adjustment were non-significant, indicating that the case workers' evaluation did not relate to the Rorschach evaluation.

When adolescents' Rorschach protocols are compared with those of adults, differences are apparent. Lucena (1948) compared the responses of 79 male adolescents from northeast Brazil with the responses of adults from a similar cultural area. The adolescents' thinking was less apt for abstraction and generalization. Affectivity of the adolescent showed greater lability and impulsiveness. Hershenson (1949) asked high-school juniors to rank the Rorschach cards according to their preference and to give reasons for their choices. The correlation analysis indicated highly affective responses to preferred cards and a lack of disphoric feeling in choosing of an achromatic card.

Use of the TAT

The Thematic Apperception Test has also been used to assess emotional characteristics of teen-agers. Ghosh (1958) administered ten unstructured inkblots and twenty cards (F) of the TAT to more than 1000 preadolescent and more than 1000 adolescent girls. Both groups revealed concern for family, and aggression was revealed in both the inkblots and the TAT story content. The preadolescent girls seemed to be happier, while the adolescent girls showed eroticism. A rise in the tendency to self-assertion was noted in the adolescent girls.

Kagan and Moss (1959) investigated achievement fantasy in terms of its reliability and validity. Three TAT protocols were administered at ages eight to nine, six to eleven, and six to fourteen, and also used data involving educational level of parents, rating of maternal concern with achievement for the first three years of the child's life, and data showing changes in IQ score during the years six through ten. Their results showed an increase in occurrence of achievement themes with age and better than chance stability of occurrence over time. They found a positive relationship between early maternal concern with achievement and both achievement fantasy and IQ gain in girls, a non-linear but generally positive relationship between achievement fantasy and IQ gain for boys and girls, and a suggestive relation between achievement fantasy and the educational level of the same-sex parent. The authors suggest that achievement fantasy is an index of the

strength of the subject's behavioral tendency to seek achievement goals
and that concern with achievement on the part of the same-sex parent
has a special influence on the child's achievement strivings.

Tests for Maladjustment

Methods of identifying maladjusted children at the ninth-grade level
have been investigated by Ullman (1952). He administered an original
forced-choice test for use by teachers, an adjustment-level-rating scale,
a sociometric test for student use, the California Test of Personality,
and the SRA Youth Inventory. Eight per cent of the children studied
were considered by teachers to be "severely maladjusted." Tindall
(1955) reported on the intercorrelations among sixteen scores indicative
of adjustment. These indicators had been administered to 66 adolescent boys in an orphanage, and included ratings by adult judges, sociometric techniques, projective techniques, and direct observation. Table
11 presents these intercorrelations, which show, in general, positive but
low relationships among the various adjustment indices. About forty-
one of these intercorrelations are significant at the 1 per cent level of
confidence, while seventeen more are significant at the 5 per cent level.
Thus, while some common variance is tapped, assessment of adjustment
by one technique has little predicted value.

Evaluation of Techniques

Much improvement in methods of assessing adjustment seems to be
needed. Although many of the current instruments are useful for research purposes, especially with large groups of subjects, their adequacy
for diagnosing individuals is doubtful. The more subjective techniques, such as the various projective tests, are being widely used in an
attempt to overcome the biases associated with the objective techniques.
The mere fact of the subjectivity, however, leaves much to the discretion of the clinician scoring the responses. It is not unusual for two
equally competent clinicians to arrive at different conclusions from the
same results of a projective technique. More research is needed in the
area of adjustment assessment, especially to develop norms for techniques used to evaluate adolescent adjustment.

EXTREME DISORDERS

Quite often the layman judges all adolescent behavior on the basis of
extreme cases, particularly since these are widely publicized. While
such extremes obviously present a very biased picture, they also indicate
the severity of the disorders that affect some adolescents. A brief

TABLE 11. Intercorrelations of adjustment indices
(r < .24 below 5 per cent level; r > .32 above 1 per cent level; N = 66)
From Tindall (1955), by permission of the author and Educational and Psychological Measurement

Indices	Self-adjustment	Social adjustment	Analytical thinking	Confidence	Sociability	Personal relations	Emotional stability	Home satisfactory	"T & S" rating	Deans' rating	Psychological rating	Guess who?	Companion choice	Rorschach	Incomplete sentences	Time sample
Self-adjustment		.66	.24	.53	.20	.62	.48	.33	.71	.26	.40	.50	.32	.26	.32	.27
Soc. adjustment			.11	.35	.15	.46	.33	.38	.42	.27	.47	.28	.27	.35	.32	.12
Anal. thinking				.33	.31	.17	.30	-.13	-.04	.13	.07	.20	.07	.11	-.04	-.09
Confidence					.50	.76	.81	.33	.03	.17	.21	.30	.22	.14	.15	.01
Sociability						.29	.32	.02	-.09	-.06	.04	.33	-.04	.11	.08	.03
Pers. relations							.79	.38	.16	.25	.31	.27	.37	.18	.21	.12
Emot. stability								.43	.01	.07	.16	.22	.24	.18	.09	.07
Home satis.									.21	-.02	.20	-.05	.13	.20	.03	.10
"T & S" rating										.55	.49	.53	.60	.29	.10	.46
Deans' rating											.58	.37	.63	.19	.10	.17
Psych. rating												.30	.49	.11	.36	.19
Guess who?													.63	.25	.13	.29
Comp. choice														.32	.11	.22
Rorschach															.09	-.09
Inc. sentence																-.10
Mean	57.0	66.2	20.8	24.9	22.1	21.6	26.4	37.2	97.5	82.6	93.8	.8	.1	15.6	125.5	6.5
S.D.	11.3	11.9	4.5	7.0	6.8	6.1	7.6	7.6	33.1	18.5	16.2	25.8	27.6	4.8	16.3	2.9

discussion of some of these extreme disturbances follows, but the reader is again reminded that these are atypical rather than typical cases.

Murderous Aggression

Easson and Steinhilber (1961), reporting on murderous aggression, found that murder and murderous violence committed by adolescents occurred where these tendencies were fostered by the parents, although such fostering is usually unconscious. In cases of murder or murderous assault, the family background of the patients showed certain definite psychodynamic patterns. In all cases one or both parents had fostered and condoned murderous assault. While this study offers strong support of our earlier discussion of the influence of the parental environment on the behavior of the child, only a very small number of adolescents engage in such extreme forms of violence.

Autism

Eisenberg (1956) re-evaluated a number of autistic children at a mean age of fifteen years, nine years after the original evaluation. The original diagnosis had been based upon the relation of two symptoms that are regarded as pathogenic for early infantile autism: extreme self-isolation and obsessive insistence on the preservation of sameness. At the time of the follow-up, thirty-four cases were at home with parents or foster parents. Of the total group of 63 subjects, three had achieved what might be called a good adjustment, thirteen a fair adjustment, and forty-six a poor adjustment. Thus, about one-third of the group was functioning at a fair to good social level. The striking disability in interpersonal relations and the severe obsessive-compulsive mechanisms remain the pathogenic feature of autism. The author suggests that in a sense the primary psychopathologic feature in infantile autism is a disturbance in social perception.

Personality Disorders

The development and psychiatric evaluation of a group of boys nine to sixteen years old who presented personality difficulties and emotional conflicts caused by fears of physical inadequacy was reported by Schonfeld (1950). Many of the variations in puberal development studied fell within the normal range. However, an apparent or actual delay in age of onset of sexual maturation, the failure of the beginning of the growth spurt, or some inadequacy in masculine development may lead to psychosomatic complaints. Although the dynamics associated with these personality disorders vary in individual boys, it would appear that castration anxieties and feelings of inadequacy play an essential role in the unconscious mechanisms involved. There do seem to be equally important conscious mechanisms in children of this age group, and they seem to be related to the boy's dependence on approval by his companions. Deviation from the group pattern, either real or felt, leads to increased feelings of inadequacy with subsequent loss of self-esteem. Although physical treatment, such as hormone induction or plastic surgery, may be most useful, the mainstay of treatment is the proper application of psychotherapy.

Mental Retardation

Adolescents who are mentally retarded often suffer undue emotional stress as a result of their basic lack in ability. Society does not wholly accept such individuals and fails to provide realistically for their proper adjustment. Fouracre (1955) suggested that these individuals need more realistic and functional programs in school, with the school working more closely with the community. Better counseling services, more realistic training programs, better social-recreational facilities, and, for the severely retarded, sheltered workshops are also needed. Failure to provide such programs will make it increasingly difficult for the retarded adolescent to adjust to our rapidly changing culture. The difficulty of finding general employment for the retarded in today's labor market will intensify the need for sheltered workshops.

Too often the atypical adolescent who is already something of a "misfit" is subjected to even greater stress by the failure of society to recognize and/or accept people who are different. Unless more professional help becomes available, such individuals are doomed to continue through life maladapted and are likely to drift into more extreme anti-social behavior. Schools and other agencies serving adolescents must be better prepared to recognize such individuals and offer programs designed to meet their needs and limitations realistically.

TREATING ADOLESCENT EMOTIONALITY

Since "the majority of young people suffer from more or less emotional stress or nervous strain during the years which intervene between childhood and adulthood" (Sadler, 1948), some emphasis must be placed on helping to alleviate this situation. Such assistance is just as important for the "normal" adolescent as for those who deviate appreciably from the norm. Sadler has written a book "directed personally to young folks" in which he discusses the various problems of adjustment and offers informal counsel toward the effective solution of these problems. His suggestions cover the areas of personal, social, and emotional development, as well as problems of educational and vocational adjustment, health, heredity, and recreation. A discussion of the role of religion and idealism in adolescence is also presented.

It is important to note the movement of the individual during adolescence from dependence on the family home toward emotional, social, and economic independence. Sexual maturation also creates a need for sound, acceptable channeling of sexual urges. Since physicians are often consulted about the problems and adjustment of adolescents and their parents, they need some simple rules and valid advice to offer. Chapman (1960) has outlined a series of rules that emphasizes the need for flexibility by both parents and adolescents as the parents gradually relinquish authority and control to the adolescent, who progressively assumes them.

Psychotherapy during adolescence was considered by Gitelson (1948) from the standpoint of the central importance of the ego ideal in the personality integration of the adolescent. He felt that character synthesis, with the therapist as catalyst and model, is the immediate goal in dealing with problems of adolescence. The most difficult problem for the therapist is created by the fact that the adolescent is emotionally alienated from all but his developmental peers, and even with these his relationships have a tenuous quality.

Group Therapy

Group therapy has been widely recommended for teen-agers, regardless of their degree of emotionality. Discussion of mutual problems with a warm, understanding adult seems to be an effective technique, and one that could readily be adapted for use in the school situation. The Commission on Group Therapy, in a "Report to the World Federation for Mental Health" (1952), indicated substantial agreement that adolescents present a special problem for group therapy. Most of the work in this field has been done with adolescent girls who appear to be favorable subjects. The report indicated that the needs of adolescents are factors that make group therapy a valuable treatment method.

The identification of adolescents in group therapy with the therapist was investigated by Briskin (1958). Twelve- to fifteen-year-olds were asked to volunteer to participate in a group that "would discuss adolescent problems." These volunteers were organized into three therapy groups, each in charge of a different therapist, and were given a special questionnaire and a group form of the Rorschach. At the conclusion of the study the questionnaire was repeated with each group. Identification was measured by the number of shifts in the direction of the therapist from the pretherapy to the post-therapy questionnaires. Although it had been hypothesized that rigidity and lability would be inversely related to identification, the results of the correlational analysis were positive in both instances.

The effects of group living in a summer camp on adolescent girls' behavior were reported by Lifshitz and Sakoda (1952). They concluded that "two factors, the development of positive attitude toward others and toward self, and the provision of leadership and situations encouraging mature behavior, help [the adolescent] to adopt more adult patterns of behavior." These same variables probably influence the apparent success of other forms of group therapy, even those that do not involve having the adolescents living together.

Permissiveness and Authority

Studies have been reported that dealt with therapy measures among institutionalized adolescents. Numbers of centers for the care and treatment of adolescent boys and girls, such as the DePeyster Cottage at Leake and Watts Children's Home, are now available (Stone, 1952). Mayer and Wolfenstein (1954) have discussed the education of children living in residential treatment centers and have concluded that some cases can successfully adjust in public schools while others need the help of an intramural school. Obers *et al.* (1933) evaluated the effectiveness of the program of Fellowship House for a group of boys most of whom came directly from institutionalized placement. All the boys appeared to have suffered severe trauma as a result of early deprivation. Part of the problem was "to determine the optimal relationship between permissiveness and authority." Although complete success was not reported, the authors do indicate significant progress. They imply the need for gradual use of permissiveness, external authority functioning for "proper guidance" and "control of internal anxiety." A study of the aggressive behavior of mentally retarded adolescent girls in a permissive classroom at a state institution was conducted by Harris and Sievers (1959). Over periods of one to two years, the positive behavior of these girls in the schoolroom tended to increase, while their negative behavior decreased. Some degree of permissiveness apparently is quite valuable in this kind of situation. Unfortunately, neither of these latter two studies indicates just how permissive the environment should be for optimal adjustment.

In general, optimal control of adolescent emotionality involves some degree of permissiveness combined with authoritative guidance. In this way the adolescent is free to explore tentative solutions to a number of situations. If he is unable to find an acceptable solution, and particularly if he becomes anxious as a result of his inability to do so, some authority figure should be available to help guide him toward the goal that he is seeking.

THE ACHIEVEMENT OF EMOTIONAL MATURITY

Achieving emotional maturity is one of the major goals of the adolescent, since such achievement represents one of the criteria of the attainment of adult status. Failure to achieve emotional maturity often means
prolongation of adolescence, in some cases well into what would
chronologically be considered adulthood. It is of course the adult
group that decides when emotional maturity has been reached by
the adolescent. Even though a teen-ager may feel mature, the adults
with whom he interacts may not consider him so.

Solomon (1948) has attempted to set the ages at which different
kinds of maturity are reached. He suggested that sexual maturity is
reached at age twelve, ritual maturity at thirteen, intellectual at fourteen, educational at sixteen, moral at eighteen, and legal at twenty-one.
Financial, economic, vocational, and social maturity are reached later.
Emotional maturity occurs in three stages. The first stage involves independence (emotional independence from parents), which comes normally at about eighteen; prematurely in rejected children or in those
with overbearing parents; belatedly, if ever, in cases of abnormal parent
fixation, oversolicitude of parents, or "smother love." The second stage
is that of "realism," which lies between overoptimism and overpessi-
mism; it is reached at an age not yet specifically determined. The third
stage of emotional maturity is "self-control," which gradually increases
from twenty to forty years of age.

The emancipated individual has been defined as one who has
achieved relative independence from adult direction (Cook, 1960).
Strang (1949) is of the opinion that "in our culture the immaturity of
adolescents is over-emphasized." She is further of the opinion that, with
proper training in the secondary school, "much can be done through
providing experiences that evoke mature behavior." Drucker (1951)
attempted to determine the traits, needs, and problems of pupils in the
early stage of adolescence by means of a Youth Inventory conducted
among 4000 junior-high-school students. He concluded that the problems that these young people recognized differed little from age
twelve to age eighteen. Their primary concerns had to do with
vocational future, improving social facility, and learning about sex
relations. These are typical goals of youth as they seek to achieve
emotional maturity.

Physical Factors

The importance of the physical factors that may be involved in
emotional maturation must be stressed. On the basis of Rorschach data
from a group of premenarcheal girls and a group of postmenarcheal

girls, Davidson and Gottlieb (1955) found "a consistent tendency for the postmenarcheal group to be more mature and better developed in intellectual and emotional function." These authors also suggest that postmenarcheal girls showed "an ability for more mature awareness of interpersonal relationships."

Early- and late-maturing boys were compared on the basis of their ratings on nine drives (Mussen and Jones, 1958). High drives for social acceptance and for aggression were more characteristic of the physically retarded than of the physically accelerated. The late-maturers' high social drive may stem from feelings of insecurity and dependence. The high aggressive drives tended to be associated with characteristics of social behavior and personality that are indicative of social and emotional maladjustment. Physical acceleration seems to be conducive of better social and psychological adjustment.

Intelligence

Bonsall and Stefflre (1955) studied adjustment of gifted children as determined by the Guilford-Zimmerman Temperament Survey. This instrument was administered to 1359 high-school senior boys in a metropolitan area. The authors concluded that the superiority in temperament found in the gifted is probably more related to the high socioeconomic level at which most of the gifted are found than to any other factor. One might, therefore, assume that an upper socioeconomic level of environment is conducive to better adjustment for teen-agers.

Taylor and Combs (1952) hypothesized that a well-adjusted individual would be able to accept more unflattering (threatening) facts about himself than would a poorly adjusted one. The subjects were given a California Test of Personality and a checklist of twenty damaging statements. These statements were likely to be true of all children and included items such as "I sometimes disobey my parents" and "I sometimes say bad words or swear." The better-adjusted children checked significantly more of these items, indicating a better degree of self-acceptance. One might conclude that the better-adjusted individual is generally more mature than the poorly adjusted one and as a result is better able to view himself honestly and realistically.

Control Patterns

Patterns of impulse control in early adolescence were explored by Livson and Bronson (1961). On the basis of their pattern of rating overcontrol and undercontrol of impulses, they found four patterns for each sex. One of the groups is characterized, for example, by moderate undercontrol and extreme lack of overcontrol. These authors attempted to ascribe personality syndromes to each of the impulse-control groups. There was some evidence to indicate that physical maturation intervened between impulse-control patterns and personality reorganization in early adolescence. Although further investigation of these patterns is needed, it might well offer a fruitful approach to measuring emotional maturity. Since there were three clusters of items (ego strength, social adjustment, and emotional expansiveness) common to both sexes, is seems likely that an "ideal" impulse-control pattern could be established for optimal emotional maturity.

Need for Better Research Techniques

Reviews of the published research on the social and emotional adjustment of the physically handicapped during adolescence have summarized the more reliable findings obtained from these studies. Most of these researchers found no differences in social and emotional adjustment between the handicapped and nonhandicapped. Norris and Cruickshank (1955) concluded that the instruments used are not sensitive enough and hence differences that probably do exist are obscured.

One could further develop the concept of the inadequacy of the instruments used to assess emotional development in childhood and adolescence. In particular, research investigations of manifest anxiety and its relationships to other factors appear to have lost considerable impact as a result of poor instrumentation, small samples, limited treatment, and attempts to measure isolated and peripheral factors. Hunt (1958) feels that significant improvements must be made in the techniques for studying the affective aspects of behavior before researchers will be able to arrive at satisfactory answers to many urgent problems of emotional development, and especially of emotional maturity.

A number of books, articles, and pamphlets are available which offer advice and counsel designed to help adolescents achieve emotional maturity. Warter (1949), for example, has written a book entitled *Achieving Maturity*, which attempts to present the findings of recent research in nontechnical language, in order to "help young people to understand themselves and their problems; particularly those problems associated with transition to adulthood." She discusses problems of bodily change, relations to family, relations to others and to the opposite sex, frustrations and feelings of inferiority, adjustive behavior, neurotic personality, schooling, and vocations. Her advice is supported by her citations and interpretations of current research literature.

The Basis of Emotional Maturity

Emotional maturity is a rather elusive factor in the adolescent's development. Maturity has various aspects, some of which may be reached early in the individual's development, and others of which may never be reached. For example, an individual who is unable to achieve successful vocational adjustment is unlikely to display adequate emotional adjustment. Emotional maturity is based on the complex interaction of a variety of adjustment patterns, and all these must reach some optimal level in order for it to be attained.

THE ADOLESCENT'S CONCERN WITH EMOTIONALITY

For a number of years the author has invited adolescent high-school students to discuss various problems with his graduate students in a seminar on adolescent behavior. Invariably the teen-agers will be asked, "Do you feel that adolescents are highly emotional and easily upset?" Most of the teen-agers respond with a qualified "yes" answer; a very common response is "Yes, but not as upset or emotional as adults seem to think we are." They also indicate that although they are aware of heightened emotionality during the teen years they are not at all sure that adulthood will not be an equally or even more emotional period.

Adolescents' Reactions to Research Methods and Findings

When one discusses research findings on adolescent conflict, the teen-agers are likely to scoff at the results. This attitude does not mean that they consider themselves free of the emotional patterns of behavior reported in these studies. Rather, they question the degree of severity of these emotional patterns, always with the feeling that they are less disturbed by these factors than the researchers would lead us to believe. Further, they point out that large numbers of their peers do not exhibit much emotional disturbance and would be generally considered well adjusted during their teen years.

The teen-age groups also express a good deal of skepticism about the methods used to collect data about adolescent behavior. They suggest that often the teen-ager cannot respond as he wishes to the types of questions found on most questionnaires or inventories. Without exception, these adolescents have felt that investigators should spend more time actually interviewing youngsters and less time with standardized tests.

Strang (1954) also emphasized this point of view. She suggested a list of topics about which teen-agers can freely write compositions. On the basis of such compositions she has related the feelings of children from different parts of the country about school, teachers, report cards, social relations, family relations, and themselves as persons. She concludes that "any teacher, spending an hour reading similar compositions written by his own class, would gain a most rewarding understanding of their personal feelings."

Positive Attitudes

Strang (1955) also reported the attitudes of a group of adolescents as indicated by compositions dealing with the topic "How it feels to be growing up." She concluded that while many of these adolescents' statements support what psychologists generally know about adolescent life, some of them suggest feelings and attitudes not sufficiently recognized in the literature. Four such areas reported by the teen-agers are: (1) satisfaction that comes from successfully completing adolescent tasks; (2) recognition that responsibility should accompany freedom; (3) eagerness to assume responsibility; and (4) insight into adults' points of view.

Feelings of Isolation

Collier and Lawrence (1951) used autobiographical materials and a series of specific questions to determine whether there is a feeling of psychological isolation among adolescents. Sixty-five per cent of their subjects reported the experience of feeling misunderstood and isolated. The social objects of these feelings were peers, parents, teachers, and siblings. The sources of relief lie in acquiring social skills and in finding that others have had similar experiences. Feeling isolated is significantly more characteristic of females than of males.

Desires for Responsibility and Recognition

One of the major difficulties involved in achieving emotional maturity during this transitional stage is caused by the adolescent's feeling that others do not perceive him as he perceives himself. The teen-ager feels that he should be allowed more responsibility than that given him by the adults with whom he functions. The following case study illustrates one aspect of this kind of situation:

George Q. is a bright sixteen-year-old who plans to become an engineer. He is greatly interested in auto mechanics and is, in fact, very skilled in this area. His father allows him to use the family car with few restrictions but will not allow him to help with any mechanical maintenance of the car. George feels quite strongly that he would like to be responsible for keeping the car in good mechanical condition. His father thinks that George is too young really to know what he's doing and tells him, "This car is a highly complex mechanism, not a toy." George's friends who own cars, however, constantly seek his assistance in working on their cars, and he is considered a "real expert" by his peer group.

Failure to gain recognition for a task completed is another problem about which the adolescent feels strongly. A common complaint is "I did what I was asked to do, yet my parents complain about the way I did it." Too often the adult becomes concerned about the adolescent's attitude toward the task and fails to realize that the task was completed. An anecdote illustrating this situation appeared in Chapter 1.

Another common complaint concerns parental failure to recognize school achievement: "My parents just assume I should get good grades and never praise a good report card" is one form of this complaint among high-school students. Here adults accept as commonplace an action that the teen-ager considers praiseworthy. Even though he is strongly motivated intrinsically toward achieving high grades, the teen-ager does like to know that his achievement is approved of by adults.

"My parents allow me a good deal of freedom, yet they frequently question my ability to handle it" is another frequently stated point of view. Joan G.'s case illustrates this point to some extent:

Joan is seventeen and quite mature. Her parents let her select her own clothes, her own friends, and allow her to set her own curfew. Nonetheless, they question her about all these things. While she does not interfere with Joan's selection of clothing, her mother does often sharply criticize Joan's choices. Her father does not approve of some of her friends and although he tells her friends are hers to choose, he comments disparagingly about her discrimination in such choices. Her parents tell her only to come home at a reasonable hour yet reprove her when they think she comes home too late. Joan expressed the feeling that "she has freedom but no responsibility." She wishes her parents would tell her exactly what their wishes are even though she might not agree with them. Then, at least, if she should break one of the rules they set, she would understand why they condemned her action. Her summary of her situation: "They tell me I am old enough to act like a mature adult but continue to treat me like a child," is most revealing.

Need for Social Skills

Adolescents are also aware that many of their emotional problems are of a temporary nature and will disappear or at least be alleviated as they develop social skills. Instruction in dancing may be of great value in allaying the anxiety of a boy who knows this skill will aid him in making a good adjustment to the opposite sex. The adults in his environment can help the teen-ager in a number of ways, yet all too often they fail to recognize his attempts to learn what he considers mature behavior patterns.

Joseph S.'s parents complain that he talks too much and is constantly trying to interrupt their conversations. They can't understand why Joseph, who had been "a nice quiet child," has suddenly become so garrulous. Actually Joseph is only trying to practice conversational skills, which he recognizes as being important in his interaction with his peer groups. He feels greater security in trying these skills out on his parents first, and their failure to recognize his actions for what they are deprives him of this much-needed opportunity.

These varied cases should give the reader some indication of the difficulties the adolescent encounters in his everyday environment in his attempts to achieve emotional maturity. It is no wonder, then, that the adolescent feels that he is in a "no-man's land" during this stage of development.

Effect of Adult Concepts

Adolescents particularly resent adults' general concept that teen-agers are beset by turmoil. In particular they are concerned about the negative picture of their age group presented by the various media of communication. Newspapers, magazines, radio, and television all seem to emphasize stories concerning adolescent antisocial behavior, especially juvenile delinquency.

There is much truth in the teen-age view. In eight years of reading newspapers in a large city, the author can recall finding very few news items concerning good deeds performed by teen-agers. However, there was at least one item a day presenting the negative behavior of some adolescent. Truly, if one relies on these sources of information, one might well believe that all teen-agers are asocial individuals, constantly in trouble and constantly agitated. In reality the negative picture so presented applies to only a very small minority of teen-agers.

Perhaps the teen-ager is right in believing that many of his emotional problems are the result of adult expectancy of emotionality at this period. Such expectancy enables many adults to explain the adolescent's behavior as "a phase kids go through." As a result the adult often fails to recognize serious problems where they do arise or sees minor problems as requiring more attention than they really warrant.

Most teen-agers welcome an opportunity to discuss their problems with any and all adults who will listen. If adults would simply attempt to communicate with teen-agers, they would find the experience most rewarding. First, they would learn that adolescents really are intelligent human beings, well aware of many of the difficulties that beset them. Second, they would realize how much they can do to alleviate the anxieties of the teen-ager. A little assurance by an adult that the adolescent is really doing the right things may be just the kind of help he needs in many situations. Third, they would discover that the more respect a teen-ager is accorded as an individual, the more he will try to live up to this standard.

REFERENCES

ANDERSON, EDWARD DYER. "Adolescent Resentment of Authority." *Minnesota Medicine,* 31, 1238-1242, 1948.

ANDREW, GWEN, and LOCKWOOD, HILDA. "Teachers' Evaluations of the Mental Health Status of Their Pupils." *Journal of Educational Research,* 47, 631-635, 1954.

ANGELINO, HENRY, DOLLINS, JOSEPH, and MECH, EDMUND V. "Trends in the 'Fears and Worries' of School Children as Related to Socio-economic Status and Age." *Journal of Genetic Psychology,* 89, 263-276, 1956.

ANGELINO, HENRY, and SHEDD, CHARLES L. "Shifts in the Content of Fears and Worries Relative to Chronological Age." *Proceedings, Oklahoma Academy of Science,* 34, 180-186, 1953.

BALEY, STEFAN. "Psychologiczna problematyka wieku dojrzewania" (Psychological Problematics of Adolescence). *Hysl Wspoicz (Warsaw),* No. 7 (50), 25-43, 1950.

BONSALL, MARCELLA RYSER, and STEFFLRE, BUFORD. "The Temperament of Gifted Children." *California Journal of Educational Research,* 6, 162-165, 1955.

BORNEMANN, ERNST. *"Jugendprobleme unserer Zeit"* (Adolescent Problems of Our Time). *Psychologische Rundschau* (Basel), 9, 77-104, 1958.

BRISKIN, GERALD J. "Identification in Group Therapy." *Journal of Abnormal and Social Psychology,* 56, 195-198, 1958.

BROOKS, SYLVIA. "Complexity of Task and Other Situational Variables as Factors in Rigidity Behavior of Fifteen-Year Olds." *Journal of Genetic Psychology,* 97, 385-403, 1960.

BURT, CYRIL, and HOWARD, MARGARET. "The Nature and Causes of Maladjustment among Children of School Age." *British Journal of Psychology, Statistical Section* (London), 5, 39-59, 1952.

BUYTENDIJK, F. "Unruhe und Geborgenheit in der Welt des Jungen Menschen" (Unrest and Security in the World of Youth). *Universitas* (Stuttgart), 13, 721-730, 1958.

CARY, MILES E. "Looking at Teen-age Problems." *Journal of Home Economics,* 40, 575-576, 1948.

CASON, ELOUSE B., *et al.* "School Practices in Promoting Mental Health." *American Council on Educational Studies,* 14 (Ser. 1, No. 40), 121-136, 1950.

CHAPMAN, A. M. "On Managing Adolescents." *Journal of the American Medical Association,* 174, 1954-1957, 1960.

CLARK, ELMER J. "Teacher Reactions toward Objectionable Pupil Behavior." *Elementary School Journal,* 51, 446-449, 1951.

COBB, HENRY V. "Role-Wishes and General Wishes of Children and Adolescents." *Child Development,* 25, 161-171, 1954.

COLLIER, REX M., and LAWRENCE, HELEN PALMER. "The Adolescent Feeling of Psychological Isolation." *Educational Theory,* 1, 106-115, 1951.

COLM, HANNA. "Help and Guidance as Discipline for Preadolescents." *Nervous Child,* 9, 131-138, 1951.

COMMISSION ON GROUP PSYCHOTHERAPY. "Report to the World Federation for Mental Health, Section III: Group Psychotherapy with Adolescents." *Group Psychotherapy,* 2, 173-176, 1952.

COOK, D. "Emotional Emancipation in Adolescence." *Journal of Teacher Education,* 11, 370-374, 1960.

CRUICKSHANK, WILLIAM M. "The Relation of Physical Disability to Fear and Guilt Feelings." *Cerebral Palsy Review,* 13(8), 9-13; 15, 1952.

DAVIDSON, HELEN H., and GOTTLIEB, LUCILLE S. "The Emotional Maturity of Pre- and Post-menarcheal Girls." *Journal of Genetic Psychology,* 86, 261-266, 1955.

DEBESSE, M. "Enkels Hedendaagse Problemen van de Jeugdpsychologie" (Some Actual Problems of the Psychology of Adolescence). *Vlaam Opvoedkundig Tijdschrife* (Antwerp), 29, 294-300, 1949.

DOHERTY, WINIFRED. "Adolescence and Psychological Disorders." *Medical Press,* 219, 508-512, 1948.

DRUCKER, A. J. "How Old, Emotionally, Are Seventh and Eighth Graders?" *Studies in Higher Education,* Purdue University, pp. 69-78, 1951.

EASSON, W. M., and STEINHILBER, R. M. "Murderous Aggression by Children and Adolescents." *American Archives of General Psychiatry,* 4, 1-9, 1961.

EISENBERG, LEON. "The Autistic Child in Adolescence." *American Journal of Psychiatry,* 112, 607-612, 1956.

EISENSTADT, S. N. "Hamered hehadash shel hanoar" (The New Youth Revolt). *Megamot* (Jerusalem), 9, 95-102, 1958.

ELKINS, DEBORAH. "How the Classroom Teacher Can Help the Emotionally Disturbed Child." *Understanding the Child,* 20, 66-73, 79, 1951.

FINN, JOSEPH P. *A Study of the Problems of Certain Catholic High School Boys as Told by Themselves and Their Teachers.* Washington, D.C.: Catholic University of America Press, 1950.

FLECK, STEPHEN, in collaboration with AILEEN DEVANNA, MARIE HAGERTY, and JANET REKATE. "Pregnancy as a Symptom of Adolescent Maladjustment." *International Journal of Social Psychiatry,* 2, 118-133, 1956.

FORNWALT, RUSSELL J. "Problem Children: School or Work?" *School and Society,* 66, 318-320, 1947.

FOURACRE, MAURICE H. "Adjusting the Exceptional Adolescent to Adult Life." *Proceedings, Conference Child Research Clinic, Woods Schools* (Langhorne, Pa.), pp. 13-23, 1955.

FRICK, WILLARD. "The Adolescent Dilemma: An Interpretation." *Peabody Journal of Education,* 32, 206-210, 1955.

GHOSH, MOLINA. "Fantasy Life of Girls at the Pre-adolescent and Adolescent Stages." *University Rejasthan Studies* (Educ.), 3, 54-82, 1958.

GITELSON, MAXWELL. "Trends in Orthopsychiatric Therapy, VI. Character Synthesis: the Psychotherapeutic Problem of Adolescence." *American Journal of Orthopsychiatry,* 18, 422-431, 1948.

GITLIN-BITENSKY, MALIA. *Hapsihologia hshevratit shel gil hahitbagrut* (Social Psychology of the Adolescence Age). Tel Aviv: Yavneh Publishing House, 1954.

GRAHAM, ALVA WHITCOMB. "Personal and Social Adjustment of High School Students." *School Review,* 55, 468-473, 1947.

HARRIS, LUCY M., and SIEVERS, DOROTHY J. "A Study to Measure Changes in Behavior of Aggressive Mentally Retarded Adolescent Girls in a Permissive Classroom." *American Journal of Mental Deficiency,* 63, 975-980, 1959.

HERSHENSON, JEANNE R. "Preference of Adolescents for Rorschach Figures." *Child Development,* 20, 101-118, 1949.

HORN, DANIEL, COURTS, F., TAYLOR, ROBERT, and SOLOMON, ERWIN. "Cigarette Smoking among High School Students." *American Journal of Public Health,* 49, 1497-1511, 1959.

HUNT, J. T. "Emotional Development in Childhood and Adolescence." *Review of Educational Research,* 28, 401-409, 1958.

IVES, VIRGINIA, GRANT, MARGUERITE, and RANZONI, JANE H. "The Neurotic Rorschachs of Normal Adolescents." *Journal of Genetic Psychology,* 83, 31-61, 1953.

JOHNSON, HARRIET C. "Teen Agers . . . a Real Challenge!" *Crippled Child,* 30(6), 13-15, 1953.

JOSSELYN, IRENE M. "Psychological Problems of the Adolescent: Part I." *Social Casework,* 32, 183-190, 1951.

KAGAN, JEROME, and MOSS, HOWARD A. "Stability and Validity of Achievement Fantasy." *Journal of Abnormal and Social Psychology,* 58, 357-364, 1959.

KEEHN, J. D. "Unrealistic Reporting as a Function of Extraverted Neurosis." *Journal of Clinical Psychology,* 12, 61-63, 1956.

KIRKPATRICK, MILTON E. "The Mental Hygiene of Adolescence in the Anglo-American Culture." *Mental Hygiene* (New York), 36, 394-403, 1952.

LENT, ADA. "A Survey of the Problems of Adolescent High School Girls Fourteen to Eighteen Years of Age." *Alberta Journal of Educational Research,* 3, 127-137, 1957.

LEONARD, CHARLES. "Tension Areas in the Adolescent." *Counseling,* 6(12), 1-4, 1954.

LEWIN, KURT. "Field Theory and Experiments in Social Psychology: Concepts and Methods." *American Journal of Sociology,* vol. 44, no. 6, 1939.

LIFSHITZ, ADELE D., and SAKODA, JAMES. "Effect of Summer Camp on Adolescents' Maturity." *Journal of Child Psychiatry,* 2, 257-265, 1952.

LIVSON, NORMAN, and BRONSON, WANDA. "An Exploration of Patterns of Impulse Control in Early Adolescence." *Child Development,* 32, 75-88, 1961.

LOWREY, LAWSON G. "Adolescent Frustrations and Evasions." In Hoch, P. H., and Zubin, J., *Psychopathology of Childhood,* pp. 267-284. New York: Grune and Stratton, 1955.

LUCENA, JOSE, ARAUJA, MARIA DA GRACA R., CAMPOS, ALDA, and LORETO, FALDINO. "O test de Rorschach en um grupo de adolescentes" (The Rorschach Test in a Group of Adolescents). *Neurobiologia* (Pernambuco), 11, 275-344, 1948.

LUCHINS, ABRAHAM S. "On the Theories and Problems of Adolescence." *Journal of Genetic Psychology*, 85, 47-63, 1954.

MANDEL, RUDOLF. *Die Aggressivitat bei Schulern* (Aggressiveness in School Boys). Bern, Switzerland: Hans Huber, 1959.

MAYER, M., and WOLFENSTEIN, C. "Diagnostic Criteria for Intramural and Extramural Schooling of Disturbed Children in a Residential Treatment Center." *American Journal of Orthopsychiatry*, 22, 351-367, 1954.

MUCHOW, HANS H. *Flegeljahre* (Early Adolescence). Ravensburg: O. Maier, 1950.

MUSSEN, PAUL HENRY, and JONES, MARY COVER. "The Behavior-Inferred Motivations of Late- and Early-Maturing Boys." *Child Development*, 29, 61-67, 1958.

NORRIS, H. J., and CRUICKSHANK, W. M. "Adjustment of Physically Handicapped Adolescent Youth." *Exceptional Children*, 21, 282-288, 1955.

OBERS, SAMUEL J., GOLDMAN, JULIA, and SUSSMAN, SARAH. "Fellowship House: A Small Group Residence of Adolescent Boys." *Mental Hygiene* (New York), 37, 66-75, 1953.

OGILVIE, FREDERICK. "The Problem of Adolescence." *Practitioner* (London), 162, 261-262, 1949.

OJEMANN, RALPH H. "Understanding Adolescents." *Children*, 1, 232-233, 1954.

PFLIEGER, ELMER F. "Pupil Adjustment Problems and a Study of Relationships between Scores on the California Test of Personality and the Mooney Problem Check List." *Journal of Educational Research*, 41, 265-278, 1947.

PITT, WILLIAM J. "Psychological Aspects of Adolescence." *Journal of Social Hygiene*, 40, 226-231, 1954.

POWELL, MARVIN. "Age and Sex Differences in Degree of Conflict Within Certain Areas of Psychological Adjustment." *Psychological Monographs*, no. 387, 1955.

RAO, C. K. VASUDEVA. "The Psychological Approach to Youth." *Antiseptic* (Madras), 45, 227-232, 1948.

REID, CHANDOS. "The Classroom Teacher and Adolescent Adjustment." *Teachers College Record*, 52, 500-511, 1951.

REMMERS, H. H., and SHIMBERG, B. *Problems of High School Youth*. Purdue Opinion Poll for Young People, Rep. No. 21. Lafayette, Ind.: Purdue University, Division of Educational Reference, 1949.

RESNICK, JOSEPH. "Towards Understanding Adolescent Behavior." *Peabody Journal of Education*, 30, 205-208, 1953.

RUBE, P. "Adolescence: I. Is There a Problem of Adolescence?" *American Journal of Psychotherapy*, 9, 503-509, 1955.

RUBE, P. "Adolescence: II. The Inner World of Adolescence." *American Journal of Psychotherapy*, 9, 673-691, 1955.

SADLER, WILLIAM S. *A Doctor Talks to Teen-agers: A Psychiatrist's Advice to Youth*. St. Louis, Mo.: C. V. Mosby, 1948.

SCHONFELD, WILLIAM A. "Deficient Development of Masculinity: A Psychosomatic Problem of Adolescence." *American Journal of Diseases of Children*, 79, 17-29, 1950.

SKUBIC, ELVERA. "Emotional Responses of Boys to Little League and Middle League Competitive Baseball." *Research Quarterly of the American As-*

sociation for Health, Physical Education, and Recreation, 26, 342-352, 1955.

SOLOMON, PHILIP. "Emotional Maturity." *Annals of Western Medicine and Surgery* (Los Angeles), 2, 12-15, 1948.

STACEY, CHALMERS L. "Worries of Subnormal Adolescent Girls." *Exceptional Children,* 21, 184-186, 1955.

STEISEL, IRA M., and COHEN, BERTRAM D. "The Effects of Two Degrees of Failure on Level of Aspiration and Performance." *Journal of Abnormal and Social Psychology,* 46, 79-82, 1952.

STONE, CLAIRE. A Residence Unit for Adolescent Boys and Girls." *Child Welfare,* 31(4), 3-6, 1952.

STÖRRING, G. E., and LÖWNAU, H. W. "Zur Problematic der Jugend in der Gegenwart" (Concerning the Problem of Youth in the Present). *Praxis der Kinderpsychologie und Kinderpsychiatrie,* 7, 1-8, 1958.

STRANG, RUTH. "Manifestations of Maturity in Adolescents." *Mental Hygiene,* 33, 563-569, 1949.

STRANG, RUTH. "How Children and Adolescents View the World." *Mental Hygiene,* 38, 28-35, 1954.

STRANG, RUTH. "Adolescents' Views on One Aspect of Their Development." *Journal of Educational Psychology,* 46, 423-432, 1955.

SZCEPANSKI, Y. "Hanoar baolam shel yamenu" (Youth in the Present World). *Ofakim* (Merhavyah, Israel), 13, 205-212, 1959.

TAYLOR, CHARLES, and COMBS, ARTHUR W. "Self-acceptance and Adjustment." *Journal of Consulting Psychology,* 16, 89-91, 1952.

TINDALL, RALPH H. "Relationship Among Indices of Adjustment Status." *Educational and Psychological Measurement,* 15, 152-162, 1955.

ULLMAN, CHARLES A. "Identification of Maladjusted School Children." *Public Health Monographs,* no. 7, 1952.

WALL, W. D. "Happiness and Unhappiness in the Childhood and Adolescence of a Group of Women Students." *British Journal of Psychology* (London), 38, 191-208, 1948.

WALL, W. D., and SIMPSON, W. A. "The Emotional Responses of Adolescent Groups to Certain Films, Part I." *British Journal of Educational Psychology,* 20, 153-163, 1950.

WALL, W. D., and SIMPSON, W. A. "The Responses of Adolescent Groups to Certain Films, Part II." *British Journal of Educational Psychology,* 21, 81-88, 1951.

WALTERS, RICHARD H., and ZAKS, MISHA S. "Changes in Responses to a Set of Personality-Inventory Items as a Function of Age." *Journal of Consulting Psychology,* 22, 458, 1958.

WARTER, JANE. *Achieving Maturity.* New York: McGraw-Hill, 1949.

WENAR, CHARLES. "The Degree of Psychological Disturbance in Handicapped Youth." *Exceptional Children,* 7, 1958.

ZINTZ, MILES V. "Academic Achievement and Social and Emotional Adjustment of Handicapped Children." *Elementary School Journal,* 51, 502-507, 1951.

CHAPTER 6

Social Development and Socialization

The process of socialization begins very early in childhood, when the child learns to conform to certain standards structured by the family social group to which he belongs. As he continues to develop, he also learns to conform to other group standards and to the general rules and regulations of the larger environment. He learns to communicate with others and learns the importance of cooperation with others in achieving various goals. His actions become directed toward behavior patterns that will gain social approval, and he learns to avoid situations that might be disapproved of socially.

As the child approaches adolescence, he has an urge to free himself as much as possible from his family ties and to associate with individuals or groups of his own age, at this stage usually with members of his own sex. The peer group now begins to set up standards and offers much of the support that the youngster previously derived from his family. As he enters adolescence, these friends play a role of great importance in the formation of his patterns of social behavior and in his social attitudes. The ways in which the group treats him and his perceptions of the way the members think he should behave in order to be acceptable to them are important factors in the formation of his social behavior patterns.

The importance of social development during adolescence is emphasized by the fact that many of the problems that confront the adolescent are social. The youngster must learn to adjust to the social norms of his culture and to meet new situations that are far more complex than those he met in his childhood days. Davis (1944) suggests that the lag of social maturity behind physical maturity is primarily responsible for the difficulty encountered by the adolescent in meeting the problems of this age successfully. Adjustment is particularly difficult in a complex civilization where the individual is expected to play many social roles.

Hess (1960) suggested that to the degree to which the period of youth acts as a subsystem of the society, it is a potential socializing influence that may be in conflict on significant points with adult society. He further proposed that the importance and self-sufficiency of teen-age society will increase in this country as well as in several other countries. As this occurs, many areas will need further study as youth seeks new goals and devises new techniques to achieve these goals.

In his book on adolescence, Fleming (1949) includes two major sections relating to social development. Part I considers the problems of adjustment in relation to the home and shows the effect of variation in the social structure of the home and in parental attitudes upon the quality of adolescent behavior. Part II surveys development in respect to the school, stressing the nature and extent of variability in the several abilities and in personal and social traits. In this section the influence of membership in a group is explored in some detail.

We must be aware, as Bayley (1956) suggested, that patterns of development are extremely complex and "individual patterns are the rule." While comparison of the adolescent with his peers is important, we must often make our final evaluation of behavior on the basis of individual performance. The fact that the peer group apparently accepts a given individual is no guarantee that that individual is well adjusted socially, and, conversely, if an adolescent does not seem to interact with the peer group, we cannot assume that this is evidence of social maladjustment.

SOCIAL BEHAVIOR IN EARLY ADOLESCENCE

Too often we think of adolescence as the period when group membership becomes all-important. Much has been written, for example, about adolescent gangs, and the term "gang" seems to have a negative connotation. Crane (1952) reports on preadolescent gangs to which a group of Australian college students recalled belonging. These gangs, like those of older adolescents, had secret signals, codes, and initiation ceremonies. The ceremonies included phallic ordeal, demonstration of skill, and social aggression. Most of these gangs engaged in socially disapproved activities. Contrary to popular belief, however, all gangs were not the product of subnormal or borderline environment, nor was gang membership a symptom of delinquency. Crane believed that gang membership served a useful purpose. The restraints of group life play a part in socializing the child by making him more willing to accept the life pattern of the adult when he grows up.

Maucorps *et al.* (1955) tested 1700 children and adolescents of both sexes, aged eight, eleven, and fourteen, who attended schools in Paris. These groups were given sociometric and parasociometric tests, the latter containing hypothetical or conditional questions such as "With

which companions would you like to spend an afternoon of leisure?"
At eleven there was a definite increase of expansiveness, a greater
amount of hostile feelings among boys, and more pronounced positive
reactions in girls when confronted with affective situations. The phenomenon of sociocentrism characterizes middle-class children.

Social Life in the Classroom

Baron (1949, 1951) tested fifth- and sixth-grade pupils of varying
levels of classroom social status with regard to personal and social
characteristics. He found significant differences in response to a number of the items, with more unfavorable responses among the lower
social-status group. The pupils with high status tended to feel more
self-confident and more adequate physically. They were also more
secure in their school relationships and were generally more emotionally stable than the low-status pupils. The average-social-status
group resembled the low-status group rather than the high-status
group. Low-status girls demonstrated a number of nervous symptoms
that were not present among low-status boys. Although there will
probably be an improvement in social adjustment and attitudes in
these groups, this study attests again to the necessity for better understanding the social life of the classroom.

Comparative retardation in development of social skills in groups
that were average in intelligence was reported by Long (1949). Her
study indicated that in general the rate of progress in socialization was
greater for the younger group. This would seem to suggest that the
earlier years are the best ones in which to cultivate social skills.

Bedoian's study (1954) of social acceptability and social rejection
among pupils in the sixth grade presents a somewhat different point of
view. He found that the under-age pupils received significantly higher
acceptance scores than either at-age or average pupils. The lower
acceptance scores were obtained by the average pupils. Pupils only
slightly under age had higher scores than those markedly under age,
but the latter still had higher scores than the other groups. One might
infer that at this age level a nonsocial ability such as intelligence is an
important factor in social acceptability. Generally, the under-age
children in a classroom are the brighter children. This latter viewpoint
is generally confirmed in a study reported by Taylor (1952), who
reported the intercorrelations between ratings by eighth-grade classmates on the Ohio Social Acceptance Scale and the following variables:
chronological age, mental age, verbal bias, and flatness of mental profiles. Groups receiving traditional and progressive types of instruction
were differentiated. Social acceptance showed no significant relationship with verbal bias or with flatness of mental profile, but there was

some positive correlation with mental age. Mental age and chronological age showed some negative correlation, and there was accordingly a tendency for the younger children in a grade to be rated as more acceptable than the older ones.

Background and Social Acceptance

Feinberg (1953) attempted to relate the background experiences of adolescent boys to social acceptance and to determine whether these experiences were characteristic of all adolescent boys or whether there were differences dependent upon their economic status. Approximately 2000 boys between the ages of thirteen and sixteen from three contrasting economic levels were administered a Personal History Questionnaire. This instrument was designed to represent six areas of adolescent adjustment. In general, Feinberg concluded that the background experiences predictive of social acceptance are for the most part common to all economic levels. Specifically, however, he found that a close family relationship is predictive of acceptance at the high and middle economic levels but not at the low level. Accepted adolescents of the high economic level are "granted" more personal freedom than those at the middle or low levels (they can spend more time away from home, i.e., overnight visits to friends, etc.). The accepted boys on both the high economic and middle economic levels were generally satisfied with their parents. The rejected boys in the high economic group were often "only" children who were not satisfied with what their parents did for them. In the middle economic group, adolescents whose mothers worked outside the home tended to be rejected. Generally, this group disliked school. For the lower economic group, the only predictor of rejection was affiliation with Boy Scouts. Feinberg felt that items descriptive of adolescent activities could be selected to predict social acceptance, and that "items predictive of social acceptance show a high degree of consistency between economic levels."

A specially prepared Adjustment Inventory was administered to a group of subjects between the ages of fourteen and sixteen. The social adjustment of the subjects varied with age in terms of dominance-submission, rejection-acceptance. Heterosexual adjustment improved with age. In some of the areas tested, subjects from low socioeconomic backgrounds showed significantly greater maladjustment than did those from the higher economic groups (Parameswaran, 1957).

Friendships among Early Adolescents

Friendship fluctuations among preadolescents were studied by Horrocks and Buker (1951). They reported a trend toward increasing stability. The onset of such stability tends to begin somewhat later with boys than with girls. Stability of friendship continues to increase up to age eighteen (Thompson and Horrocks, 1947). During early adolescence, however, friendships may be rather unstable for brief periods. A youngster who is developing more rapidly than one of his friends may find that suddenly they have little in common. As a result of this rapid development, his interests may shift and become appreciably different from those of his less mature former companion. However, this friendship is likely to be re-established when the slower-developing youngster catches up in his growth cycle and the two again have common interests.

Behavior Patterns

Generally, these studies indicate that many of the patterns of social behavior commonly associated with adolescence appear relatively early in that time span. Some of these patterns are in fact present, or at least beginning to develop, in preadolescence. At these early levels, sociability is usually same-sex-oriented, and problems related to heterosexual social adjustment are not yet apparent.

Smith and Phillips (1959) attempted to investigate the relationship between cognitive-developmental level and social effectiveness among adolescent males ranging from eleven through eighteen years of age, all of them within the normal range of intelligence. These youngsters were administered the Vineland Social Maturity Scale, the Rorschach, and the Stanford-Binet Intelligence Test. The results indicated that social effectiveness is related to developmental level in a complex fashion. Both chronological age and the context of social adaptation made significant contributions to variation in the relationships obtained.

Generally, the young adolescent has a rather pronounced feeling of insecurity that results in part from his attempts to expand his social environment. He tends to seek those whose intelligence, age, level of maturity, abilities, and socioeconomic status approximate his own, because he can feel most secure with a group whose members closely resemble himself.

Girls, because they mature earlier, are socially oriented earlier than boys. At first, they seek to form an association with only one other girl, for mutual understanding. At this stage they are more dependent on their friends than are boys and generally have much more intimate relationships. This pattern of greater intimacy among girls seems to continue up through the college years (Gronlund, 1959). A girl also prefers that her friends be attractive to boys. If they are not, she hesitates to be seen with them for fear of lowering her own status in the eyes of boys. Thus a girl's friend must be acceptable in the eyes both of other girls and of boys, whereas younger boys usually are more concerned that other boys accept their friends.

Cliques—small, exclusive, informal, face-to-face, social groups—are quite common during early adolescence and often form the basis from which secret clubs and societies develop later. The clique offers security to the young teen-agers, taking over some of the functions previously found within the family environment.

Conformity

One of the aspects of early adolescence most publicly criticized is a pattern of conformity. Young teen-agers act alike, dress alike, like the same foods and the same music. Only an unusual individual is willing at this stage of development to differ from his age-mates. Conformity represents the youngster's attempt to obtain safety and security. The more he acts like the others, the more easily he can identify with them and be accepted by them. Fear of losing group acceptance, rather than some more positive standard, may motivate an individual to conform. Nonetheless, he will conform, even to the extent of concealing his real values and real goals, in order to belong to his group. While conformity may result in at least temporary loss of individuality, it may also be a pattern of learning to get along with people by being like them.

In a study that attempted to identify socially maladjusted school children, Adams (1960) reported results which relate strongly to conformity. A Truth About People Test constructed to estimate degree of conformity toward a variety of social goals and values was administered to more than 2000 students in grades five through twelve in public and parochial schools. The test was also administered to more than 700 institutionalized delinquents. The author concluded that social adjustment is related to conformity, since the children rated as well adjusted received significantly more conforming scores than did the subjects rated as "maladjusted-shy" and "maladjusted-aggressive." Specific findings indicated that the standard school group showed more conformity than did the delinquent sample. Less conformity was demonstrated in the standard school samples with increase in age and grade level. Boys showed less conformity than girls at all levels. Greater conformity was demonstrated by those with IQ's of 80-139, while those with IQ's below 70 or above 140 showed less conformity.

When conformity is the price of group acceptance, particularly if it truly involves a loss in individuality as a result of complete subservience to the crowd, it may be quite harmful. If, however, conformity is merely a transitional stage of development, the results may be positive. In such cases conformity furthers the adolescent's identification with the peer group and helps him to attain a desirable degree of independence from the family.

SOCIAL DEVELOPMENT IN LATER ADOLESCENCE

With increasing age and increased familiarity with the social milieu, the adolescent becomes increasingly confident. As the individual develops greater self-confidence through peer acceptance and approval, he is more and more able to function on his own. Although he still wants approval and acceptance, he is no longer willing to submerge his personality as he formerly did. He now seeks to draw the attention of others of the group rather than to conceal himself among them.

As he becomes increasingly self-confident, he may even seek attention more than he seeks approval. In some cases he may even behave in a manner frowned upon by his peers, if such behavior will give him the kind of attention or recognition he seeks. His early attempts at seeking recognition may be rather crude and overzealous, and may as a result receive an unfavorable reaction. As he learns what is acceptable and what is not, he modifies his behavior accordingly. This process of socialization continues through the teen years as the individual develops into a person who can and does accept his responsibilities to society.

As the adolescent becomes more and more an individual, he again seeks the approval of the adults around him. While the young adolescent is perhaps more concerned with peer approval, the older teen-ager wants approval from both peers and adults. If he shows conformity, it is now in relation to the patterns of behavior he perceives in adults. His clubs and organizations are formally structured along adult lines rather than by peer group standards.

The older adolescent begins to find it easier to gain adult acceptance. Physically, he looks like an adult; his intellect is more oriented toward the adult world; and his social behavior is more like the behavior adults consider acceptable. Adults are perhaps still somewhat reticent about offering total acceptance of teen-age behavior, but the gap between the groups is far smaller than that existing between adult and young adolescent. The realization that the adolescent will soon be seeking a job or entering college causes most parents to try to speed up the development of adult patterns in youngsters who will soon be leaving home. More freedom and responsibility are afforded than ever before, if only in order to make the adults feel more secure when the "fledgling leaves the nest" and strikes out on his own.

Harwood (1959) has reported on the development of values and social maturity in about 1500 adolescents aged fifteen to nineteen living in Queensland. He found that social values were significantly more important for girls, and personal-social for boys. Employed groups scored higher on economic and social values, while school groups were higher on theoretical and aesthetic values. Evidence based on another scale, which measured social maturity, suggested a temporary acceleration of acceptance of responsibility among those leaving school early. However, by the age of eighteen the school group had overtaken these youngsters. Harwood also found that adolescents who regarded their sex knowledge as "satisfactory" tended to have higher social-maturity scores.

Factors Influencing Sociability

Jones (1958) investigated the factors that seem to influence high-school students' participation in extracurricular activities. Two groups, those who had "low mention" in the school newspaper, and those who had "high mention," were compared. While chronological age was not a differentiating factor, skeletal age was more advanced among "high mention" boys and among "low mention" girls. The "high mention" group was more frequently rated by adults as making a good impression on the basis of appearance. "High mention" girls were rated significantly high on expressiveness, buoyancy, poise, and prestige. On a Guess Who? Technique the "high mention" students were almost consistently above average on many prestige traits.

Pairs of friends, partial friends, and nonfriends were studied by Thorpe (1955). The pairs compared with respect to intelligence, age, neuroticism, and popularity. No differences were found in either the male-male pairs or the female-female pairs. None of the variables, with the possible exception of age, was found to be related to friendship formation. Friends tended to be more nearly the same age than non-friends. The results also seemed to indicate that cultural differences had no effect on the relationships studied.

Cannon *et al.* (1952) administered sociometric tests to elementary- and high-school pupils who had been rated on personal appearance on a scale constructed for the purpose. At all grade levels, girls scored higher in personal appearance than boys did. Girls also showed a consistent improvement in dress and grooming with age. There was a significant relationship between personal appearance and popularity for high-school girls, but not for boys or for elementary-school girls.

The results of the application of a sociogram, a classroom social-distance scale, and the California Test of Personality to a group of seventh- and eighth-graders were reported by Singer (1951). He concluded that once a group receives a total impression of an individual it is most difficult to change that impression. Impressions regarding an individual and the development of these impressions are apparently obtained in the early school grades rather than at the adolescent level. Marked success in friendship was not necessarily an indication that an individual suffers no personality difficulties. Singer also felt that the school contributes to internal as well as external behavioral development. Wardlow and Greene (1952) attempted to investigate peer status among adolescent girls. Both generalized and specific scales and measurements were used. The results indicated that peer status is situational or specific in character. Perhaps research with more precise instrumentation would determine significant characteristics not found in this study.

A study of Israeli youngsters ranging in age from eight to twenty attempted to find a relationship between participation in a gang and social maladjustment. From eight to twelve, and especially from ten to twelve, gang activities, including despotic leadership, adventurism, secrecy, etc., were found to be characteristic. There was, however, no evidence for a correlation between participation in a gang at this age and future social maladjustment. Later gangs were usually formed by maladjusted individuals. The bright and well-adjusted adolescents preferred to participate in officially recognized and open youth clubs and organizations (Wolman, 1951).

Polansky et al. (1950) attempted to separate conduct caused by deliberate attempts to influence it from conduct that is a spontaneous reaction to the behavior of someone else. The latter type of behavior is defined by the authors as "contagion," and they feel that it occurs in the absence of any "communicated intent to evolve such a change." Behavior of a group of children eleven to fifteen years old in a summer camp was observed, and sociometric tests were administered. The results showed that status in a group is an important determinant of instigating "contagion" behavior in others and also a determinant of susceptibility to such behavior.

Girl Y-Club members and nonmember girls were asked to rate one another on twelve traits of Tyron's Guess Who? without reference to membership in the organization. The Y-Club members were significantly superior to the nonmembers with respect to fathers' occupations, Otis IQ's, and school marks. The nonmembers did not, however, regard the club members in a socially unfavorable light (Keislar, 1953). Grade-point average was also found to differentiate groups of students belonging to Y-Clubs to which admission was by invitation of the members from those who belonged to clubs where invitation to membership was not required (Keislar, 1954). Less differentiation occurred between the groups in intelligence, and no differentiation was found in fathers' occupations.

Masculinity and femininity of sixth- and seventh-graders in relation to anxiety and social acceptance was studied by Gray (1957), using the Who Are They, a reputation test, a children's form of the manifest-anxiety scale, and a masculinity-femininity scale. Children of both sexes who were high in anxiety were found to show significantly more sex-appropriate behavior than children low in anxiety. High school accept-ance is more associated with sex-appropriate behavior in boys than in girls. The results are interpreted as indicating either a lack of clarity in the role expected of girls as they approach adolescence or a greater latitude in approved behavior than is tolerated in boys.

An attempt to study possible ethnic characteristics involved in friend-ships was reported by Lehrer (1954). A questionnaire was administered to a group of Jewish seventeen- to twenty-five-year-olds, in order to learn their way of choosing friends among eight photographed students. Only a small group distinguished explicitly between typical Jewish and non-Jewish faces, but although they emphasized that a person's face played no role in determining friends, they selected more Jewish photographs. Most respondents had primarily Jewish friends but were opposed to any theoretical distinction between Jews and non-Jews. Older persons and those living in Jewish neighborhoods tend more to select photographs of Jews. Generally, these findings seem to hold true in studies of other ethnic and religious groups.

The problems of young people who do not have an inner circle but who often make a heavy emotional investment in a formed group were discussed by Wittenberg and Berg (1952). These adolescents are most conspicuous in their intensive participation and often achieve what appears to be popularity and acceptance. They are, however, really successful isolates, strangers in their groups, in spite of their apparent success and popularity.

Factors in Adolescent Prestige

Keislar (1953) hypothesized that social acceptance and prestige, as measured by Guess Who? peer group ratings, show different degrees of association with ratings on other traits. Social acceptance was de-fined as the extent to which an individual's company is regarded by others as rewarding. Prestige was defined as the extent to which an individual is regarded by others as a source of cues for rewarding responses. Tenth-grade boys and girls were tested separately in order to investigate these two characteristics. Although the two character-istics were found to be clearly related, results showed that social acceptance ratings were more closely associated with the number of times an individual was chosen on two sociometric-type questions. Prestige was more closely associated with ratings on such traits as school marks, trying in school, cooperation with teachers, and serious interests. Keislar concluded that in certain areas of adolescent life social acceptance and prestige are not synonymous terms; to determine adolescent prestige patterns, measures of social acceptance are not adequate.

An experiment was conducted to explore factors associated with the acceptance of suggestions, in which the subjects were given the option of accepting or not accepting the suggestion. The tenth-, eleventh-, and twelfth-grade boys and girls involved in this study were given tasks whose difficulty varied independently of age-grade status. Age-grade status, sex of the subject, difficulty level of the task, and prestige level of the suggestion source were the variables investigated. Investigators found that acceptance of suggestions was higher for boys than for girls, and that high-prestige suggestions were accepted more frequently than those from a low-prestige source. Suggestions were also accepted more frequently on difficult items than on easy ones. Generally, except where high-pressure groups were excluded, tenth- and eleventh-graders were similar to each other but differed significantly from twelfth-graders, with the latter accepting relatively fewer suggestions. When the suggestion source was of low prestige, the three grades differed significantly in the direction of decreasing acceptance of suggestions. Girls remained higher than boys in acceptance of high-prestige suggestions, especially at the twelfth-grade level, where the boys were more resistant to high-prestige than to low-prestige suggestions. In this same grade, however, high-prestige suggestions were more readily accepted on difficult items than on easy ones, to the degree that resistance to high-prestige suggestions could be completely overcome in this group if the items were difficult enough (Patel and Gordon, 1960).

Anastasi and Miller (1949) studied prestige factors in high-school students divided by sex and by enrollment in a college preparatory course or a noncollege general course. When the pupils were asked to mark the desirable characteristics of members of their own sex, there were greater differences on the basis of the socioeconomic variables than between the sexes. Socioeconomic contrasts in prestige values were also studied by Pope (1953). A Guess Who? test consisting of descriptions of twenty-five social-behavior traits was administered to sixth-grade children in order to obtain information about possible sex and/or socioeconomic differences in prestige values. There were definite sex differences at each socioeconomic level and socioeconomic differences in the prestige values of the peer culture in several sixth-grade classes. Boys and girls of high socioeconomic status placed a higher value on conformity to adult standards and conventional rules of conduct. Boys and girls of lower socioeconomic status valued self-assertion and aggression highly.

Keislar (1959) identified high- and low-scorers on a general information achievement test among ninth-grade boys with Otis IQ's of over 100, then administered twenty-six two-choice items from the Edwards Personal Preference Schedule. High-achievement "peers" were imitated significantly more frequently than their low-achievement counterparts.

Factors Determining Friendships

Hollingshead (1949) analyzed friendship patterns among an entire high-school population and found that students tended to choose friends whose socioeconomic status is similar to their own. Neugarten (1946) reported similar findings in fifth-, sixth-, tenth-, and eleventh-graders. She concluded that choices were directed at those of the same socioeconomic level as that of the one doing the choosing, or at those of a higher level. She also found that when rejections are included in the test, children from the lowest socioeconomic homes tend to be rejected most frequently.

Rose (1956) described membership reference groups as highly valued groups that provide their members with standards of behavior and attitude. He administered a questionnaire to rural high-school students to identify the reference groups and to measure the influence of the chosen group on school participation, career plans, intimacy of family life, and peer-group popularity. The choice of a reference group seemed to be significantly associated with number of siblings, estimation of popularity among schoolmates, and plans for the period after graduation. The most frequently mentioned reference group is the immediate family. Peer popularity is associated with the desire of the individual to leave the community when he becomes adult and with optimism regarding future life chances.

A cleavage analysis of the proportion of choices on a sociometric test made by and given to students in various ways was reported by Becker and Loomis (1948). They found little or no cleavage between farm and non-farm students, with a free flow of friendship choices. "The differences in friendship choice related more to variations in behavior characteristics, personal qualities, values and moral standards displayed in the interaction between students than anything else."

Generally, it would appear that proximity, similarity of interests, and similar socioeconomic level are major factors in friendship. Early friendship is often based on physical closeness in the environment; i.e., children's friends are usually those living in the same neighborhood. Later, the major factor is probably similarity of interests and tastes, although the neighborhood friendships do maintain themselves as long as the children remain together. When an individual leaves the neighborhood to attend college, these friendships may break up. If such a break-up does come about, it is probably caused chiefly by the change in interests of the college student and partially by the discontinued physical closeness (propinquity) of the friends during the four-year period of separation.

ASSESSMENT OF SOCIAL-GROUP STRUCTURE

Since Moreno (1934) developed and administered the first sociometric test, this technique for evaluating social structure has been widely used in a variety of settings, but particularly in schools. It is a simple device for measuring aspects of sociability that the teacher either did not notice or was unable to assess easily. Basically, sociometric tests require an individual to choose a number of other individuals with whom he associates in some group activity. The number of choices the individual may make varies with the particular technique used; sometimes the number is unlimited, whereas in other cases only a small number may be chosen.

Some of the currently available sociometric tests allow the chooser to indicate those he would accept and those he would reject. The rejection end of such scales is seldom used in schools because many teachers feel that a child's rejection of another child becomes fixed if he has to indicate it in writing. On three different occasions Thompson and Powell (1951) administered a rating for measuring social status to a group of sixth-graders. They did not find any evidence of this kind of crystallization of feelings of rejection. On the contrary, the students who were most often rejected on the first administration were succeedingly less often rejected on the next two. Possibly the students who rejected these individuals at first felt somewhat guilty about the rejection and tried to be friendlier toward them or at least less rejecting.

Sociometric tests have a variety of values. Besides helping teachers become more aware of the internal structure of the class and the interaction within the subgroups, they also provide a basis for organizing classroom groups. Since they identify those pupils who help in social relations, they can be used to improve social adjustment. This author feels, however, that sociometric techniques are of quite limited value at the secondary-school level. At the elementary level, a child's close friends are likely to be of about his own age and in his own self-contained class. At the secondary level, an individual's friends may be in different home rooms, in different courses, and even in different grades. If one really wishes to measure the structure of social groups in this kind of situation, the chooser must be allowed to name anyone in the entire school that he regards as a friend. In a large school of, say, 1500 students, scoring would be most difficult. At the secondary level, sociometric devices will be most effectively used in small structured groups such as clubs or fraternities and sororities.

Other precautions should also be applied. A high acceptance score does not always indicate either good social adjustment or potential leadership qualities. A zero score (no choices) is not evidence of social maladjustment. Rather, the individual may be isolated by choice. He is often a "loner" who can operate effectively in social situations but usually feels no need for socialization. Even a high rejection score cannot be interpreted as definite evidence of social maladjustment. A well-adjusted youngster may be rejected because of his individuality in opposing the group.

The author does feel that sociometric test data derived from secondary-school youngsters is valuable for research purposes, particularly when an investigator seeks to relate social status with other variables. Although much progress has been made, school personnel, especially teachers, still need more training in these techniques before they can use the results intelligently for any given individual. The interested reader is urged to study *Sociometry in the Classroom* by Gronlund (1959) for a comprehensive, clear-cut discussion of this entire topic.

McClelland and Ratliff (1947) suggested the use of sociometric tests in the ninth grade to promote social adjustment. An analysis should be made to learn the social status of individuals and the composition of the group; then the major sources of personality weakness should be investigated. With this information, the activities of the group are so organized that each individual depends upon a part in the group and the achievement of the group is dependent upon every member. A final sociometric test should be made to determine whether greater socialization has been promoted.

McCraw and Tolbert (1953) investigated the relationship between sociometric status and athletic ability in 438 junior-high-school boys. The sociometric tests were used to indicate status in the class, the grade, and the entire school. Athletic ability was appraised through judgment ratings on an objective athletic index and through athletic experience. The relationship between sociometric status and athletic ability was fairly high, but no appreciable relationship was found between sociometric status and mental maturity. Athletic ability predominated in governing the choices of "best liked" for all three groupings.

YOUTH AND COMMUNITY ACTIVITIES

The degree to which young people have the opportunity to participate in community activities and groups may be a major factor in helping them develop toward effective adult behavior. Such participation, with the opportunities it offers for youth to interact with adults, could offer invaluable experience. Youngsters so involved would have firsthand opportunities to learn how adults react, especially in formalized group situations. Those having this type of experience would then be able to communicate information about adult modes of behavior to their peer groups. Thus, the peer group would obtain specific patterns to which to adapt and would no longer need to second-guess how adults behave.

Too often in the past, teen-agers have been denied this kind of participation, primarily because adults feel that they have little of importance to contribute. While teen-agers have not had wide experience and may not have developed the necessary values, limited participation in such activities may help to widen their experience and to develop such values. Gibbs (1953), however, cautioned against involving teen-age youth in programs and policy-making groups that require a maturity they do not possess. This point is valid if the control of the group and its decisions is completely left to the teen-agers. If, however, responsible adults whom the adolescents can respect are in charge of such groups, they will help develop proper perspectives and wholesome values.

Stein (1947) suggested that adolescents must be recognized as capable of sharing responsibility for the affairs of their communities. He has presented the nature and function of good community councils and feels that their membership should include young people who are to be treated as participating members, not as subordinates. Schools should offer courses in community affairs and the entire student body should participate in some way.

If there is no adult influence on their group activities, teen-agers, in their zeal to be like adults, may be too severe in their actions. A high-school student court usually assesses far more severe punishments on its peers who are offenders than the offense warrants or than adults would assess. This is partly due to their efforts to show adults that they can handle their own affairs, but the very severity of the penalties is actually evidence to the contrary. They need adult help in more effectively understanding concepts of justice and in developing more realistic values.

Grambs (1956) found the community group experiences of adolescents to be influenced by three variables: (1) the particular organization of the adult community with reference to helping adolescents; (2) what adolescents knew or felt about the community; (3) the mores, norms, and values that are part of the national entity. Other investigators have generally found one or more of these factors present in groups they have studied. Yet there is reason to believe that too often adolescents are limited in their knowledge about both the community and the national entity. Whether this is due to a lack of interest on their part or to the failure of the adult culture to afford the necessary opportunities is not yet fully established. Rice and Reid (1956) discussed manifestations of self-government and social responsibility in the groups of young people in a study that they conducted. This study indicated that youth seems to be excluded from active participation in the significant aspects of community life.

Function of Adult Leaders

There is some question as to how well the adults responsible for various adolescent group activities are able to evaluate the social structure of the group. Marshall (1958) compared the percentage of agreement between adult leaders' selections and club members' selections of three best friends by correlating the children's sociometric scores and the leaders' judgment of popularity. Generally, the accuracy of the leaders' judgments increased as the members improved in popularity. The shift from being below to being above the median age also influenced the leaders' judgments, which became more effective as the size of the group decreased.

The adult leader of such groups probably should be more sensitive even than the classroom teacher to social patterns within the group. Since the leader is concerned with helping youngsters adjust to their community as successful socialized individuals, it behooves him to be aware of and to understand their social behavior patterns in their own groups. Marshall (1958), in a study that attempted to predict social acceptance in community youth groups, gives some idea of how complex this task might well be. She administered a sociometric test to girls in home-economics 4-H clubs and boys and girls in agricultural 4-H groups. Her findings showed age to have a low positive correlation with sociometric status, with the groups of girls below median age actually showing negative correlations. In both groups, girls were higher than boys in sociometric status. The level of achievement in the skills or knowledge being taught to the group was also positively related to sociometric status.

If the adult leader were aware of such factors, he might be better able to organize the youngsters into meaningful subgroups. He might, for example, have those of below median age interact within their own group and thus avoid failure to be accepted by those above median age. If he recognizes the relationship between performance of skills and social acceptance, he might well spend time helping develop the skills of those who are not achieving at a high enough level. The more effectively he can help an adolescent adjust to and be accepted by his peer group at this level, the more likely that teen-ager will be to adjust effectively to the larger community later on.

Leadership Qualities in Adolescents

The casual observer has long been aware that many of those who show leadership or leadership potential during adolescence continue to be leaders as adults. Benne (1948) stated succinctly, "Leaders are made; not born." He felt that democratic leadership, in particular, requires attitudes, understandings, and skills more complex than those required by autocrats. All these can be learned, although the process may be difficult. In this vein, leadership should be seen in terms of functions to be performed in helping groups to grow and operate productively, rather than in terms of qualities inherent in one person.

While this point of view may be sound, it is still important to recognize, particularly among teen-agers, the qualities that seem to be related to leadership. Whether such qualities are learned or inherent is less important than that they be identified and that teen-agers be given opportunities to develop them.

Krumboltz et al. (1959) administered an inventory on participation in high-school activities to a group of almost 1000 aviation cadets to determine whether such activity can be used to predict later leadership ratings. The predictions on the basis of this inventory showed better than chance accuracy. Participation and honors in athletics were more predictive of future leadership than were participation and honors in other fields.

The athletic-achievement factor does seem worth further exploration. The upper 50 and the lower 50 boys of a group of more than 450 sophomores and juniors who had taken athletic achievement tests were contrasted by Biddulph (1954) for personal and social adjustment and scholastic aptitude and achievement. The high-achievement group on the athletic test showed significantly higher self-adjustment on the California Test of Personality and was superior in social adjustment as indicated by teachers' ratings and sociograms. While the mean IQ of the groups was about equal, the high athletic performance group showed superior scholastic performance as measured by grade-point averages.

Terrell and Shreffler (1958) studied leaders and nonleaders in grades one through twelve on the basis of their scores on the California Test of Personality. At the upper grade levels, the leaders had significantly higher mean adjustment scores than the nonleaders. At the lower three grade levels, the differences between leaders and nonleaders were at a chance magnitude.

Thirty-nine small groups of high-school students were studied under the hypothesis that leadership will be more stable in groups working on group-chosen tasks than in groups working on imposed tasks. Two kinds of variables were found to be significant: (1) a group process outcome; the degree of disagreement with the leader and whether or not the leader prevailed; (2) whether the task was chosen by the group or imposed by the experimenter. Some experimental rigor was sacrificed to allow for sequences of past events. In general, there was a degree of stability in leadership among the groups (Katz *et al.,* 1957).

Gifted individuals are usually considered to be more skilled in leadership than those of lesser ability. Too often there seems to be a failure to identify their leadership qualities and help to expand them. Cassel and Haddox (1959) compared the results of two groups of teen-agers, one gifted group and one typical group, on two tests, the Leadership Q-Sort Test and the Leadership Ability Test. On the Q-Sort Test there were no significant differences between the groups. On the Leadership Ability Test there was a statistical difference for decision pattern. The gifted children's scores were more similar to those of demonstrated leaders than were the scores of typical children.

Since the evidence does indicate that leadership characteristics can be identified and that leadership often maintains itself, it is unfortunate that little is done to further these characteristics. All too often, the leadership exhibited by students in their school years does not continue to be manifested in adulthood. One cause may be the failure of adults to provide teen-age leaders with opportunities to exercise and develop these skills. Roberts (1950) has written a book that suggests principles of effective organization of youth groups. She suggests the need for a balance between adult authority and youthful freedom that might lead to more effective development of various patterns, including that of leadership, in youth.

Those individuals who do have the opportunities to practice and develop leadership skills often continue to demonstrate these qualities in adulthood. A survey of the backgrounds of many of today's adult leaders reveals that many were active in group functions from early youth. Membership in Boy and Girl Scouts, 4-H, and even fraternities and sororities frequently occurs in the records of such individuals.

SOCIAL STATUS AND ADOLESCENT PROBLEMS

Josselyn (1952) discussed the heavy demands our society places on the adolescent while failing to provide him with a preconceived and carefully outlined pattern to help him meet these demands. These social pressures relate to society's emphasis upon self-development, the conflicting standards presented to children, limitations of school and free-time activities, and variations in rate of maturation in different individuals.

In a study reported by Kuhlen and Bretsch (1947), ninth-graders were tested for sociometric status and for personal problems. The top and bottom quartiles of the social-status distribution were compared with the middle half as to problems checked on the Mooney Problem Check List. Those least accepted by grade-mates checked reliably more personal problems as often present than those in the top quartile did. The items most often checked by the low groups showed predominant concern with social skills, unhappiness and lack of status, family problems, and dislike of school.

Students with high marks were compared with a group of equally intelligent pupils with low marks on twelve bi-polar trait ratings obtained on a Guess Who? technique administered to grade-mates of the same sex. The high-marks group was rated higher for both sexes on liking of school work, putting studies first, and persistence. Girls with high marks were rated as less popular with boys and as more influential. Boys with high marks were rated as more considerate (Keislar, 1955).

The finding that girls with high marks were less popular with boys recalls discussion on this point in Chapter 3. Boys generally are not much interested in social activities with bright girls who demonstrate their intelligence overtly. Such overt demonstration of brightness is more often accepted to some degree within the sex group. Nonetheless, even through the college level, it is questionable whether overt display of intellect *per se* leads to social acceptance.

Bretsch (1952) collected data on 600 ninth-grade pupils in an attempt to show the relationships between acceptability scores and pupils' self-ratings on and participation in social skills. The skills investigated included dancing, tennis, card-playing, and carrying on a conversation. Pupils whose acceptability scores fell into the highest and lowest quartiles were compared. Boys in the higher group tended to give above-average self-ratings, but for girls this trend was significant only for swimming and on the mean self-rating score. The more "acceptable" pupils reported participation in a slightly but significantly larger number of social activities. The less accepted group seemed to favor certain solitary activities.

It is self-evident that those who lack social skills are excluded from the very kinds of social participation in which such skills might be developed. This is particularly true in regard to membership in formally structured groups like fraternities and sororities. These organizations seek out those who have highly developed social skills and are already well adjusted. It is rather unfortunate that youngsters who most need such activities are usually deprived of them.

Kuhlen and Collister (1952) analyzed data from a Guess Who? test administered to a group of sixth- and ninth-graders in 1942 to detect differences between those who graduate from and those who do not finish junior high school. Generally, the drop-outs are personally and socially maladjusted individuals. They "represent a group of children who are physically unattractive, poorly groomed, lacking in social know-how, shy, withdrawing, and unhappy." The authors suggest that their data may offer a challenge to the public school to meet the social and emotional needs of pupils more adequately.

Young people sometimes engage in activities that are not approved by the adult society. In discussing these activities they themselves indicate that their reasons are socially motivated. Slater's study (1952) of the use of alcoholic beverages by teen-agers illustrates this point. Twenty per cent of the girls and 44 per cent of the boys questioned in five high schools in Utah indicated they sometimes drank alcoholic beverages, although drinking is particularly frowned upon by the Mormon group that predominates in Utah. The chief motivation was social.

That the general adjustment of the individual is a factor in acceptance was demonstrated by Greenblatt's study (1950). Seventh-grade pupils were tested with respect to school achievement, mental maturity, and mental health. Each child was given a sociometric rating determined by the degree to which he was chosen by the members of his class for social and cooperative activities. Social standing as measured by these ratings was not found to be significantly related to mental health, mental age, or achievement. However, individuals with high mental-health scores choose others with high scores, while those with low scores in mental health choose those with low scores.

Among younger adolescents an individual may sometimes be accepted by a group because he demonstrates proficiency in a single skill, even though in general he is not particularly acceptable. The case of Don C. illustrates this point.

Don C. at age thirteen was an excellent pitcher on the junior-high baseball team. He was a generally unkempt, rather rude youngster, not very well liked by adults or by girls of his own age. Boys of this age, however, admired his athletic skill and flocked around him. Most of his friends did find him irritating but seemed happy to bask in his reflected glory. By age fifteen fewer and fewer of Don's age-mates sought him out, although his athletic prowess was even greater. In the eleventh grade Don was dropped from the baseball team for poor grades. His teammates missed him for his skill but were rather relieved at his leaving, since none of them liked him personally.

This case illustrates the change in acceptance that seems to occur with age. Whereas the younger teen-ager will accept an individual because of an outstanding skill, the older adolescent seeks well-rounded individuals as friends. The social adjustment of a person like Don usually becomes poorer with age unless he can improve his behavior in areas other than athletics. More often than not, as demonstrated earlier in this chapter, those athletically endowed are also well adjusted socially and academically.

AMERICAN CLASS STRUCTURE AND SOCIALIZATION

Although our American society functions within a democratic frame of reference based on a concept of equality for all, there is no denying the presence of a social class structure. The differences among the various groups, which are usually defined as socioeconomic levels, are appreciable. Major discernible differences between these groups even in sexual behavior patterns and attitudes were evidenced by the data presented in the Kinsey reports (1948, 1953). In some parts of the United States there are still remnants of a rigidly structured caste system, in which family lineage is more important than educational and/or financial level. A caste system based upon race is also still present in our country.

Descriptions of the social classes vary from one researcher to another. Some have set up a nine-point categorization ranging from lower-lower class through upper-upper class. For our purpose we will use only a three-point category—upper, middle, and lower class—based primarily on the socioeconomic level of individuals within the groups. The relationships between social behavior and the individual's position in this kind of social structure will be discussed in the following sections.

The widely quoted study of Elmtown's youth by Hollingshead (1949) reported on the impact of the social system of a Midwestern community on its adolescents' social behavior. He examined the major areas of the school, job, church, recreation, cliques, dating, and sex, and presented the results with the statistical and verbatim materials (interviews) interwoven in the discussion. His findings supported the hypothesis that social behavior is functionally related to position in the stratified social structure. He also reported a marked diversity of behavior by adolescents in differing social classes. (Out of five socioeconomic classes listed by Hollingshead, Class I represents the high socioeconomic class and Class V the low socioeconomic class.) For example: "In the school situation the behavior patterns of classes one, two, and three are generally acceptable, whereas those of class five are tabooed." He stresses in particular the departures in actuality from the great "American dream" and concludes that "this class system is far more vital as a social force in our society than the American creed."

Class Differences in Family Patterns

Maas (1951) studied social-class differences in the family systems of preadolescents and early adolescents in relation to the alleged enduring "anxiety" among middle-class children, and also explored the findings of earlier investigators who reported a mentally healthful expression of aggression in the physically and socially freer subcultures of lower-class children. His own findings, based on interviews and observations of ten- to fifteen-year-old boys and girls in neighborhood-center clubs, disagree to some extent with previous theorizing. Lower-class families demonstrated a psychologically closed, hierarchical, and quite rigid parental relationship to their young adolescent children. These youngsters seem to form far more dependent relationships within their peer groups primarily as a result of inadequate affective communication with, fear of, and psychological distance from their parents. A considerable degree of bullying and overdependent submissiveness is characteristic among lower-class preadolescents and early adolescents. What appear to be equalitarian and flexible relationships between parents and children are found in the more open middle class. Children in this class feel that both parents are relatively equal powers and are equally accessible to the children's expression of negative feeling toward them. These children showed a wider range of relationships within the peer society and also demonstrated a less urgent dependence upon age-mates.

Westley and Elkin (1957) also found no evidence to support the view that adolescence is a period of tension for the middle-class child. Their conclusions were based on a study of adolescents in an upper-middle-class suburb of Montreal. They also failed to find any evidence that the peer group opposed parental values. Adolescent life in this community, "objectively and subjectively," is continuous with the succeeding phase of life.

Class Consciousness in Adolescents

Centers (1950) attempted to determine the nature and extent of class membership feelings among adolescents. He found class consciousness closely approximating that of adults both in distribution and in relation to occupational stratification. Generally, adolescents' class identification tends to be displaced more toward the upper middle class than does that of adults. Older adolescents conform more closely to adults in identifying themselves with the working and lower classes, which indicates a significant relationship between maturity and class consciousness. A sex difference was also reported, with girls showing more tendency than boys to identify with a higher class than that to which they belonged. Finally, he found that union affiliation by parents is not a significant influence on children of manual workers, but does influence youngsters whose parents are white-collar workers.

Himmelweit *et al.* (1952) studied the views of British adolescent boys on certain aspects of the social class system; they present a description of these boys' subjective assessment of the position of their own families within the system and the adolescents' aspirations toward social ascent. Some 60 per cent of those studied did not seem to know the meaning of the term "social class." There was a striking similarity between the views of adolescents and adults, although the former were less "sophisticated." These authors also found that knowledge concerning social class is passed on from generation to generation with surprising thoroughness. The manner of viewing the stratified system is related to these adolescents' aspirations for improved social status, with the boys showing an awareness that upward movement was implied in their vocational choice.

The responses of 100 New Zealand secondary-school boys to a questionnaire concerning social class consciousness were analyzed by Congalton (1952). Although well-defined social class consciousness was found to exist, the social classes themselves were not rigidly defined. "Generally speaking, wealth (including property and income), occupational titles, and residential districts, in that order, are considered by these boys to be criteria most indicative of social class membership."

Congalton studied social behavior traits to obtain information about whether sex and/or socioeconomic differences in prestige values of the peer culture were present at the sixth-grade level. He also reported sex differences at each socioeconomic level. Girls and boys of higher socioeconomic status seemed to place a higher value on conformity to adult standards and conventional rules. Youngsters of lower socioeconomic status placed a value premium on self-assertion and aggression (Pope, 1953).

The pattern of a close relationship between the adolescent's popularity and friendship grouping and the socioeconomic status of his parents was not found to be as marked with British adolescents as it is with American youngsters. Oppenheim (1955) reported that no differences between British grammar-school middle- and working-class boys were found in spontaneously given friendship criteria. When the boys were specifically asked about those values considered important in friendship by parents in the United States, they conformed to expectation in terms of class differences. However, these differences did not seem to lead to any consistent class bias in the actual choice of playmates.

Class Divisions in Schools and Social Groups

Because school districting tends to segregate youth of different social strata, school populations have modally different values and aspirations. Wilson (1959) investigated the hypotheses that the bulk of students in a high school provides a significant normative reference that influences the values of individuals within the school. This hypothesis was tested by comparing the educational aspirations of boys in schools with different climates of aspiration. Differences in the "contextual variable" (attributes of the membership groups) are shown to affect aspirations when relevant "personal variables" (attributes of reference persons) are controlled. The ethics of the school seemed to affect academic achievement, occupational aspirations, and political preferences.

Membership in organized groups and the function of various individuals within such groups are also influenced by social-class membership. Maas (1954) sought to find differences in the ways in which lower-class and middle-class adolescents fulfill the role of member in otherwise comparable urban neighborhood clubs. Ten paired teen-age clubs—five in slum areas and five in middle-class areas—were studied. Lower-class members directed more collaborative interactions to the adult leader, while middle-class adolescents directed more collaborative and aggressive interactions to the peer president. Lower-class adolescents directed more aggressive interaction to other members. The adult leader seems developmentally less "important" to the members in the middle-class groups than to those in the lower-class groups.

Levine and Sussman (1960) investigated social class in relation to formal group membership by means of a questionnaire administered to prospective students of an Eastern college. It was found that the higher the family income and the more gregarious the student, the more likely he would be to be invited to join a social fraternity. Youths from higher-income families, regardless of sociability, and sociable youths from low-income families were found to be more acceptable than those from low-income families who also lacked social competence. Students of lower-class origin seemed to have to reject their lower-class values if they were to find acceptance in fraternities.

Effects of Class Distinctions

Generally, the studies described here do emphasize the differences that exist in the various social classes and the effect of these differences on the developing social patterns of the teen-ager. Those who come from the "right" kind of families in general find it easier to make successful social adjustments than those whose families are from "the wrong side of the tracks." It is easier to start at the top in the social pattern than to seek upward mobility. The teen-ager becomes more and more aware of these differentiations as he broadens his range of environmental experiences and attempts to become more a part of the total society.

ADOLESCENTS' PERCEPTIONS OF SOCIAL ACCEPTANCE

Adolescents are often considered rather unrealistic in their social self-perceptions, especially in their ability to evaluate the responses of others to them. Those who are well accepted by their peers seem to underrate their degree of acceptance, whereas those who are not well accepted or are even rejected tend to overrate themselves. Ausubel (1953) suggested that adolescents have a tendency "to assume that they closely resemble the group in the degree of acceptance they accord fellow group members."

Ausubel *et al.* (1952) studied the development of socioempathic ability (perception of own and others' sociometric status) by asking third- through twelfth-grade pupils to rate their classmates on a five-point scale and to predict how their classmates would rate them. High positive correlations between measurements of actual and predicted sociometric status were found at all grade levels, representing an ability to perceive own and others' sociometric status to a highly significant degree. Children at all grade levels tended to disproportionate use of the upper portions of the rating and prediction scales, but with increasing age the distributions became noticeably more normal. There also seemed to be some evidence that the teachers show less socioempathic ability as the age of their students increases. A later attempt was made to measure the ability of high-school juniors to predict the rating given them by their classmates. Discrepancy scores were used to the degree to which these choices varied from the actual sociometric ratings. Generally, it was concluded that there was no relationship between ability to perceive one's own status and the ability to perceive the status of others. Girls demonstrated an ability to perceive their own sociometric status in relation to their social effectiveness. The individual's awareness of his own status was unrelated to teachers' ratings of "personal adjustment, scholastic competitiveness, and magnitude of academic aspirations" (Ausubel and Schiff, 1955).

Findings which indicated that attitudes toward self and others are positively and significantly related were reported by McIntyre (1952). Zelin (1954) also found significant relationships between sociometric techniques and a self-acceptance test. Correlations of .56 and .58 were found between peer acceptance and acceptance of others and a correlation of .30 was found between peer acceptance and self-acceptance. The correlation between self-acceptance and acceptance of others, however, was not significant.

Buck (1952) asked the entire student body of a small rural junior-senior high school to rate fellow students on the basis of six categories of acquaintance, ranging from nonacquaintance to strong friendship. The results indicated that the student's definition of his acquaintance pattern in the group differed from the group's definition of its acquaintance with the individual student. More than one-third of the group members underestimated themselves, and nearly two-thirds overestimated themselves with regard to acquaintance.

By now the reader has probably observed that the various research studies in this area do not show complete agreement. Although much of the evidence does seem to indicate a fair degree of individual self-awareness in relation to one's social standing, there are tremendous variations in this ability. Some of the disagreement among studies is probably due to differences in instrumentation, as well as to differences in stability of instruments. This author holds the view that teen-agers are more realistic concerning their social self-evaluations than they are generally assumed to be. However, there is still a fair degree of error in their judgments, indicating that their perceptions along these lines are not yet fully developed. One might wonder, in fact, whether any individual, adolescent or adult, is wholly aware of the way in which others view him, particularly in terms of his social functioning. Even one's best friends may be unable to define clearly their feelings about one's social standing. One must often judge this factor on the basis of overt behavior, without ever being truly aware of the real feelings of the individual being judged.

This latter point is perhaps partly substantiated by Chapin's study (1950) of sociometric "stars" who are actually isolates. (Conventional sociometric diagrams represent stars or leaders as persons most often chosen as the center of a circle of admiring friends.) When Chapin plotted number of incoming choices, number of outgoing choices, and social status in a three-dimensional model rather than on the usual two-dimensional flat surface, the "stars" appeared on the periphery rather than in the center of the total group structure. This confirms a general concept of the isolation of the leader.

Deutschberger (1947) offered some indication of the many areas involved in the development of interpersonal relationships. He suggested that an object factor above and beyond emotional determinants operates. This factor, called "Tele," is defined as "the characteristic ability of a given individual to create and enter into mutual social relationships." This factor involves such principles as discreteness, constancy, adequacy, and awareness; and distinct age and sex patternings appear in its expenditure. Deutschberger feels that Tele does not operate equally throughout the totality of an individual's social atom. There is an area in "which awareness is great, level of choice expenditure high, and perception of inter-relationships accurate." There is, however, an "unstructured region marked by tentative and token choices to which reciprocation is hit-or-miss." If such an unstructured region does exist, it would explain to some extent the difficulty of evaluating one's own social standing and that of others.

Subordination of Personal Values

The adolescent, like many adults, often tries hard to develop overt social behavior that is not based on his feelings. In order to be accepted by the peer group he may try to act as he thinks the group expects him to act. In a sense he develops a "veneer" or "façade," behind which he conceals his actual feelings. His true values and attitudes are subordinated to those of the group, although in later adolescence these may emerge even when they are not compatible with those of the group.

The adolescent does not necessarily conceal his inner feelings simply for the purpose of being certain of group acceptance. In many cases he does not know what his real values are, perhaps because they have not yet crystallized. In adults, however, the concealment is more likely to be purposeful.

The teen-ager is often well aware of his attempts to conceal his feelings and may even verbalize these feelings to a sympathetic adult listener. The following statement was made by one male member of a panel of highly intelligent fifteen-year-olds in a discussion of this problem with a group of graduate students:

"There are many things about the group to which I belong that I don't really like too much. Every time I try to express my point of view and it differs from the majority opinion, they act as if I were a real oddball. But I do like to do most of the things they do, and I guess the best thing to do is to go along with them even when I don't agree. I guess I just want to be part of the group and don't want to be labeled as 'different.' "

A fifteen-year-old girl in the same group also emphasized this point in relation to the social activities of her group:

"My friends are beginning to go out on dates and I'd rather not. I just don't enjoy this sort of thing right now. If I refuse they don't even invite me to parties and I do want to be included. So even though I don't enjoy it, I get a date when the others do. I guess you must think I'm sort of a coward, but I do want to be accepted by the group."

One might contrast these responses with those of high-school seniors who also discussed this situation with the same graduate students. One boy said:

"When I was younger I used to do a lot of things I didn't really want to do simply because the rest of the gang wanted me to do them. I didn't study too hard because none of them did, and I was almost a slave to the group demands. I still like to be with them, but other things are important too. They kid me a lot because I have an A— average, and call me the 'brain.' This bothers me occasionally, but I know I need good grades to get into engineering school, and that is more important to me than their kidding. Anyway, I'll be going to college in three months and won't see them very much."

One of the senior high-school girls indicated that clearer understanding of her own values with age had helped her change her feelings:

"A couple of years ago I went along with almost everything my friends wanted to do. I didn't really disagree with any of their ideas, but sometimes I did wonder about some of the things they wanted to do. Now as I look back I guess I just didn't know some of my own feelings. Certainly if I had had the values then that I have now, I wouldn't have been too happy about some of the things I did. I guess I might have done them anyway, just to keep on being accepted by the kids. Now, though, I really tell my friends if I disagree with them and don't always do the things they want. I guess I want to be able to respect myself and I can't do that if I give in to the gang when I disagree."

The size of the group with which the adolescent interacts may also be related to his willingness to express his own opinion. Hare (1952) asked Boy Scouts in groups of five and twelve to rate camping equipment before and after group discussions and group ratings. Boys in the larger groups failed to reach as high a level of agreement as boys in smaller groups, and leaders had less influence on group decisions in the larger group. The post-discussion questionnaire responses indicated that in large groups the members are afforded less chance to express themselves and are thus more dissatisfied with the results of discussion. As the size of the group increases, the more each member feels that his own opinion will not affect group discussion and therefore is not worth expressing in the group.

CONFORMITY AS VIEWED BY ADOLESCENTS

Adolescents are well aware of the criticism leveled against them for conformity to various patterns of behavior. They can often verbalize their feelings in this regard, and in many respects they seem rather realistic about the situation. Quite often a part of the blame is laid at the parents' doorstep, yet most adolescents deny that their behavior is an attempt to fight against their parents. Most of the adolescents who have discussed this problem in the author's classes have indicated that their parents always have more influence on their behavior than the peer group has.

As the four teen-age comments we reported show, most teen-agers will admit that they will follow specific group patterns even though they are not always in agreement with their group. Primarily, they wish to avoid being singled out in any way that might cause the group to ostracize them.

The older adolescent, who is no longer dependent on the group and who is involved in establishing his own identity, views his former rigidly conforming behavior as part of the learning experience that later allows him to develop on his own. The group provides an opportunity to explore a variety of areas that he might be afraid to attempt as an individual. There is strongly expressed agreement with the concept of "safety in numbers." Occasionally a youngster will perform as an individual, but only if the group supports, and, in fact, encourages, his activities. John R., a very bright seventeen-year-old, explained this situation as follows:

"Looking back on my experiences as a real conformist to my peer group, I sometimes feel disgusted that I was so 'sheep-like.' Yet when I start really analyzing my past behavior, I can see where I learned a lot of things without feeling too insecure. I could discuss a lot of things freely with the kids in my group, where I felt ill at ease when I tried to discuss these same things with my parents. I even think I learned a lot of things from these interactions that my parents weren't really aware of. For example, I thought my first date went rather smoothly, mostly, I think, because I picked up a lot of information about how to act in the dating situation."

To the question "Do you think that the group stifled your individuality?" John replied:

"I suppose I have to say 'yes' to that question, at least in general terms. Many times I did subordinate my own feelings and desires even though I did have a number of chances to express my ideas even when they were different. Sometimes they weren't accepted, but they were discussed and I could understand their point of view. There were other times where I thought my points were arbitrarily dismissed and I didn't like that. When they did accept one of my ideas, I knew they'd all back it up and I really had a good deal of confidence when I followed through."

To the final question, "Looking back at it now, do you think you'd act the same way if you had it to do over—knowing what you know now?" John responded:

"Generally I'd say 'yes'. There were some things I'd rather not have to do, but I'm sure I'd do them if the group felt they were important. Knowing you are accepted by the gang and being able to seek refuge with them is really important. I really learned a lot of things from the experiences of the others, and they really helped me develop. I don't interact with groups now, and mostly I'm on my own, but I think the fact that I had those experiences made my present behavior possible. It's funny, too, but my parents, who always used to criticize me for being a follower, now tell me how much I matured as a result of those group activities."

Many other adolescents expressed this same point of view in our seminars. John was perhaps atypical, since many of the older teenagers in the discussion group were still functioning as part of a structured group and felt that they would like to be involved in group activities in the future. They all felt, however, that their degree of conformity was far less than it had been earlier, and they expressed far greater willingness to disagree with the group and even to refuse to take part in some of its activities.

College students who join structured social organizations, such as fraternities, report somewhat similar experiences. As freshmen and often as sophomores they feel that they are again conformers to a high degree. There is very little resentment of this, however, since they feel that they can learn a good deal by their interactions with others, especially with the juniors and seniors with whom they might not have contact if they were not in organized groups. By the time they become juniors and seniors themselves, they assume far more active roles in the organization and again feel free to disagree with the others.

Adult Group Patterns

Despite their criticisms of this kind of conformity in adolescents, adults often follow the same kind of behavior pattern. They too join organized groups, usually to gain some status or recognition afforded by the group. A joiner's motives might even be selfish ones, i.e., he might join a group to make business contacts. However, he must still contribute to maintain the very status of the group of which he seeks to take advantage. Initially, the joiner may conform almost unquestioningly to the group's behavior pattern. Only when he feels secure and accepted does he begin overtly to express his views, especially negative ones.

Perhaps adults do remember how much they learned from earlier group behavior. This awareness may make them willing to conform again to group patterns in order to gain new experiences and as a result develop even greater individuality. No wonder it is difficult for adolescents to understand why adults who are themselves conforming to groups are so critical of similar behavior in young people. Admittedly the goals and values of the adolescent groups are usually not as well structured or positive as those of the adult group, partly because of a lower level of maturity in the members and some faulty perceptions. Nonetheless, the learning environment they provide is probably as good as or even better than that present in many adult groups.

REFERENCES

ADAMS, ANDREW A. "Identifying Socially Maladjusted School Children." *Genetic Psychology Monographs,* 61, 3-36, 1960.

ANASTASI, ANNE, and MILLER, SHIRLEY. "Adolescent 'Prestige Factors' in Relation to Scholastic and Socio-economic Variables." *Journal of Social Psychology,* 29, 43-50, 1949.

AUSUBEL, DAVID P. "Reciprocity and Assumed Reciprocity of Acceptance among Adolescents, a Sociometric Study." *Sociometry,* 16, 339-348, 1953.

AUSUBEL, DAVID P., and SCHIFF, HERBERT M. "Some Intrapersonal and Interpersonal Determinants of Individual Differences in Socioemphatic Ability among Adolescents." *Journal of Social Psychology,* 41, 39-65, 1955.

AUSUBEL, DAVID P., SCHIFF, HERBERT M., and GASSER, EDWARD B. "A Preliminary Study of Developmental Trends in Socioempathy: Accuracy of Perception of Own and Others' Sociometric Status." *Child Development,* 23, 111-128, 1952.

BARON, DENIS. "Mental Health Characteristics and Classroom Social Status." *Education,* 69, 306-310, 1949.

BARON, DENIS. "Personal-Social Characteristics and Classroom Social Status: A Sociometric Study of Fifth and Sixth Grade Girls." *Sociometry,* 14, 32-43, 1951.

BAYLEY, NANCY. "Individual Patterns of Development." *Child Development,* 27, 45-74, 1956.

BECKER, MYRON G., and LOOMIS, CHARLES P. "Measuring Rural-Urban and Farm and Non-farm Cleavages in a Rural Consolidated School." *Sociometry,* 11, 246-261, 1948.

BEDOIAN, VAGHARSH H. "Social Acceptability and Social Rejection of the Underage, At-age, and Overage Pupils in the Sixth Grade." *Journal of Educational Research,* 47, 513-520, 1954.

BENNE, KENNETH D. "Leaders Are Made, Not Born." *Childhood Education,* 24, 203-208, 1948.

BIDDULPH, LOWELL G. "Athletic Achievement and Social Adjustment of High School Boys." *Research Quarterly of the American Association for Health, Physical Education, and Recreation,* 25, 1-7, 1954.

BRETSCH, HOWARD S. "Social Skills and Activities of Socially Accepted and Unaccepted Adolescents." *Journal of Educational Psychology*, 43, 449-458, 1952.

BUCK, ROY C. "Acquaintance Positions in the Group." *Sociology and Social Research*, 37, 33-36, 1952.

CANNON, KENNETH L., STAPLES, RUTH, and CARLSON, IRENE. "Personal Appearance as a Factor in Social Acceptance." *Home Economics*, 44, 710-713, 1952.

CASSELL, R. N., and HADDOX, G. "Comparative Study of Leadership Test Scores for Gifted and Typical High School Students." *Psychological Reports*, 5, 713-717, 1959.

CENTERS, RICHARD. "Social Class Identifications of American Youth." *Journal of Personality*, 18, 290-302, 1950.

CHAPIN, F. STUART. "Sociometric Stars as Isolates." *American Journal of Sociology*, 56, 263-267, 1950.

CONGALTON, A. A. "Social Class Consciousness in Adolescents." *Victoria University College Publications in Psychology* (Toronto), No. 3, 1952.

CRANE, A. R. "Pre-adolescent Gangs: A Topological Interpretation." *Journal of Genetic Psychology*, 81, 113-122, 1952.

DAVIS, KINGSLEY. "Adolescence and the Social Structure." *Annals of the American Academy of Political and Social Science*, 238, 816, 1944.

DEUTSCHBERGER, PAUL. "The Tele-factor: Horizon and Awareness." *Sociometry*, 10, 242-249, 1947.

FEINBERG, MORTIMER R. "Relation of Background Experience to Social Acceptance." *Journal of Abnormal and Social Psychology*, 48, 206-214, 1953.

FLEMING, C. M. *Adolescence, Its Social Psychology, with an Introduction to Recent Findings from the Fields of Anthropology, Physiology, Medicine, Psychometrics and Sociometry.* New York: International University Press, 1949.

GIBBS, H. G. "Youth Participation—Fact or Folly?" *Group*, 15(3), 15-16, 1953.

GRAMBS, JEAN D. "The Community and the Self-governing Adolescent Group." *Journal of Educational Sociology*, 30, 94-105, 1956.

GRAY, SUSAN W. "Masculinity-Femininity in Relation to Anxiety and Social Acceptance." *Child Development*, 28, 203-214, 1957.

GREENBLATT, E. L. "Relationship of Mental Health and Social Status." *Journal of Educational Research*, 44, 193-204, 1950.

GRONLUND, NORMAN E. *Sociometry in the Classroom.* New York: Harper and Row, 1959.

HARE, A. PAUL. "A Study of Interaction and Consensus in Different Sized Groups." *American Sociological Review*, 17, 261-267, 1952.

HARWOOD, E. "Social Development in the Queensland Adolescent." *Australian Journal of Education*, 3, 77-87, 1959.

HESS, ROBERT D. "The Adolescent: His Society." *Review of Educational Research*, 30, 5-12, 1960.

HIMMELWEIT, H. T., HALSEY, A. H., and OPPENHEIM, A. N. "The Views of Adolescents on Some Aspects of the Social Class Structure." *British Journal of Sociology*, 3, 148-172, 1952.

HOLLINGSHEAD, AUGUST B. *Elmtown's Youth: The Impact of Social Classes on Adolescents.* New York: John Wiley & Sons, Inc., 1949.

HORROCKS, JOHN E., and BUKER, MAE E. "A Study of the Friendship Fluctuations of Preadolescents." *Journal of Genetic Psychology,* 78, 131-144, 1951.

JONES, MARY COVER. "A Study of Socialization Patterns at the High School Level." *Journal of Genetic Psychology,* 83, 87-111, 1958.

JOSSELYN, IRENE M. "Social Pressures in Adolescence." *Social Casework,* 33, 187-193, 1952.

KATZ, ELIHU, BLAU, PETER M., BROWN, MORTON L., and STRODTBECK, FRED L. "Leadership Stability and Social Change; an Experiment with Small Groups." *Sociometry,* 20, 36-50, 1957.

KEISLAR, EVAN R. "A Distinction Between Social Acceptance and Prestige among Adolescents." *Child Development,* 24, 275-283, 1953.

KEISLAR, EVAN R. "Girls' Social Groups Rate Each Other." *California Journal of Educational Research,* 4, 227-232, 1953.

KEISLAR, EVAN R. "Differences among Adolescent Social Clubs in Terms of Members' Characteristics." *Journal of Educational Research,* 48, 297-303, 1954.

KEISLAR, EVAN R. "Peer Group Ratings of High School Pupils with High and Low School Marks." *Journal of Experimental Education,* 23, 375-378, 1955.

KEISLAR, EVAN R. "The Generalization of Prestige among Adolescent Boys." *California Journal of Educational Research,* 10, 153-156, 1959.

KINSEY, A. D., POMEROY, W. B., and MARTIN, C. E. *Sexual Behavior in the Human Male.* Philadelphia: W. B. Saunders Co., 1948.

KINSEY, A. D., POMEROY, W. B., and MARTIN, C. E. *Sexual Behavior in the Human Female.* Philadelphia: W. B. Saunders Co., 1953.

KRUMBOLTZ, JOHN D., CHRISTAL, RAYMOND E., and WARD, JOE H. "Predicting Leadership Ratings from High School Activities." *Journal of Educational Psychology,* 50, 105-110, 1959.

KUHLEN, RAYMOND G., and BRETSCH, HOWARD S. "Sociometric Status and Personal Problems of Adolescents." *Sociometry,* 10, 122-132, 1947.

KUHLEN, RAYMOND G., and COLLISTER, E. GORDON. "Sociometric Status of Sixth- and Ninth-Graders Who Fail to Finish High School." *Educational and Psychological Measurement,* 12, 632-637, 1952.

LEHRER, L., "Jewish Belongingness of Jewish Youth." *Yivo Annual of Jewish Social Science* (Israel), 9, 137-165, 1954.

LEVINE, GENE N., and SUSSMAN, LEILA A. "Social Class and Sociability in Fraternity Pledging." *American Journal of Sociology,* 65, 391-299, 1960.

LONG, ALMA. "Social Development among Adolescents." *Journal of Home Economics,* 41, 201-202, 1949.

MAAS, HENRY S. "Some Social Class Differences in the Family Systems and Group Relations of Pre- and Early Adolescents." *Child Development,* 22, 145-152, 1951.

MAAS, HENRY S. "The Role of Member in Clubs of Lower-Class and Middle-Class Adolescents." *Child Development,* 25, 241-251, 1954.

MCCLELLAND, F. M., and RATLIFF, JOHN A. "The Use of Sociometry as an Aid in Promoting Social Adjustment in a Ninth Grade Home-room." *Sociometry*, 10, 147-153, 1947.

MCCRAW, L. W., and TOLBERT, J. W. "Sociometric Status and Athletic Ability of Junior High School Boys." *Research Quarterly of the American Association for Health, Physical Education, and Recreation*, 24, 72-80, 1953.

MCINTYRE, CHARLES J. "Acceptance by Others and Its Relation to Acceptance of Self and Others." *Journal of Abnormal and Social Psychology*, 47, 624-625, 1952.

MARSHALL, HELEN R. "Prediction of Social Acceptance in Community Youth Groups." *Child Development*, 29, 173-184, 1958.

MARSHALL, HELEN R. "Factors Relating to the Accuracy of Adult Leaders' Judgments of Social Acceptance in Community 'Groups.' " *Child Development*, 29, 417-424, 1958.

MAUCORPS, P. H., LAMBERT, R., and MAUCORPS, J. G. "Les manifestations primaries du comportement social chez l'enfant et l'adolescent; expansivité et polarisation" (Primary Manifestations of Social Behavior in the Infant and Adolescent; Emotional Expansiveness and Polarization). *Travail Humaine* (Paris), 18, 257-314, 1955.

MORENO, J. L. *Who Shall Survive?* Washington, D. C.: Nervous and Mental Disease Publishing Company, 1934.

NEUGARTEN, B. L. "Social Class and Friendship among School Children." *American Journal of Sociology*, 51, 305-313, 1946.

OPPENHEIM, A. N. "Social Status and Clique Formation among Grammar School Boys." *British Journal of Sociology* (London), 6, 228-245, 1955.

PARAMESWARAN, E. G. "Social Adjustment of a Group of Early Adolescent Boys." *Journal of Psychological Research*, 1, 29-45, 1957.

PATEL, AMBALAL S., and GORDON, JESSE E. "Some Personal and Situational Determinants of Yielding to Influence." *Journal of Abnormal and Social Psychology*, 61, 411-418, 1960.

POLANSKY, NORMAN, LIPPITT, RONALD, and REDL, FRITZ. "An Investigation of Behavioral Contagion in Groups." *Human Relations* (London), 3, 319-348, 1950.

POPE, BENJAMIN. "Socio-economic Contrasts in Children's Peer Culture Prestige Values." *Genetic Psychology Monographs*, 48, 157-220, 1953.

RICE, THEODORE D., and REID, CHANDOS. "Group Efforts Toward Self-government and Social Responsibility." *Journal of Educational Sociology*, 30, 75-93, 1956.

ROBERTS, DOROTHY M. *Leadership of Teenage Groups.* New York: Association Press, 1950.

ROSE, ARNOLD M. "Reference Groups of Rural High School Youth." *Child Development*, 27, 351-363, 1956.

SINGER, ARTHUR, JR. "Certain Aspects of Personality and Their Relation to Certain Group Modes, and Constancy of Friendship Choices." *Journal of Educational Research*, 45, 33-42, 1951.

SLATER, ARTHUR D. "A Study of the Use of Alcoholic Beverages among High School Students in Utah." *Quarterly Journal of Studies on Alcohol*, 13, 78-86, 1952.

SMITH, LAURENCE C., and PHILLIPS, LESLIE. "Social Effectiveness and Developmental Level in Adolescence." *Journal of Personality,* 27, 239-249, 1959.

STEIN, ABE B. "Adolescent Participation in Community Co-ordinating Councils." *Journal of Educational Sociology,* 21, 177-183, 1947.

TAYLOR, EDWARD A. "Some Factors Relating to Social Acceptance in Eighth-Grade Classrooms." *Journal of Educational Psychology,* 43, 257-272, 1952.

TERRELL, GLENN, JR., and SHREFFLER, JOY. "A Development Study of Leadership." *Journal of Educational Research,* 52, 69-72, 1958.

THOMPSON, G. G., and HORROCKS, J. E. "A Study of Friendship Fluctuations of Urban Boys and Girls." *Journal of Genetic Psychology,* 70, 53-63, 1947.

THOMPSON, G. G., and POWELL, M. "An Investigation of the Rating Scale Approach to Measurement of Social Status." *Educational and Psychological Measurements,* 11, 440-455, 1951.

THORPE, J. G. "A Study of Some Factors in Friendship Formation." *Sociometry,* 18, 207-214, 1955.

WARDLOW, MARY E., and GREENE, JAMES E. "An Exploratory Sociometric Study of Peer Status among Adolescent Girls." *Sociometry,* 15, 311-318, 1952.

WESTLEY, WILLIAM A., and ELKIN, FREDERICK. "The Protective Environment and Adolescent Socialization." *Social Forces,* 35, 243-249, 1957.

WILSON, ALAN B. "Residential Segregation of Social Classes and Aspirations of High School Boys." *American Sociological Review,* 24, 836-845, 1959.

WITTENBERG, RUDOLPH M., and BERG, JANICE. "The Stranger in the Group." *American Journal of Orthopsychiatry,* 22, 89-97, 1952.

WOLMAN, BENJAMIN. "Spontaneous Groups of Children and Adolescents in Israel." *Journal of Social Psychology,* 34, 171-182, 1951.

ZELIN, SEYMOUR L. "The Relationship of Peer Acceptance, Acceptance of Others and Self Acceptance." *Proceedings, Iowa Academy of Science,* 61, 446-449, 1954.

CHAPTER 7

Heterosexual Development

Social development was considered in the preceding chapter primarily as it occurs within groups of the same sex. This chapter discusses the development of social interaction between the sexes. While the development of social behavior among members of the same sex starts very early in childhood, the beginning of heterosexual development is particularly associated with adolescence, specifically in relation to sexual maturation. Up to the time of pubescence the members of each sex are primarily interested in associating only with individuals of their own sex. Shortly after puberty, however, there is a decided development of interest in members of the opposite sex.

The author (1955) studied age and sex differences in the psychological area of heterosexual relations, using delay in reacting to critical words as evidence of conflict. The sample included males and females ranging in age from ten to thirty years. There was a steady increase in conflict in this area, which for males reached a maximum at age fifteen, then decreased from ages fifteen to seventeen. For females, conflict increased steadily from age ten to age sixteen, with a decrease occurring between sixteen and seventeen. As indicated in Tables 8 and 9, Chapter 5, there are statistically significant differences in the increase in difference score for females between the ages of eleven and twelve, twelve and thirteen, and thirteen and fourteen, while for males these statistically significant differences appear between the ages of twelve and thirteen, and thirteen and fourteen. These tables also demonstrate a statistically significant decrease in difference scores between the fifteen-year-old and the seventeen-year-old males.

The results of this study generally support the hypotheses that emotional disturbance in the area of heterosexual relations occurs earlier for females than for males, with a difference of one year in onset of conflict being demonstrated. Boys apparently reach their peak in conflict a year earlier than girls (at age fifteen as opposed to sixteen for girls) and show a sharper decrease in conflict between fifteen and seventeen than girls do between sixteen and seventeen. Possibly the relatively easier sex adjustment that boys in our society can make as compared to girls is partially responsible for this latter finding.

A comparison was also made between the sexes to determine whether such conflict was more severe for boys or for girls at the various age levels studied. There were statistically significant differences between the sexes at ages twelve and thirteen. At both these age levels, females showed a significantly greater degree of disturbance than that manifested by the boys at the same ages. There were no significant differences at any of the other ages studied, but the results did approach significance at age seventeen, with males showing less conflict than females at that age.

Campbell (1955) studied the preferences of children at various ages for others of the same or opposite sex. At age ten or eleven, children strongly prefer members of their own sex in a variety of activities. By the age of fourteen or fifteen, girls choose boys to lead their teams, to serve on their committees, and also to accompany them to the movies. The boys at this same age choose girls for movie dates but not for the other two activities. Boys were assigned more desirable social traits in the ratings of both boys and girls. These findings are not conclusive, but they do seem to demonstrate a general trend toward increased interaction of the sexes with increasing age after pubescence.

At the beginning and at the end of a one-week session in three Junior Farm Bureau training camps, males and females aged fourteen to twenty-six were asked to designate five preferred work and play companions (Faunce and Beegle, 1948). At the beginning the choices were generally mates of like sex and like age from the same county. At the end girls preferred boys to girls, and all were willing to choose individuals from different counties. The authors report that formation of the work groups on the basis of initial sociometric choice resulted in "a superior solidarity over former camps as reflected in such indices as greater participation in discussions, larger degree of group identification, and more work accomplished."

The changes from the somewhat passive social life of the preadolescent at home into the more active contacts of school and social life were described by Tresselt (1954), who felt that the latter change comes about when the adolescent frees himself from his parents and achieves "heterosexuality." Even though interest in the other sex increases, the sexes still differ in their ideals, interests, and demands at different stages. There are particularly noticeable differences in their expectations through courtship to marriage.

SEX-APPROPRIATE BEHAVIOR

The development of sex-appropriate behavior (i.e., behavior generally considered appropriate for the individual's sex) has been a source of interest to investigators. Zuk (1958) analyzed the everyday behavior of 99 boys and girls of the Adolescent Growth Study in an attempt to investigate changes in sex-appropriateness. This study included the years from age fifteen to age seventeen. The subjects' responses to an inventory covering "things I did last week, where I went last week, what I read and radio programs I listened to" were analyzed as measures of everyday behavior. The inventory was administered a number of times over the three-year period. Sex-appropriateness was established by determining whether more boys than girls participated in each type of activity. The results generally indicated that sex-appropriate behavior increased significantly in girls from sixteen to seventeen years and seemed to become more stable in girls with increasing age. Sex-appropriate behavior seemed to be related, but to a low degree, to physical, social, intellectual, and temperament factors.

Theoretical considerations concerning sex differences in the development of masculine and feminine identifications have been suggested by a number of investigators. After setting up a number of hypotheses, Lynn (1959) reviewed the pertinent literature to see whether other studies supported his viewpoint. He concluded generally that males became more closely identified with the male role with increasing age and that the identification of females with the feminine role is less firmly developed. A larger proportion of females than males show preference for the role of the opposite sex and adopt some aspects of it. Lynn found that the male seems to identify with a cultural stereotype of the masculine role, whereas females identified more closely with aspects of their own mothers' roles. Brown (1957) reported on an extension of his earlier study concerning sex-role patterns in young children. He found that through the fourth-grade level girls showed a stronger preference for the masculine than for the feminine role. At the fifth grade this pattern changed, with girls showing a predominant preference for the feminine role.

Mussen (1961) investigated the stability over a fifteen-year period of the degree of adoption of traditional masculine or feminine sex-role interests in adolescence. Twenty seventeen-year-old boys were identified at each extremity of the masculinity-femininity scores on the Strong Vocational Interest Blank. When they were in their early thirties, the California Psychological Inventory was administered to them. Male subjects who had the highest feminine-interest scores when they were adolescents scored higher at approximately age thirty-two on the scales relating to nonmasculine interests, dominance, and capacity for status.

ADOLESCENTS AND DATING

Dating is one of the activities of adolescence that is most widely discussed by both adolescents and adults. This area is among those most affected by the approximate two-year difference in the development of the two sexes. Although a good deal has been written about dating in popular periodicals, relatively little research has been reported.

Lowrie (1948) considered that this was almost a neglected field of study. He felt that it is very important to differentiate dating from courtship (which has the implication of intent to marry) and to attempt to define various kinds of dating. He pointed out that there are many functions served by dating in the development of the adolescent's personality and in later activities in courtship. Although many colleges offer courses on marriage and the family, Lowrie felt that such courses should be given earlier in the educational program and should include more about dating. Ideally, for such information to be most useful, it should be transmitted to the individual at about the time dating begins. If it could at least be introduced toward the end of high school, it would still be valuable and might then serve as a base for later college courses in marriage and the family. "The obvious difficulty about a separate course on dating is the paucity of facts and of literature about them."

Adolescents' concern about the various aspects of heterosexual adjustment and of dating is well illustrated in a study reported by Elias (1949). He made a survey of more than 5000 high-school seniors, asking them to report conflict, confusion, or doubt about a variety of items. Table 12 presents the percentages of boys and girls so reporting on the items. Some sex differences are readily apparent. Girls seemed more concerned than boys about marriage and its success and also about intimacy with the other sex, understanding about love, and whether to become engaged. In most of the other items, responses are relatively similar for the two sexes.

Some limited resources are available for disseminating information about dating to youngsters. Science Research Associates has published a Better Living Booklet dealing with this topic. This booklet, entitled *When Children Start Dating* (Neisser, 1951) is designed to help parents and teachers better understand and help adolescent boys and girls. The actual problems of dating are prefaced by a discussion of how children learn to love and how they mature physically and emotionally. Various ways of solving problems cooperatively with their children are

TABLE 12. Percentage of 5,500 high-school seniors who checked certain problems in boy-girl relationships

From Elias (1949), *by permission of the author and The College Book Store, State College of Washington*

	Percentage	
Problem in boy-girl relationship	Boys	Girls
What makes a good marriage	13.9	32.6
Making a successful marriage	9.1	25.5
Going steady	12.0	13.3
Can't date the right person	12.7	12.5
Not enough dates	11.5	11.6
Break with (boy, girl) friend	9.0	13.4
How much intimacy to permit	6.9	14.7
Getting along with the other sex	12.2	9.5
Not having (boy, girl) friend	9.0	8.4
Understanding about love	4.4	10.5
Should I get engaged	3.1	11.5
Not attractive to the other sex	7.8	7.5
Right attitude about sex	7.9	7.3
Insufficient sex knowledge	7.6	6.9
Going "too far"	8.5	5.9
Sex problems	7.6	6.5
Uncomfortable with other sex	8.9	5.2
Wonder if anybody will want me	5.1	7.6
Learning about sex	6.4	6.4
(Boys, girls) on mind too much	7.5	5.2
Concerned about sex disease	6.4	4.1
"Necking," "smooching"	4.8	5.4
Proper sex relations	4.9	5.2
Trouble over sex relations	5.5	4.3
"Petting"	3.5	3.9
Thinking too much about sex	5.9	1.6
Embarrassed about sex	2.9	3.6
(Boy, girl) friend stepping out	3.8	2.2
Can't keep (boy, girl) friend	3.1	2.7
Too many dates	3.1	2.5
Self-abuse, masturbation	4.8	0.8
Not able to get married soon	1.8	2.7
Can't control sex desire	3.3	1.2
Quitting school to get married	0.3	0.7

suggested to parents. Although it is not particularly research-oriented, the booklet serves as a valuable starting point for discussing dating.

Influence of the Peer Group

Crist (1953) felt that "students' relationships with the opposite sex were not isolated, independent actions." There is evidence to suggest that dating is not initially engaged in because of any real heterosexual interest on the part of the individual, but rather seems to result from the expectations of the peer group. Whether or not the individual started dating at a certain age was determined primarily by the family, but the actual activity was approved by the age-mates. Thus, it can be said that "many students were initiated into dating activity through a desire to become acceptable to the group."

One cannot stress the importance of this latter fact strongly enough. Because of this kind of group pressure, many youngsters begin to date before they are really "ready" for such activities. Even prepubescent youngsters, who generally would have no sexually oriented interest in members of the opposite sex, seem to be dating. As a result, numbers of young people actually experience negative feelings about dating and develop behavior patterns that are not conducive to later success in dating.

Age at Which Dating Starts

Lowrie (1952) obtained statistics from high-school juniors and seniors and university students on the ages at which they had their first dates. He concluded that "as a rule boys and girls in these samples begin to date at approximately the same ages." The members of both sexes apparently also begin to go steady at about the same age. Because of the age differential in physical maturing, one might normally expect that boys would begin to date about two years later than girls. The fact that they date at the same ages probably reinforces the concept that group pressure is responsible for this early dating.

A small percentage of youngsters may have an occasional date before they reach adolescence, but typically dating begins at the junior-high-school level, with a steady increase in the number of dates per month from the freshman year in high school through the senior year. Punke (1944) reported that about 50 per cent of both the freshman boys and the freshman girls he studied did not have any dates. By the senior year in high school only about 20 per cent of the boys and about 12 per cent of the girls said they had no dates. The seniors dated more times per month than did the freshmen.

The child's social class also appears to be a factor in the frequency of dating and the type of dating companion chosen. The higher the social class, the more dating partners the child had; and the upper-class children generally chose partners from their own social class and their own school grade. Lower-class youngsters more often dated partners from outside the school (Hill, 1955). Hill also reported that the number of dating partners showed a steady increase from grades nine through eleven and then decreased in grade twelve. Generally, eleventh-graders had more dating partners than youngsters in any of the other grades.

After dating begins there are still difficulties involved in developing patterns of behavior to facilitate further dating. Christensen (1952) found that members of both sexes continued to feel shyness in the dating situation. Females felt that males were careless, disrespectful, and sex-driven, while males considered females inhibited, touchy, and money-minded. Both males and females agreed with much of the criticism directed toward them by the members of the opposite sex, but there were some differences related to direction of projected blame. Earlier Christensen (1948) had asked college students enrolled in marriage classes to rate twenty courtship traits as to degree of objectionability, frequency of occurrence in the opposite sex, and frequency in self. There was a .80 correlation between the ratings by the two sexes on degree of objectionability. The items considered most objectionable were generally not the ones found most frequently in the opposite sex. Males were condemned in both self- and cross-sex criticisms for necking and petting, as were females. Condemnation of opposite sex was more definite than that revealed in self-criticism. The members of both sexes agree on what is wrong with themselves but regard their own weaknesses as less serious than those of the opposite sex.

What Is Dating?

One of the difficulties this author has encountered has been in finding out just what dating is or what it means to teen-agers. Some clear-cut definition of dating would be of value particularly in attempting to determine the age at which dating starts. Such a definition, however, is probably impossible to devise. When an adult thinks about dating, he probably thinks of a situation in which a boy asks a girl to "go out" with him. Yet this is not necessarily what the teen-ager considers dating, although it may be. There is also a good deal of variation in what dating means according to the geographic locale in which the child functions, i.e., there are apparent differences between urban and rural patterns. There are also some variations according to the individual's socioeconomic level.

In urban areas dating is often defined somewhat as most adults view it—as a member of one sex inviting a member of the opposite sex to accompany him or her to some event, usually one taking place during the evening. However, this does not mean that a single couple, or even two or three couples, are going out alone. In many situations, especially for younger adolescents, a date often means going to a party where a large number of teen-agers will be together. In a sense the "dating" merely involves a boy's calling for a girl and taking her home. Much of the evening may well be spent in group activities, with the couples separating to some degree. There is also likely to be adult supervision for such a party, and such supervision is not included in adults' concepts of dating.

In rural areas even the aspect of calling for the girl and taking her home may be excluded. If a dance is held in the high school, many members of both sexes pair off after arriving at the dance, both often having come separately. Some of the couples will have agreed in advance to meet, while others will pair off at random with no previous arrangement. Part of this behavior may be caused by transportation problems, since rural homes are likely to be far apart. Part of it may result from a lesser degree of "sophistication" among rural youngsters than among urban ones. There may also be some relationship to parental practices in rural areas where social gatherings often involve large groups of varying ages.

In rural environments the dating of older adolescents may also be group-oriented. There seems to be more "double" or "triple" dating among older rural adolescents than among those from urban environments. This, again, may be related to problems of transportation. In a city, if a boy cannot use the family car to take his girl to a movie, bus or taxicab transportation is usually available. In a rural area the theater may be twenty miles away, and the youngster who owns a car probably takes his friends who do not own cars with him.

Dates also vary in terms of the purpose involved. A "coke date" may simply mean meeting a friend of the opposite sex at the corner drugstore after school to exchange pleasantries. A date may be made for a couple to go to a high-school football game with a large group. It may be made to attend an evening school dance, where again a large group is involved, with an adult driving the couple to and from the dance. A couple may go out by themselves to attend a movie or to take a walk, or a date may involve driving to the favorite "necking" spot.

It is indeed difficult to include all these activities in dating behavior. Some of them are merely oriented toward general social interaction, while others might be considered as sociosexually oriented. To generalize about dating, it is first necessary to determine what the term means to those who are being studied. Far more research is needed in this area, particularly studies in which adolescents are asked to define what dating means to them.

"Going Steady"

Another area of heterosexual functioning that is widely misunderstood is "going steady" as a major part of the dating pattern. The general interpretation of "going steady" is that a young boy and girl pair off and date only each other. This is not as formalized as an official "pinning" (i.e., a boy's giving his fraternity pin to a specific girl) or as an actual engagement, but it is often considered equally binding. Of more serious concern is the fact that this pairing-off occurs at a relatively early age. Some years ago, going steady seemed to be common only among high-school students, but today the pattern is present in junior high school as well.

As to the question whether going steady is "good" or "bad" in the total pattern of the individual's development, one can only present both sides and let the reader draw his own conclusions. Even these can be drawn only in terms of individual cases and not as broad generalizations.

ADVANTAGES. Like many of the other activities in which the young adolescent engages, going steady can be related to the attempt to seek security. This is in fact the only goal of many youngsters, who go steady with little or no real sociosexual interest involved. Many girls fear the social condemnation of their peer group if they fail to have a male companion available when the group schedules an event requiring the presence of members of the opposite sex. Such failure may be interpreted as a lack of popularity and can lower the status of the individual appreciably. Rather than take a chance that a boy will ask them for a date when they need one, many girls prefer to have a "steady" available. This may seem simply a "cold" or calculated convenience, and it often is. There is often no romantic interest, not even "puppy-love," involved in "going steady."

For boys a similar situation is present. Once a boy finds he is comfortable with one girl and does not become embarrassed in her presence, he may wish to maintain a constant relationship with her. His relationship may be based more on a feeling of personal security than on peer approval. For example, a youngster may be self-conscious about his dancing. If he finds that he can apparently dance well with a particular girl, he may try to dance only with her. He is afraid that someone else may make fun of his ability, but he knows that this particular girl thinks he dances well. He might well refuse opportunities to go out with others, seeking the companionship only of the one with whom he feels secure.

PROBLEMS. However, peer-group approval is always involved in going steady. A boy may seek to go out only with girls whom the group considers physically attractive. He may, in fact, not attempt to date a girl whom he actually likes because the peer group thinks her unattractive. Girls seem to achieve a special kind of peer-group approval if they can manage to go steady with one of the school's "ideal figures," i.e., a prominent athlete, a class officer, etc. Since many of the social activities in which a couple is involved are group activities, group approval of one's partner is quite important.

One of the major criticisms of going steady is that it limits the experience of the individual. By restricting themselves to a single constant companion, youngsters lose the opportunity of learning how to get along with a variety of people. The behavior displayed in getting along with one partner may not be appropriate in getting along with others. It is felt that both boys and girls would broaden their backgrounds by going out with a number of members of the opposite sex, and that such broader experience would be of value when marriage is being considered. Both sexes would then be more aware of the various qualities they find desirable in the other sex, and would be better equipped to recognize the "right" mate.

Some, of course, begin to go steady at an early age and continue the relationship into adulthood, when it culminates in marriage. Again, one can determine the success or failure of such a pattern of behavior only by evaluating individual cases. If the marriage succeeds, it is difficult to criticize the patterns leading to it. If the marriage fails, hindsight may indicate that too-limited dating experience may be partially responsible.

Whether going steady is as common in adolescence as many consider is somewhat debatable. Here again, one must be cautious in any generalizing about group behavior throughout this time span. The age factor is important. One can find large numbers, perhaps a majority, of high-school juniors and seniors and college freshmen and sophomores who have gone steady or are going steady. While many younger adolescents in the junior high schools do go steady, it is questionable whether these numbers reach major proportions. There has apparently been a substantial increase in the numbers going steady at the junior-high-school level, but one cannot say that a major trend has yet been established.

Again, urban-rural differences should be noted. In fact, there also seems to be a suburban pattern, which differs from both the urban and the rural pattern. If one is to believe reports appearing in various magazines and newspapers, suburban youngsters are dating at the very beginnings of adolescence, and in some cases even before puberty. These "sophisticated" youngsters attend formal dances, and patterns of going steady are readily apparent. These patterns almost resemble the early heterosexual interactions of juvenile-delinquent gangs in which early dating and going steady are an expected or even required part of membership. At best, one must consider such early formalized interaction as unhealthy, forcing youngsters into artificial situations for which they are not yet ready in terms either of maturity or of interest. This speeding up of heterosexual interaction and experience may well leave these youngsters at sixteen wondering "What's left in life to do?"

The general pattern of going steady takes place somewhat later in urban areas than seems to be the case in the suburban society. There is a good deal of heterosexual interaction at the junior-high level, with the school often sponsoring "lunch-period dances" and making its facilities available for "teen towns." However, formalized dating patterns and going steady usually do not become of major importance until the high-school years. Junior-high activities are usually closely chaperoned, and boys and girls must come to and leave these events separately.

In rural areas even less going steady is apparent, and where it occurs the couple involved usually seriously intends to continue the relationship toward marriage. The lack of transportation and the greater distances between the homes of youngsters may be partially responsible for less steady dating. The relatively smaller numbers of youngsters living in these areas may have more opportunity to know each other well and may thus feel more generally accepted. A small group of this kind may function effectively as a group, and a need to pair off may not be felt by its members.

With increased mobility of youth and with better means of communication available to them, the differences in rural, urban, and suburban patterns may be decreasing. However, this author, who until recently has always lived in urban or suburban communities, was pleasantly surprised to find striking differences still present in the relatively rural area in which he now lives. It is unfortunate that more research on this topic is not available. It would be particularly interesting to follow up these various groups in order to compare success in marriage with these earlier patterns of behavior.

"Steady" Versus "Steadily"

Another area of dating that should be briefly considered is going "steadily" as opposed to going "steady." The distinction between the two should be made clear. Going "steady" seems to mean that a young male and female go out on dates only with each other for an extended period of time and that neither will date anyone else. Going "steadily" seems to mean going out on dates quite regularly, but not necessarily with the same partner. Within this latter frame of reference, an individual may also go "steady," i.e., date the same person, but usually only for a brief time period. Regina N. stated this situation well:

"I've gone steady quite a few times. I like to go out with the same boy two or three times in a row, but that's about all. I don't like to tie myself down longer than that because I'm always meeting new boys I'd like to date. I do think it's a little better to see the same boy a few times instead of going out with a different one each time. At least I get some chance to know what he's really like, so I'll know if I'd like to go out with him again in the future."

This kind of behavior appears to offer the kinds of experiences that will be valuable later in selecting a mate. It seems much sounder than dating a different person each time, which allows only a rather superficial judgment to be made. One can obviously explore commonality of interests and tastes better after two or three contacts with a person than after just one. Perhaps it takes a relatively mature and secure person to be able to function in this way, but it does seem more likely to lead to better heterosexual adjustment.

Group-Imposed Restrictions

Sometimes the actions or requirements of one's peer group can limit such possible interaction by forcing the individual into a more restricted pattern. For example, membership in a structured organization like a fraternity or sorority may impose certain social restrictions on the adolescent. Members of such a group may interact only with members of a comparable group of members of the opposite sex who are considered acceptable to the original group.

In a large suburban high school there are twenty-seven fraternities and sororities officially active. A social-status hierarchy among these various groups is readily apparent. Two or three of the fraternities and a similar number of sororities are considered the best, with the others rated at various lower status levels. Members of the high-status fraternities will date only girls who are members of the high-status sororities. It is virtually a "sin" to date a girl who is not a sorority member, and almost as bad to date one from one of the lower-status sororities. Further, one usually may not date a member of the accepted group who has previously been dated by a fellow member of one's own group.

SEXUAL BEHAVIOR OF ADOLESCENTS

The physiological changes which take place with the advent of puberty are accompanied by increased drive in various areas, particularly in sexual behavior. Usually one would assume that, when the strength of of a drive increases, opportunities for the expression of the drive also increase. In the case of sexual behavior, the opposite condition seems to prevail. The increased or newly developed sexual-drive patterns of the adolescent do not find expanded opportunity in our society for their normal expression. These normally developing behavior patterns must, in fact, often be repressed or expressed in other than "normal" ways.

Because of societal taboos and restrictions, the adolescent frequently has a substantial number of worries and problems relating to sexual development and particularly to sexual behavior. Kirkendall (1948) found that all the sex worries or problems checked by a group of teen-age boys dealt with matters of conduct, behavior, anatomy, and/or experience. He found many individual differences, especially in comparing boys without sexual experience with those who had had such experience. The kind of experience the individual has had would presumably also be involved in determining individual differences.

Among the most comprehensive studies of sexual behavior and the problems relating to it are those of the late Dr. Kinsey and his associates (1948, 1953). Although their studies deal primarily with adult patterns of sexual behavior, a good deal of the discussion does relate to adolescence. They have reported that about 95 per cent of adolescent boys engage in activities leading to orgasm by the time they are fifteen years of age. Kinsey suggests that the actual peak of sexual capacity for males is reached just prior to adolescence, but the "peak of actual performance is in the middle or late teens." Females, however, do not experience the maximum incidences of sexual response until the late twenties. There is, therefore, an appreciable difference between the sexes in age of reaching maximum responsiveness. This poses a number of social-psychological problems. The increasing moral suppression which has come about in this country during the last hundred years has made the problem of sexual adjustment a most difficult one, especially for the younger male. Research conducted in Sweden on the incidence of premarital sex relations, as reported by Undeutsch (1950), leads to the conclusion that Kinsey's findings for the United States can be generalized to other populations. He also cites a survey done among German students that seems further to reinforce this viewpoint.

Dierkens (1957) felt that the more dangerous sexual problems for the adolescent are posed by unsatisfied curiosity, poorly understood taboos, and attitudes of withdrawal from sexual life or of overcompensation. These appear to be fairly standard problems, which confront the adolescent, and often the adult, in most civilized societies. Like most American experts in this field, Dierkens feels that only intelligent and frank sexual education will remedy the existing situation.

Berna (1953), however, found differences as well as similarities in a comparison of the sexual behavior of Swiss adolescents with that of American adolescents. He warns against uncritical acceptance of the various studies of adolescent sexual behavior. There is certainly a justification for such a suggestion in terms both of statistical errors and of problems in sampling, which have been apparent in most of the published studies of this area of behavior. In the various civilized societies there are, of course, some differences in attitudes concerning sexual behavior that result in differences in sexual expression. Nonetheless, the general categories of problems suggested by Dierkens probably do affect adolescents in most societies.

While what is usually considered as normal sex activity is prohibited to the adolescent by various cultural restrictions, less normal or even abnormal patterns are even more condemned. Even patterns that might be considered relatively normal expressions of sexuality, such as masturbation, receive disapproval and harsh condemnation. Such ridiculous statements as "masturbation leads to insanity" are widely proclaimed and have become the source of a good deal of adolescent anxiety. Any evidence of "unnatural" sex behavior, such as homosexuality, usually brings forth vehement social disapproval.

Fielitz (1958) investigated the sexual behavior of young people between the ages of sixteen and twenty in a number of large cities in Germany. He recorded the percentages of response to questions asked of some 4000 adolescents. Thirty-six percent of the boys and 27 per cent of the girls indicated that they were first told "the facts of life" by friends. Fifty-nine per cent of the boys and 53 per cent of the girls were between the ages of thirteen and fifteen when they first learned these facts. To the question "Do you think the institution of marriage is necessary or outdated?" more than 90 per cent of both sexes indicated that it was necessary. About 90 per cent of both sexes responded negatively when asked, "What do you think of a woman who does not want any children?"

Fielitz also attempted to determine what circumstances or objects stimulated the subjects sexually. Thirty-six per cent of the boys and 39 per cent of the girls indicated that alcohol stimulated them sexually, while pictures stimulated 49 per cent of the boys and only 15 per cent of the girls. Sixty-one percent of the boys had premarital sex relations, with between 28 and 44 per cent (the variation was according to the city studied) having had these relations with prostitutes. Thirty per cent of the boys said it was indispensable that a girl enter marriage as a virgin. Fielitz does not feel that youth today is sexually more corrupted and perverse than in the past, but he does feel that the temptations and allurements with which youth is confronted have increased.

Kammerer (1956) pointed out that the development of physical and emotional maturity frequently does not run parallel and also emphasized that the emotional structure of adolescents is different from that of adults. Since sexual drives are often not conscious in early adolescence, at this stage the danger of corruption by others is great. There is also a good deal of playful experimentation and exploratory curiosity; this is the stage at which many boys masturbate. Such behavior is not an indication of bad character, and punishment may only create anxiety. Mere lectures on physiology and morality are not helpful. Rather, these youngsters need to be able to confide in an experienced person who can help them gain an understanding of themselves.

The "Double Standard"

One of the major difficulties in this aspect of development is an apparent double standard in our society. Allegedly the male has greater sexual freedom than the female, and although male sexual activities may not be encouraged, they are apparently condoned. Many people, however, contend that we do not have a true "double standard." Generally, sex irregularities are not condoned in either boys or girls, although boys may be more free to make sexual advances. Such greater freedom on the part of boys, however, causes girls and their parents to be on guard constantly. Further, even the supposed greater freedom of boys may be illusory. Such extended freedom may actually cause trouble, since guilt feelings may result from any sexually aggressive act the young male may make. Thus, the greater freedom to engage in sexual exploration without greater freedom from the development of guilt feelings is not a very positive kind of freedom. The present author would generally agree with this point of view but feels that this description applies primarily to middle-class boys and not generally to lower class ones.

Sexual Deviations

Brief mention should be made of some of the conditions of deviate sexual behavior. Under various circumstances of rejection, strict parental discipline, strong societal taboos, and poor environmental influences, the adolescent may be drawn to an avoidance of the opposite sex. The insecurity that may arise from feeling inadequate and from unpleasant experiences can also contribute to the development of behavior patterns that may be considered socially unacceptable. These patterns include masturbation and homosexuality. Masturbation is rather more accepted by society, although it may cause many fears and guilt feelings to develop in the individual. Kinsey (1948) indicated that masturbation has been generally allowed as a "not too immoral" outlet among the upper social level but reported that "most of the less educated eighty-five per cent of the population still consider masturbation neither moral nor normal." Homosexuality, unlike masturbation, involves another person and in our society is a totally unacceptable pattern.

We do not suggest that homosexual experience will prevent an adolescent from ever making a good heterosexual adjustment. Repeated exposure to such experiences might well result in such failure, but a single such experience or infrequent experiences of this nature may be only a phase leading to heterosexuality. Unfortunately, the adolescent who is suffering from rejections or other difficulties may fall a victim to an adult homosexual and be enmeshed in this problem before he is really aware of its possible negative results.

Increase in Sexual Activity

Petting, premarital intercourse, and teen-age pregnancies all seem to have increased in frequency during the last two decades. The Lynds (1937) mentioned the "rise in the number of secret marriages" among the high-school population they had studied but considered this a relatively "minor school problem." Today, however, there is increasing concern about this problem in the schools. The number of teen-age marriages has increased and so has the number of illicit teen-age pregnancies. Petting appears to have become a common pattern, with Kinsey (1948) having reported that "eighty-eight percent of the male population has engaged in some sort of petting prior to marriage." Ramsey (1943) had reported earlier that about 75 per cent of his sample admitted to kissing in their teens, and a number of them had been involved in manipulation of genitalia and tongue contacts. About 25 per cent of this group admitted to having been involved in petting to a climax without, however, actual penetration. Although it is difficult to document with research, there is evidence that this latter type of behavior has appreciably increased among today's adolescents.

SEX EDUCATION

In recent years, sex education has become more and more a function of the schools. Not only is more information being transmitted through the schools, but it is being introduced at earlier ages. Some ten or fifteen years ago sex education was offered only at the high-school level, but today it is not uncommon to find the topic being introduced in the fifth or sixth grade. Even though the schools are doing more along these lines, the question constantly arises as to whether or not this is an area in which they should be involved.

Many people, particularly in the field of religion, believe that sex education should be handled primarily in the home. Since moral values are an important part of such education, the child should be taught the patterns of such values that are peculiar to his home environment.

Actually, of course, sex education must necessarily begin in the home, since the child will usually ask his first "sex" questions before the age at which he enters school. These will be "simple" questions such as "Where do babies come from?" or "Why does mommy have such a big stomach?" (a common question by a child about a pregnant mother). The way in which such questions are answered at these early ages will have much to do with the child's willingness to discuss such topics with his parents later on, especially during adolescence. If the child does not get simple, direct, and honest answers to his early questions, he is unlikely to ask questions later, probably feeling that his parents do not really know the answers or will not tell him the truth.

Even if one were to agree that ideally the home should be the basic source of sex education, it seems rather apparent that the home is not performing this function very adequately. The modern-day "enlightened" parent seems to be just as inadequate in this respect as were earlier generations. There is no denying that the emotional involvement of parents concerning this topic is a detriment when and if they try to transmit information to their children. The negative aspects of their own sex education and some of their own sexual maladjustments usually interfere with their attempts to be objective with their youngsters.

Desenberg (1947) felt that the home training that youngsters obtain does not build a sex pattern that is positively oriented toward marriage. If discussion about the normal sex act in marriage is discouraged, the youngsters are deprived of adequate education for that event. The taboos that become associated with sex expression do not facilitate positive sex adjustment in marriage. The ideal sex pattern would be one "that associates the maturing biological and psychological desire with the long-term affectional companionship and dependability of marriage."

Much of the sex education of the adolescent is gained from the peer group rather than from the parents, and, obviously, such learning is likely to be highly erroneous. Fielitz's figures, mentioned earlier, of 36 per cent of boys and 27 per cent of girls having learned the facts of life from their friends, seem rather low. Over some nine years the present author has been asking his students, undergraduate and graduate, whether they received their basic sex information at home or from their peer group. At least 90 per cent of some 6000 students have indicated that most of their information came from the peer group.

We do not mean to suggest that parents are derelict in their duties and simply make no efforts to transmit information to their children. Most parents probably do try, but for a variety of reasons their efforts are unsuccessful. Often the parent does not know how much of a response a question merits and may as a result offer either too little or too much information. Sometimes, too, parents wait too long before transmitting information, misjudging the age at which such information would be most appropriate. There have been many humorous anecdotes illustrating these points. With proper acknowledgment to whichever individuals were originally responsible for them, the author would like to repeat two of these:

Seven-year-old Johnny rushed into the house and excitedly asked, "Mommy, where did I come from?" Mother was rather taken aback by this abrupt question but felt she must discuss it. She sat Johnny down and for a full hour discussed such topics as where babies come from, etc. At the end she asked, "Well, now you know, but why were you interested in where you came from?" His simple response was "Billy said he came from Detroit, and I wondered where I came from."

The point of the anecdote is an important one. Because of her own anxiety about properly transmitting sex information to her child, this mother gave far more importance to the question than it deserved. If she had been less anxious, she might first have asked why he wanted to know, thus saving the hour's discussion. One might question the value of her discussion at this stage in the child's development, but it probably did no harm. It is doubtful if there would be much carry-over later, when the child reached pubescence.

The second anecdote illustrates the case of parents' waiting too long and assuming that the child has learned nothing during this waiting period:

Andy, a ten-year-old, had to write a short paper on his origin. He asked his mother where he came from and was told, "The stork brought you." Intrigued, he asked, "Where did you come from?" and received the same answer. "Well," said Andy, "where did Grandma come from?" and again was told that the stork had also brought her. Andy then wrote in his report, "There have been no natural births in our family for three generations."

Humorous or not, this well illustrates the failure of parents to realize that their children do pick up a good deal of sex information from their everyday environment and that their questions should always be answered honestly. Nothing is to be gained from assuming that the child is too young to understand and can wait until a later date for the requested information.

Sometimes, too, the parent bases his estimate of the best time to offer the information on the experience he himself had. With youngsters generally reaching pubescence at an earlier age than their parents did, this kind of reasoning is often erroneous. The mother of a twelve-year-old girl told this author that she was shocked when her daughter told her that she had had her first menstruation. When the author asked if she had discussed this process with her daughter, she replied: "No, I thought she was too young. I didn't have my first menstruation until I was over thirteen and thought she'd have it at about the same age." One might wonder what kind of effect the incidence of first menstruation might have on a youngster who is completely unprepared for it.

The ignorance of males concerning various aspects of sexual behavior was well documented in a study reported by Brown (1948) based on 20,000 subjects in the armed forces. These troops were addressed in small groups by a three-man panel on "Sex: Fallacies, Facts, and Problems." Questions were answered frankly and without reservation. The majority of questions revealed widespread sex ignorance. Most of the questions dealt with birth control, orgasms, sterility, craving for sex, homosexuality, masturbation, menstruation, overindulgence, pregnancy, and "sex determination." Brown felt that these results emphasize the need for frank, adult, popular sex education presented without "moralistic values." He felt that the traditional "sex lecture" is "grossly inadequate" and that our colleges and high schools should present more meaningful courses.

Frank (1951) had also suggested that traditional methods of sex education based upon shame, threat, and punishment are defeating the aspirations of parents for their children. Simple transmission of facts about sex is useless without the development of wholesome emotional attitudes. Sex education should take place continuously in the family patterns of living and in the ways in which affection is expressed or denied. He felt that our task is to show that sex is part of the relationship between people and that sex relationships depend upon the wholeness of our personalities.

Frumkin (1953) has divided sex education into two phases: providing sex information and providing sex education. Sex information, which involves teaching the biological facts, should be the province of the school. Sex education, which involves "the development of attitudes conducive to healthy living," should be handled by the home. Yet, realistically, it is difficult to separate the two aspects, even if one can actually make such a differentiation. School personnel who do attempt to transmit only the biological facts find that the student's interests go well beyond this point. The youngsters want more information of the type mentioned in the study by Brown. They are interested in and concerned about values and moral attitudes as well as about biological facts. Offering one without the other is a difficult task and perhaps an impossible one.

Most schools do not wish to delve too deeply into the value and attitudinal aspects of sexual behavior for fear of coming into conflict with the specific values and attitudes of individual parents. Since they would be involved in a highly emotionalized area, caution in this respect is probably advisable. It has been suggested that parents be invited into the schools to discuss these topics before they are discussed with the youngster. Then teachers and parents might at least develop a general framework within which to structure the discussions with the youngsters. Unfortunately, the parents who might benefit most from such discussions are least likely to attend them. They are also likely to be the parents who would disagree most with the information transmitted by the teacher.

ADOLESCENT ATTITUDES TOWARD MARRIAGE

By late adolescence, most young people of both sexes begin to look forward to marriage and to become interested in selecting mates. Although a number of colleges offer courses in "Marriage and the Family," not many high schools do so. One does not have to be contemplating an early marriage to become concerned about this topic. Even those adolescents who plan to wait until their advanced education is complete before they marry are interested in learning as much as they can about ways of insuring a happy and lasting marriage.

There are sex differences in the characteristics that are important in marriage, but there is also a good deal of similarity in the two sexes. Christensen (1947) indicated that members of both sexes "tend to emphasize about the same things when it comes to picking a partner for marriage." Both are particularly concerned about such personality traits as dependability and emotional maturity. The males he studied stressed "attractiveness, popularity, homemaking ability, education and ambition, similarity of background, prospects for normal children, and chastity."

It has been suggested that girls today are oriented less toward marriage and more toward careers than was formerly the case. Many of those who do contemplate marriage plan to combine it with their careers. It is not unusual for females to plan their job futures to include marriage and raising a family. Generally, these girls plan to "take time off" to raise their families and then return to work at about the time their children are all attending school. Many of those who married and had their children before they had ever been employed are now seeking education or training for a variety of occupations. Teaching has become attractive to many who plan to combine marriage and a career. It is a field to which they will probably be able to return after their children have grown up, and its working hours enable them to be home during most of the time that their children are there and also to share the school vacations with their children.

The results of a survey by the Girl Scout organization to determine how "adolescent girls are resolving the conflict between homemaking and career" were presented by Dixon (1958). Generally, the girls wanted to continue their education and to be employed for some time before marrying. They also expressed a preference for white-collar jobs for themselves and their husbands. Three per cent of the group said they wished to become housewives only. One-third indicated that they wanted a college education.

Some of the factors and attitudes involved in the relationships leading to marriage have been investigated. Benson (1955) studied the theory that common interests are related to marital adjustment. He found that the number of common interests *per se* had only a small relationship, the type of interests the couple have in common being more important than the number. "Mutuality of interests classified as familistic was found to be favorably related to adjustment, and mutuality of individualistic interests unfavorably related to adjustment."

Walters and Ojemann (1952) constructed tests to determine the attitudes adolescents express "when presented with a variety of situations in which they can place the woman in a superordinate, partnership, or subordinate role." When discussing their sisters, three-fifths of the group chose the partnership role. Wives were more often placed in a subordinate role. Boys placed girls in a superordinate role in the education area more frequently than did the girls themselves. Girls tended to place girls more often in the partnership role in both work and education. The partnership role tended to be somewhat more popular with girls than with boys.

The conclusions in this study seem to reflect the cultural patterns that prevail in our society. There has been a relatively rapid change in the position assigned to women both in marriage and in occupations. Some time ago, girls were expected to make a career of marriage and homemaking and generally to hold a subordinate position to their husbands. Today girls consider occupational careers other than homemaking and view marriage as a partnership in which they have an equal share.

Adolescents, especially boys, who generally view women as subordinate in marriage, are probably only partially aware of these changes. Payne (1956) found that boys in the eighth through the twelfth grades generally were opposed, at least at the verbal level, to having their wives work after marriage, while the girls expected to work after marriage. Payne felt that "the divergence of opinions could cause confusion and disappointment for the boys during the later years." The boys apparently did not anticipate a need for their wives to work outside the home. Boys evidently need help in developing a more practical orientation to the concept of wives being employed, since their viewpoint seems somewhat out-of-date.

Hoover (1950) administered an attitude scale to assess attitudes toward mixed (Catholic–non-Catholic) marriages. More girls than boys in Catholic high schools were opposed to such marriages. If the student lived in a predominantly Catholic locale and if both parents were Catholic, the negative attitude toward mixed marriage was strengthened. Students attending co-educational high schools were more opposed to mixed marriage than those attending sex-segregated schools. Generally, the brighter children from happier homes tended to oppose mixed marriage.

Early Marriages

There seems no doubt that marriages of high-school students are increasing. Most schools do not have a clear position on student marriage. Some encourage married students (at least females) to withdraw from school. There seems to be almost a fear that if the married student remains in school she will "contaminate" the others or encourage a rash of quick marriages. Other schools, however, view marriage as an acceptable situation.

The attitude of discouraging the married adolescents from completing their education is rather unrealistic. It is difficult enough for a teen-age couple to make a successful marriage without being so penalized. Many youngsters who get married do plan to continue their education, even beyond high school. Even though many of the young married girls plan to go to work to help their husbands go on to higher educational levels, they hope at least to complete high school themselves. Many girls plan to achieve a college education when their husbands have finished their education, or to attend college at the same time as their husbands. Certainly such plans are destroyed if a school does not allow these youngsters to complete their secondary education.

High-School Courses in Family Living

The need for education for family at the high-school level is becoming widely recognized. Landis (1956) has suggested that such a course would have to be given to freshmen, since many sophomores will marry.

He felt that, in view of the number of high-school students who are marrying, schools need to take a rational look at the problems involved.

Perhaps, if our schools offered courses in family living, they might change their attitude toward the married student. The recognition of a need for such courses and proper handling of them should carry over into the thinking of school authorities concerning teen-age marriages. Force (1950) has summed up some of the important facts learned from her ten-year high-school experiment in education for family living. She feels that the more immediate and visible goals of such a course, rather than its long-term aims, should be transmitted to the students. She also feels that mental health should be stressed, rather than mate selection, and that cooperation of parents and community should be elicited. If the community is involved, then the schools obviously become involved, and, hopefully, in a positive direction.

Perry (1949) felt that courses in the secondary schools should approach family living from at least three directions: through social experiences; through the individual's better understanding of himself; and through dissemination of information to high-school youth. Testing, counseling, and other procedures could usefully be employed to develop better self-understanding. Parties, dancing, and other social activities would help develop greater social adaptability. Study of such topics as courtship, heredity, first sexual adjustments in marriage, pregnancy, and preparation for parenthood would help the individual better understand physical aspects of development.

Attitude Toward Parenthood

Heron (1952) questioned adolescents about their attitudes toward parenthood. A special attempt was made to relate the idea of educational preparation for child rearing. Children ranging in age from twelve to seventeen, from both rural and industrial areas, were queried. About two-thirds of the group favored education for parenthood, and a majority, although a lower percentage, specifically supported such training in the school. Girls exceeded boys in agreement on the latter point. There were no marked differences between the area groups in this regard.

Remmers and Drucker (1951) investigated the attitude of adolescents toward problems of child management by means of Stedman's scale, Attitudes Toward Child Behavior. The scores generally related positively to age, maturation, and educational influences, and tended to be higher if either parent had had higher education. Girls received higher scores than boys, and as a result it was suggested that boys should receive more school training regarding child management.

THE ADOLESCENT'S NEED FOR ADULT GUIDANCE

No one is more aware than the adolescent himself of his need for assistance in making a good heterosexual adjustment. This extremely important area of adolescent development is one that the youngster enters with no previous experience. He must develop new skills, such as that of dancing, with which he previously was unconcerned or toward which his attitude was perhaps negative. As a result, this is the area in which the teen-ager would most welcome adult understanding and assistance. Yet, as the reader has no doubt become aware in the previous sections of this chapter, such understanding and assistance are frequently not available.

The adolescent is often rebuffed by adults even in his attempts to make relatively simple adjustments. For example, his attempts to become more involved in conversation with adults often meet with failure. The adults generally fail to realize that the youngster is trying to improve his conversational skills and is also seeking information. He wants to learn more about the ways in which adults discuss various topics and often needs some explanation of points adults find self-explanatory. In particular, many teen-agers resent their parents' unwillingness to discuss their friends, especially those of whom the adults disapprove. A youngster is told not to associate with a particular member of his peer group but is seldom allowed to discuss this individual's good qualities. Any attempt to do so is usually met with "You're not old enough to judge, so you'll simply have to abide by our decision."

When an adolescent has difficulty in discussing generalities with his parents and other adults, it is even more difficult for him to discuss important specifics, such as sexual behavior. Most teen-agers come to feel that adults usually "don't even listen" when the youngster talks to them. At most they expect to receive only a cursory response to statements or questions directed at adults. What they desire most of all is someone who really listens to what they have to say.

Here, again, there is an appreciable difference between younger and older teen-agers. It is the young teen-ager who is most eager to seek adult help, especially because he finds that the members of his peer group are as "mixed up" as he is. Yet, because of his age, he is still viewed as a child by most adults and treated accordingly. The older teen-ager, on the other hand, has succeeded in achieving rapport with adults, who are more willing to accept him because of his greater maturity. However, if the older teen-ager was discouraged in his earlier attempts to gain adult acceptance, he may avoid adults and rely exclusively on his peer group for his interaction.

The following case studies illustrate both these situations. Alice

C., now eighteen, described her difficulties in adjustment but discussed how helpful her parents had been:

"When I was about thirteen I started wanting to talk to my parents about a lot of things that were new to me. In particular I wanted to discuss some of the other kids with them to find out what qualities adults consider important in choosing friends. My parents were always patient and listened to my questions carefully. Although I think now that some of the comments I made amused them, they always responded in a serious vein. I felt I could ask them anything and be sure they'd consider my questions as important to me. I really found them very helpful in any discussion, including some excellent talks concerning sex. Here, again, they gave me their own honest viewpoint without moralizing. I do discuss a lot of things with my friends, and sometimes I feel sorry for them. It's obvious that many of them can't talk to their parents as freely as I do to mine. As a result they have to depend on each other for help, and there are many problems where this is not sufficient. Sometimes they come up with some silly and often erroneous answers because they have no adult to help them. Most of them wish they could talk to their parents but they claim their parents don't listen or don't want to talk about many things that the kids are interested in. As a result of seeing all this, I now really appreciate my parents more than ever."

Contrast this with the almost opposite situation described by Sally R., also eighteen:

"I've never been able to talk to my parents about any of the things that interest me. Even when I was a little girl I seldom got any answers. Either I was told my questions were silly or that I was too young to discuss such matters. When I reached adolescence I really was poorly prepared for some of the things that happened. I had heard the other girls talking about menstruation, but I was rather frightened when it happened to me. When I told my mother about it, she asked our physician to explain things to me. He did and I was quite satisfied with his explanation, but I can't understand why my mother couldn't have told me. I think I would have preferred to have received the information from her and before it happened. I could never discuss my friends with my parents. If they didn't like one of my friends, they'd tell me, but wouldn't tell me why. They were particularly arbitrary, it seems to me, about boys I saw, especially when I started dating. As a result of this I just don't even try to discuss problems with them. I talk to my friends about these things, even though I know some of their answers are probably wrong or at least not appropriate for me. In a way I'm rather lucky. Last year I had a teacher who really listened to me and could discuss things with me very objectively. She did really help a lot, but I still wish my parents were the ones who had helped. I know they love me but I'm sure they don't understand me. What bothers me now is my fifteen-year-old sister. She's getting the same treatment I got and I really feel sorry for her. I try to help and we do discuss a lot of things, but I think it would be much better if she could talk to our parents."

These cases may represent the two extremes; many youngsters have neither as much nor as little contact with their parents. Often teenagers feel that they can talk to their parents, but only about certain topics. Many think their parents are rather inconsistent, in that they will patiently discuss a topic on one occasion but "brush it off" on another occasion.

Perhaps the most difficult topic for youngsters to discuss with adults is sex. Too often they find that instead of getting honest, objective answers, they receive instead emotional moralizing. This is the one thing adolescents do not want. Mere verbalization of various cultural taboos is not enough: teen-agers want to know why the particular behavior is wrong, not simply that it is wrong. This criticism is leveled equally at parents and at teachers and counselors. When the discussion involves sex, most youngsters feel that communication with adults is quite poor.

Many questions dealing with sex problems might be discussed relatively easily. Adolescents, especially the younger ones, are not primarily concerned with major issues, such as sexual intercourse. They are interested in knowing whether to kiss a girl on the first date, whether to engage in necking, how to keep boys from making advances, and the like.

Jeannie C. went to a club meeting with a group of her fourteen-year-old girl friends. The conversation had centered around a dance all were attending the following week and for most of them it was to be the first date for which they would be inviting a boy. The girls were discussing whether or not to allow the boys to kiss them good night, since it would be the first date for many of them. One of the girls who had already dated a number of times assured the group that kissing was necessary if you wanted to be popular. "But," asked one girl, "suppose you don't like the boy enough to want him to kiss you?" Her friend suggested she let him kiss her anyway, since he might tell other boys she wasn't much fun and she'd have trouble getting other dates. This led to a discussion in which there was a good deal of disagreement on the topic. Jeannie later discussed the matter with her parents, who tried to help her to reach a good solution to the problem.

Too many young girls do feel that they must neck, kiss, and/or pet in order to be popular with boys. Many boys feel they must be able to "make out" on a date in order to achieve status with their peers. Even boys who are not so inclined will often verbalize fictitious adventures, in order that their friends will consider them fully masculine. Parents are particularly concerned that such activity may lead to sexual intercourse, unintentionally perhaps, if the youngsters become too aroused sexually. Therefore, they usually try to keep their youngsters from this level of involvement, frequently by inducing fear of the consequences of such an act. Such parents stress possible pregnancy, possible venereal disease contact, and other negative aspects of the situation. A wiser parent will employ a more positive approach, encouraging the youngster to have a high level of self-regard and an awareness of the implications of such activities on later dating and marital success. A secure youngster with a positive self-concept is unlikely to get involved in sexual situations that get out of control.

Sally G. was sixteen years old, very attractive, and extremely popular with boys. Some of her jealous peers kept suggesting that she must let the boys "make out" in order to be that popular. Quite the opposite was true. Boys enjoyed Sally's company and felt at ease with her. The few who did make passes quickly found out that such behavior was not acceptable. Sally would explain to a boy making such attempts that although she enjoyed his company, she would not see him again if his major interest in her was sexual. Strangely, few of the boys she had to say this to resented it and most of them kept seeing her. Sally told her mother, "I think the boys are actually relieved when I stop them. They seem to feel they have to try to show how male they are, but I think they're a little ashamed of the attempt." Sally is not a prude by any means. Rather, she is a poised, intelligent girl who knows what she wants and is capable of handling any situation well.

A girl less skilled in fending off advances might well antagonize the boys. This could be detrimental and could even lead to a bad, although undeserved, reputation. This latter kind of situation was explained to our seminar by Rick G., who was discussing a problem that his sixteen-year-old sister had had.

"My sister suddenly began to have a reputation as a girl who would let the boys make sexual advances. It got pretty bad, and almost every time she went out she came home in tears. When I found out I got real upset. I know my sister isn't that kind of girl. I talked to her about it, and began checking around. What I found out was sickening, but I realized I had done the same thing once or twice myself. One of the boys who had dated my sister had made a pass and she slapped his face. He got mad, and after he took her home, he met some of his buddies and told them how 'easy' she had been. His friends then made dates, and they, too, were quick to find that my sister wasn't that kind of girl. They didn't want to admit that they had been rebuffed and couldn't be as successful as their friends. So each one lied, embellishing his alleged experiences to make it sound better than the first boy's story. It didn't take long for my sister to get a bad reputation which even some of her girl friends believed. I knocked a few heads together and got some of the fellows to tell the truth. It helped, but rumors always persisted. Sis handled herself very well and only went out with fellows she knew well and could trust. There is no real malice necessarily involved in this kind of situation."

The young man involved might have been very much ashamed of his actions but had an even greater fear of being considered inadequate by his peers. Overemphasis on the importance of sexual prowess can easily lead to such negative behavior. If youngsters could discuss these matters freely with adults who could try to help them understand proper behavior codes, many of these problems would be far less severe.

One of the major criticisms of adults offered by teen-agers is that they have forgotten that they, too, were once adolescents. Adults will condemn behavior patterns no different from those that they themselves followed as youngsters. An adult does not have to like Rock and Roll, but to most youngsters it is no worse than the Charleston and the Big Apple were in their time, or than the Twist is now. It is not the dance *per se* that is important to the adolescent but dancing as part of the development of heterosexual behavior.

Adult criticism of such adolescents' organizations as fraternities and sororities is also disturbing to youngsters. Most of these organizations attempt to emulate the patterns of adult organizations, at least as the youngsters perceive these organizations. "My dad criticizes the rituals we have in our fraternity, but every Thursday night he puts on the weirdest uniform and heads for his lodge meeting. When he discusses some of their rituals, it's all I can do to keep from laughing." Apparently, however, this father sees no relationship between his activities and those of his son.

One might go on endlessly mentioning such specifics, but the point needs no further expansion. Although the two generations seem to be a world apart, in many ways they are really more alike than they are different.

This author is constantly amazed to find that teachers who deal daily with adolescents really know nothing about them. Each semester, after one of the teen-age panels in the seminar already mentioned has discussed some topic relating to adolescence, the students, all professional teachers, express amazement at how "sharp these kids are." They seem completely unaware that similar "sharp kids" are in their own classes every day. The difference is that in the seminar environment they listen to the youngsters and interact freely with them, without worrying about their own authority.

In this environment they also seem more willing to accept the youngsters as equals and to be interested in hearing their point of view. In the classroom, the teachers are concerned about transmitting information, maintaining discipline, etc., and apparently are not well aware of the students as individuals, thinking of them rather as members of a group.

Many adolescents are willing and eager to talk to any adult who will listen. Just give them the chance and they're hard to stop. Remember, they are not always seeking answers; they simply want to communicate. If communication can be established, many problems, even in the difficult area of heterosexual development, are easier to solve. If adults will listen, the reward is great.

REFERENCES

BENSON, PURNELL. "The Common Interests Myth in Marriage." *Social Problems*, 3, 27-34, 1955.

BERNA, JACQUES. "Das Sexuelle Verhalter de Jugendlichen" (Sexual Behavior of Adolescents). *Psyche, Heidelberg* (Heidelberg), 6, 161-171, 1953.

BROWN, D. G. "Masculinity-Femininity Development in Children." *Journal of Consulting Psychology*, 21, 197-202, 1957.

BROWN, FRED. "What American Men Want to Know About Sex." *Journal of Social Psychology*, 27, 119-125, 1948.

CAMPBELL, W. J. "Preference of Children for Others of the Same or Opposite Sex." *Australian Journal of Psychology*, 7, 45-51, 1955.

CHRISTENSEN, HAROLD T. "Student Views on Mate Selection." *Marriage and Family Living*, 9, 85-88, 1947.

CHRISTENSEN, HAROLD T. "Courtship Conduct as Viewed by Youth." *Journal of Home Economics*, 40, 187-188, 1948.

CHRISTENSEN, HAROLD T. "Dating Behavior as Evaluated by High School Students." *American Journal of Sociology*, 57, 580-586, 1952.

CRIST, JOHN R. "High School Dating as a Behavior System." *Marriage and Family Living*, 15, 23-28, 1953.

DESENBERG, BERNARD N. "Home Sex Education and Monogamy." *Marriage and Family Living*, 9, 89-92, 1947.

DIERKENS, J. "Les problems sexuels posés par l'adolescence" (Sexual Problems Posed by Adolescence). *Revue Belgede Psychologie Pedagogie* (Belgium), 19, 14-18, 1957.

DIXON, MARGUERITE M. "Adolescent Girls Tell About Themselves." *Marriage and Family Living*, 20, 400-401, 1958.

ELIAS, L. J. *High School Youth Look at Their Problems.* Pullman, Wash.: The College Bookstore, State College of Washington, 1949.

FAUNCE, DALE, and BEEGLE, J. ALLAN. "Cleavages in a Relatively Homogeneous Group of Rural Youth." *Sociometry,* 11, 207-216, 1948.

FIELITZ, FRANZ. "Natuerliches and Wiedernatuerliches im Geschlechtsleben der Grosstadtjugend" (Natural and Unnatural Aspects of the Sexual Life of Youth in Metropolitan Areas). *Psychologische Rundschau* (Basel), 9, 113-127, 1958.

FORCE, ELIZABETH S. "High School Education for Family Living." *Annals of the American Academy of Political and Social Science,* 272 (Nov.), 156-162, 1950.

FRANK, LAWRENCE K. "Newer Approaches to Sex Education." *Pastoral Psychology,* 1 (10), 19-24, 1951.

FRUMKIN, ROBERT M. "Who Should Provide Sex Education?" *Ohio Parent-Teacher,* 32, 15-17, 1953.

HERON, ALASTAIR. "Adolescents and Preparation for Parenthood." *British Journal of Educational Psychology,* 22, 173-179, 1952.

HILL, T. J. "Dating Patterns and Family Position." *Clearing House,* 29, 552-554, 1955.

HOOVER, HARRY F. *Attitudes of High School Students Toward Mixed Marriage.* Washington, D. C.: Catholic University of America Press, 1950.

KAMMERER, GERHARD. "Wie Verhalt sich der Lehrer bei sexuellen Verfehlungen von Schulern?" (How Does the Teacher Behave Toward Sexual Misdeeds of Pupils?) *Heilpadägogische Werkblätter* (Germany), 25, 98-104, 1956.

KINSEY, A. D., POMEROY, W. B., and MARTIN, C. E. *Sexual Behavior in Human Male.* Philadelphia: W. B. Saunders, 1948.

KINSEY, A. D., POMEROY, W. B., and MARTIN, C. E. *Sexual Behavior in Human Female.* Philadelphia: W. B. Saunders, 1953.

KIRKENDALL, L. A. "Sex Problems of Adolescents." *Marriage Hygiene* (Bombay), 1, 205-208, 1948.

LANDIS, JUDSON T. "Attitudes and Policies Concerning Marriages among High School Students." *Marriage and Family Living,* 18, 128-136, 1956.

LOWRIE, SAMUEL H. "Dating, a Neglected Field of Study." *Marriage and Family Living,* 10, 90-91; 95, 1948.

LOWRIE, SAMUEL H. "Sex Differences and Age of Initial Dating." *Social Forces,* 30, 456-461, 1952.

LYND, R. S., and LYND, H. M. *Middletown in Transition.* New York: Harcourt Brace, 1937.

LYNN, D. B. "A Note on Sex Differences in the Development of Masculine and Feminine Identification." *Psychological Reports,* 66, 126-135, 1959.

MUSSEN, P. H. "Some Antecedents and Consequents of Masculine Sex-Typing in Adolescent Boys." *Psychological Monographs,* vol. 75, no. 2, 1961.

NEISSER, EDITH G. *When Children Start Dating.* Chicago: Science Research Associates, 1951.

PAYNE, RAYMOND. "Adolescents' Attitudes Toward the Working Wife." *Marriage and Family Living,* 18, 345-348, 1956.

PERRY, W. D. "Some Approaches to Education for Family Living for Secondary Schools." *Marriage and Family Living,* 11, 41, 1949.

POWELL, MARVIN. "Age and Sex Differences in Degree of Conflict within Certain Areas of Psychological Adjustment." *Psychological Monographs,* vol. 69, no. 2, 1955.

PUNKE, H. H. "Dating Practices of High School Pupils." *Bulletin of the National Association of Secondary School Principals,* 28, 47-54, 1944.

RAMSEY, G. V. "The Sex Information of Younger Boys." *American Journal of Orthopsychiatry,* 13, 347-352, 1943.

REMMERS, H. H., and DRUCKER, A. J. "Teen-agers' Attitudes toward Problems of Child Management." *Journal of Educational Psychology,* 42, 105-113, 1951.

TRESSELT, MARGARET E. "The Adolescent Becomes a Social Person." *Journal of Social Hygiene,* 40, 130-134, 1954.

UNDEUTSCH, UDO. "Die Sexualitat im Jugendalter" (Adolescent Sex Behavior). *Studium Generale* (Berlin), 3, 433-454, 1950.

WALTERS, JAMES, and OJEMANN, RALPH H. "A Study of the Components of Adolescent Attitudes Concerning the Role of Women." *Journal of Social Psychology,* 35, 101-110, 1952.

ZUK, G. H. "Sex-Appropriate Behavior in Adolescence." *Journal of Genetic Psychology,* 93, 15-32, 1958.

CHAPTER 8

The Home and the Family

The home has long been acknowledged to be the basic unit within which the individual develops. In this unit, which is the primary source of socialization, the individual learns how his society functions and develops the behavior patterns that enable him to function effectively within that society. Many of the values, attitudes, and interests that are part of an individual's adult behavior had their beginnings and indeed were often fully crystallized through the early influences of the home and the family.

Yet it is within this basic unit that a good deal of the conflict between the adolescent and the adult world takes place, primarily because parents are the adults with whom youngsters have most contact. These conflict patterns usually begin at pubescence and are seldom evidenced before that time. While conflict may occur between parents and younger children, it is not as frequent or as intense as the conflict that is present during adolescence.

SOURCES OF CONFLICT IN THE HOME

English (1947) feels that adolescence is not the happy time it should be because adults often add more conflict to the period than is necessary. Adults have many concerns, among them that the adolescent will not be obedient, that he will not be a hard worker, that he will not be cooperative or grateful, and/or that he will go astray sexually. Because of these and other fears, the parent is constantly anxious and too frequently admonishes or scolds the youngster even when such action is not warranted. Rather than helping, parents may often restrict or inhibit the adolescent's strivings to choose a vocation and to obtain the proper education for it. They further restrict the youngster's attempts to emancipate himself, to make friends with his own and the opposite sex, and to integrate his own behavior.

It is completely normal for the adolescent to begin to seek emancipation from the home at this stage in his development. After he passes puberty he is in a sense already emancipated. The culture in which we live, however, prevents such emancipation from taking place at the time of pubescence. The adolescent must remain dependent on his home environment because the society is not ready to accord him adult status. Prolonged educational requirements, limited vocational opportunities, and even legal definitions keep him dependent for five to seven years after sexual maturity has been reached.

The Need for Emancipation

We are, however, well aware that the degree to which the adolescent can emancipate himself during adolescence will have a definite influence on his continued development of independence as an adult. If he is unable to gain any independence at this level, he may remain dependent on his home environment through most of his adult life. He may actually come to accept parental domination and prefer it to facing the rigors of life to which independence may expose him. If such a dependent individual marries, he may seek out a mate who will dominate him and upon whom he can depend in much the same way as that in which he depended on his parents. He may seek to maintain his former relationship with his parents after marriage, even to the extent of continuing to live with them.

Most parents tend to feel a little unhappy at seeing their youngsters grow up and need them less. They often realize that these are evidences that the youngster will soon be leaving the home, either to continue his education or to seek employment. Yet most parents also recognize that the adolescent must have enough experiences in developing independent behavior to give him a base upon which to build his later patterns of independent behavior. Although it causes them many anxious moments, wise parents try to interfere as little as possible in the youngsters' attempts to emancipate themselves.

Even in homes in which the parents do try to help the youngster, there is likely to be conflict. Parents are often inconsistent in their treatment of the teen-ager; they may treat him as an adult at one moment, and at the next moment as a child. The adolescent is himself often responsible for such treatment, since he may alternate between adult and childish behavior. When childish behavior is exhibited, the parent who is ready to give his child more independence may have some doubts of the wisdom of such a move.

Parents often put undue pressure on their children in an attempt to help them avoid some of the pitfalls they themselves have experienced in growing up. They are surprised and often hurt to find the teen-ager rejecting such attempts and persisting in having his own experiences firsthand. After he has had the experience himself, the adolescent may realize that his parents were right and were actually trying to help him. He may eventually come to accept his parents' ideas about some of the things he might well avoid, but he will not accept all their views. He will continue to seek a number of experiences for himself, and this is probably a positive kind of reaction. These experiences will help him develop patterns of behavior appropriate to adult life. He cannot and actually should not live his life vicariously through the experiences of his parents.

Parental Choice of Goals

Parents not uncommonly set goals that really are not appropriate or even realistic for their children. They may be motivated by what they consider the child's best interests, but they may, on the other hand, set such goals as a means of satisfying some basic needs of their own. In either case the goal may not satisfy the needs of the child or even be possible in terms of his abilities, interests, or temperament.

This kind of goal setting was most conspicuous in the immigrant groups that came to this country some forty or fifty years ago. These people were determined for their children to have all the advantages that they themselves had lacked. They placed a high premium on education, and the ultimate goal was for the child to become a "professional man" or at least become in some way self-employed. This was understandable, since many of these immigrants were members of minority groups, subject to the whims of their employers. As a result, they virtually forced their youngsters into vocations that they felt were important, regardless of the individual youngster's own desires. If the youngster lacked the ability to achieve the high goal set for him, the parents' disappointment in his failure often resulted in a rejection (usually unconscious) of the youngster. Again, it is difficult to be critical of such parental desires, but, carried to extremes, they do often become the source of a great deal of severe conflict with the youngster involved.

One must keep in mind the fact that parents are usually trying to be helpful even though the means they employ may bring forth a negative reaction. As adults, most of us can see in retrospect that this was true with our own parents, though we may also realize that the goals they set for us were actually inappropriate. But at the time these situations actually occur, they are not always positively perceived, perhaps because of the very immaturity the adolescent is seeking to overcome. In some cases the adult pressure is too great, and the adolescent is unwillingly propelled toward the parent-set goal. In other cases the adolescent may fight back, even employing negative means to counteract the parental pressure. Such effort may be an unconscious reaction to stress, which sometimes actually penalizes the individual, but at the time seems the best method to use.

Martin P's parents decided early in his life that he should become a dentist, and constantly pressured him toward this goal. Martin was unable to fight back directly, but he did not want to be a dentist. Although he had been an excellent student in high school, by his second year of college he was in danger of flunking out. Obviously no dental college would accept a student with such poor grades. Martin seemed as bewildered as his parents at his apparent inability to do college work. After a three-year stint in the armed forces, Martin returned to college to pursue a goal he had decided on while in the service. Parental pressure was no longer an influence. His grades were again excellent and he achieved the advanced degree of his choice.

It seems rather obvious that this apparent inability to achieve good grades in college was Martin's way of protesting against parental pressure. His own bewilderment at his inability to do better indicates that his actions were unconscious ones, since he would not admit to himself that he was trying to fail. Such an admission would probably have aroused intense guilt feelings.

Separation from the Family

A teen-ager living with his parents might reasonably be expected to make a better adjustment than one who is separated from them. Sklarew (1959) did find that adolescent boys separated early from their parents made a poorer adjustment than those who were not, but that the reverse was true of girls. Laufer (1953) discussed casework involving adolescent girls who, for one reason or another, must separate from the parents. The girls were living in a girls' club that removed them from the family environment to which they had been unable to adjust. In working with both the girls and their parents, Sklarew found that these youngsters develop a variety of problems, but that these are often not as bad as, or at least no worse than, the problems that envelop the parents. Such parents are usually subject to strong feelings of guilt, insecurity, and uncertainty that are aggravated by the separation.

The Purpose of Rebellion

Teen-age rebellion is actually not as serious a problem as is often thought. One must remember, as Gallagher (1953) has pointed out, that it is really an attempt at independence. He further stressed the necessity for such a developmental stage if the adolescent is to become a mature, responsible adult. He also suggested that the dependency parents may create is often caused by their own insecurities and anxieties and warned against overdomination and overprotection by parents.

PREADOLESCENTS AND EARLY ADOLESCENTS IN RELATION
TO THEIR FAMILIES

Preadolescents, and more especially early adolescents, are interested in learning as much about adult patterns of behavior as possible. They try to understand how adults behave, and why they behave as they do. Unfortunately, their perceptions are not always accurate and they often fail to interpret behavior as adults do. These false perceptions are partially the result of the youngster's own social, emotional, and intellectual immaturity, but they are also partly caused by the way in which adults often behave. That is, adult behavior may be inconsistent, or what seems to be positive overt behavior may actually be motivated by negative feelings. Youngsters are often aware that the behavior of adults does not always correspond to the behavior that they tell their children is proper.

Hawkes *et al.* administered a set of questions concerning the degree of involvement in family activities, treatment in homes, and relations with parents to a sample of more than 700 fifth-grade children ("Preadolescents' Views of Some of Their Relations with Their Parents," 1957). The responses indicated a considerable degree of involvement in family activities and general satisfaction with the treatment received. Girls reported more satisfactory relations with their parents than the boys did. Although various characteristics of both parents were rated favorably by the children, mothers were seen more favorably than were fathers. The same investigators also reported on "Measurement of Pre-adolescents' Views of Family Control of Behavior" (1957). The children's perceptions of parental control of their behavior were in line with that considered desirable from the point of view of mental health. There were no significant differences between the sexes. Generally, it would appear that preadolescent youngsters feel that their parents' controls of their behavior are positive and that they find the controls acceptable.

Crane (1956) asked a group of twelve- to fifteen-year-old youngsters to write essays on "The Sort of Person I Would Like to Be When I Grow Up." Boys emphasized possession of money and a secure job; girls emphasized good looks and a kind disposition. Girls were generally in greater agreement than boys. These stereotypes remain essentially the same after age thirteen. Apparently these are the characteristics that these youngsters perceive to be important to adults.

An attempt to evaluate the accuracy of parental understanding of children's feelings in regard to self-adjustment and social adjustment was reported by Langford (1954). Forty twelve-year-old children (20 boys and 20 girls) and the parents of these children were given the California Test of Personality. The parents were asked to answer the questions as they thought their children would answer them. Generally, parents underestimated the children's responses in the self-adjustment area and overestimated them in the area of social adjustment. However, their estimates were closer to those of the children in the latter area than in the former. Father-son accuracy was greater than mother-son, mother-daughter, or father-daughter accuracy. The findings of this study might lead one to conclude that adults' estimates of children's behavior are in their own way as inaccurate as children's perceptions of adult behavior.

In general, while children are preadolescent or just post-pubescent, conflict between them and their parents is relatively limited. However, if conflict is present during these early stages, it is likely to become intensified as the youngster moves further into the adolescent period. Specifically, then, the general atmosphere of the home during an individual's childhood will be a major determinant of his behavior in the home during adolescence.

THE ADOLESCENT WITHIN THE FAMILY

The family to which the adolescent belongs is the most significant determinant of his behavior, and the various standards that will guide him throughout his life are set in the home. Emphasizing this point of view, Erickson (1956) listed some of the family factors that may influence the acceptance or rejection of an adolescent. These include foreign-born parents, the majority or minority status of the religious group to which the adolescent belongs, and the parent's occupation. Broken homes, resulting from divorce, separation, abandonment, illegitimacy, or death of a parent, were also listed as major factors. Other factors included attitudes toward money, birth order, and the odd child, who may be the only boy in a family of girls or vice versa. In Erickson's frame of reference, every family unit is a unique institution, and adolescence is not a period but a process that has as its result the achieving of wholesome attitudes and habits.

Connor et al. (1954) asked female college students to respond to a questionnaire designed to discover whether the numbers of and types of expressed parent-adolescent conflicts changed between the high-school period and the time that the study was made. The similarities and differences in the backgrounds of the students and the type of adolescent conflict expressed were also evaluated. The largest single group of expressed conflicts centered about dating and mate selection. Contrary to Erickson's findings, parent-adolescent conflicts were not significantly related to student's age, education, ordinal position, family size, place of residence, or occupations of fathers and mothers.

Yoda and Kuse (1957) administered a questionnaire to junior- and senior-high-school students in an attempt to investigate parent-adolescent relationships. Their findings indicated that adolescents' feelings of independence gradually increase and that the adolescents' feelings of independence from parents reflect a variety of content. Boys evidenced stronger feelings of independence than girls did.

Family Size

Teen-age adjustment in relation to family size was studied by Landis ("Teenage Adjustments in Large and Small Families," 1954), who wished to determine how size of family affects personality development and whether a small family (one to three children) or a large family (four or more children) creates a more advantageous environment for personality development. The data indicated that size of family accounts for some notable differences in family patterns and is reflected in differences in attitudes, family experiences, achievements, and teen-age problems that carry over even into college. The results, however, were not at all conclusive as to which size of family is best suited to prepare youth for adulthood. Damrin (1949) reported no significant differences in her study of family size in relation to adjustment and school achievement of high-school girls, whereas Nye's study (1952) indicated that smaller families seem to show better patterns of adjustment between parents and adolescents. Landis (1955) reported that girls from large families seemed to be more poorly adjusted, particularly socially, than girls from smaller families, especially girls who were only children. On the other hand, boys who were only children had fewer friends than did those from larger families.

Relations with Parents

Eighteen- and nineteen-year-old boys and girls were asked to answer questions concerning their relations with their parents. Boys showed poorer relations than girls, the girls being generally more sociable. Members of both sexes had better relations with the mother. Child-parent relations, however, seem to be definitely related to the sex of children and parents (Jurovsky, 1948). The fact that children of both sexes seem to have better relations with the mother has been reported in other studies. Perhaps this is a result of the greater amount of contact youngsters have with the mother, who is more readily available than the father.

The Ethnic Background of the Home

Although it may not be as prominent a factor today as it was twenty years ago, the ethnic background of the family is still involved in the adolescent's adjustment. The social and emotional maladjustments resulting from an immigrant background often become obvious during adolescence and early adulthood rather than in the earlier years of childhood. Usually, the child whose parents adhere strongly to their original ethnic patterns of behavior lives in a neighborhood consisting of families from the same cultural background.

Every major city has subareas in which certain ethnic groups of similar background tended to congregate. A child growing up in such an area associated primarily with others like himself. If his parents were bilingual and he himself developed a slight foreign accent, these conditions were unusual. Since elementary schools are located within neighborhoods, he probably remained with a large number of his ethnic peers throughout this phase of his education.

When he enters high school, however, the adolescent generally leaves his neighborhood and enters a school in which his ethnic group is no longer the majority. He may be one of relatively few from his earlier peer group to go to high school or on to college.

As he moves out into the larger society, the adolescent becomes very much aware of his differences from the others in the new group. The once "natural" slight foreign accent now becomes a source of great concern to him. Many of the earlier behavior patterns appear unacceptable to the new group. The adolescent may withdraw from social activities where his background would make him feel ill at ease, or he may strive to identify completely with the new culture to the extent of rejecting his background. He may change his religion if he feels that it carries the stigma he now associates with that background.

The degree to which the parents adjust to the total society will relate to the adolescent's way of adjusting. If parents continue to maintain most of the behavior and value patterns peculiar to the country or culture in which they originated, they will probably transmit these patterns to their children in a rather rigid fashion. When a youngster from this rigid kind of environment reaches adolescence, his conflicts may be particularly intense. While he seeks to adjust to the values of the broader society, he is still severely limited in carrying these adjustments back into his home environment. He may have to develop two sets of values and two sets of behavior patterns appropriate for these values. It may be difficult or even impossible for him to bring these two sets of values together in a meaningful way. Thus, he may be in a state of constant anxiety as a result of his attempts to determine which values and which actions are appropriate in a given situation.

On the other hand, many foreign-born parents have themselves sought to become a part of the over-all society and to break their connection with their original background completely. Such parents encourage their children to learn the values and behavior patterns needed for being identified as an American. Such efforts may make the adolescent's adjustment easier, but they may also deprive him of exposure to some of the "richer" parts of his heritage.

Occasionally the youngster may even have some difficulty in his adjustments to the ethnic group from which he comes. Ethnic groups also have subgroupings that were originally established in the country of their origin but maintain themselves in this country. An Italian-American physician recently summed this point up as follows:

"I wanted to practice in my old neighborhood but found that my practice wasn't going too well. I figured they would accept me readily especially since my parents had lived in the neighborhood for years. When I discussed this with some of my old friends I got an explanation which I realized was true even though it shocked me. My folks had come from Sicily, but most of the others in the neighborhood had come from the north of Italy, mostly from around Rome. In their eyes I was a 'Siciliano,' basically a peasant and therefore not worthy of their association. It really surprised me to find that these old-time patterns still maintained themselves in these people despite their having been in this country for better than thirty years."

Except for a few groups, such as Puerto Ricans, immigration has been greatly reduced during the last few decades. While the old sub-areas still exist in most cities, they contain mostly older people. Generally, the young American-born adults from these immigrant family backgrounds leave the old neighborhoods and establish themselves in more heterogeneous areas. Their children, in turn, are exposed primarily to the influences of such greater heterogeneity and find it easier than their parents did to adjust to established American values. This adjustment may vary with the degree to which they maintain some identification with their original ethnic background.

General Home Relationships

Gray (1959) studied the relationships between perceived similarity to parents and indexes of personal and social adjustment of children in the fifth through the eighth grade. She used two indexes of identification: direction of identification toward or away from the same-sex parent, and distance from both parents. It was predicted and confirmed that identification with the father would be associated with adjustment in the boys, but that girls' identification with the mother would not be so associated. She interpreted her results as indicating that changed role expectancy for women today and pressure toward emancipation from parents in young adolescents were important mediating variables in determining patterns of identification in the age group studied.

Raskin (1948) expressed the view that the school tends to overlook the importance of the home in the life of the older student. Parents also tend to become more lax in their responsibilities toward their children of this age group, mistakenly assuming that the training period is at an end. Yet adolescence is a period of inner strivings and responsiveness to ideas, a period in which personal standards and ideals are formed. Very thoughtful supervision is needed; parents should study their adolescents' behavior carefully, so that they are able to offer guidance in their emotional development and in their vocational choices. Parents should also help foster heterosexual interest and contacts and help youngsters to develop a serious attitude toward sexual relations and toward marriage. This can all be done more effectively by reason and logic than by authoritarian measures.

Family socioeconomic status is a variable that seems to influence the degree and intensity of parent-adolescent conflict. Parents in the lower- , middle- , and upper-class groups vary appreciably in their treatment of their children, ranging from rigid authoritarian attitudes to an almost *laissez-faire* approach. A general democratic approach to child-rearing is found more often in both the middle- and upper-class groups than in the lower class. The degree to which the individual adolescent will rebel and the methods he will use in such a rebellion depend greatly on the kind of home climate in which he was reared.

Nye (1951) reported that the adjustment of adolescents to their parents is better among high socioeconomic subjects than among low socioeconomic subjects. Four other variables related to parental adjustment were shown actually to be reflections of socioeconomic status. These were area of residence, broken homes, size of family, and employment status of mother. Koos (1950) has also investigated socioeconomic differences in relation to family reactions to "crisis" situations. There was a broad range of description in the lower-income families, while in the middle-class family the focal point is intrafamily, i.e., in the husband-wife or parent-child relationship. The middle-class families experienced crises more frequently, reacted more severely, recovered from the experiences more quickly, and were more likely to benefit from the experiences. The lower-class family will often turn to outside help in meeting crises, but the middle-class family usually does not, both because of pride and because the kind of assistance needed is not available.

There is always a good deal of confusion in the minds of parents concerning the kinds of discipline that they can employ to control their children's behavior effectively. The kind of discipline changes as the child grows older; the parent who spanks his five-year-old probably will not consider spanking his sixteen-year-old. Moreover, the five-year-old will usually not fight back even if the punishment was unjust, but the sixteen-year-old is quick to do so, usually verbally.

Strang (1951) has attempted to ascertain just what discipline means to the adolescent. From a group of students in grades six through twelve she obtained compositions describing the attempts of parents, teachers, or other adults to correct the child's behavior. Adolescents quite frequently express a sense of injustice, especially because they feel that they are often punished before the adults know all the facts in the situation. A large number of the youngsters do, however, recognize the justice and the value of their punishments.

Sometimes a teen-ager is punished even though he has done what his parents asked of him. He is punished because of his attitude, which may have been quite negative. This point was illustrated by the brief study presented in Chapter 1. One can understand John's reaction. He had done what he was told to do, yet he was punished. His mother was so annoyed at his negative behavior that she neglected the fact that she had been obeyed. Too often parents do respond in this way because they think the child is trying to flout their authority; yet, this is not really the case.

Democratic Home Environments

The relation of type of home environment to personal and social adjustment was studied by Landis ("The Ordering and Forbidding Technique and Teen-age Adjustment," 1954) in a sample of more than 4000 high-school seniors. The child from a democratic home environment had a big advantage in personal and social adjustment as compared to a child from an authoritarian background. Authoritarian parents were more often in disagreement with their children. In most cases the girls in such families disagreed more often than the boys. Itkin (1955) studied the relationships between the students' attitudes toward their parents and their attitudes concerning the kind of control measures or supervision used by their parents. He found significant positive correlations between these two sets of attitudes, and one low correlation between attitudes toward parents and parents' attitudes toward dominance-submissiveness of the control. Generally, the results were interpreted as indicating that "students with a favorable attitude toward their parents approve of their parents' supervisory methods." Those students who object to their parents' supervisory methods have negative attitudes toward their parents.

The attitudes and opinions of a group of parents were compared with concepts of family life as presented in current professional literature (Briggs and Schulz, 1955). The subjects included authority and discipline, family relationships, adolescent independence, allowances and family money, problems of behavior and moral beliefs, and personal development. From the responses, it appeared that the majority of parents interviewed had an understanding of the emotional needs and development of teen-agers. There were evidences of both authoritarian and democratic trends, but the weight of the evidence seems to support the belief that the family is making a transition from the traditional or authoritarian pattern to more democratic attitudes.

One problem associated with this kind of transition is caused by misinterpretation of the nature of a democratic home. Too often parents seem to feel that they should allow their adolescents almost complete freedom, but this is a *laissez-faire* rather than a democratic attitude. A democratic home still imposes controls or restrictions on the child's behavior. However, such a home attempts to bring the youngster into the decision-making and allows him greater freedom of action within the limits agreed upon. A youngster who is given complete freedom to handle any and all situations as he sees fit will seldom appreciate such freedom once he gets over the initial positive reaction. Too often the parent who allows such complete freedom is inconsistent in his response when the youngster seems to take undue advantage of the situation. If, for example, such a parent allows the child free use of the family automobile, he should not be critical if the youngster takes the car on a trip that the parent thinks is too long or dangerous. Having allowed the child free use of his own discretion, parents are not in a position to question this discretion. Certainly any punishment administered in this kind of situation would be considered unjust by the youngster.

Actually, most teen-agers prefer to have their parents impose certain restrictions, although they may not always adhere to these rules. Thus, if the parents offer the child the use of the car but limit the distances traveled and the kinds of situations in which the car may be used, the youngster has a base from which to operate. He may even discuss with his parents the limits to be imposed. If he then breaks one of the rules and is punished accordingly, he will be first to agree that the punishment was justified, however little he may like it. He may even break some of the rules knowingly, but with the awareness that he will be disciplined for doing so.

What Kind of Discipline?

A final note on discipline relates to the kind of discipline the parent ought to administer and to the consistency of the discipline. Too often parents are afraid to administer certain kinds of discipline for fear of creating some emotional disturbance in the youngster, or because they fear social disapproval from their own peers. One might suggest that parents use methods of discipline that suit their own individual personalities. For example, if a parent does not feel comfortable in administering a spanking to a child, he probably should not employ this technique. If he does, he is likely to feel guilty about it and do something nice for the child by way of compensation, thus probably negating any positive effects the original punishment may have had.

More important than the actual method is the consistency of the discipline. If the youngster is made fully aware of the limits within which he may function and is consistently punished when he goes outside these limits, he is likely to recognize such punishment as deserved. If, however, he is punished on one occasion but not punished the next time he does the same thing, he may become confused. All youngsters will test the limits when they are first imposed, but once a child finds that the rules mean what they say, he can adjust well to functioning within them.

School Discipline

School teachers are quite familiar with the ideas just expressed and are often more successful in structuring the situation than parents are. The teacher is the single source of authority in the classroom, while in the home both parents are sources of authority. If the parents do not reinforce each other, neither one may be able to discipline the child effectively. Any youngster is quick to notice disagreement between the views of the two parents about controlling his behavior. Once such a situation is recognized, most youngsters are quick to take advantage of it and often cleverly play one parent against the other.

A teacher has only to be consistent in his own behavior, within the frame of reference established by school authorities. As a rule, each teacher sets the limits that apply within his own classroom, and most students adjust accordingly. After the first week of school, during which the children are busy testing the limits in the new situation, a good teacher has set the "ground rules" and made the students aware that these rules will be enforced. Once the situation is so structured, discipline problems are minimal. Further difficulty will occur only if the students find that the teacher is not consistent.

FAMILY CHANGE AND "CONFLICT PATTERN"

A good deal was written in the last decade concerning alleged changes in the structure of the American family and the resultant changes in the behavior and actions of youngsters. It has generally been suggested that our society is moving from a patriarchal to a matriarchal pattern. Mead (1947) suggested that "among long-time trends are continued insistence on free choice of marriage partners for both men and women." Further, she feels that there is an increasing acceptance of marriage as a terminable relationship, and a pronounced belief that relatives in the home, especially grandmothers, damage child-parent relationships. Mothers show increased dissatisfaction with "homemaking," which seems to have lost many of its former rewards and its high vocational status. This plight of the family is temporary and a function of general insecurity, but, more important, Mead feels that the family is undergoing irreversible changes which must be recognized if its culturally appropriate and indispensable functions are to be conserved.

Moguey (1957) has also commented on the decline of paternal authority. He feels that the role of the father is the most important factor in family stability. Although the connection is not necessarily causal, the number of broken families has increased as the traditional authority of the father has declined. Today the father's participation in the family seems to count more for family stability than did the behavior of a strict, traditional type of father. Hjelholt (1958) studied a sample of young men aged sixteen to twenty in an attempt to show that the father is "the neglected parent." Some members of the group came from broken homes, and some grew up in orphanages. Generally, the father role manifested itself conspicuously. Although some studies have shown emotional attachment to the mother, the importance of the father role emerges when social adaptation is reflected in the case of broken homes. The author quotes Hans Hoff's claim that "in the child's development his superego builds up, and social adaptation is developed, by the relationship between child and father."

Payne and Mussen (1956) administered the California Psychological Inventory to high-school boys and their parents. Analysis of the data derived from this test revealed a significant relationship between a high degree of identification with the father and perception of the father as a highly rewarding, affectionate person. Strong identification with the father was associated with perceptions of relationships with parents as highly rewarding and warm.

The relationship of teen-age adjustment to the broken-home environment was studied by Landis (1953). He administered a problem check list to more than 4000 high-school students and made his comparisons in terms of numbers and percentages of problems reported by children whose parents are living together and by those whose homes were broken by separation, divorce, or death. Problems relating to financial and living conditions were checked most often by children from broken homes. These children also checked more personal problems and family problems than did the children from complete homes. Areas relating to vocational problems, social problems, problems of boy-and-girl relationships, school problems, and problems relating to morals, religion, and the future were checked about equally by both groups.

The differences between mothers of a group of abnormal and of a group of normal adolescent girls were investigated by Handford (1954). In the abnormal ones the following qualities appeared in marked fashion: (1) the mothers pushed their daughters to fit parental plans rather than allowing them to develop as free individuals; (2) mother-daughter relationships were neurotically overbinding; (3) mothers were not frank with their daughters but were always presenting a false front; (4) the relationships between the parents were strained; and (5) the parents were anxiety-ridden. Such results are rather understandable, but the absence of such patterns in mothers of normal girls is particularly interesting.

Liccione (1955) attempted to study the changing relationships of adolescent girls to their families. Twelve Thematic Apperception cards were administered to girls nine, eleven, thirteen, fifteen, and seventeen years old. The stories were analyzed to identify themes classified as "interpersonal," "intrapersonal," and "impersonal," and also as "equilibrium" and as "disequilibrium" (tension). About 25 per cent of the more than 14,000 themes dealt specifically with the parent-child relationship. Themes on parent-child "disequilibrium" outnumbered those on "equilibrium" about five to one. At all the ages studied there was significantly greater disharmony in relationships with the mother than in those with the father. It was suggested that this greater disharmony is a function of greater interaction of mothers and daughters.

THE FAMILY AND PERSONALITY PATTERNS

The various personality, character, and emotional characteristics that are first developed in the home will in turn influence the child's continuing interaction with the home environment. If, for example, some negative character trait evolves from the child's experiences in the home environment, the presence of this trait during his adolescent years may be a source of conflict with the parents. Although they may have been responsible for the early development of this characteristic, the parents may be unwilling to accept its presence in the older child. This, in a sense, creates a vicious circle.

Brown *et al.* (1947) sampled attitudes and personal traits to reveal ten areas of affectional family relationships by means of the F-R (Family Relations) Questionnaire, which they administered to ten- and sixteen-year-old subjects. Character development was found to be most closely related to sharing family decisions, interpersonal relations, and parental attitudes toward the child's peers. The personality patterns of adolescents were significantly related to the emotional relationships and the disciplinary patterns that they experienced in living with their parents (Peck, 1958).

McGuire (1953) suggested that human personality is developed and social behavior learned in five kinds of environments. The family, the age-mates, the society, the school, and other community institutions all have a part in shaping the behavior of the individual. He also suggested that two unique elements, the biological organism and the self of the individual, play important roles in this development. He stated, "Children and youth seem to acquire from one another the experience they need to modify their personalities and supplement the approval or disapproval by older persons."

It is often difficult for adults to be aware of the personal problems of adolescents or to identify specific problems. According to Homan (1955), adolescents are most likely to seek help on problems related to school and vocational planning. She suggested that they are least inclined to seek help for more personal problems, such as those concerned with sex and family relations. The fact that adolescents do not like to be considered different or maladjusted may be the reason that they do not seek help.

THE ADOLESCENT AND THE FAMILY IN OTHER CULTURES

Earlier in this book (see Chapter 4) we presented a general discussion of adolescent development and its accompanying problems in a number of societies other than that of America. In this section, the specific problems of adolescents within the family in other societies will be discussed in more detail.

Burgess (1948) proposed that the American family presented an external picture of diversity and instability. When this picture is reviewed in the context of the change from rural to urban conditions of life, a trend is revealed from the authoritarian to the companionship type of family that currently exemplifies the American ideals of democracy, freedom, and self-expression. The apparent instability of the family is largely a symptom of this transition. Burgess felt that this changing pattern of family structure may be regarded as a vast social experiment in which adaptability becomes more significant for success in marriage and family living than does a rigid structure.

Switzerland

A comparison between two democratic societies which differ in degree and type of family control may illustrate this point. Boehm (1957) investigated social growth and conscience, the latter in terms of both rate of development and changes in content, in Swiss and American children between the ages of six and fifteen. Piaget's *"methode clinique"* was used in telling each subject stories and asking about possible actions and feelings of the children appearing in the tales, thus revealing the subjects' reasoning and attitudes. The research showed that in certain areas of social growth American children mature earlier than their Swiss counterparts. They seem to move from dependence on adults to dependence on peers earlier than do the Swiss children. At a given age our children are less subjugated to adults, and they also enjoy freedom of thought and independence of judgment earlier. In America the child's conscience becomes less egocentric at a younger age than does that of the Swiss child. The content of the conscience, however, seems to differ in these two types of societies: that of our children is less complex and is primarily geared toward social adjustment, while in Switzerland it is mainly geared toward character improvement.

France

Koskas (1949) undertook to ascertain which adolescents repudiate their families, what types of families are repudiated, and why certain adolescents accept their families while others reject theirs. A questionnaire was administered to French subjects ranging in age from fifteen to eighteen. The preliminary results revealed that 80 per cent of adolescents belonging to proletarian families do not revolt against parental authority, but only 40 per cent of the adolescents of *petit-bourgeois* families do not revolt. Of the proletarian adolescents about 20 per cent dream of the disappearance of their parents, as compared to 90 per cent of the adolescents of *petit-bourgeois* families. Eighty-five per cent of the proletarian adolescents indicated that, if their parents actually did disappear, they would work harder, but only 4 per cent of the *petit-bourgeois* adolescents so indicated.

Japan

More than 500 Japanese high-school students and their parents were asked to answer a questionnaire on the philosophy of life. The main findings indicated that in feudalistic, irrationalistic, and egoistic aspects, the social attitudes of parents did not differ significantly from those of their children in the first two years of high school. The internal consistency of the results was higher for parents than for adolescents. Generally, these results indicate that parents' influence on attitudes of their adolescents decreases when the youngster's age level increases (Yoda and Kuze, 1959).

Maloney (1951) also discussed the Japanese family structure, in which he finds the father the absolute head and the mother without status. From an early age, Japanese children are taught total submissiveness to the father, which is also expressed in the compulsive attempt to keep all interpersonal relationships free from open conflict. A study of Japanese mental patients revealed that, because of these early repressions, male patients never become violent. This was not entirely true of women patients, whose repressions were less severe because their upbringing was less rigid. Maloney felt that the universal Japanese emotional disease is neurotic conformity, and that this gives many observers a false impression that democratic institutions have been genuinely accepted in Japan.

China

Hsu (1948) described the characteristic patterns of behavior in a small semirural community in southwest China, with particular attention to patterns of family and religious life. His analyses of the culture of the community revealed the two most important influences upon the basic personality type to be authority and competition. Authority was derived from the ancestral tradition and operated through the father-son tie, while competition was carried on within a framework determined by such authority. The most important difference in personality configuration according to status occurs between the rich or highly placed and the poor or lowly placed. The end results of authority and competition are radically different for the two groups, a fact that, Hsu feels, explains the cycles of rise and fall of families and dynasties. Hsu (1949) further discussed the function and destiny of the Chinese family. The backbone of the family has been the father-son relationship, which expresses the principle of filial piety. Traditionally, a wife's duty is first and above all to her parents-in-law, and she is not supposed to remarry if widowed, although she often does. Today's youth is demanding marriage reforms, including premarital courtship and freedom in selection of mates. Many divorces are obtained on grounds of mutual consent. Although polygamy is still accepted, monogamy is on the increase. Widespread illiteracy is partly responsible for the amount of cruelty to and exploitation of women.

Russia

The function and destiny of the family in Russia from the first years after the Revolution through the late 1940's was discussed by Hindus (1949). In those early years the family was largely released from ecclesiastical and legal restraints and regulations. Registration of marriage was not required, and divorce could be obtained for the asking. Although birth-control devices and abortions were free, large families persisted and a majority of Russians held their marriages together. In 1946, new laws governing marriage, divorce, and abortion were promulgated, the primary intentions of which were to curtail divorce, subsidize family life, and increase the population. Divorces are now obtainable only through the courts, which adjudicate grounds on a discretionary basis. There is subtle encouragement to unmarried women to have children, and state financial aid is provided for them. This present system is a complete reversal of Russia's former stand.

Parent-Child Conflicts in Various Cultures

Little clear-cut research is available on specific parent-child conflicts in Japan, China, and Russia. This may be due to an unwillingness of these societies to recognize the existence of such conflicts, which are contrary to familial or ideological beliefs. In fact, leaders in these countries, particularly in Red China and Russia, commonly point to the behavior of American adolescents as an indication of the decadence of our society. Obviously, then, they would want to conceal carefully any problems of their own adolescents.

Nonetheless, one needs only to read the reports of eye-witness observers to realize that all is not serene among adolescents in these countries. Even in Russia, where governmental controls and restrictions are imposed on various aspects of behavior, there seems to be evidence of unrest in the teen-age and young adult groups.

ATTITUDES OF PARENTS AND ADOLESCENTS TOWARD ONE ANOTHER

The way in which parental attitudes influence the development of the attitudes of children has long been a source of interest. It has been suggested that many of the attitudes and/or values of young people are well structured by the age of eight or nine, and that, once established, they are difficult to change. If it is true that such patterns are well established this early in life, the home environment must be the primary factor involved in structuring them. The child is therefore directly influenced not only by the overtly expressed attitudes of the parents, but also by the general tone of the home environment, including his observations of his parents' interaction with each other and with other adults.

The general topic of attitudes and values is discussed in detail in Chapter 9. Here, we will deal briefly with the attitudes parents and adolescents have toward one another. These attitudes are not necessarily correct, since they are based on the perceptions of the individuals involved, and these perceptions are in turn colored to some degree by the emotional involvement of parents and adolescents with one another. This emotional relationship makes it rather difficult for either group to formulate an objective, unbiased point of view of the other group.

Bird *et al.* (1952) studied neighborhoods into which Negroes were immigrating to investigate the racial attitudes expressed by the white residents. About 20 per cent showed no antipathies toward Negroes, but a larger number were resentful and antagonistic, indicating that they felt that the Negroes were infringing on the rights of white people. Since there was a good deal of ambivalence in the attitude of the adults, many of the children were not exposed to a consistent and clearly evident set of evaluations of the Negro. One result of this is "that white children do not closely resemble their parents in attitudes toward Negroes even though their parents share attitudes having considerable similarity."

Research relating to the social perceptions of adolescents and their parents was reported by Hess and Goldblatt (1957). The parents and the teen-agers were both asked to express on paired-adjective rating scales their opinion of "teen-agers in general" and "adults in general." Each group was also asked to predict the ratings of the other. Parents and adolescents showed general agreement in rating "teen-agers in general" and "adults in general," although adolescents gave a more positive rating to adults than did the parents themselves. The most significant differences between the groups appeared in their predictions of each others' ratings. Parents predicted that teen-agers would rate themselves relatively high; adolescents predicted that parents would assign low ratings to teen-agers. The attitudes of mothers, as expressed by the ratings, were significantly associated with the ratings of their teen-age children, but no significant association appeared between the ratings of fathers and children. These findings are discussed in relation to the

teen-ager's concept of himself and his peers and the possible effects of
his perceptions of the reputation of adolescents upon his attempts to
establish a sense of personal identity.

The studies appear to cast some doubt on the validity of the concept
that attitudes are well defined before adolescence. While there is no
doubt of the importance of the home in the development of attitudes,
these attitudinal patterns do not seem as thoroughly ingrained as we
have often been led to believe. Apparently much basic development
of attitudes does occur during early years, but developmental patterns
are often ambiguous and poorly understood. There is, it would seem,
some flexibility at even the earlier levels, which maintains itself into
adolescence. These partially structured attitudes are further influenced
by the peer group and by adults with whom the adolescent comes in
contact outside the home.

Certainly much more research is needed if we are to attempt either
to strengthen or to weaken the role of the family in the development of
attitudes in young people. As Warnath (1955) has pointed out, "the
home thus appears indeed to be a seat of learning for the development
of social skills, and perhaps of the desire to participate in activities with
other individuals." It is important that parents be given enough information about the way in which attitudes develop and that they be
helped to implement this knowledge in ways that will help develop
healthy, positive attitudes in their children.

THE ADOLESCENT'S VIEW OF CONFLICT WITH PARENTS

A study that is well worth describing, although because it was carried
on in Poland its results are not directly applicable to our own
society, is Skorupska's "Conflicts Between Adolescents and Adults as
Viewed by the Young People" (1958). About 62 per cent of the sixteen-
and seventeen-year-olds involved in this study mentioned the frequency
of their conflicts with adults. In their own opinion, 33 per cent are
bothered by conflicts often or very often, 26 per cent seldom, and 3 per
cent not at all. Most of the conflicts occur in the home, with parents
being the adults most often involved. The mother alone, or both parents simultaneously, is involved in the conflict, seldom the father alone.
The causes of the conflicts are usually quite complex and often interrelated. Those problems most frequently mentioned as resulting in
conflict are: differences of opinion; restrictions adults put on youngsters' independence; the adults' character traits; the disobedience of the
young; and "trifles." Less frequently mentioned are: the character traits
of the young people themselves; the family's economic condition; and
poor progress in studies. The conflicts tend to arouse strong and lasting

emotions that are usually unpleasant and are often accompanied by guilt feelings and feelings of being wronged. It is most unusual for young people to remain calm and self-possessed during and as a result of such conflicts, and some feel hatred, the need for revenge, active resistance, or strong stubbornness.

According to the young people Skorupska examined, the causes of many of these conflicts lie in such character traits of the adults as lack of leniency toward young people, noisiness, talkativeness, lack of confidence in young people, and lack of knowledge about and proper judgment of them. On the other hand, the young people judge their part in the conflict more lightly. They do mention, however, as causes of conflict on their part, such features as lack of self-control, nervousness, disobedience, and lies in defense of their own freedom. Skorupska points out that the group studied is not sufficiently representative to allow any general conclusions to be drawn.

This study does serve to illustrate further the apparently great similarities of adolescents in other countries to American teen-agers. Even though Poland is under Communist domination, with the restrictions peculiar to that system, unrest among adolescents is obvious. The reader will quickly recognize most of the complaints listed as the very ones offered by American teen-agers about their own parents, varying in degree of severity. In a survey conducted by the Purdue University Opinion Poll (Remmers, *et al.*, 1949), 10,000 youngsters in high school answered questions concerning whether adolescents think their parents understand their problems. One of the questions asked was: "Do you or do you not think that most parents these days understand the problems of their teen-age sons and daughters?" Thirty-five per cent of the respondents felt that parents did understand their problems, while 56 per cent felt that they did not. Only 9 per cent were undecided. The sexes did not differ appreciably in the responses; more than 50 per cent of both boys and girls indicated a lack of parental understanding. An analysis of the data to compare high and low socioeconomic groups failed to show any significant differences.

A study by Folsom (1943) of more than 300 boys and more than 300 girls gave some of the reasons for the conflicts arising between parents and adolescents. His findings are summarized in Table 13. This table reveals that boys encounter more difficulties with their parents over use of the automobile, spending money, and school grades. Girls had greater conflicts over home duties, clubs or societies, manner of dress, and attendance at unchaperoned parties.

The teen-age panelists who address this author's seminars on adolescent behavior agree that many of the areas identified in Folsom's study remain major sources of conflict today. These youngsters generally

TABLE 13. Source of disagreement between 348 boys and 382 girls and their parents

From Folsom (1943), by permission of the author and John Wiley and Sons

	Per cent	
Source of Disagreement	Boys	Girls
Use of automobile	35.6	29.6
The boys or girls you choose as friends	25.0	27.0
Your spending money	37.4	28.8
Number of times you go out on school nights during the week	45.1	47.6
Grades at school	40.2	31.2
The hour you get in at night	45.4	42.7
Home duties (tending furnace, cooking, etc.)	19.0	26.4
Clubs or societies you belong to	5.5	10.5
Church and Sunday school attendance	19.0	18.6
Sunday observance, aside from just going to church and Sunday school	15.2	13.9
The way you dress	14.4	24.6
Going to unchaperoned parties	15.8	27.5
Any other source of disagreement	9.5	8.4
"Do not disagree"	2.0	2.1

place the major emphasis on the following areas as sources of conflict with their parents: use of family car or owning their own car; school work and grades; allowances and other financial problems; choice of friends; dating; and use of the telephone (girls particularly emphasize this). Most of the youngsters think that their parents' arguments are sound but do not think that their parents are willing to give them credit for also presenting sound arguments. The older teen-agers (sixteen- to eighteen-year-olds) are more willing to accept some of their parents' views than are the younger adolescents (thirteen- to fifteen-year-olds). Since these areas are so constantly emphasized by teen-agers, they merit some further individual discussion.

Cars—Family- or Adolescent-Owned

Most adolescents look forward to their sixteenth birthday with great eagerness and enthusiasm. One of the major reasons for such anticipation is the fact that this is the age at which they become eligible for driver's licenses in most states. The increased mobility that a car offers is associated in the eyes of most youngsters with increased independence, and both are highly desired. Parents are fully aware of this expectancy and often use the promise of a car or at least of extensive use of the family car as a kind of future bribe. "Get good grades in school and you'll be able to use the car" is a fairly common example of this kind of bribery.

Once the youngster is sixteen, he finds that the car is not readily available whenever he wishes to use it. His parents, it seems, think they have first call on the use of the car, and even though he may have a license they are reluctant to let him take the car out alone. Mother may be pleased to have her teen-ager drive her around or run errands for her but may not allow the car to be used for the youngster's social activities. Even those parents who allow their youngsters relatively free use of the car during daylight hours may prohibit use of the car after dark.

Certainly these are not mere whims on the part of the parent. Most parents are fully aware that an automobile is a complex piece of equipment that may become a deadly weapon if used improperly. They realize that the youngster may be inclined to show off and even to engage in dangerous actions in demonstrating his new skill to his peers. Their own feelings are strongly reinforced both by insurance-company statistics, which show a relatively high accident rate for drivers in the sixteen- to twenty-five-year-old group, and by the fact that the premium on automobile insurance is increased by 25 per cent if the car is to be driven by a person under twenty-five.

Yet none of these arguments is particularly convincing to the adolescent. He sees the availability of the family car as important in increasing his status in the peer group. He is also most confident of his ability and is quite certain he can handle a car as well as most adults. Many youngsters also think they know more about the mechanics of an automobile than do their parents. They will point out every newspaper article concerning an automobile accident involving adults, avoiding, of course, those involving teen-agers.

Many youngsters remember the early "bribe-technique" used by their parents on them and attempt to use the same approach. They may volunteer to perform numerous extra tasks if only they can use the car. "If I get better grades on my next report card, will you let me use the car a little more often?" is a frequent approach, and one that often works.

This author has also become aware of the differences between rural and urban areas in this respect. To the rural youngster, use of a car may be more a necessity than a luxury. The car may be useful for getting to a school some distance away or into town for any social activity. Rural youngsters seem more willing to pool their efforts so that at least one member of the group has a car available to transport the rest. Parents of these youngsters are also more willing to allow them free use of the family car. One reason for this may be the fact that the youngster is likely to have been driving and handling farm equipment even before he got a driver's license. Another may be the relatively small amount of traffic compared to that in our car-congested cities. At any rate, the urban adolescents who report to our seminars openly admit their envy when they hear rural adolescents discuss the ready availability of cars.

An even greater source of conflict appears when the teen-ager seeks to purchase his own car. Parents view such a purchase with considerable alarm, since they will be able to exercise less control than they can over the use of the family car. They are also concerned that the youngster will spend too much time either using the car or working on it and will neglect other responsibilities. In particular, parents are concerned about the effect of car ownership on schoolwork and grades. They have read innumerable "popular" articles quoting research which indicates that school grades go down when a youngster acquires a car. Then, too, most parents would prefer that the adolescent use his money for things that they consider more important, such as a college education.

These arguments also, however, often fall on deaf ears. "It's my own money, I earned it and I can spend it on a car. I'll even earn enough to pay for the insurance, and maintaining it, so it won't cost you anything." Such comments can stymie all but the strongest parents. Some youngsters try to use a positive approach: "I'll be able to run errands and take you shopping, Mom, since Dad has the family car all day." Such altruistic verbalizations are seldom followed through.

In recent years there has been an increased emphasis on teaching driver-training in the high school. Such training apparently does develop better drivers, who are more likely to be safe drivers. Recognition of these programs by automobile insurance companies has helped to reassure parents. Insurance companies now offer reductions in rates for drivers who have received such training. No one is more aware of this fact than teen-agers, who are quick to use this additional ammunition in their arguments. In this case, statistics are in their favor.

Insurance companies have also recently offered lower rates for students who have good grades in high school. Again, statistics indicate that such youngsters are relatively good risks and are generally more responsible than lower-ranking students. This gives a good student still another convincing argument for his parents. Unfortunately, it is not always the good student who is particularly eager for a car. He may be occupied with schoolwork and other activities and therefore be satisfied with occasional use of the family car. Many of the students who plan to attend college are aware that they will not be allowed to have a car at college, at least during their freshman year, and are often willing to delay car ownership until later in their college careers.

It is relatively easy to understand why this is an area of conflict; both sides have valid arguments to offer. Suffice it to say that this conflict is minimized, although still present, in the home where warm affectional relationships exist. In such an environment each side compromises, and although neither may be completely satisfied, conflict concerning a car or its use becomes intense only in an occasional particular situation.

Schoolwork and Grades

The parents' point of view concerning their youngsters' efforts in school and the results of those efforts is also usually based on positive motivation. Most parents would like to see their children reach at least their own socioeconomic level or, better still, a higher one than they have attained. They view education as a most important factor in achieving this. As a result, they are likely to be quite harsh with youngsters who do not seem to be getting what they should from the secondary-school program. In some cases, parents are unrealistic in the goals they set for their children, since children do not always possess the ability to achieve at the level desired by the parents. In such cases the child may be placed under extreme stress, and if he cannot succeed academically he is likely to encounter severe conflict with the sources of his frustration.

The bright student who is capable of a high level of achievement but fails to reach it is also likely to become involved in conflict with his parents. He may be failing to achieve at his level of ability for fear that his peer group would consider him a "brain" or a "bookworm," which are labels he wishes to avoid. He would rather risk conflict with his parents than possible disapproval by his peers. In some cases he achieves at a lower level as one means of rebelling against his parents. This may occur unconsciously, with the adolescent actually unaware of the reason for his poor grades.

Perhaps the most common, almost daily source of conflict relating to school involves homework. Parents are concerned if the youngster does not bring homework home, or if he does not spend enough time (in their eyes) on the work he does bring home. Brighter youngsters claim that they can get their assignments done in study hall during the school day, but parents feel that study-hall periods are inadequate for this purpose. Many parents today have become so concerned about homework that they criticize the schools for failing to give enough outside assignments.

Most parents want their youngsters to develop good study habits in high school so that they can feel that the youngster will continue these good habits when he goes on to college. To help accomplish this end, the parents often try to set study hours during which the adolescent is restricted to his room. With the busy schedule most teen-agers have, this is difficult to accomplish. The youngster may have many activities of which the parents approve, including music lessons, Boy Scouts or some comparable organization, athletics, and perhaps even a part-time job. Between these more or less required activities, the adolescent wants time for interaction with his peers, and time for study is secondary. Even if the teen-ager does go to his room during the assigned study period, he may do everything but study.

Our most recent teen-age panelists have indicated that they and their peers are becoming more study-oriented today than previous generations of adolescents were. Youngsters are increasingly aware of the educational requirements that must be met either to enter the job market or to gain admission to college. Not only do most youngsters know that they must complete their high-school education, but they are aware also that good grades are important. The college-bound teen-ager knows that the higher his grades are the more likely he is to be admitted to the college of his choice. Even the less able youngster who hopes to get into a trade school knows that he must successfully complete at least the ninth grade if he is to be admitted to such a school.

This greater awareness of the need for good grades has probably helped alleviate some of the tension centering around this area in the home conflicts. However, parents are equally aware of these factors and may as a result increase their pressure for high achievement on the part of the adolescent. Yet, since both groups have essentially the same perception of the situation, they are likely to understand each other's viewpoints better. As a result, it seems likely that conflict over schoolwork, although still present, is probably less severe than it was for the previous generation.

Money Problems

If the teen-ager has conflicts with his parents over money, these are usually over allowances and freedom to spend the money as the teen-ager sees fit. An allowance of some kind seems to have become almost standard in a majority of homes today, and in most cases it is instituted before the child becomes an adolescent. It is not unusual for seven- and eight-year-olds to be given a small amount of money each week to help them "learn to handle money." As the child's age increases, so does the weekly sum, since, as one parent put it, "as the youngster gets older, his cost of living goes up."

Dunsing (1956) attempted to obtain information concerning the experiences of a group of adolescents in acquiring and spending money and to compare actual with recommended practices in its use. More than 700 successful 4-H club members in grades eight through twelve were included in the study. The chief sources of spending money were allowances, doles, or irregular earnings. Irregular earnings were the most common source of adolescent spending, and the dole was least common, with more girls than boys receiving money as an allowance or a dole. Actual practices in the use of money obtained from all three sources did not seem to provide these adolescents with the most favorable learning experiences. Their practices in the use of money appeared to reflect the attitude of parents toward money.

It is hard to define just what an allowance is, since different youngsters receive this allotment for different reasons. In some cases the amount may actually be related to the "cost of living." If the allowance is meant to cover transportation to and from school and payment for school lunches, it will necessarily be higher for the high-school youngster than it was for the elementary-school child. If the youngster must pay for some clothing from the allowance, this cost will also increase as he grows older. Even if the allowance is only for social activities and entertainment, it still must increase to keep pace with the increased cost of such activities.

The purpose for which the allowance is to be used is one source of conflict. Many youngsters feel that an allowance should be made available for those things they wish to spend it on, and not to cover such necessities as transportation, lunches, or clothing. Basically, they want "pocket money" that they can consider their own with no restrictions. Many parents will disagree with such an idea, since they do not feel it helps the youngster develop "money sense." In the adult frame of reference, it is important to have the adolescent aware of the necessities as well as the luxuries, and the sum of the allowance is decided on this basis: for example, enough to cover the costs of transportation to school and school lunches, with an additional sum for "spending money." The youngster may choose occasionally to skip lunch or walk to school to increase the "spending money," and parents will not object often unless these practices are carried to extremes, i.e., the child eats no lunch at all.

Another source of conflict relating to the allowance is the reason for which it is given. In some homes the youngster is given a weekly sum with no requirement that he earn it in any way; in others, he must perform assigned routine household tasks in order to receive it, and failure to perform certain tasks may result in proportionate deductions. In other homes the child must earn his spending money outside, and is allotted all or part of his weekly earnings from a paper route or from some other part-time job. In still other homes the youngster receives no spending money at all and may even have to contribute whatever he may earn to the family.

There has been a good deal of disagreement among teen-agers themselves as to what an allowance should involve. Some feel it should be given them with no obligations. Others think they should work for it in some way, since they realize this is good training for later life. Some who have an income from a part-time job feel that they should be allowed to keep their entire earnings to spend or save as they see fit. This author has been pleasantly surprised to find that a substantial number of teen-agers do not feel that they should be paid on the basis of their performance of routine household tasks such as washing dishes or making one's bed. A number of youngsters feel that they should perform these tasks as part of their family membership, not for reward. There are also some, less altruistically oriented, who do not feel they should be paid on the basis of household tasks because money may be withheld if the assigned task is not performed. With all these differing points of view on the part of both parents and adolescents, it is easy to see why conflict arises.

Once they have money available, many adolescents feel that their parents try to control the way in which money is spent or object to the choice the youngster makes. Mary C. reported:

"When I was sixteen, my mother told me I could start buying my own clothing, at least my own skirts and sweaters. Up till then she had gone shopping with me, and although I had some choice in selection, my mother usually made the final choice. I didn't always agree with her choices, but generally I felt that she had good taste. The first time I bought two skirts and three sweaters, and when I got home my mother became quite angry. First, I had purchased too much, and, second, she thought that only one of the five choices was suitable. She took me back to the store to return the things she didn't like and helped me select replacements for some of the others. The same clerk from whom I had purchased the original clothes waited on us, and I was terribly embarrassed. My mother and I have worked out a good compromise, though. Now I can bring home two or three skirts on approval and we decide together which one I can keep. Lately I find that mother approves of almost everything I bring home. I'm not sure of whether I try to pick things that will please her, or whether my own taste is improving. Either way, I do know that many people compliment me on my clothes."

Other youngsters are not as fortunate as Mary. One girl reported that her parents let her keep the things she bought but continually made fun of them. A common complaint among girls seems to be that parents keep trying to dress them to look younger than they are.

Not only clothing, but almost any purchase the youngster makes, may be criticized by the parents. Either the youngster paid too much or he should have selected a different brand name, etc.

The parents of Bob S. told him to buy a bike to use for his paper route. They specified the amount he should spend and the equipment (lights, etc.) the bike should have. Bob picked an English bike equipped as his parents suggested and within the price limit they had set. His father criticized his choice as impractical, since "the tires are too thin for the load you have to carry" and those "hand brakes aren't as good as a coaster brake." Actually the bike held up perfectly, as Bob knew it would. Most of his friends had the same kind of bike and used theirs for deliveries, too. "I guess Dad just didn't know much about this kind of bike and would have preferred a type he was familiar with," was Bob's explanation. He did admit that he had quite a few arguments with his father about it.

Choice of Friends

Another source of frequent conflict involves parental disapproval of adolescents' choice of friends of the same sex. This kind of conflict is often a reflection of parental bias toward other groups and is also a reflection of the parents' own desire to associate with the "right kind of people." These biases may be based on the parents' religious, ethnic, or socioeconomic background. The adolescent may well have had these biases transmitted to him at an early age, but nevertheless he often chooses his friends on an individual basis without great concern about the friend's background. By later adolescence or early adulthood this kind of interaction may cease, and his friends at that level may be chosen within a biased pattern of sociability. A teen-ager may also seek temporary friendly relations with an individual whose status will enhance his own. He may not even have much in common with this sought-after friend, but he temporarily enjoys basking in reflected glory.

Joe C., a rather gangly fifteen-year-old, was interested in football but was not skilled enough to make the team. He did manage to become an assistant manager of the team, which at least made him feel a part of the group. Joe tried hard to become friendly with the team's quarterback, a seventeen-year-old boy who was a school hero. The two boys had no interests in common other than football, but Joe worked hard at getting a friendship going. He followed his friend around almost slavishly, seeming to be happy just to be near him. For a while Joe felt he was accepted by others because of this friendship and was quite pleased. His parents constantly criticized his friend as an "uncouth, uneducated boor" and asked Joe not to bring him home. The following year Joe lost interest in football and became a successful member of the school tennis team. He now had his own status as a school athlete, and his friendship with the other boy ended rather quickly. Some of Joe's new friends were younger boys who sought from their association with him the kind of status he had sought in his association with the football hero.

In such cases, parental criticism is perhaps justified or at least legitimate, because this kind of situation provides no sound basis for friendship. The parents, however, fail to realize the reasons for such a friendship and the fact that it is usually situational and temporary. Eventually most youngsters will have as their close friends those with whom they share common interests and tastes. This commonality of interests and tastes will probably mean that their friends' family backgrounds are fairly similar to their own environmentally and, often, in terms of religion and ethnic origin as well.

This is one of the areas in which overt parental criticism may result in an increase of the behavior that is criticized. If parents are critical of their youngster's choice of friends, the youngster may seek out even more friends of the same type as a means of showing his independence. He may also become critical of his parents' friends. Parents must realize that their youngster is going through a learning process, that his experiences with a variety of people help him to discern the kinds of characteristics others possess. This gives him a basis for determining the kind of characteristics he likes and dislikes in others, and also the kinds of people with whom he feels comfortable. Once he has developed such a wide experimental background, he is better equipped to choose his friends wisely and usually will choose those who are acceptable to his family. He also learns to get along with a variety of people, even some whom he dislikes, and this helps him as he increases his contacts with others in adult life.

Dating

Another major source of parent-adolescent conflict similar to the one just discussed is parental dislike of individuals dated by their youngsters. Girls usually feel that they have more severe conflict in this area than do boys. Again, parental biases concerning socioeconomic, ethnic, and religious background are apparent. The concern may be even greater than that over choices of friends of the same sex because parents fear that dating may lead to what they might consider an improper marriage.

Parents are also greatly concerned about their daughters' reputations and fear that they might become involved with boys who have poor reputations. Sometimes parents' ideas about the reputation of a boy their daughter dates are based on hearsay evidence and may not be warranted. The daughter may be more aware of what the boy is really like, but in trying to defend him to her parents she becomes involved in conflict.

This point was well illustrated in our adolescent seminar by a teen-age couple who were going steady. S., a seventeen-year-old boy, and J., a sixteen-year-old girl, discussed their families' reaction to their going steady:

S. pointed out that he was living with his mother, who worked (his father had died when he was about ten). His mother had allowed him a good deal of freedom and he was allowed to set his own hours and choose his own friends. S. was an excellent student and held a part-time job from which he was saving money for his college education. He admitted that he "had been around" and that people in his town did think him rather "loose." In his relationship with J. he felt he was a gentleman and always honest with her. He knew how her parents felt about him and could understand their attitude, but he still resented it. His own mother was not particularly critical of any of his friends, and he thought that other parents should be equally objective.

The author should point out that the twenty students in the seminar, all high-school teachers, were extremely impressed by S.'s intelligence, maturity, and enthusiasm. A number of those who had teen-age daughters wished that "my daughter had a boy-friend like S."

J. agreed with S.'s point of view. She admitted that she had been hesitant about going out with him because of all the things she had heard about him. Once, by accident, she had been on a double date with one of her friends who had brought S. as her date. J. had enjoyed being with him and when he asked her for a date, she accepted. When her parents found out about it, they were quite upset and asked her not to go out with him. J. went anyway and has been seeing S. regularly since. Her parents still object but have accepted the situation to a degree. J. resents the fact that they give S. no chance to show them what he's really like. When he calls for her, they either disappear or merely engage in brief, casual conversation.

Parents have another important fear in relation to their daughters. They are concerned that going steady may lead to sexual behavior with possible undesirable results. Accordingly, they are greatly concerned about the background and possible reputation of the boy involved in the date. They may also set limits on where the couple may or may not go, such as forbidding their going to a drive-in theater and trying to keep them from being alone together. This is not always a conscious fear on the parents' part, but even unconsciously it may bring them into conflict with the daughters, who resent their parents' apparent lack of faith in their ability to handle themselves properly.

Boys also have problems of this sort, but they usually do not involve such intense conflict as do those of girls. Parents may object to their son's girl companions, especially when the boy decides to go steady, for some of the same reasons for which they object to their daughter's choices. However, they are less likely to be as concerned about the sexual aspects of their son's dating and may even subtly encourage him in the direction of some sexual behavior.

Adolescents are usually aware of their parents' reactions to the individual they date. Sometimes they agree with these reactions, but they may continue dating a person even though they risk conflict with their parents. They may be interested in this dating companion only because of a single characteristic or pattern of behavior that they consider important, and the friendship will probably not last long.

Sally R. started going out with Bill R. when she was fourteen and he was sixteen. Sally dated other boys also, but went to all dances with Bill. She liked to dance and felt that Bill was an ideal partner, because "we look good together on the dance floor." She did not care much for his company on other occasions. She told her parents how she felt and was criticized for it. Their reactions were: "It isn't fair to Bill," and "Looking good on a dance floor isn't very important." Sally recognized the point her parents made but still went dancing with Bill. Six months later she stopped seeing him. In that six-month interval, some of her other boy friends had improved their dancing skills to her satisfaction, and she had no need for Bill. She realized later that this was selfish behavior, but at the time dancing was very important to her. She suggested that part of her conflict with her parents was due to the fact that she knew they were right, but if she had admitted that to herself, she would have stopped seeing him then and missed all the compliments of her friends on how well she danced.

One of the greatest sources of conflict in dating involves "going steady," especially in the case of younger adolescents. Most parents are thoroughly opposed to this and do not understand their youngster's reason for getting so involved (see Chapter 7). They feel (often as a result of hindsight as they look back at their own experiences) that youngsters should go out with a variety of others, so that they will learn about many kinds of characteristics rather than just those peculiar to one individual. There is, of course, a good deal of merit in this point of view, but to the youngster seeking security, the steadiness of his relationship is quite reassuring. Much of this conflict is lessened with the older adolescent group.

Use of the Telephone

A relatively new problem is conflict over the use of the family telephone. Even telephone companies have become aware of this problem and have developed small sales campaigns for private phones (not simply extensions) for adolescent youngsters. It is not now unusual, although not yet common, to see a family listing in the directory followed by the listing of the adolescent. The major complaint of parents is the amount of time a child spends on each call. It would appear that youngsters can talk for hours about seemingly trivial things, and after conversing with one friend call another for the same discussion. Parents also become angry when the child comes home from a visit with a friend and within minutes is on the phone talking to that same friend.

Adolescents fail to understand why they have conflict over use of the phone and often defend their own practice. One youngster said, "My problem isn't using the phone too much. It's trying to get my mother to cut short her hour-long conversation, so I can make a two-minute call." However, adolescent telephoning can be carried to such extremes that the adults cannot be reached by phone even in emergencies.

A number of parents have set up rules regarding when the phone may be used and for how long. In such cases parents may not allow the youngster even to accept incoming calls except during specified times. Some scheduling is probably a better solution than a private phone for the youngster, even one he must pay for himself. Such scheduling is really only part of a total family pattern of interaction and cooperation.

AN OVERVIEW

There is unquestionably a good deal of conflict between parents and adolescents concerning the situations described here and other matters as well. The question that is difficult to answer concerns the severity of these conflicts and their lasting effects. Teen-agers generally seem to be less concerned about conflicts than parents are. They regard them as part of the process of growing up and achieving independence.

One of the major difficulties involved in these conflicts is an apparent lack of communication between the two generations. This author rather likes the approach suggested by Geist (1955) to help alleviate this difficulty. He met with a group of fifteen mothers of fourteen- to seventeen-year-olds to discuss some of the topics about which parents and adolescents disagree, after having first had a meeting in which the youngsters themselves had discussed these problems. Six of these separate meetings were followed by two joint meetings at which areas of disagreement were discussed. All participants were surprised to find, in general, more agreement than disagreement between the two groups. This experiment also suggests that solutions of some serious aspects of adolescent behavior might be achieved by such group sessions.

REFERENCES

BIRD, CHARLES, MONACHESI, ELIO D., and BURDICK, HARVEY. "Infiltration and the Attitudes of White and Negro Parents and Children." *Journal of Abnormal and Social Psychology*, 47, 688-699, 1952.

BOEHM, LEONORE. "The Development of Independence: A Comparative Study." *Child Development*, 28, 85-92, 1957.

BRIGGS, VIVIAN, and SCHULZ, LOIS. "Parental Response to Concepts of Parent-Adolescent Relationships." *Child Development*, 26, 279-284, 1955.

BROWN, ANDREW W., MORRISON, JOAN, and COUCH, GERTRUDE B. "Influence of Affectional Family Relationships on Character Development." *Journal of Abnormal and Social Psychology*, 42, 422-428, 1947.

BURGESS, ERNEST W. "The Family in a Changing Society." *American Journal of Sociology*, 53, 417-425, 1948.

CONNOR, RUTH, JOHANNIS, THEODORE B., JR., and WALTERS, JAMES. "Parent-Adolescent Relationships. I. Parent-Adolescent Conflicts: Current and in Retrospect." *Journal of Home Economics*, 46, 183-186, 1954.

CRANE, A. R. "Stereotypes of the Adult Held by Early Adolescents." *Journal of Educational Research*, 50, 227-230, 1956.

DAMRIN, DORA E. "Family Size and Sibling Age, Sex and Position as Related to Certain Aspects of Adjustment." *Journal of Social Psychology*, 29, 93-102, 1949.

DUNSING, MARILYN. "Spending Money of Adolescents." *Journal of Home Economics*, 48, 405-408, 1956.

ENGLISH, O. SPURGEON. "Adolescence." *Philadelphia Medicine*, 42, 1025-1026, 1947.

ERICKSON, RALPH J. "The Adolescent Within the Family." *Journal of Child Psychiatry*, 3, 115-136, 1956.

FOLSOM, J. K. *The Family and Democratic Society*. New York: John Wiley and Sons, Inc., 1943.

GALLAGHER, ROSWELL J. "Why They Rebel." *Atlantic Monthly*, 191(6), 69-71, 1953.

GEIST, HAROLD. "Adolescents and Parents Talk It Over." *Understanding the Child*, 24, 98-102, 1955.

GRAY, SUSAN W. "Perceived Similarity to Parents and Adjustment." *Child Development*, 30, 91-107, 1959.

HANDFORD, NORAH PRUDENCE. "Mothers of Adolescent Girls." *Smith College Studies in Social Work*, 24(3), 9-34, 1954.

HAWKES, GLENN R., BURCHINAL, LEE G., and GARDNER, BRUCE. "Measurement of Pre-adolescents' Views of Family Control of Behavior." *Child Development*, 28, 387-392, 1957.

HAWKES, GLENN R., BURCHINAL, LEE G., and GARDNER, BRUCE. "Pre-adolescents' Views of Some of Their Relations with Their Parents." *Child Development*, 28, 393-399, 1957.

HESS, ROBERT D., and GOLDBLATT, IRENE. "The Status of Adolescents in American Society: A Problem in Social Identity." *Child Development*, 28, 459-468, 1957.

HINDUS, MAURICE. "The Family in Russia." In Anshen, R. N., *The Family: Its Function and Destiny*, pp. 111-124. New York: Harper and Row, 1949.

HJELHOLT, GUNNAR. "The Neglected Parent." *Nordisk Psykologi* (Copenhagen), 10, 179-184, 1958.

HOMAN, MIRIAM. "Adolescent Attitudes toward Seeking Help with Personal Problems." *Smith College Studies in Social Work*, 25(3), 1-31, 1955.

HSU, FRANCIS L. K. *Under the Ancestors' Shadow: Chinese Culture and Personality*. New York: Columbia University Press, 1948.

HSU, FRANCIS L. K. "The Family in China." In Anshen, R. N., *The Family: Its Function and Destiny*, pp. 73-92. New York: Harper and Row, 1949.

ITKIN, WILLIAM. "Relationships between Attitudes toward Parents and Parents' Attitudes toward Children." *Journal of Genetic Psychology*, 86, 339-352, 1955.

JUROVSKY, ANTON. "The Relations of Older Children to Their Parents." *Journal of Genetic Psychology*, 72, 85-100, 1948.

KOOS, EARL L. "Class Differences in Family Reactions to Crisis." *Marriage and Family Living*, 12, 77-78; 99, 1950.

KOSKAS, R. "L'adolescent et sa famille" (The Adolescent and His Family). *Enfance* (Paris), 2, 68-71, 1949.

LANDIS, PAUL H. "The Broken Home in Teenage Adjustments." *Washington Agricultural Experiment Station Bulletin*, No. 542, 1953.

LANDIS, PAUL H. "Teenage Adjustments in Large and Small Families." *Washington Agricultural Experiment Station Bulletin*, No. 549, 1954.

LANDIS, PAUL H. "The Ordering and Forbidding Technique and Teen-age Adjustment." *School and Society*, 80, 105-106, 1954.

LANDIS, PAUL H. "The Families That Produce Adjusted Adolescents." *Clearing House*, 29, 537-540, 1955.

LANGFORD, LOUIS M., and ALM, O. W. "A Comparison of Parent Judgments and Child Feelings Concerning Self-adjustment and Social Adjustment of Twelve-Year-Old Children." *Journal of Genetic Psychology*, 85, 39-46, 1954.

LAUFER, MARIE L. "Casework with Parents of Adolescents in Placement." *Jewish Social Service Quarterly*, 30, 188-196, 1953.

LICCIONE, JOHN V. "The Changing Family Relationships of Adolescent Girls." *Journal of Abnormal and Social Psychology*, 51, 421-426, 1955.

MALONEY, JAMES CLARK. "A Study in Neurotic Conformity: The Japanese." *Complex*, no. 5, 26-32, 1951.

MCGUIRE, CARSON. "Family and Age-mates in Personality Formation." *Marriage and Family Living*, 15, 17-23, 1953.

MEAD, MARGARET. "What Is Happening to the American Family?" *Journal of Social Casework*, 28, 323-330, 1947.

MOGUEY, J. M. "A Century of Declining Paternal Authority." *Marriage and Family Living*, 19, 234-239, 1957.

NYE, IVAN. "Adolescent-Parent Adjustment—Socio-economic Level as a Variable." *American Sociological Review*, 16, 341-349, 1951.

NYE, IVAN. "Adolescent-Parent Adjustment: Age, Sex, Sibling Number, Broken Homes, and Employed Mothers as Variables." *Marriage and Family Living*, 14, 327-332, 1952.

PAYNE, DONALD E., and MUSSEN, PAUL H. "Parent-Child Relations and Father Identification among Adolescent Boys." *Journal of Abnormal and Social Psychology*, 52, 358-362, 1956.

PECK, ROBERT F. "Family Patterns Correlated with Adolescent Personality Structure." *Journal of Abnormal and Social Psychology*, 57, 347-350, 1958.

RASKIN, L. E. "Starshoklasniki v semiye" (Upper Grade Students in the Home). *Semia i Shkola* (St. Petersburg, Russia), (June), 11-15, 1948.

REMMERS, H. H., DRUCKER, A. J., and HACKETT, C. G. "Youth Looks at the Parent Problem." *Purdue Opinion Panel*, 9. Report 21, 1949.

SKLAREW, BRUCE H. "The Relationship of Early Separation from Parents to Differences in Adjustment in Adolescent Boys and Girls." *Psychiatry*, 22, 399-405, 1959.

SKORUPSKA, JULIA. "Konflikty mlodziezy dojrzewajacej z osobami doroslymi w opinii samej mlodziezy" (Conflict between Adolescents and Adults as Viewed by the Young People). *Psychologia Wychowawcza* (Warsaw), 1, 206-227, 1958.

STRANG, RUTH. "What Discipline Means to Adolescents." *Nervous Child*, 9, 139-146, 1951.

WARNATH, CHARLES F. "The Relation of Family Cohesiveness and Adolescent Independence to Social Effectiveness." *Marriage and Family Living*, 17, 346-348, 1955.

YODA, A, and KUSE, T. "The Psychological Study of Parents–Adolescents Relationships." *Bulletin of Faculty Education, Nagoya University*, (3), 100-127, 1957.

YODA, A., and KUSE, T. "Seinen-ryoshin kankei: shakaiteki taido ni okeru oyako no kankei" (Parent-Adolescent Relationships and Social Attitudes). *Japanese Journal of Educational Psychology*, 6, 229-237; 266-267, 1959.

CHAPTER 9

Religion, Attitudes, and Values

Apart from the recognized fact that religion influences moral values, and to a lesser extent social attitudes, the principal reason for discussing these areas in the same chapter is that all three often create the same kinds of conflicts in adolescents. Children derive their first concepts in these areas from their parents and when, as adolescents, they begin to question the concepts they have absorbed or been taught, conflict and, often, guilt result.

RELIGION

A few decades ago concern about religion, including such specifics as church attendance and sin, was generally thought to be a major source of conflict during the adolescent years. Supposedly adolescence was a period of almost hysterical religious conversion, resulting in close attachment to the church and its various activities. Though these reports may have been correct, an almost opposite point of view seems to be prevalent today. Inside and outside the church the consensus seems to be that for some reason the grip of religion on the individual is greatly weakened or even broken during the adolescent years.

There has been a good deal of concern about this apparent loss of interest in religion by adolescents, and studies have been and are being made to attempt to determine why this is so and what can be done to reorient young people toward religion. Recently, numbers of experts have emphasized the importance of religion for youth as a help in preventing amoral or delinquent behavior. J. Edgar Hoover has been quoted as stating that church attendance would help decrease delinquency, and Judge L. L. Fawcett of Brooklyn also emphasized this point. In his study of the records over a thirty-year period of thousands of children who came before him charged with delinquency, Judge Fawcett found that only two were receiving regular organized religious instruction.

Recent articles have suggested that a present-day upswing in religious interest among adults is evidenced by the increased church attendance reported by most religious groups. If such interest is truly increasing, one would expect that young people would be more exposed than ever to religious influences from adults. There is, however, no comparable indication of increasing interest in church attendance among adolescents. There has been a recent increase in Protestant and Jewish day schools, in addition to the already well-established Catholic parochial schools. These schools reject the distinction between religious truth and secular truth in their presentation to the student of an integrated view of the Judaeo-Christian culture. It is not yet apparent whether such schools will succeed in holding the adolescent's interest in religion. Basically, the question is not one of modifying religion but of trying to make it applicable to adolescent needs in a more meaningful fashion.

Religion and the Fate of Western Culture

This may be more than merely an academic question; it may actually relate to our ultimate survival. An Army psychiatrist in the Korean conflict reported findings based on men who had been captives of the North Koreans. It was alleged that 30 per cent or more of the Americans held prisoner by the North Koreans collaborated with the enemy to some degree. Of those who refused to collaborate, many did so because of their strong religious convictions. A number of soldiers indicated that they had resisted every overture of the enemy by relying on abstract, sometimes theological convictions that had long been a part of their lives. Those who merely had a high code of ethics were found to be no more likely to resist than those operating on a less sophisticated standard. While the present author feels that the percentage of collaborators was grossly exaggerated, he feels that the emphasis on strong religious conviction was probably correct.

The armed services have increasingly recognized that development of the morality of service men is vital and have adopted crash programs to instill moral standards. It is difficult to evaluate the success of such programs. Unfortunately from a research point of view, only another major conflict might serve to structure the kind of situation in which the effectiveness of such training could properly be tested and evaluated.

The Changing Relationship of Adolescents to the Churches

There has been only rather limited research concerning the adolescent and religion. Not only do such studies show tremendous variation from one era to another, but even within a given time period two researchers might arrive at completely different conclusions. Thus, while some researchers were emphasizing the number of religious conversions of the hysterical type during adolescence, others were stressing the gradual nature of conversions when they were present at all. Some of these studies of a bygone era may have been meaningful at the time they were made, but their results are no longer applicable.

Even the place of the church in community life has been substantially altered during the past fifty years. In earlier rural and small urban communities, the churches were often the center of educational, social, and religious life, and the ministers were the best-educated persons in the community. Years ago, the church functioned as the community alter ego. Today cities are large and populations are spread out into suburban areas. The location of any particular church is seldom convenient for all its members, and the churches no longer serve as educational and social centers.

Perhaps it is appropriate to suggest that young people are still religious during adolescence but do not seem to be satisfied with traditional religious belief and ritual. There is much confusion during this period, further complicated by guilt feelings brought about by the very existence of the confusion.

CONFLICTS RELATED TO RELIGION

Remmers and Radler (1957) investigated some of the questions regarding religion that youngsters feel bring about problems and conflict. Their findings are presented in Table 14. None of the percentages in the table shows any indication of great conflict among adolescents concerning these various aspects of religion. Nonetheless, the conflicts that are present are certainly important to the youngsters involved in them. The relatively greater concern about "not living up to my religion" seems to reflect the guilt feelings that relate to questioning one's religion if the individual feels that to question it is wrong.

The role of the home and of the parents is as important in the development and practice of religion as it is in any of the areas previously discussed. The religious atmosphere of the home is naturally one of the most significant factors influencing the adolescent's religious attitudes. The child's first religious experiences and training come from the home and are later augmented by instruction through the church with which the parents are affiliated. If the home environment insists on a strict adherence to specific religious observances and imposes strict taboos, the child may be more confused in adolescence than if he comes from a more liberal home. In childhood he may readily accept all the restrictions, especially if these restrictions are common to the neighborhood in which he lives. However, when he reaches high school he may

TABLE 14. Teenagers' religious problems
From Remmers and Radler (1957), copyright © 1957 by H. H. Remmers, by permission of The Bobbs-Merrill Company, Inc.

Percentages

	Confused in my religious beliefs	Bothered by thoughts of heaven and hell	Conflict between the Bible and my school subjects	Not living up to my religion	Searching for something to believe in	Standards of "right" and "wrong"
Total	10	12	7	22	5	19
Boys	9	11	6	22	5	16
Girls	10	14	7	21	6	21
Grade 9	8	15	6	19	4	18
Grade 10	12	11	9	23	6	18
Grade 11	10	13	6	22	6	22
Grade 12	9	10	5	23	6	17
East	8	12	5	17	5	14
Midwest	11	12	7	23	6	20
South	8	14	8	26	5	21
West	6	12	8	17	4	12
Rural	9	13	7	21	4	19
Urban	11	11	6	22	7	18
Protestant	10	12	8	23	6	19
Catholic	7	14	4	19	4	14
Jewish	15	9	3	18	6	24
None	10	11	8	15	7	19
Low Income	9	13	7	21	5	18
High Income	12	11	7	23	7	19

find his classmates far less restricted and in his desire to be more acceptable to these peers he may suffer great conflict. It may be particularly difficult for him to make a good adjustment if his earlier training was based on fear and any rejection of religious principles causes him to believe that he is doomed to eternal damnation.

However, children whose parents are irreligious are not necessarily better adjusted in this aspect of adolescence. Such youngsters may feel quite insecure and actually envy those classmates who have been involved in religious experiences denied them. Again it is the children whose parents are religious but liberal in their views who seem to make the best adjustments in developing more mature religious views.

Blos (1941) has also discussed the environmental background in relation to the adolescent's concern with religion in terms of the parent's acceptance or rejection of religion. He feels that "in either case the adolescent is likely to be deeply concerned with religious concepts—either violently attracted or repelled by the dogmatic attitudes of religious institutions."

The home environment must be a living example of religious influences in operation and not one that pays mere lip service to religion. Attendance at church on Sunday followed by six days of no trace of religion is not likely to develop a good religious adjustment in the youngster. If religion in the form of various rituals is practiced regularly and sincerely by the parents, there will usually be a positive transfer of their feelings to the child that will be of value to him in making his own religious adjustment with minimal conflict.

At times the youngster strikes out against religion as a subtle means of striking out against his parents. If the adolescent is having difficulty in emancipating himself from parents who are not willing to give him the freedom he seeks, he may rebel indirectly by rejecting religion. He has come to associate the religious institution and its codes of conduct with parents and parental authority. Since he cannot react against his parents, against whom his anger is actually directed, he may instead react against religion, which he identifies with his parents. Blos feels that changing attitudes toward religion and its institutions at a later age "reflect the reactivated infantile relationships to parents or authoritative substitutes."

Rather than being a time of religious "rebirth" or "reawakening," adolescence is more likely to be a time of attempting to reconstruct or restructure religious concepts. As an individual becomes more mature and his intellect develops, he is less likely to accept blindly concepts that he had accepted literally in earlier childhood. Certain doubts are likely to develop, and many ideas will change as the teen-ager tries to fit his earlier concepts into his more expanded frame of reference. These doubts and changes in ideas will also be influenced to some degree by the part that religion has played in his environment.

AGE LEVEL AND RELIGIOUS BELIEFS AND PRACTICES

Kuhlen and Arnold (1944) attempted to study the changes in specific religious beliefs in a sample of 547 children in grades six, nine, and twelve. These youngsters were asked to respond to statements of various beliefs by indicating whether they believed the statement, did not believe it, or did not know but wondered about it. The results showed a definite change in religious beliefs during this period, with reliable differences being present on 36 of the 52 statements on the test.

Generally, these authors found that religious beliefs become increasingly abstract with age. For example, while 70 per cent of the sixth-graders accepted the statement: "God is someone who watches you to see that you behave yourself," only one-third of the twelfth-graders accepted this statement. The seniors were more likely to accept the concept: "God is a strange power working for good." This study also showed evidence of increasing tolerance on the part of the youngsters, with the percentages of subjects who indicated that Catholics, Jews, and Protestants were equally good increasing from 67 per cent in the sixth grade to 86 per cent in the twelfth grade.

An increasing dislike of church services from the sixth to the twelfth grade was evident. Nevertheless, almost two-thirds of all the groups showed concern about failing to attend church. With increasing dislike for church activities, there is likely to be a decrease in church attendance. A study by Rosander (1939) indicated that the greatest number of adolescents ceased attending church during grades ten to twelve. He suggests that failure to attend may be due to dissatisfaction with what the church has to offer, reduced parental control, or increase in other activities that lessen the available time.

For many adolescents, withdrawal from religious practices is temporary. By early adulthood they are likely to become affiliated with a church and even become active church workers. This is particularly likely to occur after marriage and the arrival of children. Some, of course, drift completely away from the church and develop other interests, while others may reject the religion of their parents for one they find more acceptable. Mull (1947) administered the revised Watson Test of Religious Thinking to freshmen and seniors in a liberal arts college. A difference did exist between the two groups, but it failed to reach statistical significance. On the basis of other evidence in this study, the author concluded that the religious thinking of the seniors is more advanced than that of the freshmen.

One must not assume that the failure to attend church is necessarily indicative of a complete rejection of religion. A youngster may not be interested in affiliation with any given religious institution, yet still feel he is religious. Remmers *et al.* (1951), in a study of a sample of 2300 replies from a nationwide poll of high-school students, found that the typical teen-age student has a favorable attitude toward the church, says prayers, and thinks of God as an omnipotent and omniscient, bodiless spirit existing everywhere. He is ready to admit that the study of certain sciences may alter his beliefs and that religious beliefs may be questioned, and he may often be perplexed by the confusion of opinions.

Confusion of opinions is a problem for many adults also. Even within a particular religion, various experts may offer different interpretations of a given concept. The interpretation may vary according to the wing of a denomination involved, or even within a wing. Perhaps it is wise to remember that most clergymen of every faith are well-educated, thinking individuals. An interpretation of a given concept may reflect the individual clergyman's perception of that concept.

Myers (1951) compared superstitious and nonsuperstitious high-school students, and also religiously and secularly oriented high-school students. Socioeconomic status, educational level of parents, and replies on factual-knowledge questions were found to be lower for the superstitious and orthodox groups than for the nonsuperstitious and secular groups. Myers found that: "The typical high-school student has a favorable attitude toward church, attends services about once a week, and says prayers once or twice a day."

IS RELIGION IMPORTANT IN ADOLESCENCE?

In any discussion of religion and adolescence the question must arise as to whether or not religion is necessary at this age level. Allport (1950) has discussed the course of development in the normally mature and productive personality. He feels that religious sentiments arise from needs, interests, temperament, rationality, and cultural response. The mature religious person can act wholeheartedly without absolute certainty, for religious aspiration is an intention to strive toward long-range goals whatever the present risks and difficulties. Allport suggests that the crux of mental health lies in one's beliefs and in the ability to integrate conflicts around a master sentiment that points beyond immediate and self-centered gratifications to large relationships, more decisive action, and deeper assurance in the realization of permanent values.

In a book edited by Anshen, Swift (1949) has suggested that anything that endangers family unity or separates man from direct dealing with his environment "weakens the hold of religion by robbing it of its function." Even when it is seemingly ignored, religion is always a part of the pattern of living. One of its major contributions has been to pass down approved ways of behaving from one generation to another. Swift felt that the strength of family life is too interlocked with the strength of religion for church and state ever to be so separated that godlessness results. Some of the means he suggested for giving greater unity to the home include decentralization of society, the revival of small communities and the creation of united neighborhoods, the wise teaching of an awareness of God, and family worship. This latter aspect is currently emphasized in the slogan "The family that prays together stays together."

The need for religion to involve more emotional appeal, since motivation for learning and growth arises from such appeal, has been stressed by Beches (1947). Religious programs are often stereotyped and fail to gain emotional response. Young people, however, demand new experiences, awareness of the presence of God, to be useful and altruistic, to participate responsibly, and to belong to a wholesome fellowship. They wish to understand accepted religious affirmations and to enjoy democratic religious authority rather than moral chaos. The Youth for Christ International had the dramatic appeal of mass meetings but, according to Beches, failed to satisfy the need for a rational faith and offended by sensational methods. If religious leaders are too busy to nurture emotion effectively, young people will be increasingly absent from church activities.

Clark (1950) drew the following conclusion from his study of "The Psychology of Religious Values": (1) genuine religious experience influences behavior; (2) women value religion more highly than men do; (3) change of religious values in college, though small, is in the direction of the prevailing religious tradition at the college; (4) religious values are important for therapy; and (5) the integration of religious values with emotional drives is due to the satisfying nature of religion, its explanation of cosmic mysteries, opportunities for merging self with higher enterprises, and the faith that such enterprises will succeed. He also concluded that the Allport-Vernon Study of Values has been the foremost instrument for its purpose. He feels that progress in research in this area will come when techniques utilizing empirical and inductive approaches are developed.

Forres (1955) also stressed religion as an important experience of individual growth and felt that the disturbed child needs spiritual

guidance in addition to psychotherapy. There is, of course, an opposing point of view among some therapists, who feel that religion is a
"crutch" for many people and is unimportant in therapy.

WHAT ARE RELIGIOUS INSTITUTIONS DOING
TO ATTRACT TEEN-AGERS?

Since the various organized religions have become very much concerned
about the increasing failure of teen-agers to attend regular services,
they have made many attempts to stimulate the youngsters' interest.
These attempts are often nonreligious in nature, designed initially
to bring adolescents into the church building.

Church-Sponsored Social Programs

Youth organizations that are more social than religious, at least in
the beginning stages, have been formed. Churches sponsor "teen
town" programs with music for dancing and free soft drinks.

Church groups have also become aware of the success of the Young
Men's Christian Association's athletic program and have started to
structure similar programs. Baseball and basketball are inducements
to the boys, while dancing lessons, tennis, badminton, etc., are available for the girls and any boys who might be interested. When a new
church building is constructed today, the plan usually includes a complete gymnasium and, if the congregation can afford it, a swimming
pool.

Gearing Religious Teaching to Adolescents

Obviously, religious groups are not interested in offering social and
athletic activities to their youngsters to the exclusion of religion. These
activities are useful in bringing youngsters into the premises; the difficult job follows. Some tolerable amount of religious teaching must be
related to the other activities, and this must be done subtly so as not to
alienate the youngsters.

Study groups are often formed, with the youngsters selecting topics
that they wish to discuss to gain better understanding. The clergyman or assistant who handles these groups must be particularly skilled
in drawing out the youngsters without simply moralizing or telling
them what is right and what wrong. He must guide them in such a
way that they seem to discover the right answers for themselves, rather
than play an authoritarian role. If such an attempt succeeds, it may
be because the youngsters like the adult leader as a person, rather than
because the doctrines he attempts to explain appeal to them.

It is most important that the religious emphasis be keyed to the teen-agers' level of understanding and functioning, without the leader's seeming to "talk down" to them. Religion must be meaningfully related to activities in which they are interested. For example, if Rock and Roll is important to teen-agers, a religious group should not attempt to ban it because it is vulgar or stirs the emotions. A more effective approach is to relate the musical beat of Rock and Roll to the beat found in many spirituals. One need only to listen to the magnificent spiritual singer Mahalia Jackson to realize how stirring a strong driving rhythm can be. If youngsters can see this kind of relationship, they may even be willing to sing a few spirituals themselves.

Organized religions have too long maintained adult standards for youngsters. In many religions there is still some sort of puberty rite, such as the Bar Mitzvah of the Jewish faith, which allegedly makes the youngster an adult member of the congregation, subject to conformity to the adult standards. We are finally becoming aware that, puberty rite or not, thirteen- to eighteen-year-olds cannot be expected fully to meet adult norms of acceptable behavior. With this realization, more clergymen and lay people are being especially trained as youth leaders, and the results do seem to be encouraging.

The adolescents themselves should be most willing to take advantage of the efforts of religious groups to recruit them. If they find that they can discuss the problems that were cited in the research studies mentioned earlier, they will be attracted. If these discussions are at their own level, and if they are free to discuss their disbeliefs as well as their beliefs without fear of moral condemnation, they will probably welcome the opportunity.

RELIGION AS VIEWED BY ADOLESCENTS

In a rather extensive survey conducted by the Moral and Spiritual Education Section of the Los Angeles Public Schools, an attempt was made to determine the attitudes of high-school seniors toward religion. Of the 3676 students who wrote anonymous essays on religious attendance, 36 per cent attend church regularly, 52 per cent attend irregularly, and 12 per cent never attend. Of 3317 students who wrote on prayer, 22 per cent pray to ask for personal benefits, 19 per cent to express thanks, 15 per cent to talk to God, 11 per cent to ask for guidance, 10 per cent to comply with habit, and 9 per cent to seek comfort. The students recommended that schools offer voluntary nondenominational religious education; that homes encourage early religious training of children; and that churches have a more reverent atmosphere during worship services and encourage more club and recreational opportunities for youth.

Most teen-agers do not actually reject religion; they simply reject some of its ritualistic aspects. They are still very much interested in religion and want to learn more about their own faith and those of others. They want particularly to know how religions differ and how they are alike. Youngsters wish to learn these things on an intellectual basis rather than on one of blind acceptance. They question religion, not because they want to become agnostic or atheistic, but because they want to accept religion in a way that is meaningful to them and that is based on their desire to be independent and free to make their own decisions. They do not want to accept a religion that tells them they are in the hands of an all-powerful, all-seeing deity who allows them no freedom of choice.

Dislike of Formal Services

The complaints of youngsters are usually related to such specific situations as church attendance. The younger child is often more willing to attend services regularly because the ritual is keyed to his level in Sunday school classes where he is with his peer group. During early adolescence, and not later than age sixteen, the youngster is expected to begin to attend church services with the adults. Most adolescents lose interest at this point, feeling that the services are not really for them but for the adults. Ken C. explained his reaction in essentially this way:

"I started going to Sunday school when I was about six. Three or four of my neighborhood friends attended with me and this was fun. The stories they told were about Biblical events and they were interesting. As I got older, I still enjoyed Sunday school, especially the discussions we had with each other as well as those we had with the teacher. But in our religion the Sunday school program ends at age fourteen, and then we were supposed to go to regular church services with our parents. I did go for about a year, but I never enjoyed it. First, it was tough to sit and listen for a couple of hours. Second, I thought the sermons were dull and often over my head. I might have enjoyed it more if I could have sat with my friends, but we had to stay with our parents. I don't have a chance to discuss religion much now. During the week my group has too many other things to consider, and we almost never discuss religion. My parents don't seem to want to discuss it either. By the time I was sixteen I wouldn't attend church any more. I'm still religious, and I pray at home, but I just can't see what I can gain from regular church services."

Many youngsters remain affiliated with a church and relatively active in church functions but do not care for regular attendance at formal services. They may be active in many of the social and athletic activities sponsored by the church and even involved in such religious activities as they enjoy.

Joe S. is president of his B'nai B'rith Youth Organization group and is a leader in many of the activities sponsored by his synagogue. Except for special occasions when the whole group is required to attend a Friday evening service, Joe has little to do with the formal ritual of his religion. The youth activities director of the synagogue is a young rabbi with whom Joe has a good deal of interaction. Joe likes this rabbi and spends a good deal of time discussing religion with him. Joe is well versed in his religion and occasionally takes an active part in the special youth services. He does not care to attend the regular adult services because "the sermons are pitched to the adult level and although I find some of them interesting, they don't usually deal with topics that interest me. Even our youth director is more rigid in his approach when he gives a sermon to the adults than he is with our group. Sometimes I have the feeling that there isn't much keyed to the teen-agers' interests in the formal aspects of my religion."

Leadership in Religious Teaching

Many religious institutions have tried to organize small study groups for teen-agers to enable them to discuss religion under the guidance of a trained leader, often a clergyman. The success of these groups varies with the ability of the leader to communicate effectively with the youngsters without resorting to dogmatic responses.

Jim P. reported his experiences with a small study group and its leader, a young divinity student. Jim and his group formed a close relationship with this young man and the study group was very successful. The leader answered most questions concerning both his own and other religions honestly, and the members of the group felt free to discuss almost any topic with him. Jim and the others learned a good deal about formal religion and about general ethical codes. Then the blow fell. One evening one of the boys started to discuss contraception and was amazed when the leader angrily told him this was not an appropriate topic. Although his religion did not forbid the use of contraceptives, apparently the young student had strong personal feelings about this matter. The ensuing tirade included comments about the evil mind of the questioner and other highly emotional statements. Needless to say, this ended the study group. As Jim put it, "He was willing to discuss general broad issues, but when it came to specific things that we were really concerned about he couldn't understand our need. He just reverted to the same kind of moralizing we always seem to get from adults."

Obviously the personality of the youth leader and/or clergyman is a major factor in his success with adolescents. If they like or admire him, they are likely to be strongly influenced by him. It is unfortunate that relatively few young men seek to enter the clergy, which is now faced with serious shortages. Religious groups are hard pressed to find clergymen to serve the adult congregation, let alone men who are capable of working with and inspiring youth.

Association with Adults in Church Activities

To encourage young people's participation in religious activities, selected youngsters are sometimes made members of such adult groups as the building committee, the membership committee, and even the finance committee. This is designed to make the young people feel that they are an integral part of the church, not set apart as a separate group. However, unless the adults are a smoothly integrated group there is some risk in this kind of situation.

Pearl C., a sixteen-year-old high-school senior, was appointed as youth representative to her church's planning committee. Pearl was appalled at the bickering and petty jealousies exhibited by some of the adults. "Some of them seemed more concerned about their own special interests than the good of the total group." In order to get out of this situation, Pearl withdrew from the youth group she was representing and ceased attending church-sponsored activities. She said, in discussing this with our seminar, "I know these kinds of things go on every day, but it was very disillusioning to find people acting this way in a religious institution."

Parent-Adolescent Conflict over Beliefs

Occasionally the more liberal attitudes of the older teen-ager bring him into conflict with the adults around him, particularly if these adults have become involved in the ritual aspects of their religion. Such adults do not accept the view that one can be deeply religious without being involved in formal ritual and regular attendance at services. They may attempt to enforce a more regular observance by their youngsters, which may lead the youngsters even further away from affiliation with the church. It is not unusual for a youngster whose parents practice extreme orthodoxy in their religion to seek a more liberal wing of that religion with which to affiliate.

Sam J. came from an extremely orthodox Jewish home and was reared in this rigid pattern. During his teens he rebelled against this pressure, claiming that he did not really understand the rituals and resented blindly following them. He married a girl who was reared in a Reformed Jewish atmosphere but could not bring himself to accept Reformed Judaism, which he considered too much the opposite extreme. Finally he and his wife affiliated with a Conservative synagogue that they felt was a good middle ground.

Too little religious emphasis in the home may also produce a negative reaction from the teen-ager. Parents who adopt an attitude of "let him select his own religion" do not give their children a base from which they can operate in comparing or evaluating religions. In protest against such extreme liberalism, a youngster may actually choose a rather orthodox religion that is completely structured and allows little room for evaluation.

The Role of Religion

There is, nonetheless, general agreement among adults and among adolescents themselves that religion can and should play an important role in the lives of adolescents. Since this period of life is marked by uncertainty and wondering, firm foundations in religion can be a steadying factor. To accomplish this end, religion must emphasize its present value in daily living, not just in some future life. It must stress the importance of loving and being loved, and must particularly stress forgiveness. This latter aspect is particularly important to youngsters who see themselves as selfish and disobedient, and who feel some guilt about their efforts to emancipate themselves from the home. Most important, the worth of the individual should be steadily emphasized. Bernard (1957) has summed this up: "The role of religion in adolescence is that of giving and in the acceptance of persistent values, improving daily living, and thus establishing a clearer outlook on life."

ATTITUDES

There has long been a general interest in the beliefs of adolescents and about their feelings toward themselves, other people, and various environmental situations. Such interest has been motivated by the desire of adults to understand youngsters better and by the hope that the identification of negative attitudes can lead to programs designed to change such attitudes effectively. This is not to suggest that there are specific attitudes peculiar to the adolescent time period, since this is unlikely. Attitudes are generally closely related to the individual's personality and are the results of previous environmental experiences. Many of the attitudes held by adults may have been fully structured relatively early in life, possibly before the age of nine.

Of particular importance in the development of a youngster's attitudes are the attitudes held by his parents. Maccoby et al. (1954) found that almost three-fourths of the boys studied planned to belong to the same political party as their fathers, and about the same percentage of the girls to the political party with which the mother was affiliated.

It is a mistake, however, to assume that parents can accurately judge their youngster's attitudes simply by relating them to their own attitudes. Young people become very much aware of the accepted social and moral attitudes expressed by their parents and by the total environment in which they live. Because of such awareness, they may pay lip service to the accepted patterns without really possessing such attitudes themselves.

Group Attitudes and the Individual

In dealing with attitudes, one must carefully assess studies that purport to discuss the attitudes of groups. Such studies are often based on the expressed attitudes of the members, which are often colored by the fact that the individual is a member of the group. In attempting to maintain his identity with the group, an individual may support verbally attitudes that he thinks the group holds. However, his own actual feelings may differ appreciably from those of the group, and these true feelings may emerge only after his need for the security offered by the group decreases.

If there is a "typical teen-ager," he has probably been best described by Remmers and his various associates, who have been studying adolescents since 1941. Their studies have involved samples of 3000 high-school students chosen to represent accurately all high-school grades, urban and rural dwellers, and different family backgrounds. These studies have been carefully structured to avoid the problem of group response and have emphasized individual responses. The data are also recorded anonymously in an attempt to free the respondent from social pressures. Remmers and Radler (1957) published a summary of their results in the book *The American Teenager*.

Some of the differences between attitudes and the actual behavior resulting from various group pressures emerge from these surveys. Most teen-agers disapprove of drinking by high-school students, yet 25 per cent of them admit to drinking. About 75 per cent disapprove of smoking, but more than one-third of the adolescents do smoke. Their disapproval is not strong enough to counteract peer pressure; when the rest of the group is smoking or drinking, it is most difficult not to go along.

Dangers of Conformity

Teen-age conformity seems to relate to acceptance of an authoritarian point of view. More than half the youngsters surveyed believed that censorship of the various media of communication is legitimate, that police should be allowed free use of wiretapping and the "third degree," and that people should be forced to testify against themselves if they refuse to do so. Seventy-five per cent of the group listed "obedience and respect for authority" as "the most important habits for children to learn."

Remmers and Radler feel that their results may indicate some of the bases for anti-intellectualism in this country. Only 15 per cent rate academic learning as "the most important thing they can get out of school." The same attitude seems prevalent at the college level, too, with 60 per cent of the students preferring popularity to brilliance. More than half believe that low grades are related to popularity, while more than 72 per cent feel that the main purpose of education is the development of a well-rounded personality and that personality is more important than grades in finding a job.

These authors feel that this conformist spirit is relatively new in our society and that it reverses the previous individualistic pattern that was the American ideal. They point out that even in intellectual pursuits group endeavor has replaced individual functioning. Research teams, in which an individual scientist may subordinate himself to the standards and goals of the group, have become common. Remmers and Radler feel strongly that we must "restore a social climate which will reward independent thinking, personal morality, and truly enlightened cooperation." Unless such a social climate can replace the present structure of going along with the crowd, "the future of our democracy is not promising."

Adolescent Attitudes Toward Peers and Parents

Harris and Tseng (1957) have reported on the results of their study of the attitudes of youngsters toward their peers and toward their parents. Using a sentence-completion test to determine these attitudes, they present results that seem to be similar to other findings. They do not find that boys go through an antigirl stage in the elementary grades as has been commonly believed. Generally girls and boys favor their peers, particularly peers of their own sex. Boys and girls also have more favorable than unfavorable attitudes toward both their parents, with positive attitudes being expressed more frequently by the members of both sexes toward the mother than toward the father. High-school boys show an increase in positive attitudes toward both parents, while high-school girls show a more pronounced increase in positive attitudes toward their fathers than toward their mothers. These authors feel that the apparent boy-girl antipathy found in the intermediate grades is "more a product of girls changing their attitude toward boys than vice versa."

Age and Honesty

A scale to measure attitude toward honest conduct was developed by Beller (1949) and was administered to nine-, twelve-, and fifteen-year-old boys from different environments. Included were boys from elementary and junior high schools, boys from an orphanage, boys from a home for neglected children, and boys from a training school for delinquents. Comparisons were made between the environmental variables and age. With increasing mental age, there was a drop in honesty, in relation to behavioral disposition. The orphanage group ranked highest while the delinquent group ranked lowest.

Democratic Values

The Bill of Rights was converted into a fourteen-item questionnaire designed to study students' attitudes toward the concepts contained in this document. The questionnaire was administered to 560 college undergraduates. The results indicated considerable disagreement and indecision regarding our basic civil liberties. They also indicated an impressive amount of ignorance concerning constitutional provisions for these rights. If we expect documents like the Bill of Rights to be meaningful to our children, the schools should offer enough information about them to help develop positive attitudes (Mack, 1956).

In a survey of high-school students, Perryman (1950) studied attitudes toward government activities. He administered a Likert-type scale of attitudes about philosophies and actual policies of government. Generally the students favored an increase in government activities over those existing at that time. The finding also indicated a more favorable attitude toward government than the students had thought they had.

FACTORS AFFECTING ATTITUDES

Some of the factors associated with attitudes have been investigated to determine what kinds of relationships might exist. Hieronymous (1951) obtained information concerning socioeconomic status, present and expected; attitude toward education; and standard-intelligence-test scores from a group of 910 ninth-grade pupils. Expected socioeconomic status showed a correlation of about .60 with present economic status and about .40 with intelligence-test results. The attitude toward education, however, correlated only .30 with present socioeconomic status, but about .50 with expected status.

This latter fact may be one of great importance in better understanding attitudes of adolescents. We often fail to recognize the influence of expected future socioeconomic status on the adolescent's present attitudes. This is a particularly crucial area in adolescence, since expectancies of future status may be quite unrealistic. Attitudes that result from possible unrealistic goals of future status may become highly negative when the individual finds the goal unattainable. Such a situation may easily lead the individual into strongly negative, prejudiced behavior.

Phillips (1950) attempted to study the relationships between the results of a social-attitude questionnaire and measures of personality, intelligence, and socioeconomic status. A questionnaire suitable for junior-high-school students was developed and administered along with the California Test of Personality to ninth- and tenth-grade students in a community near Chicago, and to eighth- and ninth-grade students from the Twin Cities area. The questionnaire consisted of 120 items, 40 for each of the three social classes—lower, middle, and upper. Generally the results indicated that members of the lower social class scored reliably lower on intelligence and personality tests than did the other two groups. A sex difference was found to exist, with higher scores reported from girls on the middle- and upper-class scales and from boys on the lower-class scale. The author also reported that "members deviating from their allegedly 'true' social class level score reliably lower on personality and intelligence tests than do the so-called 'pure' members of a given class." Certain attitudes and behavior were found to be similar in the three class levels, showing these to be relatively common and to be cohesive factors in our society.

Centers (1950) tested the hypothesis that the beliefs and attitudes of adolescents with respect to labor and collectivism exhibit the same relationships to occupational strata as do those of adults. A questionnaire was administered to 1000 students in a high school in a small Eastern city. The results indicated that the lower the parental occupational level, the greater the incidence of pro-labor and collectivist views found among the high-school students. Similar results were found in terms of class identification or affiliation. The analyses also demonstrated relationships of the attitudes to maturity and to parental labor-union affiliation.

Research dealing with some of the social attitudes of young people was conducted by the Educational Psychology Department at Warsaw University. The investigation was structured to attempt to find the factors that influence the attitudes of present-day youth. The bad influence of the environment and lack of proper care on the part of the home, school, and society were the major factors identified. Disappointment and lack of opportunity to have a good time were also influential. These young people did feel it would be possible for them to change their attitudes, provided they had greater opportunity to enjoy life. Despite the influences of their Communist-dominated environment, almost half these young people did not believe in the possibility of help by membership in a youth organization. A number of them felt that attitudes could change only if better educational methods were introduced and younger people were surrounded with greater care (Brzezinska, 1960).

The need for children to have the opportunity to experiment with their behavior and to weigh its consequences in developing their attitudes and values was stressed by Corey (1954). He felt that school children are less likely than adults to be aware of criteria for these characteristics, to anticipate conflict in what they do to support their values, and to intellectualize and verbalize. Too often the youngsters accept systems of values without critical evaluation of these systems in relation to their own welfare. Their lack of adequate experiences within the environment limits their ability to judge values intelligently.

Anderson (1952) administered personality and adjustment measures to 3200 children from nine to eighteen years of age. At each age level a group of well-adjusted, poorly adjusted, and average-adjusted children was selected on the basis of combined scores on thirteen measures. Results show sharp distinctions among the three groups on the affective index in relation to age and adjustment. Anderson suggests that there is some justification for assuming both that internal orientation toward experience has some relation to adjustment and that level of adjustment in turn modifies internal orientation.

An analysis of scores on the Thurstone Scale for measuring attitudes toward the church obtained from a sample of about 1000 students at the University of Utah was reported by Telford (1950). The Mormon students at the university were more favorable toward the church than any of the other denominational groups (which may relate to the fact that this is a Mormon-supported institution). Females were more favorable toward the church than were males, and nonveterans were more favorable than veterans. Those who were unaffiliated with any organized religion showed a closer relationship between their church attitude and use of alcohol, tobacco, and coffee than did any denominational group. Among the unaffiliated there was a direct relation between the orthodoxy of the subjects' background and the degree of antagonism they expressed toward the church.

ATTITUDES TOWARD OTHERS

A substantial amount of research has been and is being done concerning the attitudes of people toward others, especially toward minority groups. Much of this research has attempted to find the bases for intolerance in our society in an effort to determine how such intolerance can be alleviated or even eliminated. Increasingly, the schools and the individual teachers may become major factors in the prevention of intolerance and in the development of positive rather than negative attitudes toward others.

How Prejudices Develop

Radke-Yarrow and Miller (1949) attempted to determine how youngsters in the fifth through twelfth grades perceive the meaning of the word "American." To obtain the data, they questioned the youngsters about their own American group and about groups to which they did not belong—Jewish and Negro. The youngsters were also asked to express in writing the meaning of each group and to give explanations or reasons for the meaning stated. These youngsters lived in a community in which they had a minimum of personal experience with the minority groups (no Negroes lived in the community, and only one childless Jewish family). The data revealed that most of the children had a relatively low level of understanding of cultural similarities and differences among people. A number of hostile reactions were expressed by the older children toward both minority groups, very similar in content to what might be expected from youngsters in a totalitarian state. This study well illustrates the fact that youngsters assimilate through learning prejudice "which is not based on personal experience with the individual or group against which the prejudice is expressed."

Although we often think of a total American culture into which people from all races, religions, and nationalities are assimilated into a single societal pattern, this apparently does not exist. While most groups seek to be assimilated and identified as Americans, they carry over many of the patterns peculiar to their original group. In some cases (such as that of the Amish) groups wish to retain their own identity and resist Americanization, while in other cases the mainstream of American society resists the group's attempt to become Americanized (well illustrated by the treatment accorded the West Coast Japanese during World War II).

As a minority group grows in size, and particularly as its members become better educated, it may be unwilling to continue to accept the role thrust on it by the environment. In a country where "all men are created equal" everyone wishes his equality to be recognized, not only legally but in the everyday environment. The steps taken to achieve such equality may vary from "passive resistance" to overt aggression, or at least the advocation of overt aggression. The reader need only think of the present-day efforts of Negroes to achieve desegregation to realize how this works. On the one hand, we have the passive-resistance approach of the Reverend Martin Luther King and the

Freedom Riders, and at the other extreme the highly aggressive efforts of the Black Muslims, who advocate use of force to achieve their demands.

Prejudice, Montagu (1949) has suggested, usually arises from the frustration of an individual in satisfying his needs, or from his feelings of rejection. Because he feels insecure, he tries to compensate for his low status and insecurity but can usually only express his hostility toward those whom he views as unable to fight back. If he chooses to express his hostility overtly toward those more powerful, he is likely to become even more rejected and consequently more insecure. The victim whom he chooses to attack, therefore, is actually the displaced object of his wrath. If the society in which he functions condones or even approves of his acts by propagandizing against the group or individual he is attacking, he may then be ready to commit an act of aggression. He will usually find others with whom he can ally himself, thus causing him to feel less rejected, or even accepted. To maintain this acceptance he may resort to violence. As a final step, he must rationalize his prejudice in order to convince himself that his acts of aggression are not the result of prejudice or hate.

Group Stereotypes and Individual "Exceptions"

Too often young people are exposed to the stereotypes of a given group and are not aware of the group's real characteristics. If they have little or no exposure to members of that group, they are likely to accept the stereotype, even though it may be archaic and completely erroneous. When one becomes aware that a given member of the group performs in a way that is contrary to the stereotype, this can be accepted by suggesting that he is "the exception that proves the rule." One often hears it said, "So-and-so is a real person and I like him, but he certainly is different from the others in his group." Obviously, then, an individual can be accepted, but the positive traits that make him acceptable are often considered as not necessarily characteristic of his group.

Nash (1958) presented junior-high-school students with nine schematic faces varying in facial characteristics, such as height of forehead, length and position of nose, etc. These adolescents clearly revealed the stereotyped behavior reported by other investigators by identifying these pictures in terms of commonly held views of the relationship of facial characteristics with racial, ethnic, or other characteristics. The adolescents were, however, less stereotyped in their reaction than were adults.

British girls between eleven and fifteen years of age were interviewed regarding their opinions of other races. Attitudes that had originally been established on the basis of second-hand evidence changed in many cases, with the amount of change directly proportional to amount of personal acquaintance. The girls themselves indicated that acquaintance through contact was fundamental if change was to take place. Their statements concerning others related entirely to characteristics that were disturbing or reassuring, or that promised enjoyable personal relations. Generally races were thought of in the same way as individuals, and experiences with individuals were generalized to include characteristics of races (James and Tenen, 1950). These findings seem generally contrary to what we find in our own society, where individuals are often accepted, but as exceptions among their race.

Economic Bases of Prejudice

As the members of a group become more and more successful in the American society they may arouse envy, and as a result even more prejudice develops. The success of the Jews in material matters has probably strengthened the prejudice against them. The Negro today is also beginning to experience success, and has been able to compete with whites successfully for certain kinds of jobs. Not only is envy a factor but also fear, as whites become concerned that Negroes may displace them in their occupations. Whenever the in-group becomes threatened by the activities of the out-group, overt prejudice may become overtly expressed. Such overt aggression often becomes so highly emotionally involved that the individual's basic intelligence is virtually unrecognizable, as anyone who has watched television reports of the reactions of some Southerners to Negro integration must have become aware. The rather violent behavior overtly demonstrated by these few in front of obviously placed television cameras was a tragic illustration of emotional reaction's overcoming intelligent action. Even more tragic was this expression of violence by adults in front of their children, whose own developing biases could only be strongly reinforced by such behavior.

Susceptibility to Prejudice

Frenkel-Brunswik (1948) reported on the "determinants of susceptibility to racial or ethnic prejudice and allied forms of undemocratic opinions and attitudes in children." She analyzed the responses of children eleven to sixteen years of age, who were either unprejudiced or extremely prejudiced, on items covering such topics as general political attitudes, physical or moral weakness, sex role, power and money, and submission to authority. There were marked differences between the groups, with the children rated as prejudiced being illiberal, rigid, dichotomous, and punitive. The results were positively related to those obtained from the children's parents on similar material. Although these attitudes are established relatively early, the author suggests that the ethnocentrism of children is more susceptible than that of adults.

Frenkel-Brunswick (1953) also attempted to provide "documentation of children's more or less spontaneous reactions to the minority problem." Eighty-one white American gentile children (fifteen to nineteen years of age) were interviewed to ascertain their attitudes about Negroes, Mexicans, Chinese, Japanese, and Jews. On the basis of their scores on an ethnocentrism scale, these subjects were defined as "high scorers," "middle scorers," and "low scorers," with high scores indicating greater prejudice. Generally there was evidence of consistency of prejudice indicated by a correlation of .67 between interviewer's rating and ethnocentrism score. The data also demonstrated "considerable generality (rather than specificity) of prejudice." The majority of children were on the prejudiced rather than on the tolerant side, with a good deal of similarity between the middle scorers and the high scorers. There were some indications of "family influences in the area of ethnic tolerance or intolerance." The majority of the children studied favored segregation of minority groups.

Zeligs (1950) has also studied intergroup attitudes in an attempt to find the reasons for these attitudes. In 1942, 1943, and 1944 she gave the Zeligs Intergroup Attitude Test to twelve-year-old students who were of the same suburban school, same age, and same background as subjects interviewed in 1931. The reasons given for their attitudes by the 1942, 1943, and 1944 groups were similar to those given by the 1931 group. "Although customs, costumes, cleanliness, language, religion, character qualities, and civilization are still given by the children as reasons for their attitudes, the recent trends are away from prejudice because of racial and physical differences."

Opinions concerning group status among pupils, parents, and teachers of a junior high school in a poor part of "Plain City" were surveyed by Taylor (1947). This school population is composed of Spanish-Americans, Negroes, Japanese-Americans, and "Anglos." Questions were asked about equality of treatment and opportunity, and one question was directed at what the school should do. Children were more critical of school training than the adults were and made proportionately more suggestions for improvement in the school program. There was a general belief that there was equality in educational opportunity, but not in housing and job opportunities. The children attributed these inequalities to poverty or lack of education, while the adults attributed them to racial factors. Antagonism was directed mainly at the Spanish group, secondly at the Negroes.

Prejudice may result in part from a major training device employed by parents—the use of negative references to disallowed or minority groups (Mead, 1951). For example, parents may say, "Don't use bad grammar, you sound like an immigrant." As a result, prejudices form toward any person or any group unlike those accepted by the parents. This biased feeling can become highly intensified in a youngster who, feeling guilty about his resentment of his own family, takes his feeling out on others as a form of compensation. If children can be taught to be satisfied with their sex, current age, racial, religious, and national ancestry, Mead believes that improvement in majority-minority relations will result.

Gough *et al.* (1950) developed an anti-Negro attitude scale for youngsters in the third through the sixth grade. The relationship of this attitude to certain personality qualities, to generalized intolerance, and to attitude toward Jews was investigated. A positive relationship appeared between anti-Negro attitudes and the scale assessing generalized intolerance. Both the particular and generalized ethnic attitudes were found to be related to evidences of hostility, resentment, distrust, insecurity, suspiciousness, and similar characteristics, as revealed in personality test items. These findings seem to relate well to the concepts expressed by Mead in the study just mentioned.

Negroes and Prejudice

While bias toward many groups is still present in our society, it is not as obvious on the overt level as it was formerly. Anti-Semitism, anti-Catholicism, etc., still exist in our present-day America, but generally these prejudices remain below the surface. An occasional specific situation may bring the prejudice out in the open, but it usually subsides again. For example, the overt expression of anti-Catholicism reached a modern-day peak during the 1960 presidential campaigns because the Democratic candidate, Senator Kennedy, was a Catholic. After he was elected President, the overt anti-Catholic attitudes subsided, though they arise sporadically on specific issues involving federal funds for parochial schools. The fact that Kennedy was elected despite such overt display of bias was indeed a victory of reason over bias; it is highly unlikely that a Catholic candidate could have been elected to this high office thirty years ago.

Today the greatest amount of overtly displayed prejudice is directed at the Negro, particularly the Southern Negro. This is not to suggest that there is no bias toward the Northern Negro, but simply that it is covertly or more subtly expressed. There is no officially planned segregation of schools in the North, but nonetheless there are many schools comprising only Negro students. Unwritten neighborhood covenants serve to keep Negroes from certain residential districts in most Northern cities. Despite all this, Negroes do have upward mobility in the North and do move into all-white neighborhoods. There is usually a flare-up when such an event occurs, but this generally subsides, and although Negroes are not completely accepted by their white neighbors, they are at least tolerated, especially if they are well educated and in the professional class.

The Southern Negro is, however, often the object of direct overt expression of prejudice. Despite the Supreme Court decision, only token integration of carefully selected Negro students has taken place in the schools in most Southern states. Reactions have been so strong as to lead to violence, as in Little Rock and other strongholds of segregation. Obviously it takes more than a legal edict to eliminate segregation, and such an edict may serve only to bring prejudice to the surface. As long as the Southern Negro "knew his place," he was "accepted" by the Southern whites. Once he was declared equal to those who had thought themselves superior, he became a threat to them socially and economically. Reaction to such threat is almost certain to be aggressive.

Despite segregation and less than good educational environment in "separate but equal" schools, Southern Negro children have values very similar to those of Northern white children. This was well demonstrated in a study by Hughes and Thompson (1954), which analyzed essays written by Northern white children in a nonsegregated school and Southern Negro children in segregated schools. Both groups equally prized knowledge, achievement, and economic value highly. The white students put significantly greater emphasis on happiness, security, and independence and a much lower value-emphasis on justice and group unity. The Negro pupils were strongly critical of segregation and were concerned with social justice in this connotation.

The Social Problem Analyses, Advanced Series, which deals with attitudes toward Negro problems, was administered to tenth-grade pupils. Less favorable attitudes toward Negro problems appear among children from a lower socioeconomic background as compared with a higher one, among boys as compared with girls, among new-stock Americans, and among those of average intelligence compared with those of higher intelligence (Hayes, 1953).

These latter factors illustrate a point briefly discussed earlier. The equality and with it the economic opportunity offered the Negro in an integrated society is an immediate threat to the group showing the most negative attitude and is probably one of the basic causes of these attitudes. Economically, the lower group, representing unskilled and semiskilled occupational levels, will be competing for jobs against Negroes long before the middle or upper economic groups will be involved in such competition. This competition also is evident earlier against males than against females, and against those of less than average rather than of high intelligence.

The real source of concern is whether or not the attitude toward the Negro can be changed in a reasonably short time. Mayo and Kinzer (1950) attempted to determine if such changes in attitude toward Negroes have taken place with the passage of time. A Test of Racial Attitudes was administered to the students of three high schools for white children and four high schools for Negro children in Tennessee in 1940 and in 1948. The 1940 sample consisted of 460 whites and 467 Negroes; the 1948 sample tested 456 whites and 626 Negroes. Although the members of both white and Negro groups expressed more favorable opinions of the Negro in 1948 than in 1940, they were even further from agreement on issues involving interracial relations. Apparently these greater differences resulted from the fact that the attitudes of the Negro students had shifted more than those of the white students between 1940 and 1948.

Blood (1955) suggested that discrimination can exist without prejudice. In a study of store managers, the author demonstrated that discrimination ("overt behavior which deprives groups of equal access to social facilities such as jobs and accommodations") may be practiced by persons who are not actually prejudiced (possessing an attitude "involving an adverse judgment of the . . . characteristics of members of a group"). This may of course be possible, but practice of discrimination would seem likely to lead to prejudice. If numbers of those who are being discriminated against attempt to fight the discrimination, they become a threat to the discriminator, who may fear that their efforts will jeopardize his position and may thus develop highly negative emotional reactions to them, which become in essence prejudice.

BIAS WITHIN GROUPS

Seldom discussed, but nonetheless present, is the bias that exists within racial, religious, ethnic, and socioeconomic groups. These biases are not necessarily based on fear, as are between-group prejudices, although they often do have a psychological basis. They may rather be based on geographic differences, differences within a religion, and differences in degree of skin pigmentation within a given race. Such biases are also unlikely to result in overt physical violence, but they may still result in highly negative emotional responses.

Ethnic Groups

Perhaps the oldest of these types of bias are those within ethnic groups that originated in the "old country" from which the group originally emigrated. These were generally biases based on geographic differences, with urban-dwellers "looking down" on the peasants or rural-dwellers. Although the descendants of the two groups may now live in the same urban area in this country, they still tend to maintain their old-world reactions to each other. The Irish, for example, still refer to "lace curtain" or "shanty" Irish, designations based on family backgrounds in Ireland, regardless of present status.

Religions

Biases within a religion are perhaps more apparent in America today than was true in Europe a generation ago. One reason for this is that more divisions within religions exist here than did in Europe. Within one European country, one wing of a sect predominated; in another country, a different wing was dominant. When members of one denomination from different countries came to America, they often clashed. The Orthodox Jews, for example, came from Russia, Poland, etc.; but the German Jews who came to this country were generally members of the Reformed wing. Even today Orthodox Jews practically deny that Reformed Jews are members of the same religion. Reformed Jews consider strict orthodoxy archaic and cannot understand the behavior of those who practice it. To make matters even more confused, Conservative Judaism has gained much popularity in America today as a sort of middle ground. Neither the Reformed or the Orthodox group accepts its tenets, and in turn its members frown on theirs.

Protestantism is composed of a large number of denominations. Members of the various sects often regard their own sect as the true representative of Protestantism and disapprove of some, if not all, of the others. In addition to the differences between Episcopalians and Methodists, Methodists and Baptists, etc., there are also differences in ritual and functioning within each of these groups. For example, the Missouri Synod, although having a large membership, is not the official Lutheran organization. Lutherans who are not members of this group often react negatively to it when discussing its relation to their own branch of their religion.

Even in the more uniform structure of the Roman Catholic church, differences in interpretation of a given edict may be offered by different priests. It is not unusual for two equally well educated, devout Catholics to take opposite sides on a particular issue. An illustration of this can be found in the newspaper reports of Cardinal Spellman's comments concerning the Supreme Court decision forbidding a state to require prayers in the public schools. Many prominent Catholic clerics and lay people took issue with the Cardinal's point of view.

The failure of most people to realize that within-religion biases exist was brought home to this author recently in a very striking fashion. He was attending a meeting at which a group of college students and other adults, whose goal was to help fight prejudice, were presenting a discussion. Their main theme dealt with various illustrations of bias between racial and religious groups, and it was obvious that much work had gone into their program. During the discussion period that followed their presentation, a member of the audience asked, "Isn't it true that there may be as much bias within groups as there is between groups?" He illustrated his question with some comments about his own religious group. The panel moderator quickly responded, "That may be true of your group, but it certainly isn't true of us Protestants." Needless to say, the remark of the moderator completely negated any positive effects the original panel discussion might have had.

Races

Biases within a racial group can be illustrated by an examination of some of the reactions of Negroes to Negroes. In some geographic areas a dark-skinned Negro "looks down" on one whose skin is lighter, while in other areas the opposite is true. Negroes as a group are usually proud of any outstanding achievement of an individual member of their race, but if his achievement brings him into regular contact with whites he may be thought to be "too good for his own people." Recently this author spent some time in a large Northern city where Negro parents were protesting because their children attended a school having only Negro teachers. These parents reflected the attitude that Negro teachers would not offer their children as good an education as would white teachers, despite the fact that these teachers had been carefully selected and were rated as superior to many white teachers by their white supervisors.

The Class System

Socioeconomic differences are, of course, related to our class system, which in some areas actually resembles a caste system. Mere acquisition of wealth alone is not sufficient to gain membership to various clubs or organizations. One must have come from "the right kind of family," and this is even more important than financial status. Economic mobility is easier to achieve than is social mobility. It is perhaps democratic for people to say they are "middle class," but many don't really believe it or are at least striving to move up.

The socioeconomic factor was discussed in Chapter 6. As previously suggested, parents of the upper socioeconomic class prefer that their youngsters' associates be members of the same class. Parents of a low socioeconomic group also may not be pleased if their youngsters associate with those of a higher level. Such a youngster may be told that he "thinks he's too good for his family."

How Within-Group Biases Affect Adolescents

All these biases affect the behavior of adolescents whose homes transmit the biases. A child reared in a Reformed Jewish home will look askance at the behavior of a youngster reared in a rigidly Orthodox home, especially if the latter youngster wears a skull cap in public. An Orthodox Jewish youngster is shocked to hear that the adolescent from the Reformed Jewish environment has not had a Bar Mitzvah. An Episcopalian youngster who dates a Baptist girl may be goaded or teased by his peers in his church group. "Lace curtain" Irish families are not enthusiastic when their youngsters associate with children from "shanty" Irish backgrounds. Such behavior might lower their status among their own peer group.

A friend of this author's recently married a girl who in the eyes of his family was of a "peasant" class. The young lady was as well educated as her husband, and her family was wealthier than his, but his grandparents had come from an urban center of the country of their origin and hers had come from the rural area. Although the couple themselves had no difficulty in adjusting, they seemed to be constantly arbitrating arguments between their families.

We do not suggest that such within-group biases are as serious as biases between groups. Yet it is hard to see how much can be done about between-group bias when obvious within-group bias exists. However, members of the group within which bias exists may have much in common despite their differences, while two unrelated groups who are prejudiced against each other may have little or nothing in common.

CAN ATTITUDES CHANGE?

A question of major concern is whether attitudes can be changed, or at least modified, particularly during the adolescent years. If it is true that the adolescent's attitudes are a reflection of his past and present environment, is the development of these patterns rigidly fixed or is there some degree of flexibility within which change or modification is possible? Obviously, the answer will vary according to the individual and his specific environmental background, but some data is available concerning changes in group and individual attitudes.

Martin (1954) has discussed the development of values in relation to learning theory and identification. He proposed that attitudes are often learned initially through imitation of adults. This imitative behavior is reinforced by the approval of the adults. Persons other than the parents, including teachers and members of the peer group, are involved in such development. As the child grows older he is also influenced by such media as books, newspapers, radio, and television. If all these environmental factors react on the individual in much the same way, and he also experiences behavioral situations that make them more meaningful, attitudes are likely to become strongly fixed.

The older the individual becomes, the more his attitudes resemble those of the adults around him, especially those of the group with which he identifies. As this resemblance increases, attitudes are likely to be far more difficult to change. Thus, attempts to change attitudes should probably begin relatively early, certainly by the beginning of the junior-high-school years.

What the School Can Do

If the school is to become involved in attempts to change attitudes, something more than simple subject-matter content is needed. Sister Mary Agnes (1947) asked 70 high-school girls who had volunteered to read two books about Negroes whether their attitudes toward Negroes had changed. In general, the group had better attitudes than a control group. However, the results did not prove that the better attitude was directly related to the reading. The very fact that these girls volunteered to read the books may have indicated a desire on their part to try to change their attitudes.

Changes in attitudes toward world peace after a seven-week unit of study on the United Nations were reported by Klee (1949). The changes were in a positive direction, favoring the principles embodied in the United Nations Charter. Of 218 changes recorded, 33 students listed the school course as a major factor in 192 changes. Class discussion was also a major reason given for the change.

Horton (1953) used on high-school students a polling technique in which items from the Bill of Rights were paraphrased. About 20 per cent of the students consistently gave "antidemocratic" responses. A course in civics "was not at all significant in terms of the individual's attitudes toward allowing greater freedom for minority groups." Those who were better informed, however, generally demonstrated lesser degrees of prejudice.

Too often youngsters' responses to attempts to modify behavior relate to the personality of the individual attempting the modification. Students may really attempt to change a negative attitude if they like the individual who is trying to guide them. If, on the other hand, they dislike the adult, they may feel that he is not being honest in his attempts to change their attitudes, and their views may become even more negative.

Effects of Personal Contacts

Personal contact with individuals or groups against whom one is biased has been recommended as useful for bringing about changes in attitude. This approach may be useful, but only if the personal contact occurs under extremely favorable conditions, where the group discriminated against can appear in a "good light." Yet even if a change in attitude does result, it is not necessarily generalized. The individual or small group with whom the contact has been made may be seen in a more positive fashion, but a negative attitude toward the over-all group may still persist.

Influencing Group Attitudes

Kelley and Volkart (1952) studied twelve groups of urban Boy Scouts in an attempt to determine resistance to change of group-anchored attitudes. These youngsters were exposed to contra-norm communication in the form of a talk on the unimportance of camping and forest lore in Scout training. Attitude change was measured by tests under conditions of private and public expression before and after the talk. Resistance to change did not seem any greater under public than under private conditions. Greater resistance to change was manifested by Scouts who value their membership more highly, and this relationship is more evident under private than under public conditions. Apparently the stronger one's identification to a group, the stronger the resistance to any change that seems contrary to that group's aims. Lewin (1947) feels that the Boy Scout organization fosters frontier ideals such as self-reliance and individual initiative, which have lost much of their meaning in our highly interdependent society. A democratic society must provide for both self-expression and social intercourse, and present-day scouting falls far short with respect to policies of social participation and the building of understanding of national and international policies. If Lewin's thesis is correct, it might partially explain the failure of the Boy Scouts to be a more potent force in fighting prejudice.

Cook (1947) believed that the designation for the development of good will among associations of individuals should be "intergroup education," rather than "intercultural education" or "education for better human relations." The author discusses in detail his analyses of recent studies dealing with the process of socializing children and the nature and control of prejudiced attitudes. He also discusses the conflicting role of the school, which on the one hand is a reducer of ethnic tensions and on the other hand a transmitter of community bias patterns. He feels that the function of the researcher is "to assist in the understanding of intergroup relations in and about the school, to analyze their effects on individuals and the community, and where possible, to bring these behaviors by experimental action into line with democratic ideals."

Communicating Positive Attitudes

A good deal of work obviously remains to be done in fighting prejudice and in preventing the development of negative attitudes. Much has been accomplished, but even more is needed. Perhaps greater exposure of groups to one another will result in the acceptance of more individuals, until ultimately the major part of the group is accepted. In times of stress, such as during World War II, bias is relatively minimal as all groups strive toward a common goal. Southern-born Marines were not likely to refuse air cover during an attack because the support fighter squadron had Negro pilots. In times of peace or at least relative calm, there seems to be no single goal to so integrate people. If we can orient our adolescents to a dedication to the basic principles of democracy and can set goals that all could reach cooperatively, we will have done much toward eliminating prejudice. Such a program does, however, require the constant guidance of liberal, non-prejudiced adults who are capable of successfully communicating such goals to adolescents.

ATTITUDES AS VIEWED BY ADOLESCENTS

Young people are greatly concerned about their attitudes toward others and about the attitudes others express toward them. As the youngster moves into the teen years, his environment is broadened and he comes into contact with many different kinds of individuals. Such experiences often become a source of disturbance to a youngster, especially if he finds that the attitude he held in relation to certain kinds of people is not compatible with the way these people function in situations in which he has direct contact with them. With increasing age he tends to become more liberal in his attitudes but does not necessarily change them.

Group Biases

Often a youngster will not express his attitudes openly if they seem contrary to those of his peer group but will instead overtly verbalize attitudes approved by the group. On the other hand, the difference between an individual's attitudes and those of the group may become wide enough to cause him to break with the group.

John J., a high-school senior, is a member of one of the "better" fraternities in his school. He is planning to drop out of this organization after nearly three years of membership, even though he is slated to be the next president. John explained his feelings: "When I first joined the group (I was fourteen) I felt it was important. The members of the fraternity felt it was the best organization in the school and that their status was obvious to others. They had many attitudes toward other groups which I really didn't like, but I went along with them because I liked the status. This year they passed a new rule, and this was too much for me. They voted not to have any further contact with another fraternity because it was too 'low status' and our association with them might lower our own status. Well, I grew up with a lot of the fellows in that other group and they're still my friends. I spoke out against the resolution but when it passed I decided to resign. I've had too many pleasant experiences with some of the other group and I don't think they are 'low status.' My own fraternity brothers think I'm a traitor, but I'd rather be a traitor than that kind of snob."

Adult Biases

The expanding environment of the youngster may often bring him into direct contact with individuals or groups against whom his parents have expressed very strong biases. If these contacts are negative, they will tend to reinforce the parental point of view and intensify his own prejudice. If, on the other hand, his contacts are positive, he may come into conflict with his parents.

Rick C. was reared in a very small town in the Pacific Northwest, where he remained until he was eighteen. He was constantly exposed to anti-Semitic prejudice, although no Jewish people lived in his town. His first exposure to any Jew came when he was assigned to an Air Force crew and found that two of his fellow crew members were Jewish. His first reaction was one of shock, since these two seemed to be as pleasant as anyone he had met. His continued interaction with them was highly positive, and a very close friendship arose. Rick visited the homes of his friends on furloughs and found their families to be just as pleasant as any of the adults he knew at home. When Rick went home on a furlough he told his parents about these friends, and his father went into a violent vituperative tirade. In the argument that followed, Rick told his father he was narrow-minded. After his discharge from the Air Force, Rick elected to attend the college that one of his Jewish friends attended and did not immediately return home. Today Rick is active in his own religion but still maintains these early service friendships. He visits his family occasionally but will never discuss religion or racial problems with them.

Young teen-agers usually fail to understand their parents' biases toward people in a socioeconomic group lower than their own and will mingle with members of these groups as long as they have common interests. Yet they are often enough exposed to members of these groups to avoid those who fit the stereotypes presented by their parents. Thus, their positive interactions seldom go beyond those individuals with whom they have had positive contacts.

Mike C. explained his feeling to our seminar in this way. "I'm on the football team with Bill, who is a Negro. He's one of the nicest guys I know and we're good friends. I don't like any of the other Negro boys in school, but Bill is an example to his race—more like a white man than a Negro." To the question, "Do you feel more sympathetic toward Negroes as a result of your friendship with Bill?" he responded, "Not too much. I think most of them are lazy and shiftless." In further defense of his point of view he added, "I've talked this over with Bill and he says he's ashamed of a lot of the members of his race, too."

Adolescents seem to be able readily to identify prejudice as it is directed toward them or toward others. They feel that the adults around them, both parents and teachers, show their biases rather openly. They admit that they do not necessarily agree with the adults but are often impressed by the repetition of these adult feelings. They are likely to be highly influenced by the attitudes of adults whom they like.

Joanne C. told our seminar that her own prejudice against a certain ethnic group came from a teacher whom she greatly admired. In some of her private contacts with this teacher, she had been exposed to some highly prejudiced remarks. Although Joanne was at first shocked at these statements, she felt that a person as bright and well-rounded as this teacher would not make such remarks unless they were really justified. As a result, Joanne accepted her statements and began to repeat them to others. Even now, as a mature adult, she says, "I worshipped that teacher and even today I find it hard to accept the fact that her statements were those of a bigot."

MORALS AND VALUES

The development of moral behavior and moral values during adolescence, like the development of attitudes, is closely related to the environmental experiences of the individual. Burstin (1953) asked subjects ranging in age from eight and a half to sixteen to respond to the question: "Imagine that you possess a magic charm which would enable you to change the world. What would you change?" In tracing the general lines of social-moral development through childhood and adolescence, the author identified three more or less distinct stages of development. The first is a preoccupation with concrete material things; the second, a concern with values; and the third, a phase of self-discovery in which the adolescent becomes aware of his own unique personality and of his individual responsibility and role in society.

Development of Values

Specific moral values in youngsters aged three to fifteen years were also studied by Wallon (1949). These youngsters were asked to recall examples of kindness, wickedness, dishonesty, bravery, and shame in their experience. Children from three to seven showed less variety in their responses and fewer sex differences than did the older group. The boys from seven to fifteen cited more social situations; the girls, more incidents involving sentiment. Boys' worlds were masculine and they said little about girls, but girls attributed more evil to boys than to their own sex. Both bravery and dishonesty were largely attributed to men by both sexes, while shame was more often associated with women. Dishonesty was viewed for the most part in terms of relations with individuals. Men more than women were viewed as the instruments of both good and bad transactions. Differences in response were found to depend on age, sex, and experience.

Stendler (1949) administered to children in the eighth and ninth grades a test consisting of five stories describing acts of stealing from private persons and from corporations. The majority indicated that stealing private property was more serious, except in cases when punishment from a corporation was feared, or when the theft would slow up production. Of the reasons given, 24 per cent were classified as amoral (refraining from stealing only because of fear of punishment); 12 per cent of the children had absolute standards; and 66 per cent gave a relative moral judgment.

This latter response is almost to be expected when so many adults feel that it is all right to get what you can from a large corporation while considering it dishonest to steal from an individual. The many attempts to operate coin telephones without using money, the "cheating" on income tax, etc., are everyday illustrations. In a recent issue of the *Chicago Tribune Sunday Magazine* (July 15, 1962), thefts of "honest" people from their corporate employers were documented, with indications that such thefts cost business millions of dollars per year. All too often we read of kindly "little old ladies" who have embezzled large sums from their employers ostensibly to "do good" for others. Since youngsters are readily exposed to such happenings, either through hearing one of their parents brag about a "shrewd deal" or by reading of these events in newspapers, it is not remarkable that they respond in like fashion.

Imamura (1959) administered the Moral Diagnosis Form of forty questions about the child himself, his family, his friends, and society to seventh- and eighth-grade children. These youngsters generally considered "to be courageous" as a fundamental consideration in their moral behavior and had a better understanding of what is good than what is bad. Because of their unwillingness to admit their own mistakes, they misjudged their own behavior oftener than that of other members of the family, friends, and society. The author reported that "to be courageous" is often "regrettably mixed up with to be stubborn."

Each school group has a double standard of morality that Muller identifies as (1) inner morals, underlying the general mores, dictated by individual conscience; and (2) outer morals, determined by processes between members of the group and the outer world. Individuals must sacrifice their personal advantages and their personal morals in favor of the group. The group, in turn, protects the student against the teacher, the school, and all other groups (Muller, 1949/50).

Havighurst and Taba (1949) reported on the results of a cooperative investigation aimed at studying the character and personality of sixteen-year-olds in a Midwestern American community. Five traits—friendliness, honesty, loyalty, moral courage, and responsibility—are discussed in some detail. Honesty is the most widely and unquestioningly accepted trait. Telling the truth and respect for property were stressed, while disapproval is expressed against such acts as borrowing things without permission and using small sums of the family's money without permission. Some compromise may be attempted when protecting a friend conflicts with being honest and truthful toward school authorities.

These authors found that beliefs relating to loyalty seemed to be confused and uncertain, with loyalty to friends often being subordinated to other values. When conflicting loyalties are involved, reactions are even more uncertain. Moral courage is usually defined as defending and protecting one's rights and the rights of others. Yet there is often a "hesitancy about raising questions of rightness and wrongness in criticizing peers for fear of being regarded as a prig." Generally, Taba found that students who rebelled showed more moral courage than those who more generally followed acceptable standards.

Standards of responsibility were found to be highly developed and practiced in a variety of practical circumstances. Punctuality, completing jobs, duties toward home, and duties toward school are taken seriously. Generally, responsibility "toward work outside the school was taken more seriously than responsibility toward school work or school activities."

A good deal of acceptance of stereotyped beliefs was found in this study, and high agreement with statements expressing middle-class codes of conduct was typical. "Individual positions deviating from the generally accepted code are feared and shunned." A lack of readiness to face conflict of choices was also noted. When the items expressed a conflict of values, there was hesitancy in taking a position; but when the items stated a specific position, the responses were generally positive.

Relation of Values to Environment

The studies of values have related to various environmental and educational situations. The Allport-Vernon Study of Values was administered by Karn (1952) to male students specializing in engineering. The groups of civil-, metallurgical-, electrical-, chemical-, and mechanical-engineering students varied appreciably in their economic, aesthetic, and political values. These differences in values scores may reflect basic differences in motivation among the specific fields of engineering, or "they may be the result of specialized curricular features or teaching within the various departments of engineering."

Responses to an open-end questionnaire on dares obtained from rural youth in grades four to twelve by Witryol and Calkins (1958) were analyzed and interpreted in terms of marginal social values. The proportion of dare categories reflecting challenges to various forms of authority increased in magnitude from the childhood to the adolescent years. Direct challenges to physical danger dropped sharply with age and were emphasized more by boys than by girls. Social aggression toward the opposite sex was predominantly a female value until grade nine, when it reached a peak and then dropped off until at grade twelve the male and female proportions were essentially the same. Witryol and Calkins interpret these and other dare categories as marginal social values that provide a special type of motivation when incentives possess properties of negative threat as well as positive prestige values.

From two groups of ninth-grade students who differed in social class but were equated for IQ, race, nationality, religion, and sex, data were collected pertaining to their expressed values. The factors investigated included purposes, feelings, attitudes, interests, beliefs, thinking, action, and aspirations. Statistically, the data failed to indicate any significant differences in value patterns between the groups. The range of difference within each group proved to be greater than the difference between groups (Rothman, 1954). This latter finding offers further confirmation of the point expressed in the previous discussion of within-group prejudice.

Amado (1951) described the standards and habits of a group of twelve- to sixteen-year-old youngsters who meet at a Parisian café-bar, and whom he considers maladjusted. Their principle is to live without any responsibilities for the alleged purpose of being artistically creative. Their code demands living outside their homes and having no steady domicile. When they need money the girls will practice prostitution while the boys sell themselves as homosexuals. Amado views this adolescent group as a caricature of the numerous Bohemian societies and of the existentialists on the Left Bank of the Seine.

Trent (1958) has also described atypical teen-age groups, in this case institutionalized delinquents, in attempting to explore and compare the expressed family, peer, and self values of three ethnic groups. Twenty Negro, 20 white, and 20 Puerto Rican boys were matched on several variables. The qualities and achievements described by the subjects in a structured interview were defined as values. There were no significant differences between ethnic groups in expressed family, peer, or self values, nor were there differences in value-conflict scores. Self and family values were strongly oriented toward materialism and personal gratification. Outer-directed character traits, such as helping others, were the most frequently mentioned peer values. Generally it was concluded that such subjects need help in discovering personal values that are meaningful to themselves and in gaining an appreciation and acceptance of nonmaterialistic, moral, and spiritual values.

Teaching Values in the Schools

The Educational Policies Commission (1951) has reaffirmed the responsibility of the public schools for the teaching of moral and spiritual values. Current social trends point up the necessity for increased attention to moral education, and the development of an adequate program demands clarification of the essential values of American life. Substantial agreement exists among the American people regarding certain moral values, the most basic of which is the supreme importance of the individual personality. There is, however, no similar agreement as to the ultimate sanction of this value system.

Eysenck (1960) has suggested that moral values are learned and are to be explained by facts and principles of modern learning theory. He tested the hypothesis that conscience is a conditioned response formed by pairing conditioned stimuli (those producing socially less desirable behavior) with unconditioned stimuli (usually parental control techniques) immediately after the conditioned stimulus. Stimulus generalization is the concept used to explain the association of conditioned stimuli and fear-anxiety responses. Eysenck suggests the application of this theory to child rearing, but questions the possibility of developing a uniform process of character education because of differences in individual personalities.

MORALS AND VALUES AS VIEWED BY ADOLESCENTS

By the time a youngster reaches adolescence, he usually has a well-developed knowledge of what is right and what is wrong in specific situations. He has also learned some general moral concepts of right and wrong, but these are frequently learned through conditioning, special training, or parental instruction. Unfortunately, much of this learning is not meaningful. A child may know that a certain response in a given behavioral situation is wrong but he probably does not know why. A very young child, for example, learns not to cross the street alone because he will be punished if he does. Thus, he has learned it is wrong to cross the street because punishment results, rather than because there might be danger involved in crossing the street without exercising proper caution. He learns caution later, when he is older and can comprehend the danger.

Even for the older child, the explanations of the positive or negative aspects of a situation are often related to a specific fact without emphasis on the total pattern. If an eight-year-old asks his father why he stops for a stop sign, he will probably be told that "it's the law." The actual function of the stop sign in relation to the flow of traffic is seldom explained. Thus, even as adults, many stop at stop signs only because they are afraid of the punishment involved if they are caught, not because they are aware of the purpose of the stop sign.

Therefore, as the youngster grows older he is likely to respond to situations calling for moral decisions in terms of specifically learned responses. If he has not learned a specific response appropriate for a given situation, he is often unable to generalize from other responses because he is unaware of their relationship with the present situation. Then, too, because the child is afraid of punishment for doing the wrong thing, he may suffer severe emotional conflict when confronted by a situation in which he is uncertain of the correct response. His fear of doing the wrong thing may be so great that he will make either no response at all or an inappropriate one.

Confusions Resulting from Adult Inconsistency

Most adolescents are quick to recognize their lack of knowledge of the reasons that certain responses or patterns of behavior are wrong. They are also fully aware of the inconsistencies between what adults verbally indicate to be right or wrong and the actual behavior of adults themselves.

HONESTY. For example, a child of eight or nine can recognize the inconsistency involved when, after his mother has told him never to lie, she tells him to tell the door-to-door salesmen that she is not home. The adolescent is perhaps even more aware of these inconsistencies because his perception of how adults actually behave is appreciably sharper than that of a younger child.

Arthur C. discussed a situation in which he felt he had been mistakenly criticized for unethical behavior. Arthur had bribed some of his friends to vote for him in a club election. His father found out about this and severely reprimanded him for behaving in an immoral manner. Arthur realized that what he had done had not been completely honest, but he had seen his father perform in much the same way. Not long before, his father, who was a restaurant owner, had been running for councilman. During the pre-election period he was constantly "buying" free drinks for his patrons and occasionally "picking up" the check of a prominent customer. Since his father did not usually do such things, Arthur felt they were done in order to help get votes. When Arthur tried to explain to his father that he was imitating his behavior, he was told, "Politics is an adult game, not for kids."

BUSINESS DEALINGS. Frequently, adolescents are aware that adults who overtly appear to be highly moral in their behavior in civic and social affairs are almost amoral in their business dealings. This ability of adults to compartmentalize their behavior is confusing to youngsters.

Roberta C. had an uncle whom her friends considered the very model of an ethical, upstanding citizen. He was a leader in charity drives, active in service organizations, and a heavy contributor to the local orphanage. Roberta, however, was aware of another facet of her uncle's behavior. She knew that during the past year he had undersold his competitors at a substantial loss (which he could well afford) and driven them out of business. One of the competitors had committed suicide, and while her uncle sympathized, he had no real remorse, even stating, "A guy without guts doesn't belong in this business." Roberta always felt rather guilty when her friends told her how lucky she was to have such a "great guy" as her uncle.

Some adolescents feel that if one has enough money, others will excuse his unethical behavior. Basically there is the assumption that wealth can buy one a good reputation, or at least that people may forget the immoral acts by which the money was acquired. While this is not necessarily true, it does occur, and the youngster therefore is able to cite various examples.

William R. felt that there were many people who are today con-

sidered only in a positive way who do not deserve their "good" reputation. He cited the case of Andrew Carnegie as an illustration of his
point. "Today we think of Carnegie as a great philanthropist—particularly when we see libraries bearing his name all over the country.
Certainly he did make a major contribution through his wealth. I
think, however, that much of his wealth was ill acquired. Maybe not
illegally, but he sure used unethical methods to achieve his ends, some
of which resulted in a good deal of human suffering. Today, though,
we seem to act as though the end justified the means. Almost like saying, as long as he used the money for good purposes, who cares how it
was acquired."

SEXUAL MORALS. It is the moral aspects of sex that produce in most
adolescents considerable emotional upset. Adolescents continually
worry about having premarital sexual relations and are threatened with
various dire penalties ranging from venereal disease to pregnancy that
could result from such activities. Yet they are constantly exposed to
books and stories of adults who engage in premarital and extramarital
relations. If adults indulge in such behavior, knowing it is morally
wrong, why should the adolescent refrain?

Louise C., a sixteen-year-old senior, lived in a wealthy suburban
community composed of young executives and professional people.
She described some of the adult behavior she had observed that disturbed her, while pointing out that such behavior was not typical of
her community. One of the families in the neighborhood had many
parties, with their swimming pool as the main attraction. Louise had
observed some of the parties and had seen considerable "necking and
petting" between men and other men's wives. Although Louise felt
that her parents and most of their friends would never engage in such
behavior, she still was upset to see adults acting in this way. It was
completely inconsistent with what she had been taught. Further, she
liked these people and had spent many pleasant afternoons at their
house. She had always thought them to be "real nice people" and was
greatly disillusioned by what she had seen.

Example Versus Precept

In general, the problem can be summed up in the question frequently
asked by teen-agers: "Why don't adults practice what they preach?"
Children and adolescents are more likely to learn from living examples
of adult behavior than from verbalized preachment. Obviously, then,
if adults want a youngster to develop good moral behavior, they must
set the example with their own behavior. If a child has been reared
in a home where parents do practice what they preach, he will readily
develop as his parents want him to. He will then be able to resist

effectively the environmental stimuli that might encourage him to misbehave.

Arnold R. came from a very secure home environment and grew up with a strong admiration for his parents and the way they behaved. He would constantly strive to emulate their behavior and to be as much like them as possible. In high school his friends occasionally wanted to engage in activities he thought immoral or dishonest. When he refused to go along with some of these activities, his friends considered him "chicken," but this didn't bother Arnold. He explained, "I don't have to do things I think wrong, things that I'd be ashamed of and would make my parents ashamed of me. I'm not 'chicken' at all. I have my own standards of behavior and my real friends respect them. I don't care to have friends who can't accept me and my beliefs."

AN OVERVIEW

The general area of religion, morality, and attitudes is one of the most confusing ones for the adolescent to manipulate. Many of his attitudes and values are transmitted to him by adults and are often sources of conflict when he is in an environmental situation that seems contrary to the things he has been taught. Then, too, the growing adolescent sees many contradictions in the behavior of adults as related to the way in which these adults expect him to behave. Adolescents have been told what is right and what is wrong, but are particularly concerned about why certain things are right and others wrong. They are not willing to accept religion blindly simply because it is the religion of parents or because of a fear of the consequences of rejecting religion. They want to learn more about religion, particularly about its positive aspects rather than about those that cause anxiety.

The fact that adolescents question religion, question certain moral values, and question the attitudes of adults can lead to positive development on their part. Moral conduct must be based on a desire to seek good for its own sake rather than because of imposed authority. Mere knowledge alone is not sufficient, since knowledge of right and wrong will not insure ethical behavior. A religion, to be meaningful to adolescents, must not only emphasize love and brotherhood but must offer the individual opportunities for self-realization.

If a youngster is to develop a positive philosophy of life, he must be able to perceive religion, moral values, and attitudes in a meaningful way. He must understand the relationships and interrelationships of these areas as they relate to his own developing frame of reference in the society in which he is growing up. If his previous environmental experiences have been too rigidly structured to allow him to explore these areas on his own, his philosophy of life will in turn be inflexible, and a good deal of conflict will result as he tries to relate it to his everyday behavior. If his early training has been a fear-oriented one, he is likely to feel intense guilt whenever the environmental situation forces him to function in a way that is contrary to his rigid beliefs.

REFERENCES

AGNES, SISTER MARY. "Influence of Reading on the Racial Attitudes of Adolescent Girls." *Catholic Educational Review*, 45, 415-420, 1947.

ALLPORT, GORDON W. *The Individual and His Religion: A Psychological Interpretation*. New York: Macmillan, 1950.

AMADO, GEORGES. "Ethique et psychologie d'un groupe d'adolescents inadaptes" (Ethical Standards and Psychology of a Group of Maladjusted Adolescents). *Evolution Psychiatrique* (Paris), no. 1, 3-30, 1951.

ANDERSON, JOHN E. "The Relation of Attitude to Adjustment." *Education*, 73, 210-218, 1952.

BECHES, ISSAC. "Emotions in the Religious Development of Young People." *Religious Education*, 42, 281-284, 1947.

BELLER, E. K. "Two Attitude Components in Younger Boys." *Journal of Social Psychology*, 29, 137-151, 1949.

BERNARD, HAROLD W. *Adolescent Development in American Culture*. New York: World Book Co., 1957.

BLOOD, ROBERT O., JR. "Discrimination without Prejudice." *Social Problems*, 3, 114-117, 1955.

BLOS, P. *The Adolescent Personality: A Study of Individual Behavior*. New York: Appleton-Century-Crofts, 1941.

BRZEZINSKA, ZOFIA. "The Attitude of Today's Youth towards Life." *Psychologia Wychawawcza* (Warsaw), 3, 150-166, 1960.

BURSTIN, J. "Aspects de l'evolution sociomorale de l'adolescent" (Aspects of the Socio-moral Development of the Adolescent). *Enfance* (Paris), 6, 97-146, 1953.

CENTERS, RICHARD. "Children of the New Deal; Social Stratification and Adolescent Attitudes." *International Journal of Opinion and Attitude Research* (Mexico), 4, 315-335, 1950.

CLARK, WALTER H. "The Psychology of Religious Values." *Personality*, Symposium No. 1, 45-62, 1950.

COOK, L. A. "Intergroup Education." *Review of Educational Research*, 17, 266-278, 1947.

COREY, STEPHEN M. "Attitudes, Values and Aversions." *Teachers College Record*, 56, 121-128, 1954.

EDUCATIONAL POLICIES COMMISSION. *Moral and Spiritual Values in the Public Schools*. Washington, D. C.: National Educational Association of the United States, 1951.

EYSENCK, H. J. "Symposium: The Development of Moral Values in Children: VII. The Contribution of Learning Theory." *British Journal of Educational Psychology*, 30, 11-21, 1960.

FORRES, H. "Begegnung mit religios entwurzelten Jugendlichen" (Encounter with Religiously Uprooted Youngsters). *Praxis der Kinderpsychologie und Kinderpsychiatrie* (Goettingen), 4, 303-305, 1955.

FRENKEL-BRUNSWIK, ELSE. "A Study of Prejudice in Children." *Human Relations* (London), 1, 295-306, 1948.

FRENKEL-BRUNSWIK, ELSE, and HAVEL, JOAN. "Prejudice in the Interviews of Children: I. Attitudes toward Minority Groups." *Journal of Genetic Psychology*, 82, 91-136, 1953.

GOUGH, H. G., HARRIS, D. B., MARTIN, W. E., and EDWARDS, MARCIA. "Children's Ethnic Attitudes: I. Relationship to Certain Personality Factors." *Child Development*, 21, 83-91, 1950.

HARRIS, DALE B., and SING CHU TSENG. "Children's Attitudes toward Peers and Parents as Revealed by Sentence Completions." *Child Development*, 28, 401-411, 1957.

HAVIGHURST, R. J., and TABA, H. *Adolescent Character and Personality*. New York: John Wiley & Sons, Inc., 1949.

HAYES, MARGARET I. "Attitudes of High School Students toward Negro Problems." *Journal of Educational Research*, 46, 615-619, 1953.

HIERONYMOUS, A. N. "A Study of Social Class Motivation: Relationships between Anxiety for Education and Certain Socio-economic and Intellectual Variables." *Journal of Educational Psychology*, 42, 193-205, 1951.

HORTON, R. E. "Freedom, Fascism, and Fear." *Purdue University Studies in Higher Education*, no. 80, 43-54, 1953.

HUGHES, JULIUS H., and THOMPSON, GEORGE G. "A Comparison of the Value Systems of Southern Negro and Northern White Youth." *Journal of Educational Psychology*, 45, 300-309, 1954.

IMAMURA, KEN-ICHIRO. "Chugakusei no dotoku ishiki ni tsuite" (On the Conscience of Japanese Junior High School Students: Their Moral Awakening). *Japanese Journal of Educational Psychology*, 7, 79-83, 1959.

JAMES, H. E. O., and TENEN, E. "How Adolescents Think of Peoples." *British Journal of Psychology*, 41, 145-172, 1950.

KARN, HARRY W. "Differences in Values among Engineering Students." *Educational and Psychological Measurement*, 12, 701-706, 1952.

KELLEY, HAROLD H., and VOLKART, EDMUND H. "The Resistance to Change of Group-Anchored Attitudes." *American Sociological Review*, 17, 453-456, 1952.

KLEE, LORETTA E. "How Do You Feel about World Peace? A Study of Some Changes in Expressed Attitudes of Senior High School Students." *Journal of Educational Research*, 43, 187-196, 1949.

KUHLEN, R. G., and ARNOLD, M. "Age Differences in Religious Beliefs and Problems during Adolescence." *Journal of Genetic Psychology*, 65, 291-300, 1944.

LEWIN, HERBERT S. "The Way of the Boy Scouts: An Evaluation of an American Youth Organization." *Journal of Educational Sociology*, 21, 169-176, 1947.

MACCOBY, ELEANOR E., MATTHEWS, RICHARD E., and MORTON, ANTON S. "Youth and Political Change." *Public Opinion Quarterly,* 18, 23-39, 1954.

MACK, R. W. "Do We Really Believe in the Bill of Rights?" *Social Problems,* 3, 264-269, 1956.

MARTIN, W. E. "Learning Theory and Identification: The Development of Values in Children." *Journal of Genetic Psychology,* 84, 211-217, 1954.

MAYO, GEORGE DOUGLAS, and KINZER, JOHN R. "A Comparison of the 'Racial' Attitudes of White and Negro High School Students in 1940 and 1948." *Journal of Psychology,* 29, 397-405, 1950.

MEAD, MARGARET. "Race Majority–Race Minority." In Hughes, M. M., ed., *The People in Your Life: Psychiatry and Personal Relations by Ten Leading Authorities,* pp. 120-157. New York: Alfred A. Knopf, 1951.

MONTAGU, M. F. ASHLEY. "Some Psychodynamic Factors in Race Prejudice." *Journal of Social Psychology,* 30, 175-187, 1949.

MORRIS, J. F. "The Development of Moral Values in Children: II. Development of Adolescent Value Judgments." *British Journal of Educational Psychology,* 28, 1-14, 1958.

MULL, HELEN K. "A Comparison of Religious Thinking of Freshmen and Seniors in a Liberal Arts College." *Journal of Social Psychology,* 26, 121-123, 1947.

MULLER, KARL. "Die Gruppenmoral der Schulklasse" (Group Morals within the School Class). *Kölner Zeitschrift zur Sociologie und Sozial Psychologie* (Cologne), 2, 84-87, 1949-1950.

MYERS, M. S. "The Role of Certain Religious Values for High School Youth." *Studies in Higher Education, Purdue University,* no. 79, 79-85, 1951.

NASH, H. "Stereotyped Associations to Schematic Faces." *Journal of Genetic Psychology,* 93, 149-152, 1958.

OKAJI, ICHIRO. "Studies on Characteristics of Adolescents' Attitudes toward Life." *Japanese Journal of Educational Psychology,* 6, 7-13, 1958.

PERRYMAN, J. NELSON. "Up-state New York Student Attitudes toward Government Activities." *Public Opinion Quarterly,* 14, 336-338, 1950.

PHILLIPS, E. LAKIN. "Intellectual and Personality Factors Associated with Social Class Attitudes among Junior High School Children." *Journal of Genetic Psychology,* 77, 61-72, 1959.

RADKE-YARROW, M., and MILLER, J. "Children's Concepts and Attitudes about Minority and Majority American Groups." *Journal of Educational Psychology,* 41, 449-468, 1949.

REMMERS, H. H., MYERS, M. S., and BENNETT, E. M. "Some Personality Aspects and Religious Values of High School Youth." *Purdue Opinion Panel,* 1951.

REMMERS, H. H., and RADLER, D. H. *The American Teenager.* Indianapolis: Bobbs-Merrill, 1957.

ROSANDER, A. C. "Age and Sex Patterns of Social Attitudes." *Journal of Educational Psychology,* 30, 481-496, 1939.

ROTHMAN, PHILIP. "Socio-economic Status and the Values of Junior High School Students." *Journal of Educational Sociology,* 28, 126-130, 1954.

STENDLER, CELIA BURNS. "A Study of Some Socio-moral Judgments of Junior High School Children." *Child Development*, 20, 15-28, 1949.

SWIFT, ARTHUR L. "Religious Values." In Anshen, R. N., *The Family: Its Function and Destiny*, pp. 393-405. New York: Harper & Brothers, 1949.

TAYLOR, TRAVIS H. "Intergroup Relations at Cosmopolitan Junior High." *Journal of Educational Sociology*, 21, 220-225, 1947.

TELFORD, C. W. "A Study of Religious Attitudes." *Journal of Social Psychology*, 31, 217-230, 1950.

TRENT, RICHARD D. "The Expressed Values of Institutionalized Delinquent Boys." *Journal of Genetic Psychology*, 92, 133-148, 1958.

WALLON, GERMAINE H. *Les notions morales chez l'enfant* (Moral Ideas in the Child). Paris: Presses Universitaires de France, 1949.

WITRYOL, SAM L., and CALKINS, JAMES E. "Marginal Social Values of Rural School Children." *Journal of Genetic Psychology*, 92, 81-93, 1958.

ZELIGS, ROSE. "Reasons Given by Children for Their Intergroup Attitudes." *Journal of Genetic Psychology*, 76, 145-161, 1950.

CHAPTER 10

Adolescent Interests

Knowledge of the interests of adolescents is a major factor in understanding their behavior and its development. Many of the activities in which an individual is or will be engaged evolve from specific interests or combinations of them. While we are often aware of the importance of interests, we generally think of them only in terms of specifics. We know, for example, that certain interests or interest patterns can be related to future specific vocational fields, but we often fail to relate these interests to present activities not directly connected with vocations.

Interests and motivation are very closely related, and generally an individual will work harder to achieve goals that interest him than he will toward those which do not. In that they help propel an individual toward a goal, interests actually are motivators. Since we are concerned with certain aspects of controlling behavior, it is particularly important that we understand the development of these types of motivators, including the way in which interests can be stimulated and related to specific situations in the environment. If, for example, we knew how to stimulate a high level of interest in mathematics, we could be sure our students would be highly motivated to learn that subject.

CAUSES OF VARIATION IN INTERESTS

The study of interests is difficult because of biological and cultural variations among individuals, variations related to geographic locale and other environmental aspects, and variations resulting from sex. There are also major variations in interests from one decade to another, and interest changes that result from technological changes. For example, some twenty years ago bowling was considered a lower-class activity, and bowling alleys were dirty places with indolent, often semialcoholic pin boys. Today, bowling is a highly acceptable sport, with millions of people interested in it. This change has resulted partly from technological improvements—the automatic pinsetter, air conditioning, etc. Bowling has become a family sport in which women and children take as active a part as men.

In vocational areas, advanced technology has created jobs that require interests appreciably different from those necessary a decade ago. Technological changes have also given people more leisure time in which to explore a variety of activities and to develop more precise long-term interests. Aids have been developed that enable those with strong interest but limited skills to function in the area of their interest. For example, if one has a strong interest in art but is not skilled in structuring basic designs, paint-by-number kits are available and the budding artist has only to fill in a pre-structured basic design.

Physical traits may limit an individual's ability to participate in an area in which he is interested. A teen-ager may have a strong interest in basketball yet be too short to become a member of a team. He may still partially satisfy this interest by participating as team manager, or he may simply be content to be a spectator. Even activities which call for little physical action may be prohibited because of some minor physical defect. Color blindness, for example, would certainly prevent one from becoming a painter.

Despite these variations, the exploration of the development of interests is still useful. If, in fact, we remain constantly aware of the variations and how they affect the individual, we can do more to help manipulate his behavior. In examining a youngster's lack of interest in reading, we must first determine whether it results from lack of adequate intellect, lack of properly developed skills, lack of motivation, etc. If we can establish the cause of the lack of interest and can develop a skill or a behavior pattern to overcome that cause, the interest will usually be easier to develop. If a youngster is not interested in reading because his reading skill is poor, his interest in reading can be increased by improving his skill.

Substitute Interests

Although knowledge of the individual's present interests is important, these cannot always be judged on the basis of what they seem to be. It is sometimes advisable to examine some of the aspects of the situation in which the individual is currently functioning and also to investigate his past interests. An individual may be currently oriented to a goal that will really not satisfy his major interests, but which he feels is the best he can achieve. Knowledge of his earlier interests may help us to understand his present actions and also alert us to the frustrations that he may face.

Walter was enrolled in a course designed to train him as an X-ray technician and was considered one of the best students in the class. He seemed greatly interested in and enthusiastic about his studies and his future work. Occasionally he seemed rather depressed, but since he held a part-time job to help pay for his school it was assumed that he was merely tired. When his depression worsened, Walter was referred to a counselor to attempt to find the basis of his difficulty. In the sessions that followed Walter finally admitted that his major interest was in the field of medicine and that he wanted to become a physician. He knew that he was intelligent enough to accomplish this, but was also aware that finances were not available even for college premedical training. Although he recognized that he could not hope to achieve his goal, he still wanted to be involved in the field of medicine. He selected the program leading to training as an X-ray technician as a means of partially satisfying his desires. Although pleased that he would be functioning in the general field of his choice, he had become depressed at having to accept a lower occupational level than that demanded by his interests.

Particularly in working with adolescents, it is necessary, although difficult, to differentiate between expressed interests and actual interests. The expressed interests may result from the youngster's attempts to be like the others in his peer group, while his actual interests may be appreciably different. Sometimes, too, an expressed interest is a means of concealing an actual interest that cannot be satisfied at the moment. A youngster who cannot dance may express a lack of interest in girls, professing instead a great interest in sports. If he is given some help in developing his dancing skill to the extent of feeling comfortable, his real interest in girls will emerge.

PREADOLESCENT INTERESTS

Although interests that appear in childhood are quite unstable and often related more to fantasy than to reality, they are worth investigating. In individual cases an early interest sometimes continues, becomes intensified with age, and strongly influences the functioning of the individual when he reaches adulthood. Many of the younger child's interests are related to the immediate environment and not necessarily related to any meaningful future patterns of behavior. Any given event may stimulate the interest of youngsters, but another event will cause this interest to be replaced by another. Thus, when Colonel John Glenn successfully orbited the earth, many youngsters began to act the role of astronaut. Only a few months earlier, these same youngsters emulated baseball players, such as Roger Maris.

Although the play interests of children are influenced by such events, certain patterns seem to continue from one generation to another. These interests are usually longer lasting than those stimulated by a major event. Girls still play with dolls and tea sets, and boys still play cowboys and/or "cops and robbers." While these play activities may be dropped for a period of time, they usually re-emerge. For example, when the television program "Captain Video" was popular, many youngsters played spaceman, but when this interest waned they became cowboys again.

Sex-Appropriate Concerns

The fact that some of these early interests are culturally approved and maintained helps account for their recurrence over the years. Parents typically buy their youngsters sex-appropriate toys and encourage their use. Little girls get dolls and tea sets; little boys are given trucks, guns, and eventually athletic equipment. As they grow older, children are even more directed toward sex-appropriate activities and discouraged from participating in those that are not sex-appropriate. An eleven-year-old girl who wants to play baseball is considered a "tomboy" and discouraged by adults as well as by her male age-mates at least from active participation in this sport. A boy who wants to play with dolls or plays "house" with little girls is considered a "sissy" and encouraged to engage in more masculine activities. This kind of attitude carries over into adulthood; certain occupations are considered appropriate for males and others for females. We have viewed with suspicion a female who chooses to become an engineer or plumber, and we are frequently wary of the male who chooses to become a beautician or even a primary-grades schoolteacher.

Rosenberg and Sutton-Smith (1960) conducted an investigation to compare male and female differences in games played. Of the total check list, 18 items differentiated boys from girls and 40 differentiated girls from boys. When these data were contrasted with traditional concepts of masculine-feminine play and with earlier data, the results indicated that girls today evidence greater interest in masculine activities than they did formerly. These authors felt that their study presented further evidence to support those theories which emphasize the increasing masculinity of the feminine self-concept.

Some of this apparent increase in masculinity of the female may have resulted from the job upheaval of the World War II era. In order to maintain production, many industries had to employ women to perform tasks previously handled only by males. Not only were women successful in taking over these jobs, but in those requiring greater precision of movements, they were actually superior to men. As a result women became aware that they could compete successfully with men in occupations that had once been completely closed to them. In situations where women work alongside men, they find it most effective to rely for advancement on proficiency at the job rather than to try to take advantage of their sex. As a result they frequently demonstrate characteristics of a masculine type. This general change is beginning to carry over into our schools, with an increasing demand that girls be given the opportunity to take courses in manual training and industrial arts from which they were previously barred.

Youngsters are aware of this change, particularly if their own mothers are employed in a "masculine" type occupation. Little girls find they can work as well with saws and hammers in building things as many boys can. Even some of the toys now available for girls are those that were once considered only appropriate for boys, and many toys are made to be sold to both sexes.

Interest Categories

Amatora (1960) investigated interests during preadolescence and found that 90 per cent of the interests recorded by students in twelve schools in ten states fell into ten categories. Although these interest categories varied in intensity with age and sex, they did tend to recur in all parts of the United States. The ten categories were: things owned, good life, vocation, relatives, travel, school, pets, money, education, and health. These interest categories occur at a variety of ages, and most of them continually recur from age to age, varying in degree of intensity at different ages.

ANALYSES OF ADOLESCENT INTERESTS

Van Dalen (1949) analyzed the play of junior-high girls in seventh, eighth, and ninth grades by means of two indexes, a Strength Index and a Physical Fitness Index. Girls in the high groups on both indexes exceeded girls in the corresponding low groups in both total number of play activities and total time devoted to play activities. Girls in the low groups showed more interest in playing musical instruments, bicycling, and playing with pet animals than did those in the high groups. The high groups displayed a preponderance of physical activities involving competition and subordination of individualism. The question of whether these girls were more interested in physical activities because of their strength, or whether their interest in physical activities led to greater strength, is not fully answered; it would seem that either could be the case.

Van Dalen (1947) also reported on a differential analysis of the play of adolescent junior-high-school boys. The boys who were high on the

Strength Index and the Physical Fitness Index exceeded to a marked degree those with low scores in number of play activities and time devoted to them. Boys in the lower group on the Strength Index participated in games that had a lower degree of organization than those in which the high groups participated. Again, as with the girls, the direction of the interest factor is not fully established.

Seventh- and eighth-grade children were asked to describe freely their three greatest interests. Their responses were categorized into eight classifications: education, good life, health, money, objects, relatives, travel, and vocational, with about a quarter of the responses scattered among other miscellaneous interests. "Possession of objects" was of highest interest for both grades and both sexes, with "vocation" and "good life" chosen next. An analysis of sex differences showed boys to be relatively more interested in "vocation" and "good life," while girls were more interested in "objects" and "relatives." Cars and bicycles were mentioned frequently as the specific objects in which they were interested (Amatora, 1957).

Canonge (1948) reported on the results of a questionnaire concerning the interest of students aged fourteen to seventeen at male centers of vocational training in France. Ninety per cent of these youths sought the company of young girls, with 39 per cent expressing this as a most ardent interest. Dancing was listed as a major interest, not so much for itself, but for the opportunity it afforded to meet girls. Other major interests included reading, games, work, and friendship.

Harris (1949), to make a further investigation of sex differences in the life problems and interests of adolescents, repeated an earlier study done by P. M. Symonds and compared the earlier results with his own. Changes in the relative significance accorded fifteen issues, considered as both problems and as interests, showed increased concern with love and marriage, family relations, mental health, and study habits. Sex differences were as great in 1957 as in 1935, reflecting the greater interest of boys in recreation and money, and of girls in social relationships and personal attractiveness. In recent years, girls also emphasize an interest in love and marriage and in family relationships. The more recent study showed less consistency between the order of issues considered as problems and their order considered as interests.

Stability of Interests

Along with increasing age from childhood through adolescence, an increase in the stability of interests seems to occur. The unstable, constantly shifting interests of the younger child eventually develop into the stable long-term interests of adolescence and adulthood. Once interests stabilize, they become meaningful in relationship to future activities, including vocational selection, and in motivating present activities in interest-oriented areas. Once we know an interest is relatively fixed, it becomes easier to help direct or guide the individual into the areas in which this interest can be most effectively used.

The Kuder Preference Record is an instrument that is widely used to assess interests, and it has also been widely employed to determine the stability of interests. Fox (1947) administered the Kuder Preference Record to ninth-grade pupils. After a two-month interval, during which an intensive guidance program was carried out with these youngsters, the test was repeated. Correlations between the initial and the final tests ranged from .85 to .42 for boys, and from .85 to .54 for girls. The order of stability of interests for boys was: scientific, musical, artistic, mechanical, computational, social service, clerical, literary, and persuasive. The order for girls was: social service, literary, scientific, musical, artistic, clerical, computational, mechanical, and persuasive. Jacobs (1949) also used the Kuder scores to measure stability of interests at the secondary-school level and found correlations high enough to suggest that a large portion of pupil interests had not changed in a period of seventeen months. Comparison of the correlations with reported reliabilities of the various Kuder scores, however, indicates that some changes in interest patterns have occurred, the greatest changes appearing on the scientific and clerical scales. With the exception of increase in persuasive interests by the boys, there is no notable evidence of sex differences with respect to stability of interests.

The Kuder Preference Record was administered to students in the ninth grade on the assumption that their interests would remain constant to the twelfth grade. The highest interest area remained the highest for 52 per cent of the students; the lowest interest area remained the lowest for 43 per cent. However, for 80 per cent of the students the highest interest area at ninth grade remained among the three highest at twelfth grade; for 76 per cent the lowest area remained among the three lowest (Mallinson and Crumrine, 1952). Strong (1953) did extensive follow-up studies on the interest scores on his inventory and found the scores to be very stable after the age of seventeen. In the follow-up after eighteen years, less than 10 per cent of all A ratings changed to C, and less than 5 per cent of the C ratings changed to A. Interests generally were more stable among college students than among high-school students.

While these studies generally indicate that there is increased stability of interests from the junior-high-school age through the college age, it is inadvisable to assume this will always be true in an individual case. Interests may never become permanently fixed, and changes in interests may take place well into adulthood. An interest that an individual thought was strong may prove not to be when he becomes involved in a situation relating to the interest. The continual broadening of the environment may make him aware of previously unknown areas, and his interests may shift accordingly. Generally, too broad interests narrow down to more precise and specialized ones as an individual becomes more involved in the area of his choice. He often finds he cannot do everything within the area and so decides to do only a specialized part of the total task. For example, a young man entering the field of law may find it too difficult to keep up with all the latest developments in the total field. In order to function more efficiently, he may find it necessary to specialize in only one aspect of law, perhaps corporation law. Lack of certain characteristics may also lead him to a specialized field. He may not have the personality characteristics, such as persuasiveness, that are required for a successful trial lawyer, and may therefore choose to specialize in an area of law that is oriented to research and does not require appearing in court.

MEASURING INTERESTS

Interest inventories were mentioned in Chapter 1, in the discussion of research techniques. Like most inventories, these are usually long questionnaires on which the individual answers questions about himself. The questions are usually indirect, to prevent the individual from discovering which items relate to which major interest area. The interests so measured may be compared to those found in a group that functions in that area to determine how closely the youngster's interests parallel those of the group.

Interest inventories are most often used in choosing occupations by determining the resemblance of an individual's interests to the interests of those already in that field. Three of the most commonly used inventories of this kind are the Strong Vocational Interest Blank, the Kuder Preference Record, and the Lee-Thorpe Occupational Interest Inventory. Each of these inventories has a different approach to measuring interests and a different way of relating interests to occupations. Nonetheless, all result in more or less the same sort of measurement and generally can fulfill the same functions.

Attempts have been made to relate interests to academic achievement. Correlations between interests and grades are generally quite low, offering little predictive value. Strong (1943) found that interest scores did seem to relate to persistence in an area even if they do not predict grades. There are "studiousness" keys made for the Strong Blank that Mosier (1937) found to correlate with grades to some degree in certain areas. This technique requires constant restructuring for each new situation, and its over-all value is questionable. While we might

338 THE PSYCHOLOGY OF ADOLESCENCE

be willing to assume that a student will earn far better grades in courses in which he is interested than in those in which he is uninterested, we cannot substantiate this theory with the instruments presently available.

Generally, the responses to paper-and-pencil interest inventories tend to be more "honest" than those to paper-and-pencil personality inventories. An individual may wish to conceal certain personality characteristics but usually has no reason to conceal his interest patterns. Nonetheless, the individual's personality may be an important factor in his response to interest inventory items. Darley and Haganah (1955) include a report by Block and Peterson on the relationship between personality and interest scores of 100 Air Force officers. Personality characteristics of these men were related to scores on each Strong scale. Those with high mathematical scores tended to be introspective, lacking in social poise, lacking confidence in their own ability, sympathetic, and nonaggressive. These are not necessarily indicators of good or poor adjustment, simply descriptive characteristics often found in association with a strong interest in mathematics. An individual with these personality traits might make an effective adjustment as a mathematician, whereas similar traits would not be appropriate for a dean of students.

Interests may be assessed by inventories other than those mentioned, by open-ended questionnaires, or by interviews, any of which methods may be effective. In some cases one approach may be used more successfully on one individual than on another, while in other cases a combination of these approaches will be most effective. Generally, information about the expressed interests of students can be highly valuable in educational as well as in vocational guidance.

Today, even theories about interests are changing appreciably. The point of view that interests result from chance conditionings is giving place to the belief that interests are related to needs and adjustment patterns. This change in thinking and the necessity for research to develop an effective theory of interest development are currently being stressed by vocational counselors and others involved in investigating interests. Such research may eventually lead to extensive changes in interest-testing and to the development of techniques far more precise than those currently available.

INTERESTS AND INTELLIGENCE

Lack of interest in a given area is often misinterpreted as lack of ability. There is a conception—or perhaps a misconception—that very bright individuals are unskilled in mechanical tasks or lack manual skills. If this is true, the lack of skill is probably due to lack of interest rather than to lack of ability *per se*. That is, a very bright child may not be interested in building things and thus have very little experience with tools. If, however, an interest in building can be developed, the bright child will probably be more skilled than an equally interested child of lesser intellect.

Some interest areas do seem not to appeal particularly to very bright youngsters, and some seem to rank low for all intelligence levels. Leach (1954) investigated the question of whether first choices of interest areas differ for ninth-graders of different intellectual ability. Generally, he concluded that the persuasive interest ranks relatively low in popularity in all intelligence groups. He also found that the "outdoor interest ranks highest in the lowest and average intelligence groups and second in the below-average group." The group with superior intelligence gave the computational interest its highest score.

An interest test and a sociometric questionnaire were administered to more than 700 high-school students in an attempt to study the relationships of interests and leadership among adolescents. Cliques were delineated by means of criteria based on the number and reciprocity of choices. A leader and a follower were selected from each of 21 boys' cliques and 28 girls' cliques. Comparisons were made between leaders and followers within the cliques. Girl leaders were significantly higher than followers in science interests, athletic leadership, attractiveness, prestige, prominence, and style setting. Boy leaders showed significantly higher social interests than followers did and were rated higher in acceptability, athletic leadership, popularity, and prominence. Leaders in general seem to be more sensitively distinguished from followers by the social responses of others to them than by their sociometric or interest test behavior (Marks, 1957).

LEISURE-TIME ACTIVITIES

Adolescents are often accused of making poor use of their leisure time by not engaging in meaningful activities during such periods. Ulich (1959) conducted an investigation in Germany to determine whether or not pupils aged ten to nineteen would be capable of meaningful leisure-time activities. The data were gathered from interviews with the mothers of 456 secondary-school students, not from the pupils themselves. The findings were generally interpreted as supporting a five-day school week (concerning which there had been a great deal of controversy) and as justifying a need for leisure time. Eighty-one per cent of the mothers felt that the children were capable of meaningful activities during their free time.

Today many youngsters feel that they have too little leisure time because of the many formalized activities in which they must take part. With music lessons, homework, baseball or some other sport, and club meetings, little time is left for real leisure. If the youngster has a spare-time job, there is even less time, if any. Franklin and Remmers (1960) found that one-third of the 2000 teen-agers they questioned complained that they had too little leisure.

Recently the present author was discussing this lack of leisure time with a well-known pediatrician in a large Midwestern hospital center. The doctor pointed out that a large number of the young teen-agers with whom he came in contact were victims of this overemphasis on planned activity. Many of them had nervous habits, such as tics, which, he felt, resulted from the constant pressures to which they were exposed. He felt strongly that youngsters should have time to just "lie around and do nothing."

Quite often, leisure-time activities include participation in games and sports. Sehgal (1953) reported on a study of the recreational interests of boys and girls aged twelve to sixteen. According to results of the questionnaire he administered, games and sports were the most popular recreational activities of this age group. Movies were equally popular with both sexes. Leisure-time activities may be limited by a variety of factors, including lack of money and lack of environmental opportunity, which are actually socioeconomic factors. MacDonald *et al.* (1949) collected data on the leisure activities of children in four socioeconomic levels and attempted to relate leisure activities to socioeconomic class. Those children whose behavior differed from the pattern of their socioeconomic level were found to interact with children from other levels. Thus they were apparently prepared in their thinking and feeling for "upward mobility."

Hollingshead (1949) investigated the informal activities of adolescents in relation to their socioeconomic status. Going to the movies and visiting each other's homes were the activities most frequently engaged in by the upper class (Class I). Reading habits differed according to sex as well as to social class, with Class II girls and Class V boys borrowing the greatest number of books while Class II boys and Class V girls borrowed the fewest. Although raising pets was popular in all groups, it was most popular in Classes III and IV.

HEALTH INTERESTS AND PHYSICAL ACTIVITIES

Interests in health and physical activity are apparent among teen-agers. As was pointed out in Chapter 2, adolescents are very much interested in and concerned about health problems ranging from possibly serious disabilities to such conditions as acne. They are interested, in particular, in enhancing their appearance; for example, girls will engage in dieting to achieve some ideal physical condition. Boys may become interested in weight lifting and other exercises designed to improve the masculine physique. One of the major interests of teen-agers is in sports, particularly team activities. When not actually playing baseball, boys will spend time discussing their various baseball heroes and quote batting averages incessantly. Girls who are not actively involved in sports themselves are likely to be spectators for the sports in which the boys are participating. Swimming is popular with both sexes, especially since this activity is one that they can enjoy together. Tennis, another sport in which both sexes can participate, seems to be gaining popularity.

Youngsters today are more likely to engage in rather well-organized team activities than in the informal "pick-up" games of a few decades ago. Baseball is an example, with Little League teams for younger children and Pony League and Babe Ruth League teams for adolescents. These leagues are structured along adult lines and formalize the activity of the youngsters. The rules are stressed and training is as important as the game itself. Increasing numbers of youngsters have become involved in this particular organized activity, and the leagues have grown in number throughout the United States.

There has been a good deal of criticism of formally organized leagues, which are often accused of failing in their major function. Supposedly, youngsters should be taught to be good sports and to play according to the rules. Unfortunately, the main stress seems actually to be on competing to win. As a result, the less skilled youngsters on a team may never get to play for fear that their ineptness may cost a game. In some areas, parents have taken over the game, and it is not unusual for them to humiliate an umpire or coach in front of the youngsters. Adults are primarily responsible for these failings in such organized activities, and youngsters cannot be blamed for reacting to the situations as they do.

The health interests of youngsters are important to them, and there is evidence to suggest that not enough information is available to satisfy these interests. Remmers *et al.* (1954) analyzed the responses given by a representative sample of high-school students to questions about "health practices" and "health insurance," and to "questions dealing with beliefs, superstitions, and misconceptions in matters of health." Generally, a higher proportion of urban students have medical, dental, and eye examinations, and more urban pupils and more of the "high" income group carry "health insurance." Urban pupils of higher grades, upper income level, and with mothers who have higher-level education give more correct responses to true-false questions on beliefs and misconceptions. Schaller (1960) devised an inventory for determining health needs and interests of high-school students and after proper validation administered it to 500 students, 100 parents, 20 health educators, and 17 doctors. The conclusions indicated that there was a common core of interest among high schools, with the expressed needs of boys and of girls differing markedly. Interest was shown particularly in habit-forming substances, and in the importance of activity and rest. Courses on the structure and functioning of the human body, community health services and facilities, etc., appear to be least desired.

MASS MEDIA AS ADOLESCENT INTERESTS

Over the years adults have been highly critical of the alleged effects of various forms of communication on the development of youngsters. Comic books, television, radio, and newspapers have all been considered to be sources of information that influence the behavior of adolescents negatively. Youngsters' tastes in mass communications were analyzed by Lyness (1951) from the results of a questionnaire administered to youngsters in grades five, seven, nine, and eleven regarding their reading, radio-listening, and movie-going. Boys generally preferred an "adventure and violence" pattern, while the girls showed a preference for "love, private life, and glamour." Neither sex showed much interest in "educational" content, but boys did like magazines dealing with popular science and mechanics. The third-graders emphasized humor, fantasy, and adventure; they showed little interest in love, private life, or glamour and even less interest in educational themes.

Lyness (1952), in a further investigation of the place of mass media in the lives of youngsters, found that even in pretelevision days mass media contaminated the leisure time of students in the third grade through the eleventh. With increasing age there was an increase in the attention given newspapers, magazines, and radio, but movie attendance changed very little. When the respondents were asked which medium they would keep if they had to give up all but one, they chose radio. Today they would probably choose television.

Books, Newspapers, and Magazines

Reading interests have been analyzed at most grade levels in attempts to determine what topics interest youngsters most. Carsley (1957) studied the interests in books of ten- and eleven-year-old children by means of a questionnaire administered to about 2000 youngsters. At these levels, youngsters enjoyed listening to the teacher read aloud more than they did silent reading; listening to other children was least enjoyable. The home was generally the most satisfying environment for the private reading of books. In low socioeconomic areas there was less home reading than school reading. Films, television, and radio appeared to exert a considerable influence on children's reading.

The nature of the home environment does seem to be a major factor in reading interest. Generally, youngsters of average to high socio-economic levels read more extensively than those of below average levels. This is apparently related to the availability of reading material in the home and to the attitude of the parents toward reading. Homes of higher socioeconomic levels are more likely than those of lower levels to have a greater variety of good books and magazines available. Parents on the higher levels are also usually better educated and more interested in reading themselves and are more likely to furnish a better grade of reading material for their youngsters.

Anderson (1948) administered a questionnaire to seventh- and eighth-grade pupils in order to study their leisure-time reading interests. At every age level, a greater percentage of girls than boys liked to read. Girls ranked fiction first, followed by comic books, biography, animal stories, Western stories, and music. Boys ranked comic books first, followed by fiction, animal stories, biography, and Western stories. More girls than boys had a favorite book. Of the 67 magazines listed as favorites, *Life* magazine ranked highest. In newspaper reading, both boys and girls ranked comics first and general news second.

Bernstein (1955) asked ninth-grade students to read two stories of equal readability, one of which was much more interesting than the other. Comprehension of these stories was tested by means of both objective and free-response questions. Interest was found to be associated not only with superior comprehension but also with greater reading speed. Apparently those who read quickly with good comprehension are more interested in reading than are those who read slowly with limited comprehension.

The reading interests of English adolescents living in India were studied by Mar (1955). A questionnaire was administered to English boys and girls in the upper four classes of Delhi schools. The findings indicated that both boys and girls read fiction most often, with Dickens a popular author. Girls read more plays and poems, while boys read more about sports and games. Both read popular magazines and daily newspapers.

The attitudes of youngsters eleven to sixteen years old in British grammar schools toward twelve novels read as part of the school English syllabus were recorded by Whitehead (1956). The results showed few sex differences, and factors inherent in the novel itself proved most important in determining attitudes toward it (rather than age, sex, teacher, etc.). A preference was shown for novels "written in easy language, dealing with themes that are relatively immature emotionally, in which they find it relatively easy to identify with the hero or heroine, and in which the element of wish fulfillment is comparatively open." Unfavorable attitudes expressed toward *A Tale of Two Cities, Gulliver's Travels, Pilgrim's Progress,* and *The Cloister and the Hearth* supported the conclusion that these books were unsuitable for young-sters of the age group studied.

Young teen-agers enjoy stories of families, of life in other lands, and of adventure (Frank, 1954). Historical backgrounds are also quite in-teresting to these youngsters. Stories about animals, about the teen years, and about careers are popular. Biographies, science, and books telling how to do things rank high in interest appeal, as do books about school and sports. Science fiction, mysteries, and, to some degree, poetry are also appealing; so are comic books. Teen-age reading gen-erally is apparently quite diversified and covers an extensive number of areas.

Norvell (1950) felt that sex differences were a dominant factor in the selection of reading material. Girls will often read boys' books, but boys almost never like girls' books. Girls not only read more than boys, but their interests are more homogeneous. Boys generally prefer more nonfiction than girls, with major interests in biography, history, adventure, mechanics, inventions, and tales of athletic skills. Girls prefer stories dealing with home and school life, and while they do read adventure stories they prefer those that are rather light reading. Girls read and like drama and poetry much more often than boys do.

A study of the reading interests of tenth- and eleventh-grade young-sters fifteen to seventeen years of age was made by Patel (1953), with particular emphasis on determining which parts of the newspaper they found most interesting. Boys chose as most important foreign news, scientific news, and comics, while comics, social events and the women's section were considered important by girls. Comics were most fre-quently selected as the preferred topic by both.

Wall (1948) concluded that his studies showed the importance of newspaper reading in the lives of both adolescents and adults. Read-ing habits are developed in the early and middle teens, although the attitudes formed toward the press in this period are hardly serious or critical. Wall recognized the influence of environmental factors in the determination of reading habits but offered no suggestions for improving of reading habits under specific educational direction.

Comic Books

Comic books have often been considered to have negative effects on the development of youngsters, but there has been little research evi-dence to substantiate this point of view. Comic books are widely read for much the same reasons as those for which books are read, and most youngsters do not feel negatively toward them. Some comic books, such as Classic Comics, present worthwhile material to youngsters in a palatable form, and a youngster may even be encouraged to read the original story upon which the comic book was based. At any rate, one might take the position that reading comic books is better than not reading at all.

Butterworth and Thompson (1951) studied factors related to age-grade trends and sex differences in youngsters' preferences for comic books. They administered a questionnaire to elementary- and high-school children to determine preferences, age-grade trends, sex differences, and characteristics of comic books. The boys generally selected comic books with masculine "adventure," "violence," and "success for hero" characteristics. Girls chose books characterized as "feminine," "adolescent," "romance," and "humor."

Blakely (1958) studied reading of comic books among seventh-grade children as related to certain other variables. The results were analyzed as to type of comics read and frequency of reading comic books. Children who differed in either or both of these variables did not differ correspondingly in tested reading ability. Neither did they differ in achievement level in language, spelling, or general school achievement. Further, no differences in intelligence or in number of behavior problems appeared to be related to types of comic books or to frequency with which they are read.

Frank (1949) tried in a pamphlet to answer some of the questions that parents raise about the effects of comic books, radio, and motion pictures upon their youngsters. She pointed out that comic books, in part, follow somewhat the same pattern that children's reading has followed in the past except for the recent addition of crime and horror comic books, which have created much criticism. Since more than 50 million comic books are sold yearly and each is probably read by more than one reader, it is obvious that the comic-book problem can be important. Frank felt that "many of the recent attacks on the comics have made parents anxious as a result of scare headlines. This is unfortunate because anxious parents may do more damage to their children than comic reading." Parents probably cannot prevent their children from reading comic books, but they might be able to help them select those that are relatively "good."

Leisure-time language activities of high-school pupils were studied by means of check lists and diary records of radio listening, and monthly records of voluntary book reading (Sterner, 1947). Interest *per se* rather than the specific medium seems to be what attracted pupils to these language activities. The author also concluded that one cannot predict how much time a student will devote to one medium from knowledge of the pupil's activity in another medium. Factors such as age, sex, intelligence, etc., are only slightly related to youthful choices of interests, media, or specific titles within media.

Radio

Although radio is apparently less important among the interests of young people than it was some two decades ago, primarily because of the advent of television, it is still one of the major areas of interest. Disc jockeys obviously plan much of their programming for the tastes of the teen-age audience, as evidenced by the recent emphasis on Rock and Roll, which for a time was all one could hear. Even though television has cut into this area to some extent, many youngsters still listen to radio more hours per day than they watch television. With car radios and transistor sets they can listen almost anywhere, while television viewing is still restricted to the home.

McKellar and Harris (1952) studied radio preferences of 1400 students aged eight to fourteen, using questionnaires to gather the data. Given a choice between radio and cinema, they preferred radio almost three to one. Program preferences favored "entertainment," such as humorous productions and light music, over "serious" broadcasts of talks, classical music, and historical events. McKellar and Harris felt that the influence of radio upon young people has not been fully assessed; socially undesirable effects have probably been overstated, and constructive, educational values underemphasized.

The impact of radio on teen-agers is reflected in sales of phonograph records. Most of the records sold during the Rock and Roll craze were brought to the attention of teen-agers by radio disc jockeys. Most of the teen-agers' Rock and Roll ideals, such as Elvis Presley, Connie Francis, etc., owe their fame in part to the influence of disc jockeys on teen-agers. If there were at one time other kinds of radio programs that influenced the teen-ager, most of these are now defunct. Radio today is primarily devoted to music, with occasional news and sports events interspersed.

Television

Just as there was great concern over the impact of radio on the younger generation of the era in which radio first became popular, so is there great concern today over the impact of television. Concern has been particularly expressed about the great amount of violence and borderline immorality allegedly present in many television programs. Television has further been criticized for failing to emphasize the classics and also for failing to keep people well informed on current events. However, at the same time, educational television stations are being licensed throughout the nation, and educational television is fast becoming a part of the school classroom. Although it is inconsistent and often erratic, television is fast leaving its infancy and is, in fact, entering its own "adolescent period."

Maccoby (1951) compared the behavior of youngsters four to seventeen years old in homes owning television sets with that of those in homes without sets. She found that children spent two and one-half to three and one-half hours a day viewing programs. She also found that television brings families into close physical proximity but restricts social interaction that might interfere with viewing. Children in set-owning homes tended to spend less time with playmates, and parents had difficulty getting them to leave the set to eat their meals and go to bed. Television also seemed to be substituted for radio, music, and reading. Parents in general seemed to approve of it and commonly used it as a "pacifier" for their children.

Seagoe ("Children's Television Habits and Preferences," 1952) felt that "television has a major impact on the child audience," with radio and movie attendance sacrificed in favor of viewing television. She also found that low socioeconomic status was positively related to television viewing. The children involved in her study generally preferred adventure, comedy, and family programs, but their favorite program was not necessarily the one seen most frequently. In a report on "Some Current Research in Television for Children," (1952), Seagoe suggested the use of a score sheet by which an adult might judge how good any television program or movie is for children. She felt that parents and teachers must help children understand and appreciate programs, should set up listening groups to evaluate programs, and should take active stands in the encouragement of good programs.

Scott (1953) recorded the responses of second- through eighth-grade children in the East San Francisco Bay area who had television in their own homes or who observed it in the homes of others. Sixty-two per cent of the viewers could identify the specific products advertised and 16 per cent could not. Eighty-five per cent of his sample (both high and low-economic groups) watched television for an average of sixteen hours a week. Sixty-one percent chose their own programs with no adult help whatsoever. Fifty-nine per cent indicated that they preferred TV to any task. While 63 per cent reported acquiring information from television that helped them in school, only 25 per cent had ever reported such information at school.

Although these studies offer valuable information concerning the impact of television, they were done when it was a relatively new phenomenon. Many homes were still without sets, and a homeowner who had one usually could count on nightly guests. A youngster who had a set in his home would gain popularity with peers who had none. The very newness of the medium, which offered viewers entertainment previously unavailable to them, was a major factor in this intense interest. Correspondingly, other media suffered, with radio and movies being relegated to secondary positions and even newspapers becoming less important in transmitting news.

Today, some ten years later, the situation seems to have changed appreciably. Now almost everyone owns a television set, and color television is becoming increasingly popular. As the medium became increasingly accepted, some of its initial appeal wore off, and audiences became more and more sophisticated. Many of the formerly popular entertainers went off the air as audiences refused to accept simple slapstick as a substitute for comedy. Viewers were quick to realize that television news coverage, although often "on the spot," seldom offered the details to be found in newspapers. Reruns and old movies drove many to return to movie theaters for fresh entertainment, and movie makers, in turn, became more "quality-oriented" to maintain and encourage this trend. Radio, too, has regained some of its old status, but it cannot hope to compete fully with the video portion of television.

Modern-day television programs are still under attack for an overabundance of violence and other unsatisfactory features, including the commercials, but the medium is definitely "growing up" in its coverage of world-wide news events of great importance. The recent successful orbiting of the Telstar communication satellites has made it possible for international television to develop fully. Such technological improvements bring added hope that television will pass through its adolescence quickly and reach full adult status, offering to the viewer the very best that we and other nations can present. If this medium does have a major impact on our society and is capable of forming or changing attitudes, programming must be carefully structured for a positive total effect.

The study by Witty and Kinsella (1958), although now some years old, deserves mention for its extensive analysis of the specific viewing interests of youngsters. A number of the programs mentioned in the analysis are still being shown today, either as a continuation of a regular series or as reruns, while others are no longer being presented. The data in Table 15 show the ten favorite programs of youngsters in grades one to three, four to six, seven to eight, and nine to twelve in 1958.

The ten programs chosen as favorites by ninth- through twelfth-grade pupils are listed in Table 16. This analysis presents the favorite programs of boys and girls separately, showing some of the sex differences in viewing preferences.

TABLE 15. The ten favorite TV programs of youngsters in 1958 (by grades in the Chicago area)

From Witty and Kinsella (1958), by permission of The National Council of Teachers of English and Paul Witty and Paul Kinsella

	Grades 1-3	Grades 4-6	Grades 7-8
1	Zorro	Zorro	American Bandstand
2	Bugs Bunny	Shock Theatre	Shock Theatre
3	Mickey Mouse	Father Knows Best	Dick Clark Show
4	Blue Fairy	Disneyland	Maverick
5	Disneyland	Maverick	Gunsmoke
6	Lassie	Dick Clark	Father Knows Best
7	Susie	Colt 45	Playhouse 90
8	Shirley Temple	American Bandstand	Steve Allen
9	Superman	Cheyenne	Ozzie and Harriet
10	Mighty Mouse	Leave it to Beaver	Have Gun—Will Travel

This study repeats previous studies made in 1950, 1951, and 1952. In 1950, 43 per cent of the students had TV sets at home; in 1951, 68 per cent had them; in 1952, 88 per cent reported sets at home; and in 1955 and 1958, 97 per cent had TV sets at home. In 1950 the youngsters devoted 21 hours per week to TV; in 1951, 19 hours. In 1955 the sixth study in the survey showed that the average was 24 hours; in 1957, 22

TABLE 16. Ten favorite TV programs of boys and girls in the ninth through twelfth grades (Chicago area)

From Witty and Kinsella (1958), by permission of The National Council of Teachers of English and Paul Witty and Paul Kinsella

	Girls	Boys
1	American Bandstand	Shock Theatre
2	Dick Clark Show	Maverick
3	Father Knows Best	Gunsmoke
4	Shock Theatre	Zorro
5	Playhouse 90	American Bandstand
6	Maverick	Dick Clark Show
7	Ozzie and Harriet	Have Gun—Will Travel
8	Dinah Shore Show	Sports
9	Movie	West Point Story
10	Steve Allen	Sergeant Bilko

hours; and in 1958, 20 hours a week. That high-school students watch television less than elementary students is evidenced by their average of only 13 hours a week in 1958.

The increasing preference from elementary- through high-school years for programs like the Dick Clark Show and American Bandstand is definitely in line with the development of increasingly heterosexual interests. These programs are specifically aimed at teen-agers and present the music that most teen-agers prefer. They also show the latest dance steps and allow youngsters to develop their dancing skills in the privacy of their homes.

Witty and Kinsella also point out that very few teachers considered the unfortunate characteristics of certain television programs a primary source of children's misbehavior. The teachers questioned did feel, however, that too many crime and Western programs are presented. Teachers thought that there should be greater emphasis on opera, travelogues, great plays, good music, news, and science programs. Parents, too, felt that they would prefer their youngsters to be exposed to more travelogues, plays, science, and good music. The programs that parents considered desirable for their children are listed in Table 17.

TABLE 17. Desirable programs for children suggested by parents in 1958
From Witty and Kinsella (1958), by permission of The National Council of Teachers of English and Paul Witty and Paul Kinsella

Program	Type
Mickey Mouse Club	Combination
Disneyland	Variety-animated
Lassie	Animal
Captain Kangaroo	Variety-children
Mr. Wizard	Science
Ding Dong School	Preschool
Blue Fairy	Fantasy
Shirley Temple	Fairy tales
Father Knows Best	Family situation
Leave it to Beaver	Family situation

When one compares Tables 15 and 17, some agreement between the parents' preferences and the youngsters' favorite programs is apparent. The authors of these studies strongly recommended that teachers and parents work with commercial agencies to develop more desirable and provocative offerings for children.

Now, five years later, few if any of the suggestions offered by these various researchers have been put into effect. Newton Minow, chairman of the Federal Communications Commission, has publicly called television a "vast wasteland'" and has indicated that some federal intervention could occur if programming is not upgraded. Nonetheless, there have been a great many outstanding programs that have offered invaluable experiences to adolescents in connection with their studies. A youngster studying Shakespeare has had the opportunity to see excellent productions of *Hamlet, Macbeth,* etc., presented by the finest actors of our time. Librarians claim that television has actually stimulated youngsters' reading and that adolescents are withdrawing more books than ever.

Much research is still neeeded before we can be truly aware of the extent of television's impact on adolescents. If one could truly determine what variables would develop positive characteristics in youngsters, programmers might be better able to relate those variables to their attempts to upgrade the medium. The recent increased use of educational television also creates a need for extensive research, including long-range follow-up studies, to evaluate its relation to education in general.

Movies

Movie attendance is still a major interest of youngsters, just as it was in the pretelevision era, but television has probably reduced the frequency of movie attendance to some extent. Before television became available in the home, Fleege (1945) studied the movie attendance of boys in Catholic high schools. The average boy attended 1.2 times per week, and none of the group involved indicated that he never went to the movies. Almost 50 per cent indicated that they attended movies primarily for entertainment, enjoyment, pleasure, and amusement. More than 25 per cent stated that they attended movies simply to pass the time or to have something to do. These are, of course, the expressed reasons of these youngsters and may not be the real reasons. The adolescent may not really be able to analyze his true reasons for attending movies, whatever they may be, and may express the more or less accepted reasons.

Fleege also attempted to analyze the influences of movies on high-school boys. About 30 per cent of the respondents said that movies did inspire them to try to be like the hero, or influenced their action, behavior, and conduct. About 10 per cent felt that movies influenced their attitudes, and another 10 per cent indicated that movies gave them new ideas. Movies also influenced them in regard to manners, social relations, morals, vocations, and self-improvement. Imitation seems to be the single factor most apparent in their responses.

The reactions to a film shown to 200 boys and an equal number of girls were studied by means of interviews, examinations, and clinical analysis. Results indicated a good deal of identification with and projection into the situations presented on the part of the young spectators (Lanz-Stuparich, 1952). The author suggested that serious consideration be given this matter by those responsible for influencing the lives of these future citizens. Philippon (1952) also investigated the influence of movies on children and adolescents. He felt that the most serious problems are fatigue, remembrances, and influence on the subconscious and conscious mind. He was most concerned about the danger of nervous and mental disturbance from films and thought that all youths who frequent movies more than once per week should be given psychiatric supervision. While it may be partially true that too frequent movie attendance is related to some kind of emotional disturbance, which might be increased by movies, this would seem to be a fairly extreme viewpoint.

Keilhacker (1955) stressed the need for more research relating to movies and their effects on the reactions of youngsters. He felt that it was impossible for an adult to predict the reactions of youngsters to movies from his own reactions to the same movies. The reactions of adolescents are also different from those of children. To children, movies usually represent an imaginary world; for adolescents, movies are also an area in which they may try to determine their own future.

The need for more research in this area is probably greater today than ever before. More and more movies are being billed as "For Adults Only," but many teen-agers manage to see these. Particular concern has been expressed about the effects of some recent foreign films that vividly portray immorality and even obscenity. The American film-maker is also involved in "reality-oriented" films that show the seamier side of life, including various kinds of perverted behavior. The negative effects of such films on young audiences have been widely proclaimed, but there has been little or no research to reinforce or negate such claims.

Theater

Herrfahrdt (1956) reported on the development of theatrical interests in German girls ranging in age from thirteen to nineteen. The girls sixteen or older showed very high interest in the theater. With increasing age, comedies have less appeal and modern "realistic" plays become more popular. Local opera houses also seemed to help stimulate theatrical interest. Among the particular favorites of these youngsters were classics that they had previously read and discussed in school.

There has been even less research in this area than in the area of the movies. Many American children have no opportunity to attend the theater, and its influences, if any, are probably fewer than those of movies or television. However, many plays are made into movies or appear on television, so that even a nontheater-goer may be exposed to them. Some of these plays, such as O'Neill's *The Iceman Cometh*, are intended only for adults; when they are presented in a theater, the restriction against youngsters' attending can be enforced. *The Iceman Cometh,* however, has been shown as a "Play of the Week" on television, giving adolescents the opportunity to see it if their parents permitted. Even though the television performance was preceded by the announcement that it was for adults only, it is safe to assume that many parents, unfamiliar with the play's content, were willing for their adolescents to see the work of a man who is considered a great playwright.

OTHER AREAS OF TEEN-AGE INTEREST

Kohlman (1951) studied the interests of teen-agers and children in class discussion by high-school girls. Children's play interests, emotional expression of needs, physical health habits, etc., were among the topics explored. There were different interests in the different classes. For example, interest in the child-child relationship was strongest for the freshman group, while the junior and senior groups showed more interest in emotional expression. The sophomores evidenced more interest in children than did the other three classes. The author feels that family-life education could help to effect happier sibling relationships through greater understanding of the teen-agers' interests in younger children.

Lantagne (1958) administered an inventory to 4000 high-school students in an attempt to determine their interest in problems of marriage and parenthood. He found a significant interest in marriage and in parenthood among these students, with a considerable variation by sex in certain items, but also considerable similarity of interest for boys and girls. Boys were interested in prevention of juvenile delinquency, while girls were interested in pregnancy problems. Generally, the girls showed a greater over-all interest in marriage and parenthood than the boys did. There were no significant differences in the percentage of interest as related to religious belief.

THE ADOLESCENT VIEWS HIS INTERESTS

Adolescents are often very much aware what their major interests are and are concerned about the relationship of these interests to their present and future patterns of behavior. They are also aware of the apparent instability of their interests, frequently expressing concern at their inability to "stick" to a given pattern. They are only vaguely aware, however, that some of their interests may be unrealistic or result from social pressure rather than from personal needs. Youngsters frequently have difficulty in differentiating their interests into primary and secondary patterns that separate those that may be related to future goals from those that are more or less in the hobby category. Many are also concerned because they seem to have a considerable miscellany of interests rather than any major specific interests.

The Peer Group's Relation to Interests

It is particularly difficult for some youngsters to give up certain childhood interests. However, if no one in the adolescent peer group has a similar interest, a youngster may feel uncomfortable about maintaining the interest. For example, a child may have devoted much time to developing a collection of "baseball cards" (cards with baseball players' pictures and statistics concerning performance) and may have found many other children with whom he shared this interest. When he reaches adolescence his interest in baseball may increase, but his card collection may be considered childish by his peer group. Although he may feel rather unhappy at giving up an activity on which he spent so much time and effort, the negative reaction of his peers will probably cause him to drop it.

The peer reaction will not always cause the youngster to discontinue an interest pattern; but it may, instead, cause him to continue the interest secretly for a time. Later, when peer pressure is lessened, the interest may reappear on the overt level.

From the time he was about nine years old, Ronald G. was greatly interested in collecting and cataloguing insects. He devoted a good deal of time to this project and frequently brought his displays to class to discuss them with the other students. When he entered the eighth grade he became a member of a small group of boys, none of whom shared this particular interest. He found that they thought it rather odd and called him "buggy" Ronald. Since he liked this group and shared other interests with them, he decided to conceal his interest in insects, and the group assumed that he had dropped it completely. At the twelfth-grade level, he enrolled in a zoology course where this interest was quite acceptable, and Ronald again brought his collection to class. It was quite obvious from his exhibit that he had continued to work extensively on this collection during the years when he seemed to have discontinued it.

Perhaps more difficult is the necessity some teen-agers feel to appear to have interests that they do not really possess. Young teen-agers and particularly teen-agers who reach pubescence late are often placed in this awkward position.

Janice C., a fourteen-year-old, explained how she had to make believe she had a certain interest: "I do go out on dates with boys but I really don't enjoy it. I'm just not too interested in boys right now." When asked why she dated if she didn't like it, she replied, "I was accepted as a member of a sorority, and it seems all the girls do is talk about boys and dating. At first I didn't join these conversations, but the others started to make fun of me. I want to be liked by them, so I started pretending to be interested in boys, too. Then some of the other girls wanted me to double-date with them or come to their parties where boys were invited. I managed to make excuses the first few times, but I felt I better try to attend or they'd realize I was just making up the things I had told them. I don't date too often, just enough so they'll believe I'm interested in boys. The only thing is I worry now that I might not enjoy dating when I'm older since it's not very pleasant right now."

Certainly peer-group influence is a major factor, to the extent that false interests may develop as the individual seeks acceptance. Occasionally a youngster may try to get the others to accept one of his interests, and he may be successful in doing so. If, however, the group shows any resistance or acts as if the idea presented is rather peculiar, the youngster is unlikely to push the attempt. He may instead follow the paths previously suggested: conceal his interest; or drop it entirely and follow the interests of his group even if they are not his own. Obviously, a youngster is willing to do these things only if most of his interests are similar to those of the peer group. If they are completely different, he is likely to leave that group and seek one whose interests are more compatible with his own.

Discovering Major Interests

The apparent lack of major interests is one of the sources of concern mentioned previously. This author seriously doubts that very many adolescents actually lack major interests, despite their claims that this is the case. Sometimes a youngster simply needs a little help in identifying his major interests and, once they are identified, he is quick to realize that they were there all the time, even though they perhaps had not crystallized.

Doug Z. went to see his high-school counselor, and the following discussion occurred:

Counselor. What is the trouble, Doug? Something seems to be bothering you.

Doug. Yes sir! I'm entering my junior year next year and I don't really know what courses I want or even the program to choose.

Counselor. That's not unusual, Doug. A lot of the other students want this same kind of advice.

Doug. Really? Gee, I'm surprised to hear that. I've been sort of worried because most of the fellows seem to know exactly what they're interested in and I really don't know what my interests are.

Counselor. I'm not sure if I understand that, Doug. You must be interested in something.

Doug. That's just it—I seem to be interested in everything equally. I like animals, I like sports, I like building things, I like all my courses in school—I mean I really like everything. I just think that by now I should be more interested in some things than in others. That's why I came to see you; thought maybe you could help.

Counselor. Well, I can try. Let's give you a couple of interest tests and see if we can find anything.

A week later Doug came back to the counselor, after having taken a battery of interest, aptitude, temperament, and ability tests.

Doug. Well, I'm back to get the results. I really had trouble making some of those choices about things I like to do. Can we talk about it now?

The counselor discussed Doug's abilities and aptitudes with him, pointing out a high mechanical-scientific aptitude. Then he went on to discuss the interest tests.

Counselor. Doug, according to these profiles, your highest interests are in mechanical, scientific, and mathematical areas. This seems to be in line with your aptitude and ability.

Doug. Gee, that's funny. I've thought for a long time I'd like to be an engineer but didn't think I was interested enough.

Counselor. Doug, although you originally said you liked everything, aren't there some things you spend more time doing than others?

Doug. Well, yes, I guess so. I do spend some time in Dad's workshop building things, but I just seem to build all kinds of little gadgets —nothing specific.

A few sessions later Doug indicated that the interviews and tests had all been very helpful.

Doug. I guess I just needed a little help in tying things together. I see now how a lot of the things I did really weren't different at all—just different parts of a single interest. I really know what I like now and have decided on the courses and program that will be most interesting to me.

AN OVERVIEW

There is a need for far more research on interests, particularly if they are to be used effectively as motivators of behavior. We must learn in particular how to help youngsters develop interests that are realistic and related to their abilities and aptitudes. The development of interests that are not merely educationally or vocationally oriented will become increasingly important; with more leisure time becoming available to all, interests oriented toward enjoyment of everyday living are also needed. More attention might be given toward developing interests in hobbies, music, art, woodworking, etc.—activities in which the individual can profitably be engaged during his leisure hours. Since many workers today do not feel any real sense of pride in their workday achievements, it is even more crucial that they should gain satisfaction from leisure-time activities that provide some outlet for their abilities and relief from the boredom of their jobs.

Despite the obvious importance of vocational interests, this area has not been discussed in this chapter. The discussion of vocational interests is included in Chapter 11, which deals with the development of vocational plans. While many of the interests described in the present chapter do relate to vocational choice, the author feels that vocational interests need more intensive treatment.

REFERENCES

AMATORA, SISTER MARY. "Free Expression of Adolescents' Interest." *Genetic Psychology Monographs,* 55, 173-219, 1957.

AMATORA, SISTER MARY. "Interest of Pre-Adolescent Boys and Girls." *Genetic Psychology Monographs,* 61, 77-113, 1960.

ANDERSON, ESTHER, M. "A Study of Leisure-Time Reading of Pupils in Junior High School." *Elementary School Journal,* 48, 258-267, 1948.

BERNSTEIN, MARGERY R. "Relationship between Interest and Reading Comprehension." *Journal of Educational Research,* 49, 283-288, 1955.

BLAKELY, W. P. "A Study of Seventh Grade Children's Reading of Comic Books as Related to Certain Other Variables." *Journal of Genetic Psychology,* 93, 291-301, 1958.

BUTTERWORTH, ROBERT J., and THOMPSON, GEORGE G. "Factors Related to Age-Grade Trends and Sex Difference in Children's Preferences for Comic Books." *Journal of Genetic Psychology,* 78, 71-96, 1951.

CANONGE, FERNAND. "Intérêts et curiosités des éleves de centres d'apprentissage" (Interests and Curiosities of the Pupils of Vocational Training Centers). *Enfance* (Paris), 1, 304-315, 1948.

CARSLEY, J. D. "The Interests of Children (aged 10-11) in Books." *British Journal of Educational Psychology,* 27, 13-23, 1957.

DARLEY, JOHN G., and HAGANAH, T. *Vocational Interest Measurement: Theory and Practice.* Minneapolis: University of Minnesota Press, 1955.

FLEEGE, U. H. *Self-revelation of the Adolescent Boy.* Milwaukee: The Bruce Publishing Company, 1945.

FOX, WILLIAM H.   "The Stability of Measured Interests."   *Journal of Educational Research,* 41, 305-310, 1947.

FRANK, JOSETTE.   "Comics, Radio, Movies—and Children."   *Public Affairs Pamphlet,* no. 148, 1949.

FRANK, JOSETTE.   *Your Child's Reading Today.*   New York: Doubleday & Co., 1954.

FRANKLIN, R. D., and REMMERS, H. H.   *Report of Poll 57 of the Purdue Opinion Panel: Youths' Attitudes re Elections, Competition, Discipline, Status, Spare Time, Driving, Grandparents, and Health.*   Lafayette, Ind.: Purdue University, Division of Educational Reference, 1960.

HARRIS, DALE B.   "Sex Differences in the Life Problems and Interests of Adolescents."   *Child Development,* 30, 453-459, 1959.

HERRFAHRDT, ILSEMARIE.   "Beitrag zur Entwicklung des Interesses am Theater bei 13- bis 19-jahrigen Schulerinnen" (Development of Theatrical Interest in 13- to 19-year-old School Girls).   *Psychologische Beitraege* (Meisenheim/Glan), 2, 390-408, 1956.

HOLLINGSHEAD, A. B.   *Elmtown's Youth.*   New York: John Wiley & Sons, Inc., 1949.

JACOBS, ROBERT.   "Stability of Interests at the Secondary School Level."   *Educational Records Bulletin,* no. 52, 83-87, 1949.

KEILHACKER, M.   "Le cinéma et les réactions des enfants et des adolescents" (Movies and the Reactions of Children and Adolescents).   *Cahiers Pedagogique* (Paris), 14, 67-75, 1955.

KOHLMAN, ELEANORE L.   "Teen-age Interests in Children."   *Journal of Home Economics,* 43, 23-36, 1951.

LANTAGNE, JOSEPH E.   "Interest of 4,000 High School Pupils in Problems of Marriage and Parenthood."   *Research Quarterly of the American Association for Health, Physical Education, and Recreation,* 29, 407-416, 1958.

LANZ-STUPARICH, MARIA.   "Les adolescents et le cinéma" (Adolescents and the Cinema). In Baumgarten, Franziska, *Le psychotechnique dans le monde moderne* (Psychotechnology in the Modern World), pp. 557-561. Paris: Presses Universitaires de France, 1952.

LEACH, KENT W.   "Intelligence Levels and Corresponding Interest Area Choices of Ninth Grade Pupils in Thirteen Michigan Schools."   *Journal of Experimental Education,* 22, 369-383, 1954.

LYNESS, PAUL I.   "Patterns in the Mass Communications Tastes of Young Audiences."   *Journal of Educational Psychology,* 42, 449-467, 1951.

LYNESS, PAUL I.   "The Place of the Mass Media in the Lives of Boys and Girls."   *Journalism Quarterly,* 29, 43-54, 1952.

MACCOBY, ELEANOR E.   "Television: Its Impact on School Children."   *Public Opinion Quarterly,* 15, 421-444, 1951.

MACDONALD, MARGHERITA, MCGUIRE, CARSON, and HAVIGHURST, ROBERT J.   "Leisure Activities and the Socio-economic Status of Children."   *American Journal of Sociology,* 54, 505-519, 1949.

MCKELLAR, PETER, and HARRIS, RALPH.   "Radio Preferences of Adolescents and Children."   *British Journal of Educational Psychology,* 22, 101-113, 1952.

MALLINSON, GEORGE GREISEN, and CRUMRINE, WILLIAM M. "An Investigation of the Stability of Interest of High School Students." *Journal of Educational Research*, 45, 369-383, 1952.

MAR, EVELYN. "An Investigation into the Reading Interest of Adolescents." *Studies in Education and Psychology* (Delhi), 4, 35-38, 1955.

MARKS, JOHN B. "Interests and Leadership among Adolescents." *Journal of Genetic Psychology*, 91, 163-172, 1957.

MOSIER, C. I. "Factors Influencing the Validity of a Scholastic Interest Scale." *Journal of Educational Psychology*, 28, 188-196, 1937.

NORVELL, G. W. *The Reading Interests of Young People.* Boston: D. C. Heath and Co., 1950.

PATEL, A. S. "Newspaper Reading Interests of Secondary School Children." *Journal of Educational Psychology* (Baroda), 11(1), 34-43, 1953.

PHILIPPON, O. "L'influence du cinéma sur l'enfance et l'adolescence, l'enquête nationale française" (The Influence of Moving Pictures on Children and Adolescence, National French Inquiry). *Nouvelle Revue Pedagogique*, 7, 526-530, 1952.

REMMERS, H. H., HORTON, R. E., and MAINER, R. E. "Attitudes and Knowledge of Youth Related to Health." *Purdue Opinion Panel Report*, 13(3), 9, 1954.

ROSENBERG, B. G., and SUTTON-SMITH, B. "A Revised Conception of Masculine-Feminine Differences in Play Activities." *Journal of Genetic Psychology*, 96, 165-170, 1960.

SCHALLER, WARREN E. "Health Needs and Interests as a Basis for Selecting Health Content in Secondary Schools." *Research Quarterly of the American Association for Health, Physical Education, and Recreation*, 31, 512-522, 1960.

SCOTT, LLOYD F. "A Study of Children's TV Interests." *California Journal of Educational Research*, 4, 162-164, 1953.

SEAGOE, M. V. "Children's Television Habits and Preferences." *Quarterly of Film, Radio, Television* (Berkeley, Calif.), 6 (2), 143-152, 1952.

SEAGOE, MAY V. "Some Current Research in Television for Children." *California Journal of Educational Research*, 3, 151-153, 1952.

SEHGAL, J. C. "An Investigation into the Recreational Activities of Adolescents." *Studies in Educational Psychology* (Delhi), 2, 41-48, 1953.

STERNER, ALICE P. "Radio, Motion Picture, and Reading Interests: A Study of High School Pupils." *Teachers College Contributions to Education*, no. 932, 1947.

STRONG, E. K., JR. *Vocational Interests of Men and Women.* Stanford: Stanford University Press, 1943.

STRONG, E. K., JR. "Validity of Occupational Choice." *Educational and Psychological Measurement*, 13, 110-121, 1953.

ULICH, EBERHARD. "Concerning the Leisure Time Activities of Adolescent Pupils." *Psychologische Rundschau* (Basel), 10, 180-190, 1959.

VAN DALEN, D. B. "A Differential Analysis of the Play of Adolescent Boys." *Journal of Educational Research*, 41, 204-213, 1947.

VAN DALEN, D. B. "A Differential Analysis of the Play of Junior High School Girls." *Journal of Educational Research*, 43, 22-31, 1949.

WALL, W. D. "The Newspaper Reading Interest of Adolescents and Adults, Part III." *British Journal of Educational Psychology*, 18, 87-104, 1948.

WHITEHEAD, F. "The Attitudes of Grammar School Pupils towards Some Novels Commonly Read in School." *British Journal of Educational Psychology*, 26, 104-111, 1956.

WITTY, P., and KINSELLA, P. "Children and TV: A Ninth Report." *Elementary English*, 35, 450-456, 1958.

CHAPTER 11

Vocational Interests, Planning, and Guidance

The development of vocational interests and the relationship of these interests to vocational plans have been widely investigated. With the rapid development of the field of vocational counseling, it has become increasingly important to know how and why vocational interests develop, and particularly to determine how these interests may best be related to the choice of an occupation. The speed of technological change today leaves little room for the unskilled laborer, and it is increasingly necessary to help the individual identify the field in which he can function most effectively within the limits of his abilities, aptitudes, and interests. It is no longer advisable to try to orient an individual toward a single specific occupation, since such an occupation may not be available ten years hence. Rather, the individual must be oriented toward an occupational area within which specific vocations may constantly change. We are told that the typical production-line worker today may have to be retrained at least three times in the next two or three decades to keep up with the advances in his field. To meet this challenge, to be able to make these changes effectively and with minimal effort, the individual must have a broad base from which he can operate. Until relatively recently, we could teach a youngster a single operation of a given machine without being concerned about his understanding of the total function of that machine. In the future he may need to understand all about that machine and its relationship to a variety of other machines, with only slight concern about any specific operation.

EARLY VOCATIONAL INTERESTS

Very young children often discuss what they want to be, but the occupations they select are usually unrelated to those in which they will actually become interested later on. Little boys want to be cowboys, locomotive engineers, pilots, spacemen, etc., while little girls think of becoming dancers, nurses, teachers, or mothers. These interests are very much related to the kinds of toys we give youngsters and the kinds of books we read to them, and are not to be seriously considered as indicators of later vocational choice. It is interesting to note, however, that at the earlier age levels girls' choices are more limited than are those of boys. The socioeconomic, intellectual, and educational factors that may finally influence an individual's occupational choice do not operate during early childhood, and all children generally make similar choices. The total environmental background of an individual child does have some influence, however. Rural youngsters mention agricultural occupations more frequently than business fields, while city children seldom mention agricultural occupations.

As the youngster approaches adolescence, the childhood "fantasy" interests begin to shift toward more reality-oriented interests that relate to their view of the occupational choice. A study by this author (1955) indicated that the beginning of serious concern about one's future vocation occurs at about the age of twelve and continues up into the adult years, with increasing concern being shown with increasing age. In early adolescence, however, interests are reality-oriented in that they include actual adult occupational fields, but not in the sense that the youngster is actually suited for the occupational goal he professes a desire to achieve.

ARE ADOLESCENTS' VOCATIONAL CHOICES REALISTIC?

Numerous studies have indicated that many adolescents are quite unrealistic about their vocational goals. Far more youngsters, for example, choose professional occupations than will actually enter those occupations, while relatively few choose the types of skilled labor in which many of them will eventually engage. Dufty (1960) analyzed the data on vocational choices from a questionnaire administered to more than 1300 thirteen- to fourteen-year-old high-school boys. Their level of vocational aspiration was found to be "considerably above the likely level of attainment." Professional occupations and adventurous occupations were overselected in terms of the ability of the labor force to absorb them and in terms of the pupils' intellectual level. Generally, the chief reason for the choice made was the "intrinsic nature" of the work. Among those choosing unskilled jobs, "pay orientation" was found to be important, while for those choosing professional and white-collar jobs, "security" was most valued. Stubbins (1948) studied the personal data and occupational choice of more than 200 veterans and found that about 62 per cent made appropriate choices, while about 26 per cent were unrealistic. Those with more education made more realistic choices.

Carp (1949) felt that high-school boys were realistic about occupations. She compared the "desired" and "expected" occupations of boys fourteen to eighteen years old with their fathers' and grandfathers' occupations. The relationship between these occupations and the "expected" occupations of the youngsters led her to conclude that these youngsters had realistic occupational goals. Dresden (1948) presented "subjective, individual, and nonstatistical" evidence to support her contention that data obtained from questionnaire surveys are often misleading. She believed that the true vocational goals are much closer to the individual's abilities than he is willing to record on a questionnaire.

Dresden's criticism is a valid one. Frequently, the wording of a questionnaire may influence the individual's response. For example, if the question reads, "What occupation would you like to enter?" the respondent may indicate a field he would like, while being fully aware that it is not the one he will actually enter. Powell and Bloom (1962) asked two questions of the tenth-, eleventh-, and twelfth-grade students involved in their study of occupational choice: first, "What occupation would you like to enter, assuming that you have financial resources, ability, and freedom of choice?" and, second, "What occupation do you really expect to enter?" The responses to these two questions and the significance of the differences in these responses are presented in Table 18. A further analysis of these data by grade level showed that 59 per cent of the tenth-graders, 63 per cent of the eleventh-

TABLE 18. The percentage of students who prefer and plan to enter certain vocational levels
From Powell and Bloom (1962), by permission of the authors and Dembar Publications

| | Boys | | Girls | |
	Occupation preferred	Occupation planned	Occupation preferred	Occupation planned
Professional	64.9*	49.3	69.7	53.0*
Clerical, Sales	6.6	9.9**	23.2	30.9**
Service	1.3	1.3	1.6	1.4
Agriculture	5.4	4.7	.6	.6
Skilled	12.5*	7.9		
Semi-Skilled	3.1	9.5**		
Unskilled	.8	.9		
Armed Services	3.2	7.7	1.4	1.4
Housewife			1.6	5.5*
No Response	2.0	9.0*	1.9	7.14*

*Significant difference at .01 level between Preferred and Planned Vocation
**Significant difference at .05 level between Preferred and Planned Vocation

graders, and 67 per cent of the twelfth-graders plan to engage in the occupation they prefer.

If the planned occupation differed from the preferred one, the youngsters were asked to indicate why they did not expect to enter the preferred occupation. These results are presented in Table 19. Some of

TABLE 19. Reasons given for not entering the preferred occupation (percentages) *From Powell and Bloom (1962), by permission of the authors and Dembar Publications*

	Boys	Girls
Inadequate finances	7.90	15.39
Ability for chosen work	5.79	9.40
Lack of ability for chosen work	2.63	5.98
Choice of parents	11.05	2.56
Preparatory work for job	3.16	12.82
Opportunity in chosen work	4.74	5.98
Like chosen work	18.42	10.26
Marriage	0.00	12.82
High pay	4.74	.86
Security	2.10	.86
Undecided	15.79	6.84
No reason	6.32	6.84
Armed services	10.53	0.00
Miscellaneous	3.16	6.84
Related field	3.68	2.56

the reasons given suggest that the youngsters are realistic about the field that they actually select, or at least about the reasons why they will not enter the preferred field.

The total data from this study, however, support the concept that vocational choices are unrealistic. No more than 40 per cent of the graduates among the high-school population studied will enter college, and a number of these (about 15 per cent) will not graduate. About 50 per cent of those males who graduate from high school will enter the skilled and semiskilled occupations. Obviously, then, both the relative lack of preferred and planned choices of these occupations and the preferred and planned choices of the professions are quite unrealistic. Girls appear to be as unrealistic as boys in regard to the professions but are more realistic in their choices of the clerical and sales occupations.

Schmidt and Rothney (1955), who followed approximately 350 high-school students from tenth grade to approximately six months after graduation, suggest that vocational choices varied a good deal during this period. If this is so, the realism of a youngster's choice at any given time would be rather difficult to assess truly, since any choice would be subject to change. Porter (1954), however, found a high consistency among what high-school senior boys prefer to do, what they plan to do, and what they actually do.

Causes of Unrealistic Choices

If there is, however, a lack of realism in the vocational choices of youngsters, why is this so? The reasons are many and varied, but one of the major ones is ignorance of the preferred field. Relatively few adolescents are truly aware of all the details relating to success in the field they choose. They are often even unaware of the academic requirements they must meet in order to enter the field. For example, a youngster may decide that he wishes to become a psychologist. He probably thinks that he will be qualified to function in that field when he receives his Bachelor's degree. He will find, however, that he has almost no opportunity to enter the field without an advanced degree, usually the Ph.D. He may be unwilling or unable to pursue this advanced goal and as a result may turn to some other field. If he were well acquainted with the total field, he might be aware that for some occupations within psychology, such as school psychology or psychometry, a Master's degree is sufficient.

Another factor is the status accorded an occupation. Such a field as medicine is chosen by many youngsters not because of any great desire to serve humanity, but because the field has high status value and offers an opportunity for rapid social advancement. Often parents try to guide their youngsters into these high-status fields in order that the youngsters may achieve a higher social status than the parents were able to achieve. Being the parents of a professional person enables them to feel that they have also gained status.

Financial remuneration is an important factor in job choice that may also lead to unrealistic choices. Often youngsters have an inaccurate idea of the actual income that they would be able to achieve in a given field. For example, the fields of engineering have been widely advertised as offering unlimited financial opportunities. Only a casual look at the classified advertisements is needed to see that there is a demand for engineers, and that high salaries are available. A closer look, however, often shows these high salaries are only for those with highly specialized skills, and that the average engineer is not likely to be eligible for these jobs. The high salaries and unlimited opportunities are for only a few, while the majority, though earning adequate salaries, seldom amass wealth.

Youngsters may make an unrealistic choice of an occupation because they are unrealistic in their appraisals of themselves. The interests they profess to have may not be real interests, or they may overvalue an aptitude in which they have only minor proficiency. Many youngsters fail to evaluate realistically their own level of intelligence and choose occupational goals that they are intellectually incapable of reaching.

Lack of realism in vocational choice does not always mean that youngsters choose goals that they are incapable of reaching. Actually, many youngsters choose occupations at a lower level than that which they are capable of achieving. Sometimes this may be necessary for financial reasons; a youngster may be unable to afford the education required for the field he prefers. In other cases, one may settle for a less demanding occupation because it seems to offer more security with less effort than would higher levels. Today many college students marry and have families, and such added responsibilities may lead the individual to take a job that seems attractive rather than continue on to an advanced degree.

Whatever the reason, and regardless of whether the choice is beyond the individual's ability or at a lesser level than he could achieve, frustration is likely to result. The person who is unable to reach a desired goal that is beyond his level will probably have difficulty in adjusting to some other occupation. One who selects an occupation at a level below that on which he is capable of performing is likely to become bored and dissatisfied with his vocation. He may, however, find that it is too late for him to attempt a change and thus be stuck in a field that is neither challenging nor motivating to him.

VOCATIONS PREFERRED BY ADOLESCENTS

Regardless of the degree of realism involved, most youngsters have made a vocational choice by the time they reach the junior year of high school. Porter (1954) stated that by the senior year of high school there was a high degree of consistency among the boys between what they planned to do and what they actually did. Powell and Bloom (1962) investigated these choices in a sample of about 1000 tenth-, eleventh-, and twelfth-grade high-school students. Table 18 (page 363) indicates the general categories into which their responses fell. The specific fields preferred within these various categories are also interesting.

The boys named 50 different occupations, 33 of which were ranked in the professional category. The specific occupations selected by the boys were: engineering, 23.3 per cent; medicine and automotive mechanic, 5.6 per cent; research, 4.1 per cent, aviation and the business world, 3.4 per cent each. Most boys had no clear-cut idea of what "to enter the business world" meant, except that it involved a white-collar occupation. Such jobs as electrician, carpenter, and television serviceman were also mentioned. Three fields were most often preferred by girls, with 21.6 per cent choosing office work; 15 per cent, teaching; and 13.7 per cent, nursing. The job of airline hostess ranked fourth, and was preferred by 4.1 per cent. Of the 35 different vocations mentioned by the girls, some 33 are classified as professional in the *Dictionary of Occupational Titles*. Among the professional vocations named were journalism, modeling, dramatics, fashion design, interior decoration, physical therapy, law, library work, and social work.

The analysis in Table 18 of vocations youngsters actually plan to enter shows that significantly fewer boys expect to enter occupations categorized as professional and skilled. About 9 per cent frankly admitted they had no idea of their vocational future. Of the others, 18.6 per cent expected to become engineers; 5.4 per cent, to become auto mechanics; 4.7 per cent, to enter the business world; 4.5 per cent, to enter the sales field; 4.1 per cent, to become semiskilled factory workers; and 7.7 per cent, to enter the armed services. More girls expected to enter the clerical and sales fields and fewer to enter the professions than preferred to; 29.8 per cent planned to do clerical work; 16.9 per cent, to teach; 12.8 per cent, to become nurses; and 5.5 per cent, to become housewives.

Reasons for Choices

Attempts have been made to determine the reasons for youngsters' preferences. In a study sponsored by the *Scholastic Magazine* in 1945, more than 90,000 youngsters were asked to respond to the question "Which of the following comes closest to being your ultimate aim in life?" The results indicated that 4 per cent had as their ultimate goal to make a lot of money. About 15 per cent wanted to be prominent and respected members of their community, while another 20 per cent wanted "to reach the top in some field of work and become famous." "To live a simple but secure and happy life without making a lot of money or becoming famous" was chosen by 44 per cent of this group as their ultimate aim in life. Another 10 per cent chose "to serve society and help improve the health or welfare of my fellow men," while the last 7 per cent indicated that they did not know their ultimate aim.

In the more recent study by Powell and Bloom (1962), students were asked to indicate the specific reasons why they chose the vocation they listed as their preferred one. The results for grades ten, eleven, and twelve combined are presented in Table 20. There were some grade trends that seemed interesting. Boys, for example, showed an increase from 1.3 per cent in the tenth grade to 5.7 per cent in the twelfth grade in selecting a job because of interest in people. This might be interpreted as indicating an increasing social consciousness with increasing age. There was a statistically significant increase between the

TABLE 20. The percentage of total reasons given as a basis for the selection of certain vocational areas

From Powell and Bloom (1962), by permission of the authors and Dembar Publications

Motivating factor	Boys	Girls
Interest in work	36.2	27.4
Ability to do the work	6.1	4.3
Interest in people	3.4	15.2
Personal advancement	7.0	3.9
Offers security	11.9	6.0
Service to others	5.3	17.4
Adventure and travel	4.3	5.1
Creative idealism	5.3	4.0
Plan to marry	.1	5.8
Armed services	2.7	.6
Previous experience	3.6	2.6
Variety within the work	1.5	.6
Need education	.4	1.4
Religious	.9	.6
Social prestige	.6	.7
Same work as father	3.3	.5
Parental influence	1.6	1.0
Miscellaneous	2.5	1.9
No reason given	5.2	2.9

eleventh and twelfth grades in the frequency with which boys gave "service to others" as a reason for desiring a particular job. A substantial increase in the desire for travel and for adventure was apparent among the eleventh-grade boys. Among girls, both the job preferences and the reasons for these preferences seem to indicate a greater social awareness than the boys showed. The interest in working in a social atmosphere seems to become most pronounced for girls by the time they reach the eleventh grade.

Contrary to what many laymen believe, with increasing age there was actually a decrease in the desire for financial security. For girls, there was an indication that the ability to do the work becomes increasingly important from the tenth to the twelfth grade. Girls also tended to choose occupations that are compatible with marriage. Nursing and teaching, for example, are often chosen as occupations that one can continue after marriage. Teaching, in particular, is mentioned because "the vacations are the same as the children's school vacations so you can spend time with them."

An interest in the work is generally considered more important by boys than by girls. Girls place more emphasis than boys do on an interest in people and a desire to be of service to others. Finally, girls appear to be more influenced by the desire for security than are the boys.

Ultimate Goals

Powell and Bloom also asked these high-school students to respond to the question "What is your ultimate goal with regard to vocational objectives?" Of the boys, 21.4 per cent indicated their major goal was to enter a specific occupation, while 13.1 per cent wanted to "own their own business." About 12 per cent wanted to "become a personal success in their position"; 11 per cent wanted "financial success and security"; about 5 per cent wanted to "do the job well." Fifteen per cent of the boys had not yet formulated their ultimate goals. Of the girls, 37.6 per cent expressed the desire to enter a specific occupation; 9.3 per cent were desirous of "doing the job well"; 8.1 per cent expressed the desire for personal success and advancement; 7.6 per cent wanted to be of service to others. Eighteen per cent did not yet know their ultimate goals.

FACTORS AFFECTING OCCUPATIONAL CHOICE

Young people have a number of ideas about occupations. Although some of their ideas may be quite erroneous, they will have some effect on the attitude the youngster develops toward a given occupational area and may also strongly influence his interests in this area. Youmans (1956) analyzed the responses of more than 1200 boys to test the hypothesis that "Position in the social structure . . . is more important in formulating the occupational expectations of youth than are such factors as the home, the schools, work experience, and type of community." This factor, measured by the occupational level of the father, did show the highest degree of association with the young people's occupational expectations of all these variables measured.

Edmiston and Starr (1948) administered a questionnaire covering twenty-seven factors that might affect choice of vocation to youngsters in grades seven through eleven in an attempt to determine their attitudes toward occupations. Boys generally desired more independence in jobs than girls did. "Service to mankind" was of the greatest importance for the entire group, while "demands responsibility" and "adventure" were of least importance.

Family Financial Status

Good wages as a major factor in job choice has been investigated by Dittmer and Payne (1948). Their survey of male high-school and college seniors supports Durant's hypothesis that those who mention good wages as an important feature of a job come from lower socio-economic levels than those who do not mention this factor. When students in the sample were asked about their wage expectations, both individuals who did not and those who did mention "good wages" gave nearly equal figures.

While the financial aspects of a certain occupation may be quite attractive to an individual, his own financial status may be a major factor in determining whether he may reach that occupational goal. Wiegman (1955) had asked students in 1950 to estimate their prospects of college attendance, including the role of their financial resources in relation to these prospects. A definite relation was found between rank in class and prospects of college attendance. These students were later given a follow-up to find out how accurate their estimates had been. Of those who were sure they would attend, 76 per cent actually did. Of those who were not sure, 41 per cent did attend, as did 19 per cent of those who felt they were financially unable and 7 per cent of those who had not been originally interested in attending college. The data did indicate, nevertheless, that the financial barrier prevented a substantial number of capable students from enrolling in college.

Strong ("Amount of Change in Occupational Choice of College Freshmen," 1952) found that students selecting occupations with high prestige values were less likely to change than those choosing occupations with less prestige value. Those freshmen who did not make changes by their sophomore year also scored higher on the appropriate Vocational Interest Test scale than those who changed their choices. Apparently high prestige value is an influential factor in stabilizing interest in an occupation.

Intelligence

A major factor in vocational selection is intelligence, and ignorance of intelligence scores required for training in a vocation may cause an individual to be seriously misled. Today, more than ever before, one must exceed certain intelligence minimums in order to be admitted to various occupational fields, particularly those requiring advanced education. These are not called IQ minimums but specific "cut points" on admissions tests; practically, however, they relate almost directly to intelligence. Admission to colleges and especially to professional schools is often largely dependent on the individual's ability to exceed the cut point on these tests. It has been said that many individuals currently functioning successfully in professional fields would not even be admitted to the training programs in those fields if they had to pass the entrance tests required today. Since these tests are almost completely weighed in the direction of intelligence and/or achievement, they often eliminate people who might well succeed in the field if they were given the opportunity to try. The justification is that high standards of selection do help insure that most of those admitted to a program will succeed. It is doubtful, however, that one can assume that all who fail to be admitted would be unsuccessful, although as a generalization this might be sound in a majority of cases.

Just how realistic the cut points assigned for admission to various fields are is also difficult to assess. Is it valid to assume that the cut point should be much higher for a person seeking an advanced degree in physics than for one seeking an advanced degree in elementary education, if we are seeking the best person in each field? Perhaps their specific aptitudes might be appreciably different, but should not their over-all intelligence be comparable? Various professional training schools sometimes seem to raise their cut points simply to show that their field is tougher or requires greater ability than some other field, and not actually in order to attract truly qualified students.

At present, little is being done to equate various other factors with these test results. Interest, motivation, and various personality characteristics are assessed as secondary factors, if at all. There is, however, no guarantee that the individual who has a high IQ and even is a "straight A" student will necessarily be the most successful practitioner in the field. While medical-school records, for example, seem to indicate that today's students, who are carefully selected on the basis of the medical school's admissions tests, receive better grades and are better students than those who preceded them, there is no evidence to suggest that they are better doctors than their predecessors were. This emphasis on intelligence and achievement is insufficient really to predict success in the field, though it may predict academic success.

It is particularly difficult for youngsters, even those who are truly aware of their own capabilities, to make occupational choices without thorough knowledge of the academic barriers they must overcome. A youngster may know that he has a high IQ and may demonstrate his ability with excellent academic achievement, but he must be made aware that this does not guarantee admission to the field of his choice unless he can also pass the various admissions tests successfully. Obviously, the youngster who is a bright high-achiever is likely to gain admission to the program he chooses. However, one who is only slightly above average in intelligence but achieves at a high level (perhaps because of extremely high motivation and willingness to put forth a good deal of effort in his work) may find the path to his chosen goal blocked by his inability to reach a high enough level on the admissions tests. The fairness of this is questionable, but certainly these barriers do exist and young people must be made thoroughly aware of their presence.

It must be acknowledged that certain occupations do require a higher level of ability than others do. Obviously, a person planning an occupation that requires college training must be more intellectually gifted than an individual who will become a semiskilled laborer. Schmidt (1953) attempted to relate primary mental abilities and occupation choices in a group of tenth-grade students. These students were asked to express their occupational choices at three different times during the academic year and were also given the Primary Mental Abilities Test near the end of the year. The ten occupations most frequently chosen were: secretary, teacher, nurse, artist, machinist, auto mechanic, doctor, draftsman, engineer, and bookkeeper. In relation to the occupations chosen, students tended to make higher than average scores on "approximately half of the tests of Primary Mental Abilities which purport to measure abilities required for those occupations."

Sweeney's study (1954) suggests the dangers of using intelligence alone as a criterion for job selection. He administered the California Test of Mental Maturity and the Kuder Preference Record (Vocational) to more than 1000 high-school senior boys, many of whom were also given the Minnesota Speed of Reading Test. Generally, Sweeney found that interests appear to be more closely related to temperament, other abilities, and personality than to intellectual factors. These findings are important if high intelligence is to continue to be, as it currently is, a major factor in admission to many occupational fields. Despite the importance of the other factors mentioned, it would be well worth while to explore various means of helping youngsters develop vocational interests that are closely related to their intelligence.

Personality

The relationships between various personality and/or temperament traits and specific occupations are not as well established as those between intelligence and occupations, but such relationships apparently do exist. An analysis of personality characteristics is usually a part of the testing programs used by industrial firms in executive selection and is usually considered as valuable as any other tests that may be used. Such characteristics as sociability, aggressiveness, vigor, emotional stability, etc., either singly or in various combinations, are probably closely related to success in many fields. Generally, however, a comprehensive analysis of personality traits or characteristics is noticeably missing from the selection procedures involved in admission to the advanced educational training required for many fields. As we have previously pointed out, admission to most advanced graduate programs is based on some sort of intelligence and/or achievement test, and little or no attention is given to personality or character traits. It is not unusual for students admitted on this basis to be eliminated from these programs later because of personality problems that become apparent to their advisors. Others, whose defects are not obvious, manage to complete their academic training satisfactorily, only to find that they do not possess the temperament traits necessary for success in their chosen field.

Nathan S. was a brilliant student in high school and college and was admitted to medical school, where he maintained an "A" average. When he completed medical school and finished his internship, he decided to apply for training in psychiatry. It was relatively obvious to the screening committee that Nathan did not relate well with others and that he was unlikely to be successful in that field. The committee indicated in its report that he should avoid private practice, in which he would have to work closely with patients on a personal basis. Nathan was persuaded to go into medical research, where he has been very successful. However, he still feels that he could have been equally successful in psychiatry and is apparently still unaware of his own personality problems.

Small (1953) attempted to explore the personality factors involved in vocational choice by comparing the selections made by well-adjusted adolescent boys with those made in the same category by disturbed subjects. The better-adjusted boys seemed consistently more realistic in their job choices than the disturbed subjects were. A job-concept interview was found more effective than the Thematic Apperception Test or the case history in assessing the fantasy or needs content of vocational choices. The better-adjusted subjects showed needs connected with environment involvement, while the poorly adjusted subjects showed needs associated with environment-avoidance.

Although a few tests, such as the Kuder Preference Test (Personal), are designed to relate personal characteristics to occupations, relatively little use is made of these in public-school vocational-guidance programs. Many guidance counselors and most teachers are unaware of the relationships that exist between personality characteristics and various occupations and are usually not well enough trained even to assess personality adequately. Barahal (1953) felt that vocational counselors should at least be sensitive to the need of referring to psychiatrists or psychologists students or clients who exhibit deep emotional problems that prevent an adequate vocational adjustment. He also felt that the psychiatrist treating such a client should, in turn, use the services of vocational counselors to facilitate the total adjustment of the individual.

Cawley (1947) administered the Strong Vocational Interest Blank for Women and the Bernreuter Personality Inventory to junior and freshman college women and to high-school junior girls. Part of each of these groups was retested two years later with the Strong Blank. Intelligence-test scores and scores on tests in reading and English were drawn from the school's files. Cawley found that bright girls in high school develop vocational interests better suited to individual circumstances earlier than do those who are not as bright. She also found that characteristics of personality accompany certain patterns of interests, e.g., "ambiverts" are most likely to develop interests in social relations; "introverts" maintain the highest level of interest in the literary and fine arts, etc. More masculine girls tended to go to work after high school, while more feminine girls went to college, but both groups displayed a trend toward greater femininity over the two-year period between the tests.

On the evidence currently available, a good deal of research is needed to relate personality characteristics more closely to specific occupational areas, perhaps in much the same way as interests have been related to these areas. Since particularly good training is required to assess personality, vocational counselors would need careful teaching in order to use the assessment instruments presently available and any new ones that may be developed. With their present limited training, most vocational counselors probably should not become deeply involved in personality assessment, since they are generally not well qualified to interpret the results of the tests, especially those of the projective techniques.

Socioeconomic Factors

It has been relatively well established that a high positive relationship exists between socioeconomic status and intelligence, and that there is also a positive relationship between intelligence and the possible occupational level an individual is capable of achieving. Since occupational level and socioeconomic status both relate positively to intelligence, one would expect to find that they also relate positively to each other. A number of research studies have demonstrated that such a positive relationship does exist and that it is generally relatively high.

Pierce-Jones ("Vocational Interest Correlates of Socioeconomic Status in Adolescence," 1959) attempted to construct a measure of socioeconomic status indirectly from items on the Kuder Vocational Preference Record. After this instrument was developed, it was administered, along with the Kuder Vocational Preference Record, to more than 350 subjects in order to relate socioeconomic status with adolescent interests (Pierce-Jones, "Socioeconomic Status and Adolescents' Interests," 1959). Subjects on a high socioeconomic level preferred complex social activity, highly creative artistic pursuits, and scientific, literary, and business activities that confer responsibility and prestige and demand high ability. They generally rejected outdoor, mechanical, and routine clerical work, and were indifferent to selling, social-welfare tasks, and office work. Subjects on a low socioeconomic level tended to prefer agricultural, mechanical, domestic-service, and routine clerical tasks, and generally rejected social welfare and exacting business, literary, and aesthetic tasks. They did not appear to develop as clear "like-dislike" patterns as did the subjects on the higher socioeconomic levels.

Hyman (1956) also studied the relationship between the vocational interests of a group of high-school seniors and their intelligence-test scores. Social status, determined on the basis of the father's occupation, was related to results of the intelligence test and the interest test. The author concluded the social status and intelligence interact to influence ". . . the attempts at identification with various occupational levels which are revealed by vocational interests. . . ."

Moser (1952) studied the effect of the amount of schooling of parents on the vocational preferences of high-school students, and also the effect of the number of books and magazines in the home on these preferences. Data on a sample of almost 500 high-school students were collected and analyzed. (Dates and locale of the study were not reported.) He reported that the highest percentage of college attendance was found among parents of students preferring literary, computational, and social service activities. The lowest percentage of college attendance by parents was found in the group showing clerical, musical, and mechanical preferences. A similar relationship was found between number of books in the home and vocational preferences. The investigator concluded that "the cultural atmosphere of the home, the parental background, and hence parental example and training play an important part in influencing young people in their vocational preferences and selections."

The occupation of the father has been considered a major factor in determining the youngster's occupational preference. Samson and Stefflre (1952) studied the vocational objectives in relation to the occupations of parents of more than 1000 senior-high-school students who had been given a thorough vocational guidance service. It was concluded that the adolescent's objective was not unrelated to the parental occupation at any occupational level. It is possible that youngsters choose the occupation that their father is engaged in, or one similar to it, because it is the field about which they know the most.

Another socioeconomic problem involved in vocational choice may penalize a youngster. Parents at the various socioeconomic levels usually have expectancies for the occupational level they wish their children to achieve. Parents at the high socioeconomic levels expect their children to achieve at least a comparable level, and most of their children will do so. If, however, such parents have a child who has only average ability and is therefore incapable of achieving the high occupational goal set by his parents, the parents may fail to help the child to make a realistic occupational choice. Similar problems may confront a very bright child from a low socioeconomic level. His parents may see little value in higher education and encourage the youngster to leave school early. He is thus prevented from securing the education that he needs to reach the occupational goal of which he is capable. On the other hand, parents who want their child to reach a professional occupational level may be unable to assist the youngster to finance the required educational training.

Work Experience

Work experiences of youngsters in part-time jobs seem to be related to some extent to the type of permanent employment they will eventually hold. These relationships are rather low and often reflect a geographic condition. For example, children of farmers often do part-time agricultural work in the rural area in which they live. That a number of them later become farmers suggests a relationship between the part-time job and the later vocation. However, opportunities for farm youngsters to engage in nonagricultural jobs are limited. Today it is increasingly difficult for adolescents to find much choice among part-time or summer jobs. As a result, the relationships between these jobs and the child's later permanent employment are probably less meaningful today than they were twenty or thirty years ago.

Bateman made a study of "The Effect of Work Experience on High-School Students' Vocational Choice" (1949). The vocational interests of workers and nonworkers (measured on the Kuder Preference Record) were compared by matching boys and girls employed on part-time jobs with an equal number of nonworkers in terms of age, grade, sex, intelligence, and father's occupation. The workers and the nonworking students did not differ greatly in their interest patterns.

Work experience does seem to have some effect on scholastic achievement. Bateman (1950) studied the scholastic achievement of 263 pairs of working and nonworking high-school students matched for sex, grade, school, father's occupation, and IQ. The grade-point average of working students was found to be reliably lower than that of nonworking students. Bateman had previously analyzed the difference between working and nonworking eleventh- and twelfth-graders who were matched on school, sex, grade, and father's occupation, and found no significant differences in intelligence ("The Effect of Work Experience on High-School Students as Revealed by the Bell Adjustment Inventory," 1949). When the four scales of the Bell Adjustment Inventory were administered to these two groups, two reliable differences were found. On both the emotional and the social scale the eleventh-grade girls who worked had reliably lower average scores than their nonworking classmates.

Ethnic or Racial Factors

The ethnic and/or racial background of an individual may be a major factor in his choice of an occupation. All of us have heard that many professional schools allegedly set up quotas that allow only minimal numbers of students with certain racial or religious backgrounds to be admitted to their programs. Although the evidence that might confirm such rumors is limited, most people agree that biases are present. Thus, a youngster may not attempt to pursue the occupational goal that he really prefers and is capable of achieving because he feels that his cultural, racial, or religious background may prevent his admission to that occupation.

Davis (1949) summarized and interpreted the data from a study made for the Committee on Discrimination in College Admissions of the American Council on Education. These data were gathered by the Elmo Roper organization on a nation-wide sampling of 10,063 white high-school seniors of the class of 1947. Intensive interviewing was also done with a sample of more than 5000 white high-school seniors from cities of more than 500,000 population. The data are discussed in connection with demand for college education, potential demand, and factors in successful admission to college. Thirty-five per cent of the class of 1947 wanted to go to college that fall, and an additional 20 per cent hoped to go but were hindered by financial shortages. The two major barriers appeared to be economic difficulties and social or family backgrounds that worked against the development of a conviction that college was worth while. Analysis of the data on the acceptance of submitted applications indicated discrimination against Jewish students living in the Northeast and in large cities.

Cultural background currently creates more difficulties in the choice of jobs for Negroes than for any other group. Differences in the interests of Negro and white lawyers, physicians, and life-insurance agents have been found with the Strong Vocational Interest Blank for Men. Strong ("Interests of Negroes and Whites," 1952) felt that if Negroes in these three vocational groups are not equal to the whites in ability, quality of performance, and success, then the test scores will be lower. Negroes may also have different interests from those of whites, or react to the interest test items in terms of ambition rather than of their genuine interests. If Negroes are really different from whites in their interests, which we are not ready to accept as a fact, then their interests must be measured from a Negro, not a white, point of reference.

A study done in Washington, D. C., by Mundy (1949) points up the limited occupations readily available to the young Negro. Mundy examined almost 3000 work permits issued to Negro boys over a two-year period and an additional number issued to white boys, all between fifteen and seventeen years old. He found that 90 per cent of the Negro boys were employed as messengers, helpers, porters, busboys, dish-washers, and stock boys. White boys also held these positions, but the ratio was considerably lower than for Negroes. The white boys had a monopoly on such desirable jobs as clerk, usher, stuffer, salesman, and other, comparable positions. Mundy concluded that the schools are not doing an effective job of vocational placement for Negro boys.

Bryant (1949) analyzed the results of a questionnaire sent to rural and urban high schools in Texas, as well as to 6000 Negro workers in fifteen selected occupational areas. The results revealed that secondary schools for Negroes trained largely for the professions and that pupils in these schools do not take advantage of the few vocational courses offered. The most common occupations for Negroes in Texas are chauffeur, domestic worker, and service worker; 42.9 per cent of all Negro workers are in such jobs. Directly or indirectly, the labor unions are believed to have been instrumental in relegating Negro workers to low-paying, unskilled occupational areas. Nevertheless, opportunities are available to Negroes in building, industry, printing, agricultural, and commercial trades. Bryant felt that Negro high schools in Texas should place greater emphasis on vocational education through in-school and on-the-job training.

The jobs that are easily available to whites are not necessarily available to Negroes. That this situation does exist, no matter how unjust it may be, must be recognized particularly by vocational counselors who work with Negro clients. This is not to suggest that, because discrimination exists, counselors should discourage Negro students from choosing occupations in which they are capable of functioning. Rather, the counselor should help make the Negro client fully aware of the difficulties while encouraging him to choose an occupation in which he can make full use of all his abilities, interests, and aptitudes. One may hopefully assume that if more and more Negroes, despite discrimination, will accept the challenges and train for the occupations in which they are capable of succeeding, their performance will prove their worth to employers and/or colleagues.

Perhaps the ultimate integration of Negroes into schools that are today predominantly white will help alleviate these current problems. As Negro pupils demonstrate that, given the opportunity, they can compete successfully with white students academically, it should become increasingly obvious that they are capable of competing vocationally. Such integration will also require high-school vocational counselors to work more closely with Negro students on proper job selection. While it is probable that Negroes will continue to encounter discrimination in admission to some colleges and to certain occupations, as Jews, Catholics, and individuals from foreign backgrounds still do, successful performance in these fields should ultimately reduce such discrimination to a minimum.

THE PROCESS OF VOCATIONAL DEVELOPMENT

Before we discuss vocational testing and counseling, some mention should be made of the attempts of investigators to develop a theory of vocational development and behavior. Super *et al.* (1957) have attempted to construct such a theory along developmental lines and to identify factors which might influence vocational development. Table 21 presents an outline of the stages in vocational life in which the behavior depicted at each stage is based on the potential developed in the preceding stages. The development is a process that "continues through time and is manifested in a sequence of vocational behaviors, occurring throughout the life span of an individual."

TABLE 21. Vocational life stages

This table presents, in outline form, a synthesis of the ideas of Buehler (1935), Miller and Form (1951), and Ginzberg and associates (1951). It gives a brief description of the nature of the vocational behavior which seems characteristic of each life stage and it indicates the approximate age limits of the stages. As additional data on each life stage and substage are gathered, Table 21 may be filled in more fully with the details of vocational behavior that may be expected at each life stage, showing the sequences through which vocational development passes.

From Super et al. (1957), by permission of the authors and Bureau of Publications, Teachers College, Columbia University

1. *Growth stage (birth–14)*

   Self-concept develops through identification with key figures in family and in school; needs and fantasy are dominant early in this stage; interest and capacity become more important in this stage with increasing social participation and reality testing. Substages of the growth stage are:

FANTASY (4–10)	Needs are dominant; role playing in fantasy is important.
INTEREST (11–12)	Likes are the major determinant of aspirations and activities.
CAPACITY (13–14)	Abilities are given more weight, and job requirements (including training) are considered.

2. *Exploration stage (age 15–24)*

Self-examination, role tryouts, and occupational exploration take place in school, leisure activities, and part-time work. Substages of the exploration stage are:

TENTATIVE (15–17)	Needs, interests, capacities, values, and opportunities are all considered. Tentative choices are made and tried out in fantasy, discussion, courses, work, etc.
TRANSITION (18–21)	Reality considerations are given more weight as youth enters labor market or professional training and attempts to implement a self-concept.
TRIAL (22–24)	A seemingly appropriate field having been located, a beginning job in it is found and is tried out as a life work.

3. *Establishment stage (age 25–44)*

Having found an appropriate field, effort is put forth to make a permanent place in it. There may be some trial early in this stage, with consequent shifting, but establishment may begin without trial, especially in the professions. Substages of the establishment stage are:

TRIAL (25–30)	The field of work presumed to be suitable may prove unsatisfactory, resulting in one or two changes before the life work is found or before it becomes clear that the life work will be a succession of unrelated jobs.
STABILIZATION (31–44)	As the career pattern becomes clear, effort is put forth to stabilize, to make a secure place in the world of work. For most persons these are the creative years.

4. *Maintenance stage (age 45–64)*

Having made a place in the world of work, the concern is now to hold it. Little new ground is broken, but there is continuation along established lines.

5. *Decline stage (age 65 on)*

As physical and mental powers decline, work activity changes and in due course ceases. New roles must be developed; first that of selective participant and then that of observer rather than participant. Substages of this stage are:

DECELERATION (65–70)	Sometimes at the time of official retirement, sometimes late in the maintenance stage, the pace of work slackens, duties are shifted, or the nature of the work is changed to suit declining capacities. Many men find part-time jobs to replace their full-time occupations.
RETIREMENT (71 and on)	As with all the specified age limits, there are great variations from person to person. But complete cessation of occupation comes for all in due course, to some easily and pleasantly, to others with difficulty and disappointment, and to some only with death.

TABLE 22. Outline of vocational-development tasks in chronological order

The idea for this table was adapted from Stratemeyer, Forkner, and McKim (1947).

From Super et al. (1957), by permission of the authors and Bureau of Publications, Teachers College, Columbia University

Preschool Child
1. Increasing ability for self-help
2. Identification with like-sexed parent
3. Increasing ability for self-direction

Elementary-school child
1. Ability to undertake cooperative enterprises
2. Choice of activities suited to one's abilities
3. Assumption of responsibility for one's acts
4. Performance of chores around the house

High-school adolescent
1. Further development of abilities and talents
2. Choice of high school or work
3. Choice of high-school curriculum
4. Development of independence

Young adult
1. Choice of college or work
2. Choice of college curriculum
3. Choice of suitable job
4. Development of skills on the job

Mature adult
1. Stabilization in an occupation
2. Providing for future security
3. Finding appropriate avenues of advancement

Older person
1. Gradual retirement
2. Finding suitable activities for skills to occupy time
3. Maintaining self-sufficiency insofar as possible

Using Havighurst's frame of reference (1953), Super and his associates have outlined a series of vocational developmental tasks (Table 22). This list generally indicates that until adolescence most of these tasks are related only indirectly to later work. During adolescence the tasks become more directly related to vocations, particularly after youngsters enter high school. Throughout the adult period, these tasks are directly related to vocations. The authors view this process of development as a dynamic one in which new behavior is based on old. Development results from the "occurrence of additions to and modifications of the existing behavior pattern."

Super and his associates feel that, in order to understand this progressive development of vocational behavior, some of the determinants of such behavior must be examined. Among these determinants are "concepts of roles and self," "personal factors," and "situational factors." The first of these, concepts of roles and self, relates to the development of the individual's self-concept particularly as it concerns occupational role-taking, i.e., a vocation is viewed favorably or unfavorably as it is considered appropriate or inappropriate to the self. Personal factors that influence individual vocational behavior include intelligence, special aptitudes, interests, values, attitude, and personality. Situational factors are those external to the individual that influence his choice, such as "religious background, atmosphere of the home, and parental attitudes toward schooling."

This attempt to structure a theoretical framework for the development of vocational behavior is not, of course, the only one, or necessarily even the best one. Even if one were to accept this theory as a general framework, much expansion and/or revision would be needed as research studies explore areas about which only limited information is presently available. Much more research is needed, particularly in the areas of the role factors and the situational factors as they relate to this theoretical structure.

VOCATIONAL TESTING

Many of the tests that are administered to help determine the individual's suitability for a given occupation have already been discussed in other chapters in this book. Intelligence tests, achievement tests, personality tests, and interest tests have been described and their advantages and disadvantages discussed. The present discussion attempts to show how these test results are related to one another in helping to determine the occupational field for which an individual is best suited. This use of tests is based on the assumption that an individual will probably function most effectively in an occupation that makes full use of his intelligence, personality characteristics, etc., as they effectively relate to one another. Suppose, for example, that an individual wants to become an accountant. Intelligence tests reveal that his intellect is more than adequate. Aptitude and achievement tests indicate that he has high ability in mathematics. The interest test shows interest in working with details. The temperament test indicates that he likes to work alone and is emotionally stable. All these factors interrelated would seem strongly to confirm his occupational choice. If, however, an individual with the same interest and temperament patterns has an IQ of 80 and low mathematical aptitude, a different picture is presented. Despite his desire to become an accountant, it is very un-likely that such an individual could succeed even in the academic work required for admission to that field.

Interest Tests

Even though a battery of tests is ordinarily used to determine the individual's suitability for an occupation, counselors may not consider the results of all tests equally important. Generally it appears that vocational counselors make more use of the interest test results than of any of the others. This may be justified if the results of the interest test are interpreted to the client after he has been appraised in terms of his abilities and aptitudes. The client can then be shown whether or not his interests are realistic in terms of his ability to perform in the areas of his greatest interest. In a sense, the interest-test results can be used as a final means of confirming whether or not the individual is suited to the vocation he has chosen. If the interests related to his chosen field rate low on the test, this does not necessarily mean that he should be dissuaded from entering that field. Rather, it may indicate that he is not really aware of the requirements or activities involved in the field, or that he has chosen it for reasons other than actual interest, perhaps as leading to something in which he is interested. Then, too, while his interest in an area may be low, his ability or aptitude in that area may be high, indicating that he can succeed in the area even though he is not highly enthusiastic about it. An individual may, for example, wish to become a physician. His high-school interest scores may show high scientific and social-service interests but very low interest in mathematics. Since the high scientific and social-service interests do relate to medicine, they seem to confirm his choice. However, mathematics is required in the training leading to admission to medical school, and a counselor noting the low interest score in this area might feel that the apparent lack of interest in math might keep the individual from achieving his ultimate goal. This is possible, but the interest test results alone do not give the answer. If the youngster has demonstrated high mathematical aptitude and achievement, he will probably pass the required courses even if he does not like them. If, however, he has low mathematical aptitude and has achieved poorly in previous courses, he will probably not do well enough in the required courses to be admitted to medical school. It is the function of the counselor to present these results in a manner that will enable the student to understand how these factors interrelate.

Since interest tests are considered important by counselors, some discussion of them beyond that presented in Chapter 10 seems appropriate. Jackson (1947), for example, attempted to determine how vocational interests as measured by the Kuder Vocational Preference Record are related to certain aspects of available personnel data. His findings seemed to indicate that vocational interest was unrelated to intelligence and was also unrelated to success in an appropriate vocational course. Further, the interest scores seemed to be unrelated to scholastic average. The vocational interests were significantly related to courses selected in the ninth grade, and the interests expressed by the selection of courses in the ninth grade persisted through college.

If interest-test results are to be meaningful in vocational counseling, it must be assumed that these tests are valid and cannot be contaminated by "faking." Generally, "faking" is not considered likely to occur when the client taking the test really wants to assess his own interest. Cross (1950) has demonstrated that "faking" on the Kuder Vocational Preference Record is possible "when an applicant for a job has any idea of what job he is being considered for." If this situation exists, his "scores should be interpreted in the light of knowledge that faking is possible if he desires to fake."

"Faking" is probably not a serious problem in the use of interest tests with high-school students. At this level a more common problem is poor preparation of the students for taking the test. Too often students are given an interest test when they have little or no idea why the test is given. If the results are to be meaningful, the students should be made completely aware of what the test is, why it is being given, and what they can expect to learn from the results. With this kind of preparation, most students will take the test carefully, with few, if any, attempts at "faking." Actually, students should be well prepared for all the tests they take, particularly those that will be used in vocational counseling. The results are useful and meaningful only when the person tested has put forth his maximum effort.

Intelligence and Aptitude Tests

The importance and usefulness of intelligence tests have also been discussed earlier in this book (Chapter 3), and it seems readily apparent that knowledge of an individual's potential is important in the selection of an appropriate vocation. However, knowledge of the individual's general intelligence score may not be sufficient for determining his suitability for a given vocation, since this score does not indicate his specific abilities. Aptitude tests are generally used to determine the specific areas in which the individual has capabilities. If, for example, a youngster has an IQ of 150, he would seem capable of entering the field of physics. If, however, his aptitude test scores in physics and mathematics were extremely low, it would be unlikely that he would be well suited for that field. If such aptitude tests were not available to the counselor, he might well recommend physics as an appropriate field, on the assumption that a youngster with an IQ of 150 would be capable of success in the academic courses required.

Bennett *et al.* (1952) have attempted to determine whether aptitude testing does "prove out" in counseling practice. They analyzed questionnaires returned by 1700 persons who had been given the Differential Aptitude Test while they were in high school. The results were sorted according to the post-high-school activities of these individuals, and the average D.A.T. score was determined for each of the career groups. Although several varieties of talent appear within each career group, the conclusion was that individuals do tend to enter occupations for which their abilities fit them. It is important, therefore, that students be made aware of their true abilities and the ways in which these abilities relate to various occupational fields.

VOCATIONAL GUIDANCE

It is not our purpose to explore in detail the field of vocational guidance. If the reader wishes further information, many excellent books are available (Johnson *et al.,* 1961; Mortensen and Schmuller, 1959; Peters and Farwell, 1959). A brief discussion of the field is included here because more and more youngsters are being exposed to some degree of formal vocational counseling during their high-school careers. As Humphreys (1950) has pointed out, there are few decisions in a young person's life as important as his choice of a future occupation. Helping youngsters make wise choices can be greatly facilitated by the assistance of sympathetic adults, whether they be parents, teachers, or professional guidance counselors. Any assistance these adults can offer a youngster in helping him better understand himself, his abilities, his interests, his personality, the job world, the educational opportunities, etc., will help the youngster to make a wise choice. Basically, then, vocational guidance as we view it here involves anything that can be done to help make a youngster aware of how his various characteristics relate to success in occupational fields.

Vocational Orientation

Before successful vocational counseling can be given, youngsters must be informed about the many occupations available to them. Very often a youngster's choice is based to some degree on his knowledge of a specific occupation, but he may be completely unaware of a number of closely related occupations. He may have no information at all about many occupations for which he is suited as well as or better than he is for the one he has chosen. In many cases even his knowledge of a given occupation is erroneous or biased, as a result of his having been exposed to only a few people in the field.

TIMING OF ORIENTATION. This author strongly feels that there is a great need for vocational orientation in our schools before the student reaches the high-school level, at which he may be required to make an occupational choice (Bush and Powell, 1955). Even if the youngster is not required to choose a specific occupation at this point, he should at least know enough about his vocational goal to be able to choose the high-school program that will be most appropriate. The decision to enroll in a college preparatory program, a commercial program, or an industrial arts program must usually be made by the time the student enters the ninth grade. To change a program after that time is often difficult. Once a student has committed himself to a high-school program, a change may necessitate his making up many prerequisites and could add as much as a year to his high-school career.

The primary function of personnel in a vocational orientation program would be to transmit occupational information that would help youngsters gain a clearer picture of the variety of occupations available. Information on occupations should include educational and training requirements, availability of jobs, financial remuneration, advancement afforded by specific jobs, and the relation of the occupation to other occupations. All this should have been provided by the time students complete junior high school. Early transmission of such information is of particular value to those students who plan to leave school early. If they were truly aware of the requirements of various occupations, many of them might recognize the value of completing school in order to be better qualified for the occupations they choose.

AVAILABLE MATERIALS. The present-day failure of our schools to transmit such information successfully cannot be blamed on lack of adequate materials. Materials offering information about general occupational fields and about specific occupations within these fields are available for the asking. Many of these are free or involve only minimal costs that any school system could easily absorb. Information available ranges from professional occupational files, such as those developed by Science Research Associates, Chronical Guidance Publications, and others, to simple job descriptions presented in comic-book form. Most large industrial organizations have material describing the various kinds of jobs involved in their plants and offices, and most of this material is available to schools in large quantities. Federal agencies, such as the Department of Labor, Department of Commerce, etc., also have materials describing in detail tremendous varieties of vocations. Some business organizations, such as life insurance companies and drug firms, have sponsored series of popular-magazine advertisements that are designed to help parents and youngsters become more familiar with the occupational opportunities in medicine, nursing, teaching, and other fields.

ACCESS TO VOCATIONAL MATERIALS. Although all these materials are readily available, very few of them can be found in most elementary and junior high schools. Many high schools have the more professional occupational files but seldom possess the other materials mentioned. Even when a school has these various materials, they are often not made directly available to students. Often they are placed in the school library, where the librarian simply considers them an additional burden.

Even if students had ready access to these materials, either teachers or counselors would be needed to discuss them with the youngsters. Occupational materials should at least be made available to teachers so that they could discuss occupations intelligently with their students. This author feels strongly that vocational information can become an integral part of almost every course taught in our schools. If, in fact, youngsters understood how a particular course related to or was required by a given occupation, they might see more value in the course and be motivated to achieve at a higher level. For example, a youngster planning a career in physics may see little value in a course in English grammar and composition. If either the English teacher or the physics teacher were to make clear to him that writing precise research reports is a major part of the work involved in his chosen field, he might well be motivated to work harder in the English course. Teachers and counselors could not only help youngsters understand how various courses relate to each other in aiding them to reach their occupational goals, but could also help them determine the correct required course sequences and the appropriate electives.

TEACHER OR COUNSELOR? Bacquet et al. (1954) indicated that occupational information is transmitted more effectively by counselors than by teachers. In their study in France, occupational information was presented in four Paris upper primary classes (ages thirteen to fourteen) by the regular teachers through booklets and discussion. This was supplemented in four other classes by films and lectures by counselors. Questionnaires concerning occupations were then administered to both groups. An analysis of the results indicated that the group lectured by the counselors made more clear-cut choices, had a better understanding of the occupations, and were less influenced by prestige factors than the group exposed only to the teachers.

Baxter (1951) also emphasized that occupational information is necessary for eighth-graders, since they commonly experience difficulty in choosing proper curricula in high school. He felt that a good program should involve occupational information, tests of interests and abilities, individual conferences, field trips, and conferences involving teachers and parents. He felt that such a program would be effective in guiding the selection of goals, in increasing educational effectiveness, and in educating parents so that they might help their youngsters to select occupations.

"CAREER DAYS." Many high schools have "career days" on which people representing various occupations are invited to discuss their occupations with students. While the idea may be a sound one, in actual practice "career days" leave much to be desired. Too often the fields represented are largely professional, and little emphasis is placed on the unskilled, semiskilled, and skilled trades. Youngsters often have such tight schedules that they do not have an opportunity to attend all the discussions. Often they will choose to hear about a field in which they think they are interested but fail to attend the discussion relating to the occupation they will actually enter. The author has heard many of those presenting information discuss only the positive aspects of an occupation without mentioning any barriers or difficulties a youngster might encounter. Nonetheless, "career days" can be a most valuable means of disseminating occupational information and, if properly structured, could be most useful at the junior-high-school level. It is particularly important that both the positive and negative sides of the picture be presented. Thus, if a youngster is impressed with the status or financial position of the person representing an occupation, he will be made aware of the steps involved in reaching this level and the obstacles that may prevent him from achieving this goal.

STUDENT ATTITUDES. In one of their recent reports based on the Purdue Opinion Panel, Franklin et al. (1960) discussed "Youths' Attitudes Toward Industrial Relations." This study pointed up the lack of realism among these youngsters concerning vocational choice, with 58 per cent of the respondents aspiring to be professionals, whereas 52 per cent of those expecting to achieve such occupations will be disappointed. Although these adolescents tend to respect both union and management leaders, they have very little knowledge of industrial relations. They tend to favor government intervention in labor disputes and are generally pessimistic about the future of collective bargaining. This study, like a number of those previously discussed, offers further evidence of young people's lack of information about the world of work.

Counselors and Counseling

Most modern-day high schools do include vocational and educational counseling among their responsibilities. In most schools, tests that are useful in counseling are administered to the student body almost as a matter of course. In fact, the National Defense Education Act offers a subsidy to assist schools in purchasing these tests as a means of encouraging the development of counseling programs. A testing program of this nature is, however, effective only to the degree to which the counselors interpreting the test results to the students are effective. Unfortunately, there are large numbers of counselors in our high schools today whose skills and training are at best minimal. The requirements set by many state departments of education for certification of guidance counselors are of a relatively low level, and many schools designate as guidance counselors individuals who do not meet even these requirements. Such an individual, although he may be a "warm person who relates well to youngsters," is ill equipped to interpret standardized test results.

USE OF COUNSELORS. Even if a high school is fortunate enough to have well-trained, effective guidance counselors, it is unlikely to have enough of them to be of real service to all the students. Too often the counselor spends most of his time with the "problem cases" who are referred to him and has little time left for the nonproblem students who are in the majority. While one cannot deny that such "problem" youngsters need help, it is not certain that the counselor is the person best suited to provide it. Perhaps these time-consuming cases might best be referred to other special personnel, such as school psychologists or psychiatrists. Then the counselor would be better able to devote his efforts to helping the majority with their relatively "easy" educational-vocational problems.

It is, of course, always easy to be critical of public-school counselors, but it should be pointed out that great strides are being made in this area. Colleges are intensifying their counselor-training programs and in many cases are requiring internships. State departments of education are raising their standards and are requiring counselor candidates to obtain advanced degrees. School systems are also demanding greater competence among the guidance personnel and are offering better salaries to those who possess such competence. The National Defense Education Act also makes funds available to help schools pay for qualified people and assists colleges to offer various institutes and training programs to help increase the number of counselors.

While all these gains are important, their true effect is not yet felt in the schools. Some of the wealthier school districts can attract highly trained professionals, but what of schools in average or poor socio-economic areas? In most of these, guidance services are still minimal or even nonexistent. Thus, even today, a large percentage of high-school students has little or no exposure to vocational counseling or guidance. Others have probably had no more than one session with a counselor, and that consisting of a rather casual discussion of stand-ardized test results during the youngster's senior year.

College personnel are particularly aware of the lack of counseling so apparent in their college students and are rather critical of many high-school guidance programs. Peebles (1946) reported on the nature of the guidance that college students should have to help them make a satisfactory adjustment to college. An analysis of four ques-tionnaires administered to almost 500 freshmen in six selected Mid-western colleges showed considerable variation in precollege guidance facilities and information. Students considered parents as most helpful and seldom mentioned high-school guidance counselors. If there were written sources of information, these students knew little about them. Peebles urged that an active program be designed and brought to the student; "it is not sufficient to set up precollege guidance services and then sit back and wait for students to take advantage of them."

COUNSELING IN THE COLLEGES. This latter comment might well be ex-panded to include guidance services available to college students. Many colleges and universities do have guidance services available and engage in large guidance testing programs. Unfortunately, many stu-dents are completely unaware of the existence of these services and therefore fail to take advantage of them. Quite often the only students who do benefit from these services are those who are sent to a counselor because they are having some difficulties. The author worked in such a college guidance center for some years, but most of his clients were people from the local community who paid a fee for this service. Few college students, for whom the service was free, ever took advantage of the counseling center. Where this kind of situation exists, the col-leges are in no position to criticize the high schools' failures.

Guidance Research

The need for research in guidance in the schools is a most important one. While there is often a good deal of research going on in relation to the total field of guidance, there is little within school systems. All too many high-school guidance programs seem to have been structured on a hit-or-miss basis, with little or no investigation of what students really need. It is strongly recommended that school counseling personnel survey the youngsters in the school in order to determine the kind of program that will most effectively meet their needs.

Gemelli (1947), writing about the development of vocational-guidance programs in Italy, stresses the need for continued study of the youngsters after they have completed their schooling. He further stresses that guidance should not only be based on the analysis of individual skills and abilities, but should also include diagnosis of personality. These analyses and diagnoses must all be considered in relation to the social conditions under which skills and personality traits may best be utilized. Such a program would also call for a strong emphasis on continuing active research, including extensive follow-up studies.

The present-day inadequacy of high-school counseling programs has been emphasized by a number of investigators. Leonard's study (1949) of graduates of vocational high schools, one year after graduation, showed that less than one-third of these graduates were employed in the trades for which they had been trained, and less than one-half were even employed in the field for which they had been trained. The need for more adequate vocational guidance and placement is stressed. Jahoda (1949) asked thirteen- and fourteen-year-old youngsters to imagine that they had started work the day before and to write a theme describing their experience. On the basis of an analysis of these themes, he concluded that the present methods of preparing children for occupational life are inadequate, and that there is a need for continuous vocational guidance. Ward (1949) has also stressed the widespread inadequacy of community services for fitting the right man to the right job and has suggested that out-of-school guidance facilities be organized to serve the needs of the community as a whole.

Gellman (1952) felt that the needs for a vocational adjustment service are not suitably met by the run-of-the-mill vocational guidance programs. He felt that use of a work trial situation would be helpful in providing an observational basis for determining the behavior of the individual under varying working conditions. Moss (1951) has described a trainee acceptance center that is designed to allow each child to work in conditions that foster rather than make difficult the development of a healthy personality. Such a program involves cooperation among industries, schools, and employment services to make the transition from school to job easier and will provide adequate vocational counseling.

Job Placement

Usually no attempt is made by the counselor who helps a youngster determine his vocational choice actually to aid him in finding a job.

Although some high schools, especially vocational training schools, do work with various industries in placing their students, they are in the minority. There appears to be a general feeling among high-school guidance counselors that their work is over when they have helped the youngster decide on the most suitable occupation. The problem of getting him placed in that occupation is one that must be solved by the youngster himself. Counselors are often unwilling even to furnish the test results used in counseling the youngster to an employer who might find such results useful. The same problem also exists in many community vocational counseling services.

Employment services also fail to make use of counseling facilities in their attempts to place youngsters. Often a youngster is placed in a job that he claims to prefer but for which he will be unsuited. Some of the larger private employment services have testing and counseling programs designed to aid them in placing the right person in the right job, and apparently these have been quite successful. The United States Employment Service also offers some testing and counseling for clients who are uncertain of their vocational goals. There is, therefore, a good deal of evidence that vocational counseling services and placement services should be closely interrelated. It is rather difficult to understand why public-school guidance programs do not involve job placement services, but it seems likely that they will ultimately be forced to do so in order to insure the effectiveness of the guidance program. High-school vocational-guidance counselors do often aid college-bound students in selecting the most appropriate college and in helping them gain admission to it. It should not be difficult for them to offer comparable employment selection services to those who are not college-bound, and it would be quite easy to enlist the cooperation of various businesses and industries. Business and industry would probably welcome such interaction, since it would assist them in getting the right worker for the right job, thus eliminating much of the present hit-or-miss selection.

Parents and Vocational Counseling

Many of the earlier studies indicated that parents were a major influence in determining the vocation selected by their youngster. The author feels that this is less true today than it was a few decades ago. Many parents today apparently try not to influence their children. They constantly verbalize the idea that a young person "should choose any occupation he likes as long as it makes him happy." This thought is also obvious to the youngsters. In a questionnaire that more than 2000 adolescents filled out before being tested and counseled, the question "What do your parents want you to be?" was answered by about 85 per cent with "Anything I want to be." The author believes that parents do not really feel this way, but that they are afraid of being accused of over-directing their youngsters. Actually, the failure of parents to discuss occupations with their youngsters for fear of unduly influencing them may actually penalize the youngsters.

James C. was referred to a vocational counseling center by his father, who was a physician. James, who was seventeen, had no idea what vocation he might enter. Although test results indicated that he had a high I.Q., he was achieving poorly in school and seemed completely unmotivated. In the discussion that followed the interpretation of the test results, James indicated that he had given some thought to medicine as a career but really knew very little about the field. The counselor thought this odd, since James' father was an M.D., but the youngster said his father wouldn't discuss the field with him and even discouraged this choice. At a later appointment with the father, the counselor mentioned this point. The father agreed that he did not discuss his field with the boy for fear of influencing him. He admitted that he would be pleased if James did enter the medical profession but felt it "must be his own decision." The counselor was later able to get father and son together in a discussion in which the father expressed his preference to James. Immediate rapport was established between them since they shared this same interest. James did finally enter medical school, and his father now tells all his patients not to hesitate in helping their children select vocations.

While many private vocational counseling services do include parents in their guidance procedure, most high-school guidance services do not. In some schools, parents may be furnished with some of the guidance information but are not personally included in the discussions. Ryden (1951) described a high-school counseling program in which parent-student-counselor conferences were held for members of a sophomore class. He concluded that the students counseled in this way made more progress in realistic planning for an educational and vocational future than did students whose parents were not included. This procedure also tended to keep the school and the home from giving the student conflicting counsel.

The school system with which the author was associated did not directly include the parents in the counseling procedure but did attempt to establish communication with them. After a youngster had been counseled, a rather extensive report, including test results and a summary by the counselor, was sent to the parents. One night each week, guidance offices were opened to parents who wished to discuss these reports. The vocational-information files were also made available to the parents so that they could familiarize themselves with occupations that their youngsters might be contemplating. Parents became so enthusiastic about this operation that they literally overwhelmed the counseling staff. Regardless of the exact procedure, it does seem advisable to make every effort to include the parents in the counseling of their youngsters.

Special Problems in Counseling

In any school system there are youngsters who need special counseling well beyond what the majority of students may require. These special cases include those who are physically, mentally, and emotionally handicapped, for whom special testing may be needed before they can be adequately counseled. The degree as well as the kind of impairment must be carefully considered so that the youngster may be helped to reach an occupational goal within the limits of his capability. The counselor must know what occupations are open to the handicapped and have extensive knowledge of sheltered workshop facilities for those too handicapped to function in other occupational environments. These kinds of special problems have been recognized, and attempts have been made to orient counselors to handle them effectively. More vocational rehabilitation centers are available, at which counselors especially trained for this purpose aid in guidance.

There are, however, other special problems confronting guidance counselors, which are less obvious and for which few if any special provisions have been made. Discrimination in admission to college and/or various occupations, for example, is often ignored by counselors. Certainly a counselor should not attempt to keep an individual from planning to enter an occupation because he may encounter discrimination. Rather, the counselor should explain clearly to the youngster the problems he may encounter, so that if he still chooses to enter that field he will be fully aware of what he faces. Such awareness might, of course, cause the individual to change his goal, but this might be a sound decision if he felt he would be unable or unwilling to try to overcome the obstacles to his original choice.

NEGROES. The individual's social-cultural background may also present special problems that the counselor must be able to handle. Nowhere is this more apparent than in the case of the American Negro. Johnson (1947) has pointed out that the Negro population, which is still transitional, "lives on many planes of American culture." Negro youth should be given a socially realistic education; the primary responsibility for their guidance rests on the school. They should be accepted for what in some cases they are, "culturally retarded and marginal, in terms of the culture to which they are in the process of assimilating." Their education should give them understanding of their own social world and a knowledge of the broader world around them. If such an education can be offered, Johnson believes that in time a new race will evolve, even better adapted to modern civilization than other Americans, "who remain in a world and a day of change bound by the chains of custom, and whose greatest pride is in the deeds of their ancestors." It is indeed unfortunate that relatively few of the limited number of vocational counselors who deal with Negro students are presently capable of functioning in a way compatible with Johnson's thinking. Too often the white counselor working with the Negro cannot really understand the environment in which the Negro lives and the special problems that face him. While we do not suggest that Negro children should be assigned only to Negro counselors, some Negro counselors should be available in schools that contain mostly Negro students. A Negro counselor could probably offer valuable assistance to the white counselor on the special problems of the Negro client.

SCHOOL-LEAVERS. Each year large numbers of students drop out of our secondary schools for a variety of reasons. While the problems of the drop-out will be discussed in detail in Chapter 13, some mention of the occupational difficulties he faces should be made here. While there is evidence to suggest that those who complete school get better jobs (Cantoni, 1955), such knowledge is of no value to the individual who decides to leave school early or is compelled to do so. Roberts (1947) concluded that "there is a widespread inadequacy of vocational guidance for boys and girls who are products of the present American educational system."

Naville (1949) used the term "vocational illusion" for the notion that the child or adolescent fashions to himself of the trade he plans to enter before he has actually been able to have contact with it. He studied the role of this illusion in the vocational maladjustment of children and adolescents who left school early and entered industry. According to answers furnished to questionnaires, the majority of these young people had formerly had anticipatory illusions of a most varied kind concerning work. They had been induced to go into the shop of their parents or an older friend, but most of them were dissatisfied with the work and even resentful toward the foreman.

Jahoda (1952) also found that in the majority of cases the determination of a vocational choice is determined by the informal influence of parents, relatives, and friends. Institutional agencies usually come into the situation after job attitudes have hardened, and the youngster is willing to consider only a rather narrow range of jobs. Conferences held when the adolescent is leaving school seldom change the choice already made. Jahoda concluded that there should be earlier, fuller, and more realistic job information and an attempt to prevent choices from becoming fixed too early. Such earlier counseling would be particularly valuable to those who plan to leave school before finishing. The majority of those leaving school do so before they have had any counseling. If adequate counseling were offered in time, some drop-outs might be dissuaded by a realistic presentation of the difficulties that they will encounter in seeking jobs without having completed their education.

Such an approach would necessitate early identification of potential drop-outs and the development of counseling programs designed to encourage those who are able to remain in school to do so. Those who insist on leaving will need special counseling to help them find jobs for which they will be qualified within the limits of their abilities. Many of those who leave school early regret having done so; appropriate guidance at the right time might prevent others from acting unwisely.

Those who do or must leave school early should be encouraged to seek out-of-school guidance services. Johnson and Legg (1949) studied conditions of youth employment in Louisville, Kentucky. They interviewed more than 500 boys and girls, fourteen to nineteen years of age, all of whom were out of school and working or wanting to work. These authors concluded that "the combined efforts of school, industry, and employment agencies in the community will be required to give the best possible education to all its young people, supplemented with effective counseling and guidance services both in school and out."

THE ADOLESCENT'S CONCERN WITH SELECTING A VOCATION

Perhaps no one is more aware than the adolescent himself of the many difficulties facing him in his selection of an occupation, however inaccurate or unrealistic his perceptions concerning occupational fields may be. There does seem to be some evidence that indicates increasing clarification of self-concepts in at least some vocational areas (O'Hara and Tiedeman, 1959). Adolescents today are generally more knowledgeable concerning vocations than were those of a decade ago, but with the increasing complexity of occupations today, even this increased knowledge is often minimal.

The constant publicity to which youngsters are currently exposed concerning problems confronting them educationally is often misleading or discouraging to youngsters. For example, teen-agers are being constantly harangued about the great difficulties they will encounter in seeking admission to college. While college admission is and will continue to be increasingly selective, the picture is not as dark as it is presented to be. Despite the increasing number of enrollments, there are still many openings for students in colleges across the country. A youngster may not be able to gain admission to the college that is his first choice, but he can probably be admitted to any number of equally good though perhaps less well-known colleges. Overemphasis of these difficulties may actually keep some students from applying to the school of their first choice, and, as a result, some of these schools may still have openings when school starts in the fall.

Randy J. had planned to seek admission to a major Eastern university for preprofessional training. He was told by his counselor that his chances of being admitted to this college were minimal and was encouraged to go elsewhere. As a result, Randy did not even apply to his first choice but went instead to an excellent small Midwestern university. At the end of a successful freshman year, he wrote to the Eastern university to request permission to transfer there. He was admitted as a sophomore and was amazed when the director of admissions asked him why he hadn't come there as a freshman. Randy enjoyed his experience at the smaller school, but feels he would have preferred to spend the freshman year at his present school. He is not resentful of his high-school counselor, since he feels that the advice was offered honestly on the basis of the apparently erroneous information available to the counselor.

Results of Inadequate Information

Lack of adequate information concerning occupations is perhaps the most frequent complaint of youngsters. They feel that they have little opportunity to get an accurate picture of both the positive and negative aspects of the field in which they are interested. Teen-agers indicate that teachers and counselors offer little assistance and seem to know no more about various occupations than the youngsters do. Actually, until an individual has entered an occupation, he seldom realizes how little he knew about it. The greatest number of complaints usually comes from people out in the field who have learned from experience that the job is not what they thought it would be.

Because they lacked adequate information about the occupation they chose, young adults may find themselves in occupations that they do not like, or for which they are really not suited. When they become aware of their error in choice, it is often too late to change fields, and many will spend their lives working in occupations in which they are not happy. These young adults tend to be most critical of the schools for failing to provide them with adequate information and counseling.

Robert C. came to a vocational counseling center to seek help. He was twenty-eight years old and had been an engineer for five years. Although he was doing well financially, he was unhappy with his work and thought he wanted to make a change. Engineering, and particularly the detailed desk work he had to do, left him dissatisfied. He also felt he had little opportunity to work with people, since most of his work was rather solitary. After a battery of tests was administered and interpreted to him, he indicated that he might like to teach science in high school. This appeared to be a sound choice, and after much soul-searching, Robert decided to make the change. He had to make some financial readjustments, but since he was unmarried this was not difficult. A few years later, Robert visited the counselor to tell him how much he liked his new field and how he wished he had entered it originally rather than spending five years in a field he disliked.

If Robert had had a wife, and perhaps children, he might have found it extremely difficult to give up his relatively good income in engineering to accept an appreciably lower salary in education. He was fortunate also in being able to change his job without having to be completely re-educated. Since he had received substantial academic background in science as part of his engineering training, to go into teaching he needed only the few education courses required for certification. Usually, however, a change in occupation is more difficult to make; extensive retraining or further education is likely to be necessary.

The author has worked with large numbers of students who decided to change fields after their education was well along. He has seen third-year medical students leave medical school to train for other occupations and helped counsel graduate students to change to fields other than the one for which they were studying. In some cases these students were forced to add two or three years of college to their programs in order to get the background required for admission to the new field. When occupational goals must be changed at the eleventh hour, part of the time spent in training for the field originally chosen may be wasted, and the individual may be delayed from entering his field at the age at which he might be most productive physically.

Attitudes Toward High-School Counseling

Most young people feel that they received very little assistance from vocational counselors in making their vocational choices. Very few of them, in fact, felt that the counselors influenced their decisions in any way, and even fewer changed their choices as a result of counseling. Most youngsters feel that they had only minimal contact with their counselors, which often involved nothing more than setting up the high-school program and little if any discussion of vocations. Many claim never to have seen the results of the various tests administered to them for purposes of vocational-educational counseling. Those who have seen the results often indicate that these were not adequately interpreted. It is not unusual for students to be completely unaware of whether or not vocational counseling is available in their schools.

Of those who have received counseling, many feel that it was offered too late. They may find that they have not taken some of the courses required for admission to their field because they were not given the necessary information at the time when it would have been most useful. Since many high-school programs are rather rigidly structured, the youngster may have to continue in postgraduate work to take the courses he needs. Had this knowledge been available to him at the time he planned his high-school program, these courses could have been included in it.

The quality of the counseling is often quite obvious to the youngsters. They recognize the counselor's lack of information about occupations and his inability to answer specific questions. While they may realize that the counselor cannot possibly be informed on every aspect of every available occupation, they do feel that he should know where they can find such information. There is also a feeling that counselors tend to overemphasize occupations in which they themselves are interested and fail even to discuss those that they consider low level or uninteresting.

Joanne D. was discussing her high-school counselor with this complaint: "She doesn't talk about occupations at all; she's really a college placement counselor. She tells us which colleges have nice social environments, and seldom discusses their academic standards." Joanne felt that this kind of information might be of value to some students, but it was not the kind of counseling most of them sought. Although she was going to college, she felt that the counselor offered no services that would be of any use to students who were not. While the counselor did discuss test results with the students, Joanne felt that these results were presented in isolation, with no discussion of their relationship to occupational choice.

Certainly one of the functions of a good vocational counselor is assisting students to select a college that offers a program leading to their vocational goal. However, this should be preceded by assistance in making the proper vocational choice.

Parents and Vocational Selection

Almost all teen-agers have some comment to make concerning their parents' effort or lack of effort to assist them in making an occupational choice. Most of their complaints indicate extremes, i.e., parents either do not discuss vocations with their youngsters at all, or they select occupations for the youngsters without giving them any choice in the matter. Not many teen-agers feel that their parents have helped them sufficiently or even that the parents have enough knowledge about vocations to help them. The case of James C., cited earlier in this chapter, well illustrates how a youngster may be penalized by the failure of his parents to discuss his occupational goals with him.

For the parents to make the choice for the youngster is perhaps worse than for them to offer no advice at all. The parental preference may be based on variables that should not necessarily be major factors. If the parents wish to have their children achieve a higher status level than they have achieved, they may try to direct the youngsters into occupations offering higher status. They may try to steer their youngsters into the field that they themselves wish they had been able to enter. These reasons are often unrealistic in terms of the youngster's capabilities, and he may be forced to try for an occupational goal that he cannot reach. His failure will greatly frustrate the parents and will probably result in many emotional problems for the youngster himself.

Teen-agers will resent such parental pressure and may even select an occupation different from the one the parents prefer simply as a means of showing independence. If the parental controls are too rigid and the youngster cannot make his own choice, he may even fail the courses required for admission to the field the parents prefer. This will probably keep him out of that field, but it may also penalize him in others. Even if the individual can and does achieve the vocational goal his parents have set for him, he may be very unhappy in his work, no matter what remuneration it affords. Obviously, neither extreme is helpful.

Most teen-agers welcome the opportunity to discuss their occupational preferences with their parents, in order to find out what their parents think of the choices and what choices might appeal to their parents. If the school vocational counselor can also be brought into these discussions, he can present a picture of the youngster's abilities and aptitudes based on test results and help both the parents and the youngster to relate these talents to suitable occupations.

Desire for Information

Most teen-agers realize that the lack of realistic information already discussed presents their greatest problem. Often the author has asked a youngster, "Have you even considered X occupation as one you might be interested in?" All too often the response has been, "I've heard of it and it sounds interesting, but I don't know very much about it or where to get the information." When the author has pointed out to teen-agers who profess to be interested in the field of psychology that a Ph.D. is necessary really to function in that field, the reaction has been one of complete surprise. Most of them are also relatively unaware of the many specialities to be found in a general field and the substantial differences among these specialties. Even college students who have taken a number of courses in a certain field are often unaware of the necessity for advanced study. Many have received the Bachelor's degree with a major in a field only to find that there is little or no employment available to them. The individual who is unwilling or unable to pursue an advanced degree may feel that he has wasted four years of his life.

Students often agree with the criticisms of "career days" presented earlier. They feel that too few occupations are represented and that a biased picture of fields discussed is presented. Teen-agers do approve of having "career days" but feel that they should be made more useful.

Teaching as a Vocational Choice

Frequently youngsters are influenced against an occupation they might have chosen by comments made by people in that occupation. The field of teaching is perhaps most affected by this kind of situation. When the author asked high-school students if they would consider teaching as a career, he often received such an answer as: "I did consider it, but most of my own teachers seem to think I'm foolish. They keep telling me about poor salaries and big classes, and seem to always be complaining." This is probably overstated, but it has some basis. Youngsters are also exposed to constant criticism of teachers by laymen, by magazine articles, and even by their parents. As a result, they do not view teaching as a highly desirable choice.

On rare occasions a counselor may be able to show a youngster the value of combining teaching with the occupation he has selected.

Sandra V. wanted to become an artist and seemed to have a good deal of talent. Her high-school counselor approved of her choice of becoming an artist, but suggested that she take enough education courses to qualify her to teach art. Sandra seemed shocked at the idea of teaching, and asked the counselor why he would suggest such a thing. He discussed the difficulties involved in achieving success in art, and suggested that teaching would allow her an opportunity to continue her art interest in her spare time while she earned an adequate income. Sandra followed this advice and became an art teacher. She continued to paint and eventually began to sell her work. Although her income as an artist is far greater than her teacher's salary, she found that she

THE PSYCHOLOGY OF ADOLESCENCE

wanted to keep on teaching. She felt she could help encourage other talented youngsters with whom her teaching brought her in contact. Sandra now recommends that her students also get a teaching certificate.

AN OVERVIEW

One could continue discussing the youngsters' criticisms of school guidance programs indefinitely and find that many of them are valid. Adolescents want as much realistic information as they can possibly get about themselves, about various occupations, and about the relationships between their abilities, aptitudes, interests, etc., and occupational requirements. All of them would like to find occupations in which they could use their talents in satisfying ways. They would welcome all the assistance they could get in making wise decisions but are very much aware that such assistance is seldom available.

Although great strides have been made in the field of vocational counseling during the last fifty years, there is still a good deal to be done. There is a tremendous need for expanded college programs to train guidance counselors, in order to increase the number and the effectiveness of such counselors. The schools particularly need to establish the functions of counselors on a better basis and to relate their services to the total school program. To help counselors function more effectively, better measuring instruments will have to be developed, and more specific information about various occupations must be made readily available. Finally, more extensive longitudinal studies must be initiated if we are to determine the long-range effectiveness of vocational-guidance programs.

REFERENCES

BACQUET, R., CHAUDAGNE, H., LARCEBEAU, J., and LEON, A. "Une expérience d'information dans des classes de fin d'études primaires" (An Experiment in Occupational Information in Upper Primary Classes). *Bulletin de l'Institut National d'Etude du Travail et d'Orientation Professiennelle* (Paris), 10, 3-27, 1954.

BARAHAL, G. D. "Personality Problems and Vocational Planning." *Personnel Guidance Journal*, 31, 224-226, 1953.

BATEMAN, RICHARD M. "The Effect of Work Experience on High School Students' Vocational Choice." *Occupations*, 27, 453-456, 1949.

BATEMAN, RICHARD M. "The Effect of Work Experience on High School Students as Revealed by the Bell Adjustment Inventory." *Journal of Educational Research*, 43, 261-269, 1949.

BATEMAN, RICHARD M. "The Effect of Work Experience on High School Students' Scholastic Achievement." *Occupations,* 28, 353-356, 1950.

BAXTER, LINDLY C. "Vocational Guidance for Elementary-School Pupils." *Elementary School Journal,* 51, 343-345, 1951.

BENNETT, GEORGE K., SEASHORE, HAROLD G., and WESMAN, ALEXANDER. "Aptitude Testing: Does It 'Prove Out' in Counseling Practice?" *Occupations,* 30, 584-593, 1952.

BRYANT, IRA B. "Vocational Education in Negro High Schools in Texas." *Journal of Negro Education,* 18, 9-15, 1949.

BUEHLER, C. "Der Menschliche Lebelslauf als psychologisches Problem." *Acta Psychologia* (The Hague), 1, 45-48, 1935.

BUSH, C. L., and POWELL, M. "Vocational Orientation in Junior High School." *NEA Journal,* 44, no. 8, 1955.

CANTONI, LOUIS J. "Stay-ins Get Better Jobs." *Personal Guidance Journal,* 33, 531-533, 1955.

CARP, FRANCES MERCHANT. "High School Boys Are Realistic About Occupations." *Occupations,* 28, 97-99, 1949.

CAWLEY, SISTER ANNE MARY. "A Study of the Vocational Interest Trends of Secondary School and College Women." *Genetic Psychology Monographs,* 35, 185-247, 1947.

CROSS, ORRIN H. "A Study on Faking on the Kuder Preference Record." *Educational and Psychological Measurement,* 10, 271-277, 1950.

DAVIS, HELEN E. *On Getting into College: A Study of Discrimination in College Admissions.* Washington, D. C.: American Council on Education, 1949.

DITTMER, RICHARD W., and PAYNE, STANLEY L. "Who Wants 'Good Wages?'" *Public Opinion Quarterly,* 12, 488-489, 1948.

DRESDEN, KATHERINE W. "Vocational Choices of Secondary Pupils." *Occupations,* 27, 104-106, 1948.

DUFTY, N. F. "Vocational Choices of 13-14 Year Old Males in Relation to Intelligence and Reasons for Job Choice." *Australian Journal of Education,* 4, 38-56, 1960.

EDMISTON, R. W., and STARR, C. H. "Youth's Attitudes toward Occupations." *Occupations,* 26, 213-320, 1948.

FRANKLIN, R. D., GRAZINO, S. G., and REMMERS, H. H. *Report of Poll 59 of the Purdue Opinion Panel: Youths' Attitudes toward Industrial Relations.* Lafayette, Ind.: Purdue University, Division of Educational Reference, 1960.

GELLMAN, WILLIAM. "Facilitating Vocational Adjustment." *Jewish Social Service Quarterly,* 29, 143-147, 1952.

GEMELLI, AGOSTINO. *L'orientamento professionale dei Giovani nelle scuole* (Vocational Guidance of Youth in School). Milan: Societa Editrice "Vita e Pensiero," 1947.

GINZBERG, E., et al. *Occupational Choice.* New York: Columbia University Press, 1951.

HAVIGHURST, R. J. *Human Development and Education.* New York: Longmans, Green & Co., Inc., 1953.

HUMPHREYS, J. ANTHONY. *Helping Youth Choose Careers.* Chicago: Science Research Associates, 1950.

HYMAN, BERNARD. "The Relationship of Social Status and Vocational Interests." *Journal of Counseling Psychology,* 3, 12-16, 1956.

JACKSON, JOSEPH. "A Note on the Crystallization of Vocational Interests." *Journal of Social Psychology,* 26, 125-130, 1947.

JAHODA, GUSTAV. "Adolescent Attitudes to Starting Work." *Occupational Psychology* (London), 23, 184-188, 1949.

JAHODA, GUSTAV. "Job Attitudes and Job Choice among Secondary Modern School Leavers, II." *Occupational Psychology* (London), 26, 206-224, 1952.

JOHNSON, CHARLES S. "The Guidance Problems of Negro Youth." In Harms, B. E., *Handbook of Child Guidance,* pp. 587-598. New York: Child Care Publications, 1947.

JOHNSON, ELIZABETH S., and LEGG, CAROLINE E. "Louisville Youth and Their Jobs." *Social Service Review,* 23, 39-50, 1949.

JOHNSON, W. F., STEFFLRE, B., and EDELFELT, R. A. *Pupil Personnel and Guidance Services.* New York: McGraw-Hill Book Co., Inc., 1961.

LEONARD, REGIS J. "Occupational Experiences of Trade School Graduates." *Occupations,* 28, 28-31, 1949.

MILLER, D. C., and FORM, W. H. *Industrial Sociology.* New York: Harper & Row, 1951.

MORTENSEN, D. G., and SCHMULLER, A. M. *Guidance in Today's Schools.* New York: John Wiley & Sons, Inc., 1959.

MOSER, WILBUR E. "The Influence of Certain Cultural Factors upon the Selection of Vocational Preferences by High School Students." *Journal of Educational Research,* 45, 523-526, 1952.

MOSS, R. MAURICE. "From School to Work." *Child,* 16, 25-27, 1951.

MUNDY, PAUL. "The Young Negro Worker in Washington, D. C." *Journal of Negro Education,* 18, 104-113, 1949.

NAVILLE, PIERRE. "La crise de 'l'illusion professionnelle' chez l'enfant et l'adolescent" (The Crisis of the 'Vocational Illusion' in the Child and the Adolescent). *Enfance (Paris),* 2, 41-53, 1949.

O'HARA, ROBERT P., and TIEDEMAN, DAVID V. "Vocational Self Concept in Adolescence." *Journal of Counseling Psychology,* 6, 292-301, 1959.

PEEBLES, CLARENCE M. "Counseling Precollege Students in the Secondary Schools." In Hamrin, S. A., and Endicott, F. S., *Improving Guidance and Personnel Services through Research: A Report of the Tenth Annual Conference on Guidance and Personnel Work held at Northwestern University, July 18, 19, 20, 1946,* pp. 71-78. Evanston, Ill.: School of Education, Northwestern University, 1946.

PETERS, H. I., and FARWELL, G. F. *Guidance: A Developmental Approach.* Chicago: Rand McNally, 1959.

PIERCE-JONES, JOHN. "Vocational Interest Correlates of Socio-economic Status in Adolescence." *Educational and Psychological Measurement,* 19, 65-71, 1959.

PIERCE-JONES, JOHN. "Socio-economic Status and Adolescents' Interests." *Psychological Reports,* 5, 683, 1959.

PORTER, J. RICHARD. "Predicting Vocational Plans of High School Senior Boys." *Personnel Guidance Journal,* 33, 215-218, 1954.

POWELL, M. "Age and Sex Differences in Degree of Conflict within Various Areas of Psychological Adjustment." *Psychological Monographs,* vol. 69, no. 2, 1955.

POWELL, M., and BLOOM, V. "Development of and Reasons for Vocational Choices of Adolescents through the High School Years." *Journal of Educational Research,* 56, 126-133, 1962.

ROBERTS, ANDREW. "School-Leavers Show Lack of Vocational Guidance." *Occupations,* 26, 171-174, 1947.

RYDEN, A. H. "Including Parents in Counseling." *Occupations,* 29, 587-590, 1951.

SAMSON, RUTH, and STEFFLRE, BULFORD. "Like Father . . . Like Son?" *Personnel Guidance Journal,* 31, 35-39, 1952.

SCHMIDT, JOHN L., and ROTHNEY, JOHN W. M. "Variability of Vocational Choices of High School Students." *Personnel Guidance Journal,* 34, 142-146, 1955.

SCHMIDT, LOUIS G. "Primary Mental Abilities and Occupational Choices." *Journal of Educational Research,* 47, 297-300, 1953.

SMALL, LEONARD. "Personality Determinants of Vocational Choice." *Psychological Monographs,* 67(1), no. 351, 1953.

STRONG, EDWARD K., JR. "Amount of Change in Occupational Choice of College Freshmen." *Educational and Psychological Measurement,* 12, 677-691, 1952.

STRONG, EDWARD K., JR. "Interests of Negroes and Whites." *Journal of Social Psychology,* 35, 139-150, 1952.

STUBBINS, JOSEPH. "Lack of Realism in Vocational Choice." *Occupations,* 26, 410-418, 1948.

SUPER, D., CRITES, J., HUMMEL, R., MOSER, H., OVERSTREET, P., and WARNATH, C. *Vocational Development: A Framework for Research.* New York: Bureau of Publications, Teachers College, Columbia University, 1957.

SWEENEY, FRANCIS J. "Intelligence, Vocational Interests and Reading Speed of Senior Boys in Catholic High Schools of Los Angeles." *California Journal of Educational Research,* 5, 159-165, 1954.

WARD, ROSWELL. *Out of School Vocational Guidance: The Organization, Operation, and Development of Community Vocational Guidance Service.* New York: Harper & Row, 1949.

WIEGMAN, ROBERT R., and JACOBSON, PAUL B. "How Well Did They Know?" *Journal of Higher Education,* 26, 267-270, 1955.

YOUMANS, E. GRANT. "Occupational Expectations of Twelfth Grade Michigan Boys." *Journal of Experimental Education,* 24, 259-271, 1956.

CHAPTER 12

The Adolescent and the School Curriculum

Aside from the home, the school is the agency that has most contact with the adolescent. Almost one-half the youngster's day is spent in the environment of the school, which is charged with helping him accumulate knowledge and develop skills that will enable him to become a competent adult citizen. Currently, a good deal of criticism is being leveled against the schools for alleged failure to accomplish these aims. These charges have been directed both at the educational programs and at the personnel whose function it is to implement them. This chapter deals primarily with academic programs as they relate to adolescent functioning, while Chapter 13 deals with the interpersonal relations and the psychological environment of the schools. Although most writers on adolescent psychology do not concern themselves with the curricular aspects of secondary education, this author believes that familiarity with the schools' programs is important in gaining understanding of the adolescent's problems in school.

The youngster's formal education starts, of course, well before he reaches adolescence, by which time most youngsters have been exposed to at least six years of elementary school. By the time the youngster reaches junior high school, many basic skills will be developed, as well as many patterns of school-related behavior, such as study habits. Teachers in the secondary schools have therefore found it easy to blame the failure of many of their students to perform adequately on the poor background training these youngsters received in the elementary schools. If the elementary schools did not prepare a youngster properly, which may sometimes be the case, simply condemning them for this failure does not solve the student's problems. Rather, the secondary schools should have programs available to enable such a youngster to overcome the deficiencies in his background and to function effectively in his work in the secondary school. There is, unfortunately, no consistency in the planning of such programs, if they are offered at all, in the secondary schools throughout our nation. Not only is there tremendous variation among school systems in different geographic locales; there are also substantial differences among secondary schools in the same school system. One high school in a district may have excellent remedial programs, while another within the same district may have none. Since youngsters are assigned to schools on the basis of neighborhood boundaries rather than on the basis of one school's ability to satisfy their needs better than another, a school offering remedial programs could conceivably have fewer students needing such assistance than does a school where no such programs are available.

Before discussing the specific problems of adolescents relating to various kinds of school functioning and adjustment, it is necessary to survey school programs in general. In the following sections, the aims and goals of education and the content and organization of curriculums are discussed in order to familiarize the reader with some of the major difficulties confronting the schools. Some understanding of these problems will also indicate why youngsters encounter some of the difficulties that hamper or impede their learning.

AIMS AND GOALS OF SECONDARY EDUCATION

There has been a dearth of research that directly relates aims of education to individual development. This may indicate that the learner and his needs are generally ignored or rejected in determining institutional goals. Woodruff (1958) suggested that objectives ought to be concerned less with need as it is psychologically defined and more concerned with what the student ought to have, a view that seems to be popularly accepted. It is not, however, in accord with Havighurst's thesis (1958) that research is likely to affect educational change in periods when the concept of human nature is undergoing drastic revision or when society is under heavy pressure for social change. Actually, most of the recent studies take societal demands as a point of departure. In analyzing theories of adolescence, Muuss (1958) found that American concepts were more psychologically oriented, while European views reflected the impact of physiological studies to a greater degree. The view an individual holds concerning adolescent development, whether it is psychologically or physiologically oriented, will usually be reflected in his viewpoint concerning educational goals.

The success of the American high school in meeting the nonacademic goals of the nineteenth century was documented by Commager in a recent book (1958). He suggested a need for new objectives that recognize the lengthened period of professional training, lessened vocational needs, and the educative forces of mass media and other opinion-shaping agencies. He analyzed the school's undue emphasis on instilling patriotism as a holdover from the time when there was a need to Americanize an immigrant population. Skaurud (1956) supported this view in his study of trends during the last half-century that indicated a major goal in the study of history to be the development of a desire for the democratic way of life. Potter (1955) analyzed the educational programs of transitional societies and concluded that schools defend the *status quo* by avoiding controversial issues and failing to teach students to examine social issues critically.

Defining the Function of the Schools

One of the problems facing secondary education seems to be that of defining the areas that are legitimate objects and functions of the school and separating them from those that properly belong to other institutions. The question of whether families depend too much on the school to serve situations that have previously been best served by the home was investigated by the Rockefeller Brothers' Fund (1958). Generally, the secondary schools do appear to have assumed or been forced to assume functions that should belong to other institutions. At present this trend appears to be continuing, with even more tasks that properly belong elsewhere being assigned to the schools. Although recent studies (Conant, 1959; Bush, 1958) have affirmed the success of secondary schools in general education, they have also emphasized the need to clarify the specific objectives of specialized education. Bush (1958) suggested that there is a unique strength in a comprehensive high school dedicated to the dual purpose of general and specialized education. This view has been strongly supported in the Yearbooks of the American Association of School Administrators (1958) and the Association for Supervision and Curriculum Development (1956).

In attempting to identify the goals of general education, Skaurud (1956) examined national committee reports written since 1900. He observed two major objectives of the study of American history: (1) to develop a desire for the American way of life; and (2) to develop a desire to apply the scientific method to problems of American life.

There has generally been a paucity of research in connection with goals of general education. As a result, it has been difficult to structure criteria against which high schools could evaluate their programs of general education. French and others (1957) did propose a comprehensive list of goals for the high school, in which they identified specific levels of behavior competence (within the areas of self-realization, human relationships, economic efficiency, and civic responsibility) in order to give additional meaning and clarification to general aims. They sought specific aspects of behaviors so that high schools might be able to evaluate their general education programs.

Some recent studies of educational aims have offered fresh perspec-

tives. Pace (1958) defined the integrating potentials of educational objectives and offered new approaches to their classification. Goodlad
(1958) called for an over-all conceptual system to help determine priori-
ties in objectives, feeling that the development of such a system would
help the high school find its unique function. Dreiman (1957) proposed
that it was the function of the high school to help students "to be
excited about ideas, to be unawed by power, to be unafraid of controversy, and not to be content with themselves." Although many of these
"new" ideas have a good deal of merit, they have not as yet been widely
accepted or put into general practice.

Who Should Control the Schools?

The development of educational objectives appears to have been increasingly influenced by private and public groups. Valid or not, their
proposals have received a good deal of national coverage, which has in
turn encouraged other groups and individuals to jump on the band-
wagon. Bayles (1958) found that many of the disputes over the aims of
the schools are actually group conflicts over control of the schools. He
felt that the teaching profession should become active in striving to
realize the ideal of free inquiry in the school and particularly should
rid itself of the tendency to avoid conflicts. Smith (1956) has pursued
the same issue, urging that the lines between professional autonomy
and legitimate public authority be drawn more explicitly. Unfortunately the present trend seems to be toward more interaction of lay
people with the schools. School-board members are usually lay people,
but, in addition, educators have involved members of the communities
in a variety of lay committees. While there may be some public-rela-
tions value in including laymen in school affairs, all too often these
committees become influential in determining school policy. Reisman
(1956) reported on the dangers of relying too heavily on lay opinion for
educational direction, since the layman's view often differs substantially
from that of the professionals. Deam (1957) found, for example, that a
sampling of school-board members in Virginia was more conservative
than were social-science teachers in setting limits for discussing controversial issues. Cook (1955) conducted a survey of aims considered significant by parents, students, and English teachers, and found that parents and students laid more stress on formal language studies than
teachers did, and less stress on understanding of mass media of communication. Although Woodruff (1958) has insisted that it is not in
keeping with American traditions to have educators formulate educational aims, there is no evidence to indicate that any group of nonedu-
cators would be more competent than educators in such formulation.
The author knows of no major business or industry that allows its

basic policies to be strongly influenced by laymen, even though these laymen, as stockholders, may own a portion of the business. It is unfortunate that the stockholders in education—the taxpayers—do not allow the educational administrators to function with the autonomy allowed major industrial leaders.

CURRICULUM CONTENT AND ORGANIZATION

Major contributions to research in curriculum content and organization have been made by a number of organizations and foundations, yet there is still a minimum of basic research in orientation and selection of curriculum content. Although the title of a recent ASCD Yearbook (1956) was "What Shall the High School Teach?" the candid conclusion indicated that there was no answer to this question at the present time. The orientation of the school curriculum is generally a reflection of social requirements, which are constantly changing. These changes are in turn reflected in special emphases of the schools. An example is the recent concern with the academically talented, about whom the research has increased tremendously since the Russians successfully orbited the first Sputnik. As the problems of juvenile delinquency have had a greater impact on society, the emphasis on research in this area has also increased (see Chapter 14), creating a demand for extensive adjustment of curriculums to meet effectively the needs of those who might become delinquent. Conant (1959) emphasized subject matter courses in a comprehensive high school and recommended a specific curriculum for the academically talented; improved counseling services; extension of the foreign-language program; ability grouping; and emphasis on English composition. Other recommendations in his report were for a diversified program for the development of marketable skills; special consideration for very slow readers; an academic inventory; an academic honors list; a developmental reading program; a summer-school program; required courses in science, mathematics, English, and social studies; and a home-room program. In essence, the report called for an intensive re-evaluation of the functions of the schools and a tremendous expansion and intensification of programs that are now relatively minimal in their effectiveness.

Further complicating the situation in education today is the lack of uniformity among the states in requirements for high-school graduation. Some states require four years of English and some, three years; whereas others require only two years, or even one. Similar differences exist in history, science, mathematics, and social studies curriculums. There is a good deal of evidence that some students enroll in many more courses than are required, but many will take only the required minimums.

Requirements relating to certification of teachers also vary widely from state to state. Perhaps as a result of this variability, there is little reciprocity among the states in honoring one another's teaching certificates. It is not unusual for a teacher with a number of years of experience in one state to find that he must take one or more additional courses in order to be certified to teach in another state. Currently a national organization is attempting to develop standards of teacher training at the college and university level, so that any individual who receives a certificate from any of the approved institutions participating in a standard program will be able to teach in all states in this country.

The preceding survey of the situation as it exists today is a minimal one that omits many problems. Even on the basis of this presentation, however, the reader should be quite aware of the need for tremendous effort to improve our educational programming. With the confusion that exists in the minds of the professional "experts" as to the best program to enable youngsters to learn most effectively, it is easy to undertand why so many lay or nonprofessional "experts" tend to be publicly critical of our current programs.

SUBJECT MATTER IN SECONDARY SCHOOLS

Numerous studies have been made in recent years concerning various problems that confront youngsters in specific areas of subject matter at the secondary-school level. As was pointed out earlier, some of these problems are already well developed by the time the youngster completes his elementary-school program. While secondary-school personnel have long been aware of this situation, until recently they have not been concerned about remedying it. They have, in a sense, taken the children as they come and pushed them on as far as possible. Many of the efforts of the elementary schools to improve their programs have not been followed through in the secondary schools. This failure has been, until recently, most obvious in the area of reading.

Reading

For a number of years, youngsters in the elementary grades have been divided into reading groups that gave each youngster the opportunity to learn at his own pace and within the limits of his own ability. In many schools such grouping continued through the sixth grade, but it usually ended at the seventh-grade level, when all the youngsters were "lumped" into their various classes regardless of reading level. Apparently it was assumed that the elementary-school grouping procedure was aimed at making all the youngsters alike by the time they reached junior high school. In fact, the exact opposite is true. As a result of such grouping, youngsters are more different in their reading skills in the sixth grade than they were in the first grade, since the fast group has progressed rapidly, the average group has progressed at an average rate, and the slow group has progressed slowly. Thus, at the end of six years of elementary-school grouping, the gap between the fast and slow groups is far greater than it was at the first-grade level.

REMEDIAL COURSES. Until relatively recently, students whose reading skills were poorly developed by the time they entered high school had to struggle along as best they could. Those who went on to college did have some opportunity to receive help in a remedial reading program. After World War II, most colleges and universities set up extensive remedial reading programs for those whose reading skills scored below par on a standardized reading test. The need for such programs was quite obvious, since about one-half of entering freshmen classes were found to be in need of remedial reading. Recently, however, many colleges have dropped or greatly curtailed these programs and have suggested that these reading skills should be developed at an earlier level. During the same period, many secondary schools have developed programs that, in essence, continue the grouping pattern used in the elementary schools. Many of these are multiple-track programs, in which youngsters are grouped in each field of subject matter according to ability, but the main emphasis is on the development of better reading skill. More secondary schools than ever before have developed remedial reading programs, and more classroom teachers are being trained in the methods of teaching reading effectively at the secondary level. Bullock (1956) has suggested the need for more individualized instruction, more differential assignments, and more primary-grade reading material at an adolescent interest level.

Aukerman (1948) studied good and poor eleventh-grade students to determine whether differences existed in their reading status. Students who differed by at least one letter grade were paired with subjects matched on the basis of intelligence, sex, age, grade level, subject, hour of recitation, and teacher. English, American history, chemistry, and mathematics were the subject areas investigated in this study. In all four fields good students were significantly superior to poor students in general reading ability; and in American history, they were better in specific reading ability. Good and poor students were not significantly different in either general or specific vocabulary ability, which suggests that knowledge of words is less important than reading ability as a whole. That some kind of remedial work is needed was made clear by Traxler's study (1950) of the scores made by a group of students on the Cooperative English Test, Form C, Reading Comprehension. Of the 36 students from four independent schools who were tested, only 3 exhibited a gain in comprehension each year. Traxler suggested that variations from year to year in growth of reading achievement, or any other skill learned in school, bear a close relationship to instruction, guidance, and the process of inward maturing. Lee (1951) studied 630 Negro pupils in the ninth grade and 382 in the twelfth grade in three Southern states to determine the relationship between reading competence and (1) mental ability; (2) general reading attainment; (3) interest in school activities; and (4) socioeconomic background. The correlation between "education of grandparents and parents" and competence in interpretation was .417. Interest and competence in reading correlated .264. The influence of general reading ability was not clear-cut but was related to "apprehending the literal meaning of passages and in drawing inferences from nonemotive material." The correlation of reading competence with the American Council on Education Psychological Examination was .589.

Since there is now an increasing emphasis on programs to continue the development of reading skills up through the secondary school, as well as on remedial programs, the question of the effectiveness of these programs becomes pertinent. High-school developmental reading programs are relatively new, and a good deal of follow-up study must be done to evaluate their effectiveness. Blake (1954) conducted a follow-up study to determine the academic success over a period of four and a half years of 122 control-group students and 128 probationary students who were required to take a course in study and reading skills. He concluded that the students were benefited academically, and that the majority of them recognized the benefits which they received. While there will doubtless always be a need for remedial reading, many of the reading problems one encounters in the secondary schools might well be eliminated or alleviated by increasing emphasis on developmental reading programs in which the youngsters would continue to be grouped according to their reading ability. This grouping pattern should be followed in all courses involving a good deal of reading, such as English, social studies, history, and geography. The reading level of the youngster should also be taken into consideration in such areas as mathematics, since a youngster must be able to read and understand problems in order to solve them.

Brownell (1953) investigated the influence of reading training in the area of social studies on the students' ability to think critically. He used his own ninth-grade classes as experimental and control groups, with twenty-four pairings on the basis of intelligence and of reading, which was taught an average of two hours a week for twenty-eight weeks. Changes in critical thinking were measured by the Watson-Glaser Critical Thinking Appraisal. The data tentatively suggest most significant gains in the experimental group, although the evidence did not demonstrate conclusively that these greater relative gains were caused by training in reading alone. In such situations it is always difficult to appraise whether reading ability *per se* improves or whether the youngster is more motivated as a result of his closer contact with the instructor in the remedial situation.

READABILITY OF STUDENT COMPOSITIONS. Lorge and Kruglow (1950) investigated the readability of compositions written by pupils in the eighth and ninth grades who were applying for admission to the Bronx High School of Science in New York. The compositions were rated by means of the Lorge Readability Formula, which takes into account the structural elements of written expression. The intelligence of the youngsters was measured by a test made up of arithmetic items, vocabulary items, and proverb-matching items. With educational level held fairly constant, as it was, there was not a significant relationship between readability of compositions and intelligence-test scores. However, applicants for admission to this high school are usually a very select group of the brightest eighth- and ninth-grade students in New York City, and their compositions might be expected to have a high level of readability. It is doubtful that the same result would have occurred with a sample of youngsters who were less able intellectually.

LITERATURE. The objectives for the study of literature have not yet been clearly defined, although courses in literature are required of students in nearly all high schools. Currently, educational theorists propose two possible approaches: (1) "to study techniques of literature and the facts surrounding its production" and/or (2) "to produce through literature a series of controlled responses in students that will culminate in basic concepts about human living, relationships, and understanding of the role of man" (Carlsen, 1961). There has not been sufficient research to demonstrate the worth of either approach, nor has the educational value of the study of literature been clearly substantiated. Moulton (1959) reviewed the professional writings on the teaching of literature from 1925 to 1955. She identified two general treatments of the subject: (1) as a humanistic discipline and (2) as training for citizenship, with the recommendations strongly favoring the second point of view. Of the 161 descriptions of classroom practice that she examined, only eight were reports of controlled experimentation. Moulton strongly recommends more controlled experimentation to determine objectively the real results of varying emphases in the teaching of literature.

A review of professional studies published from 1950 to 1957 on the teaching of poetry was done by Stensland (1958). The objectives most frequently mentioned were to "increase vicarious experience, to provide enjoyment, and to give moral training." Despite these stated objectives, the methods of teaching poetry that were usually recommended were the study of historical and literary backgrounds, the study of versification, and the discussion of the experience or theme of a poem. The study of meaning through such processes as defining words, unraveling figures of speech, and explaining allusions was also strongly recommended. There is obviously a notable discrepancy between the objectives sought and the methods used. Overemphasis on such methods is likely to lead to boredom or other negative feelings that are not conducive to the enjoyment of poetry.

Whether or not the study of literature as generally presented is effective has been questioned by a number of investigators. Russell (1958) demonstrated that much reading matter by itself has little effect on a person's deeper feelings and behavior. Reaction to a particular book depends upon the kinds of content and upon the background, interests, and personality of the reader. Carlsen and Grimes (1959) analyzed novels about Texas that were written for adolescents and found that the action usually took place on ranches in Western Texas, generally giving the reader a highly stereotyped picture of that region. Carpenter (1957) discussed the image of the adolescent presented in American fiction and concluded that the adolescent was treated either as a confused individual simply waiting for maturity or as a symbol of the confused characteristics of our total society. Smith (1958) studied children's books about foreign countries and found little that would give American young people a picture of contemporary daily life in those countries.

There has been a good deal of disagreement among the experts concerning use in the classroom of books that present a picture of individuals who transgress the moral precepts of society. Apparently some educators feel that the presentation of such themes would be disturbing to youngsters. Calitri (1959) demonstrated, however, that the individual adolescent is fully aware of "goodness" and "badness" and every mixture of the two in his environment. Literature could serve as a medium by means of which students could be encouraged to discuss openly the problems of human experience. Cook (1957) specified three functions to be served by books: (1) Each selection must fit into a plan for a systematic presentation of literary or social values. (2) Each selection must have some teaching value (these values are not necessarily measurable). (3) The selections must be made with due regard to the maturity level for which they are intended.

Youngsters seem to be reading more today, and the importance of literature as a medium of communication is increasingly recognized. "Its function in the schools is to continually awaken young people to ideas, experiences, attitudes, and feelings" (Carlsen, 1961). Unfortunately, many of the books presented to young people offer only limited, and sometimes distorted, views of human life. There is need for further research to determine how literary appreciation grows by developmental stages, and a need for a development of reading material appropriate for such stages. Research is also needed to determine methods of teaching literature that will foster development of reading skills. Perhaps most important is the need to develop materials keyed to the interests of youngsters in contemporary affairs.

Mathematics

The space race with Russia has caused increasing emphasis on the need for improving instruction in mathematics. Even more important, perhaps, is the emphasis on attracting more youngsters to mathematics courses in the high schools. For many years now, the majority of students have avoided taking more than the minimum required high-school courses in mathematics, and have continued this avoidance in their college careers. Mathematics would appear, generally, to be one of the least-liked subject-matter areas in the curriculum. Just when this dislike begins is hard to pinpoint, but apparently it arises during the youngster's elementary-school career and is reinforced as he moves into secondary school. There have been many reasons offered for this dislike, including an overemphasis on content, too much emphasis on mere computation, and the traditional step-by-step methodology, which inhibits the more able youngster. It has been suggested also that most elementary-school teachers, who are basically generalists, do not like mathematics themselves and do not fully understand the concepts underlying the material they teach. Poffenberger and Norton (1959) demonstrated that the teacher is an influential source in determining the student's attitude toward mathematics. They questioned 390 college freshmen to determine factors relating to attitudes toward mathematics and found that two of the most influential were previous teachers and parental expectations. Malone and Freel (1954) measured the attitudes of 800 junior- and senior-high school students toward mathematics. An analysis of the results indicated that the students recognized the practical value of mathematics and indicated a desire for a more thorough presentation of the subject. No significant differences in attitudes were found between the different grade levels included in this study.

Hotyat (1952), in a comparison of sixth-grade and ninth-grade pupils, suggested that a number of weak points is apparent in the mathematical thinking of adolescents. He found fragility of concepts either on the operational (i.e., functional) side or on the essentially generic side of a number of concrete perceptual situations, and also found a great deal of difficulty in selecting a method of demonstration. There was also evidence of difficulty in translating mathematical thinking into symbolic notation, and there were errors of reasoning in connection with seeking the proper demonstration. On the whole, Hotyat found that the weak points in the mathematical thinking of adolescents decrease as one goes from the lower classes to the higher.

Four hundred and sixty-nine high-school students were tested to determine their conceptions of mass, weight, and volume (Elkind, 1961). The results indicated that while 87 per cent of the students had attained abstract conceptions of mass and weight, only 47 per cent had an abstract conception of volume. The percentage of students having an abstract conception of volume increased significantly between the ages of twelve and eighteen, with a significantly higher percentage of boys than girls attaining this abstract conception. Generally, there was a low but positive correlation between IQ and the attainment of the conception of volume.

Elkind interpreted the results of his study in the framework of Piaget's genetic theory of intelligence. This theory proposes that the operational and structural readiness for the attainment of the volume conception appear just at the onset of the study of formal structure in mathematics and the adoption of adult roles. These latter two events produce an attention of interest and opportunities for spontaneously attaining quantity conceptions of which the formation is now dependent upon the particular role the young person adopts. This conclusion was found to be consistent with the relation of age, sex, and IQ to the attainment of an abstract conception of volume.

Hoffman (1955) selected 90 boys and girls between the ages of twelve and seventeen and divided them into three IQ groups based on the Wechsler-Bellevue Intelligence Scale: 50–85, 86–115, and 116–up. These subjects were presented several series of drawings designed to test their ability to form concepts from perceptual material. The concepts studied included size, symmetry, depth, thickness, acuteness, and solidity. Hoffman found that the subjects' scores on the conceptual tests correlated higher with verbal than with nonverbal Wechsler scores, "in spite of the nonverbal nature of the conceptual problems." Smith (1959) studied the significance of maturity and other variables in relation to an understanding of the limit concept. Three hours of special instruction in limits were given to certain seventh- through twelfth-grade classes, while other classes, equated for mental age, were given no instruction. The findings on a limits test showed experience to be important, and significant gains in conceptualizing limit occurred at all levels. Chronological age was not a related variable, but mental age was positively correlated with limits test scores.

CHANGES IN MATHEMATICS TEACHING. A number of new approaches and techniques in teaching mathematics have recently been employed in the schools. Although some of these newer approaches have not been thoroughly investigated, studies are currently being done to determine their effectiveness. Zoll (1957) investigated the relative merits of varying amounts of application in plane geometry. Each of three teachers taught both experimental and control classes that were equated for geometric aptitude, intelligence, and arithmetic and algebraic competence. The statistical analyses revealed no significant differences with varying amounts of application between the experimental and control classes. There were no differences among the experimental classes in regard to their ability to solve "originals," knowledge of facts and principles, or ability to apply facts and principles in practical problems. Zoll felt that the ability to apply geometric facts and principles seemed to be associated with individual males of good ability and mathematical competence.

Kenney and Stockton (1958) equated three groups of more than 100 each and compared three approaches to teaching percentage. One approach emphasized drill, the second emphasized understanding and reasoning, and the third approach was a combination of the first two. The results of a test administered to these groups showed evidence of progress in the upper three-quarters of all classes. Although there appeared to be advantages in the composite and understanding approaches, the evidence was inconclusive. Griff (1957) used three heterogeneous interest groups of plane geometry students to study the effect of one-level and three-level assignments that were varied quarterly through the school year. A test of functional competence was administered, as well as class quizzes, and the results indicated that the students did more and better work in a one-level approach. Hines (1957) reported that students who did out-of-class work seemed to achieve better than those who did not do homework.

An informal study indicating that use of small groups provided a good learning situation for algebra, geometry, and business mathematics was reported by Ivie et al. (1958). However, they reported that the superior students showed limited desire to progress and that some students felt the need for class activities.

The effect of systematic home-school cooperation on the achievement of eighth-grade students was investigated by Ilioff (1957), who found a consistently positive effect between increased parental understanding and pupil achievement. This latter finding is an important one, since many parents today are completely unfamiliar with the approaches now used to teach mathematics. They are distressed that their youngsters do not do some of the things they themselves did, such as memorizing the multiplication tables. It would appear that schools should make an attempt to apprise the parents of the methods being used, so that parents may better understand what their youngsters are doing.

SEX DIFFERENCES IN MATHEMATICAL ABILITY. There is a widely held misconception that boys are superior to girls in mathematics at all grade levels. Many teachers believe this to be true and are likely to require less of girls than boys in mathematics. Further, girls are seldom encouraged to enroll in advanced mathematics courses, since it is assumed that they are not capable of functioning successfully in such courses. Recent investigations have indicated, however, not only that girls are often equal to boys in mathematics achievement, but that in some cases they are even superior to boys. McCutcheon (1957) analyzed achievement in eighth-grade mathematics and science in relation to a number of variables, using experimenter-designed pre-tests and post-tests in mathematics and an intelligence test. A total of 378 teachers answered questionnaires, and 6471 students participated in the study. The statistical analyses showed the following findings: (1) With adjustments for initial differences, there were no sex differences in final achievement. (2) Girls scored higher on the pre-tests, post-tests, and intelligence tests. (3) Significant differences in achievement in intelligence among the upper, middle, and lower 5 per cent were noted. Pruett (1960) studied the mathematics achievement of about 45,000 ninth-grade students in Indiana. Girls did better work than boys in mathematics, and the better mathematics students were found in schools with large enrollments.

Powell *et al.* (1962) investigated sex differences in mathematics achievement in grades three through eight. When the students were divided into five IQ groups (75–94, 95–104, 105–114, 115–124, and 125–up), sex differences in arithmetic achievement were noted. Boys generally excelled in arithmetic fundamentals, while girls excelled in arithmetic reasoning. These trends reversed at different grade levels, but boys were never superior to girls in either of these aspects of arithmetic. In the general analysis (all IQ groups added together), no sex differences were apparent in either fundamentals or reasoning.

The evidence offered by these recent studies should bring about a much-needed change in the views concerning sex differences in achievement in mathematics. Since the evidence does indicate that girls are not inferior to boys in this subject-matter area, it would appear that girls should be encouraged to enroll in more advanced mathematics courses in high school and college. Such encouragement would probably influence more girls to seek occupations in which knowledge of mathematics is essential. At present most girls seem to believe that they are not capable of entering occupations of this sort, and this belief has often been reinforced by teachers who still consider girls less capable in mathematics than boys are.

Science

Not only mathematics but science also has been emphasized since the advent of the space age as an area of increasing importance. Some experts seem to believe that little or nothing was being done in high schools with regard to science courses until the time of Sputnik I. However, the National Education Association Research Division (1958) provided figures indicating that, of 1,250,000 high-school graduates in 1957, about 175,000 had taken four years of science, and 480,000 more had completed three years of science. More than half the schools in the United States were engaged in revision and expansion of their science curriculum before the first Russian satellite was orbited. Generally, the evidence indicated that the senior high schools were doing a more comprehensive job in teaching science and in improving methods than had been assumed. The junior high schools, however, do not seem to have been as active in building and revising science curriculums, and there is apparently a need for improvement at this level.

Badley (1953) felt that scientific interest should be noted early, that provisions should be made for effectively guiding such interest, and that junior-high-school students possess an eagerness for knowledge which needs understanding and encouragement. He suggested that the classroom teacher has the greatest opportunity and responsibility for such guidance, with assistance from guidance specialists if such personnel are available. Johnson (1953) indicated that at the high-school level, too, the classroom teacher is most effective in orienting students toward science. Foshay (1953) suggested that the school has a twofold task in guiding youngsters toward science: (1) to help children toward a personal security that will permit them to be original; and (2) to help them give form to their original inquiries.

The general interest of youngsters in science was discussed by Lentlke (1956) from the results of a questionnaire administered to about 1500 high-school students in Germany. Boys were most interested in mathematics, science, and physical education. As they grew older, the boys selected more sciences than languages, and biology was particularly popular. Knepp (1950) had also found that high-school students were particularly interested in articles dealing with human biology.

BIOLOGY. Stone (1959) reviewed and evaluated current textbooks and courses of study for high-school biology. She found that little attention was paid to recent developments, and only minor attention to theories and unifying concepts. Howard (1958) found that present-day textbooks in biology differ in their emphases from those used forty and eighty years ago. In the past, biology books emphasized factual objectives and memorization of unrelated facts. Today the books emphasize functional information and interrelationships among living things. Tyrell (1958) found that teachers today consider biological principles, conservation, essential life processes, and human physiology to be the most important areas in biology.

The effectiveness of various teaching methods in high-school biology was studied by Newman (1957). In this study the lecture-discussion method was used, with three variations. In one approach, no reading assignments were made in or out of class; in the second approach, outside readings were assigned; and in the third approach, textbook reading was done in class. All three groups of students involved in the study showed gains. No method was significantly superior to the others with students who scored high on intelligence and reading comprehension, but in the group that read textbook assignments in class, students with low intelligence and reading comprehension showed more significant improvement than such students did in the other two situations.

CHEMISTRY. There has been a good deal of criticism of the methods that have been used to teach chemistry, especially of those which emphasized memorization. Fonsworth (1957) attempted to achieve reflective thinking by applying the methods of science to problems of daily life and human affairs. Both the teachers and the students involved in this study cooperated in selecting problems and methods of solving them. Fonsworth found gains with this approach (based on IQ, a critical thinking test, and a standardized chemistry achievement test) with respect to growth in mental ability and the application of abilities required in critical thinking. There were also significant gains in the use of the scientific method in solving chemistry problems.

The ability to understand and apply the scientific method in chemistry is apparently more closely related to intelligence than to any parts of a chemistry achievement test. Porter and Anderson (1959) studied the relationships of specified abilities in chemistry to each other and to intelligence and found that the top and middle intellectual groups were not always superior to the lower group in achievement. In terms of the total test, the intellectually superior students did achieve more than the middle or lower groups.

The methods of performing experiments prescribed in high-school chemistry laboratory manuals were compared with pupil-devised methods of studying the same problems by Mark (1958). After the students had performed a set of ten experiments, their acquisition of factual information and their ability to interpret chemical knowledge were measured through a standardized chemistry examination. At the beginning of the second semester a standardized chemistry aptitude test was given as a pretest. The groups did not differ significantly at the start and did equally well on the factual test. The experimental group was significantly superior, however, in ability to interpret chemical knowledge.

PHYSICS. The effectiveness of two different methods of instruction in high-school physics with students of high and low intelligence was investigated by Garside (1959). About 700 students were divided into thirty groups using traditional methods and thirty using Harvey White physics films. The students were placed in upper-ability and lower-ability groups. Regardless of the method of instruction, the highly intelligent students achieved at a significantly higher level than the students of low ability. The groups were then equated for intelligence by means of covariance, a statistical statement used when two scores are summed to make a composite; no significant difference was found between the film and the traditional group, but retention was higher for the traditional group.

Hubbard (1958) investigated the effect of three teaching methods in a high-school physics course on the achievement of the students. One group was taught by television only; a second group was taught by television supplemented by a physics teacher; and the third group was taught by the same teacher, using only traditional classroom approaches. No one method was more effective for any one ability level, nor was there any general superiority of one method over the others.

O'Connor (1959) investigated the process by which high-school physics students solved laboratory problems. His groups were small and his findings only tentative, but his approach is an interesting one. He checked the steps toward the solution of problems by direct observation and by tape recordings of students "thinking aloud." His tentative findings indicated that pupils of high ability solved more problems than those of lesser ability, although the problem-solvers were not restricted to any ability group. Those who solved one problem did not necessarily solve the others, and there were no common patterns of solution or of failure to find a solution among the problems, ability groups, or all students. O'Connor concluded that mental ability and quantitative conceptualizing were not sufficient bases for selection of potential scientists.

Social Studies

Relatively few experimental research studies have been conducted in the field of social studies, partly because of the difficulty of obtaining objective data related to the general goals of the area. This field is also somewhat obscured by the effects of various out-of-school activities that influence youngsters' behavior. Hill (1954) attempted to test the hypothesis that the organized study of selected materials pertaining to social class assists youngsters in formulating attitudes toward social justice and democracy and would also help them in choosing their friends. In no case, however, did the experimental groups appear to benefit more than the control groups. Extra-curricular activities and interactions might well eliminate any differences that an in-school program seems to bring about.

The development of the social-studies curriculum over the last fifty years was traced by Cruikshanks (1957), who felt that the evidence indicated that textbooks are major determinants of the curriculum. Textbooks have been widely criticized in the past for their failure to include enough information about specific countries and people and their tendency to perpetuate stereotypes. Recent investigators (Takaki, 1954; and Deodhar, 1954) examining textbook content have found that current texts allot more space to discussions of foreign countries and have better balanced content and a more objective approach than do the older texts.

Rehage (1951) compared programs of social studies planned by pupils and teachers with those directed by teachers, using two matched eighth-grade groups in his sample. The results indicated that the time spent in student-teacher planning did not result in any loss in achievement of the commonly accepted goals of social-science instruction. Rehage also studied the development of insight into the principles of group planning, changes in the internal structure of the group, and group productivity. Although some differences favoring the teacher-student planning group did appear, they did not appear often enough to justify any claim for the superiority of this method.

Subject-Matter Research

In all the fields of subject matter discussed, experimental research is clearly needed to determine effective methods of presentation, especially methods that will help students qualitatively. Some of the newer approaches currently being tried in the schools, such as the team approach, may prove effective but are not yet developed to the point at which they can be thoroughly evaluated. There is a particular need for research studies relating to measurement of achievement or change beyond the level of factual information. Most important, perhaps, is the need for better reporting of research, so that areas needing further investigation can be more readily identified.

EVALUATION OF STUDENTS

The general use of tests, including their various advantages and disadvantages, has been discussed in various chapters in this book (see Chapters 1, 3, 4, and 10). The use of these instruments in the schools requires a little further treatment.

Standardized Tests

One of the major tasks confronting the secondary school is that of properly evaluating student progress. Although many kinds of standardized tests, as well as teacher-made examinations, are used regularly, there is reason to believe that these are not used as effectively as they might be or even that they are misused. Part of the difficulty lies in the fact that while most of the instruments employed are group tests, the results are used directly to evaluate individuals. Worcester (1948) reported a misuse of intelligence-test scores that illustrates this point. A group test dependent on reading ability may be given to all students, including those deficient in reading. If the low score received by a youngster with a reading deficiency is considered meaningful by itself, he may be seriously penalized. Provision must be made for intensive study of those making low scores.

One of the prime difficulties in the use of achievement tests is the failure to relate the test results to a previous evaluation. Kvaraceus and Lanigan (1948) had retested elementary-school children with different forms of the Advanced Iowa Every-Pupil Test at half-year intervals over a two-year period. They found regular gains in reading comprehension, vocabulary, and work-study skills, and some "regressions" in arithmetic and language tests over one of the test intervals. Individual pupils tended to maintain relatively the same rank from one half-year to the next. The authors concluded that "adequate interpretation of an individual performance at any one given testing period is not possible unless reports of previous testing are available."

Parsley and Powell (1962) substantiated this point of view in a study of academic gain during the school year and academic loss over the summer vacation. The subjects were given the California Achievement Test Battery at the beginning of an academic year, at the end of the same academic year, and at the beginning of the following academic year. Contrary to hypothesis, the students did not show losses in achievement over the summer but in many instances showed gains. These findings present interesting implications in relation to the possibility of a twelve-month school year and suggest the desirability of reconsidering the time needed at the beginning of a new school year to review previously learned material. Parsley and Powell (1960) discussed the need for such a semi-annual achievement testing program in an article that also describes the application of such a program in the study of academic gain during the school year and academic loss over the summer vacation.

Another difficulty in the use of standardized achievement tests is the overlap of content in tests purporting to measure achievement in different areas. Spaulding (1951) reported results obtained from administering the Progressive Achievement Tests to ninth-graders in an attempt to study the reliability of the tests and the correlations between the parts. Reliability for all tests except that of reading comprehension was high. Intercorrelations among the entire battery of tests ranged from .250 to .914, indicating more overlapping of content in some of the major parts than is desirable for diagnostic purposes. Parsley and Powell (1962) felt that the same objection could be made to the California Achievement Test Battery. A qualitative inspection of their data seemed to indicate that the Reading Comprehension Test and the Arithmetic Reasoning Test measured the same thing, since the students ranked about the same on both tests.

Teachers must necessarily be quite cautious in their use of the diagnostic profiles that most tests offer. While the total test may be highly reliable, any given part may be far less so. For example, a subtest designed to measure arithmetic fundamentals may consist of 60 items and may have a reliability of .85. If the student's score on this test is very low, one might correctly assume he is weak in this area. If one then tried to determine which specific fundamental area is weakest— addition, subtraction, multiplication, or division—he would be treading on thin ice. Each of these areas would be measured on a 15-item test, which is too short, no matter how high its reported reliability, to be a truly appropriate basis for diagnosis.

A further disadvantage of achievement-test scores is that they offer no means of determining the subject's motivation. A low test score might result from lack of interest in the test or failure to understand its purpose. A youngster who has a low score on the test may achieve at a higher level in actual classroom performance because his motivation is greater. Stockstill et al. (1959) found significant differences between the Differential Aptitude scores of motivated and unmotivated students in the ninth grade. Generally the girls scored higher than the boys, with the motivated girls performing best. That girls often do perform better than boys on such tests may also result from differences in motivation, such as girls' stronger desire to conform to all school situations, including tests.

The biggest problems facing most school systems are determining what instruments are most effective and structuring an effective testing program. Lindquist (1951) has suggested some criteria upon which an effective high-school testing program might be based. He suggests that, for purposes of guidance, individualization of instruction, and valuation, we must use a number of tests, each of which measures a broad trait or ability of the pupil. The traits to be measured are those whose development is a fundamental objective of the whole program of secondary education. The tests should collectively describe all important aspects of the pupil's educational development. It is also important that all the tests be administered to all high-school pupils periodically, rather than on a "one-shot" basis.

Teacher-Made Examinations

Most teachers have relatively limited technical knowledge about test construction, yet they must constantly develop tests to evaluate the progress of their students. The kind of test (true-false, multiple choice, or essay) that is most effective may vary with the content of the course and with the teacher's goals. A teacher may not know which kind of test is most appropriate for a given course of study and may as a result fail to evaluate what he seeks to evaluate. Many teachers feel that objective examinations must be used to avoid any subjectivity in scoring, but such tests may be inappropriate for the kind of knowledge the teacher seeks to measure. An essay test usually gives the student wide opportunity to show the various facets of his knowledge, whereas the objective examination may allow him to demonstrate only retention and recall of factual information.

In many high schools, departmental examinations, rather than tests constructed by individual teachers, are administered. Such examinations presuppose a certain uniformity in instruction which may not in fact exist. A teacher may successfully teach his students to understand general concepts related to certain subject matter, only to find that the objective departmental examination does not give them an opportunity to demonstrate such understanding. Even if all the teachers of a particular subject help make up the departmental examination, the total examination may not adequately measure the functioning of achievement of the students in various classes. In general, teachers need more and better background in the area of tests and measurements, with particular emphasis on the construction of tests. Such training would enable them to construct more effective instruments and to ascertain more accurately the times at which they should be given.

Perhaps the greatest error that most teachers make is the failure to use their own tests as learning devices, not merely as evaluative instruments alone. Many authorities agree that teacher-made tests should be used primarily for learning and secondarily for evaluation. After a test has been scored, it should be returned to the students for discussion. This enables the student to find out which items he missed, as well as what the right answer should have been and why. If the test is not returned, the student does not know what mistakes he made, and, being unable to correct his errors, will in fact perpetuate them.

Symonds (1952) suggested that the objective significance of evaluation by the teacher and self-evaluation by the pupil is often destroyed by needs of individuals to justify, exalt, defend, enhance, punish, or depreciate themselves. Such distortions destroy the validity of marks and point to the need for better understanding between pupils and teachers. Lack of mutual understanding may cause both teachers and students to feel the need of enhancing or depreciating themselves and of periodically adopting adjustments prejudicial to their best interests. For example, too often teachers do not return examinations for discussion because they do not wish to defend their reasons for considering a given answer the correct one. Students, on the other hand, fail to raise their questions in discussions for fear that the teacher may interpret their remarks negatively.

Academic Grades

The academic grade that is recorded in the student's permanent record file represents the teacher's final evaluation of the student's work. The ways in which final grades (or even the interval grades assigned during a term) are determined vary considerably. The final grade may be purely an arithmetical average of the interval grades, or it may represent a general over-all appraisal by the teacher. Final grades and/or interval grades may be based on examinations, term papers, oral reports, etc., or on the teacher's purely subjective judgments. It has been suggested that grades are too often based on these subjective judgments rather than on more objective measures. The alleged superiority of girls over boys in terms of the grades is considered evidence of such subjectivity. Supposedly, teachers grade youngsters as much on their general behavior as on their achievement. Since girls seem to be more socially conforming, they are less likely to disrupt the classroom situation and are rewarded for this behavior in their grades. While this may be true to some degree, it is not safe, on the basis of the evidence presented earlier, to accept it as a generalization. Some authorities feel that the reverse of this situation is true in the high schools, where boys are believed to be given higher grades because they need them in order to attend college, while girls are graded lower because college is less important to them. This, too, seems to be a misconception. There is no doubt that, for one reason or another, grades do reflect teachers' subjective judgments, but there is no real evidence to indicate that such subjectivity is entirely good or entirely bad.

A far more serious problem than subjectivity in grading is posed by the differences in grading standards in different school systems and at different levels within a school system. For example, a grade of "A" is given a numerical value of 4 in some systems, but of 1 in others; an "A" also is sometimes defined as 90-99 and sometimes as 85 and up. Students transferring from one system to another may find it difficult to have their records meaningfully evaluated, and colleges, whose applicants' marks represent all four methods, may have still more difficulty in making fair appraisals.

Generally, it seems quite clear that better grading procedures should be developed, and perhaps uniform procedures should be used in all schools. Perhaps Hadley's study (1954) entitled "A School Mark—Fact or Fancy?" sums up the inadequacy of present-day grading. Using scores on achievement tests for the basic skills, the final or term average mark, and a ranking on an acceptance scale, the author concluded that of the 158 pupils who were most liked, 50 per cent were assigned marks higher than measured attainment. Of the 118 least-liked pupils, 50 per cent were marked lower than their actual attainment and 19 per cent were marked higher. Hadley further concluded that 307 who were assigned intermediate positions had an even chance of being marked above or below their actual attainment.

FACTORS RELATING TO ACADEMIC ACHIEVEMENT

Intelligence

All evidence to date indicates that there is a relatively high positive correlation between intelligence and achievement. While it is true that this high correlation is partially a function of the tests used to measure these characteristics (intelligence tests actually appear to be high-level achievement tests), the correlation is nonetheless a meaningful one. Generally, the bright students achieve at a much higher level than do the dull ones. Those of average ability usually achieve better than those who are dull and poorer than those who are bright, although there is considerable overlapping. Substantial numbers of students, for various reasons, achieve at a level lower than that at which they are capable of functioning, and these youngsters are often pointed out as indicating that the high correlation between intelligence and achievement is a fallacy. However, there is a number of factors, including emotional problems and inadequate development of skills, that may prevent such under-achievers from reaching their proper level.

The importance of intelligence in relation to achievement is most notable at the high-school level. In most school systems the average IQ of the high-school students is slightly higher than that of elementary-school students. This is generally true because the duller students are not capable of functioning academically at the level necessary for success in high school and usually drop out of school or attend a technical school. Eifer (1952) analyzed the age, sex, and ability data on pupils in grades 8.5, 10.5, and 12.5 in twenty-six high schools in Los Angeles County. He found that there were "considerably more retarded than accelerated pupils," with a significantly larger percentage of boys in all IQ levels. There was a particular tendency for the slow-learning, over-age male pupils to drop out of school before their senior year. Acceleration was not widely used, with only about one-fifteenth of the boys and about one-ninth of the girls (in the very rapid learning groups) having been accelerated. About "four percent of the bright boys and almost two percent of the bright girls have been retarded one or more years." Barrett (1950) found differences in the intelligence of students electing a two-year terminal course and those selecting the regular four-year course in a commercial high school. The two-year students were on the average eight months older and from four to eight points lower in IQ than the four-year group. There was considerable overlap, and Barrett felt that such factors as cultural background, social adjustment, and economic necessity may affect the selection of courses almost as much as intelligence does.

THE SUBNORMAL STUDENT. While schools are generally concerned with the ability of all their pupils, the greatest concern is expressed toward the mentally subnormal and the gifted. In recent years, special programs have been designed to help those at the extremes of the intellectual range function effectively within the limits set by their intelligence. At the secondary-school level, the emphasis on the gifted is greater, since a large percentage of the subnormal youngsters do not attend high school. Those who do are usually placed in special classes for the "slow-learner" or the "educable subnormal," and such special programs may be useful for youngsters at this extreme. It has been said that, since the general high-school curriculum is usually geared at a slightly above average IQ level, little or no provision is made for those who are not dull enough for the "slow-learning" classes but are nonetheless below average in intelligence (roughly, those with IQ's between 75 and 90). It is often these latter youngsters who drop out of school without having developed skills that will make them employable.

Even where special classes are made available to those classified as "educable" the programs designed for these youngsters may not offer them adequate opportunity to function as effectively as they might, even within their intellectual limitations. It is true that in our high schools many of the classes for "slow learners" or "educable mentally handicapped" youngsters offer little more than custodial care. The teachers are often "warm, sincere" individuals who have had little or no training in methods and techniques for successfully teaching these children. Until recently, there were very few textbooks available that could satisfy the interests of these youngsters with material written for their low reading level. These youngsters are often excluded from the industrial-arts programs in which they might learn low-level but useful skills, since it takes too much time to train them and teachers often feel that they might not be "bright" enough to learn the necessary safety precautions. Many of the trade schools also exclude these youngsters by requiring that students seeking admission to their programs must have successfully completed at least the ninth grade in school.

PROGRAMS FOR THE GIFTED. Currently, the major emphasis in American education seems to be directed at offering more effective educational programs for intellectually gifted youngsters. This emphasis is usually justified by the statement that these youngsters have the most to contribute to our future society, and it is therefore important that they develop their capacities and begin to achieve at a high level early in life. These concepts are by no means new; special provisions have been made for the gifted for many decades, but usually on a smaller scale than at present. With today's more sophisticated measuring instruments it is easier to identify gifted youngsters than it was two or three decades ago. Within limits, however, the general approaches toward the education of the gifted have not changed appreciably. The gifted youngsters are either accelerated, homogeneously grouped, or given special enrichment programs within the heterogeneous classes. Acceleration is not as frequently employed today as it was twenty or thirty years ago. Educators feel that, while acceleration may move a child up to a level where he can function most effectively academically, he may fail to adjust socially and emotionally if placed with youngsters a year or two older chronologically. This author questions the validity of the evidence on which such a conclusion is based. However, acceleration is only infrequently employed. Currently, enrichment and homogeneous groupings are the approaches most frequently used.

Abramson (1959) set out to investigate the relationship between ability grouping in high school and subsequent success in college. Graduates of four different high schools, who had completed at least two years at a liberal arts college, were studied. Three intelligence levels (115–124, 125–134, and 135–160) were studied in the samples selected from each of the four schools. One of the high schools had placed gifted students in heterogeneous classes and left enrichment to the discretion of the teacher; the second had provided some honors classes for superior pupils; the third had offered a more extensive program of "honors school" for its extremely able students, and the fourth was a special school for gifted children who were admitted only on the basis of a special examination. The graduates of these varied school programs showed no significant differences in performance during the first two years of college. Abramson feels that no superiority of preparation for college can be claimed for either the special high school or the "honor class" program as contrasted with the programs that group students heterogeneously. General achievement of students, when judged by grade-point averages, is associated with level of intelligence rather than with the type of program.

Advanced placement programs that allow gifted youngsters to combine the last two years of high school with the first years of college have also been structured in recent years. There is as yet no consensus as to the effectiveness of these programs. Many administrative and supervisory problems must be worked out before the success of such programs can be adequately evaluated. Haskew (1956) described an experimental program in which 28 exceptionally able high-school students attended a special five-week seminar that pooled high-school and college facilities for advanced instruction in chemistry. Among the objectives of the program were to expedite the careers of students, to challenge and absorb them with intensive instruction in one field, to provide advanced orientation to college instruction, and to interest college faculty members in able high-school youngsters. This trial effort was to be expanded and evaluated at a later date.

The author feels that there is no conclusive evidence to indicate that any specific approach to educating the gifted is more effective than what has been done in heterogeneous classrooms. This is not to suggest that one or another of these methods cannot be effectively used, but simply to emphasize the failure to demonstrate such effectiveness through adequate research. One might almost accept the view that the intellectually gifted will generally succeed academically regardless of, or perhaps in spite of, the approach employed by any given school.

Personal Factors

Numerous personal and personality characteristics appear to be related to academic success. It has been suggested, for example, that students generally achieve at a higher level in those subjects they like than in those they dislike. Dean (1950) asked 1694 pupils, divided into sex groups and equated for chronological age and composite achievement, to express their first, second, and third choices of subjects. These choices were then compared with achievement on a standardized test battery. The results indicated a decided trend toward preference for subjects in which achievement was high, although the relationship was not sufficiently conclusive to predict success on the basis of liking or vice versa. If such a relationship does exist, it has important educational implications. Particularly, it suggests the value of helping students develop a liking for courses that will be important in their later educational careers. One of the most difficult problems confronting teachers is interesting students in a subject that will be important in their future educational plans but seems unimportant to them at the time they are enrolled in the course.

Angelino and Hall (1960) used the S-O Rorschach Test (a group form of the Rorschach) to study temperament attributes of high- and low-achieving bright students from grades seven through twelve. The results indicated that "low-achievers show a lack of tact and the presence of rigidity, two attributes not found in high-achievers." Astington (1960) hypothesized that prediction of academic performance of grammar-school candidates in England would be improved if personality qualities were considered along with achievement scores. Personality was measured by teachers' ratings for six qualities, classmates' ratings on sociability, and a questionnaire for appraising introversion-extroversion. The sample included 300 boys in five primary schools in a county borough and 700 boys in a grammar school in the same town. At all levels the academically successful boys received higher ratings than the unsuccessful boys. Grammar-school teachers' ratings of persistence, independence, and interest showed an average correlation of .60 with achievement scores, but the ratings by primary-school teachers showed low correlations. Apparently, personality assessments are more useful in predicting achievement at the grammar-school than at the primary-school level.

Resnick (1951) reported on the results of a study of the relationship between the average marks of high-school students and various measured factors of adjustment, such as school environment, socioeconomic status, emotional stability, study habits, intelligence quotients, and mental health. The correlations between high-school grades and the tests were: Symonds' Adjustment Questionnaire, .17; Bell Adjustment Inventory, −.07; Lewerenz and Steinmetz Orientation Test, .55; Thorpe Mental Health Analysis Test, .24. The correlations indicate that, for the most part, the pupils achieving higher grades also secured higher mean test scores, indicating a tendency toward more satisfactory adjustment.

Malpass (1953) used a sentence-completion test, a school picture test, and a personal document test to provide evidence regarding the eighth-grade pupils' perception of school situations. These instruments were analyzed to score the pupils' attitudes on a five-point scale ranging from positive to negative, and the scores were related to results of the Stanford Achievement Test. There was little or no correlation between the attitude score and the Stanford Achievement Tests in arithmetic and reading. There were, however, significant correlations between the perception tests and mean semester grades. These latter correlations appeared to indicate a positive relationship between the attitudes revealed in the perception of school situations and current academic success. Bene (1959) also studied attitudes toward school among middle-class and working-class grammar-school students in Britain. He supported the findings of Hollingshead that working-class children are not as much interested in reading as are middle-class children. Bene also supported the observations of Davis and Havighurst that working-class children are not as willing as middle-class children to spend the years of their youth in school in order to gain higher prestige and more social rewards as adults.

The hypothesis "that high achievers would have more predominant and extensive future time perspective than low achievers and that a positive relationship would be found between optimism and extensiveness of future time perspective" was investigated by Teehan (1958). Seventh- and eighth-grade boys, divided into a group of low-achievers and a group of high-achievers and equated for age and socioeconomic status, were used in this study. The time-perspective criteria used included: (1) ratings of twenty-five thoughts or conversations the subjects had engaged in during the past two weeks in terms of present, past, or future content; (2) a story-completion technique; and (3) writing a story in response to each of three Thematic Apperception Test cards. The TAT responses were rated on a five-point optimism scale. Results of the statistical analyses generally confirmed the hypothesis. Apparently youngsters who have a good perspective of the future can relate present studies to later needs and achieve at a higher level as a result of such perception.

Causes of Under-Achievement

Recent investigations have indicated that a fairly large percentage of students at various IQ levels can be classified as under-achievers. Two studies by the author and others (both 1962) indicated that between 20 and 25 per cent of some 700 second- through eighth-grade pupils in an urban Midwestern community were under-achieving. These youngsters had been divided into five IQ categories: 75–94; 95–104; 105–114; 115–124; and 125–up; and the same percentage of under-achievement was found in each category. The same authors are presently attempting to investigate various causes of under-achievement in this same sample. Several other investigators, using a variety of approaches, have been studying this problem.

Some of the causes of the decrease in achievement level among Dutch secondary school students have been investigated by de Graaf (1951). He felt that increased democratization of the secondary school produces emotional conflicts in a growing number of students. These conflicts include differences in the cultural level of the home and the school environment, which enhance a fear of failure and result in too much intellectual authority of the child at home. De Graaf believes present methods of formal education must be adapted to the basic issues of adolescent psychology if these conflicts are to be resolved.

A sentence-completion test was used to study the relationship between scholastic under-achievement and certain personality factors (Kimball, 1952). The subjects were 20 adolescent boys of high intelligence who were failing in their school work. Kimball found that more of these boys had negative relationships with their fathers than did the youngsters in a control group. The under-achievers' aggressive feelings were a source of guilt and anxiety more frequently than were those of the control group. The under-achievers were also less able to express these negative feelings directly. Kimball (1953) later reported on more detailed case studies of the same youngsters. She concluded that in general these under-achievers had poor father relationships, were passive and feminine, and were unable to express their negative feelings directly.

Dowd (1952) also studied under-achievers in the highest decile in scholastic aptitude as measured by the A.C.E. These poor achievers were compared to the best achievers in the same aptitude range. Personality questionnaires revealed no differences between the two groups. High-school records showed that whatever factors operated to depress achievement in college had operated similarly before the students entered college. Under-achievement was significantly more frequent among males than females. Among the factors that were the same for both groups were age at college entrance, extracurricular activities, part-time employment, concern over finances, and size of high-school graduating class.

Present-day knowledge of the causes of under-achievement is still minimal. Apparently numerous factors influence the level at which a youngster achieves, and these factors are probably related in a number of complex ways. A youngster who under-achieves will never fulfill his capabilities unless he can be helped to more effective achievement. There is a great need for research to determine why a youngster may be an under-achiever and, particularly, to determine how he can be helped.

HIGH-SCHOOL ACHIEVEMENT AND SUCCESS IN COLLEGE

Although many colleges today administer some kind of admissions examination as a major part of their admission procedures, the single best indicator of success in college seems to be the student's record of achievement in high school. There are some limitations involved in this statement, since there are qualitative and quantitative differences among high schools. Bledsoe (1954) analyzed data from the annual reports of the Georgia Accrediting Commission for the year 1952-53. Results showed that students who were members of larger graduating classes in high school tended to make significantly higher average marks during the first years of college than did students who attended small and middle-sized high schools. This is probably true because the larger graduating classes come from urban or large suburban areas where the standards for grading are higher. Many a valedictorian from a small high school finds that he is only a "C" student in the more competitive college environment, which brings together many valedictorians.

The records made in the University of Wyoming by students entering from fully accredited high schools were compared with those made by students who came from substandard schools. Ability as measured by tests was held constant, as were such factors as the type of community from which the students came and the distance of this community from the University. Students from accredited schools remained in the university longer and returned from absences more frequently than students from nonaccredited schools. There was little difference between the two groups in grades earned or college honors achieved. Entrants from nonaccredited schools had a better record in regard to probation and dismissal (Orr, 1949). Possibly the student from the nonaccredited school realizes the problems he faces and works harder to make up for his poorer academic background.

Many state universities must admit students from the lower academic ranks in high school because their state charters require them to do so. Generally the poorer students fail to survive in college and often withdraw before the end of their first year. Munger (1955) compared college students who ranked in the upper third of their high-school graduating classes with those in the lower third in an attempt to measure their "collegiate persistence." The subjects were placed in "persistence" groups according to the number of semesters for which they had enrolled and the point at which they withdrew or graduated. A significant relationship was found between first-semester grades and persistence, although aptitude scores were not significantly related to persistence. Students in the upper third of their high-school class showed significantly greater persistence than did those in the lower third.

All these studies would seem to indicate that colleges and universities are justified in trying to be more selective in their admission requirements. When large numbers of poorer students (who have to be admitted) fail and drop out, much time and effort are wasted by both the students and the faculty. The poor student may have taken a place that might have been filled by a more able student. For a university to lose as many as one-quarter of its entering freshman class is even economically unsound, since a large faculty and extensive facilities must be available even to those who will not survive.

The belief is generally held that students who attend private high schools will be more successful in college than those who attend public high schools. Davis and Frederiksen (1955) made comparisons between public-school and private-school students with respect to achievement (as measured by grades) at Princeton University. The method of analysis of covariance was employed to permit comparison of two or more groups with respect to achievement in college while holding constant the effect of ability. On the average, the public-school graduates made a higher academic average for the freshman year in relation to ability as measured by the Scholastic Aptitude Test (Verbal Section) than did the private-school graduates. The same was true for the sophomore year, when ability was measured by the average grade of the first term of the freshman year, by the College Board Aptitude Test, or by a measure based on secondary-school rank in class.

Baker *et al.* (1955) factor-analyzed fifteen high-school and university achievement variables and produced two factors. "One of these factors can be called first-semester-academic-success factor and the success-in-the-university variables are almost pure measures of this factor. The second factor seems to be concerned solely with the high school situation." These authors concluded that success within the high school seems to be almost twice as important as coming from a relatively successful high school. Vaughan (1947) had indicated that success in college did not seem to relate to the requirement of fifteen academic units set by most high schools. He suggested that success in college depends more upon general ability than it does upon a set program of high-school subjects.

These studies indicate that a number of students who are not really capable of success in college do, nonetheless, enter college. More broadly, the question to be considered is whether those who generally go to college are academically superior to those who do not. Phearman (1949) studied the school records and the returns on a questionnaire sent to graduates of 94 high schools and compared those graduates who went to college with those who did not. The frequencies of the various reasons given for not going to college were similar to those found by Bell in 1938, with the economic factor being important in both studies. As a group, those who entered college were academically superior to those who did not. College attendance was found to be related to size of family, father's occupation, and parents' education. Of those enrolled in college, 67.4 per cent of the boys and 33.1 per cent of the girls had all expenses paid by parents. A comparison of their median percentile ranks showed that the boys in college were slightly superior academically to the girls.

PROGRAMS FOR STUDENTS NOT PLANNING COLLEGE CAREERS

It was stated earlier that many high-school programs are geared primarily for those who plan to enter college. This may be justified in a high school having a large percentage of college-bound students, but it is not appropriate in one from which relatively few students will enter college. The vocational-training programs available are at best limited, and many youngsters fail to avail themselves even of these limited programs. A number of the factors involved in this kind of failure have been mentioned earlier and include overemphasis on academic subjects, rigid state requirements, and poor educational and vocational counseling. It is not our intention to discuss vocational-training and industrial-arts programs in detail, but merely to suggest the need for further development and expansion of such programs in a reality-oriented frame of reference. They would meet the needs of considerably more than half the youngsters in our present secondary-school populations, for most of whom such training is currently unavailable. Much research is needed in this area to determine the various kinds of vocational-training programs that would effectively satisfy the needs of youngsters. There is also a major need for trained teachers in this area, since even fewer colleges today are offering teacher-training programs in industrial arts.

THE ADOLESCENT LOOKS AT THE ACADEMIC PROGRAM

To get a clear picture of the youngster's view of his secondary-school experience, one must often wait until he has completed high school. He is then in a position to determine whether or not the education he received is of any real value to him either at the next level of education or in his job. While many high-school students offer criticisms of their courses, as a general overview of the entire program these are perhaps less meaningful than are those of the high-school graduate. The criticisms of certain aspects of the school situation by students in attendance may, however, be meaningful, especially as these relate to the students' failure to understand specific situations or requirements.

Required Courses

One of the major objections that high-school graduates have made to their educational program involves the rigidity of the requirements. Quite often they fail to see the need for certain required courses that seem to bear no relationship to the academic or vocational career that they plan to seek. They are also particularly concerned with the rules that prevent them from taking courses which they feel would be of value. For example, many college-bound youngsters would like to take typing in high school because they feel that this skill would be useful in college. They find, however, that in many high schools the typing courses are restricted to business students. Business students, on the other hand, may find that they cannot enroll in certain English literature courses that might interest them, because these are available only to college-preparatory students.

The most difficult problem relating to requirements of a specific program confronts the youngster who decides to change his program after the second or third year in high school. Such a change may require enough additional work to add a year or more of school to the youngster's program. The case of Ruth R. illustrates this point:

Ruth had enrolled in the business program when she entered high school because she felt she would be unable to afford to attend college and should prepare for a job. When she was in her junior year of high school, one of her uncles offered to help her go to college. Ruth immediately asked to have her program changed to the college-entrance program. When the new program was set up, Ruth found that she had to attend high school for an extra year in order to make up required courses. She did so, and later successfully went on to college. She feels that the extra year was wasted and says, "If someone had told me how difficult it was to make the change, I think I would have started in the college prep program. I could have gone to business school afterward if the opportunity to go to college hadn't arisen. What really made me mad was the counselor I had to see when I wanted to change my program. She told me that I should have taken the college prep course in the first place because with my grades I could have gotten a scholarship easily. The only benefit I got from a year and a half of the business program is that I can type."

Even the youngster who is enrolled in the proper program can often see no value in some of the required courses. For example, many high schools still require youngsters to take two years of Latin. Most adolescents view this with distaste and would prefer to take a modern language instead. Often they are told, however, that Latin is required for entrance to college, or for admission to medical school, only to learn later that this is not actually true in most colleges today. Many people learned that "all Gaul is divided in three parts," but cannot see that this is of any value in the occupations they now pursue.

Sometimes a student is not allowed to take as an elective a course that would be of great value to him in his college work because the course is restricted to youngsters who are not college-bound. Many youngsters planning careers in engineering feel, and properly so, that they would benefit greatly by a course in machine shop or auto mechanics. They usually find that these courses are available only to those in the industrial program. In all fairness, it should be pointed out that most teachers of auto-mechanics courses would welcome the presence of pre-engineering students and that they resent the restrictions as much as the youngsters themselves do.

Many youngsters attending college feel that their high-school programs gave them insufficient background for the college programs they enter. Quite often they are required to take in college courses that they could have taken in high school, had they been properly counseled. Michael J. reported his problem in this respect:

"In our college preparatory program we were required to take math up through intermediate algebra, but trigonometry, advanced algebra, and calculus were all electives, and I wasn't encouraged to take them. In college I had to take one year of math, so I took college algebra and trig. These were really high-school-level courses, and I could have taken more advanced math in college if I'd known. Advanced algebra and calculus would have been more useful to me at the college level."

Youngsters who do not attend college also are often quite critical of the programs they took in high school, indicating that these offered only minimal training for the jobs they planned to enter:

Roy C. wanted to be an automobile mechanic and was enrolled in the industrial program in high school. He had two courses specifically related to his plans—automobile maintenance and automobile mechanics—and felt that both were a waste of time. He commented, "In the auto mechanics course we got to change mufflers and tail pipes, spark plugs, and other minor parts. We never really worked on engines, although the teacher demonstrated engine work for us. I really can't blame the teacher, since most of the 'goof-offs' were put in the course. The school treated this program like it was a catch-all for all the dullards and behavior problems. As a result the few of us who really wanted to learn didn't have much chance."

Industrial-arts programs have also been criticized for the rigidity within the program that fails to allow youngsters to show more initiative. The author recently visited an industrial-arts display in which all the youngsters had made the same thing: cedar chests. When he asked one of the boys why this was so, he was told that the instructor had required it, and that he also made the students all work step by step at the same pace. A number of the boys indicated that the cedar chest was useless to them and felt that they should have been allowed to build something that interested them. They also resented having to follow the pace set by the instructor. One boy felt that he could have completed three projects in the time spent on one.

Apparently, girls are more satisfied with their non-college preparatory programs than boys are. Generally, girls can learn enough shorthand and typing at least to enable them to get jobs. The brighter girls are quite critical of the slow pace set in many of these courses, feeling that they are held back by the teacher's efforts to adjust the pace for the slower youngsters. Girls who enroll in home-making classes feel that these courses too teach only minimal skills, and that they could be greatly improved.

Tests and Grades

Many students express discontent with the kinds of tests they take and particularly with the grades they receive. High-school students are particularly critical of the various standardized tests they must take. The criticism is not directed at the tests themselves, but rather at the failure of the school to transmit the results of these tests to the student. Youngsters are also critical of the fact that they are often given standardized tests but have no knowledge of the purpose of the test or of what it is supposed to measure. Kitty C. described her reaction to her own school testing program:

"When I was a junior in high school we were told that we would take a battery of tests for two consecutive days. We weren't told what the tests were or how the results would be used. I really didn't work too hard on them, and on one particular test, the one they gave late in the afternoon, I just put down the first answer that occurred to me. A year later I asked to talk to one of the school counselors about my plans to go to college. He got the test folder and started looking through the results. He told me that my intelligence test score was rather low, and thought this was odd in view of my excellent grades.

He told me that on the basis of the IQ score I wasn't college material, but he realized from my grades that something must have gone wrong on the test. I told him how I had taken the test and he understood my point. However, he pointed out that normally that test score would go on my transcript, which would be sent to the college I wanted to attend. Only then did I realize the importance of the test, a year too late. Fortunately, he arranged for me to be retested and I really worked at the test that time. The result was forty points higher than the first test. If only I had been told the first time what the test was for, I'm sure I would have done very well."

Teacher-made tests also come in for a good deal of criticism. Bender and Davis (1949), by means of a questionnaire, surveyed student opinion regarding testing practices. The results indicated that students thought that true-false or multiple-choice tests were preferable if there had been no opportunity to study for the examination. They considered the essay type of test the one that enabled them to show their knowledge to the best advantage. These youngsters were very much interested in having advance notice of testing and in the return of test papers for correction of errors. The failure of teachers to return test papers is frequently criticized, since most youngsters do want to find out what items they missed and to learn the correct answers.

The criticism that is perhaps most frequently offered concerns the failure of tests to question youngsters' actual understanding of the questions. Most tests, they feel, require them to memorize information and simply "regurgitate" the information. They feel that even easy tests often require only a repetition of memorized facts and give no opportunity for the student to demonstrate his understanding of these facts. Although many students do prefer essay tests, they are fully aware of the subjectivity of the teacher in scoring these tests. One student put it this way: "I always hope the teacher reads a real poor test first, then the others look good by contrast. If he reads the best one first, the rest will look worse than they actually are." While this statement may not be completely accurate, there is a good deal of truth in it. A teacher is likely to use the first two or three papers he reads as a rough standard against which the others are compared.

The concern about the teacher's subjectivity is also directed toward school marks. Youngsters generally feel that the grade they receive in a course should be "objective" and based purely on their record of achievement. High-school students feel, however, that teachers are more subjective than objective in their grading practices and that they include behavior judgments in their grading. Norman J. discussed this problem with our seminar:

"I always have trouble with my grades and think my teachers are unfair. As far as classwork is concerned I'm always receiving one of the top two or three grades on my exams. Yet my report card usually lists only B's, while some of the kids who get slightly lower test marks than I do get A's. The teachers say that they give me B's to encourage me to work harder, as they know I can. They claim that if I got A's I'd start to 'goof off.' Even if this were true I don't think it's fair. Actually I think they give me B's to punish me for clowning around in class. I guess I do deserve to be reprimanded for my behavior, but lowering my grade doesn't seem to be the fair way to do it. I want to go to college and I need the A's on my record."

One might question the value of using lower-than-deserved grades as a means of motivating the student toward higher achievement. Such an approach leaves it purely up to the teacher to determine just when the youngster is working as hard as he should. A very bright youngster may be achieving better than any other students in the class, but in the teacher's judgment he still may not be working up to capacity. Using grades in this way may actually have a negative result, since the youngster may come to feel that he will never reach the standard set by the teacher and may decide to settle for the "B's."

Anderson and Steadman (1950) asked eighth-graders to give their reaction to use of a report card for reporting grades. These youngsters reported that the achievement record was useful in helping them understand their strong and weak points and in forming their educational goals. They preferred three or more reporting periods in the school year. They felt that the achievement record needed better interpretation to their parents, since the parents demonstrated frequent discontent with their youngster's achievement records. Conferences between the parent and the teacher were recommended as a good means of interpreting the report card.

Study Habits

College students are most critical of the failure of high-school teachers in helping them develop study habits that would be of value to them. They also feel that there should have been courses designed to help them study more efficiently, and particularly to read more efficiently. Those youngsters who do possess good study habits at the college level usually developed these habits on their own while in high school or junior high school.

Genevieve T. had been a straight "A" student in high school, but in her first semester in college she was able to achieve only a "C" average. She realized that, although she studied three or four hours a day, her study habits were ineffective. The college she attended offered a noncredit course in Improvement of Study, and she enrolled in this course. As a result of her success in learning better study methods, her grades went up, and she found that she could drop about one hour a day from the time devoted to study. She feels that the high school should have offered a course comparable to the one she took in college. Her conclusion was, "I guess the work in high school wasn't too challenging and I had to put forth relatively little effort to get 'A's.' "

The failure of the high school to challenge students to work as effectively as they might is a frequent criticism made by bright youngsters. If they could be made to realize that the competition will be more intense at the college level, they might be more concerned about developing their study skills and receiving higher grades. Brighter youngsters often express the view that their high-school work was too easy. This opinion has been reinforced by the opinion of foreign-exchange students who attend our American public schools. These youngsters almost always state that high-school programs are far easier here than in their native countries. After spending a year in a school in this country, some of them find it difficult to readjust to the higher level of work expected in their own schools.

Vocational-Training and Industrial-Arts Programs

Since the majority of high-school students does not plan to attend college, the criticisms of students who do not expect to continue formal education are particularly important. Many of them do feel that the general high-school program tends to favor those who are college-bound and fails to provide for the youngster who will terminate his formal education when he completes high school. Particularly, they are concerned with the barely minimal training offered by the vocational-training and industrial-arts courses in most high schools. Generally, they indicate that they must spend too much time in academic courses and have too little time available for specific training.

These youngsters are fully aware of the difficulties that will confront them when they seek employment with only the barest minimum of a salable skill. They would prefer to spend far more time actually learning to operate various kinds of machines and equipment and less time learning the "theory" of these machines. They are often quite critical of the equipment that is available to them in their high schools, much of which is antiquated war surplus, quite unlike the equipment they will be operating in a modern factory. Even within these limits, they feel that they are too restricted in the things they are allowed to do and that most of the courses are taught "by the book." Further, they recognize that many of the teachers who teach industrial arts are not highly trained and often have only "book knowledge" of the area in which they are instructing.

Generally, then, it would appear that relatively large numbers of high-school students are dissatisfied with their programs, regardless of whether they plan to continue their education beyond high school or not. Many of the problems are intensified for those youngsters who will not even complete their high-school education. These youngsters are usually fed, with no skills, into a labor market where it is extremely difficult for them to find work. The "drop-out" will be discussed in greater detail in the next chapter.

AN OVERVIEW

The author realizes that this chapter presents a rather pessimistic picture of our present-day educational structure. This is not to suggest, however, that educators are pleased with the existing situation. Today, more new ideas are being discussed than ever before, and more research is in progress. Team-teaching, programmed learning, and a variety of other "new" methods are being introduced into our schools in the hope of improving programs.

Although art, music, home economics, and similar subjects were not discussed in this chapter, there has been an increasing emphasis on improving the teaching of such subjects in the high schools. Generally, the trend seems to be in the direction of producing a well-rounded individual who will appreciate the cultural aspects of his environment even if he does not actively engage in them.

The author does feel that far more useful research must be done to help determine the most effective learning environment. Particularly, he feels that colleges and universities must greatly improve their methods of selecting and training those individuals who will become the teachers of tomorrow.

REFERENCES

ABRAMSON, DAVID A. "The Effectiveness of Grouping for Students of High Ability," *Educational Research Bulletin,* 7, 169-182, 1959.
AMERICAN ASSOCIATION OF SCHOOL ADMINISTRATORS. "The High School in a Changing World." *Thirty-sixth Yearbook.* Washington, D. C.: The American Association of School Administrators, a Department of the National Education Association, 1958.
ANDERSON, ROBERT H., and STEADMAN, EDWARD R. "Pupils' Reactions to a Reporting System." *Elementary School Journal,* 51, 136-142, 1950.

ANGELINO, HENRY, and HALL, RICHARD L. "Temperament Factors in High- and Low-Achieving High School Seniors." *Psychological Reports,* 7, 518, 1960.

ASSOCIATION FOR SUPERVISION AND CURRICULUM DEVELOPMENT. "What Shall the High Schools Teach?" *1956 Yearbook.* Washington, D. C.: The Association for Supervision and Curriculum Development, a Department of the National Education Association, 1956.

ASTINGTON, E. "Personality Assessments and Academic Performance in a Boys' Grammar School." *British Journal of Educational Psychology,* 30, 225-236, 1960.

AUKERMAN, ROBERT C., JR. "Differences in the Reading Status of Good and Poor Eleventh Grade Students." *Journal of Educational Research,* 41, 498-515, 1948.

BADLEY, TED. "The Early Guidance of Scientific Interest." *Education,* 73, 448-452, 1953.

BAKER, ELIZABETH C., BAKER, G. A., ROESSLER, E. B., and SHONTZ, H. B. "Factor Analysis of High School Scholastic Experience and Success in the First Semester at the University of California at Davis." *College and University,* 30, 351-358, 1955.

BARRETT, HARRY O. "Differences in Intelligence between Two- and Four-Year Course Pupils in a Commercial High School." *Journal of Educational Research,* 44, 143-147, 1950.

BAYLES, LEWIS A. "Freedom and Power in a Multigroup Society as Related to the Control of Education." Unpublished doctoral dissertation, Ohio State University, 1958. Abstract: Dissertation Abstracts 18, 953-54, no. 3, 1958.

BELL, H. M. *Youth Tell Their Story.* Washington, D. C.: American Council on Education, 1938.

BENDER, WILLIAM, JR., and DAVIS, ROBERT A. "What High School Students Think about Teacher-Made Examinations." *Journal of Educational Research,* 43, 58-65, 1949.

BENE, EVA. "Some Differences between Middle-Class and Working-Class Grammar School Boys in Their Attitudes toward Education." *British Journal of Sociology,* 10, 148-152, 1959.

BLAKE, WALTER S., JR. "Does Compulsory Training Help Students on Probation?" *Personnel Guidance Journal,* 33, 94-96, 1954.

BLEDSOE, JOSEPH C. "An Analysis of the Relationship of Size of High School to Marks Received by Graduates in First Year of College." *Journal of Educational Sociology,* 27, 414-418, 1954.

BROWNELL, JOHN A. "The Influence of Training in Reading in the Social Studies on the Ability to Think Critically." *California Journal of Educational Research,* 4, 28-31, 1953.

BULLOCK, HARRISON. *Helping the Non-reading Pupil in the Secondary School.* New York: Bureau of Publications, Teachers College, Columbia University, 1956.

BUSH, ROBERT N. "Clarity of Aim for the American High School." *California Journal of Secondary Education,* 33, 449-52, 1958.

CALITRI, CHARLES. "*Macbeth* and the Reluctant Reader." *English Journal*, 48, 254-61, 1959.

CARLSEN, G. ROBERT. "Literature in the Secondary School." *Review of Educational Research*, 31, no. 2, 173-178, 1961.

CARLSEN, G. ROBERT, and GRIMES, WILLIAM L. "Not Every Texan is a Cowboy." *Texas Outlook*, 43, 10-12, 1959.

CARPENTER, FREDERIC I. "The Adolescent in American Fiction." *English Journal*, 46, 313-319, 1957.

COMMAGER, HENRY STEELE. "A Historian Looks at the American High School." In Chase, Francis S., and Anderson, Harold A., eds., *The High School in a New Era*, pp. 3-19. Chicago: University of Chicago Press, 1958.

CONANT, JAMES B. *The American High School Today: A First Report to Interested Citizens.* New York: McGraw-Hill Book Co., 1959.

COOK, LUELLA B. "Criteria for selecting and evaluating reading material in literature." In Robinson, Helen M., ed., *Materials for Reading*, pp. 133-137. Supplementary Educational Monographs, no. 86. Chicago: University of Chicago Press, 1957.

COOK, STANLEY S. *A Comparative Study of Aims Held by Parents, Students, and Teachers for an English Program in a Suburban High School.* Unpublished doctoral dissertation, Wayne University, 1955.

CRUIKSHANKS, ANDREW N. *The Social Studies Curriculum in the Secondary School: 1893-1955.* Unpublished doctoral dissertation, Stanford University, 1957.

DAVIS, JUNIUS A., and FREDERIKSEN, NORMAN. "Public and Private School Graduates in College." *Journal of Teacher Education*, 6, 18-22, 1955.

DEAM, CALVIN W. *Opinions of Virginia Schoolmen Concerning the Treatment of Controversial Issues.* Unpublished doctoral dissertation, Indiana University, 1957.

DEAN, STUART E. "Relation of Children's Subject Preferences to Their Achievement." *Elementary School Journal*, 51, 89-92, 1950.

DE GRAAF, A. "Enkele hoofdoorzaken van de daling van het prestatievermogen van leerlingen op de middlebare school" (Some Major Causes of the Decrease in Achievement Level of Secondary School Students). *Psychologische Achtergronden* (Groningen), no. 15/16, 22-36, 1951.

DEODHAR, SHYAMA. *The Treatment of India in American Social Studies Textbooks: 1921-1952.* Unpublished doctoral dissertation, University of Michigan, 1954.

DOWD, ROBERT J. "Underachieving Students of High Capacity." *Journal of Higher Education*, 23, 327-330, 1952.

DREIMAN, DAVID B. "Fundamentals for Today's High Schools: A Layman's Point of View." *Educational Forum*, 22, 95-103, 1957.

EIFER, GORDON. "Grade Placement of Secondary School Pupils in Relation to Age and Ability." *California Journal of Educational Research*, 3, 31-36, 1952.

ELKIND, DAVID. "Quantity Conceptions in Junior and Senior High School Students." *Child Development*, 32, 551-560, 1961.

FONSWORTH, EMILE C. *The Use of the Reflective-Thinking Approach in the Teaching of High School Chemistry.* Unpublished doctoral dissertation, Ohio State University, 1957.

FOSHAY, ARTHUR W. "Foundations for Guidance toward Science." *Education,* 73, 431-433, 1953.

FRENCH, WILL, *et al. Behavioral Goals of General Education in High School.* New York: Russell Sage Foundation, 1957.

GARSIDE, LEONARD J. *A Comparison of the Effectiveness of Two Methods of Instruction in High School Physics as Measured by Levels of Achievement of Students of High and Low Intelligence.* Unpublished doctoral dissertation, University of Wisconsin, 1959.

GOODLAD, JOHN I. "School Scene in Review." *School Review,* 66, 391-401, 1958.

GRIFF, ERNEST R. "The Comparative Effectiveness of One-Level and Three-Level Assignments in Plane Geometry." *Mathematics Teacher,* 50, 214-16, 1957.

HADLEY, S. TREVOR. "A School Mark—Fact or Fancy?" *Educational Administration Supervision,* 40, 305-312, 1954.

HASKEW, L. D. "Advanced Study for Exceptionally Able High School Students." *Exceptional Children,* 23, 50; 89, 1956.

HAVIGHURST, ROBERT J. "The Influence of Social and Psychological Research on Secondary Education in the United States." In Bereday, George Z. F., and Lauwerys, Joseph A., eds., *The Secondary School Curriculum Yearbook of Education, 1958.* Yonkers, N. Y.: World Book Co., 1958.

HILL, THOMAS JORDAN. *Experimental Study of Selected Instructional Material in Social Class at the Secondary Level.* Unpublished doctoral dissertation, University of Florida, 1954.

HINES, VYNCE A. "Homework and Achievement in Plane Geometry." *Mathematics Teacher,* 50, 27-29, 1957.

HOFFMAN, HERBERT N. "A Study in an Aspect of Concept Formation, with Sub-Normal, Average, and Superior Adolescents." *Genetic Psychology Monographs,* 52, 191-239, 1955.

HOTYAT, F. "Les faiblesses de la pensée mathematique chez les adolescents" (Weak Points in the Mathematical Thinking of Adolescents). *Enfance* (Paris), 5, 273-300, 1952.

HOWARD, CUBIE W., JR. *A Comparative Analysis of the Objectives and Content of Biology Instruction in the Secondary Schools in Three Periods as Revealed by Representative Textbooks in the Field during Those Periods.* Unpublished doctoral dissertation, Indiana University, 1958.

HUBBARD, GEORGE W. *The Effect of Three Teaching Methods on Achievement in a Senior High School Physics Course.* Unpublished doctoral dissertation, University of Oklahoma, 1958.

ILIOFF, LOUIE B. *The Effect of Certain Teaching Practices Involving Systematic Home-School Cooperation upon the Achievement of Eighth Grade Pupils in Mathematics.* Unpublished doctoral dissertation, Pennsylvania State University, 1957.

IVIE, CLAUDE, FOWLER, EUGENIA, and GRAHAM, VIRGINIA. "Grouping in the Normal Mathematics Class." *Mathematics Teacher,* 51, 450-452, 1958.

JOHNSON, PHILIP G. "A High School Teacher's Opportunity for Guidance toward Science." *Education,* 73, 439-442, 1953.

KENNEY, RUSSEL A., and STOCKTON, JESSE D. "An Experiment Study in Teaching Percentage." *Arithmetic Teacher,* 5, 294-303, 1958.

KIMBALL, BARBARA. "The Sentence-Completion Technique in a Study of Scholastic Underachievement." *Journal of Consulting Psychology,* 16, 353-358, 1952.

KIMBALL, BARBARA. "Case Studies in Educational Failure during Adolescence." *American Journal of Orthopsychiatry,* 23, 406-415, 1953.

KNEPP, THOMAS H. "The Reading Choices of High School Biology Students" *Turtox News,* 28, 140-143, 1950.

KVARACEUS, W. C., and LANIGAN, MARY A. "Pupil Performance on the Iowa Every-Pupil Test of Basic Skills Administered at Half-Year Intervals in the Junior High School." *Educational and Psychological Measurement,* 8, 93-100, 1958.

LEE, MAURICE A. "Nature and Causes of the Difficulties of High School Pupils in Reading and Interpreting Four Kinds of Materials." *Journal of Negro Education,* 20, 499-512, 1951.

LENTLKE, HANS MARTIN. "Eine Erhebung an Hohern Schulen uber das Interesse an den Schulfachern, Insbesondere an der Biologie" (High School Students' Interests in School Subjects, Especially Biology). *Psychologische Beitraege* (Meisenheim/Glan), 2, 308-326, 1956.

LINDQUIST, E. F. "Some Criteria of an Effective High School Testing Program." *American Council of Educational Studies,* 15, Ser. 1, no. 46, 17-33, 1951.

LORGE, IRVING, and KRUGLOW, LORRAINE. "The Relationship between the Readability of Pupils' Compositions and Their Measured Intelligence." *Journal of Educational Research,* 43, 467-474, 1950.

MCCUTCHEON, GEORGE JAMES. *An Analytical Study of Achievement in Grade Eight General Science and in Grade Eight General Mathematics in Minnesota Public Schools.* Unpublished doctoral dissertation, University of Minnesota, 1957.

MALONE, WILLIAM H., and FREEL, EUGENE L. "A Preliminary Study of the Group Attitudes of Junior and Senior High School Pupils towards Mathematics." *Journal of Educational Research,* 47, 599-608, 1954.

MALPASS, LESLIE F. "Some Relationships between Students' Perceptions of School and Their Achievement." *Journal of Educational Psychology,* 44, 475-482, 1953.

MARK, STEVEN J. *Experimental Study Involving the Comparison of Two Methods of Performing Experiments in High School Chemistry.* Unpublished doctoral dissertation, Pennsylvania State University, 1958.

MOULTON, DOROTHY E. *The Teaching of Literature in the Senior High School: A Historical and Critical Study of Recent Trends Based Upon an Analysis of Selected Professional Publications, 1911-1955.* Unpublished doctoral dissertation, University of Michigan, 1959. Dissertation Abstracts, 20: 1962.

MUNGER, PAUL F., and GOECKERMAN, ROBERT W. "Collegiate Persistence of Upper- and Lower-Third High School Graduates." *Journal of Counseling Psychology,* 2, 142-145, 1955.

MUUSS, ROLF E. H. *Theories of Adolescence: An Analysis of Selected American and European Positions.* Unpublished doctoral dissertation, University of Illinois, 1957. Abstract: Dissertation Abstracts 18, 500-501; no. 2, 1958.

NATIONAL EDUCATION ASSOCIATION, RESEARCH DIVISION. "Mathematics and Science." *NEA Research Bulletin,* 36, 67-73, 1958.

NEWMAN, EARL N. *A Comparison of the Effectiveness of Three Teaching Methods in High School Biology.* Unpublished doctoral dissertation, University of Oklahoma, 1957.

O'CONNOR, THERENCE T. *The Problem-Solving Process of High School Students in Physics.* Unpublished doctoral dissertation, New York University, 1959.

ORR, HARRIET KNIGHT. "A Comparison of Records Made in College by Students from Fully Accredited High Schools with Those Having Equivalent Ability, from Second and Third Class High Schools." *Journal of Educational Research,* 42, 353-364, 1949.

PACE, C. ROBERT. "Educational Objectives: The Integration of Educational Experiences." *Fifty Seventh Yearbook, Part III, National Society for the Study of Education,* pp. 69-83. Chicago: University of Chicago Press, 1958.

PARSLEY, K. M., and POWELL, M. "Twice-a-Year Achievement Testing Lessens Guesswork." *Ohio Schools,* 38, no. 8, 15, 1960.

PARSLEY, K. M., JR., and POWELL, M. "Achievement Gains or Losses during the Academic Year and over the Summer Vacation Period: A Study of Trends in Achievement by Sex and Grade Level among Students of Average Intelligence." *Genetic Psychology Monographs,* 66, 285-342, 1962.

PHEARMAN, LEO T. "Comparisons of High School Graduates Who Go to College with Those Who Do Not." *Journal of Educational Psychology,* 40, 405-414, 1949.

POFFENBERGER, THOMAS M., and NORTON, DONALD A. "Factors in the Formation of Attitudes toward Mathematics." *Journal of Educational Research,* 52, 171-176, 1959.

PORTER, MARJORIE R., and ANDERSON, KENNETH E. "A Study of the Relationship of Specified Abilities in Chemistry to Each Other and to Intelligence." *Science Education,* 43, 12-19, 1959.

POTTER, ROBERT E. *The Role of the School in a Transitional Society.* Unpublished doctoral dissertation, University of Illinois, 1955.

POWELL, M., O'CONNOR, H. A., DEUTSCH, M., and PARSLEY, K. M. In press. "Are There Really Sex Differences in Achievement?" *Journal of Educational Research.*

POWELL, M., O'CONNOR, H. A., and PARSLEY, K. M. In press. "Further Investigation of Sex Differences in Achievement." *Journal of Educational Research.*

PRUETT, ROLLA GRANCIS. *The Achievement in Mathematics and Science of Ninth Grade Pupils in the Schools of Indiana.* Unpublished doctoral dissertation, Indiana University, 1960.

REHAGE, KENNETH J. "A Comparison of Pupil-Teacher Planning and Teacher Directed Procedures in Eighth Grade Social Studies Classes." *Journal of Educational Research,* 45, 111-115, 1951.

RESNICK, J. "A Study of Some Relationships between High School Grades and Certain Aspects of Adjustment." *Journal of Educational Research,* 44, 321-340, 1951.

RIESMAN, DAVID. *Constraint and Variety in American Education.* Lincoln: University of Nebraska Press, 1956.

ROCKEFELLER BROTHERS FUND. *The Pursuit of Excellence: Education and the Future of America. Panel Report V of the Special Studies Project.* Garden City, N. Y.: Doubleday and Co., 1958.

RUSSELL, DAVID H. "Some Research on the Impact of Reading." *English Journal,* 47, 398-413, 1958.

SKAURUD, MARVIN H. *A Survey of the Changing Trends in the Senior High School American History Curriculum during the Last Half Century.* Unpublished doctoral dissertation, University of Minnesota, 1956. Dissertation Abstracts 16: 691-92; no. 4, 1956.

SMITH, B. OTHANEL. "Basic Issues in American Secondary Education—1956." In Halverson, Paul, ed. *Frontiers of Secondary Education I,* pp. 17-30. Syracuse: Syracuse University Press, 1956.

SMITH, DORA V. "Children's Books around the World." *Elementary English,* 35, 81-92, 1958.

SMITH, LEHI TINGEN. *The Role of Maturity in Acquiring a Concept of Limit in Mathematics.* Unpublished doctoral dissertation, Stanford University, 1959.

SPAULDING, GERALDINE. "The Use of the Progressive Achievement Test at the Ninth Grade Level in Independent Schools." *Educational Research Bulletin,* No. 56, 75-77, 1951.

STENSLAND, ANNA LEE. *Current Issues in the Teaching of Poetry in Secondary School.* Unpublished doctoral dissertation, University of Wisconsin, 1958.

STOCKSTILL, KIAH, JR., FRYE, ROLAND, and STRITCH, THOMAS M. "Comparison of Differential Aptitude Test Scores for Junior High School Students." *Psychological Reports,* 5, 765-768, 1959.

STONE, DOROTHY F. *Modern High School Biology.* Science Manpower Project Monograph. New York: Bureau of Publications, Teachers College, Columbia University, 1959.

SYMONDS, PERCIVAL M. "Pupils' Evaluation and Self-Evaluation." *Teachers College Record,* 54, 138-149, 1952.

TAKAKI, TORI. *The Treatment of Japan and Peoples of Japanese Descent in Senior High School American History Textbooks.* Unpublished doctoral dissertation, University of Michigan, 1954.

TEEHAN, JOHN E. "Future Time Perspective, Optimism, and Academic Achievement." *Journal of Abnormal and Social Psychology,* 57, 379-380, 1958.

TRAXLER, ARTHUR E. "Reading Growth of Secondary-School Pupils during a Five-Year Period." *Educational Records Bulletin,* no. 54, 96-107, 1950.

TYRELL, JOHN A., JR. *A National Survey of the Opinions of Biology Teachers as to the Most Important Areas in High School Biology and an Achievement Test in These Areas.* Unpublished doctoral dissertation, Boston University, 1958.

VAUGHN, WILLIAM J. "Are Academic Subjects in High School the Most Desirable Preparation for College Entrance?" *Peabody Journal of Education,* 25, 94-99, 1947.

WOODRUFF, ASAHEL D. "Educational Research and the Curriculum." *School Review,* 66, 402-417, 1958.

WORCESTER, D. A. "A Misuse of Group Tests of Intelligence in the School." *Educational and Psychological Measurement,* 7, 779-781, 1948.

ZOLL, EDWARD JOSEPH. *The Relative Merits of Teaching Plane Geometry with Relative Amounts of Applications.* Unpublished doctoral dissertation, New York University, 1957.

CHAPTER 13

The Adolescent and the School

The academic curriculums described in the previous chapter are obviously of major importance in considering how the adolescent relates to the school. Actually, however, these are only a part of a total school environment that also includes social and emotional situations and a strong emphasis on interpersonal relations. A student's ability to function academically may be influenced by his ability to adjust to this total environment.

In building the curriculum it is therefore important to be aware of many factors that may affect the pupil. Maclean (1949) has presented and discussed three major assumptions in curriculum-building. First, he proposes that we must know whom we are teaching before we know what, when, and how to teach. Second, we must know all about the student's background (home, groups, society, and culture) before we know what, when, and how to teach. Third, he suggests that "we cannot know what, how, and when to teach until we can identify and project not only the current and probable future needs of students individually and in common, but the needs of our dynamic and emerging society to have them trained for active service in and to that society." If these are the sound bases for curriculum-building that they seem to be, far more research is needed for the development of strong curriculums.

Tyler (1950) proposed that "any tested concept of educability is dependent upon the kind of educational opportunities that are available." In this sense, schools may be evaluated according to the extent to which they achieve their goals as defined in terms of existing conditions. Tyler points out that the education of children in American schools is affected by a number of factors other than the ability of the child or the apparent efficacy of the teaching or the system. Among these factors are the emphasis on verbal media of communication, the conflict between lower-class children and middle-class teachers, and the limits in areas of experience with which schools commonly deal. Others are lack of attention to the organization of behavior in learning and the failure to take account of emotional learning.

452

The problems of education in the age of technology and mass society were discussed by Geiger (1952), who has concluded that there is "no cause to fear that the world of technology makes our children un-childlike. It is only that from the beginning they are at home in it." Loss of "humanism" he considers only a matter of definition based on an antiquated Renaissance concept. Geiger felt that youth today are closer to life than the allegedly well-bred youth of two generations ago. Generally, the viewpoint expressed by Pinto (1955) has wide support. He proposed that the secondary school should not only screen out the most capable students for more advanced studies, but that its most important role should consist in reflecting the most formative period in the personality of the adolescent.

Even the relatively rigid structure of the Soviet system assumes that the primary role of the teacher is that of guiding the student toward creative effort. According to Danilov (1950), the teacher's task in the Soviet school is to expose the learner to basic knowledge and to direct him toward a thorough assimilation of this knowledge as well as toward the skill of applying it to life situations. The teacher is, of course, also expected to guide the pupil toward formulation of a dialectic-materialistic ideology and a Communist morality. From these aims ensue the following educational principles: a Communist ideation in all the educational material; a link between theory and practice; a thoroughness of the educational process; and a balance between collec-tivization and individualization. One need not be sympathetic to the aims of such Communistic indoctrination in order to recognize an attempt to relate the educational system to the total environment, albeit a rigidly structured one.

Learning is dependent upon interaction among the students in the class, since such group membership affects motivation; upon the direc-tion of attention; and upon the activities of the student. Group ex-pectancies influence the individual's need to learn, while the group provides a proving ground for self-realization and for testing social con-cepts and conduct. The cultural adaptation of the learner is likewise influenced by the group. Thelen and Tyler (1950) feel that it is there-fore necessary to deal simultaneously with school achievement problems and group process problems.

Trow et al. (1950) also discussed the class as a group and indicated that teachers could profit greatly from an understanding of the basic sociopsychological concept of the group and the consideration of intra-group relationships offered by social psychology. These authors assert that group phenomena definitely affect the learning process. Motiva-tion is affected by goal determination, a supportive atmosphere, and the extent to which individuals in the class are accepted as participating members. The teacher may have to function in several roles and must be alert to the cues indicating the need for each role.

MENTAL HYGIENE AND THE SCHOOLS

The mental health of school youngsters has become a major consideration in the development of a positive learning envoirnment. Evidence available to date indicates that students who have difficulty in adjusting to the school are likely to be ineffective students. Their emotional problems will generally interfere negatively with their attempts to learn. School personnel are now expected to recognize early symptoms of mental and social maladjustment and to try to set up programs of prevention and/or remedy. Volz (1950) believes that this job can be best achieved "through the establishment of case work units in the school . . . the remedial school case worker is an experienced teacher with additional training in social case work." Spock (1950) surveyed mental-health efforts in the schools and the variety of approaches being developed. He recommended as most effective a combined approach involving a psychiatric team, clinical psychologists, counselors and counseling teachers, social workers, and nurses.

The common purposes of education and psychiatry were discussed by Hinsie (1950), who suggested that the psychiatrist is becoming an educator and the educator a psychiatrist. Modern schools stress methods of learning rather than methods of teaching, and the older doctrine of extrinsic motivation is becoming supplanted by that of intrinsic motivation. Hinsie described three basic structures of mind. The first is the personality framework of the individual, which is established before birth. The second consists of five phases of emotional growth. The third comprises the training and experiences of the child's emotions at the hands of the parents. Hinsie felt that there are great advantages to be gained by the close cooperation of teachers and psychiatrists.

Practices in meeting pupils' adjustment needs were surveyed through a questionnaire sent to the superintendents of schools in 110 cities with populations of between 50,000 and 300,000 (Nolan, 1948). Information was obtained regarding administrative and coordinating units concerned with the clinical services available, and the duties and qualifications of such specialists as social workers, school psychologists, and attendance workers. There was a marked tendency toward consolidation of special services in the interests of administrative efficiency. About one-half of the cities responding had some form of guidance clinic, and psychological service played an important part in most of these clinics. Social workers, school psychologists, and attendance workers were becoming increasingly concerned with the study of the child in all his relations to the community. Hertzman (1948) presented the results of a survey that demonstrated the feasibility of a quick evaluation of student personal problems on a mass basis. Students who might not be reached in any other way can and should be helped through the schools.

In classrooms that promote mental health, the pupils choose appropriate goals and have the opportunity to make progress toward these goals (Strang, 1954). The teacher helps the pupil set the limits, and teacher and pupils express approval of desirable behavior. In this setting, the group is frank in accepting differences of opinion and the teacher is sensitive to the individual pupils and their needs. Thus, the teacher is able to establish constructive, friendly relations with the pupils. Vaughan (1955) proposed that a mental-health program in the school system must be concerned with the individual emotions and physical well-being of all the children and adults making up the school community. In allocating responsibility for providing mental-health protection for school-age children, various states and communities differ in policy and practice. Vaughan discussed details of the Massachusetts program, which takes a broad view of the problem and endeavors to cope with it on a state-wide basis.

Korman (1948) presented a discussion of psychological practice on Soviet school children. He suggested that one of the basic reasons for giving students of pedagogical institutes psychological practice in the schools is to train them in the individual approach to students. The teacher must have a knowledge of child psychology, the ability to put that knowledge into practice, and the ability to understand the personality of each child. Students who are doing practice observation are advised to select for observation two children, one doing well, the other not. Korman felt that the following categories should be used in observing these children: interests; relationships of the child to his work; relationships of the child to other persons; traits of will; intellectual activity; capabilities and inclinations; attentiveness; peculiarities of feeling; and temperament.

An attempt to examine differences in psychological functioning and classroom effectiveness was reported by Jackson and Getzels (1959). They studied two groups: adolescents who were satisfied with their recent school experiences and adolescents who expressed dissatisfaction with their experiences. They administered a student opinion poll to 531 seventh- through twelfth-grade students in a private school, and identified two groups of students, one group one and one-half standard deviations above the mean score for the poll, and the other the same degree below. "Satisfied" and "dissatisfied" boys and girls were compared on the basis of IQ, achievement test scores, various personality tests and inventories, and teachers' ratings. The satisfied group did "better" than the dissatisfied group on all test variables. There were no significant differences between the two groups in either IQ or achievement. The teachers rated the satisfied boys significantly higher than the dissatisfied boys in leadership, desirability, and studiousness, but there were no significant differences in the teachers' ratings of the satisfied and dissatisfied girls. An analysis of the students' Adjective Check List indicated that dissatisfied boys "seem to project the causes of their discontent upon the world around them so that adults are seen as rejecting and lacking in understanding (extrapunitive)." The girls apparently are more intropunitive, since they are "more likely to be self-critical, turning blame for their dissatisfaction inward."

Social and Emotional Hygiene

Myklebust (1948) presented a general discussion of the stages of social development in children and suggested that public schools should consider it their duty to foster social development to the same degree as individual and scholastic development. Ivins *et al.* (1949) proposed a method whereby the curriculum of a school can be analyzed to learn whether or not the needs of the students are being met. Their conclusions emphasized that schools must give more attention in the future to making students socially competent. The content and methodology of education must therefore be changed to harmonize with present-day knowledge. Amundson (1954) reported on an experiment in group discussions and other guided interpersonal relationships in the homerooms of adolescent students. One of the most significant conclusions was that teachers who participated in the project became more observing of interpersonal relationships, leadership qualities, and isolation and rejection than they had been previously.

The Rosenzweig Picture-Frustration Study was administered to two groups of girls in grades five to eight: one group in a progressive school, the other in a traditional school. An attempt was made to control the groups for age, socioeconomic status, intelligence, and personality adjustment. Results indicated that both groups were within the normal range on the Group Conformity Rating Category for this study. However, pupils in the traditional school tended toward overconformity, while pupils in the progressive school differed significantly in the opposite direction (Mensh and Mason, 1951).

School anxiety is usually only a symptom and may have various causes, but the effect is always interference with optimal learning in school. The child without anxiety has confidence in his ability to succeed and in the continued acceptance and trust of teachers and fellow students should he fail to be perfect. Widmer (1955) feels that this suggests the means of preventing and curing school anxiety. Artificial production of anxiety by teachers or parents through threats, punishment, or excessive demands should never be used.

While the present author generally agrees that there is a need for greater emphasis on mental hygiene in the schools, he feels that a note of caution should be offered. One should not expect present-day teachers to be expert mental hygienists or therapists. Their training in these areas at best is minimal; certainly it is inadequate for any attempts at therapy. This does not mean that any teacher cannot structure a classroom environment that is conducive to good mental-hygiene practices. However, it is quite unlikely that a teacher will be able to cause any great improvement in the temperament of a seriously disturbed youngster; and he may, in fact, make the situation even more serious. The author would be pleased if all teachers were able at least to recognize symptoms of maladjustment and refer the children so identified to some qualified person or agency for further diagnosis and/or therapy. To accomplish even this end, our teacher-training institutions must help develop these skills in their students, as well as offer inservice training to those already teaching.

Identifying Problem Youngsters

The problems involved in identifying in the classroom youngsters who may be emotionally disturbed are complex and varied. There are very few measuring instruments available that a teacher can administer, score, and interpret simply. Although paper-and-pencil personality tests are available for use, there is reason to doubt their value in the classroom situation for diagnosing an individual's problems. Chency (1949) administered a questionnaire concerning school and part-school problems to more than 1500 high-school students, with results indicating that these students have important problems that have been discussed only superficially, if at all. The problems he identified on this questionnaire fell largely into the areas of selecting a vocation, training for a vocation, marriage, and getting along with people. Chency indicated that the questionnaire could be a most useful instrument for identifying the problems of high-school students.

Danielson and Rothney (1954) attempted to determine the differential value for counseling purposes of high-school students' structured and unstructured autobiographies. Two groups of juniors were asked to write autobiographies, one structured, the other unstructured. The autobiographies were read by counselors, and the problems were noted and categorized. The structured form seemed to elicit a significantly greater total number of problems and a significantly greater number of educational problems, while the unstructured form elicited a significantly greater number of family problems.

Even if special instruments are not used, there are various available sources of information on all pupils that might be used for isolating problems. Fisher (1955) suggests that a good cumulative record for each child may be a great help in solving the problem of individualizing instruction. In the cumulative record folder the teacher may find records of a youngster's developmental history and may be able to perceive many factors that seldom come to light in the classroom. However, Fisher felt that the interpretation of the data in the cumulative record is a task for trained educators. She suggested a number of ways in which teachers can be helped to contribute effectively to the development of a good cumulative record.

Teachers probably base most of their judgments of a youngster's adjustment on their observations of actual behavior in the classroom. Unfortunately, their judgments of adjustment may be based on gross overt patterns rather than on careful observation that would make them aware of less obvious problems. As has been suggested, teachers often feel that the loud "overactive" child is the one who is emotionally disturbed and are likely to consider the "nice quiet" child well adjusted. An observation of this sort relates only to the effect of a child's behavior on the class environment, rather than to the adjustment of the child himself. In actual fact, the "nice quiet" youngster may be seriously withdrawn emotionally, while the "overactive" youngster may be a generally well-adjusted individual simply responding to a momentary impulse. Present-day teachers are increasingly aware of withdrawal and its possible meaning, but still fail properly to identify withdrawn behavior.

Wandt and Ostreicher (1954) questioned the validity of sampling classroom behavior even by trained observers. Two seventh-grade classes, one of high learning ability, the other of low ability, were observed for seven forty-five-minute periods in each of six school subjects. A group of fourteen rating scales was used by each of two observers to assess the social-emotional climate of the classroom as influenced by teachers and students. The social-emotional climate varied systematically with both classes and with the three observed teachers. Even when the class group was held constant, initial observations were found to be unreliable indexes of the average climate. However, it seems likely that the classroom teacher could make observations more effectively than an outside observer could. With a little training in systematic observation, the teacher who is with his students each day for a school year could identify many potential problems.

Psychological Training of Teachers

If the teacher is expected to diagnose or identify emotional disturbance, he must be well oriented in the psychology of human development and in the psychology of learning. He must have a deep understanding of developmental psychology to help the individual child who presents a problem in the classroom. Farnsworth (1955) outlined psychiatric principles useful to the teacher, comprising the attitudes of the good teacher concerning himself and his pupils. He discussed the role of the teacher in promoting pupil maturity and other positive aspects of teacher-pupil relationships, with special stress upon love and affection, and also emphasized the teacher's concern for the emotional development of the pupil. Farmer and Rossman (1951) described experiences gained from teaching the Bullis course, "Human Relations in the Classroom," and the background and method involved in this approach. They asserted that the classroom situation provides an excellent setting for the development of sound mental-health principles. The teacher in this setting should have an appreciation of emotional problems in children, and particularly in adolescents, since individual problems may develop particular significance at this age. The successful teacher should know the problems of the adolescent and understand how to assist him in resolving them. Wenzl (1953) pointed out, however, that the high-school teacher can do justice to his job only when he uses "psychology" in evaluating the effectiveness of his teaching. Despite his psychological attitude toward the student and his needs, the teacher can be successful only if he takes into account such problems as the overload of the material to be learned and the exorbitant demand for memory. He must also be concerned with the presentation of problematic material and with various test situations.

Anderson (1950) proposed that certain aspects of the multiple task of the teacher plainly demand that he have an understanding of the learning process and be able to guide or direct the learning of his individual students. Generally, teachers should be familiar with the characteristic nature and direction of learning that is primarily motor, intellectual, or social in type. Anderson felt that study of the psychology of learning could contribute to building appropriate curriculums and to evaluation, as well as to methodology.

THE TEACHER AND THE PUPILS

The previous discussion shows that the teacher plays a major, if not the major, part in structuring the school environment as it relates to the individual student. Teachers must assume a variety of roles, including those of referee, judge, social counselor, disciplinarian, friend, etc., but the most important one often appears to be that of "foster parent." Crane (1954) discussed the way in which American teachers function as "foster parents" to their pupils. He suggested that educators must consider a child as a total personality instead of as a recipient of intensive drill in one small segment of human experience. Generally, the child spends as many of his waking hours in school as he does at home, and he is often in contact with the teacher even more than with his parents.

Teachers' Background and Behavior

Many critics of education feel that today's teachers do not understand the problems peculiar to the various socioeconomic classes and are not, therefore, equipped to deal with these problems. Murray (1951) summed up such feelings in his comment that teachers as a rule are unaware of the implications of social class in their methods and curriculums. He felt that most teachers proceed implicitly on the assumption that all students are middle-class. This works a hardship on the lower-class students, who have different learning opportunities, rewards, and punishments. Curriculum and procedural planning should meet the needs of students at all social levels.

Currently, the concern over the background of teachers has become greater because an increasing number has had only emergency training. Grant (1950) investigated the background of a group of emergency-trained teachers in Britain and attempted to elicit information regarding personal and family matters, former employment, education, attitudes toward teaching, hobbies and interests, and self-appraisal of personal qualities. The results revealed that the candidates were mature, experienced in living, and highly motivated toward teaching as a profession, although their academic backgrounds were sometimes weak. The trainees were generally persons of good character and more than average ability. The majority of those who seek to become trained as teachers in emergency training programs in this country also seem to be sincerely interested in the profession. Most of them hold bachelor's degrees in some liberal-arts or science field and have had experience in fields other than education. Academically, they appear to be good students, and they seem to make effective teachers. There is a need for more follow-up study of emergency-trained teachers and especially for comparing them to teachers trained in standard programs.

Aden (1955) urged that teachers adopt a philosophy before they teach. Yet even the best teachers will be met by obstacles, including deficiencies of pupils, noneducative and anti-educative influences, and, lastly, the socially advanced age at which most children begin school. He pointed out that the teacher can inhibit and redirect a child's reactions even if he cannot change the child's basic psychological pattern. The teacher can thus fit the child into the current pattern of culture into which he was born. Frank and Frank (1954) felt that, in classrooms and schools where children are permitted and expected to talk, play, and work freely at their own level, teachers have ample opportunity to develop codes for work and play through which children can grow strong as persons. These authors discuss the many different ways in which the teacher can indirectly influence the child. The classroom atmosphere is created by the teacher's attitudes as well as by his or her words. Since each school is bound to get its share of disturbance, the teacher must make it fairly evident that such disturbance does not mean absence of values and order in his own behavior. If he does not, the unsureness and anxiety of the orderly children will increase.

Teacher-Student Relationships

The relationship that exists between the teacher and the students is a basic factor in determining the general climate of the classroom. It is therefore important to determine the various bases for such relationships as both the teachers and the pupils perceive them. Michael et al. (1951) administered a questionnaire to eleventh- and twelfth-grade students in an attempt to measure the attitudes of these students toward the behavior or practices of teachers. The factors that contributed to classroom enjoyment were ranked as follows: (1) teacher's methods of teaching; (2) teacher's personality; (3) confidence in teacher's knowledge of subject; (4) good mark obtained in the course; (5) short assignments; and (6) no special emphasis on discipline. The girls, but not the boys, generally indicated that they would undergo strict discipline and lengthy assignments to attain a high mark. All the students indicated a preference for teachers who allow voluntary answers over those who call upon specified individuals. They also prefer those teachers who participate in extracurricular school activities to those who do not, even though the latter may be better classroom teachers. No systematic relationship was found between the students' scholastic averages and their attitudes as expressed on the questionnaire.

Kaback (1955) felt that the degree of personal satisfaction which any teacher derives from his role is closely associated with his own personal needs. Once the teacher has become aware of the nature of his own reactions to his adolescent students, he can then begin to fathom the complex relationships that develop between his own physical, emotional, social, and intellectual needs and the needs for security and adequacy in adolescents. Emotional and personal needs must also be met if good adjustment is to follow. The teacher must be aware that the social needs of adolescents include a strong need to be identified with a group.

If teachers are to be expected to evaluate the adjustment of their students, some indication of the validity of such ratings is important.

Ausubel *et al.* (1954) obtained teachers' ratings of "adjustment and aspirational traits" for a class of high-school juniors and related these to self-reports and to objective and projective measurements of these same traits. The ratings had high split-half reliabilities. Rorschach scores, teachers' ratings, and scores of the Minnesota Multiphasic Personality Inventory were not significantly intercorrelated, except for the last two with respect to girls. High level of anxiety (measured by the Illinois Personality Inventory) was associated with poor adjustment in girls but not in boys. Generally, the teachers' ratings were more meaningful and psychologically valid for girls than for boys. The validity of teachers' ratings of aspirational traits was "highly questionable." It does appear, however, that teachers' ratings of the current behavior and adjustment of pupils are relatively valid, though there is, of course, room for improvement.

A study to determine whether changes in teachers' attitudes toward pupils occur during teacher training and early teaching experience was reported by Callis (1950). He concluded that the Leeds Teacher Attitude Inventory, which was used in his study, should be further investigated as to its efficiency in predicting teacher-pupil relations. He further concluded that there are significant differences among teacher-training candidates according to their major curriculum, and that these differences are present in about the same magnitude at the beginning of professional training as at the end of it.

Hoyt (1955) tested various hypotheses regarding the effect of what teachers know about junior-high-school students on these pupils' classroom achievement and attitudes. He concluded that teachers' use of test information and other appraisal data significantly increased their knowledge of pupils' characteristics. This knowledge by itself, however, was not joined to any increase in pupil achievement. There was a definite tendency for increase of teacher knowledge of pupil characteristics to improve pupil attitudes toward teachers.

Pupils' Ratings of Teachers

There have been many reports of studies in which pupils have rated teachers on a variety of characteristics. Most of these studies have dealt with the ratings of relatively mature students. Amatora (1954) proposed that significant benefits may be realized from ratings of younger pupils, and administered the Diagnostic Teacher Rating Scale to fourth-through eighth-grade pupils to investigate this contention. She concluded that elementary-school pupils are fairly stable in their ratings of teachers and exhibit a satisfactory degree of both agreement and discrimination. Amatora suggested that elementary-school teachers might utilize this rating information as a first step toward improvement of their relations with their pupils. Witryol (1950) analyzed the "free" responses of sixth-graders and twelfth-graders to questions about what type of behavior they thought would evoke praise or blame from teachers. The ten most frequent praise categories and the ten most frequent blame categories, in parallel form, were combined in the form of paired comparisons and administered to pupils, experienced teachers, and teachers in training. The results demonstrated an extremely high degree of consistency of judgment throughout the populations studied. Students' perceptions of teachers appear to remain relatively stable from about the sixth through the twelfth grade.

Seidman and Knapp (1953) attempted to determine the students' perception of their teachers' likes and dislikes. Teachers in parochial schools were asked to state what they liked and disliked in students' behavior; individual behavior; preparation of assignments; and person state which factors in their behavior they thought teachers liked and disliked. The responses were divided into four categories: interpersonal behavior, individual behavior, preparation of assignments, and person ality. No significant differences were found between student and teacher responses in like categories relating to interpersonal and indi vidual behavior. The students thought that preparation of assignments was more important to teachers than teachers indicated it to be, and the opposite was true of personality. The only significant difference in dislike was in personality, which teachers mentioned more frequently than students did.

Gage *et al.* (1955) devised three tests of teachers' understanding of pupils, which were administered to more than 100 fourth-, fifth-, and sixth-grade teachers. Their pupils were then asked to rate the teachers on a forced-choice and on a free-choice rating scale, and these scales were correlated with the teachers' scales. One significant correlation was found—between teachers' accuracy in predicting interpupil prefer ences and pupils' judgment that their teacher "knows which pupils you like best in class" ($r = 28$). This accuracy score was also found to correlate .33 with accuracy in predicting pupils' problems and .27 with the mean socioeconomic status of the class. The authors interpreted this as "indicating some relationship between transparency of inter pupil preferences and pupils' 'social class' status."

A questionnaire based upon the Likert Techniques was administered by Amos (1952) to 150 Negro and white ninth-grade pupils and to 75 white teachers in Michigan. He was attempting to determine the ac curacy with which children could predict the attitudes of white teachers toward Negroes. White pupils were more successful in predicting the attitudes of teachers and were less ego-involved than the Negroes. The Negroes judged teachers as more prejudiced and rejecting that they actually were. However, when socioeconomic status was held constant by matching a white and Negro factory group, the differences obtained were more related to social class than to race, and it was concluded that no significant differences existed.

Teachers' Characteristics That Students Like

A number of attempts have been made to determine what characteristics students like most in their teachers. One study of this type on a very large scale was done by Witty (1947) based on data secured from a popular radio program (Quiz Kids). Witty had suggested that the program award a scholarship to the teacher most effectively and convincingly described in a pupil's composition entitled "The Teacher Who Has Helped Me Most." Some 12,000 youngsters from grades two through twelve responded. The responses were divided into three age groups (up to nine, nine to fourteen, and fourteen and up). A preliminary analysis revealed that twelve traits occurred frequently. "Cooperative, democratic attitude" ranked highest for the youngest group and was not lower than second in any age group. Kindliness, consideration for the individual, patience, and wide interests also ranked high.

Serebrinsky (1946) asked boys and girls twelve to fifteen years old and boys and girls sixteen and older to respond to a check list of eighteen traits of teachers. They were asked to indicate the three traits that they considered indispensable to a good teacher. The five leading traits, in order of frequency, were: justice-fairness, culture, friendliness, comprehensibility, and activity. The order of preferential responses was considered to be independent of age or sex. The same subjects checked four traits from two lists of twenty that they considered to be descriptive of the desirable student. The leading traits indicated were studiousness, obedience, teachableness, intelligence, and activity. Leeds (1954) reported the reactions of about 1000 fourth-, fifth-, and sixth-grade pupils to ascertain aspects of teacher behavior. Some 200 teachers were rated by their students on a fifty-item questionnaire designed by Leeds. The findings indicated that affective, personal, and human factors provided the basis for differentiating teachers well liked by pupils from those greatly disliked. To be appreciated and liked, the teacher must exhibit behavior stemming from a personality basically well adjusted and characterized by a sincere liking for children, a kind and pleasant disposition, and a balanced outlook of life.

It is truly difficult to picture the ideal characteristics for success in teaching. The various youngsters in a class all respond to a teacher in their own ways and as a result of their own backgrounds. A teacher may, therefore, be "loved" by some members of a class and be "hated" by other members of the same class. In one school a teacher may be considered too "strict," while the same teacher when transferred to a different school may be considered "lenient." Youngsters obviously may be influenced by home factors, peer reactions, and even gossip in responding to a particular teacher. The size of the class may also be a major factor. A teacher may be well liked by a class of twenty students with whom she can interact freely but be unable to interact and communicate effectively with a class of forty.

There are some attempts being made currently to determine the ideal characteristics of teachers and to develop instruments that will identify those possessing these characteristics. Should they succeed, we will have, in essence, standardized teachers. The author hopes this will never occur, since he feels that contact with a variety of different types of teachers is important to youngsters. If the students can adjust to different teacher personalities and continue to function effectively, they will learn valuable patterns of behavior that will be useful to them in adult life, in which they will be required to interact with all types of people.

Do Teachers Cause Maladjustment?

Snyder (1947) reviewed scientific studies in an attempt to discover the extent of maladjustment among teachers and its effects on pupils. Although there is no more maladjustment among teachers than there is in the general population, Snyder felt that its existence in teachers was more important because they affect the adjustment of others. Teachers' maladjustments are caused by job-associated frustrations and personal emotional problems. Children dislike teachers who demonstrate personal emotional maladjustment. Adjusted teachers, Snyder indicated, have an important influence on the adjustment of the child. Gladstone (1948) took issue with Snyder on the preceding statement, which suggests its converse—that maladjusted teachers cause maladjustment in their pupils. He found this to be untrue with a large percentage of maladjusted teachers. Sometimes persons who have experienced maladjustment can better sympathize "or realize the effects of irritating or therapeutic measures." Gladstone urges that we "beware of paper and pencil tests of adjustment" in drawing conclusions about these interrelationships.

The present author feels that a maladjusted teacher may increase difficulties experienced by a child already emotionally disturbed. He doubts, however, that a maladjusted teacher does much damage to those youngsters who are basically well adjusted. Fortunately, most youngsters adapt to the personality of whatever teacher they have at a given time. For example, if youngsters have a maladjusted teacher in the eighth grade, they may appear to show maladjusted behavior in that teacher's classroom; but if the same youngsters have a well-adjusted ninth-grade teacher, they adapt to that teacher also and seem well adjusted. The disturbed youngster often fails to adapt to different teachers and may be influenced negatively by either maladjusted or well-adjusted teachers, or by both.

Parent-Teacher Relationships

About two decades ago, relatively few parents had much interaction with teachers, but today the picture is changed. Large numbers of parents are as well educated as or better educated than teachers and no longer stand in awe of them. Consequently, teachers can no longer always count on parental support for the way they handle and teach youngsters. Lay groups have been formed all over the country that attempt, if not to control, at least to have a strong voice in school policies. As a result, many teachers feel that they are being undermined by parents who freely criticize the schools in the presence of their youngsters. A good many misunderstandings have arisen, in which parents have tried, often successfully, to have a teacher's decision overruled, and a good deal of tension exists as a result of such situations. Kaplan (1950) discussed findings based on more than 500 individual parent-teacher conferences supplementing report cards in the elementary schools. He found tensions detrimental to parent-teacher relationships centering in three areas. Parents frequently misunderstand or fail to agree with the school program. Both parents and teachers tend to protect vested interests. Finally, parents who reject, overprotect, or misunderstand their children, and teachers who do not know how to deal with children, endanger good parent-teacher relationships.

Discipline in the School

A thorough perusal of the available research literature on school discipline reveals that little scientific investigation has been done in this area. A number of the studies that have been made are concerned with juvenile delinquents or are in the field of learning theory. Strang (1938) stated that "from 1885 to 1937 . . . there were few references to objective studies in the published articles on discipline." Since that time there has been a number of articles in popular magazines, but relatively few in professional or research journals. Douglas (1945), Krantz (1935), and Owens (1929) wrote on the administrative procedures related to discipline in the public schools, but showed little concern for the effect of discipline on the adjustment of the disciplined pupil. Most of the investigators had indicated that far more boys than girls are considered behavior problems and thus are more often disciplined in school. Eaton (1956) stated, "The data clearly revealed not only that there was more problem behavior among boys, but also that there were more boys involved in almost all types of behavior problems."

A few studies have attempted to determine whether differences exist between children who need discipline and those who do not (Hales, 1940; Tallent, 1956). Generally, these investigators have found that youngsters needing discipline show lower average IQ's than those who do not. Tucker (1938), in reporting personality differences based on standardized test results, stated, "In general, the personality traits of the troublesome child are less desirable than those of the average child of his age." There also seems to be some evidence indicating that more children with behavior problems come from low socioeconomic backgrounds than come from high ones, although these findings are generally inconclusive.

Principals' ratings of the disciplinary effectiveness of 82 secondary-school teachers were related to observational data on 38 practices in the teachers' classroom procedures. The results of correlational analyses tended to support the conclusions that enriching a lesson by the use of visual aids, routinizing various classroom procedures in a mechanical way, and "enthusiastic" teaching are all closely related to effective discipline (Celler, 1951).

Radina (1950) has analyzed the motives of children's violations of discipline during lessons in the Soviet educational system. He proposed that out of the humanitarian principle of respect for the learner as well as out of the stringent demands made upon him stems the most vital need of education—the individual approach toward each student. Such an approach is possible only if the teacher understands the motives underlying the student's behavior. This entails the fullest recognition of the fact that the child's violation of discipline is not related to external stimuli but to his inner experiences. The teacher must have thorough insight into the personality characteristics of each child and must institute corrective measures in the light of these characteristics. Reproof and punishment are ineffectual, according to Radina.

Powell and Bergem (1962) compared tenth-, eleventh-, and twelfth-grade "conforming" and "nonconforming" boys (matched for IQ) in order to determine how the two groups differed. "Nonconformers" were youngsters who were sent to the administrative offices for discipline three or more times during the academic year. Generally, the nonconformers tended to show poor social adjustment (on the California Test of Personality) and were more impulsive (on the Thurstone

Temperament Schedule) than the conforming boys. The reading scores of the nonconformers (on the California Reading Achievement Test) were also poorer, as were their academic grades. The problem young-sters were also more often absent or tardy than were the nonproblem group. The conforming boys generally came from higher socioeconomic homes, had better-educated parents, and attended church more fre-quently than the nonconformers. The nonconforming youngsters held part-time jobs, owned their own cars, smoked, and stayed around "hang-outs" far more often than the youngsters in the conforming group.

Ten suggestions to teachers for helping pupils develop responsibility for self-discipline were offered by Rockwell (1950). These were: allow-ing the youngsters to arrange the classroom; planning each day's activ-ities with the pupils; reviewing the day's activities with the class; planning a program to meet pupils' needs; permitting the pupils to evaluate themselves; helping youngsters set their standards high enough; providing for the acceptance of each child; making the class-room a learning laboratory; giving personality to the classroom; and realizing the effect of the teacher's personality on the class.

Many secondary schools do attempt to give students some part in establishing disciplinary procedures. Some schools have student courts that determine the discipline to be administered to violators of the school's behavior codes. Such student courts must, however, be under the direction of a responsible teacher. If not, they tend to be far harsher in the administration of discipline than either teachers or administrators are. Students do seem to respond well to discipline administered by their peer group, and in this sense student courts can be most effective. Apparently student-school interaction in developing codes of behavior is more effective than simply having the school author-ities develop these codes.

One must constantly be aware that most youngsters who are con-sistent discipline problems are probably rather maladjusted. Mere administration of punishment, including such a severe measure as expulsion, is not likely to solve these youngsters' problems. Consistent misbehavior should be looked upon as an indicator of emotional dis-turbance, and the youngster referred for diagnosis and/or treatment. One must also be able to differentiate between those youngsters who are consistently in difficulty and those who may occasionally create "spur-of-the-moment" disturbances. A very bright youngster may sometimes be considered a behavior problem, but he may not be emo-tionally disturbed. His disruption of the classroom is likely to result from his having completed his work sooner than the rest of the students and having nothing to keep him occupied. If the teacher offers this

type of youngster some interesting extra activity, his apparent misbehavior often ceases.

THE DROP-OUT

Although the problem of the youngster who leaves school before he has
completed his education is not a new one, it is one of the most serious
that today's educator faces. The problem is perhaps more serious today
than it was previously, because today employment for those who leave
school early is relatively unavailable. The youngster who leaves school
early usually has no salable skills and is suited only for unskilled labor
jobs, which are extremely scarce. Even the armed forces show no
enthusiasm about accepting the enlistment of such youngsters and in
fact often recommend that they return to school and complete their
education before enlisting. Industrial training programs usually accept
only those who have completed high school, and the trade schools
generally admit only those who have successfully completed the ninth
grade.

Although laymen generally think that only the intellectually dull
youngsters drop out of school, because of their inability to perform
academically, the evidence does not support this view. Fairly substantial numbers of youngsters of average or above-average intelligence, as
well as a number of intellectually gifted youngsters, leave school before
graduation. Regardless of ability level, the youngster who leaves
school early is generally at a major disadvantage and seldom has an
opportunity to work up to the level of his potential.

Reasons for Dropping Out of School

A great many investigators have attempted to determine the factors
that may relate to a youngster's decision to leave school. Gragg (1949)
surveyed two school systems and concluded that school retardation,
male sex, low verbal intelligence, lack of participation in extra-class
activities, and broken homes were factors that were clearly evident
with school drop-outs as opposed to those who graduate. Thomas
(1954) found the activity factor to be most closely related to whether or
not a student finishes high school. He reported that the correlation between grades and number of activities is almost as high as that between
IQ and grades. Arnholter (1956) studied two groups of students who
had started high school together and were matched by age, sex, and
IQ, one group having dropped out of school, and the other group
having graduated. The two groups were compared in performance on
the California Mental Health Analyses and the Rotter Incomplete
Sentence Blank. There was fairly conclusive evidence that drop-outs

show less well-adjusted personalities as measured by these instruments. Penty (1956) found that the drop-out rate was 14.5 per cent among good readers and 50 per cent among poor readers. The peak of drop-outs occurred at the tenth grade. Penty made an intensive study to compare poor readers who drop out and poor readers who continue to graduation. In each group there was a marked disparity between reading age and mental age. Other factors, such as emotional adjustment, home security, and enjoyment of extracurricular activities, served to encourage pupils to remain in school even though they had reading difficulties. Hecker (1953) investigated the reasons why youngsters in Kentucky left school and listed the following: (1) frequent grade failure, particularly in the first grade; (2) regression in scholarship of the school-leavers as they progressed through the grades; (3) failure or lack of opportunity to participate in extracurricular activities; (4) the feeling that the school did not provide a program for work experience. The youngsters felt, after having left secondary school, that such subjects as business, shop experience, and home economics were the most needed or desired.

No single source of data alone is sufficiently reliable to determine the factors that influence leaving school. Pregnancy and employment were, however, persistent and potent causes of leaving the secondary schools of Maryland (Moore, 1954). Although there was evidence of a definite relationship between certain factors in the school and dropping out, Moore believed that the school can help only indirectly in abolishing the persistent reasons for students' dropping out of school.

Over-all, it would appear that drop-outs tend to be less intelligent, less able academically, less well adjusted, less active, and from a poorer environment than the individuals who complete their education. To most of the drop-outs, the schools seem to offer little or no opportunity to satisfy their felt needs. Although many of them regret it later, dropping out seems at the time to be the best thing to do.

Although it is not directly related to school problems, a study by Wattenberg (1948) concerning delinquent behavior during the summer months should be mentioned here. He compared delinquency rates during the school year with delinquency rates during the summer when school is not in session and reported two contrasting patterns. For some children, school seems to give rise to conditions that increase chances for getting into trouble, and certain school situations encourage the development of feelings that result in destructive aggression. Most children, however, are prevented by the school from forming definite patterns of delinquency. Without school organization, some children find undirected leisure a frustrating experience that expresses itself in delinquent acts. Apparently, then, for most youngsters the school and its discipline provide a cohesive force that keeps them functioning in socially acceptable patterns of behavior.

Helping the Drop-Out

It is quite difficult to determine just what is being done to help the drop-out, either to encourage him to remain in school or to assist him after he has dropped out. Research in this area is complicated by unfortunate actions by school authorities, some of which are conducted unofficially. For example, some youngsters are apparently encouraged, or at least not discouraged, in dropping out when they feel that the school does not really have anything to offer them. Further, if a drop-out wishes to return to school at a later date, he is usually accepted without enthusiasm, and no special effort is made to structure a program that will be of use to him. School authorities will probably officially deny that such practices occur, but the author has had a substantial number of experiences with youngsters who have been "victims" of circumstances of this kind.

Wetzel (1955) reviewed the research over the last two decades and found that, even with the increased length of attendance, each year only 60 per cent of the seventeen-year-old population of our country graduates. He discussed what is being done and what might be done to assist young people to complete their education. Adult-education programs are discussed, including the type of training they could offer that might be of value to the youngster who leaves school early and later wishes to add to his education. Generally, it appears that psychological problems are closely involved in a youngster's decision to complete or not to complete his education. The cost of such education in relation to the monetary returns it would offer also appears to be a major point in helping the youngster make his decision.

An attempt was made by Hastings High School to work on the dropout problem. With the presence of four or more of ten characteristics indicative of the prospective drop-out as a guide, a total of about 300 prospective drop-outs was identified. A counselor attempted to establish a close personal relationship with each of these. About 113 dropped out of school, 43 graduated, and 125 were still in school at the time that the results were published. Jaques (1956) felt that the personal counseling had helped to retain many of them. One cannot be certain, however, that those who continued might not have done so even without the counseling.

Crocker and Powell (1961) described an attempt to identify prospective school-leavers in junior high school and the efforts of the school and a community guidance organization to help these youngsters remain in school. In general, this attempt was a failure, with all but one or two of the youngsters leaving school early. The authors concluded that too little assistance was offered and that it came too late. They strongly recommended that efforts be made to identify potential school-leavers earlier in their educational careers in order to help them solve the problems that may cause them to leave school.

Fox and Parrotte (1947) described the night-school program in an institutional environment. There were only two requirements for attendance: the inmates must have the desire to attend school regularly and they must be willing to work. These youngsters were all over sixteen years of age, but there was no age limit or specified IQ, both of which the day school required. Fox and Parrotte maintained that attendance at night school as well as attendance at day school facilitates rehabilitation of the retarded individual.

In general, one must conclude that relatively little has been done to assist the school-leaver effectively. There is an increasing stress on attempts to identify those who may leave and to offer them proper guidance. Such guidance is aimed primarily at encouraging them to remain in school and is of little value to those who drop out anyway. Some provision must be made to give better preparation for employment to those who will actually drop out. This would necessitate the development of special vocational-training programs in which such youngsters could learn salable skills. Adult-education courses must be expanded to give those who dropped out without such skills the opportunity to gain them outside of the regular school environment. Most important, perhaps, would be the need to develop better methods of identifying potential drop-outs early enough that they may be referred for early treatment of their problems.

EDUCATIONAL GUIDANCE

In Chapter 11, attention was directed to vocational counseling and guidance in the schools. Counselors are, however, usually designated as educational and/or vocational, and as much of their effort should be directed toward the educational aspects as to the vocational, although obviously the two are interrelated. Hand (1955) pointed out that the problem of responsibility in guidance has not been satisfactorily resolved in many schools. Guidance is regarded as a separate function, supplementary to the instructional program. Hand attempts to show that instruction is really inseparable from guidance, the reason that separation of instruction from guidance continues to exist, and the role of specialized personnel.

Elementary-School Guidance

There is currently an increasing emphasis on the development of guidance and counseling programs at the elementary-school level. There is still some disagreement as to what kind of personnel should be involved in these programs, but generally it is agreed that the classroom teacher would play the major role. Kawin (1955) felt that it was logical for the school to engage in a conscious effort at guidance as early as possible in the life of the child, starting with his entrance into school at kindergarten or first grade. Just as every teacher is constantly guiding children, so every good school has guidance constantly going on, whether or not the program is labeled as such. The good teacher must observe and study each child in order to understand him as he is, a unique individual.

At the present time, most of the guidance in the elementary school is handled by the classroom teacher, with occasional assistance from the school principal. Relatively few elementary schools have full-time guidance counselors assigned to them, although a school system may have such a person available as a consultant to serve all the schools in the system. This kind of consulting service does seem to be increasing appreciably, although it is difficult to find many counselors who are trained to function at this level. College teacher-training programs are increasing their emphasis on training classroom teachers to be more effective as counselors, rather than concentrating on the training of specialized personnel.

Secondary-School Guidance

Griffiths and Scott (1955) proposed that the high-school counselor is in a key position in the life of the school and that a cooperative counselor-teacher relationship is essential. The teacher has numerous opportunities to observe pupil behavior, and both the teacher and the counselor should study and interpret these observations and jointly plan a course of action. In this kind of interaction, occasions for formal counseling and in-service education will be recognized.

Wimmer (1948) reported a survey made of guidance procedures and practices at the secondary level. She analyzed the data in terms of the percentage of 447 schools "using certain methods to treat specific topics and to provide specific services to educational, vocational, and personal adjustment." The results of the study indicated that the counselor plan is the most generally used and that the guidance activities are most frequently carried on by home-room teachers and counselors. The schools were generally concerned with all the problems of their students. Guidance materials were most frequently made available through the counselor or the library.

A wise guidance program for college preparation begins early in the child's educational experience with evaluation of the individual and encouragement toward his maximum development. Traxler (1951) mentions the following areas of guidance: (1) appraisal of general scholastic aptitude; (2) the discovery of broad abilities and interests; (3) identification of weaknesses in fundamental skills that may interfere with educational success; (4) guidance in the selection of secondary-school subjects that will best provide a broad foundation for college and for life; (5) guidance in the development of personal qualities and improving adjustment; and (6) counseling of students. These six areas should be equally applicable to all students whether they are college-bound or not. We suggest that one need only change Traxler's fourth point to read "guidance in the selection of secondary-school subjects that will best provide a *sound* foundation for work and for life."

Various approaches toward counseling students for scholastic adjustment were discussed by Stromswold and Wrenn (1948). They defined scholastic adjustment in terms of the over-all personal adjustment of the student rather than in the narrow terms of satisfactory school achievement. To aid the counselor, they describe five categories of causes of maladjustment. These are: (1) misclassification resulting from discrepancies between the student's abilities and his educational or vocational aspirations; (2) inadequate educational background; (3) inadequate study habits and skills; (4) inadequate use of time; and (5) nonacademic problems such as personality disturbances, financial difficulties, etc. These authors briefly describe the technique and direction of the counseling process appropriate to each of these categories.

Walker (1955) attempted to determine the accuracy of counselors' judgments in predicting the occupational and educational performance of former high-school students. Data concerning 60 male students were given to 25 counselors five and six years after the students had left high school. The counselors were asked to estimate the occupational and educational performance of these students after leaving school, and these estimates were compared with the students' actual performance. Educational performance was predicted more accurately than job performance. Predictions of both school and job performance were more accurate for bright students than for dull ones. The school performance of dull students was underestimated, but there was no consistent direction of error in the predictions of job performance for these students.

Cantoni (1955) reported the long-term effects of a guidance experiment conducted in the Flint, Michigan, public schools during the years 1939–1943. A follow-up completed in 1953 demonstrated that, as compared with a control group, the experimental group of high-school graduates had made important gains in emotional adjustment, educational level reached, cultural status, and occupational status. Apparently these gains stem from the high-school program of guidance and counseling. This is unfortunately one of the few instances in which an experimental study has been structured and an effective follow-up carried out. There is a major need for more research of this kind if we are to determine the most effective means of guiding students to optimal over-all adjustment.

Qualifications of Counselors

An attempt was made to construct and validate a test designed to measure the professional knowledge of secondary-school counselors (Schuyler, 1948). Schuyler felt that such counselors need more extensive training in the principles of psychology and mental hygiene, a better understanding of the various techniques of counseling, and more training in the use and principles of statistics. While she acknowledged that professional knowledge is only one characteristic of the ability to counsel, she felt that it could be measured and that it is related to success and competence in counseling. Today, some fourteen years later, counselors still appear to be poorly trained in the use and principles of statistics, although their training in measurement has been considerably improved.

Guidance in Relation to the Community

Seymour (1955) commented on two reasons that the school administrator needs competent guidance services. First, the pupils need counsel in making choices that draw from them their highest potential; second, the school needs help in determining the best possible organization and program. It is essential that the ingredients of a good guidance program achieve these major objectives. Each administrator must consider the guidance program in relation to the particular problems of his school and of the total community. The latter aspect is most important, since a particular school must train its youngsters for effective participation in the community in which they live. The community's geographic location, its character—agricultural, industrial, or residential—and even its political structure may be important factors in determining the guidance program of its schools.

Youngsters must be familiarized with community resources as part of their school program. Sobel (1949) described a project carried on by eighth-graders in a large city school of mixed racial and ethnic composition and varying socioeconomic status. Work committees wrote radio and motion-picture scripts, made scrapbooks, and wrote essays concerning various facilities, types of neighborhoods, etc. A series of lectures by a policeman, a school nurse, a social worker, the school guidance counselor, and others gave additional information. Sobel felt that the project contributed to the students' understanding of the community and its function. Such a program might also help youngsters understand the economic problems of their community and guide them in selecting occupations that are needed in the community.

Finally, there is a definite need for increased interaction between parents and counselors. Too often the parents are able to gain only second-hand knowledge of a counselor's discussions with their children. Counselors should always be available to parents who wish to discuss their youngsters. They should, in fact, invite parents to come in for conferences, not just in those cases where some difficulty has arisen, but in all cases. Parents would probably support guidance programs far more actively than they do at present if they were made a part of the program. Such interaction would also help parents and counselors agree on a common direction in which both could guide the youngster, thus avoiding some of the contradictions that presently exist. Parents are, after all, part of the over-all community whose needs the school is attempting to meet and satisfy.

NON-CLASS ACTIVITIES

In any discussion of the adolescent and the school, some mention should be made of organized learning experiences held under the auspices of the school but generally not as an integral part of the formal academic curriculum. Faunce (1954) has defined non-class activities as "the less formal phases of the school program, usually offered either during an activity or homeroom period or outside class hours, and generally not credited in terms of the usual Carnegie units." There is a good deal of confusion about what constitutes non-class activities, but they apparently include such projects as helping interpret the school program to the public, providing enrichment for the gifted, and offering vocational opportunities outside the school day. Although some of these activities seem to duplicate the formal curriculum, they do appear, nevertheless, to make a distinct contribution to adolescents' education. They offer learning experiences that are distinguished from the formal curriculum by their flexibility and adaptability to students' interests and needs (Brown, 1956; Brown, 1957; Hunt, 1956).

Most educators strongly approve of encouraging students to participate in non-class activities, since they believe that there is a relationship between failure to participate and dropping out of school (Livingston, 1958). There is some concern lest so much time be spent in non-class activities that attention to the formal curriculum will suffer. However, McCaslin (1958) found that the majority of actively participating students who were absent from class more frequently in order to attend non-class activities received higher grades, had higher achievement ratings, and were less often absent from school than those who participated in few non-class activities. Generally, it seems inadvisable to regulate the number of activities in which a student may participate. Hughes and McAllister (1956) recommend that the school's guidance facilities should be used to help those students who do overparticipate make wiser choices.

Too often participation in non-class activities may become related to social status. Gordon (1957) found this to be true in the high-school social system that he studied. He indicated that students of low status are often excluded from participation. This study emphasizes the complexity of the relationship of non-class activities to the total school program. More information must be gathered concerning the fundamental factors influencing participation.

If non-class activities are to be successful, the school faculty must be strongly involved and genuinely interested. Ryan *et al.* (1956) have indicated that such whole-hearted support is seldom found. Teachers often resent being assigned as advisers for non-class activities unless they receive extra pay or a reduced work load. Court opinions have established the authority of school boards to make such assignments as long as they are made on a reasonable and nondiscriminatory basis (Garber, 1955; Unruh and Beck, 1955). However, enforced assignments are not likely to lead to successful activities, and extra pay for extra work seems to be a far more effective approach (*Nation's Schools,* 1956).

There do appear to be some promising trends in the programs of non-class activities, including a conscious effort to relate the objectives of non-class activities to the general objectives of education (Rennicke and Hearn, 1955). There are also efforts to link non-class activities to projects sponsored by local community and civic clubs, with the objective of better community understanding of these activities (Gerich *et al.,* 1955). Generally, a program of non-class activities seems essential to complement the formal curriculum. Additional research is needed in all areas of extracurricular activities to strengthen the present programs and to provide better means of coordinating non-class activities with other educational programs provided by the schools.

ADOLESCENTS LOOK AT THEIR SCHOOL EXPERIENCES

Appraisal of Teachers

Teen-agers are quite willing to discuss their teachers with members of their peer group and with adults who are not directly part of the school. Most youngsters tend to like most of their teachers, but they can almost always identify the teacher they dislike and can clearly state the reasons. They are prompt to admit, however, that their individual liking or disliking of teachers is not always a reflection of the whole class's reaction to the same teacher. One youngster may violently dislike a teacher, but essentially because of the teacher's personality. Basically, youngsters like a teacher who is competent in his field, maintains discipline fairly, and is an interesting person. They prefer teachers who allow class discussion and who will let the students express their own opinions even if the teacher does not agree with those opinions. Usually, they like any teacher who shows a real interest in adolescents and who is willing to help them explore their problems. Perhaps one of the most popular characteristics in a teacher is a sense of humor. However, they do not like the "comedian" who is always joking, often at the expense of the class. Sarcasm is particularly disliked, although most youngsters do seem to enjoy an occasional display of cynicism by the teacher. The teacher's sense of humor need not be particularly apparent in the classroom if the youngsters have had the opportunity to see it expressed in out-of-class activities.

Most teen-agers are quick to identify the teachers with whom they can communicate easily and those with whom they cannot. They particularly dislike teachers who allow no student response in class and do not wish to discuss problems with teen-agers outside the class. Youngsters prefer teachers who will either respond to a question with a direct answer or help the student find the answer. They do not approve of those who treat their questions as though they were silly or insist that the student is responsible for finding his own answers and make no attempt to guide or help him. The teacher's ability to communicate is most important in his attempts to transmit knowledge of the subject he teaches to the students. Youngsters are particularly critical of those teachers who fail to do this. They feel that, even though the teacher knows the subject, his failure to communicate his knowledge penalizes them. They do not always blame the teacher for this failure but instead sometimes blame the method he employs, which they often feel is imposed on the teacher by the school system.

Lynn R. had a teacher in a foreign-language course who did not seem able to communicate with the class. She indicated that she was getting very little from the course despite her desire to learn the language. Lynn felt that the teacher knew his material but suggested that the method he used to present it was ineffective. She felt that there should have been more opportunity for the students to ask questions about certain meanings and certain grammatical considerations. Lynn stated that most of the students liked this teacher and felt that he was capable of doing a far better job. The youngsters in his class actually were sorry for the teacher, who, they assumed, was forced to follow a teaching method, prescribed by the school, with which he did not feel comfortable. In this case, they condemned the school rather than the teacher.

Although most students dislike a teacher who is a harsh disciplinarian, they do like teachers who are consistent in their behavior. They prefer that the teacher let them know relatively early in the term just what he expects from them. They wish to know what he expects of them academically and are particularly interested in finding out what kind of homework he plans to assign. They want some of this information spelled out in detail so that no misunderstanding will arise later as a result of their having been uninformed. For example, if an English teacher assigns themes or term papers, the students want to know which topics are acceptable and which are unacceptable. The students would like the teacher to define clearly the style he prefers them to follow and the outline procedure he expects them to use. If they know generally what a teacher wants and that he means what he says, they will usually be well behaved in his classes. If they find that a teacher is inconsistent, they will be constantly testing the limits to see how much they can get away with. If, for example, a teacher assigns homework but fails to collect the papers regularly, many students will not bother with the assignments. If the teacher "cracks down" on them they will turn in their work, but once he "eases up" again their work ceases.

Adolescents expect teachers to be fair in their treatment of all the youngsters in a class and do not like teachers who show favoritism or rejection to certain students. Adolescents are quick to criticize a teacher for being too harsh with less capable youngsters or for having "teacher's pets" among the brighter youngsters. Teachers who are objective in their handling of the students are more readily accepted by students than are those whose subjective judgments are obvious. Although the students may laugh if a teacher makes a joke at their expense, they do not like this kind of behavior and much prefer to be "laughed with" rather than "laughed at."

Most youngsters are aware of the problems a teacher faces when the class is heterogeneously structured. They realize that the teacher has to communicate with youngsters with low ability, average ability, and high ability, all in the same room. However, they generally expect the teacher to cope with this problem effectively and are disappointed if he does not. Roger G. discussed this kind of situation with our seminar.

"Our social-studies teacher is a nice guy but he isn't too good a teacher because he doesn't get through to half the kids. I know our class has kids of different ability levels but I think he should be able to help all of them. Actually I think that only about half of the kids really understand him. The slower kids keep falling farther behind, and the bright kids can't go ahead as fast as they'd like to. It seems to me that he could sort of group us like we used to be grouped in elementary school, and work with each group at its own ability level. By trying to work with the whole class, I think he penalizes both the smarter and the slower kids. I know our school doesn't go in for ability grouping, but I don't think anyone would stop him from informally grouping us in class."

The Teacher and Non-Class Activities

Most youngsters feel that their teachers should be more willing to participate in non-class activities. They further feel that they should be allowed to request the teacher they prefer as sponsor of these activities instead of having a sponsor assigned. They are quite disappointed when teachers whom they like seem unwilling to become involved in these activities, since such activities give the student an opportunity to get to know the teacher better in an informal setting. They indicate that the advisers assigned by the school are often uninterested in the activity and are of little assistance, even failing to be present at the meetings. Many students feel that too many teachers not only fail to participate in non-class activities but are openly hostile to such activities. This hostility does not necessarily result from the teachers' feeling that they will be forced to participate but seems rather to be a more generalized disapproval. Social clubs are considered by teachers as breeding grounds for snobbery, while academic clubs (math clubs, etc.) are frowned on by many teachers as being only for the "brains." Students feel that the teacher criticisms of social clubs are unwarranted and based more on the teacher's personal biases than on fact. If these organizations do become as exclusive as the teachers report them to be, the failure of teachers to interact with them may be responsible.

Sarah H. was president of one of her high-school social clubs. For three years, one of the teachers had served as faculty adviser and had actively interacted with the group. Without seeming to be authoritarian, this teacher had guided the group quite effectively and had succeeded in moving it to function in a highly democratic fashion. This was most obvious when new candidates were considered for membership. The faculty adviser helped in this selection and was able to persuade the membership committee to consider all the candidate's qualifications rather than a single qualification such as socioeconomic status. At the time that Sarah became president, the faculty adviser left the school for another position. A new adviser was assigned, but she had little interest in the group and attended the meetings without participating. Without any guidance, the membership committee selected only those youngsters who had high socioeconomic status and eliminated some potentially fine members because they "didn't dress well," "couldn't afford the various activities," and for other arbitrary reasons. Sarah felt that snobbery was becoming apparent despite her own efforts and was planning to resign from the club in protest. She was quite bitter about the uninterested attitude of the new adviser and blamed her for the change in the youngsters' behavior.

Many adolescents do agree that teachers should receive extra remuneration for participating in non-class activities but are afraid that many teachers would become involved only for this reason rather than because they have a real interest in the group or its activities. They would prefer to have teachers volunteer because of a real interest in the youngsters and their goals. Finally, the youngsters feel that they should be allowed some voice in the selection of advisers rather than having them assigned by the school administrator alone.

Reactions to Guidance and Counseling

Most students who successfully complete a high-school education do feel that they have benefited from the school's counseling program. Jensen (1955) asked a random sample of 20 per cent of 8000 high-school students to respond to a questionnaire that attempted to measure their feelings about counseling that they had received. Generally, the feeling of these students was positive toward the help they had received in all areas. They felt that the counselors were most helpful in assisting them to appraise themselves and least helpful in assisting them to make progress toward realistically chosen goals.

Kittredge (1955) administered a questionnaire to two groups of youngsters some three years after graduation. One group had IQ's between 120 and 171; the other had IQ's between 90 and 109. Both groups were asked for their reactions to the effectiveness of the guidance program of the school district in which they had been students. The superior students generally expressed satisfaction with their high-school guidance program, but there was little indication that they were treated differently from the average students except in academic programming. These bright youngsters felt that the guidance programs helped them in various phases of individual development and in preparation for college work. They felt that the programs were weak in the adult-pupil relationship with regard to the students' personal and social problems.

There is little documentation concerning the dull students' reactions to guidance. The paucity of documentation exists because few dull youngsters reach high school, where guidance might be available. It does appear, however, that such youngsters are generally dissatisfied with what little help they do receive. These youngsters seem to feel that counselors do not want to "waste time" on them and would rather counsel the bright students. Many duller youngsters feel that they need both educational and vocational counseling more than the bright students do and resent being deprived of this service.

Maher (1952) attempted to determine what type of counseling youngsters preferred. He questioned more than 1600 high-school junior and senior boys and girls, attending both public and private schools. He found that the juniors preferred a more directive type of counseling than the seniors wanted, and that girls generally preferred a more directive type than the boys did. Students attending private schools tended more toward directive procedures than did those attending public schools, but students attending small private schools tended to choose less directive procedures than did those in medium-sized and large private schools.

Probably the major criticism of guidance programs is centered around the insufficiency of counseling. Many youngsters indicate that they have seen a counselor only once or twice during their high-school careers. Substantial numbers of youngsters say that they would have liked to consult counselors more often but usually were unable to make appointments because the counselor was too busy with others. Students also seem to prefer full-time to part-time counselors. Apparently they are less at ease with a counselor who may also be one of their teachers than with one identified only as a counselor. Nevertheless, most adolescents do think their teachers should be better informed in the area of guidance, at least to the extent of advising them on where they may find information that will be of value to them. Particularly, they feel that classroom teachers should have more occupational information available that they can discuss intelligently with interested students.

Numbers of youngsters feel that there should be more emphasis on guidance in the junior high schools. While they do not want to make a vocational choice at that time, they would like information that would help them make one later. Particularly, they would like to have various test results explained to them so that they might begin to appraise themselves and to identify their own strengths and weaknesses. They would also like more information that would help them to familiarize themselves with occupations about which they have little knowledge. Those who have experienced group guidance sessions consider that these are adequate for the junior-high level but prefer that they be organized by trained guidance counselors rather than by class-room teachers.

Parental Influences on Attitudes Toward School

As more and more parents become involved in school activities through parent-teacher associations and lay committees, the general attitude of the public toward the schools seems to deteriorate. Open criticisms of school practices and of teachers are common in the press and other communications media. Teachers are no longer held in awe and are in fact widely criticized for their apparent weaknesses. Young-sters are very much aware of this attitude, and it might be assumed that they would take advantage of it in their own relations with teachers. While the author is somewhat displeased by the constant negative criticisms of education by the public, he has been glad to note that most students are not overly affected by this situation. Not only do they continue to function effectively in class, generally learning more than did these same critical adults when they were students, but they con-tinue to view teaching as an occupation with relatively high status.

Anderson (1954) attempted to determine the attitudes of four social-class groups toward various occupations. Seven occupations ranked higher than college teaching in the judgment of the groups. These were surgeon, physician, college president, judge, architect, dentist, and electrical engineer. Parents of the upper two classes considered teach-ing more suitable for their children than did parents of the lower two classes. Those who are engaged in teacher training quickly become aware that many upper-middle- and lower-upper-class youngsters enter this field, but they also find numbers of lower-class youngsters who view the teaching profession as a means of raising their own social status.

Richey and Fox (1951) studied responses of a sample of almost 4000 students in 74 Indiana high schools and found that parents were more influential than teachers in the matter of vocational choice. About 30 per cent of the boys and 48 per cent of the girls rated teaching as less desirable than other occupations requiring the same amount of train-ing. The students generally felt that the community has no right to control the out-of-school behavior of teachers.

The author has found that, although many adolescents see need for improvement in their own school, they are generally displeased with the constant criticisms directed at the schools by adults. The youngsters feel that adults should actively support school programs and work with the school authorities and teachers to help bring about useful changes.

The Drop-Out's Reactions

Most youngsters who drop out of school do so because they do not believe that the school is meeting their needs. Many of them are quite bitter about the school's failure to give them the sort of training that would enable them to gain employment when they leave school. The dull youngsters consider that the school's emphasis on academic subjects penalized them, since their failure to perform in an acceptable manner in these courses deprived them of the opportunity to continue in shop or manual-training courses. Many of them also feel that if they had received adequate counseling and some encouragement they would at least have tried to remain in school. They generally seem to have the impression that counselors are not interested in them because they cannot do as well as the brighter youngsters, especially those who are college-bound.

Those of average or better-than-average intelligence who left school early are not particularly bitter about their school experiences, but they, too, feel that little attempt was made to encourage them to remain in school or even to warn them of the difficulties that would confront them when they sought employment. (The author has found that this attitude is not always justified. Many of these youngsters are warned but usually fail to heed the warning.) Those who seek to return to school a year or two later feel that the schools do not want them back and will not try to set up appropriate programs for them.

Peter J. came to the university counseling center shortly after his discharge from the Marine Corps. Peter reported that he had left school at the age of sixteen and had sought employment. He could get only unskilled laboring jobs and after a year decided to enlist in the Marine Corps. The recruiters suggested he complete school, but when he refused they allowed him to take a battery of tests. He did quite well on all these tests and was accepted into the Corps and sent to radar school. He completed this program at the top of his class and would have been eligible for a college engineering training program if he had held a high-school diploma. At this point, he decided to get some counseling assistance. The test battery administered at the counseling center confirmed the results of the Marine Corps tests. It was suggested that he return to high school to complete his education, but he indicated that he had already tried this. "They didn't really know what to do with me," he stated, "and I wasn't happy back with those young kids." On the basis of his test scores and some very strong recommendations by the Marine Corps, Peter was allowed to enter a nearby college as an unclassified full-time student. Two years later, he had achieved a straight "A" average and was granted full standing in the junior class. The following semester he transferred to an engineering college, where he is still maintaining an "A" average. Although Peter resents the years he lost, he does not really blame his high school. He feels an attempt should have been made to persuade him to finish but doubts that he would have done so. "I guess I just had to grow up the hard way," he said of his experiences. He does feel that schools should make some attempt to encourage drop-outs to return by offering programs that will meet their needs, or at least to encourage them to attend adult education courses.

AN OVERVIEW

Despite their readiness to recognize the flaws that exist in their high-school programs, most youngsters do feel that their schools do a good job of preparing them for their next goal. They regard most teachers as good teachers who are sincerely interested in their students. There is obviously room for improvement, but an encouraging note is apparent. Today more bright youngsters are choosing to go into teaching at both public-school and college levels. These youngsters, aware of the needs that were not satisfied in their own school careers, may work harder to satisfy more adequately the needs of the generations they will teach.

One of the greatest problems at the present time is the lack of meaningful controlled experimentation in education. Researchers must be encouraged to undertake studies that will lead to better methods of training teachers and more effective methods of teaching. Future teachers will need more help than ever, especially in the complex area of teacher-student relationships.

REFERENCES

ADEN, ROBERT C. "Teachers as Inhibitors and Redirectors." *Peabody Journal of Education*, 33, 27-30, 1955.

AMATORA, SISTER MARY. "Teacher Rating by Younger Pupils." *Journal of Teacher Education*, 5, 149-152, 1954.

AMOS, ROBERT T. "The Accuracy of Negro and White Children's Predictions of Teachers' Attitudes toward Negro Students." *Journal of Negro Education*, 21, 125-135, 1952.

AMUNDSON, CARL L. "Increasing Interpersonal Relationships in the High School with the Aid of Sociometric Procedures." *Group Psychotherapy*, 6, 183-188, 1954.

ANDERSON, G. LESTER. "What the Psychology of Learning Has to Contribute to the Education of the Teacher." *Journal of Educational Psychology*, 41, 362-365, 1950.

ANDERSON, WILLIAM F. "Attitudes of Parents of Differing Socioeconomic Status toward the Teaching Profession." *Journal of Educational Psychology*, 45, 345-352, 1954.

ARNHOLTER, ETHELWYNE G. "School Persistence and Personality Factors." *Personnel Guidance Journal*, 35, 107-109, 1956.

AUSUBEL, DAVID P., SCHIFF, HERBERT M., and ZELENY, MARJORIE P. "Validity of Teachers' Ratings of Adolescents' Adjustment and Aspirations." *Journal of Educational Psychology*, 45, 394-406, 1954.

BROWN, WILLIS. "What about Extra-Class Activities?" *Education*, 78, 94-99, 1957.

BROWN, WILLIS. *Extra-class Activities in Aviation, Photography, Radio for Secondary School Students: Suggestions for School Administrators and Sponsors.* Washington, D. C.: U. S. Department of Health, Education and Welfare, Office of Education, Bulletin No. 11, 1956.

CALLIS, ROBERT. "Changes in Teacher-Pupil Attributes Related to Training and Experience." *Educational and Psychological Measurement*, 10, 718-727, 1950.

CANTONI, L. J. "Long-Term effects of the Flint, Michigan, Guidance Experiment." *Psychological Reports*, 1, 359-362, 1955.

CELLER, SIDNEY L. "Practices Associated with Effective Discipline: A Descriptive Statistical Study of Discipline." *Journal of Experimental Education*, 19, 333-358, 1951.

CHENCY, TRUMAN. "A Method of Identifying Problems of High School Students." *Occupations*, 27, 387-390, 1949.

CRANE, GEORGE W. "Teachers Are 'Foster Parents.'" *Education*, 75, 46-52, 1954.

CROCKER, M., and POWELL, M. "Too Little and Too Late." *The Vocational Guidance Quarterly*, 9, 266-268, 1961.

DANIELSON, PAUL J., and ROTHNEY, J. W. "The Student Autobiography: Structured or Unstructured?" *Personnel Guidance Journal*, 33, 30-33, 1954.

DANILOV, M. A. "O sisteme printzipov obuchenia v sovetskoi shkole" (Concerning the System of Educational Principles in the Soviet School). *Sovetskaya Pedagogika* (Moscow), no. 4, 115-128, 1950.

DOUGLAS, HARL R. *Organization and Administration of Secondary Schools.* (1st ed., rev.) New York: Ginn & Co., 1945.

EATON, M. T., *et al.* "Problem Behavior in School." *Journal of Educational Psychology*, 47, 350-357, 1956.

FARMER, HESS, and ROSSMAN, WILLIAM B. "Helping Teachers Appreciate Emotional Problems in Children." *American Journal of Psychiatry*, 108, 375-380, 1951.

FARNSWORTH, DANA L. "Emotions and Learning." *Harvard Educational Review*, 25, 95-104, 1955.

FAUNCE, ROLAND C. "Schools for Adolescents: Nonclass Experience." *Review of Educational Research*, 24, 66-73, 1954.

FISHER, MILDRED L. "The Cumulative Record as a Tool." *Yearbook of the Association for Supervision and Curriculum Development*, 147-173, 1955.

FOX, WILLIAM W., and PARROTTE, IRENE. "Continuation School for Boys and Girls over Sixteen Years of Age in the Institution Environment." *American Journal of Mental Deficiency*, 52, 148-152, 1947.

FRANK, LAWRENCE, and FRANK, MARY H. "Teachers' Attitudes Affect Children's Relationships." *Education*, 75, 6-12, 1954.

GAGE, N. L., LEAVITT, GEORGE S., and STONE, GEORGE C. "Teachers' Understanding of Their Pupils and Pupils' Ratings of Their Teachers." *Psychological Monographs,* 69, no. 406, 1955.

GARBER, L. O. "Extra-classroom Duties without Extra Pay." *Nation's Schools,* 56, 72-73, 1955.

GEIGER, T. "Fragen de jugendbildung im zeitalter der technik und de massengesellschaft" (Problems of Education in the Age of Technology and Mass Society). *Psychologische Praxis,* 11, 63-78, 1952.

GERICH, J. P., *et al.* "What Are Some Promising Administrative Practices in the Large High Schools?" *Bulletin of the National Association of Secondary School Principals,* 36, 11-16, 1955.

GLADSTONE, ROY. "Do Maladjusted Teachers Cause Maladjustment? A Review." *Journal of Exceptional Child,* 15, 65-70, 1948.

GORDON, C. W. *The Social System of the High School: A Study in the Sociology of Adolescence.* Glencoe, Ill.: The Free Press, 1957.

GRAGG, WILLIAM LEE. "Some Factors Which Distinguish Drop-outs from High School Graduates." *Occupations,* 27, 457-459, 1949.

GRANT, PETER J. T. "The Social and Educational Background of Emergency Trained Teachers and Reasons for Their Choice of the Profession." *British Journal of Educational Psychology,* 20, 164-174, 1950.

GRIFFITHS, MARGARET, and SCOTT, BERNICE. "Guidance Specialists as Resource Persons. The High School Counselor." *Yearbook of the Association for Supervision and Curriculum Development,* 113-126, 1955.

HALES, L. "A Mental Health Survey of One Thousand High School Students in Salt Lake City, Utah." *Educational Abstracts,* V, 1940.

HAND, HAROLD C. "Relationships of Guidance to Instruction." *Yearbook of the Association for Supervision and Curriculum Development,* 3-11, 1955.

HECKER, STANLEY E. "Early School Leavers in Kentucky." *Bulletin of Current School Services, College of Education, University of Kentucky,* 25, (4), 1-74, 1953.

HERTZMAN, JACK. "High School Mental Hygiene Survey." *American Journal of Orthopsychiatry,* 18, 238-256, 1948.

HINSIE, LELAND E. "A Psychiatrist Looks at Educational Practice." *American Council on Education Studies,* 14 (ser. I, no. 40), 90-103, 1950.

HOYT, KENNETH B. "A Study of the Effects of Teacher Knowledge of Pupil Characteristics on Pupil Achievement and Attitudes towards Classwork." *Journal of Educational Psychology,* 46, 302-310, 1955.

HUGHES, O., and MCALLISTER, E. S. "What Extra-Class Activities Should Be Included in the Senior High School Program?" *Bulletin of the National Association of Secondary School Principals,* 49, 99-104, 1956.

HUNT, GLADYS B. "Enrichment through the Student Activities Program." *Peabody Journal of Education,* 34, 98-102, 1956.

IVINS, WILSON H., FOX, WILLIAM H., and SEGEL, DAVID. "A Study of a Secondary School Program in Light of Characteristics and Needs of Youth." *Bulletin of the School of Education of Indiana University,* 25(6), 1-68, 1949.

JACKSON, PHILIP W., and GETZELS, JACOB W. "Psychological Health and Classroom Functioning: A Study of Dissatisfaction with School among Adolescents." *Journal of Educational Psychology*, 50, 295-300, 1956.

JAQUES, WILLIAM T. "Hastings High School Works on the Drop-out Problem." *Personnel Guidance Journal*, 35, 39-40, 1956.

JENSEN, RALPH E. "Student Feeling about Counseling Help." *Personnel Guidance Journal*, 33, 498-503, 1955.

KABACK, GOLDIE R. "An Examination of Teacher Reaction to Adolescent Needs." *Education*, 76, 242-245, 1955.

KAPLAN, LOUIS. "Tensions in Parent-Teacher Relationships." *Elementary School Journal*, 51, 190-195, 1950.

KAWIN, ETHEL. "Guidance Specialists as Resource Persons. Preschool and Elementary School Guidance." *Yearbook of the Association for Supervision and Curriculum Development*, 101-113, 1955.

KITTREDGE, MICHAEL HERBERT. "Superior Graduates Look at Their High School Guidance." *California Journal of Educational Research*, 6, 178-180, 1955.

KORMAN, T. A. "O psikhologicheskoi praktike studentov v shkole" (Psychological Practice on School Children). *Sovetskaya Pedagogika* (Moscow), no. 3, 54-62, 1948.

KRANTZ, LAVERNE. "Administrative Procedure for the Control of Discipline in the High School." *American School Board Journal*, XCI, 48, 1935.

LEEDS, CARROLL H. "Teacher Behavior Liked and Disliked by Pupils." *Education*, 75, 29-37, 1954.

LIVINGSTON, A. HUGH. "High School Graduates and Drop-outs: A New Look at a Persistent Problem." *School Review*, 66, 195-203, 1958.

MCCASLIN, RICHARD E. *A Study of Extra-curricular Activities in Three Secondary Schools of Baltimore County*. Unpublished doctoral dissertation, University of Maryland, 1958.

MACLEAN, MALCOLM S. "Adolescent Needs and Building the Curriculum." In Williamson, E. G., ed., *Trends in Student Personnel Work*, pp. 27-39. Minneapolis: University of Minnesota Press, 1949.

MAHER, TRAFFORD P. *The Attitude of High School Juniors and Seniors Toward Counseling Procedure with Reference to Certain Personality Factors and Personal Problem Frequency*. Washington D. C.: Catholic University of America Press, 1952.

MENSH, IVAN N., and MASON, EVELYN P. "Relationship of School Atmosphere to Reactions in Frustrating Situations." *Journal of Educational Research*, 45, 275-286, 1951.

MICHAEL, WILLIAM B., HERROLD, EARLE E., and CRYAN, EUGENE W. "Survey of Student-Teacher Relationships." *Journal of Educational Research*, 44, 657-673, 1951.

MOORE, PARLETT L. "Factors Involved in Student Elimination from High School." *Journal of Negro Education*, 23, 117-122, 1954.

MURRAY, WALTER I. "The Concept of Social Class and Its Implications for Teachers." *Journal of Negro Education*, 20, 16-21, 1951.

MYKLEBUST, R. "Korleis skulen kan fremja den sosiale utviklinga hos barn og ungdom" (How Can the School Further Social Development in Children and Adolescents?). *Norsk Pedagogisk Tidsskrift* (Oslo), 32, 129-145, 1948.

NATION'S SCHOOLS. "Opinion Poll: Eighty Per Cent of Superintendents Think That Teachers Should Receive Extra Pay for 'Extra' Responsibilities." *Nation's Schools*, 58, 56-57, 1956.

NOLAN, WILLIAM J. "A Survey of Practices in Meeting Pupil Adjustment Needs." *Journal of Educational Research*, 42, 268-278, 1948.

OWENS, ALBERT A. "The Behavior-Problem Boy." *Journal of Educational Research*, XX, 166-180, 1929.

PENTY, RUTH C. *Reading Ability and High School Drop-outs*. New York: Bureau of Publications, Teachers College, Columbia University, 1956.

PINTO, GIOVANNI. "I problemi psicopedagogici della scuola media visti da uno psicologo" (The Psychopedagogical Problems of the Secondary School as Seen by a Psychologist). *Difesa Sociale* (Rome), 34, 72-83, 1955.

POWELL, M., and BERGEM, J. "An Investigation of the Differences Between 10th, 11th, and 12th Grade 'Conforming' and 'Non-conforming' Boys." *Journal of Educational Research*, 56, 184-190, 1962.

RADINA, K. D. "Analiz motivov narusheniia det'mi distsipliny na urokakh" (An Analysis of Motives of Children's Violations of Discipline during Lessons). *Sovetskaya Pedagogika* (Moscow), 1, 22-26, 1950.

RENNICKE, D., and HEARN, H. C. "Some Basic Trends in School Activities." *School of Education, Indiana University*, 27 (4), 1951.

RICHEY, ROBERT W., and FOX, WILLIAM H. "A Study of Some Opinions of High School Students with Regard to Teachers and Teaching." *Bulletin of the School Activities*, 26, 147-148, 1955.

ROCKWELL, JACK G. "Pupil Responsibility for Behavior." *Elementary School Journal*, 51, 266-270, 1951.

RYAN, LEO, *et al.* "School Life in the Academic High Schools." *High Points*, 38, 5-24, 1956.

SCHUYLER, HELEN K. "The Professional Knowledge of Secondary School Counselors: Its Measurement and Significance." *Transactions, Kansas Academy of Science*, 51, 340-343, 1948.

SEIDMAN, JEROME M., and KNAPP, LEDA B. "Teacher Likes and Dislikes of Student Behavior and Student Perceptions of These Attitudes." *Journal of Educational Research*, 47, 143-149, 1953.

SEREBRINSKY, BERNADO. "Los maestros que los alumnos prefieren" (Teachers whom Students Prefer). *Review of American Education*, 1, 13-15, 1946.

SEYMOUR, HOWARD C. "An Administrator Looks at Guidance Services." *Education*, 75, 433-438, 1955.

SNYDER, WILLIAM U. "Do Teachers Cause Maladjustment?" *Journal of Exceptional Children*, 14, 40-46, 1947.

SOBEL, MORTON J. "Familiarizing Children with Community Resources." *Elementary School Journal*, 50, 223-229, 1949.

SPOCK, BENJAMIN. "Schools Are a Fertile Field for Mental-Health Efforts." *Child*, 15, 10-11; 39, 1950.

STRANG, RUTH. "Contributions of Research to Discipline and Control." *Thirty-seventh Yearbook of the National Society for the Study of Education,* Part II, 1938.

STRANG, RUTH. "Characteristics of a Classroom Which Promotes Mental Health." *Nervous Child,* 10, 363-367, 1954.

STROMSWOLD, STANLEY A., and WRENN, GILBERT C. "Counseling Students toward Scholastic Adjustment." *Educational and Psychological Measurement,* 8, 57-63, 1948.

TALLENT, N. "Behavioral Control in Intellectual Achievement of Secondary School Boys." *Journal of Educational Psychology,* 47, 490-503, 1956.

THELEN, HERBERT A., and TYLER, RALPH W. "Implications for Improving Instruction in the High School." In Henry, N. B., ed., *The Forty-ninth Yearbook of the National Society for the Study of Education. Part I. Learning and Instruction,* pp. 304-335. Chicago: University of Chicago Press, 1950.

THOMAS, ROBERT JAY. "An Empirical Study of High School Drop-outs in Regard to Ten Possibly Related Factors." *Journal of Educational Sociology,* 28, 11-18, 1954.

TRAXLER, A. E. "Guidance Toward College Preparation." *School and Society,* 73, 113-116, 1951.

TROW, WILLIAM CLARK, ZANDER, ALVIN C., MORSE, WM. C., and JENKINS, DAVID M. "Psychology of Group Behavior: The Class as a Group." *Journal of Educational Psychology,* 41, 322-338, 1950.

TUCKER, LOUISE E. "A Study of Problem Pupils." *Teachers College Record,* XXLI, 1938.

TYLER, RALPH W. "Educability and the Schools." In *American Association for the Advancement of Science. Centennial. Collected Papers Presented at the Centennial Celebration, Washington, D. C., September 13-17, 1948.* Washington: American Association for the Advancement of Science, 1950 (issued by Yale University Press, New Haven, Conn., 1950).

UNRUH, A., and BECK, N. "State Controls over Extracurricular Activities." *Clearing House,* 30, 244-246, 1955.

VAUGHAN, WARREN T., JR. "Mental Health for School Children." *Children,* 2, 203-207, 1955.

VOLZ, HORACE S. "The Role of the School in the Prevention and Treatment of Delinquent and Other Abnormal Behavior." *School and Sociology,* 71, 21-22, 1950.

WALKER, JOHN L. "Counselors' Judgments in the Prediction of the Occupational and Educational Performance of Former High School Students." *Journal of Educational Research,* 49, 81-89, 1955.

WANDT, EDWIN, and OSTREICHER, LEONARD M. "Validity of Samples of Classroom Behavior." *Psychological Monographs,* 68(5), no. 376, 1954.

WATTENBERG, WILLIAM. "Delinquency during Summer Months." *Journal of Educational Research,* 42, 253-267, 1948.

WENZL, ALOYS. "Psychologie des unterrichts an hoheren schulen" (Psychology of Teaching in High Schools). *Psychologische Rundschau (Basel),* 4, 184-192, 1953.

WETZEL, PAUL W. "What Are We Doing for School Drop-outs?" *American School Board Journal,* 131(4), 29-31, 1955.

WIDMER, KONRAD. "Gedanken zum problem der schulangst." (Thoughts on the Problem of School Anxiety). *Heilpadagogische Werkblätter* (Germany), 24, 194-203, 1955.

WIMMER, NANCY E. "Guidance in Secondary Schools." *School Review,* 56, 343-349, 1948.

WITRYOL, SAM L. "Age Trends in Children's Evaluation of Teacher-Approved and Teacher-Disapproved Behavior." *Genetic Psychology Monographs,* 41, 271-326, 1950.

WITTY, PAUL. "An Analysis of the Personality Traits of the Effective Teacher." *Journal of Educational Research,* 40, 662-671, 1947.

CHAPTER 14

Juvenile Delinquency

It is not our purpose to try to present a complete discussion of delinquency, since it would be virtually impossible to include all the studies conducted in this field. For more comprehensive coverage of this topic, the reader is referred to any one of a number of sources (Glueck, 1959; Merrill, 1947; Kvaraceus, 1945, 1954). We hope only to make the reader aware of the many difficulties involved in studying this extremely complex field. Although a good deal is known about the incidence and the possible causes of delinquency, little has been done to solve or alleviate this problem, for reasons that may be better understood after reading this chapter.

THE GENERAL NATURE OF THE PROBLEM

Behavior that deviates from the norm can be found in individuals from early childhood to late adulthood and is not necessarily peculiar to any given age range. Yet the layman generally thinks of adolescence as the period during which the greatest amount of deviant behavior is apparent. This attitude is strongly reinforced by the constant publicity concerning the apparent increase in juvenile delinquency, and juvenile delinquency is associated primarily with adolescents. The term "juvenile delinquency" is popularly used, in fact, to describe a wide range of disapproved behavior. It is not unusual to hear a group of adolescents called "delinquents," though they may be relatively normal youngsters.

Legal Aspects

Such widespread use of the term is not justified. Juvenile delinquency refers only to the behavior patterns of youngsters who have broken a law. In the Report to the Congress on Juvenile Delinquency (1960), the term was defined as "behavior which society does not accept and which it feels justifies some kind of admonishment, punishment, or corrective measures in the public interest." In a strictly legal sense, the term should be applied only to those adjudged delinquent by a juvenile court. This strict definition, however, fails to include the behavior of those youngsters who commit delinquent acts but are not caught. Even if we use only the strict legal definition, there is tremendous variation in laws concerning exactly what constitutes a delinquent act and considerable variation in the age beyond which an individual is tried as an adult offender. While many states set this upper age limit at eighteen, others set it at sixteen or seventeen. The severity of the offense may also determine whether the youngster is tried in a juvenile court or as an adult. In some states, for example, a youngster accused of murder is tried in an adult criminal court, and in others the juvenile court can waive jurisdiction and allow a juvenile to be tried for a felony in an adult criminal court.

It has been estimated that about one million youngsters come to the attention of the police annually (Hornbostel, 1953), but of this number only about one-half million are actually handled by the courts. In 1958, between 1.5 and 2 million youngsters under eighteen were dealt with by the police. These figures include traffic violations, which, although technically considered delinquent acts, are not usually included in analyses of data relating to delinquency. Of the group handled by the juvenile courts, only about 40,000 or 50,000 (about 10 per cent) are committed to institutions for delinquents. Most of the research studies that have been made concerning delinquency have involved primarily the latter group—the institutionalized delinquents—and many of the conclusions have been based on these studies. It is, however, difficult to assume that the relatively small proportion of delinquents who are institutionalized are truly representative of all delinquency or even of that larger group that is handled by juvenile courts. For example, while ten youngsters may have committed the same delinquent act, only five of them may have been caught. Of these five, only one may be committed to a public correctional institution, while the other four may be placed in private institutions, referred for psychiatric treatment, or placed on probation. The only one of the original group who is available for research is the institutionalized one, and the mere fact that he was the only one so incarcerated may indicate that he is not representative either of the original ten or even of the five who had appeared in court.

Only recently have investigators been able to base studies on data other than that available in the correctional institutions. Data have now been released by some of the larger juvenile courts, and as a result the studies based on this broader information have brought forth some new information about delinquency. Nonetheless, even these data include only youngsters who have officially appeared in a juvenile court.

They do not include those who have made unofficial appearances in court, those who have simply been reprimanded by a police officer, or the large number who commit delinquent acts but are not caught. We do not wish to detract from the value of the many excellent studies in this area but simply to point out that the samples in many of them are not representative of the total population of youngsters who have committed one or more delinquent acts.

The Increase in Juvenile Delinquency

A great deal of concern has been and is being expressed concerning the apparently great increase in juvenile delinquency during the decade 1950–60. In a recent Children's Bureau publication (1960), it was pointed out that "increases in both police arrests of juveniles and juvenile court delinquency cases have far outstripped increases in the population of children age ten through seventeen years." The most recent increase in delinquency has not been as great as in previous years and is proportionately only slightly higher than the increase in the population of youngsters. However, a sizeable increase in delinquency for those in the ten-to-seventeen age group is predicted for the future.

It is difficult to determine whether these figures indicate that delinquency today is actually far more common than it was a few decades ago, or whether other factors may account for this apparent increase: for example, more efficient law enforcement and better reporting of data, as well as the increase in the number of juvenile courts. In the report to Congress (1960) it was suggested that the increase is not the result of such factors but is real, and that the problem is actually greater today than it was previously.

During the period from 1948 to 1958, there was a 50 per cent increase in the population of youngsters in the ten- to seventeen-year age group. During the same period, the rate of reported juvenile delinquency doubled. If the 1958 rate remains static, it is expected that in the next ten-year period between 4 million and 5 million different children will appear in juvenile court for delinquent acts that they have committed. Even if we deal only in these numbers, regardless of the proportion of the population they represent, the seriousness of the problem is quite apparent.

Analysis of expenditures and costs for juvenile-delinquency services offers further evidence of the scope of the problem. The Department of Health, Education, and Welfare (1960) made such an analysis for four selected services: public services, detention services, training schools, and probation services. These figures are minimal, since they represent only samplings of these various services or cannot even be estimated. It is, for example, impossible to estimate the cost of optimum organization and staffing for supplying police services for juvenile delinquents. The cost of some 2200 juvenile officers in large units providing special services is approximately $8,000,000 (assuming an annual salary of $3600). The 1958 operating budget for 21 detention institutions in 14 states was $11,400,000. Training-school expenditures for 1957-58 for 139 training institutions were $61,100,000, while the estimated capital program requirements for training-school facilities needed in 9 states in the next five-year period are $168,400,000. The cost of probation services for 1958 was $19,288,800, with most of the probation officers carrying a triple work load. Had enough probation officers been available, the additional cost would have approximated $38,988. Even if we were to double all these amounts, the figure would probably not approximate the true cost of these services as they presently exist in our nation, much less the cost of such services if optimum conditions were met.

Sex Differences in Delinquency

On the basis of most of the figures presently available from juvenile courts and other agencies that deal with delinquents, boy offenders outnumber girl offenders by about four to one. It is possible that juvenile-court authorities are less severe in their punishment of girls than of boys, and/or that girls may be classified as unofficial delinquents more often than boys are. The most frequent offenses of boys are stealing, malicious mischief, and truancy, while for girls appearance in court is usually for being ungovernable, for running away, or for sexual promiscuity. There are often catch-all categories; "being ungovernable" may include a variety of different offenses.

Wattenberg and Saunders (1954) reported on a series of comparisons between all boys and all girls against whom complaints were received by the Youth Bureau of the Detroit Police Department in 1952. There were 4533 young people involved in this study, of whom 3451 were boys and 1082 were girls, all aged ten to seventeen. For girls the recorded offenses were incorrigibility, sex offenses, truancy, and shoplifting. For boys the offenses were burglary, assaults, and destruction of property. The recreation patterns for the boys were active "excitement-hungry" ones, while the girls chose less vigorous, more socially aimless patterns. The family backgrounds showed a high percentage of broken homes, alcoholic parents, and quarreling in the home. Girls were more closely associated with their parents but were bitter about them; boys were more independent and less bitter. More girls than boys had difficulties in getting along with grownups. Few girls had jobs, while more boys were financially independent. Wattenberg and Saunders felt that the differences in the development of misconduct can be traced to cultural differences in the way the sexes are treated. Girls appeared to be more emotionally involved and disturbed, but boys outnumbered girls in the number of offenses by three to one.

Is Delinquent Behavior Peculiar to the Adolescent?

Before beginning our discussion of the factors involved in delinquency, there is need for further clarification of whether or not deviant behavior adjudged as delinquent is peculiar to the adolescent time period. That it is not will become apparent in the discussion that follows. Much of the behavior that leads to delinquency develops during childhood, and youngsters commit delinquent acts long before they reach pubescence. Fenton's study (1935) of institutionalized delinquents indicated that 57 per cent of the group began their delinquent careers before the age of ten, while 64 per cent of the delinquents studied by Glueck and Glueck (1933) committed their first delinquent act before that age.

Why, then, does the layman usually think of the juvenile offender as being an adolescent? The simplest explanation is that juvenile courts have limited age jurisdiction and within this frame of reference are more likely to deal harshly with an adolescent than with a child. Penal or correctional institutions for juvenile offenders seldom admit a youngster under the age of twelve, and juvenile-delinquency studies of inmates of these institutions therefore involve only youngsters between twelve and eighteen years of age. Thus, if one inspects only the records of juvenile courts or correctional institutions, delinquent behavior seems to reach a peak at about age fifteen. If, on the other hand, one examines all court records relating to criminal acts, the peak in criminal behavior appears to be reached in the late teens or early twenties.

FACTORS RELATED TO DELINQUENT BEHAVIOR

While knowledge of causes may be useful in developing the ability to control a problem, in some cases the causes are extremely complex and not subject to control. Then, too, there is often a complex interrelationship between causes, and effective treatment of one cause does not necessarily alleviate the effects of other causes. It is also possible to treat a problem without fully understanding its causes, as evidenced by the successes of medicine in treating or preventing disorders whose causes are not fully understood. We therefore use the term "factors" rather than "causes" or "causal factors," since the latter terms might imply relationships that do not actually exist.

Many of the factors relating to delinquency have been identified within broad frameworks as psychological, social, and biological. Each of these categories is important, and specific factors within each have been identified and associated with delinquency. These three categories are not unrelated; in fact, their interrelationships are quite complex. One might well consider delinquency as a problem based on the combination of these biological, social, and psychological factors. While the biological factor seems less closely associated with delinquency than the other two factors, it is nonetheless impossible to suggest that any one of the three is generally more important than others, although this may be established in the case of a single individual. For example, suppose there are two brothers living in the same home, both of them physically healthy. One becomes delinquent; the other does not. Since the physical and social factors seem to be comparable, the factor associated with the delinquency is probably psychological.

Stott (1960) has criticized the attempts of investigators to dichotomize psychological and sociological delinquency. In order to determine to what extent delinquency is purely cultural, he investigated the prevalence of psychological factors in 415 Glasgow boys under fifteen years of age who were on probation and a control group of 404 boys from the same public schools. He found that the probationers from high-delinquency areas were as maladjusted as those from "good areas," i.e., they were not simply conforming to a delinquent environment. The delinquents were, however, consistently less well adjusted as the geographic density of delinquency increased. "It is suggested that this in turn is only one of several consequences of unfavorable ecology."

In a number of investigations of the relationship of biological factors to delinquent behavior, attempts have been made to identify possible genetic patterns of such behavior. Penrose (1955) suggested that the application of genetics to complex social phenomena such as crime and delinquency has not proved highly successful. Despite the evidence showing a preponderance of criminality in favor of the male sex of about five to one, no study has yet demonstrated a direct hereditary connection. There are several studies of families that seem to indicate possible genetic influences, but other interpretations can also be applied. Studies of physical traits, use of twins, and even experiments in sterilization have attempted to relate heredity to crime, but with little success. Penrose concludes that the question of the relation of heredity to crime is still unresolved. There is at present little reason to be concerned about possible hereditary aspects of delinquency.

Childhood Development and Delinquency

As we stated previously, much of the development of the behavioral patterns that lead to the commission of delinquent acts often takes place well before the child has reached pubescence. Rich (1954) considered "childhood as a preparation for delinquency" and discussed the behavior of a growing person as being the result of numerous factors that operate throughout the life of the individual. The child begins early to develop certain characteristics, and these become more fixed as his age increases. Rich felt that the acceptance of the child by the parents is the most important factor in obtaining the security necessary for his emotional development; he considers the importance of the family as paramount. A second major factor is accomplishment, while a third factor is the influence of the companions with whom the child associates. Rich also considers the school important in determining and directing the child's development. The failure of any one or of all these factors may lead to maladaptive patterns of behavior that may result in the commission of delinquent acts.

Kaufman (1955) has investigated sources of predelinquent character in his study of cases referred by the Boston Juvenile Court to the Judge Baker Guidance Center and of cases on which he consulted for the Massachusetts Society for the Prevention of Cruelty to Children. He states, "The problem of delinquent and predelinquent character . . . is multiply determined." Using an essentially psychoanalytic framework, he suggests that "we consider the deprivation of adequate parent figures, the disturbances in psychosexual development, . . . and the ego and superego disturbances as essential components of the character structure of the delinquent." All these factors or disturbances are associated with early development and are usually present before the child reaches pubescence.

What Conditions Produce Delinquency?

Several of the conditions that have been regarded as producing juvenile delinquency have been discussed by Hirschberg and Noshpitz (1955). They feel that some of the conditions that are commonly regarded as producing delinquency really have little or no over-all influence. These conditions include poverty, inadequate housing, inadequate play facilities, cultural conflict between the foreign-born parent and his native-born child, lack of a supporting figure on whom the boys could model themselves, and physical or mental abnormality. The forces that they feel do produce delinquency are to be found in family background, type of personality, the social setting, and a general relation to the restraining influences of home, church, community, and state. These factors operate during childhood, even though the delinquent act may not be committed until later. Hirschberg and Noshpitz regard as contributing factors the undue publicity given the delinquent by the popular press, the prolonged schooling of boys who are unwilling or unable to profit from book-learning, and the social instability found in areas where racial groups clash.

In popular publications a good deal has been written about adolescent gangs, apparently on the assumption that gang membership is necessarily undesirable and is closely related to delinquency. While some gangs may engage in delinquent acts, gang membership *per se* cannot be directly associated with delinquency. Crane (1951) indicated that preadolescent gangs are not necessarily the product of a subnormal environment but also occur in environments where insufficient outlets for adolescent feelings and energies exist. The essence of the behavior of such gangs, as he views them, is a testing of the restrictions placed by adult mores. In place of the adult barrier, the gang develops its own system of mores, which gives it cohesiveness and protects its identity as an in-group. The gang may play a considerable part in the boys' socialization.

As an outgrowth of his earlier studies, Crane (1955) advanced the hypothesis that "boys who lack a secure anchorage in the family life (namely, affectionate relationship with the father) . . . are those most likely to be found in gangs." Since it has also been noticed that "children moved away from gang membership from the age of twelve," the question was asked whether children of this age are "beginning to make satisfactory identifications upon which to base their learning of the adult role." To find the answer to this question, Crane asked boys and girls aged ten to fourteen to "record the person they would most like to be like when they reach adulthood." The results did indicate that with increasing age boys showed increasing identification with an adult male with whom they had close contact. Crane suggests that a boy's membership in a gang is "evidence of the lack of affectionate attachment to an adult male." He adds, however, that no permanent harm is done if the child is able to form this kind of attachment before he reaches the age of fourteen.

The police records of 344 boys eleven years old and of 3787 others who had passed their twelfth birthday were studied by Wattenberg (1953). The younger group came in greater proportion from poorer socioeconomic levels and were more dependent on their parents for spending money. In comparison with the older group, the eleven-year-olds included proportionately more members of gangs and fewer "lone wolves." These younger boys were reported to get along better with their classmates at school and to express fewer hostile feelings toward adults than the older boys did. The latter aspect may be only a demonstration of a more conventional pattern of verbal report. This study also demonstrates that gang membership is apparently well developed before the youngster reaches pubescence. Since identification with the gang is important to the youngster, particularly as it is a substitute for other identification, he is likely to follow the dictates of the gang very closely. If the gang is involved in the commission of delinquent acts,

the youngster needing this kind of identification will follow the delinquent pattern in order to maintain it. Wattenberg and Faigenbaum
(1953) have concluded "that delinquency is frequently the product of
generalized personality disorganization of some type." Since such personality disorganization usually develops over a long period of time,
the factors leading to such disorganization are probably operating during childhood.

THE HOME ENVIRONMENT AS A FACTOR IN DELINQUENCY

The home-family environment of the youngster has already been mentioned as possibly a major factor in determining whether or not he will
develop personality characteristics and behavior patterns that may
lead to delinquent behavior. This aspect of delinquency has been
widely investigated, and most of the studies do support the view that
disorganization and/or deterioration of the home environment is
closely related to delinquency. Glueck (1953) investigated 400 possible
related factors in a systematic study of 500 delinquents who were carefully matched with nondelinquents in IQ, ethnic derivation, age, and
residence area. The family backgrounds and home climates of the delinquent group were markedly inferior to those of the nondelinquent
group.

Cass (1952) attempted to devise a method for measuring certain parent-child interaction variables and ascertaining the degree of interdependence of these variables. The indexes of parent-child conflict and
of the child's social adjustment are in some way related to the specific
combination of one of the variables, parental awareness, with another
variable, parental control. A group of 21 seriously maladjusted adolescent residents of the Ohio State Bureau of Juvenile Research were
paired individually with a group of adolescents rated as well adjusted,
by age, race, sex, and father's occupational level. Cass concludes
that the two variables mentioned, as reported by the child, seem to
have considerable importance in the total parent-child relationship.
Children who manifest social maladjustment tend, in general, to be
those who report more maternal control and whose mothers are less
aware of their needs than is the case with children who are better adjusted socially.

A study of 83 neurotic and delinquent girls aged fourteen to nineteen, of whom approximately three-fourths were thieves, was reported
by O'Kelly (1955). The social histories of these adolescents revealed
many disturbing influences. In one-third of the cases, the child had
been separated from the mother for six months or more during the
first five years; in one-fifth of the cases, the child had been grossly re-

jected by the mother before committing an offense. These factors occurred more frequently for the thieving than the nonthieving delinquents. Only 24 per cent of the thieves had normal relationships with their mothers as compared with 76 per cent of the nonthieves. Apparently loss of or rejection by the mother is specifically associated with thieving. While there was no corresponding association between sexual delinquency and lack of maternal affection, there did seem to be a fairly close association between sexual delinquency in the mother and in the daughter, with daughters of sexually immoral mothers tending to have similar problems. The relationship with the mother is apparently a more important factor in thieving than the relationship with the father. Sexual delinquency, on the other hand, may be indicative of a disturbed relation with the father. The reports dealing with the child's development during the early years were more frequently unsatisfactory in the thieving than the nonthieving group, which suggests that the thieves had a strained relationship with the mother from the beginning.

Broken Homes

ABSENCE OF ONE PARENT. Evidence available from a variety of studies seems to indicate a definite relationship between delinquency and broken homes. The general description of a broken home in most of the studies emphasized the physical absence of one of the parents. Within this frame of reference there are a number of reasons for the break, including death, divorce, separation, and desertion. Recent investigations of this problem have attempted to determine whether a break caused by death results in reactions appreciably different from those resulting from a break with both parents living. Monahan (1957) did not feel that there would be any major difference between children from socially broken homes and orphaned children, although the former now predominate. He felt that "the fact of a break in the home rather than the nature of the break may be of more crucial importance to the child insofar as official delinquency is concerned."

Bartlett and Horrocks (1958) attempted to determine in what ways the needs status of adolescents from homes where one parent is deceased might differ from that of those from homes where both parents were living. The Experimental Form of the Horrocks-Lucas Needs Questionnaire was administered to 461 eighth- through twelfth-grade students. The data were factor-analyzed, and seven factors were isolated. Three factors—heterosexual striving versus satisfaction from parents, socioeconomic factor, and death of mother as related to childbirth—showed significance. Only the factor of heterosexual striving versus satisfaction from parents showed any significant relationships

between needs and numbers of parents deceased. Bartlett and Horrocks concluded that "this factor indicated that the adolescents from
homes where one parent is deceased tend to receive less recognition and
affection from adults." Their apparent striving for recognition by the
opposite sex may represent an attempt to compensate for this lack
of adult recognition and affection.

The correlation between broken homes and delinquency seems to
be significant, even though a causal relationship has not yet definitely
been established. Smith (1955) felt that one must consider the effects
of the psychologically broken home as well as those of the structurally
broken home, since the psychologically broken home may have even
more damaging effects on a youngster's personality. A broken home
is not an isolated phenomenon, and even though a home may not be
broken the family may be disintegrated because of a variety of conditions. Smith considered it extremely doubtful that a child will become
involved in delinquent behavior without the existence of strong deviation pressures in his environment. Higher rates of delinquency are
thus usually found in areas having higher than normal rates of broken
homes, and such rates are found most often in socially disorganized
urban areas. In such areas poverty and disrespect for law prevails, and
in general both broken homes and delinquency are more prevalent in
areas inhabited by lower-class families. Smith suggests that high delinquency rates among children from broken homes can be explained
in terms of the differential treatment they receive both from the law
and from social agencies as compared to that given to those from complete homes.

THE PSYCHOLOGICALLY BROKEN HOME. The influence of the psychologically broken home as a factor involved in delinquency needs a good
deal of further research, since there may be as many psychologically
broken homes as physically broken ones, or even more. It is, of course,
much more difficult to identify a psychologically broken home and to
judge the degree to which such a home environment has deteriorated.
A study of high-IQ delinquents by Caplan and Powell (1962) offers
some evidence of the influence of a psychologically broken home on
delinquent behavior. The evaluations of the home backgrounds of
these bright youngsters did indicate a good deal of deterioration in
the home situation. In a number of cases, the psychological disturbances of the parents or their accompanying behavior patterns led
directly to the youngsters' referral to the court. Actually the referrals
were made by these parents, who charged the children with "being
ungovernable" or "uncontrollable," despite the fact that they might
not have committed any act that would have brought them into contact with the police. One must assume that only a very strong emo-

tional upheaval in the home environment could bring a parent to prefer charges against his or her own child.

Quite frequently couples stay together "for the sake of the children." While it may be true that a poor home environment where both parents are present is better than a poor broken-home environment, one may still question the validity of this reason for a couple's remaining together. If the emotional stress is serious, it is constantly reinforced by the continual contact of two conflicting adults living in the same environment, and such an environment must react on the children. They in turn will necessarily become emotionally involved, even to the extent of "taking sides" with one parent against the other. Actually both parents may be rejecting their children emotionally, despite their claim that they remain together for the children's sake. If the situation has reached this extreme, one might well question the wisdom of the parents' remaining together unless they are willing to seek psychiatric or psychological help in solving their problems.

Socioeconomic Status

The results of early studies of juvenile delinquency seemed to show a strong relationship between juvenile delinquency and socioeconomic status. Generally, it appeared that delinquents came primarily from low socioeconomic home environments. This seemed to be particularly true of institutionalized delinquents. Although there was some evidence to indicate that youngsters from high socioeconomic backgrounds also committed delinquent acts, such youngsters were seldom institutionalized and were usually unavailable for study. Many laymen considered this further evidence that the rich were able to "buy" their children out of court, but this was not a fair interpretation. Most juvenile-court judges would prefer to allow delinquent youngsters the opportunity to get private treatment or to be placed in a good private school. Unfortunately, parents from low socioeconomic areas could not afford such treatment or placement, and their children were necessarily remanded to state-supported institutions for treatment. With the present-day increase in delinquency, it is more apparent that delinquents come from all socioeconomic levels, but the largest number still are from low socioeconomic environments.

Blue (1948) attempted to establish relationships between juvenile delinquency, race, and socioeconomic status. Using census data for the city of Detroit, he calculated the following partial correlation coefficients: .52 for race and delinquency, holding economic status constant; and −.59 for economic status and delinquency, holding race constant. Blue felt that these results supported the hypothesis that economic status is more closely related to juvenile delinquency than is race.

Nye *et al.* (1958) also investigated the relationship between socio-economic status and delinquency. An anonymous delinquency check-list was administered to more than 2000 boys and girls in grades nine to twelve in three Western cities and three Midwestern communities. These authors had hypothesized "that there is no significant difference in the amount of delinquent behavior of boys and girls in different socioeconomic strata." The results of the study did not offer sufficient evidence to reject this hypothesis. Since this study did not generally involve youngsters who had actually been arrested for delinquent acts, it would seem to support the view that delinquency occurs at all levels. Whether youngsters respond truthfully when their responses are anonymous, and whether they admit to acts they have really not committed, is always difficult to assess.

If one accepts the thesis previously suggested—that the physically and/or psychologically broken home may be a factor in delinquency—delinquency may reasonably be expected to occur at every socio-economic level. Homes broken through divorce, death, or separation are not peculiar to any one economic level but are common to all. The emotional strains leading to a psychologically broken home are also common at all economic levels. It is possible that parents of middle and high socioeconomic status who conflict with each other may remain together for reasons related to their status level, while parents from lower socioeconomic strata may be quicker to separate. Those who do remain together physically, though a serious emotional rift exists, may do so because divorce is not condoned in their own status group, because it is against their religion to separate, or for any number of other reasons.

SOCIAL MATURITY AND DELINQUENCY

Social workers and others who have direct contact with juvenile delinquents often comment that these youngsters appear to be more socially "mature" than nondelinquents of the same age levels. This should not be surprising, however, since, as we have already indicated, young delinquents often operate as part of groups when they commit delinquent acts. They are often members of clubs where they have opportunity for interaction with their sex-mates and also with members of the opposite sex who are members of the club's "auxiliary." If the group of which a boy is a member is interested in girls, the youngster is likely to show overt interest in girls. One might well question whether such apparent social maturity is positive or whether it is really a reinforcement of other negative patterns of behavior.

If delinquent youngsters appear to be more socially mature and socially accepted, this is generally true only in their immediate peer groups, which usually consist of other delinquents. If one studies them in the total peer environment or studies their apparent views of themselves, it becomes evident that they are not well liked and that they have negative feelings about their relationships with others. Peters (1957) administered the Semantic Differential Scales and a modified Science Research Associates Youth Inventory to delinquents and to nondelinquents. The results indicate that a definite relationship exists between an individual's feelings about himself and his feelings about others. Delinquents, as compared with nondelinquents, hold more negative feelings toward themselves and others.

McDavid and Schroder (1957) attempted to investigate the differences in intepretation of positive (increase in self-evaluation) and negative (self-devaluation) events by individuals who respond "appropriately" as opposed to those who respond "inappropriately" to social approval and disapproval. These authors proposed that a delinquent population does not make adequate discriminations between positive and negative social events. Obviously, the poorer the discrimination, the less effective social reward would be as a rehabilitating force. They administered the Situational Interpretation Test to 750 adolescent males in summer camps and high schools and to 160 juvenile delinquents committed to reform schools. The results indicate that delinquents' interpretations of positive events tend to be more self-negative, and those of negative events more self-positive as compared to interpretations by nondelinquents. Generally, the delinquents did not differentiate between negative and positive social events.

Trent ("Socioempathetic Ability in a Group of Institutionalized Delinquent Boys," 1957) attempted to duplicate Ausubel's procedure in comparing delinquents he studied with the nondelinquents of the original study. He hypothesized that "the perceptions of the delinquent, as compared to the non-delinquent, would tend to show more distortions and self-deception which may result from his own needs and the attitudes he holds toward the individuals in the group." The findings did indicate that the delinquent youngster's perception of his own sociometric status in a group tends to be distorted. However, his perception of the sociometric status of others was superior to that of the nondelinquent group. Trent suggested that "an individual's perception of his own sociometric status may not affect the accuracy with which he perceives the status of others." Trent made a study of "The Relationship of Anxiety to Popularity and Rejection among Institutionalized Delinquent Boys" (1957), which involved 63 boys organized into two cottage groups. The results indicated that popularity was positively related to rejection. Subjects who were chosen more frequently tended to be rejected more frequently. The more anxious subjects were less popular, and the over-all results of the study seem to support the contention that more anxious youngsters tend to be less popular within child populations.

Trent (1959), in another study, asked the same delinquent boys to rate themselves and others on a five-point scale. The youngsters were also administered the Children's Manifest Anxiety Scale. Anxiety was found to be negatively related to accuracy of perception of own status. The less anxious enjoyed significantly higher social status than the more anxious, supporting the thesis of Trent's previous study of anxiety. He also found that the greater the social status, the more accurate the perception of own status. Subjects who overestimated their own status tended to overestimate the status of others.

Generally, the results of these various studies indicate that the juvenile delinquent is not "popular" with his over-all peer group, although he may appear to be popular in his small immediate peer group. The delinquent does not actually view himself as well liked socially but seems to feel that others are rather negative in their responses to him. He, in turn, develops negative attitudes toward others and is generally negatively oriented to positive social events. Part of his apparent social maturity may be an attempt to seek social adequacy by close interaction with his delinquent peers.

INTELLIGENCE AND DELINQUENCY

Intelligence has probably been the most thoroughly investigated of all the factors that seem to be associated with delinquency. Despite the number of investigations, however, no definite conclusion has yet been reached concerning the exact relationship between intelligence and delinquency.

Comparisons of Delinquents and Nondelinquents

Most of the early studies reported that delinquents were significantly below average in intelligence. Merrill (1947) reported that 11.6 per cent of a sample of 500 youngsters from the California courts were mentally deficient. This figure is well above the percentage of defectives in the normal population. Even though some youngsters may test below their actual capability as a result of the emotional tensions usually accompanying their delinquency, this high percentage is confirmed by other findings. Kvaraceus (1945) reported that 10.4 per cent of all public-school children referred for guidance are mentally deficient, while the Gluecks (1934) had reported that 13.1 per cent of a sample referred to the Judge Baker Foundation Clinic for diagnostic study were mentally deficient. The New Jersey Juvenile Commission

(1939) reported that 13 per cent of the youngsters committed to juvenile training schools in that state had IQ's under 70.

The figures quoted for the average intelligence among delinquents are generally significantly lower than the average intelligence reported for nondelinquents. Kvaraceus (1945) studied a group of unselected New Jersey school children and found their average IQ to be 103, as compared with an average IQ of 89 among 761 children referred to a central guidance service as problem children. Glueck (1934) compared 1000 clinic-referred delinquents with more than 3000 school children. She found that only 41.6 per cent of the delinquents had average intelligence or better (IQ of 90 or above), while 79 per cent of the school children had average or above-average IQ's.

There is evidence which indicates that juvenile delinquents are not representative of the whole child population in social status and in a number of other variables that relate to intelligence. Delinquents appear in disproportionate numbers from low socioeconomic groups, Negro families, foreign-born parents, etc. The unofficial delinquent whose name seldom appears in official police or court records is generally from a higher socioeconomic level. Merrill (1947) has also found a difference between the IQ's of those who appear in juvenile court only and those who are committed to institutions following a court appearance. The court samples' average IQ was 85; that of youngsters committed to institutions was 82.

There have been many criticisms of these earlier research studies. One of these is that they failed to consider the usefulness of the test applied to the sample studied. Davis (1950) reported on an experimental study of school children of varying socioeconomic background who were given standard intelligence tests and a test to measure untaught responses to problems in daily life outside the schools. The differences between the high and low socioeconomic groups that appeared on the intelligence-test results were not present in the results of the daily-life-problems test. Davis concluded that standard tests did not really measure the problem-solving abilities of youngsters from low socioeconomic environments. The emotional state of a youngster being tested in a court environment, previously mentioned, may also result in his failure to achieve as well as he might on a standard test.

A major criticism of the early studies concerned their apparent failure to compare samples that realistically related to each other. Institutionalized delinquents are not representative of the whole population of those adjudged delinquent and are even less representative of the total population of adolescents. Nonetheless, they were often compared with such populations, with the results inevitably indicating that the institutionalized group was inferior. As a result, it was proposed that comparisons should be made of delinquents and nondelinquents with socioeconomic status held constant. Lichtenstein and Brown (1938) had found that 10 per cent of the 658 grade-school children from a high-delinquency area had IQ's below 70. If this figure is used as a control percentage, one has a basis for comparing delinquents and non-delinquents, thus equated for socioeconomic background. Merrill (1947) had studied delinquents and nondelinquents from the same communities and did not find a significant difference in IQ for the two groups. She did find, however, that there were twice as many delinquents as nondelinquents in the group with IQ's below 70.

Studying delinquents and nondelinquent controls from the same areas and the same public schools, Burt (in Glueck, 1959, p. 81) found that only 1.2 per cent of the control group was in the 50-to-70 IQ range, while 7.6 per cent of the delinquents had IQ's in this range. In the above-115 IQ group he found only 2.5 per cent of the delinquents, as opposed to 8.5 per cent of the nondelinquents. Charles (1936) also found differences between the IQ's of delinquents and nondelinquents of the same socioeconomic status. He found that about 30 per cent of the white boys and 47 per cent of the Negro boys among the delinquents he studied had IQ's of less than 70. The public-school group involved in this study indicated that slightly more than 1 per cent of the white boys and about 3.5 per cent of the Negro boys had IQ's below 70.

This kind of matching may be more precise than earlier methods, but it still leaves many cultural factors unaccounted for. Two families may live in the same neighborhood and have similar socioeconomic status but at the same time present cultural variations. In one family the parents may be foreign-born, while in the other family they may be native-born. Their religions and value systems may also differ appreciably. To control even these aspects of cultural variation, studies have been structured to compare delinquent youngsters with their own nondelinquent siblings. Healy and Bronner (1936) compared 105 delinquents with a like number of nondelinquent siblings matched for age and sex. Their results (which excluded those with IQ's below 70) generally favored the nondelinquents. This study and a similar one reported by Shulman (1929) indicate that delinquents appear to rate lower in intelligence tests, even when the cultural factors are equated.

Dinitz et al. (1957) also found differences in intelligence between delinquents and nondelinquents. They used the delinquency vulnerability (D.E.) and social responsibility (R.E.) scores on the California Psychological Inventory, and the delinquency proneness (D.P.) index based on the combination of these two scores (D.E. + R.E.), as measures of delinquency vulnerability. These instruments were administered to 126 sixth-grade boys who were nominated by teachers as being "insulated" against delinquency and to 101 sixth-grade boys in the same school nominated by the same teachers as headed for involvement with the law. California Mental Maturity records and the results of the Stanford tests in reading and arithmetic were available on these students. The authors found a significant difference in intelligence between the two groups. They also reported significant differences on the reading test favoring the nondelinquents, and approximately the same differences on the arithmetic test. The authors felt that the motivational aspect seemed to be of the greatest importance in explaining reading deficiencies among delinquency-prone subjects.

Significant Areas of Intelligence

In briefly summarizing some of these findings, the Gluecks (1950) conclude that the delinquents and nondelinquents resemble each other in "originality, creativity, banality, intuition, phantasy, and over-verbalizing intelligence." The delinquents seem to have somewhat lesser skills in observation and "show less potential capacity for objective interests." They also report that larger proportions of delinquents are "unrealistic thinkers and lack common sense." Woodward (1955) presented a general discussion of the role of intelligence in delinquency, involving a detailed review of the literature. She found a divergence of opinion as to the significance of low intelligence in delinquent behavior. The average IQ of delinquents in the United States and in Britain is about 92, with the possibility that their scores are deflated by cultural factors. Woodward felt that improved tests and sampling methods have resulted in a rise in the "tested intelligence" scores of delinquents in America over the past forty years. Her important over-all conclusion is that low intelligence is a negligible factor in delinquency.

Harrington and Davis (1953) attempted to test the hypothesis that delinquents are characterized by a relative inability to engage in abstract thinking (which is a dimension of intelligence). The subjects included 33 male high-school students and 29 delinquent boys, equated for age and IQ. A list of ten proverbs was administered, and the subjects were asked to explain what each proverb meant. Their responses were rated for degree of abstractness by four psychologists working independently, and all ratings were transformed into comparable scores. The results did not support the hypothesis. There was no significant difference between the groups in ability to abstract the general principle from the proverbs. This would seem to indicate that this dimension of intelligence is not related to delinquency.

Present-Day Appraisals of the Intelligence Factor

Although there is need for further research in the area of intelligence as it relates to delinquency, much of the present-day evidence seems to indicate that, if other factors (socioeconomic, race, etc.) are held constant, intelligence is a less important factor than had been previously assumed. Nonetheless, it seems safe to assume that disproportionately large numbers of delinquents will continue to come from the lower IQ groups for reasons which do relate, directly and indirectly, to their low level of intellectual functioning. One of these reasons, for example, may be the failure of our public schools to offer programs keyed to the needs of children with low IQ's. Inability to "keep up" with average and above-average youngsters is likely to cause frustration that may ultimately lead these youngsters to leave school either as truants or as drop-outs. Since jobs are not readily available to them, they have little to do when they are out of school and intentionally or accidentally may become involved in delinquent behavior. This is not to suggest that low intelligence *per se* leads directly to this kind of situation. Actually, the school environment's failure to satisfy their needs may be only the precipitating factor in the delinquent behavior to which home and other environmental factors have made them prone. The Caplan and Powell (1962) study of high-IQ delinquents further emphasizes this point at the opposite extreme. The school was often the only environment in which these bright youngsters could function effectively and satisfy their needs. It is not intelligence or lack of it that relates directly to delinquency, but rather the failure of the environment to offer situations wherein an individual can gain satisfactions no matter what his IQ is.

OTHER FACTORS STUDIED

Many factors other than those already mentioned have also been studied, as investigators have sought to locate factors that relate somehow to delinquency. Although these studies have been limited and the findings sometimes inconclusive, they are briefly presented in this section to emphasize further the complexity of the problems of juvenile delinquency.

Church Attendance

Since J. Edgar Hoover suggested that regular church attendance by youngsters might cut down on delinquency, there has been some argument concerning the validity of this statement. In a study of delinquent repeaters and nonrepeaters, Hewitt and Jenkins (1946) found that regular church attendance differentiated these groups, with the nonrepeating group attending regularly. Wattenberg (1950) also reported that church attendance "generally reduces tendencies toward juvenile misconduct." Church attendance is, however, an indicator of general family morale rather than an entity in itself, and it reflects the parents' attitudes and feelings toward religion.

Leisure Time

Some decades ago the use of leisure time was not considered a problem for youngsters, especially those living in rural areas. The youngster did his share of the family work and helped earn his share of the family income. To a lesser degree this is still true of rural youth today, but urban youngsters do not have much opportunity to contribute work or income to the family. Society has not kept pace with the increase in leisure time available to youngsters and has failed to provide the institutions and facilities needed to make productive use of it. In most urban areas recreational facilities are limited, and those that are available are often inaccessible to certain groups, particularly those from low socioeconomic backgrounds. Grygier (1955) concluded, after an extensive review of the literature, that the actual validity and reliability of the findings of studies relating to leisure time are "very uncertain." On the basis of his study of 100 London delinquents aged twelve and a half to fourteen and a half, with at least two convictions for serious offenses, he proposed that a more rigorous pursuit of reliable information be made, particularly in assessing the sociopsychological aspects of leisure behavior. Grygier viewed the leisure pursuits of delinquents as "a part of an interaction between the individual and his environment, between his needs and his deprivations or satisfactions." Only when these points are related to investigations into social and personality factors can knowledge of leisure-time pursuits be of much help in diagnosis, therapy, and vocational guidance.

Mass Media

Even though delinquency was present long before comic books—or movies, radio, and television—became widely known, there is today a great deal of concern about the effects of these media on behavior. Wertham (1948) stated his belief that comic books produce a great deal of serious delinquency. Committees have been set up to "screen" comic books in a number of cities, and those considered "bad" because of their emphasis on violence have been banned from public sale.

Even in 1933, when these various mass media did not have as widespread influence as they do today, Mann (1933) suggested that they tended to glorify the criminal or immoral girl. All four media, it has been said, offer knowledge of techniques of committing crime or delinquent acts. Hoult (1949) compared the comic-book reading of 235 delinquents ten to seventeen years old with that of a control group and found statistically significant differences in the number of comic books read. Both groups read the same number of "harmless" books, but the delinquents read many more "questionable" books. While it is possible that overt physical behavior of a delinquent type may result from reading comic books, this is likely to occur only in cases in which there is already a developed pattern of deviant behavior. Generally, however, most people tend to overestimate the importance of comic books as a major factor in delinquency.

Personality Characteristics

Investigators have been identifying personality characteristics that apparently relate to delinquent behavior, and in some cases have attempted to determine if there is such a thing as a "delinquent personality." Zakolski ("Studies in Delinquency, I," 1949), attempted to determine the personality structure of delinquent boys and that of nondelinquent boys. He wished to discover whether a method for predicting delinquency, based on the differences in the two groups, could be found. Using the results of several standardized tests, he found that the delinquent and nondelinquent are similar in many ways. Since society does, however, distinguish sharply between these two groups, the traits in which differences are shown become significant. The delinquent boy is less intelligent; his health adjustment is poorer; he is less well adjusted socially; his school abilities are poorer; and his family relations are poorer. "The delinquent boy," Zakolski concluded, "presents a psychological deficit."

Monachesi (1950) studied four groups of boys to compare personality characteristics of delinquents (institutionalized and noninstitutionalized) and nondelinquents. The study included 85 nondelinquent boys of various socioeconomic levels attending public secondary schools and 160 boys attending denominational schools. The two groups of delinquents included 73 boys on probation or in the County Home School in Minnesota and 123 boys in the Minnesota State Training School for Boys. The personality adjustment of the boys was measured with the Minnesota Multiphasic Personality Inventory. Monachesi found that, contrary to general assumptions, the personality patterns shown by the delinquent boys do not seem to differ in many essentials from those of nondelinquents. The delinquent boys who were placed on probation were not greatly unlike those who were committed to the State Training School.

NEUROTIC PATTERNS. Peterson et al. (1959) administered two "delinquency" scales to 116 delinquents and 115 matched nondelinquents. When the results were factor-analyzed, three major groupings that seemed related to delinquency emerged: "psychopathic personality"; a "neurotic" dimension, including "impulsive anti-social behavior";

"regret, depression and other negative affect," and "inadequacy." The authors felt that the first two factors were related to family dissension and the last factor, to school difficulties. Peterson and Quay (1961) further investigated personality factors in delinquency in a study involving the use of four questionnaires that differentiated delinquents and nondelinquents. These questionnaires were administered to 203 training-school inmates and to 203 high-school boys. The items in each questionnaire were intercorrelated over the entire sample, and four separate factor analyses were made. After the resulting first-order factors were interpreted, the relations among them were examined, and a second-order factorization was performed. The following findings were isolated: (1) Psychopathy and neuroticism factors that had been previously isolated were almost identically reproduced in the present study. (2) A factor called "inadequacy" that had appeared in the previous study did not appear in this study. (3) Differences in item content from questionnaire to questionnaire occasioned differences in meaning of first-order factors, but many of the latter could be subsumed under second-order concepts of psychopathic and neurotic delinquency. (4) Most of the remaining first- and second-order dimensions seemed to refer to a history of delinquent behavior, but the authors considered the possibility of test-taking defensiveness in their interpretations.

Ohwaki (1952) presented the development of the delinquent personality in the following phases: personal social environment of reformatory boys; dynamics of the social situation; intelligence; interests; and emotional-character study. The Kraeplin-Uchida Addition Test, the Mueller-Lyer Illusion, and the Thematic Apperception Test were used to measure these phases. Loss of parents, poverty, excessive fears and anxieties, and decreased image-duration as a result of lack of attention are characteristics of the delinquent group. The intelligence level of these delinquents was found to be higher than that of prewar delinquents.

Kaufman et al. (1959) felt that adolescence has a particular impact on girls with delinquent character formation. They suggested that the normal girl has stability, which, with the experience of being able to count on her environment as a source of help, enables her to cope with the various problems of adolescence. The delinquent girl, however, has the experience of tension or trouble arising from her environment as a source of concern to her and cannot rely on her environment to help meet her needs. The stresses of adolescence, which act as pressures toward growing up, become a threat to the delinquent girl, and these pressures become related to her fears of separation and loss and to sado-masochistic concepts of relating. The authors felt that as a result the delinquent girl has available only the relatively few ego devices of denial and the repetition compulsion of antisocial behavior as methods of coping with tensions.

Kay (1954) attempted to study the reactions of delinquents, neurotics, and stable nondelinquents (the control group) to experimentally induced frustration. He hypothesized that the frustration tolerance of the control group could be differentiated from that of the remaining two groups, and that neurotics manifest a significantly greater amount of nonadaptive motor behavior than either of the other two groups. Results based on the use of the Rosenzweig Picture-Frustration Test and finger-maze tests confirmed both hypotheses. Members of the control group demonstrated significantly higher tolerance of frustration than did either of the other groups, and there were also marked differences among the groups as to their ways of resolving the frustration situation. While only a few of the controls and neurotics terminated the experiment on their own initiative, almost half the delinquents did. According to his data, Kay felt that the instability of these delinquents is the result of a disturbance of normal interpersonal rather than of intrapersonal relations. He further concluded that the delinquent population should not be regarded as a homogeneous group, and that the various types of delinquents—normal, neurotic, or aggressive—should therefore be placed in different schools. Merrill (1947) also suggested that low frustration tolerance is an important factor related to delinquency. She views frustration tolerance as one of the reasons for which one youngster becomes delinquent while another from similar environmental circumstances does not. Kvaraceus (1945) contends that frustration of basic psychological needs results from unstable home life, poverty, and disorganized community controls. In a discussion of his study he wrote, "The inquiry, therefore, seemed to involve largely an analysis of the life story of the children as individuals and the searching out of the nature of the frustrating influences."

IS THERE A "DELINQUENT PERSONALITY"? Although there is more research evidence available concerning the personality factors that might be related to delinquency, the studies summarized serve adequately to illustrate the general conclusion concerning this area. Specifically, it is quite apparent that the "delinquent personality" has yet to be identified, and it is doubtful that it will be identified in the near future. Even the specific relationships between personality characteristics and delinquency have not yet been well established, or in some cases even identified. The fact that delinquents and nondelinquents appear to be more similar than different in personality makeup requires even more intensive study to determine what real differences may exist. Even where a characteristic such as frustration tolerance does seem to differ in the delinquent and nondelinquent groups, it is difficult to determine how this characteristic can be changed. The development of the ability to tolerate frustration is a task that begins early in childhood and is influenced by various environmental considerations. One would need to identify at an early age those youngsters who need assistance in this area, and even then it might be difficult to determine how the pattern of tolerance could be strengthened.

MEASUREMENT AND PREDICTION OF DELINQUENCY

Tests of almost every known type have been administered to delinquents and nondelinquents in an attempt to identify characteristics and factors related to delinquency. The main purpose of these various research studies has been to determine what the major factors are, and particularly how their presence can be identified in a youngster before he actually commits a delinquent act. Several of the investigators have attempted to devise new instruments that will predict potential delinquent behavior early enough to prevent delinquency.

Use of Tested Instruments

The Minnesota Multiphasic Personality Inventory has been used in a number of studies of delinquents. Recently Hathaway and Monachesi (1952) administered this test to more than 4000 ninth-grade school children and checked the results against local police and court records to identify those with records of delinquency. The MMPI profiles of those identified as delinquents indicated that high scores on the Pd (psychopathic deviate) and Ma (hypomania) scores (alone or in combination), low Mf (masculinity-femininity) scores among boys, and low Hy (hysteria) scores among girls were prevalent.

Deri (1954) discussed the use of the Szondi Test in the differential diagnosis of delinquents based on chiefly qualitative data. She felt that use of the over-all score pattern of the Szondi, rather than isolated signs, is the sensible approach to diagnosis. The Szondi does not directly show a "delinquency pattern," but the picture it gives of behavorial impulses and their controls can lead to useful insight into the dynamics of various kinds of delinquency. Deri discussed the Szondi records of 13 murderers, 50 thieves, and 25 juvenile truants, and presented 13 "murderer" profiles and "typical" profiles for other delinquent groups. While this is an interesting study, it must be pointed out that the Szondi Test has been roundly criticized by experts and would certainly be suspect as a major instrument for diagnosing delinquents.

Young (1956) reported the results derived from a study in which she administered sixteen Thematic Apperception Test cards to 34 delinquent boys and 34 delinquent girls. Although she admits that the sample is a small one, her findings showed the following patterns: Delinquent boys most frequently refer to the paternal figure as advising the child. More than one-third of the boys described the death of the father and 20 per cent specified that the son shot the father. Generally the delinquent boys admired the father more than the mother but saw more good than bad in both their parents. Delinquent girls, on the other hand, tended to depict undesirable rather than desirable traits in both parents, especially in the mother. Both boys and girls viewed the mother as the more punitive parent, as the person who requires work, study, or practice, and as the one from whom the child runs away. The themes that seemed to reveal needs of the subjects were described by the majority and included succorance and/or love; heterosexual behavior; aggressive behavior; intragressive-dejection syndromes; desire for material possessions; achievement; and failure. About 62 per cent of the plots were unhappy ones, although one-third of them were changed to have happy endings.

The foregoing studies involve the use of tested instruments for measuring personality structure to determine patterns of responses peculiar to delinquents. Since they were all designed to help identify various personality problems, they are of value in the study of delinquency. To date, however, none of them has been demonstrated to be adequate for the prediction of delinquency, especially since they cannot always be appropriately used with young children. The findings from these studies represent a major step in identifying factors that relate to delinquency after the youngster has been declared officially delinquent. What is to be desired, however, is an instrument that could be administered to youngsters in order to determine which of them are delinquency-prone.

Attempts to Develop Predictive Instruments

Glueck and Glueck (1950) developed the Glueck Social Prediction Table, which is based on five interpersonal family factors that were found to have sharply differentiated 500 delinquents from 500 nondelinquents ("supervision of boy by mother; discipline of boy by father; affection of mother for boy; affection of father for boy; and cohesiveness of the family"), and also on character-structure patterns derived from the Rorschach ("social lability") and on temperament traits determined by psychiatric interviews ("adventurousness, extroversion, and emotional instability"). Black and Glick (1952) applied this table to a group of 100 Jewish boys confined to the Hawthorne–Cedar Knolls School in New York State, in an attempt to determine whether they could have been identified as delinquents five years earlier. They found that 91 per cent of the group could have been thus identified. Since Jewish children were not a part of the original Glueck samples, these findings seemed to indicate that the table was useful beyond the limits of the standardized population. Thompson's study (1952) of 100 boys who had originally been included in the Cambridge-Somerville Youth Study indicated that 91 per cent of these boys could have been identified as either potential delinquents or true nondelinquents. Other studies (New Jersey Research Bulletin No. 124, 1955; Rexford *et al.,* 1956) have offered further evidence of the apparent validity of the Social Prediction Scale.

Although they are useful, the Social Prediction Scales are quite technical and there is some question as to the adequacy of the sample involved in their development. Shapelin and Tiedeman (1951) commented on this point. They feel that the table can be used only by trained psychologists and social workers. This approach doubtless needs improvement and simplification, and the Gluecks appear to be making attempts to achieve these ends (Glueck, 1956).

The Kvaraceus Scale (Kvaraceus Delinquency) is another major attempt to devise an effective instrument for predicting delinquency. This scale is composed of 75 multiple-choice items, and an attempt is made to differentiate between the responses of delinquents and nondelinquents to these items. These items measure differences in areas related to personality structure, home and family background, and school experiences. High positive scores characterize delinquents, while high negative scores characterize nondelinquent youngsters. Separate scoring keys are used for boys and for girls. Kvaraceus has also developed a KD Proneness Checklist, which covers the same areas as the Proneness Scale and is designed to be used by teachers and professional workers. Kvaraceus felt that more predictive validity studies were needed to confirm the value of these instruments, and he reviewed and summarized studies reported up to that time in which the KD Proneness Scale and Checklist had been used (Kvaraceus, 1956). Although these studies generally appeared to support the validity of the instruments, there was considerable overlap in the criterion groups. The Scale and the Checklist showed low positive correlations with each other, suggesting that they are independent estimates of delinquency-proneness.

A number of other instruments has been used in an attempt to predict delinquency (Weeks, 1943; Durea, 1939; Zakolski, "Studies in Delinquency, II," 1949; Reckless *et al.,* 1957), but none of them has yet been sufficiently validated to be widely accepted. Wilkins, Hill, and Gibbons (1955) commented on predictive methods as they are used in the treatment of delinquency. Wilkins felt that they were valuable for three reasons: (1) they are workable methods; (2) they can be constructed within a particular framework of three matrices—information, control, and decisions—with no causal hypothesis needed; and (3) they involve the use of experimentation suitable for studying human behavior (which Wilkins labels "quasi-experimental" design). Hill offered the view that predictive methods are defective since they only show that delinquents fail, never why they fail. He felt that more study of cause and effect media is needed to improve the treatment of delinquents. Gibbons interprets the value of predictive measures for the psychiatrist and suggests what the psychiatrist himself can contribute to them. They all agree that the social sciences are still in need of "universal" laws, similar to those of the physical sciences, that can be applied to continuous research.

PREVENTION AND/OR TREATMENT OF DELINQUENCY

Even if a scale can be developed that will enable us to predict delinquency proneness perfectly, that will only be the first step toward the prevention of delinquency. The job of working with the youngsters so identified in order to change their behaviors to a more positive set of goals would then become a major one. At present we cannot set down specific standards or patterns of action that will prevent delinquency. In fact, many of the older ideas concerning prevention of delinquency have been abandoned, since attempts to put them in practice proved ineffective. For example, slum clearance was long regarded as of major importance in preventing delinquency. However, slums have been cleared, and new housing developments have replaced deteriorating neighborhoods only to have new slum areas elsewhere replace the old, and delinquency continues.

Beck, in three studies (all 1954), stressed the need to awaken public conscience to combat those evils in the community which cause delinquency. He felt that delinquency control should not be directed at parent-child relations but should demand civic action, since it is a social, economic, and cultural problem. Helping parents to understand and enjoy children is important in preventing delinquent behavior, but Beck felt that social action is needed to develop an ideal community to which people could adjust ideally. He felt that middle-class social institutions fail to repress or channelize constructively the hostility that delinquents put into action.

While prevention of delinquency may be our ultimate goal, its achievement obviously lies somewhere in the future. We must, of course, strive constantly to reach this goal as soon as possible. Research toward this end is essential. Until the goal is reached, however, we are confronted with the problems and treatment of those who are presently delinquent. For them prevention is too late; the need is for immediate and successful treatment geared toward at least preventing repetition of delinquent behavior. Since recidivism is common among delinquents today, most present-day treatment obviously does not accomplish this aim. To date, many kinds of treatment have been employed, each with some degree of success. We cannot yet say, however, that any single method is better than any other, or that any specific combination of methods is most effective.

Shelley (1956) proposed that supervision in a probation and parole setting should recognize the cultural, economic, emotional, and educational frustrations suffered by many adolescent offenders. Furthermore, he felt that it is necessary to distinguish between the basically extroverted "acting-out" delinquent and the neurotic delinquent. He discusses techniques for treating the psychopathic personality, the situational delinquent, the gang member, and the neurotic offender. Shelley believes that it is the function of the officer to help the youthful probationer or parolee to find substitute satisfactions, and that if the youngster is fortunate enough to do so, he will feel less frustrated and will have less need for aggression and rebelliousness. For many young people, the relationship with the caseworker will be the deciding factor in redirecting aggression into acceptable behavior patterns. Curran (1955) also described the activities of various kinds of agencies in dealing with juvenile delinquency. Among the agencies he mentions are Bellevue Hospital in New York City, the New York City Retention Home for Boys, the George Junior Republic, the Chicago Area Project, and the Cambridge-Somerville Youth Study. Many types of therapy also are needed to meet the many causes of delinquency. Curran stated that "a high percentage of juvenile delinquents can be salvaged if one uses a combination of individual and group therapy in special wards of psychiatric and state hospitals and in psychiatrically oriented reformatories."

Residential Treatment Centers

There is currently a large number of residential centers in which juvenile delinquents are placed by courts. These include reformatories, state training schools, state forestry camps, private schools, and other facilities supported by various civic or religious groups. Most of these centers purport to have a residential treatment unit, but the size and effectiveness of the units vary. In general, the state reformatories and training schools are very poorly staffed for social or psychiatric services. Even those that are fairly well staffed are usually overcrowded, and some youngsters may be released while still "in treatment" in order to make room for newcomers. The private agencies are often better staffed and better able to control the size of their delinquent populations. Coltharp and Weber (1952) have indicated that a residential treatment unit in a state school helps increase public awareness that delinquents have emotional problems. Its presence would provide for group therapy, individual therapy, and on-the-spot counseling, all of which could be most helpful to the delinquent youngsters. They recognize, however, that there may be strong resistance to such a unit from the regular staff.

Grunhut (1955) reported the results of a study of 100 delinquent boys (under punitive detention) in a New Detention Center near Oxford, England. He employed the case-study method to evaluate the program at the center in the light of: (1) what types of boys are sent there by the magistrates; (2) how different individual offenders respond to the new treatment; and (3) what criteria should be applied in the selection of boys for this type of rehabilitation. His conclusions indicated that: (1) moderate past criminal experience does not preclude a fair prospect of success following detention; and (2) detention in the center seems to produce a "crimeless" period following release (88 per cent of those released had not been reconvicted after three months), which must be exploited quickly to help the boy make a permanent social adjustment.

Caditz (1959) administered the Minnesota Multiphasic Personality Inventory and the Edwards Personal Preference Scale to 94 boys committed to a state training school, first prior to their entry and again after they had been institutionalized for approximately six months. The same tests were also administered to an unselected group of sophomore high-school boys, who also were retested about six months later. The findings indicated that the training-school experience was not effective in modifying the significant differences that were found between the delinquents and the nondelinquents before the delinquents entered the training school. Further, Caditz reported that the delinquents' and nondelinquents' basic personality needs as measured by the EPPS did not differ. When the results of the second test were compared with the results of the first test, both groups showed improvement in terms of lower MMPI mean scores. Comparisons within the delinquent subgroups indicated that boys from broken families differed from the nondelinquents more than did boys from intact families. However, the boys from broken homes seemed to benefit more from the training-school experience (in terms of better personality organization and stability) than those from intact homes. Finally, Caditz concluded that the variable considered as the most appropriate measure of specifically delinquent traits, the Pd (psychopathic deviate) scale of the

MMPI, was not materially affected by the delinquent's training-school experience. The latter finding was more pronounced in the case of boys who did not come from broken homes.

Caditz (1961) attempted to test the hypothesis that experience in a forestry-camp would cause delinquent boys to become more like non-delinquents. Three groups were established for this purpose. The experimental group consisted of 17 boys, assigned to a youth forestry camp, who were judged to be no major security risk (average age sixteen and a half years). One control group included 94 boys (average fifteen and a half years) who were confined to a training school, and the second control group consisted of 97 high-school sophomores. All three groups were given the MMPI and retested five or six months later. On the first testing, the forestry group scored significantly lower on the false scale than the training-school group. The Pd (psychopathic deviate) scale was the only one on which the forestry-camp boys scored significantly higher than the nondelinquent controls, and in no instance did the forestry group score sigificantly higher than the training-school boys. In the retest, the forestry camp boys scored significantly lower on the Pd scale than did the training school boys but remained significantly higher in their scores than the nondelinquent group. The Hy (hysteria) and the Pa (paranoia) scales also became significantly lower for the forestry group than for the training-school group. Caditz concludes that "for at least one type of delinquent boys the forestry camp experience is associated with improvement in social attitudes and level of emotional maturity."

A prediction table was constructed from background variables and responses to an attitude scale by Freeman and Weeks (1956). This table was applied to a sample of 171 delinquent boys assigned to Highfields and a control group of 58 delinquent boys assigned to Annandale Farms. Highfields is a residence for delinquent boys which has no barred windows, or locked gates, or guards, and which features a permissive atmosphere and group therapy. Annandale Farms is a modern, minimum-security institution. In general, the Highfields program resulted in greater likelihood of successful treatment. However, further research is necessary on other factors influencing success or failure of treatment in addition to the background variables and attitudes considered in this study.

A follow-up study of girls who had been discharged from Laurelton State Village during a ten-year period from 1936 to 1946 was conducted by Hartzler (1951). Of the 30 girls on whom the follow-up was actually done, 17 were rated as successful; 8, as unsuccessful; and 5, as partially successful. Three factors seemed to distinguish between the successful and unsuccessful girls: (1) degree of delinquency, both prior to admission and during institutionalization; (2) length of time on parole; and (3) type of home to which they returned.

The last factor identified in the Hartzler study, the type of home to which the youngster returns, is a major factor in whether the effect of institutional therapy carries over when the youngster is released. All too often a youngster who has shown progress in therapy must return to the poor environment that initially gave rise to his delinquent behavior. Some are able to cope with this environment as a result of insights gained from the therapy. Others, unfortunately, do not reach this point in their treatment and may again be negatively influenced by their home or neighborhood environment. This danger is well recognized, and whenever it is possible a youngster is placed in a foster home instead of being returned to his former environment.

Bloom (1955) described the residential treatment and grammar-school education provided for boys of superior intellect at Red Hill School, a residential treatment center at Maidstone, Kentucky. Here the formality of academic and social education is combined with the necessary informality of proper psychotherapy. Adult-child intimacy is encouraged, since the school accepts boys for four years or more. Bloom felt that the permissive atmosphere of the school, the informality of the adult-child relationships, and the opportunities presented for spontaneous activities all combined to make this type of treatment desirable for the behavior problems encountered at Red Hill.

Group Therapy

Because most of the institutions that house delinquents are inadequately staffed, there is often little opportunity for individual therapy. Some attempts have been made to develop group therapy programs on a fairly regular basis. Gersten (1952) examined and evaluated the changes in observed behavior and in intellectual, emotional, and social adjustment in a group of institutionalized male juvenile delinquents who participated in approximately twenty weekly sessions of group therapy. The author found that this experimental group gained in intellectual performance, school achievement, emotional security, social maturity, and adjustment, as measured by standardized tests and ratings of group records. More extensive experimentation along these lines would obviously be valuable.

Philip and Peizotto (1959) worked with an experimental group of 43 delinquent boys who were given brief group therapy with the object of reducing their hostility. A matched control group received no therapy during the three-and-one-half-week period of this study. Both groups were given a modified Thematic Apperception Test at the beginning and at the end of the experiment, in order to test the hypothesis that the experimental group would show a reduction in hostility. The results of the TAT comparisons confirmed this hypothesis at the 5-per-cent level of significance. Changes in the hypothesized direction of the TAT scores for the other four variables—need for achievement, blandness, insecurity, and guilt—occurred, but did not reach an acceptable level of significance.

These studies do appear to demonstrate the possible effectiveness of group therapy with delinquents, even if the therapy cannot be carried to a conclusion before the youngster is released from the institution. Conceivably, such group therapy could be attempted at out-patient clinics in high-delinquency areas. At any rate, the evidence indicates that group therapy can be employed with some effectiveness in institutions, even those in which individual treatment is also available.

THE NEED FOR MORE RESEARCH

The reader must by now be well aware that a good deal of research has been conducted in an attempt to determine which factors seem most related to delinquency, how delinquency might be predicted, and what might be done to prevent it; but he must also be aware that, despite all the findings of these various studies, little has been done to alleviate the problem, which, in fact, continues to increase in intensity. The inadequacy of the samples involved in many of the earlier studies, the lack of proper measuring devices, and even the failure of juvenile courts to make their records available to investigators, are among the reasons for the failure to solve the problem.

Various subtle factors also seriously limited the early investigators. The failure of courts to penalize delinquents from average and high socioeconomic backgrounds in the same ways that they penalized those from lower socioeconomic backgrounds made it impossible for the researchers to get representative samples. The unwillingness of private agencies and treatment centers to allow researchers to study their records left only the records of public institutions for study. Schools have been particularly unwilling to provide information concerning students who have become delinquent, probably for fear that the school might be found to have contributed to the frustrations that brought about delinquent acts. It is still quite difficult to obtain school and/or court records for use in investigating possible racial differences related to delinquency, for fear, one supposes, that the evidence might show some evidence of discrimination.

The factor of discrimination was partially demonstrated in a study by Axelrad (1952), who compared 300 Negro and white delinquents in the same institution. The study was designed to determine whether the courts were committing Negro and white children on the same basis and whether the two groups differed on family constellations. (The family constellation refers to the structure of the family and the youngster's place within that structure. It describes the relationships of the various members of the family with the adults and with each other.) The results disclosed that Negro children are committed younger, for less serious offenses, with fewer previous court appearances, and with less prior institutionalization. Negro children came from more unstable homes and from homes with a different kind of pathology from that of the white delinquents. Further research in this area is greatly needed, if only to control possible discrimination by the courts.

Despite the fact that the relationship of intelligence to delinquency has been frequently studied, the results are still inconclusive. Recent studies have almost completely changed the concepts accepted twenty-five years ago. A recent study of average- and high-IQ delinquents by Caplan and Powell (1962) opens a whole new field of investigation of the intelligence factor as it relates to school achievement and other behavioral patterns of this kind of delinquent.

Finally, if the current research aimed at developing better instruments for predicting delinquency is successful, a whole new field of research will be opened. There will be a tremendous need for studies dealing with methods of preventing delinquency and/or changing the behavior of those who appear to be delinquency-prone. With the increased cooperation of the community, the police, the courts, and the schools, future researchers may well find the answers we so desperately seek. Once these answers are found, they will then have to be put in practice in the lives of children.

ADOLESCENTS VIEW DELINQUENCY

No group is more aware of juvenile delinquency than the millions of nondelinquent youngsters in this country. Although a large majority of them are well-behaved youngsters who are relatively well adjusted to their environment, they feel that they suffer from the behavior of those who become delinquent. These "normal" youngsters particularly resent the loose use of the term "delinquent" by adults, who seem to apply it to all adolescents. As has been mentioned in other connections, they resent the fact that newspapers and other communications media devote much space or time to the problems of delinquency but seldom discuss the positive behavior of the majority of adolescents.

Delinquency Penalizes All Adolescents

Many youngsters feel that, because of the behavior of a few, they are subjected to more restrictions, such as curfews, than are necessary. They complain that even minor acts which they consider just "horseplay" are considered by adults as evidence of delinquent behavior. Most of them feel that law-enforcement officers are so delinquency-conscious that they automatically assume the worst when they encounter a youngster engaged in some relatively harmless act. One youngster summed up the feeling of his group with this explanation:

"On Saturday nights we all meet at the soda fountain after we take our dates home. About the time we get there a police car pulls up and parks until we've left. Nothing has ever happened, but they act like they expect a 'rumble' or something. It seems to us they'd be better off patroling some of the high-crime neighborhoods instead of wasting their time watching us. We'd understand it if we had made some trouble, but we never have."

Because most adolescents are fully aware of the seriousness of the problem of juvenile delinquency, they feel that adults do have a right to be concerned, just as they are concerned about adult criminality. Adults do not, however, generalize in the same way about adult criminals. Adults are not generally suspicious of the behavior of all other adults because of the acts of a few individuals, but teen-agers feel that they are all viewed with suspicion because of the well-publicized behavior of a few delinquents.

If a youngster does get into a borderline situation that might bring him into contact with the police, he usually fears that he will not get a fair chance. Generally the police are quite lenient with youngsters involved in minor difficulties and often let them off with a simple warning. There are, no doubt, occasions when a youngster is treated more harshly by the law-enforcement officials than his behavior warrants, but these instances are rare. There is, however, a widespread feeling of resentment against the police by teen-agers. Even though the feeling may not be justified, it is often reinforced by particular situations. One of our panelists described such a situation in which he was involved and explained his peer group's reaction when he told them about the following incident:

"About a month ago, I was with my dad when he ran a stop sign. A policeman stopped him and was going to give him a ticket. Dad explained that he'd never broken the law before, and the officer finally let him go with just a warning. Last week I was driving the car, and started to go through a stop sign which I almost didn't see because of a parked car. I stopped about ten feet beyond the sign but not quite in the intersection. A police car pulled up and out stepped a policeman. I tried to explain about the parked car, which was still there, but he wouldn't listen. He said, 'You probably weren't going to stop at all, but must have spotted our cruiser at the last minute. All you kids are alike, always breaking the laws. It's time you got a lesson.' Then I got a ticket and had to go to court. About ten adults ahead of me paid similar fines and no comment was made. When I got to the window the clerk said, 'When are you kids going to realize you can't just run around breaking laws?' and gave me a thorough tongue-lashing. My dad also bawled me out, but I reminded him about his ticket. Then he actually saw the point and agreed that the police were sometimes over-zealous in dealing with teen-agers. Dad knows I wouldn't maliciously go through a stop sign. When I told the kids in school about it, some of them had had similar experiences, and most of them felt that they were discriminated against by the police."

Actually, most juvenile courts do not consider traffic offenses as delinquent behavior in the strict legal sense and seldom include the traffic violations in their court statistics concerning delinquency. How-ever, many teen-agers are unaware of this and feel that a court appear-ance for a traffic violation identifies them as delinquents. While there may be some justification in the statement of one teen-ager, "When I said I didn't have the car registration, the police acted like I'd stolen the car," one must also agree that there is some justification in the atti-tude of the policeman. Car theft is common among delinquent young-sters, and the police are probably right in being suspicious if a young-ster cannot offer proof of ownership.

Many youngsters are particularly concerned about accidental delin-quency, i.e., being involved in a delinquent situation in which they take no active part but are considered guilty by association. Sal G. described this kind of situation:

"One of my buddies was walking home the other night when another kid we know pulled up in a new car and offered him a ride. This kid said it was his father's new car and he was just checking it out. About five minutes later a police car pulled them over and arrested both of them. When he found out it was a stolen car, my buddy tried to tell the police what happened but they wouldn't listen. Fortunately, the other kid told them what had happened, and they apologized to my buddy and let him go. Sure, we can understand the policeman's point, but it just seems that they think we're all liars."

Nondelinquents' Attitudes Toward Delinquents

Most teen-agers will avoid youngsters whom they know are delin-quents, not so much because they are afraid of getting involved with them as because they do not like that sort of youngster. They are fully aware of the way in which delinquent behavior reflects on them and tend to reject youngsters they consider responsible for this. While such rejection may further frustrate the delinquent and even cause him to become involved in more negative behavior in an attempt to gain status, one cannot blame the nondelinquent youngsters for their behavior. Ron D., a teen-ager from a high-delinquency area, told our seminar about a situation of this kind in which he had been involved:

"One of the kids we knew just came back from six months in the State Training School, and started bragging about how he'd really had a 'good deal.' None of the kids I know would even talk to him and he got real mad. He told us we were a bunch of sissies and would never be worth much. He said he'd show us who the big shot was. Next day he came in wearing a new watch which he said he bought with money he got from rolling a drunk, and offered to take some of us with him next time he did the same thing. When everyone refused, he got real mad. That afternoon he stole a car and brought it around to give us rides. No one would go and he roared off. The police caught him and he's now back in the State School."

One of the teachers in the seminar asked Ron whether he thought they'd been fair to the boy. The teacher suggested that if Ron and his group had been nicer to him, the youngster might not have committed the robberies in order to gain status. Ron thought this over, then responded:

"I guess that's possible. Maybe we should have given him a break, but we didn't like his bragging. Anyway, in our neighborhood a kid can't afford to be seen with anyone who has a record. If he gets into trouble, the cops come to pick you up too because you're a friend of his. Maybe it is rough on these kids, like you say, but the law will be breathing down your neck. Actually it's kids like that who make it rough on us, so why should we worry about them?"

Rehabilitation Problems of Delinquents

This kind of reasoning may be valid, but it creates difficulties for the youngster who has been delinquent and is trying to keep out of further trouble. He feels that he is rejected by those with whom he seeks to be friendly and by society in general. Such youngsters feel that the school authorities in particular reject them, and even though they are able to re-enter school they feel that no one really wants them there. Unfortunately, this is often quite true. School personnel often feel that a youngster who is readmitted to school after he has committed a delinquent act is likely to be a troublemaker and frequently set up unusually harsh standards to which such a youngster must conform. It may be true that many of these delinquents only return to school because the law compels them to and that they may cause a good deal of disturbance in the school. With all these problems confronting him, it is indeed difficult for a youngster to rehabilitate himself, and those who succeed deserve much credit.

Other elements of society also tend to reject a youngster who has a "record." The armed forces will allow such a youngster to enlist only under very special circumstances. Relatively few employers are willing to "take a chance" with such a youngster and usually do so only grudgingly. The youngster employed under such circumstances is likely to feel that suspicion is constantly directed at him.

Ray T. was released from a state training school for boys to which he had been committed for six months. When he went back to school he found that most of his old friends avoided him, and few of the teachers even spoke to him. Ray enrolled in an auto-mechanics course, and this, he feels, saved him. The auto-mechanics teacher knew nothing about Ray's past and was impressed with his knowledge of cars and his willingness to work hard. Ray was generally unhappy with the rest of the school environment and thought of quitting, but decided to stick it out because of the auto-shop program. When some of the other students learned of his skill, they asked him to help them with their own cars, and Ray was happy to oblige. In return, some of the boys offered to help Ray with his other subjects, and he welcomed their assistance. When his other teachers noted his improved work, they began to take an interest in him. Ray graduated successfully and has a good job as an auto mechanic in a garage.

This happy ending in Ray's case does not necessarily follow for others in similar circumstances. The author had occasion to discuss Ray's case with his former teachers. They agreed that they had originally been unfair to him, but when they realized he was different they were quick to help. However, they still thought most delinquents not worth the effort and simply viewed Ray as the exception that proved the rule. Fortunately for Ray, he had a skill that enabled him to show ability in some area. Unfortunately, however, few delinquents have such skills or the opportunity to acquire them.

Recently a young former delinquent addressed our seminar about the problems he had in rehabilitation. He was particularly critical of the training school to which he had been sent, feeling that he had actually been set back educationally while he was there and had therefore been penalized when he re-entered his old high school. He described his experience in this way:

"I'd always been a fairly good student in school even though I got in trouble. At the state training school I was put in a tenth grade, but I soon found they were doing sixth-grade work. All the teachers were very poor and didn't even know the subjects they taught. When I got out at the end of a year they sent my old school a note saying I'd successfully completed the tenth grade, and my school put me in the eleventh grade. I was really lost. Finally I told the principal what had happened and asked if I could repeat the tenth grade. He was nice enough to agree, and explained my situation to my teachers. Everyone was very helpful (I think because of my previous good record in school). I finally graduated with a high-B average and I'm attending college now. I really resent losing that year. I know it was my own fault that I got in trouble, but I don't think it's right to have such poor school programs in state schools. A lot of the fellows I knew there were so discouraged that they didn't even go back to school when they got out."

AN OVERVIEW

It seems rather obvious that the delinquent is penalized in many ways for his negative behavior. Instead of getting the status he seeks from his peers, he is rejected. One cannot condemn the nondelinquents for their failure to accept those with a record of delinquency. If we expect to enlist the aid of the "normal" teen-ager in helping to rehabilitate those who get into trouble, we must first change our adult attitudes toward both delinquents and nondelinquents.

REFERENCES

AUSUBEL, D. P. "Sociempathy as a Function of Sociometric Status in the Adolescent Group." *Human Relations, 8,* 75-84, 1955.

AXELRAD, SIDNEY. "Negro and White Male Institutionalized Delinquents." *American Journal of Sociology,* 57, 569-574, 1952.

BARTLETT, CLAUDE J., and HORROCKS, JOHN E. "A Study of the Needs Status of Adolescents from Broken Homes." *Journal of Genetic Psychology,* 93, 153-159, 1958.

BECK, BERTRAM. "Juvenile Delinquency—Why and How." *Journal of Social Hygiene,* 40, 210-221, 1954.

BECK, BERTRAM. "New Approaches to Juvenile Delinquency." *National Parent-Teacher,* 49(1), 26-28, 1954.

BECK, BERTRAM. "What We Can Do About Juvenile Delinquency." *Child Welfare,* 33, 1, 3-7, 1954.

BLACK, BERTRAM J., and GLICK, SELMA J. "Recidivism at Hawthorne—Cedar Knolls School." *Research Monograph No. 2,* New York: Jewish Board of Guardians, 1952.

BLOOM, LEONARD. "Some Aspects of the Residential Psychotherapy of Maladjusted or Delinquent Children." *British Journal of Juvenile Delinquency,* 6, 41-49, 1955.

BLUE, JOHN T., JR. "The Relationship of Juvenile Delinquency, Race, and Economic Status." *Journal of Negro Education,* 17, 469-477, 1948.

CADITZ, SYLVAN B. "Effect of a Training School Experience on the Personality of Delinquent Boys." *Journal of Consulting Psychology*, 23, 501-509, 1959.

CADITZ, SYLVAN B. "Effects of a Forestry Camp Experience on the Personality of Delinquent Boys." *Journal of Clinical Psychology*, 17, 78-81, 1961.

CAPLAN, N., and POWELL, M. "Study of Delinquents with High IQs." Unpublished, 1962.

CASS, LORETTA K. "Parent-Child Relationships and Delinquency." *Journal of Abnormal and Social Psychology*, 47, 101-104, 1952.

CHARLES, C. M. "A Comparison of the Intelligence Quotients of Incarcerated Delinquent White and American Negro Boys and of Groups of St. Louis Public School Boys." *Journal of Applied Psychology*, 20, 499-510, 1936.

COLTHARP, RALPH W., and WEBER, GEORGE H. "A Residential Treatment Unit within a State School for Delinquents: An Experiment." *Psychiatric Quarterly Supplement*, 26, 149-160, 1952.

Comparisons of Expenditures and Estimated Standard Costs for Selected Juvenile Delinquency Services. Children's Bureau. No. 10. Washington, D. C.: U. S. Department of Health, Education and Welfare, 1960.

CRANE, A. R. "A Note on Pre-adolescent Gangs." *Australian Journal of Psychology*, 3, 43-46, 1951.

CRANE, A. R. "Pre-adolescent Gangs: A Socio-psychological Interpretation." *Journal of Genetic Psychology*, 86, 275-279, 1955.

CURRAN, FRANK J. "Specialized Techniques in the Treatment of Juvenile Delinquency." *Journal of the American Medical Association*, 157, 108-113, 1955.

DAVIS, ALLISON. "Tests of Children of Varying Socio-economic Levels." *New York Times*, March 23, 1950.

Delinquency Prevention: The Size of the Problem. Children's Bureau. No. 4. Washington, D. C.: U. S. Department of Health, Education and Welfare, 1960.

DERI, SUSAN K. "Differential Diagnosis of Delinquents with the Szondi Test." *Journal of Projective Techniques*, 18, 33-41, 1954.

DINITZ, SIMON, KAY, BARBARA, and RECKLESS, WALTER C. "Delinquency Proneness and School Achievement." *Educational Research Bulletin*, 36, 131-136, 1957.

DUREA, M. A. "The Differential Diagnosis of Potential Delinquency." *American Journal of Orthopsychiatry*, 9, 394-398, 1939.

FENTON, N. *The Delinquent Boy and the Correctional School*. Claremont, Calif.: Claremont College, 1935.

FREEMAN, HOWARD E., and WEEKS, ASHLEY H. "Analysis of a Program of Treatment of Delinquent Boys." *American Journal of Sociology*, 62, 56-61, 1956.

GERSTEN, CHARLES. "Group Therapy with Institutionalized Juvenile Delinquents." *Journal of Genetic Psychology*, 80, 35-64, 1952.

GLUECK, SHELDON. "The Home, the School and Delinquency." *Harvard Educational Review*, 23, 17-32, 1953.

GLUECK, SHELDON. *The Problem of Delinquency*. Boston: Houghton Mifflin, 1959.

GLUECK, SHELDON, and GLUECK, ELEANOR T. *Five Hundred Criminal Careers.* New York: Alfred A. Knopf, 1933.

GLUECK, SHELDON, and GLUECK, ELEANOR T. *One Thousand Delinquents: Their Treatment by Court and Clinic.* Cambridge, Mass.: Harvard University Press, 1934.

GLUECK, SHELDON, and GLUECK, ELEANOR T. *Unraveling Juvenile Delinquency.* Cambridge, Mass.: Harvard University Press, 1950.

GLUECK, SHELDON, and GLUECK, ELEANOR T. "Early Detection of Future Delinquents." *Journal of Criminal Law, Criminology and Police Science,* vol. 47, no. 2, 174-182, 1956.

GRUNHUT, M. "Juvenile Delinquents under Punitive Detention." *British Journal of Delinquency,* 5, 191-209, 1955.

GRYGIER, TADEUSZ. "Leisure Pursuits of Juvenile Delinquents: A Study in Methodology." *British Journal of Delinquency,* 5, 210-228, 1955.

HARRINGTON, ROBERT W., and DAVIS, ROBERT H. "A Note on Juvenile Delinquents and the Ability to Abstract." *Child Development,* 24, 285-286, 1953.

HARTZLER, ETHEL. "A Follow-up Study of Girls Discharged from the Laurelton State Village." *American Journal of Mental Deficiency,* 55, 612-618, 1951.

HATHAWAY, STARKE R., and MONACHESI, ELIO D. "The Minnesota Multiphasic Personality Inventory in the Study of Juvenile Delinquents." *American Sociological Review,* 17, 704-710, 1952.

HEALY, W., and BRONNER, A. F. *New Lights on Delinquency and Its Treatment.* New Haven: Yale University Press, 1936.

HEWITT, I. E., and JENKINS, R. I. *Fundamental Patterns of Maladjustment.* Springfield, Ill.: Department of Mental Hygiene, State of Illinois, 1946.

HIRSCHBERG, J. COTTER, and NOSHPITZ, JOSEPH. "Comments on Sociopsychological Aspects of Juvenile Delinquency." *American Medical Association Journal of Diseases of Children,* 89, 361-373, 1955.

HOULT, T. F. "Comic Books and Juvenile Delinquency." *Sociology and Social Research,* 33, 279-284, 1949.

KAUFMAN, IRVING. "Three Basic Sources for Pre-delinquent Character." *Nervous Child,* 2, 12-15, 1955.

KAUFMAN, IRVING, MAKKAY, ELIZABETH S., and ZILBACH, JOAN. "The Impact of Adolescence on Girls with Delinquent Character Formation." *American Journal of Orthopsychiatry,* 29, 130-143, 1959.

KAY, BRIAN. "Reactions of Delinquent and Other Groups to Experimentally Induced Frustration." *British Journal of Delinquency,* 4, 245-264, 1954.

KVARACEUS, WILLIAM C. *Juvenile Delinquency and the School.* New York: World Book Co., 1945.

KVARACEUS, WILLIAM C. *The Community and the Delinquent.* New York: World Book Co., 1954.

KVAKACEUS, WILLIAM C. "Forecasting Juvenile Delinquency." *Journal of Education,* 138(4), 1-43, 1956.

LICHTENSTEIN, M., and BROWN, A. W. "Intelligence and Achievement of Children in a High Delinquency Area." *Journal of Juvenile Research,* 22, 1-25, 1938.

MCDAVID, JOHN, JR., and SCHRODER, HAROLD M. "The Interpretation of Approval and Disapproval by Delinquent and Nondelinquent Adolescents." *Journal of Personality*, 25, 539-549, 1957.

MANN, ARTHUR. "The Children's Hour of Crime." *Scribners*, 93, 313-315, 1933.

MERRILL, M. A. *Problems of Child Delinquency*. Boston: Houghton Mifflin, 1947.

MONACHESI, ELIO D. "Personality Characteristics of Institutionalized and Non-institutionalized Male Delinquents." *Journal of Criminal Law and Criminology*, 41, 167-179, 1950.

MONAHAN, THOMAS P. "The Trend in Broken Homes among Delinquent Children." *Marriage and Family Living*, 19, 362-365, 1957.

NEW JERSEY JUVENILE COMMISSION. *Justice and the Child in New Jersey* (Trenton), 82, 1939.

NEW JERSEY RESEARCH BULLETIN NO. 124. *Predicting Juvenile Delinquency*. Trenton, N. J.: State Department of Institutions and Agencies, 1955.

NYE, F. IVAN, SHROT, JAMES F., and OLSON, VIRGIL J. "Socioeconomic Status and Delinquent Behavior." *American Journal of Sociology*, 63, 381-389, 1958.

OHWAKI, YOSHIKAZU. "Cooperative Researches on the Personality of Juvenile Delinquents." *Tohoku Psychologica Folia* (Sendai), 13, 1-46, 1952.

O'KELLY, ELIZABETH. "Some Observations on Relationships between Delinquent Girls and Their Parents." *British Journal of Medical Psychology*, 28, 59-66, 1955.

PENROSE, L. S. "Genetics, and the Criminal." *British Journal of Delinquency*, 6, 15-25, 1955.

PETERS, JAMES SEDALIA II. "Socio-economic Egocentricism in Delinquents and Non-delinquents." *Studies in Higher Education, Purdue University*, no. 85, 1-21, 1957.

PETERSON, DONALD R., and QUAY, HERBERT C. "Personality Factors Related to Juvenile Delinquency." *Child Development*, 32, 335-372, 1961.

PETERSON, DONALD R., QUAY, HERBERT C., and CAMERON, GORDON R. "Personality and Background Factor in Juvenile Delinquency as Inferred from Questionnaire Responses." *Journal of Consulting Psychology*, 23, 395-405, 1959.

PHILIP, B. ROGER, and PEIZOTTO, HELEN E. "An Objective Evaluation of Brief Group Psychotherapy on Delinquent Boys." *Canadian Journal of Psychology*, 13, 273-280, 1959.

RECKLESS, W. C., DINITZ, S., and MURRAY, E. "The 'Good' Boy in a High Delinquency Area." *Journal of Criminal Law and Criminology*, 48, 18-25, 1957.

Report to the Congress on Juvenile Delinquency. Children's Bureau. Washington, D. C.: U. S. Department of Health, Education and Welfare, 1960.

REXFORD, EVEOLEEN N., SCHLEIFER, MAXWELL., and VAN AMEROGEN, SUZANNE TAETS. "A Follow-up of a Psychiatric Study of Fifty-seven Antisocial Young Children." *Mental Hygiene*, 196-214, 1956.

RICH, GILBERT J. "Childhood as a Preparation for Delinquency." *Journal of Educational Sociology*, 27, 404-413, 1954.

SHAPELIN, J. T., and TIEDEMAN, D. V. "Comment on the Juvenile Delinquent Prediction Tables in the Gluecks' *Unraveling Juvenile Delinquency.*" *American Sociological Review,* 16, 544-548, 1951.

SHELLEY, JOSEPH A. "Dynamics and Treatment Needs of Adolescence." *Journal of the National Probation and Parole Association,* 2, 106-115, 1956.

SHULMAN, HARRY M. *A Study of Problem Boys and Their Brothers.* Albany: New York State Crime Commission, 1929.

SMITH, PHILIP M. "Broken Homes and Juvenile Delinquency." *Sociology and Social Research,* 39, 307, 1955.

STOTT, D. H. "Delinquency, Maladjustment and Unfavorable Ecology." *British Journal of Psychology,* 51, 157-170, 1960.

THOMPSON, RICHARD E. "A Validation of the Glueck Social Prediction Scale for Proneness to Delinquency." *Journal of Criminal Law and Criminology,* 43, 451-470, 1952.

TRENT, RICHARD D. "The Relationship of Anxiety to Popularity and Rejection among Institutionalized Delinquent Boys." *Child Development,* 28, 379-384, 1957.

TRENT, RICHARD D. "Socioemphathic Ability in a Group of Institutionalized Delinquent Boys." *Journal of Genetic Psychology,* 91, 99-108, 1957.

TRENT, RICHARD D. "Anxiety and Accuracy of Perception of Sociometric Status among Institutionalized Delinquent Boys." *Journal of Genetic Psychology,* 94, 85-91, 1959.

WATTENBERG, W. W. "Church Attendance and Juvenile Misconduct." *Sociology and Social Research,* 34, 195-202, 1950.

WATTENBERG, W. W. "Eleven-Year-Old Boys in Trouble." *Journal of Educational Psychology,* 44, 409-417, 1953.

WATTENBERG, W. W., and FAIGENBAUM, DAVID. "Patterns in Delinquency." *Journal of Clinical Psychology,* 9, 78-81, 1953.

WATTENBERG, W. W., and SAUNDERS, F. "Sex Differences among Juvenile Offenders." *Sociology and Social Research,* 39, 24, 1954.

WEEKS, H. A. "Predicting Juvenile Delinquency." *American Sociological Review,* 8, 40-46, 1943.

WERTHAM, FREDERIC. "The Comics—Very Funny!" *The Saturday Review,* May 29, 1948.

WILKINS, LESLIE T., HILL, C. P., and GIBBONS, T. C. N. "Symposium on Predictive Methods in the Treatment of Delinquency." *British Journal of Delinquency,* 6, 82-98, 1955.

WOODWARD, MARY. "The Role of Intelligence in Delinquency." *British Journal of Delinquency,* 5, 281-303, 1955.

YOUNG, FLORENCE M. "Responses of Juvenile Delinquents to the TAT." *Journal of Genetic Psychology,* 88, 251-259, 1956.

ZAKOLSKI, F. C. "Studies in Delinquency: I. Personality Structure of Delinquent Boys." *Journal of Genetic Psychology,* 74, 109-117, 1949.

ZAKOLSKI, F. C. "Studies in Delinquency: II. Prediction of Delinquency in Boys." *Journal of Genetic Psychology,* 74, 119-123, 1949.

Index of Authors

534

Havighurst—*cont.*
327, 358, 381, 403, 407, 447
Hawkes, G. R., 251, 282
Hayes, M. L., 308, 327
Healy, W., 508, 531
Hearn, H. C., 477, 489
Hecker, S. E., 470, 487
Heist, P., 122, 140
Henry, W. E., 126, 140
Henton, C. L., 37, 71
Heron, A., 238, 245
Herrfahrdt, I., 352, 358
Herrold, E. E., 488
Hershenson, J. R., 162, 178
Hertzman, J., 455, 487
Hess, R. D., 23, 27, 181, 212, 266, 282
Hewitt, I. E., 510, 531
Hieronymous, A. N., 300, 327
Hilden, A. H., 82, 107
Hill, C. B., 517, 518, 533
Hill, T. J., 221, 245, 423, 447
Hillway, T., 16, 27
Himmelweit, H. T., 94, 107, 203, 212
Hindsman, E., 108
Hindus, M., 265, 282
Hines, V. A., 418, 447
Hinsie, L. E., 454, 487
Hinton, R., 92, 108
Hirschberg, J. C., 498, 531
Hjelholt, G., 260, 282
Hobart, C., 23, 27
Hoffman, H. N., 417, 447
Hofstaetter, P. R., 140
Hogben, H., 30, 71
Hogben, L., 71
Hollingshead, A. B., 192, 201, 212, 340, 358
Homan, M., 262, 282
Honigman, I., 115, 142
Honzik, M. P., 82, 84, 107, 108
Hoover, H. F., 237, 245
Horn, D., 157, 178
Hornbostel, V. O., 493
Horrocks, J. E., 21, 22, 27, 184, 185, 213, 215, 501, 502, 529
Horton, R. E., 313, 327, 359

Hotyat, F., 416, 417, 447
Hoult, T. F., 511, 531
Howard, C. W., 421, 447
Howard, M., 152, 176
Hoyt, K. B., 462, 487
Hsaio, H. H., 90, 106
Hsu, E. H., 117, 140
Hsu, F. L. K., 5, 27, 121, 140, 264, 282
Hubbard, G. W., 422, 447
Hubble, D., 52, 71
Hughes, J. H., 308, 327
Hughes, O., 477, 487
Hummel, R., 405
Humphreys, J. A., 385, 404
Hunt, G. B., 476, 487
Hunt, J. T., 171, 178
Hunter, T. A., 41, 71
Hurlock, E. B., 10, 27
Hyman, B., 375, 404

Ilioff, L. B., 418, 447
Imamura, K., 319, 327
Itkin, W., 257, 282
Ives, V., 161, 178
Ivie, C., 418, 447
Ivins, W. H., 456, 487

Jackson, C. M., 71
Jackson, J., 383, 404
Jackson, P. W., 95, 107, 455, 488
Jacobs, R., 336, 358
Jacobson, P. B., 405
Jahoda, G., 391, 395, 396, 404
James, H. E. O., 305, 327
Janis, I. L., 129, 140
Jaques, W. T., 471, 488
Jenkins, D. M., 490
Jenkins, R. I., 510, 531
Jennings, E., 108
Jensen, A. R., 127, 141
Jensen, K., 32, 71
Jensen, R. E., 481, 488
Joffee, N. F., 52, 69
Johannis, T. B., 281
Johnson, C. S., 394, 395, 404

Index of Subjects

Abilities, mental, 77-78; motor, 44-45, 47, 60-61; and vocational choice, 362-365

Academic achievement, attitudes toward, 102-103; and college achievement, 435-437; and college admission, 104, 436; and family conflict, 272-273; and intelligence, 96-97, 428-431; and personality, 431-433; sex differences in, 9, 90-92; and work experience, 376-377 (see also Under-achievement)

Academic grades, 427-428, 441-442

Acceptance (see Social Adjustment)

Accidents, 44

Achievement tests (see Measurement)

Acne, 49, 67

Adjustment, age differences in, 144-145; and family relationships, 239, 247-259, 260-280; and intelligence, 97-99, 130, 170; measurement of (see Measurement); in other societies, 149-151; physical factors in, 51-52, 63-64, 169; as a school problem, 454-459, 465-466; sex differences in, 144-145; and acceptance, 200; sex-social (see Heterosexual relations) (see also Emotionality; Social adjustment)

Adolescence, age differences in, 9-10; cultural impact on, 2-3, 5, 8-9; definitions of, 1-2; economic impact on, 7; frames of reference for, 20-24; methods of studying, 12-16; negative reactions to, 24-26; in

Adolescence—cont.
other cultures, 2-5 (see also specific cultures); prolongation of, 6-8; purposes of studying, 11; sex differences in, 8-9; techniques of studying, 16-20; theories of, 2; time span of, 1-2, 6-11; universality of, 3-5

Adult leaders, 196 (see also Teachers)

Adults, adolescents' view of, 23-24

Age, of entering school, 8; relation to sex differences, 10

Aggression, 155, 165, 168

Alcohol, use of, 298, 302; and personality, 119-120; and sexual behavior, 229; and social adjustment, 200

Allowances, 273-276

Amish youth, 120-121

Anxiety, and academic achievement, 456-457; age differences in, 154; and intelligence, 98-99; and sex-appropriate behavior, 190; sex differences in, 154; and sexual behavior, 228; sources of, 153-154

Appearance, 63, 68-69

Aptitude tests (see Vocational testing)

Athletic ability, 45, 52, 59, 194, 197

Athletic interests, 341

Attitudes, and conformity, 298-299, 315-316; toward democracy, 300; factors affecting, 297, 300-317; parental influence on, 265-267, 297-298; and prejudice, 302-312; to-

547